GRAMMAR EXPLORER 2

Paul Carne
Series Editors: Rob Jenkins and Staci Johnson

NATIONAL GEOGRAPHIC LEARNING | CENGAGE Learning

Australia • Brazil • Japan • Korea • Mexico • Singapore • Spain • United Kingdom • United States

Grammar Explorer 2

Paul Carne

Publisher: Sherrise Roehr

Executive Editor: Laura Le Dréan

Managing Editor: Eve Einselen Yu

Senior Development Editors: Mary Whittemore, Eve Einselen Yu

Development Editor: Maureen Sotoohi

Associate Development Editor: Alayna Cohen

Assistant Editor: Vanessa Richards

Senior Technology Product Manager: Scott Rule

Director of Global Marketing: Ian Martin

Marketing Manager: Lindsey Miller

Sr. Director, ELT & World Languages: Michael Burggren

Production Manager: Daisy Sosa

Content Project Manager: Andrea Bobotas

Print Buyer: Mary Beth Hennebury

Cover Designer: 3CD, Chicago

Cover Image: BRIAN J. SKERRY/National Geographic Creative

Compositor: Cenveo Publisher Services

Student Book 2: 978-1-111-35110-6

National Geographic Learning
20 Channel Center Street
Boston, MA 02210
USA

Cengage Learning is a leading provider of customized learning solutions with office locations around the globe, including Singapore, the United Kingdom, Australia, Mexico, Brazil and Japan.

Cengage Learning products are represented in Canada by Nelson Education, Ltd.

Visit National Geographic Learning online at **ngl.cengage.com**

Visit our corporate website at **www.cengage.com**

HW:

14-4 phrasal verbs

p. 384

Printed in the United States of America
1 2 3 4 5 6 7 8 9 10 17 16 15 14

CONTENTS

UNIT 3 Health and Fitness 58

Nouns

UNIT 4 Going Places 86

Pronouns, Prepositions, and Articles

National Geographic images introduce the unit theme—real world topics that students want to read, write, and talk about.

UNIT 8 Consumer Society

Comparatives and Superlatives

▲ Cars in a scrap yard in Canada.

Lesson 1
page 206
Comparative Adjectives and Adverbs

Lesson 2
page 213
Comparisons with *(Not) As . . . As* and *Less*

Lesson 3
page 220
Superlative Adjectives and Adverbs

Review the Grammar
page 227

Connect the Grammar to Writing
page 230

205

Units are organized in **manageable lessons**, which ensures students **explore, learn, practice,** and **apply** the grammar.

Each lesson begins with the ***Explore*** section, featuring a captivating National Geographic article that introduces the target grammar and builds students' knowledge in a variety of academic disciplines.

LESSON 1 Comparative Adjectives and Adverbs

EXPLORE

CD2-28 **1 READ** the article about consumer societies. Notice the words in **bold**.

What is a Consumer Society?

A *consumer* is a person who buys things, and a *consumer society* is a society that encourages people to buy and use goods.[1] Some people think that a consumer society provides people with **better** lives. People in consumer societies tend to live **more comfortably**. They eat a **wider** variety of food. They go to restaurants **more often**. They also buy a lot of products, maybe more than they need.

Products such as TVs, cell phones, and computers used to be luxuries.[2] Today people can buy these things **more easily than** ever before. The market for these goods is growing **faster** all the time. Consumer societies encourage people to buy **bigger** and **better** products. For example, **"smarter"** phones come out every year. In a consumer society, people are often buying **newer** and **more advanced** products. This creates a lot of waste. Nowadays, many people are thinking **more seriously** about the effects of consumer societies on the environment, and they are trying to become **more responsible** consumers.

[1] **goods:** items that can be bought or sold
[2] **luxury:** something that is expensive but not necessary

206

Comparisons with *(Not) As . . . As* and *Less* LESSON 2

EXPLORE

CD2-30 **1 READ** the excerpt from a discussion between the professor of a business class and a guest speaker. Notice the words in **bold**.

Online Reviews: ★ or ★★★★?

Professor: So, Dennis, what changes have you seen in marketing recently?

Dennis: Well, as you know, customers love to post online reviews of products these days. These reviews are now just **as important as** traditional advertising. Maybe even more important. TV advertising is **as useful as** it was before, of course. On the other hand, newspaper ads[1] are much **less**

Professor: Hmm. That who **aren't**

Dennis: Really? I'm online revi write revie there migh shoppers a **as** they use ads. If a cu **enthusiast**

[1] **ad:** short for advertisement
[2] **endorse:** to say that you support
[3] **enthusiastically:** to do somethin

▼ A billboard, a traditional form of advertising

LESSON 3 Superlative Adjectives and Adverbs

EXPLORE

CD2-31 **1 READ** the article about a problem on Mount Everest. Notice the words in **bold**.

Mount Everest:
The Highest Garbage Dump in the World?

Most people know that Mount Everest is **the highest** mountain in the world. However, there is another fact that many people don't know: it has become one of **the dirtiest** mountains in the world.

Mount Everest is one of **the toughest** and **most exciting** mountains to climb on Earth. It is not **the coldest** or **the windiest** place on Earth, but it comes close! These challenges make it one of **the most attractive** mountains for serious climbers. Since 1952, over 3500 climbers have reached the top. Unfortunately, most of them have left equipment and trash on the mountain.

In fact, trash is now one of **the biggest** threats to the environment on Mount Everest. Local organizations have brought tons of trash down from the mountain. One of **the most interesting** projects handed over more than a ton of tin cans, glass bottles, and old climbing tools to artists in Nepal. The artists used the trash to create works of art. Then, they sold the art to raise money for local charities.[1] **The least expensive** work of art cost $17, and **the most expensive** one cost $2400.

[1] **charity:** an organization that raises money to help people

► The consumer society produces a lot of waste, even in the Himalayas. Here, a climber collects trash on Mount Everest.

220 COMPARATIVES AND SUPERLATIVES

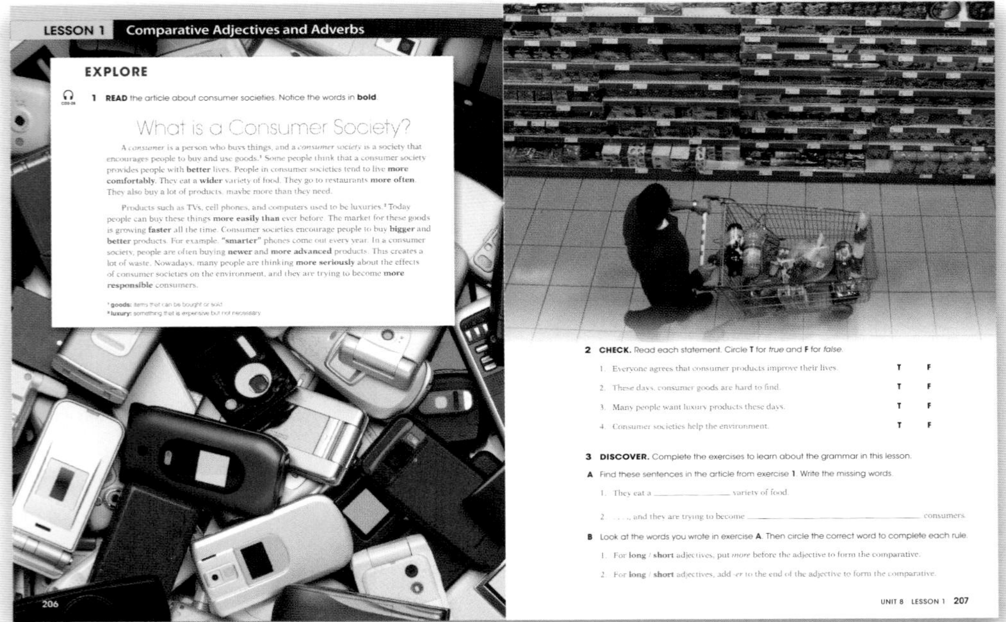

LESSON 1 Comparative Adjectives and Adverbs

EXPLORE

1 **READ** the article about consumer societies. Notice the words in **bold**.

What is a Consumer Society?

A *consumer* is a person who buys things, and a *consumer society* is a society that encourages people to buy and use goods.[1] Some people think that a consumer society provides people with **better** lives. People in consumer societies tend to live **more comfortably**. They eat a **wider** variety of food. They go to restaurants **more often**. They also buy a lot of products, maybe more than they need.

Products such as TVs, cell phones, and computers used to be luxuries.[2] Today people can buy these things **more easily than** ever before. The market for these goods is growing **faster** all the time. Consumer societies encourage people to buy **bigger** and **better** products. For example, **"smarter"** phones come out every year. In a consumer society, people are often buying **newer** and **more advanced** products. This creates a lot of waste. Nowadays, many people are thinking **more seriously** about the effects of consumer societies on the environment, and they are trying to become **more responsible** consumers.

[1] **goods:** items that can be bought or sold
[2] **luxury:** something that is expensive but not necessary

206

2 **CHECK.** Read each statement. Circle **T** for *true* and **F** for *false*.

1. Everyone agrees that consumer products improve their lives. **T F**
2. These days, consumer goods are hard to find. **T F**
3. Many people want luxury products these days. **T F**
4. Consumer societies help the environment. **T F**

3 **DISCOVER.** Complete the exercises to learn about the grammar in this lesson.

A Find these sentences in the article from exercise **1**. Write the missing words.

1. They eat a ______ variety of food.
2. . . . , and they are trying to become ______ consumers.

B Look at the words you wrote in exercise **A**. Then circle the correct word to complete each rule.

1. For **long** / **short** adjectives, put *more* before the adjective to form the comparative.
2. For **long** / **short** adjectives, add *-er* to the end of the adjective to form the comparative.

UNIT 8 LESSON 1 207

In the ***Explore*** section, students discover how the grammar structures are used in the readings and in real academic textbooks.

2 **CHECK.** Read each statement. Circle **T** for *true* or **F** for *false*.

1. Dennis thinks that online reviews are not very important in marketing. **T F**
2. Newspaper ads used to be more effective. **T F**
3. Some marketing people have a negative opinion of online reviews. **T F**
4. Customers with problems are more likely to write online reviews. **T F**
5. Online shoppers won't buy a product if they see a negative review. **T F**
6. Positive online reviews aren't very valuable. **T F**

3 **DISCOVER.** Complete the exercises to learn about the grammar in this lesson.

A Look at each phrase from the discussion in exercise **1** on page 213. Does the phrase mean *equal* or *not equal*? Circle the correct answer.

1. as useful as — **equal** / **not equal**
2. less effective than — **equal** / **not equal**
3. aren't as positive as — **equal** / **not equal**
4. not as harmful as — **equal** / **not equal**
5. as valuable as — **equal** / **not equal**
6. as enthusiastically as — **equal** / **not equal**

B Look at the phrases from exercise **A**. Then answer the questions.

1. What word follows comparisons beginning with *as* + adjective? ______
2. What word follows comparisons beginning with *less* + adverb? ______

MAOCHANG

214

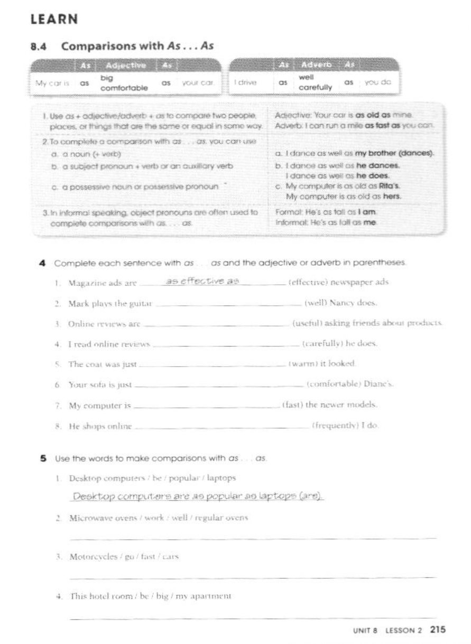

LEARN

8.4 Comparisons with *As . . . As*

	As	Adjective	*As*	
My car is	as	big comfortable	as	your car.

	As	Adverb	*As*	
I drive	as	well carefully	as	you do.

1. Use *as* + adjective/adverb + *as* to compare two people, places, or things that are the same or equal in some way.	Adjective: Your car is **as old as** mine. Adverb: I can run a mile **as fast as** you can.
2. To complete a comparison with *as . . . as*, you can use a. a noun (+ verb) b. a subject pronoun + verb or an auxiliary verb c. a possessive noun or possessive pronoun	 a. I dance as well as **my brother (dances)**. b. I dance as well as **he dances.** I dance as well as **he does.** c. My computer is as old as **Rita's.** My computer is as old as **hers.**
3. In informal speaking, object pronouns are often used to complete comparisons with *as . . . as*.	Formal: He's as tall as **I am**. Informal: He's as tall as **me**.

4 Complete each sentence with *as . . . as* and the adjective or adverb in parentheses.

1. Magazine ads are ___as effective as___ (effective) newspaper ads.
2. Mark plays the guitar ______ (well) Nancy does.
3. Online reviews are ______ (useful) asking friends about products.
4. I read online reviews ______ (carefully) he does.
5. The coat was just ______ (warm) it looked.
6. Your sofa is just ______ (comfortable) Diane's.
7. My computer is ______ (fast) the newer models.
8. He shops online ______ (frequently) I do.

5 Use the words to make comparisons with *as . . . as*.

1. Desktop computers / be / popular / laptops
Desktop computers are as popular as laptops (are).
2. Microwave ovens / work / well / regular ovens
______
3. Motorcycles / go / fast / cars
______
4. This hotel room / be / big / my apartment
______

UNIT 8 LESSON 2 215

The ***Learn*** section features clear grammar charts and explanations followed by controlled practice of the grammar forms.

In the ***Practice*** section, students practice the grammar using all four skills through communicative activities that prepare them for academic work.

PRACTICE

9 Use the words in parentheses to complete the conversation with comparative adjectives or adverbs. Add *than* where necessary. In some cases, more than one answer is possible.

Matt: My phone is working (1) worse than ______ (badly) ever! And it's (2) ______ (old) all the other phones I see, too. I want a (3) ______ (modern) phone.

Lara: Take a look at my phone. It was (4) ______ (cheap) my last phone, and I'm much (5) ______ (happy) with it. When I'm traveling, I listen to music (6) ______ (often) I do when I'm at home, so I wanted a phone with a (7) ______ (big) memory card.

Matt: Wow, it's much (8) ______ (nice) mine! The screen is a lot (9) ______ (large), too. I want one like that!

Lara: Yeah, you need a big screen, because you watch videos on your phone (10) ______ (frequently) I do.

10 Look at the charts comparing three laptop co[…] the comparative form of the adjectives and a[…]

Product Details	T400
Screen size	15 inches
Weight	5.5 pounds
Amount of time on the market	18 months
Cost	$565

Customer Ratings	T400
Starts quickly	★★★
Runs reliably	★★★★★
Operates quietly	★★★★
Displays pictures well	★★★

1. (large / small) The screen of the T400 is la[…] smaller than ______ the XJ7's.
2. (light / heavy) The XJ7 is ______ the T400.
3. (new / old) The A-50 is ______ the XJ7.
4. (cheap / expensive) The T400 is ______
5. (quickly / slowly) The T400 starts ______ the A-50.

PRACTICE

8 Complete the sentences with the superlative form of the adjectives and adverbs in parentheses. Use *least* if *not* is included in the parentheses.

1. **Kelly:** I think people are too concerned about having (1) the most modern ______ (modern) cell phones. Cell phones contain some of (2) ______ (rare) minerals on Earth, but many people just throw their old cell phones away when they buy a new one. This is (3) ______ (one of the / bad / thing) you can do! But if you recycle your old cell phones, it's (4) ______ (one of the / good / thing) you can do.
2. **Amir:** My cell phone is (5) ______ (important / thing) I own. It's (6) ______ (convenient / place) I have to keep information.
3. **Brad:** My new cell phone is a piece of junk! It was (7) ______ (not expensive) phone in the store. What a mistake! Also, the salesperson in that store was one of (8) ______ (not helpful / salesperson) I've ever spoken to.

9 **EDIT.** Read the article about trash in the desert. Find and correct eight more errors with superlatives.

Cameron's Camels

The Arabian Desert in the Middle East is one of the ~~most hot~~ hottest environments on Earth, and it has the less amount of rainfall. But to the camel, it is home. The camel is one of the most strong animals in the world. Camels can go for many days with only a little food and water. When they do find water, they probably drink the most quick of any land animal. Adult camels can drink about 25 to 30 gallons (95–114 liters) in ten minutes. Unfortunately, finding water is not the seriousest problem camels face. Most dangerous threat to camels comes from humans. Tourists in the desert leave trash behind. Camels think the trash is food and eat it. This is very dangerous for the camels, because it can kill them.

One of the most polluted part of the desert is outside the city of Abu Dhabi. Each year, many […]

[…]25

Students use their new language and critical thinking skills in the ***Apply*** section.

10 APPLY.

A Work with a partner. Use the words in parentheses to write superlatives. Then choose the correct answer to complete each fact on the quiz.

General Knowledge Quiz

1. ______ is the highest mountain ______ (high / mountain) on Earth.
   a. Mount Kilimanjaro b. Mount Everest c. K2
2. ______ is ______ (fast / animal) in the world.
   a. the camel b. the zebra c. the cheetah
3. ______ is ______ (long / river) in the world.
   a. The Nile River b. The Amazon River c. The Yangtze River
4. ______ is ______ (wide / ocean) on Earth.
   a. The Pacific Ocean b. The Atlantic Ocean c. The Indian Ocean
5. ______ is ______ (small / continent).
   a. Africa b. Antarctica c. Australia
6. ______ is ______ (large / animal) on Earth.
   a. the elephant b. the blue whale c. the giraffe
7. ______ is ______ (cold / place) on Earth.
   a. Antarctica b. Alaska c. Canada
8. ______ is ______ (close / planet) to the sun.
   a. Mars b. Venus c. Mercury

B Check your answers at the bottom of this page. How many of your answers were correct?

C With your partner, write six more general knowledge facts like the ones from the quiz in exercise **A**. Use superlative adjectives and adverbs.

1. The Nile River is the longest river in the world.

D Use the facts from exercise **C** and quiz your classmates.

A: This is the largest country in South America.
B: Is it Argentina?
A: No.
C: Is it Brazil?
A: Yes, it is!

Answers: 1. b Mount Everest; 2. c the cheetah; 3. a The Nile River 4. a the Pacific Ocean; 5. c Australia; 6. b the blue whale; 7. a Antarctica; 8. c Mercury

226 COMPARATIVES AND SUPERLATIVES

UNIT 8 Review the Grammar

Charts 8.1, 8.3–8.7

1 READ & WRITE.

A Read the information about the Greendex survey, and look at the chart. Then complete each sentence according to the information in the chart. Use the comparative or superlative form of the adjective or adverb in parentheses. For some sentences, more than one answer is possible.

Greendex™

The Greendex is a survey of 1000 consumers in several countries. It asks consumers how they spend their money. Each consumer receives a score. High scores indicate "green," or environmentally friendly, attitudes. Low scores indicate environmentally unfriendly attitudes.

Greendex: Rankings

	Overall	Housing	Transportation	Food	Goods
Americans	44.7	31.5	54.9	57.0	44.2
Brazilians	55.5	48.9	67.1	57.5	53.8
British	49.4	35.9	62.7	62.2	47.1
Canadians	47.9	35.1	57.8	60.9	45.7
Chinese	57.8	48.2	69.0	63.7	56.8
Germans	51.5	40.3	61.9	61.9	47.1
Indians	58.9	51.4	67.3	71.1	57.3
Japanese	48.5	35.3	65.9	54.7	52.7
Mexicans	53.9	48.0	62.2	53.6	54.5
Russians	53.1	44.1	66.4	60.4	47.9

Transportation

1. The Chinese make *the greenest* (green) choices.
2. Americans are ______ (green) consumers.
3. British consumers make ______ (green) choices than Canadian consumers.
4. Mexican consumers are ______ (green) Japanese consumers.

Food

5. The British are ______ (concerned) the Chinese.
6. Indians are ______ (concerned) consumers.
7. Russians are ______ (concerned) Brazilians.
8. American

Review the Grammar UNIT 8

Goods

9. Canadians don't buy goods ______ (responsibly) Mexicans do.
10. Indians buy goods ______ (responsibly).
11. Germans buy goods ______ (responsibly) Brazilians.
12. Americans buy goods ______ (responsibly).

B In your notebook, write four or five sentences based on the housing data from the Greendex chart in exercise **A** on page 227. Use comparative and superlative adjectives and adverbs. Use the sentences from exercise **A** to help you.

Mexicans make greener housing choices than Canadians.
Indian consumers are more concerned about green housing than German consumers are.

Charts 8.1–8.7

2 EDIT. Read the article about the results of the Greendex survey. Find and correct eight more errors with comparatives and superlatives.

The Greendex Survey: Some Overall Conclusions

- According to a recent Greendex survey, people in India were the ~~most green~~ *greenest* consumers in the world. They scored lower in transportation than the Chinese were, but they scored the highest than the Chinese in three other categories.
- Mexicans were more concerned about green transportation as green food or goods. For them, the low score of all was in the housing category.
- Germans scored highly in the transportation category than they did in the food category. However, they were least concerned about housing than goods.
- The Japanese were one of the least concerned nationality overall. They had one of the most bad scores in the housing category.
- Americans had the lowest overall score of all the nationalities in the survey. Food was the only category in which Americans did not score lower then the other nationalities.

228 COMPARATIVES AND SUPERLATIVES

Charts 8.1–8.4, 8.6

3 LISTEN & SPEAK.

A Listen to a professor discussing the Greendex survey with her students. Then complete the students' opinions about the survey. (CD2-33)

Martin:

1. Most people think that their country is ______ the results show.
2. Many people think they buy goods ______ they really do.
3. We like to think we're trying ______ we can to be green.

Karin:

4. Life in the United States is much ______ without a car.
5. Cars that use less gas are becoming ______ in the United States.
6. Attitudes about the environment aren't changing ______ people think.

Andrew:

7. Most people want to make life ______ for themselves and their families.
8. Everyone wants an ______ life.

B Look at the sentences from exercise **A**. Then listen again. Do you agree or disagree with the students' ideas and opinions? Why, or why not? Write notes on your own ideas and opinions in your notebook. (CD2-33)

C Work with a partner. Share your ideas and opinions from exercise **B**. Use comparatives and superlatives.

I agree with Martin's opinion about goods. People don't shop as carefully as they think they do.

Charts 8.1–8.7

4 WRITE & SPEAK.

A Look at the items in the box. Then rank the items from 1 to 8, with (1 = the least important and 8 = the most important).

____ a. a big car	____ d. a smart phone	____ g. plastic bags
____ b. stylish clothing	____ e. meals in restaurants	____ h. a gold watch
____ c. a computer	____ f. a TV	

B In your notebook, write six sentences about the items from exercise **A**. Use comparatives and superlatives and your own ideas and opinions.

I think a computer is less important than a smart phone.

C Work with a partner. Share your rankings from exercise **A** and your opinions from exercise **B**.

UNIT 8 REVIEW THE GRAMMAR 229

Review the Grammar gives students the opportunity to consolidate the grammar in their reading, writing, listening, and speaking.

INSIDE A UNIT

Connect the Grammar to Writing provides students with a clear model and a guided writing task where they first notice and then use the target grammar in one of a variety of writing genres.

Connect the Grammar to Writing

1 READ & NOTICE THE GRAMMAR.

A Before you buy something, do you compare it with similar products? Discuss your shopping habits with a partner. Then read the text.

The Best Sleeping Bag

I needed to buy a new sleeping bag for a winter camping trip. So, I went to a camping store and compared three different brands[1] of sleeping bags: Ultra Comfort, Snowy Down, and Northern Trek. I wanted to look at each sleeping bag very carefully. For winter camping, the Snowy Down had the highest rating. But in some ways, the other two sleeping bags were better. Of the three sleeping bags, the Snowy Down was the warmest, but it was also the most expensive. The Northern Trek cost less than the Snowy Down, but it was just as expensive as the Ultra Comfort. The Ultra Comfort was warmer than the Northern Trek. Finally, the Ultra Comfort was lighter than the other sleeping bags, so it was easier to carry.

I decided not to get the Northern Trek for camping outside. It wasn't as warm as the other sleeping bags. But we were having a mild winter, so I didn't need the warmest kind of sleeping bag. So I looked more closely at the lightest sleeping bag, the Ultra Comfort. That's the one I chose.

[1] **brand:** the commercial name for a product

GRAMMAR FOCUS

In exercise **A**, the writer uses comparatives and superlatives to discuss three sleeping bags.

*The Ultra Comfort was **warmer than** the Northern Trek.*

*. . . it was just **as expensive as** the Ultra Comfort.*

*Of the three sleeping bags, the Snowy Down was **the warmest** and **most expensive**.*

B Read the text in exercise **A** again. Underline the comp[...]
Then work with a partner and compare your answers.

C Work with a partner. Complete the chart with informati[...]

Product Details	Ultra Comfort	Sno[...]
Cost	*as expensive as the Northern Trek*	
Warmth		*the war[...]*
Weight		

Write a Product Review

2 BEFORE YOU WRITE. Think of a product that you plan to buy. Compare three different brands of this product. Complete the chart with information about each brand. Use the chart from exercise **1C** as a model.

Product Details	Product #1	Product #2	Product #3
Cost			

3 WRITE a review comparing the three different brands of the product you chose. Write two paragraphs. Use the information from your chart in exercise **2** and the article in exercise **1A** to help you.

WRITING FOCUS Correcting Run-on Sentences

A run-on sentence is an error that happens when two independent clauses are connected without a connecting word or correct punctuation.

✗ *I enjoyed my winter camping trip next year, I'll invite a few friends to join me.*

To correct a run-on sentence, you can divide the run-on sentence into separate sentences.

✓ *I enjoyed my winter camping **trip. Next** year, I'll invite a few friends to join me.*

You can also use a comma and a conjunction (*and, but, or*) between the two independent clauses.

✓ *I enjoyed my winter camping **trip, but** next year I'll invite a few friends to join me.*

4 SELF ASSESS. Read your review and underline the comparatives and superlatives. Then use the checklist to assess your work.

☐ I used comparative adjectives and adverbs correctly. [8.1, 8.2, 8.3]

☐ I used comparisons with *less* and (*not*) *as . . . as* correctly. [8.4, 8.5]

☐ I used superlative adjectives and adverbs correctly. [8.6, 8.7]

☐ I checked for and corrected run-on sentences. [WRITING FOCUS]

ACKNOWLEDGMENTS

The authors and publisher would like to thank the following reviewers and contributors:

Gokhan Alkanat, Auburn University at Montgomery, Alabama; **Dorothy S. Avondstondt**, Miami Dade College, Florida; **Heather Barikmo**, The English Language Center at LaGuardia Community College, New York; **Kimberly Becker**, Nashville State Community College, Tennessee; **Lukas Bidelspack**, Corvallis, Oregon; **Grace Bishop**, Houston Community College, Texas; **Mariusz Jacek Bojarczuk**, Bunker Hill Community College, Massachusetts; **Nancy Boyer**, Golden West College, California; **Patricia Brenner**, University of Washington, Washington; **Jessica Buchsbaum**, City College of San Francisco, California; **Gabriella Cambiasso**, Harold Washington College, Illinois; **Tony Carnerie**, English Language Institute, University of California San Diego Extension, California; **Whitney Clarq-Reis**, Framingham State University; **Julia A. Correia**, Henderson State University, Arkansas; **Katie Crowder**, UNT Department of Linguistics and Technical Communication, Texas; **Lin Cui**, William Rainey Harper College, Illinois; **Nora Dawkins**, Miami Dade College, Florida; **Rachel DeSanto**, English for Academic Purposes, Hillsborough Community College, Florida; **Aurea Diab**, Dillard University, Louisiana; **Marta Dmytrenko-Ahrabian**, English Language Institute, Wayne State University, Michigan; **Susan Dorrington**, Education and Language Acquisition Department, LaGuardia Community College, New York; **Ian Dreilinger**, Center for Multilingual Multicultural Studies, University of Central Florida, Florida; **Jennifer Dujat**, Education and Language Acquisition Department, LaGuardia Community College, New York; **Dr. Jane Duke**, Language & Literature Department, State College of Florida, Florida; **Anna Eddy**, University of Michigan-Flint, Michigan; **Jenifer Edens**, University of Houston, Texas; **Karen Einstein**, Santa Rosa Junior College, California; **Cynthia Etter**, International & English Language Programs, University of Washington, Washington; **Parvanak Fassihi**, SHOWA Boston Institute for Language and Culture, Massachusetts; **Katherine Fouche**, The University of Texas at Austin, Texas; **Richard Furlong**, Education and Language Acquisition Department, LaGuardia Community College, New York; **Glenn S. Gardner**, Glendale College, California; **Sally Gearhart**, Santa Rosa Junior College, California; **Alexis Giannopolulos**, SHOWA Boston Institute for Language and Culture, Massachusetts; **Nora Gold**, Baruch College, The City University of New York, New York; **Ekaterina V. Goussakova**, Seminole State College of Florida; **Lynn Grantz**, Valparaiso University, Indiana; **Tom Griffith**, SHOWA Boston Institute for Language and Culture, Massachusetts; **Christine Guro**, Hawaii English Language Program, University of Hawaii at Manoa, Hawaii; **Jessie Hayden**, Georgia Perimeter College, Georgia; **Barbara Inerfeld**, Program in American Language Studies, Rutgers University, New Jersey; **Gail Kellersberger**, University of Houston-Downtown, Texas; **David Kelley**, SHOWA Boston Institute for Language and Culture, Massachusetts; **Kathleen Kelly**, ESL Department, Passaic County Community College, New Jersey; **Dr. Hyun-Joo Kim**, Education and Language Acquisition Department, LaGuardia Community College, New York; **Linda Koffman**, College of Marin, California; **Lisa Kovacs-Morgan**, English Language Institute, University of California San Diego Extension, California; **Jerrad Langlois**, TESL Program and Office of International Programs, Northeastern Illinois University; **Janet Langon**, Glendale College, California; **Olivia Limbu**, The English Language Center at LaGuardia Community College, New York; **Devora Manier**, Nashville State Community College, Tennessee; **Susan McAlister**, Language and Culture Center, Department of English, University of Houston, Texas; **John McCarthy**, SHOWA Boston Institute for Language and Culture, Massachusetts; **Dr. Myra Medina**, Miami Dade College, Florida; **Dr. Suzanne Medina**, California State University, Dominguez Hills, California; **Nancy Megarity**, ESL & Developmental Writing, Collin College, Texas; **Joseph Montagna**, SHOWA Boston Institute for Language and Culture, Massachusetts; **Richard Moore**, University of Washington; **Monika Mulder**, Portland State University, Oregon; **Patricia Nation**, Miami Dade College, Florida; **Susan Niemeyer**, Los Angeles City College, California; **Charl Norloff**, International English Center, University of Colorado Boulder, Colorado; **Gabriella Nuttall**, Sacramento City College, California; **Dr. Karla Odenwald**, CELOP at Boston University, Massachusetts; **Ali Olson-Pacheco**, English Language Institute, University of California San Diego Extension, California; **Fernanda Ortiz**, Center for English as a Second Language, University of Arizona, Arizona; **Chuck Passentino**, Grossmont College, California; **Stephen Peridore**, College of Southern Nevada, Nevada; **Frank Quebbemann**, Miami Dade College, Florida; **Dr. Anouchka Rachelson**, Miami Dade College, Florida; **Dr. Agnieszka Rakowicz**, Education and Language Acquisition Department, LaGuardia Community College, New York; **Wendy Ramer**, Broward College, Florida; **Esther Robbins**, Prince George's Community College, Maryland; **Helen Roland**, Miami Dade College, Florida; **Debbie Sandstrom**, Tutorium in Intensive English, University of Illinois at Chicago, Illinois; **Maria Schirta**, Hudson County Community College, New Jersey; **Dr. Jennifer Scully**, Education and Language Acquisition Department, LaGuardia Community College, New York; **Jeremy Stubbs**, Tacoma, Washington; **Adrianne Thompson**, Miami Dade College, Florida; **Evelyn Trottier**, Basic and Transitional Studies Program, Seattle Central Community College, Washington; **Karen Vallejo**, University of California, Irvine, California; **Emily Young**, Auburn University at Montgomery, Alabama.

From the Author: It has been an honor to work with National Geographic material in the preparation of this book. My thanks are due to my excellent development editors Maureen Sotoohi and Eve Einselen Yu, to Laura LeDréan, Tom Jefferies, Mary Whittemore, and the entire team at National Geographic Learning. The project has benefited from the expertise and enthusiasm of many experienced reviewers, and their contribution is also greatly appreciated. Finally, it has been an absolute privilege to work alongside my fellow authors, Daphne Mackey, Amy Cooper, and Sammi Eckstut. Hats off to you all!

Dedication: To Vicky, my wife and best friend, for her timeless love and support; to my wonderful sons, Thomas and Robin, for keeping me going; and last but not least, to my beloved border terrier, Bodhi, for his patience (sometimes!) and unflagging optimism throughout.

Text and Listening

4: Exercise 1. Sources: National Geographic Magazine, November 1999; http://lionguardians.org/the-lion-guardians. **20:** Exercise 2. Source: http://news.nationalgeographic.com/news/2008/08/photogalleries/wip-week96/index.html. **26:** Exercise 1. Source: National Geographic Magazine, June 2010. **33:** Exercise 1. Source: http://www.culturalsurvival.org/current-projects/community-radio-project. **38:** Exercise 10. Source: http://newswatch.nationalgeographic.com/2012/05/21/ng-explorers-help-record-xyzyl-language. **39:** Exercise 1. Source: http://video.nationalgeographic.com/video/specials/nat-geo-live-specials/chin-interview-nglive. **44:** Exercise 9. Source: National Geographic Magazine, November 1998. **51:** Exercise 8. Source: National Geographic Magazine, July 2007. **54:** Exercise 3. http://www.atlasobscura.com/places/ancient-stepwells-india. **54:** Exercise 4. http://www.mandatory.com/2012/05/07/10-guys-who-survived-wild-animal-attacks/4. **60:** Exercise 1. Sources: http://www.sangomaza.co.za; http://www.ancestralwisdom.com/sangoma.html. **68:** Exercise 1. Source: National Geographic Magazine, February 2009; http://www.webmd.com/diet/acai-berries-and-acai-berry-juice-what-are-the-health-benefits; http://environment.nationalgeographic.com/environment/enlarge/chinese-ginseng.html. **73:** Exercise 8. Source: http://education.nationalgeographic.com/education/media/fresh-fruits-vegetables/?ar_a=1. **74:** Exercise 1. Source: http://www.bbc.co.uk/sport/0/football/18887653. **78:** Exercise 7. Source: http://www.news.com.au/breaking-news/eight-glasses-of-water-a-myth-academic/story-e6frfku0-1226385483550. **82:** Exercise 4. Source: http://www.nationalgeographic.com/explorers/bios/jenny-daltry. **88:** Exercise 1. Source: http://www.bbc.co.uk/news/world-radio-and-tv-16833168. **96:** Exercise 1. Sources: http://www.bbc.com/travel/slideshow/20120801-blue-holes-of-the-bahamas; http://www.seadragonbahamas.com/divingseasonsofthebahamas.html. **101:** Exercise 10. Sources: http://www.nationalgeographic.com/explorers/bios/catherine-jaffee. **103:** Exercise 1. Source: National Geographic Magazine, March 2011. **108:** Exercise 9. Sources: http://www.huffingtonpost.com/2012/07/14/kent-couch-lawn-chair-balloonist-tandem-flight-iraqi-fareed-lafta_n_1673162.html; http://www.couchballoons.com. **122:** Exercise 1. Sources: http://news.nationalgeographic.com/news/2010/04/100402-aral-sea-story; http://www.britannica.com/EBchecked/topic/31983/Aral-Sea. **128:** Exercise 11. Sources: http://earthobservatory.nasa.gov/Features/WorldOfChange/decadaltemp.php; http://www.nasa.gov/topics/earth/features/warmingpoles.html. **130:** Exercise 1. Sources: http://ngm.nationalgeographic.com/2011/08/robots/robots-photography#/12-paro-robotic-seal-family-714.jpg; http://online.wsj.com/news/articles/SB10001424052748704463504575301051844937276. **136:** Exercise 1. Source: http://www.theatlantic.com/technology/archive/2012/02/heres-what-humbert-humbert-looks-like-as-a-police-composite-sketch/252866. **140:** Exercise 8. Sources: http://www.census.gov/prod/2013pubs/acs-22.pdf; http://www.laalmanac.com/LA/la10b.htm. **143:** Exercise 11. Source: http://www.reuters.com/video/2012/07/06/ugandan-student-makes-a-billion-through?videoId=236379211&videoChannel=2602. **144:** Exercise 1. Source: http://www.economist.com/node/18277141. **152:** Exercise 3. Source: http://www.dailymail.co.uk/news/article-2135299/Brit-bought-cut-price-island-Seychelles-50-years-ago--lives-blissful-solitude.html. **158:** Exercise 1. Sources: http://www.smh.com.au/articles/2006/03/29/1143441187263.html; http://animals.nationalgeographic.com/animals/mammals/koala. **172:** Exercise 2. Source: http://news.nationalgeographic.com/news/2012/08/120831-venus-two-faced-cat-genetics-animals-science. **173:** Exercise 3. Sources: http://www.pbs.org/wgbh/nova/bowerbirds/trail.html; http://www.theguardian.com/science/neurophilosophy/2012/jan/19/1. **174:** Exercise 1. Sources: http://news.nationalgeographic.com/news/2007/10/photogalleries/primate2-pictures/photo3.html; http://www.livescience.com/10268-surprise-hidden-yellow-tailed-monkey-colony-discovered.html. **178:** Exercise 1. Sources: http://www.bbc.com/future/story/20120622-space-a-travel-guide; http://www.cnn.com/2013/08/15/travel/virgin-galactic-250000-ticket-to-space. **192:** Exercise 1. Sources: http://water.epa.gov/type/oceb/habitat/coral_index.cfm#important; http://www.coris.noaa.gov/about/hazards; http://www.pmel.noaa.gov/pubs/PDF/sutt3748/sutt3748.pdf; http://www.nytimes.com/2012/07/14/opinion/a-world-without-coral-reefs.html. **198:** Exercise 11. Source: http://www.nwf.org/News-and-Magazines/National-Wildlife/Animals/Archives/2010/Kermode-bear.aspx. **200:** Exercise 2. Source: National Geographic Magazine, November 2011. **220:** Exercise 1. Source: http://www.cnn.com/2013/01/15/world/asia/everest-trash-art. **225:** Exercise 11. Source: http://www.cameronscamelcampaign.com. **227:** Exercise 1. Source: http://environment.nationalgeographic.com/environment/greendex. **234:** Exercise 1. Source: http://newswatch.nationalgeographic.com/2013/02/25/carnivorous-plants-glow. **240:** Exercise 11. Source: http://www.desertmuseum.org/kids/oz/long-fact-sheets/Saguaro%20Cactus.php. **242:** Exercise 1. Source: National Geographic Magazine, April 2011. **250:** Exercise 1. Source: National Geographic Magazine, January 2011. **256:** Exercise 10. Source: http://news.nationalgeographic.com/news/2009/05/090504-sunderbans-tigers-video-ap.html. **260:** Exercise 1. Source: http://www.epa.gov/air/noise.html. **264:** Exercise 1. Source: http://news.nationalgeographic.com/news/2011/01/pictures/110105-underwater-sculpture-park-garden-cancun-mexico-caribbean-pictures-photos-science. **271:** Exercise 1. Sources: http://www.nydailynews.com/news/world/felix-baumgartner-broke-sound-barrier-skydive-article-1.1255164; http://www.euronews.com/2012/10/24/felix-baumgartner-life-on-the-edge. **279:** Exercise 1. Sources: https://www.youtube.com/watch?v=8lThsSJU328; http://www.nationalgeographic.com/explorers/bios/kakani-katija/. **286:** Exercise 12. Source: http://ngm-beta.nationalgeographic.com/archive/a-monkey-that-knows-no-bounds. **288:** Exercise 4. Source: http://www.nationalgeographic.com/explorers/bios/barrington-irving. **308:** Exercise 1. Source: http://www.bbc.co.uk/news/mobile/world-europe-isle-of-man-15773388. **210:** Exercise 1. Source: http://www.inspirationgreen.com/the-trash-people-of-ha-schult.html. **358:** Exercise 13. Source: National Geographic Magazine, May 2011. **376:** Exercise 6. Source: http://education.nationalgeographic.co.uk/education/thisday/jun3/father-canning-laid-rest/?ar_a=4. **376:** Exercise 6. Source: http://www.encyclopedia.com/topic/Nicolas_Appert.aspx. **382:** Exercise 1. Sources: http://www.nationalgeographic.com/explorers/bios/tan-le/; http://www.ted.com/talks/tan_le_my_immigration_story.html. **396:** Exercise 1. Source: http://news.nationalgeographic.com/news/2013/08/130808-moche-priestess-queen-tomb-discovery-peru-archeology-science. **399:** Exercise 5. Source: National Geographic Magazine, June 2005. **404:** Exercise 1. Source: National Geographic Magazine, September 2004. **417:** Exercise 6. Source: http://photography.nationalgeographic.com/photography/photo-tips/uig-bay-evening-richardson. **419:** Exercise 6. Source: https://sites.google.com/site/fatherofgarbology/garbology. **426:** Exercise 1. Source: http://www.franckgoddio.org/projects/sunken-civilizations/heracleion.html. **431:** Exercise 9. Source: http://news.nationalgeographic.com/news/2007/09/070919-sunken-city_2.html. **434:** Exercise 1. Sources: http://www.telegraph.co.uk/science/science-news/8582150/Kon-Tiki-explorer-was-partly-right-Polynesians-had-South-American-roots.html; http://www.cla.calpoly.edu/~tljones/polynesia.%20science%202010.pdf. **454:** Exercise 3. Sources: http://outofedenwalk.nationalgeographic.com/; http://www.outofedenwalk.com/. **454:** Exercise 3. Source: http://ngm.nationalgeographic.com/2006/03/human-journey/shreeve-text.
Definitions for glossed words: Sources: *The Newbury House Dictionary plus Grammar Reference*, Fifth Edition, National Geographic Learning/Cengage Learning, 2014; *Collins Cobuild Illustrated Basic Dictionary of American English*, Cengage Learning 2010, Collins Cobuild/Harper Collins Publishers, First Edition, 2010; *Collins Cobuild School Dictionary of American English*, Cengage Learning 2009, Collins Cobuild/Harper Collins Publishers, 2008; Collins Cobuild Advanced Learner's Dictionary, 5th Edition, Harper Collins Publishers, 2006.

Photo

Inside Front Cover, left column: Dr. K. David Harrison/Living Tongues Institute for Endangered Language, ©Jim Webb/National Geographic Creative, ©Nav Dayanand, ©Claire Bangser, ©Michael Christopher Brown/National Geographic Creative, **right column:** ©Sandra Lynn Kerr, ©Mark Thiessen/National Geographic Creative, ©Marco Grob/National Geographic Creative, ©Australia Unlimited/National Geographic Creative, ©AFP/Getty Images.

2–3: ©Valdrin Xhemaj/epa/Corbis; **4:** ©Carol Beckwith & Angela Fisher/Photokunst; **5:** ©Chris Johns/National Geographic Creative; **11 left:** ©Robin Smith/Getty Images, **right:** ©Vitalii Nesterchuk/Shutterstock; **12:** ©Jodi Cobb/National Geographic Creative;

(*continued on page C1*)

The Present

▶ A bride wears paint on her face to prevent bad luck during a traditional wedding ceremony in the village of Donje Ljubinje, Kosovo.

EXPLORE

CD1-02

1 **READ** the article about weddings among the Afar people of Djibouti. Notice the words in **bold**.

An Afar Wedding

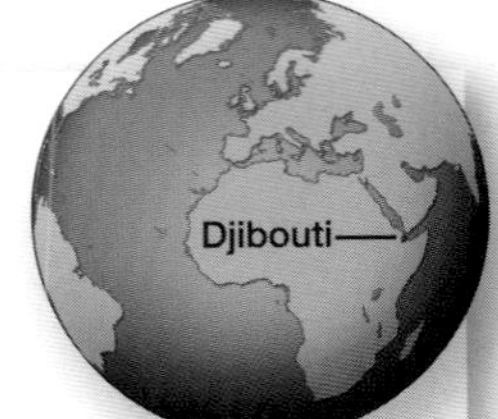

What is an Afar wedding ceremony like?

The actual wedding ceremony is only for men. The bride[1] **does not go** to this ceremony. Instead, her father **represents**[2] her. The women **celebrate**[3] in a different place. They **sit** and **talk** about the bride's life. The women's ceremony often **includes** a lot of dancing.

What happens next?

After these separate ceremonies, the bride and groom[4] **meet** with their families and friends. Sometimes this party **lasts** all night. The next day, the bride and groom **invite** their families to their new home. They **eat** a traditional[5] meal. A typical meal is goat with rice.

What do the bride and groom wear?

Often they both **dress** in traditional clothes, but the bride sometimes **wears** a western-style dress. Some brides **wear** a lot of gold jewelry.

Who pays for the wedding?

In the Afar culture, the man **pays** for the wedding. He also **provides** a home for his new wife, but they **do not live** there together until three days after the wedding.

[1] **bride:** a woman on her wedding day
[2] **represent:** to act in the place of someone
[3] **celebrate:** to have a party or a meal to mark a special occasion
[4] **groom:** a man on his wedding day
[5] **traditional:** based on things that people have done in a certain way for a long time

▶ This Afar bride wears gold jewelry for her wedding.

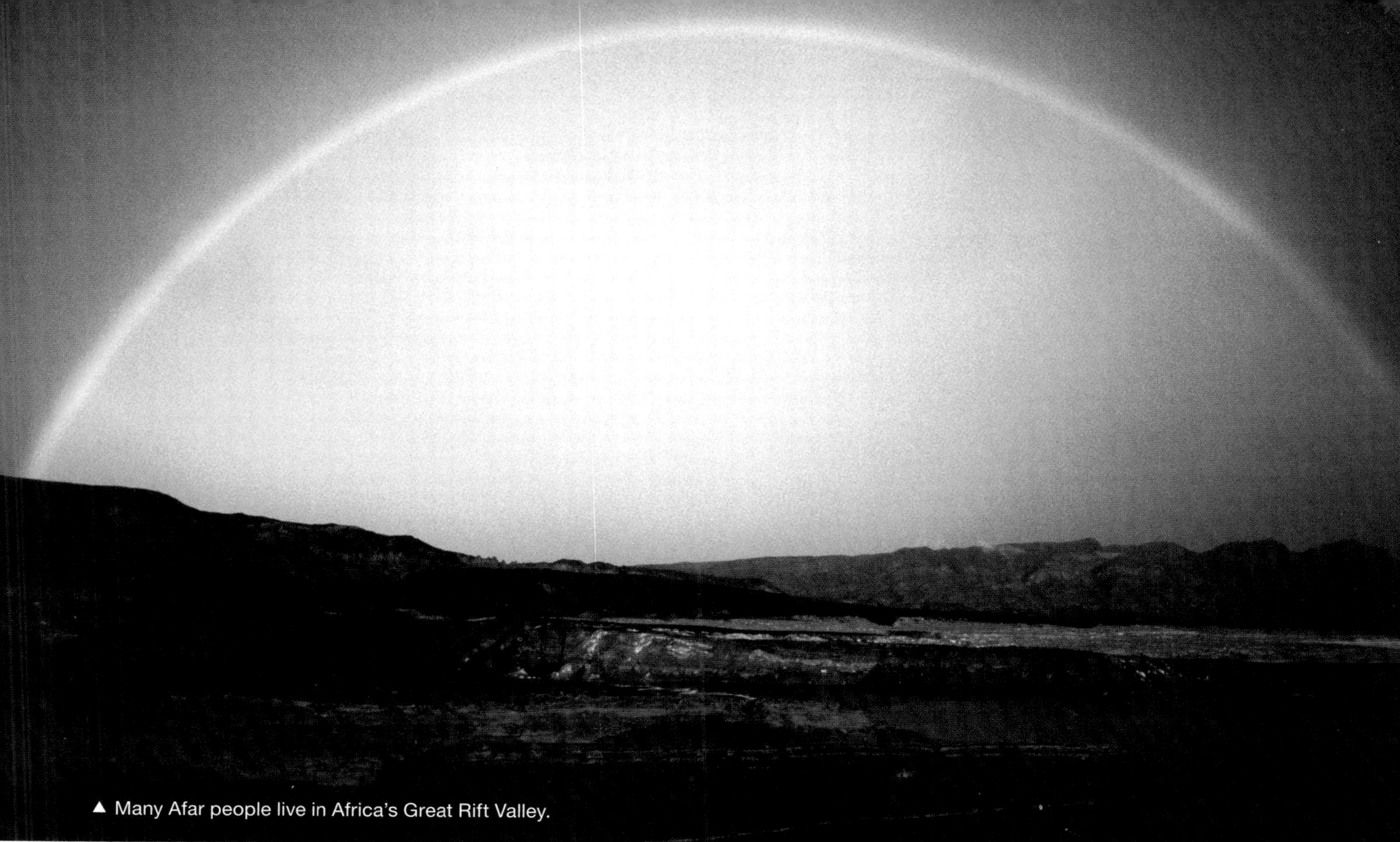
▲ Many Afar people live in Africa's Great Rift Valley.

2 CHECK. Read the statements. Circle **T** for *true* or **F** for *false*.

1. The bride and groom go to the wedding ceremony together. **T** **F**
2. Women dance to celebrate the wedding. **T** **F**
3. Sometimes the bride does not wear traditional clothing. **T** **F**
4. The family eats a traditional meal. **T** **F**
5. The bride's father pays for the wedding. **T** **F**

3 DISCOVER. Complete the exercises to learn about the grammar in this lesson.

A Look at these sentences from the article in exercise **1**. The subject of each sentence is underlined. Write ***S*** if the subject is singular. Write ***P*** if the subject is plural.

1. ______ The bride **does not go** to this ceremony.
2. ______ Instead, her father **represents** her.
3. ______ The women **celebrate** in a different place.
4. ______ They **sit** and **talk** about the bride's life.
5. ______ The women's ceremony often **includes** a lot of dancing.

B Notice the verbs in **bold** in the sentences in exercise **A**. How are the verbs in the sentences with a singular subject different from the verbs in the sentences with a plural subject? Discuss your answer with your classmates and teacher.

LEARN

1.1 Simple Present: Affirmative and Negative Statements

Affirmative		
Subject	Verb	
I/You/We/They	**eat**	a lot.
He/She/It	**eats**	a lot.

Negative			
Subject	*Do Not/Does Not*	Base Form	
I/You/We/They	do not don't	eat	a lot.
He/She/It	does not doesn't	eat	a lot.

1. Use the simple present to talk about: a. habits and repeated actions b. facts and general truths c. how often something happens	a. We **eat** dinner at 7:30. b. The mail **doesn't come** on Sundays. c. Jim **visits** his uncle twice a year.
2. **Be careful!** Don't forget to add *-s, -es,* or *-ies* to verbs when the subject is *he, she, it,* or a singular noun.	✓ Rosa **teaches** math. ✗ Rosa teach math.

See page **A1** for simple present spelling rules.

REAL ENGLISH

Contractions are usually used in conversation and informal writing.

*He **doesn't** watch TV.*
*We **don't** like pizza.*

4 Complete each sentence with the correct form of the verb in parentheses.

1. At an Afar wedding the families __________ (eat) a traditional meal.
2. An Afar bride __________ (not attend) the actual wedding ceremony.
3. The women __________ (dance) during their celebration.
4. The bride and groom __________ (invite) their friends and family to a party.
5. The bride's parents __________ (not pay) for the wedding.
6. The wedding __________ (not end) on the first day.
7. A groom __________ (provide) a new home for his bride.
8. They __________ (not live) together immediately.

5 **SPEAK.** Work with a partner. Take turns making affirmative or negative statements. Use the subjects and verbs from the chart below.

The groom pays for the wedding. The bride doesn't go to the wedding ceremony.

Subjects	Verbs
the bride the wedding guests the groom the bride's father they she he	dance eat go live pay sing wear

1.2 Simple Present: Questions and Answers

Yes/No Questions			Short Answers
Do/Does	Subject	Base Form	
Do	I/you/we/they	sing?	Yes, I **do**. / No, I **don't**.
Does	he/she/it		Yes, he **does**. / No, **he doesn't**.

Wh- Questions				Short Answers
Wh- Word	*Do/Does*	Subject	Base Form	
What	do	I	sing?	Popular songs.
When		you		Every Saturday night.
Why		they		They love music.
Who	does	she	visit?	Her father.
How often		she		Twice a year.
How		he	**celebrate?**	He has a party.

Who or *What* as Subject			Short Answers
Wh- Word	Verb		
Who	**teaches**	this class?	Professor Ortega.
What	**makes**	you happy?	My family.

1. *Yes/No* questions ask for answers of *yes* or *no*.	A: **Do you speak Russian?** B: Yes, I do. / No, I don't.
2. *Wh-* questions ask for specific information. The answer is a person, place, thing, or other piece of information.	A: **Where** does Jeff live? B: In Sydney.
3. *Who* or *What* can be the subject in a *Wh-* question. When *Who* or *What* is the subject, the verb is always in the third person singular form (*-s/-es* form).	A: **Who** teaches math? (*Who* = subject) B: Arlene.
4. **Be careful!** When *Who* or *What* is the subject, do not use *do* or *does* with the main verb.	✓ **Who** teaches this class? ✗ **Who** does teach this class?

6 Complete each question. Use the words in parentheses and the simple present.

1. ___Do all brides wear___ (all brides / wear) white dresses?
2. ______________ (what / people / give) the bride and groom?
3. ______________ (the bride's mother / cut) the wedding cake?
4. ______________ (the bride and groom / have) a party after the ceremony?
5. ___Who does the bride dance___ (who / the bride / dance) with first?
6. ___What the bride and groom___ (what / the bride and groom / do) after the wedding? do after the wedding?
7. ______________ (what / the guests / do) at the wedding?
8. ______________ (who / pay) for the wedding?

7 SPEAK. Work with a partner. Take turns asking and answering the questions from exercise **6**. In your answers, talk about weddings in your own culture or country.

A: *Do all brides wear white dresses?*

B: *No, they don't. Some brides wear red dresses.*

1.3 Frequency Adverbs with the Simple Present

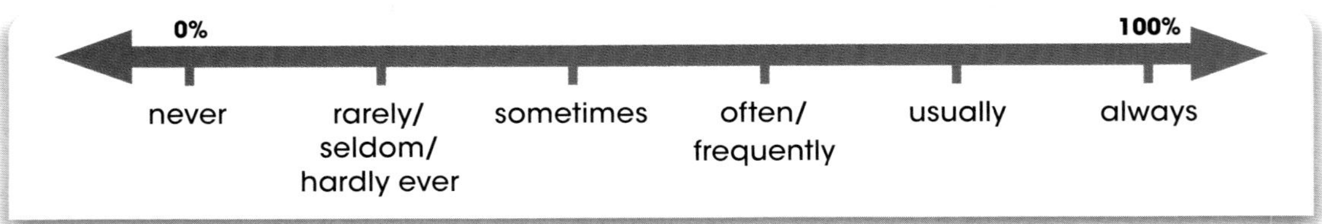

1. Frequency adverbs are often used with the simple present. They tell how often something happens.	I **usually** enjoy parties. I don't **always** remember his birthday. Do you **sometimes** eat at restaurants?
2. Frequency adverbs usually come after the verb *be*. They usually come before other verbs.	I am **sometimes** early for class. Jenny isn't **often** late. Wedding guests are **usually** happy.
3. *Sometimes, usually, frequently,* or *often* can come at the beginning or end of a statement.	Brides wear red dresses **sometimes**. **Usually** Western brides wear white.
4. *Ever* is common in questions about frequency. It means *at any time*. It is not usually used in affirmative statements.	A: Do you **ever** eat at restaurants? B: No, I **never** do. / Yes, I **often** do.

8 Rewrite each statement or question using the adverb in parentheses. Place the adverb in a correct position.

1. (usually) I am with friends on my birthday.

   I am usually with friends on my birthday.

2. (hardly ever) Marco is on time for parties.

   Marco is hardly ever on time for parties.

3. (never) My parents forget my birthday.

   My parents always forget my birthday.

4. (always) Children aren't happy at birthday parties.

   Children never aren't happy at birthday.

5. (often) Does your sister send you photos?

   Does often your sister send you photos?

6. (sometimes) Jackie buys unusual presents for her family.

   Jackie buys sometimes parents for her family?

   Someties

7. (rarely) In the United States, brides wear red dresses.

8. (frequently) I go back to my hometown.

9. (seldom) Carlos talks to his brother on the phone.

10. (ever) Do you visit your cousin in Spain?

PRACTICE

CD1-03

9 Complete the converse

simple present. Then list

Ghana

Valerie: Tell me, Kofi ?

(people / usua

Kofi: Well, I am Asa

(not celebrate) d, we celebrate on the

day of the week For example, I was born

on a Friday, so I ways / wait) until the

first Friday after celebrate.

Valerie: Oh, that's interesting. When (4) ______________ (*krada* / start)?

Kofi: In the morning. For the Asante, a new day (5) ______________ (never / begin) at midnight. The day (6) ______________ (always / start) at sunrise.

Valerie: What (7) ______________ (you / usually / do) to celebrate *krada*?

Kofi: Well, for children, parents (8) ______________ (often / prepare) a special breakfast for *krada*. They (9) ______________ (usually / make) a dish called *oto* from sweet potatoes and eggs. They (10) ______________ (always / fry) the *oto* in palm oil. Later in the day, the child has a party. At the party, children (11) ______________ (usually / eat) meat with rice and a sweet dish called *kelewele*.

10 **SPEAK.** How do people usually celebrate their birthdays in your culture? In your family? Share your answers with a partner.

A: *In my country, we usually cook a big meal for our friends.* B: *Really? That's a lot of work!*

11 Complete the exercises.

A Read the statements. Then add a frequency adverb from the box to make true statements about yourself and your family. You can use some frequency adverbs more than once.

always	ever	hardly ever	never	often	rarely	seldom	sometimes	usually

1. We don't ^usually^ give each other expensive presents.
2. I send my parents a card on their wedding anniversary.
3. We get together as a family.
4. I am late for family parties.
5. My family has big celebrations.
6. My parents are happy to see me.
7. People in my family aren't quiet during meals.
8. We spend weekends together.

B Work with a partner. Share your statements from exercise **A**. Ask and answer questions about your statements.

A: *We don't usually give each other expensive presents.*

B: *Do you ever give each other expensive presents?*

A: *Not often. We usually buy something small or go out for dinner.*

12 **EDIT.** Read the conversation. Find and correct seven more errors with the simple present and frequency adverbs.

Kenji: How often ~~your family does get~~ does your family get together?

Raoul: We get together about two or three times a year, but it's not always easy. My brother lives on the West Coast, and my sister often is away on business trips.

Kenji: So, where you meet when you get together?

Raoul: Well, we go usually to my parents' house. We tries to get home to celebrate their wedding anniversary every year. Sometimes, my brother and I visit each other on our birthdays. Once every two or three years we take a vacation together. I'd like to do it every year, but it cost a lot of money.

Kenji: Have you a good time with your brother and sister?

Raoul: Oh, yes, most of the time. We have sometimes a few arguments, just like any family.

13 LISTEN, WRITE & SPEAK.

A Look at the photos and read the captions. Then work with a partner and answer the questions.

1. Where are the people in each picture?
2. What is the name of each activity?
3. Would you like to do these activities? Why, or why not?

▲ Bungee jumping is a popular vacation activity. Here a woman bungee jumps from a cliff in Ukraine.

▲ A boy jumps from a high tower on Pentecost, Vanuatu. This is called *land diving*. He uses vines as a rope.

CD1-04

B Put the words in the correct order to make questions. Then listen to the radio show and take notes to help you answer each question.

1. the tower / climb / the boys / do / why ____________________

   ____________________ Notes: ____________________

2. the boys / how / jump / do / off the tower ____________________

   ____________________ Notes: ____________________

3. digs / the ground / who / below the tower ____________________

   ____________________ Notes: ____________________

4. do / the boys / get killed / rarely / why ____________________

   ____________________ Notes: ____________________

CD1-04

C Listen to the interview again. In your notebook, write the answers to the questions from exercise **B**. Then work with a partner and compare your answers.

14 APPLY.

APPLY. Work in a small group. How do people in your country celebrate the change from childhood to adulthood? Is there a special ceremony? Discuss your answers.

A: *In my country, your 20th birthday is special. It means you're an adult. We celebrate with a big ceremony.*

B: *Really? Do you wear special clothes?*

A: *Yes. Women usually wear traditional clothes. Men usually wear suits and ties.*

EXPLORE

CD1-05

1 READ the article about Diwali. Notice the words in **bold**.

Diwali

What are these women doing?

These women in India **are getting** ready for *Diwali*. Diwali is an important holiday for Hindus. It is also called the Festival of Lights. Diwali **happens** in late October or early November every year.

What do Hindus do during Diwali?

People **like** to have new clothes for Diwali. The women in the photo **are wearing** new *saris*.[1] They **are lighting** sparklers and **placing** them around their home. They **want** their family to have a successful future. The women **hope** that the sparklers attract Lakshmi, the Hindu goddess of wealth and success. The star-shaped design on the floor is a *rangoli*. It also **helps** to attract the goddess.

Hindus **believe** that Lakshmi **visits** people's homes during Diwali. In the Hindu religion, a visit from Lakshmi is a very good thing. It **means** a happy future for the family.

[1] **sari:** a traditional form of dress for women in India and other south Asian countries

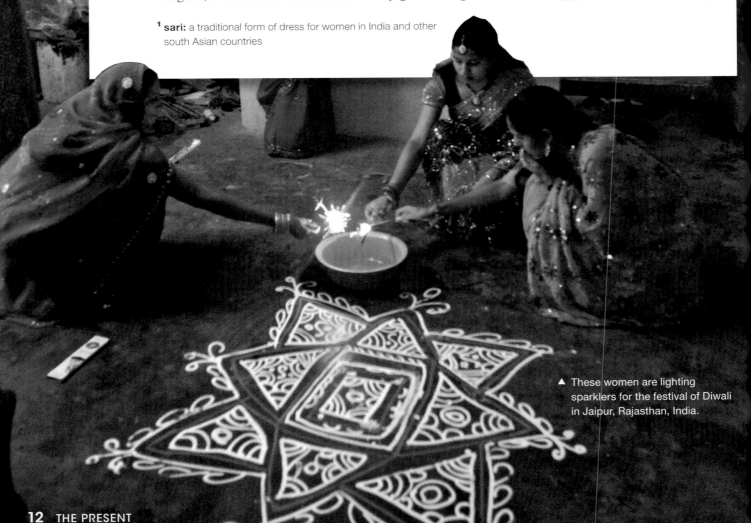

▲ These women are lighting sparklers for the festival of Diwali in Jaipur, Rajasthan, India.

2 CHECK. Read the questions. Then write short answers.

1. What is another name for Diwali? the Festival of Lights
2. When does Diwali take place? ____________
3. What are the women in the photograph wearing? ____________
4. Where is the *rangoli*? ____________
5. Who is Lakshmi? ____________
6. What does a visit from Lakshmi mean? ____________

3 DISCOVER. Complete the exercises to learn about the grammar in this lesson.

A Look at these sentences from the article in exercise **1**. Check (✓) the correct description of each **bold** verb.

	Happening Now	Generally True
1. These women in India **are getting** ready for Diwali.	✓	___
2. People **like** to have new clothes for Diwali.	✓	___
3. The women in the photo **are wearing** new saris.	✓	___
4. They **are lighting** sparklers . . .	✓	___
5. They **want** their family to have a successful future.	___	✓
6. The women **hope** that the sparklers attract Lakshmi . . .	___	✓

B Work with a partner. Compare your answers from exercise **A**. What do you notice about the verb form that describes actions that are happening now?

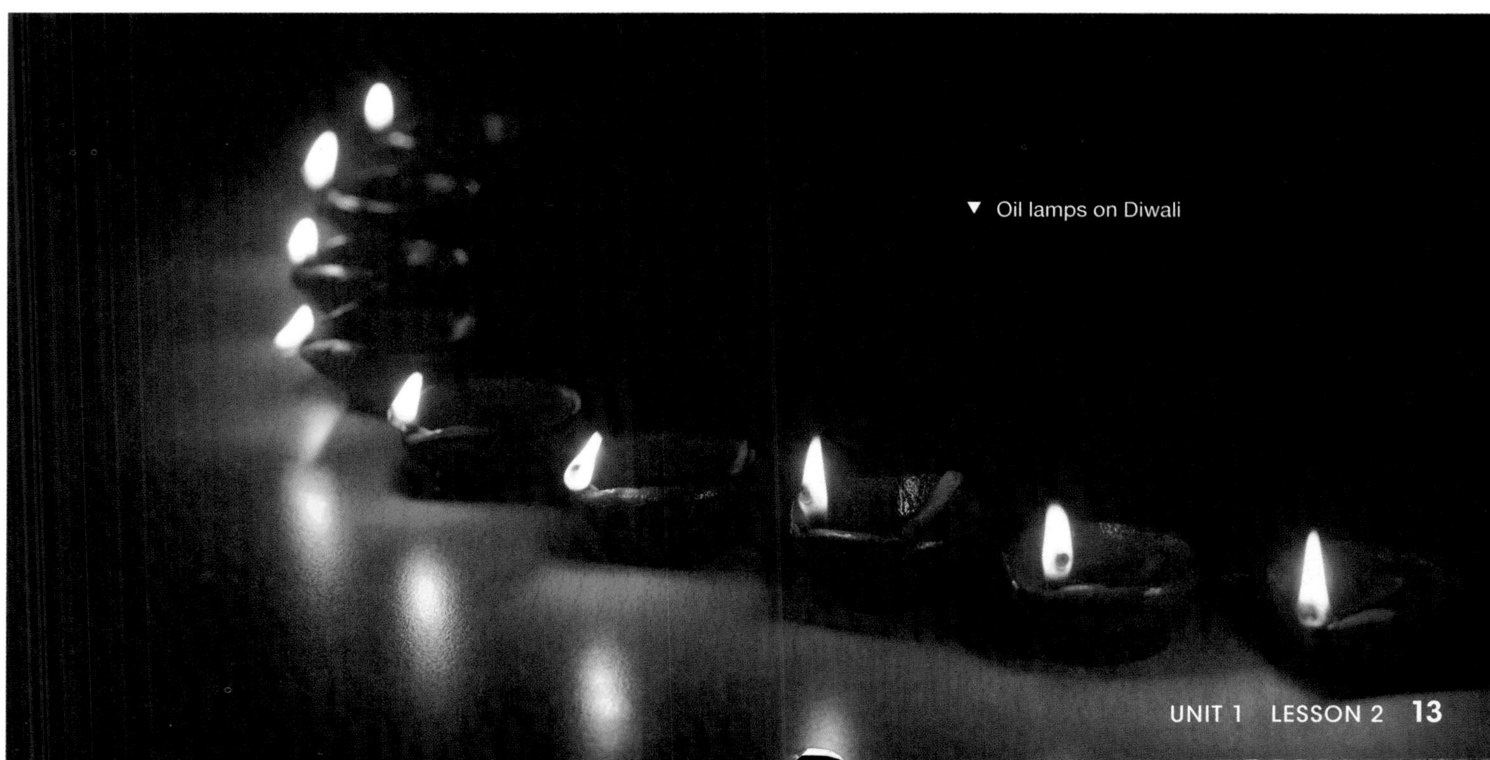

▼ Oil lamps on Diwali

LEARN

1.4 Present Progressive: Affirmative and Negative Statements

Affirmative		
Subject	*Be*	Verb + *-ing*
I	am 'm	studying.
He/She/It	is 's	working.
You/We/They	are 're	eating.

Negative		
Subject	*Be* + *Not*	Verb + *-ing*
I	am not 'm not	studying.
He/She/It	is not isn't / 's not	working.
You/We/They	are not 're not / aren't	eating.

1. Use the present progressive* to talk about: a. actions in progress now, at the moment of speaking b. actions in progress at the present time, but maybe not at the moment of speaking	a. Look! They**'re dancing** in the street. b. My class **is studying** world history this semester.
2. **Remember:** Use the simple present to talk about: a. habits and repeated actions b. facts and things that are generally true c. how often something happens	a. Dave and I often **take** a walk after dinner. b. It **snows** a lot in Finland. c. I **meet** with my boss twice a week.
3. Some adverbs and time expressions commonly used with the present progressive are: *now, at the moment, this year,* and *these days.*	It **is raining** at the moment. Susie **is working** hard these days.

* The *present progressive* is sometimes called the *present continuous.*
See page **A1** for spelling rules for the *-ing* form of verbs.

4 Complete each sentence with the present progressive form of the verb in parentheses.

1. The women are lighting (light) sparklers.
2. They are drawing (draw) pictures on the floor.
3. Usha isn't celebrateing (not / celebrate) the holiday with her family.
4. She is studying (study) in England this year.
5. I'm not prepareing (not prepare) the food for the party.
6. Alberto is helping (help) in the kitchen at the moment.
7. He is washing (wash) the dishes right now.
8. We are getting (get) the house ready for the party.

5 Circle the correct form of the verb to complete each sentence.

1. Thousands of people **attend** / **are attending** the festival this year. The hotels are full!
2. Every November people **celebrate** / **are celebrating** a special holiday in Mexico.
3. My grandmother usually **organizes** / **is organizing** the celebrations in my family.

4. The Chinese New Year **marks** / **is marking** the end of the winter season.

5. Right now I **make** / **am making** a cake for the party.

6. My father **makes** / **is making** beautiful cakes to celebrate special events.

7. We **have** / **are having** a party for my grandparents every summer.

8. Everyone **dances** / **is dancing** right now.

1.5 Present Progressive: Questions and Answers

***Yes/No* Questions**			**Short Answers**
Be	Subject	Verb + *-ing*	
Am	I	helping?	Yes, you **are**. / No, you**'re not**.
Is	he		Yes, he **is**. / No, he**'s not**.
Are	you		Yes, we **are**. / No, we**'re not**.

***Wh-* Questions**				**Answers**
Wh- Word	*Be*	Subject	Verb + *-ing*	
What	am	I	doing?	You**'re studying**.
	is	he		He**'s singing**.
	are	they		They**'re cooking**.
Why	is	she	crying?	She**'s watching** a sad movie.

***Who* or *What* as Subject**				**Short Answers**
Wh- Word	*Be*	Verb + *-ing*		
Who	is	dancing	with Carmen?	Her father.
What		happening?		John's leaving.

1. **Remember:** *Who* or *What* can be the subject in a *Wh-* question. When *Who* or *What* is the subject, the verb is always in the third person singular form (*-s*/*-es* form).

A: **Who's** playing the piano?
B: Marta.

6 Use the words in parentheses to complete the questions or answers. Use the present progressive.

1. A: Hi, Ana. (1) What are you doing (what / you / do)?
   B: I (2) am buying (buy) a plane ticket online.

2. A: (3) Where are living (where / you / live) these days?
   B: I (4) am renting (rent) an apartment near the university.

3. A: (5) Why is your computer making (why / your computer / make) a noise?
   B: (6) It's not working (it / not work) properly.

4. A: (7) Is your phone ringing (your phone / ring)?
   B: Yes, it is. Thanks. My (8) brother is calling (brother / call) me.

7 SPEAK. Work with a partner. Ask and answer the questions in numbers 1 and 2 in exercise **6**. Use your own answers, not the answers in the book.

1.6 Action and Non-Action Verbs

1. Action verbs describe physical or mental actions.	Action: She **studies** hard every night. Non-Action: I **want** to go to the dance.
2. Non-action* verbs do not describe actions. They describe states, conditions, or feelings. Here are some common categories of non-action verbs: a. **Feelings:** *dislike, hate, like, love, miss* b. **Senses:** *feel, hear, see, smell, sound, taste* c. **Possession:** *belong, have, own* d. **Appearance:** *appear, look, seem* e. **Desires:** *hope, need, prefer, want* f. **Mental States:** *believe, think, understand*	 a. I **love** to dance. b. The soup **smells** delicious. c. He doesn't **own** a car. d. Ted **looks** tired today. e. I **want** some coffee. f. She **understands** Japanese.
3. Non-action verbs are not usually used in the progressive.	✓ They **own** a house and an apartment. ✗ They are owning a house and an apartment.
4. It is possible to use the progressive form with some non-action verbs, but their meaning changes. Some common examples are: *have, think, look, smell,* and *taste.*	Non-Action / Action He **has** a headache. / He **is having** lunch. I **think** this book is great. / I **am thinking** of the answer. The food **tastes** good. / She **is tasting** the food.

* *Non-action verbs* are sometimes called *stative verbs.*

8 Complete the conversations with the verbs in parentheses. Use the simple present or the present progressive.

1. **Eric:** (1) ______ you ______ (like) your new home in Italy?
   Jane: Yes, I really (2) ______ (love) it, but I (3) ______ (think) about the United States a lot.
   Eric: What (4) ______ you ______ (miss) most?
   Jane: Oh, family get-togethers, probably.
2. **Sally:** Why is Nikki taking so long at the bakery?
   Christina: She (5) ______ (taste) the different kinds of cakes. She (6) ______ (want) the perfect cake for her wedding.
3. **Mark:** That's a nice camera.
   Tim: Thanks, but it (7) ______ (not / belong) to me. It's my sister's.
   Mark: (8) ______ you ______ (have) your own camera?
   Tim: No, I (9) ______ (not own) a camera.
4. **Maria:** (10) ______ you ______ (have) fun tonight?
   Barbara: Not really, I (11) ______ (have) a headache.

PRACTICE

9 Look at the photos and read the captions. Then complete the conversation with the words in parentheses. Use the simple present or the present progressive form of the verbs.

▲ The New Zealand rugby team does the *haka* before a match.

▲ Maori dancers from New Zealand perform the *haka,* a traditional war dance.

Todd: Hey, Steve, (1) what are you doing (what / you / do)?

Steve: (2) ______________ (I / read) a magazine. Look at this photo of the New Zealand rugby team . . . (3) ______________ (they / look) scary!

Todd: (4) ______________ (what / they / do)?
(5) ______________ (they / dance)?

Steve: (6) ______________ (they / perform) the *haka*. It's a Maori war dance.

Todd: (7) ______________ (they / do) it before every game?

Steve: Yes. (8) ______________ (it / help) them get ready for the game mentally, and (9) ______________ (they / believe) that it frightens the other team.

Todd: Interesting. (10) ______________ (it / work)?

Steve: Maybe in the past, but (11) ______________ (it / never / surprise) anyone now. (12) ______________ (the other team / usually / pay) no attention. But, (13) ______________ (the fans / love) it, and (14) ______________ (the *haka* / always / provide) an opportunity for great photos!

10 WRITE & SPEAK.

A Use the words to make *Yes/No* and *Wh-* questions. Use the simple present or the present progressive.

1. what holidays / you / enjoy What holidays do you enjoy?
2. what / your classmates / do / right now ______________
3. what / you / want / for your birthday ______________

4. you / do / anything interesting / these days Are you doing ?

5. you and your friends / like / soccer Do you and your friends

6. you / often / work / on weekends Do you often work on weekend

7. what / your class / study / this week What do your class study?

8. where / you / usually / have / lunch Where do you Usually have lunch?

B Work with a partner. Ask and answer the questions from exercise **A**.

A: *Which national holidays do you enjoy?* B: *I like Thanksgiving. How about you?*

CD1-06

11 Complete the conversations with the words from the box. Use the simple present or present progressive. Then listen and check your answers.

~~do~~	have	not believe	not look	talk	think
hate	need	not feel	not want	taste	

Conversation 1

Midori: Hi Sally, how (1) ___are___ you ___doing___?

Sally: I'm OK. How about you?

Midori: Great. You know, I usually (2) ___hate___ big crowds, and I (3) ___think___ people are too noisy in big groups. Well, guess what: right now I'm in New York City at the Thanksgiving Day parade!

Sally: You are? I (4) ___believe___ it!

Midori: Yes, I am! And I (5) ___am having___ a wonderful time!

Conversation 2

Angela: Mmm . . . this soup (6) ___taste___ delicious! Do you want some?

Kara: No, thanks.

Angela: Are you sure? It's really good.

Kara: No, thanks. I (7) ___don't feel___ well, and I (8) ___don't want___ you to get sick.

Conversation 3

Mike: Hi, Kemal. Are you OK? You (9) ___don't look___ very happy. What's the matter?

Kemal: Oh, I . . .

Andy: Hey, Mike, do you have a minute? I (10) ___need___ to ask you something.

Mike: Sorry, but Kemal and I (11) ___am talking___ right now. Can I talk to you later?

12 READ & WRITE.

A Read the paragraph. Underline the verbs in the simple present and circle the frequency adverbs.

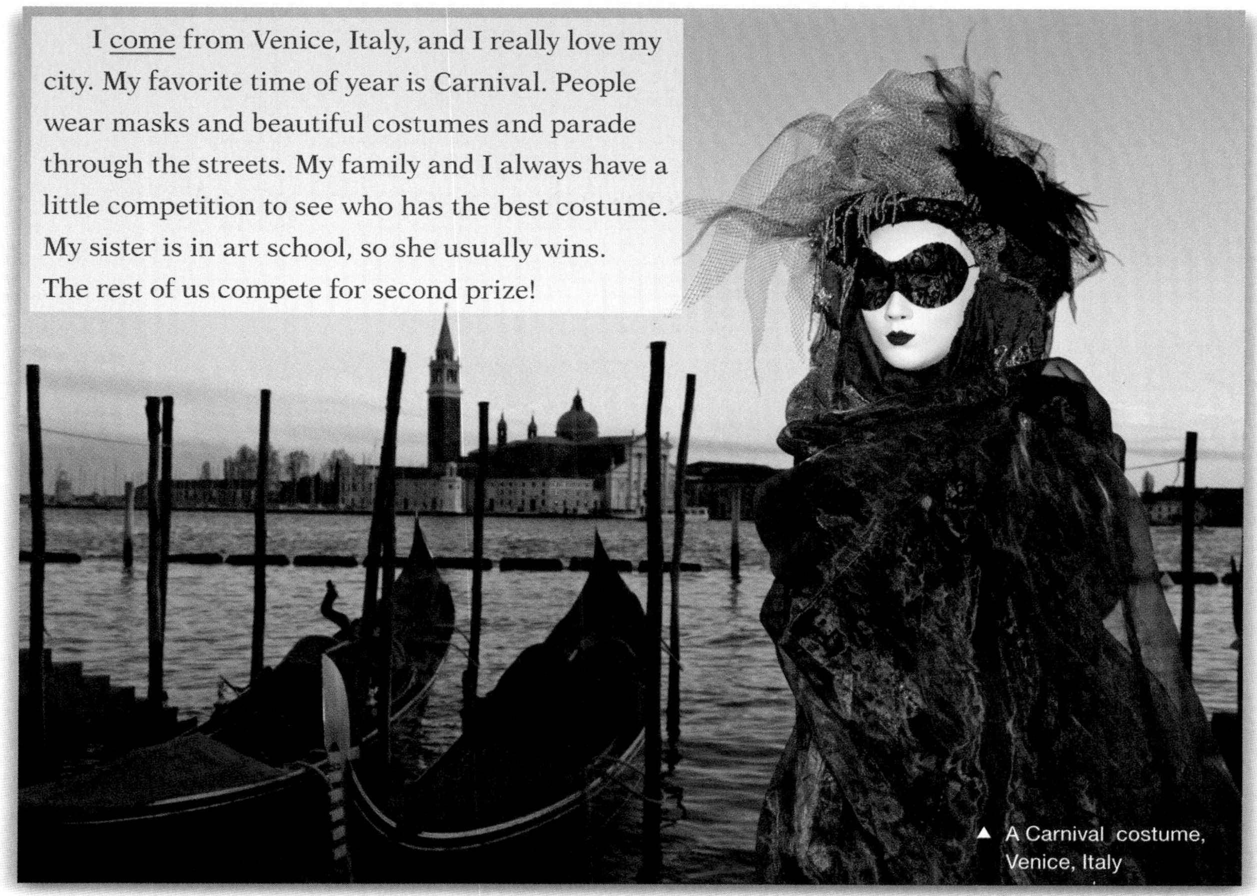

I come from Venice, Italy, and I really love my city. My favorite time of year is Carnival. People wear masks and beautiful costumes and parade through the streets. My family and I always have a little competition to see who has the best costume. My sister is in art school, so she usually wins. The rest of us compete for second prize!

▲ A Carnival costume, Venice, Italy

B In your notebook, write a paragraph of five or six sentences about an event in your country or culture. Use the simple present and frequency adverbs.

13 APPLY.

A Write questions to ask a classmate about what he or she is doing this week, this month, this semester, or this year. Use the present progressive.

Questions	Answers
Where are you living these days?	

B Work with a partner. Take turns asking and answering your questions from exercise **A**. Take notes on your partner's answers in the chart.

C Tell the class about your partner. Use the information from the chart in exercise **A**.

Charts 1.1–1.6

1 Complete the conversation with the words in parentheses. Use the simple present or the present progressive.

Silvana: Hey Christine, it's the 4th of July . . . (1) Why are you sitting (why / you / sit) here in the library?

Christine: I (2) __________ (work). I (3) __________ (have) an important assignment to finish.

Silvana: But Americans (4) __________ (always / celebrate) Independence Day!

Christine: Well, things are different this year. I (5) __________ (usually / visit) my brother and sister, and we (6) __________ (have) a barbecue, but they're not around this year.

Silvana: Oh, (7) __________ (what / they / do) this year?

Christine: Matt (8) __________ (take) a computer course in San Francisco, and my sister Denise (9) __________ (work). She's a doctor.

Silvana: Oh, that's too bad!

Christine: Yeah, and she often (10) __________ (work) on weekends and holidays.

Silvana: Well, listen, I (11) __________ (not do) anything special today. (12) __________ (you / want) to get something to eat later?

Christine: Great idea! I (13) __________ (hear) the new Thai restaurant on Tucker Street is really good. (14) __________ (you / like) Thai food?

Silvana: I (15) __________ (love) Thai food! Give me a call when you are ready.

Charts 1.1, 1.3, 1.4

2 **EDIT.** Read the paragraph about *La Tomatina.* Find and correct five more errors with the simple present, the present progressive, and frequency adverbs.

La Tomatina

In my town, Buñol, Spain, the local people are organizing a festival called *La Tomatina* every year. It always is starting on the last Wednesday in August, and it last for a week. *La Tomatina* is a food fight. Every summer, thousands of local people and visitors gets together to throw tomatoes at each other. Yes, that's right—tomatoes! And I'm not talking about just a few tomatoes. *La Tomatina* is using around a hundred tons of tomatoes every year. These days the festival is becoming so popular that other countries start to organize their own events similar to *La Tomatina*.

▲ A man lies in tomatoes at *La Tomatina* in Sutamarchán, Colombia.

Charts 1.1–1.6

3 LISTEN to an excerpt from a lecture about *La Tomatina*. Write the missing words.

CD1-07

Professor: . . . Now, let's look at the next slide, and you will see what (1) I am talking about. Yes, there we are. Now, look at the young man in this photo. (2) ______________ in tomatoes almost up to his waist. And do you see what's happening . . . ?

Student 1: (3) ______________ more tomatoes at him!

Professor: Yes, Kim, that's right. And he's smiling about it.

Student 1: Are you sure? (4) ______________ he's smiling.

Professor: Hmm . . . well, I guess you're right. But (5) ______________ he is complaining?

Student 1: No, (6) ______________ to get away. He's just waiting for the tomatoes to hit him.

Professor: Yes, that's right. (7) ______________ a good time.

Student 2: So, (8) ______________ us that people actually do this for fun? They get covered in tomatoes! What's the point of that?

Professor: You know, Philip, that's a very good question. We live with so many laws and rules. . . . Sometimes, (9) ______________ to feel that there are no rules. Many ancient celebrations (10) ______________ a time like this. For a few hours or a couple of days, no one (11) ______________ to obey the usual rules. I mean, you can't just go to Buñol and start throwing tomatoes in January, right?

Charts 1.1–1.6

4 SPEAK. Work in a small group. Discuss your answers to these questions.

1. Does *La Tomatina* sound like something you would like to go to? Why, or why not?
2. Tell the other members of your group about a special festival or celebration in your town or city.

▼ *La Tomatina*, Buñol, Spain

Connect the Grammar to Writing

1 READ & NOTICE THE GRAMMAR.

A Does your culture have any traditional sports events? Discuss the event(s) with a partner. Then read the text.

The Kila Raipur Sports Festival

In February, my family and I usually go to the Kila Raipur Sports Festival. Kila Raipur is a town near my home in India. It's January now, and we are planning our trip. We are looking forward to this tradition. Each year, thousands of people attend the festival.

At the festival, people race huge tractors.[1] Men sometimes lift bicycles with their teeth. In this photo, men are racing carts pulled by oxen. This is everyone's favorite event.

[1] **tractor:** a vehicle that a farmer uses to pull machinery

GRAMMAR FOCUS

In the text in exercise **A**, the writer uses the simple present to talk about repeated activities and events and facts.

*In February, my family and I usually **go** to the Kila Raipur Sports Festival.*
*Kila Raipur **is** a town near my home in India.*

*At the festival, people **race** huge tractors. Men sometimes **lift** bicycles with their teeth.*

B Read the text in exercise **A** again. Underline the verbs in the simple present. Circle the frequency adverbs. Then work with a partner and compare your answers.

C Complete the chart with information about the Kila Raipur Sports Festival.

2 BEFORE YOU WRITE.

A Complete the chart with information about a traditional sports event in your culture. Use the chart from exercise **1C** as a model.

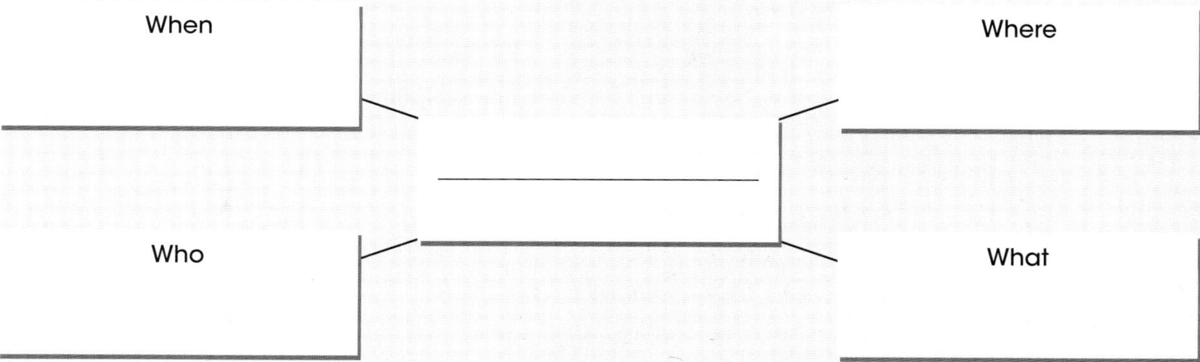

B Look at the information in your chart from exercise **A**. Place a *1* next to information that you want to include in your first paragraph. Place a *2* next to information that you want to include in your second paragraph.

3 WRITE two paragraphs about a traditional sports event in your culture. Use the information from your chart in exercise **2A** and the text in exercise **1A** to help you.

WRITING FOCUS Capitalizing Proper Nouns

Proper nouns are the names of specific people, places, and things. Some examples of proper nouns are the names of:

- streets, cities, states, countries, and continents
- days of the week, months, and holidays
- people and special events

*In **February**, my family and I usually go to the **Kila Raipur Sports Festival**. **Kila Raipur** is a town near my home in **India**.*

4 SELF ASSESS. Read your paragraphs and underline the simple present and circle the frequency adverbs. Then use the checklist to assess your work.

- ☐ I used the simple present for facts. [1.1]
- ☐ I used the simple present for repeated actions and events. [1.1]
- ☐ I put the frequency adverbs in the correct place. [1.3]
- ☐ I capitalized proper nouns. [WRITING FOCUS]

UNIT 2 Survival

The Past

▼ The Parthenon, Acropolis, Athens, Greece

EXPLORE

CD1-08

1 READ the article about a project to protect lions in Kenya. Notice the words in **bold**.

The Lion Guardians Project, Kenya

Cattle[1] are basic to the lives of the Maasai people of Kenya. In fact, the Maasai have a saying, "Without the land and the cattle, there are no Maasai people." In 2006, Maasai cattle herders[2] in Kenya **had** a problem. Lions regularly **killed** their cows. The herders **sent** warriors[3] to hunt and kill the lions. Many lions **died**. The Maasai **were** a big threat to the survival of lions in Kenya.

A local organization, Living with Lions, **wanted** to save lions. They **helped** train Maasai warriors to protect lions, not kill them. The warriors **learned** to track the lions with modern technology. They **warned** herders before the lions **got** near their cows. The warriors **didn't kill** any more lions. Instead, they **became** Lion Guardians.[4]

The Guardians **persuaded** the herders not to hunt the lions. They **gave** each lion a Maasai name, and **taught** the herders and villagers about them. Local people **began** to see the lions as individuals. Now, there are more than 30 Lion Guardians. Because of the Guardians' work, the number of lions that die in their part of Kenya is falling fast.

▼ A lion in the Maasai Mara Game Reserve, Kenya

[1] **cattle:** cows and bulls
[2] **herder:** a person who cares for a large group of one kind of animal
[3] **warrior:** a fighter or soldier
[4] **guardian:** a person who protects other people or property

2 CHECK. Read the statements. Circle **T** for *true* or **F** for *false*.

1. Cattle are not important to the Maasai people. **T** **F**
2. The Living with Lions organization wanted to protect the lions. **T** **F**
3. Cattle herders educated Maasai warriors about lions. **T** **F**
4. Lion Guardians use technology to protect cattle. **T** **F**
5. Local people learned more about lions from the Lion Guardians. **T** **F**

3 DISCOVER. Complete the exercises to learn about the grammar in this lesson.

A Find the simple past form of these verbs in the article from exercise **1**. Then write them in the charts.

Group A		Group B	
Present	Simple Past	Present	Simple Past
kill	killed	have	had
die	died	send	sent
want	wanted	get	got
learn	learned	become	became
persuade	persuaded	teach	taught

B Look at the simple past forms of the verbs in Group A. Compare them with the verbs in Group B. How are they different? Discuss your answer with your classmates and teacher.

◀ A Maasai man uses a cell phone to help guard his cattle.

LEARN

2.1 Simple Past: Affirmative and Negative Statements

Affirmative		
Subject	Verb	
I/He/She	**helped**	the animals.
You/We/They	**went**	to Africa.

Negative			
Subject	*Did Not/ Didn't*	Base Form	
I/He/She	**did not**	**help**	them.
You/We/They	**didn't**	**go**	to China.

1. Use the simple past for: a. a completed action or event b. a regular or repeated action or event in the past c. past states or feelings	a. She **called** me yesterday. b. I **worked** every day last week. c. He **felt sick** this morning.
2. To form the simple past, add *-ed* or *-d* to the base form of most regular verbs.[1]	play → **played** dance → **danced**
3. **Be careful!** Many common verbs have irregular past forms.[2]	eat → **ate** make → **made** go → **went** see → **saw**
4. The simple past forms of *be* are *was* and *were*. Do not use *did not* or *didn't* with *was* and *were* in the negative.	It **was** warm. It **wasn't** cold. They **were** at work. They **weren't** at home. ✓ I **wasn't** late for class yesterday. ✗ I didn't was late for class yesterday.

[1]See page **A2** for spelling rules for the simple past.
[2]See page **A4** for a list of irregular verbs.

4 Complete each sentence with the simple past form of the verb(s) in parentheses.

1. Herders in Kenya weren't (not be) able to protect their cattle.
2. For years, lions killed (kill) many cows in Kenya.
3. The herders sent (send) warriors to hunt the lions.
4. Living with Lions started (start) a new program in 2007.
5. At first, some Maasai weren't (not be) happy about the program.
6. The organization gave (give) every Guardian a cell phone.
7. When a Lion Guardian saw (see) a lion nearby, he called (call) his neighbor.
8. The Lion Guardians project didn't change (not change) the situation in Kenya immediately. It took (take) time.
9. Scientists studied (study) the lion population.
10. The Lion Guardians didn't save (not save) all the lions.

2.2 Simple Past: Questions and Answers

Yes/No Questions			Short Answers
Did	Subject	Base Form	
Did	I/he/she/it	help?	**Yes**, she **did**. / **No**, she **didn't**.
	we/you/they		**Yes**, they **did**. / **No**, they **didn't**.

Wh- Questions				Short Answers
Wh- Word	*Did*	Subject	Base Form	
When		you	**call**?	This morning.
Why	**did**	she	**leave**?	Because she had a meeting.
Who(m)		they	**see**?	Nick and Sarah.

Who or *What* as Subject		Short Answers
Wh- Word	Verb	
Who	**called**?	My sister.
What	**happened**?	I missed the train.

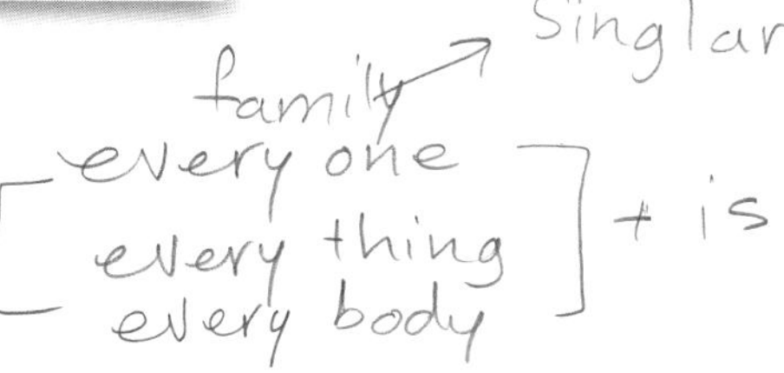

1. *Whom* is sometimes used as the object in very formal speaking or writing.	**Whom** did you ask?
2. **Remember:** *Who* or *What* can take the place of the subject in a *Wh-* question. When *Who* or *What* is the subject, do not use *did*.	✓ **Who** called? ✗ Who did call?

5 Complete the short conversations with the words in parentheses. Write simple past questions and then write the answers.

1. A: Did your phone ring (your phone / ring) just now?
   B: Yes, it did.
2. A: Did your parents give (your parents / give) you any money last month?
   B: No, they didn't.
3. A: Did the teacher sent (the teacher / send) you an e-mail?
   B: No, he didn't.
4. A: Did your friend pay (your friend / pay) for your lunch yesterday?
   B: Yes, he did.
5. A: Did you do anything fun (you / do) anything fun last night?
   B: No, I didn't.
6. A: Did I disturb you? (I / disturb) you?
   B: No, you didn't.

REAL ENGLISH

Time expressions such as *last night, last week, six months ago,* or *in 2011* are often used with the simple past.

I saw Kim ***two days ago.***
She swam every day ***last year.***

7. A: Did it rain (it / rain) yesterday?

   B: Yes, it did.

8. A: Did we have (we / have) homework last night?

   B: Yes, we did.

6 **SPEAK.** Work with a partner. Take turns asking and answering the questions from exercise **5**. Use your own answers, not the answers in the book.

7 Complete the conversations. Use the words in parentheses to write simple past questions.

1. A: Why did you go (you / go) to Kenya?

   B: Because we wanted to see the wildlife there.

2. A. How often did you see (you / see) lions when you were in Kenya?

   B: Almost every day.

3. A: Who the camera belonged to (the camera / belong to)?

   B: It belonged to our guide. → rule

4. A. Did Katye write (Katya / write) in her journal last night?

   B: Yes, she did.

5. A. Who gave (give) the presentation yesterday?

   B: Sheila.

6. A. When did the plane arrive (the plane / arrive)?

   B: A few minutes ago.

PRACTICE

8 Complete the conversation with the words in parentheses. Use the simple past.

Amy: (1) Did you read (you / read) Jinny's e-mail about the whale rescue?

Josh: No, I didn't. (2) What did she say (what / she / say)?

Amy: Well, the whale (3) came (come) too close to the shore, and some fishermen (4) found (find) it in their net.

Josh: That's terrible! (5) Did it survive (it / survive)?

Amy: Yeah, it did, but according to Jinny, the rescue (6) took (take) about an hour.

Josh: So, (7) Did she take (she / take) any photos of it?

Amy: Yes, (8) She took (she / take) a lot. (9) She sent (she / send) a few of them with her e-mail. They're amazing!

▲ Emperor penguins crowd together to keep warm.

9 LISTEN & WRITE.

CD1-09

A Listen to an interview with a nature filmmaker. Then complete the questions from the interview with the verbs in parentheses. Use the simple past.

1. How long ___did it take___ (it / take) to make your last nature film?
2. Why ___did you choose___ (you / choose) Antarctica?
3. So, what ___did you see___ (you / see)?
4. Why ___did they walk___ (they / walk) so far?
5. When ___did the females return___ (the females / return)?

CD1-09

B Listen again and check your answers.

C Read the summary of the last part of the interview. Then complete the paragraph with the verbs in the box. Use the simple past.

begin	~~climb~~	come	crowd	fall	keep	lay	return	survive	walk

The emperor penguins (1) ___climbed___ onto the sea ice and (2) ________ 50 miles to mainland Antarctica. The females each (3) ________ one egg and (4) ________ to the sea. The males (5) ________ the eggs safe through the terrible winter. They (6) ________ together to keep warm. The temperature (7) ________ to −40 degrees Fahrenheit, but the males (8) ________. In the spring, the females (9) ________ back. Then the sea ice (10) ________ to melt.

CD1-09

D Work with a partner. Compare your answers from exercise **C**. Then listen again and check your answers.

▸ A giant panda bear eating bamboo

10 EDIT. Read the conversation. Find and correct seven more errors with the simple past.

Rolf: Hi, Jun. Did you finish~~ed~~ your assignment about animal survival yesterday?

Jun: Hi, Rolf. Yes, I did. I write about giant pandas in China.

Rolf: That's an interesting choice. How did it go?

Jun: Oh, it didn't went very well.

Rolf: What did go wrong?

Jun: Well, I did a lot of research, but I didn't found much new information. Everyone else's assignments were at least five pages, but my assignment was only two pages.

Rolf: What Professor Blake said?

Jun: She didn't say anything—she just look at me.

Rolf: Well, don't worry too much. I gave her the shortest assignment last week and got the highest grade in the class. She sayed it was excellent!

11 APPLY.

A Write interview questions to ask a classmate about a recent project or assignment. Use the words in the box to help you.

Did you . . .?	What did you . . .?	Where did you . . .?	Who did you . . .?
When did you . . .?	Why did you . . .?	How did you . . .?	

B Work with a partner. Ask and answer your questions from exercise **A**. Take notes on your partner's answers in your notebook.

A: *What did you write about?* B: *I wrote about sports in schools.*

C Write a paragraph of four or five sentences about your partner's assignment or project.

Alain wrote a paper about sports in schools. He did a lot of research. He asked all his friends for their opinions. He also interviewed the football and baseball coaches.

EXPLORE

CD1-10

1 **READ** a radio interview with a woman who works to help Maya languages survive in Guatemala. Notice the words in **bold**.

Community Radio in Guatemala

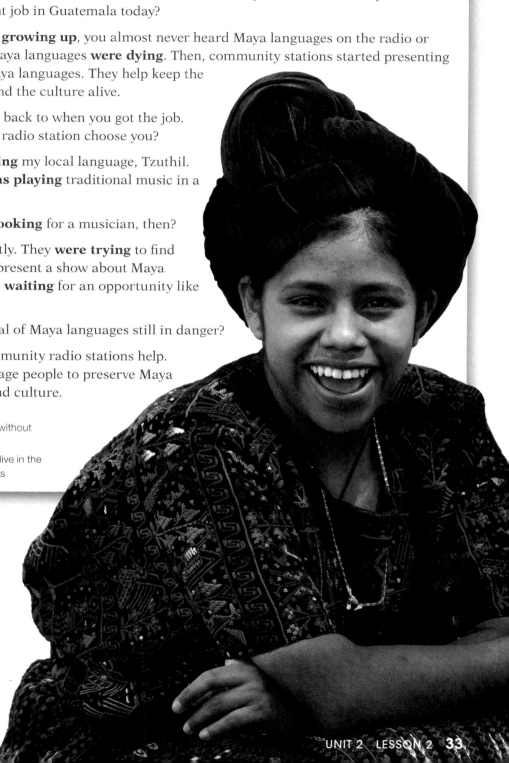

Interviewer: So, Angelica, you work as a volunteer[1] at a community[2] radio station. Why is that an important job in Guatemala today?

Angelica: When I **was growing up**, you almost never heard Maya languages on the radio or TV. Some Maya languages **were dying**. Then, community stations started presenting shows in Maya languages. They help keep the languages and the culture alive.

Interviewer: Now, let's go back to when you got the job. Why did the radio station choose you?

Angelica: I **was teaching** my local language, Tzuthil. Oh, and I **was playing** traditional music in a band.

Interviewer: **Were they looking** for a musician, then?

Angelica: No, not exactly. They **were trying** to find someone to present a show about Maya music. I **was waiting** for an opportunity like that.

Interviewer: Is the survival of Maya languages still in danger?

Angelica: Yes, but community radio stations help. They encourage people to preserve Maya languages and culture.

[1] **volunteer:** a person who does work without being paid for it

[2] **community:** a group of people who live in the same area and have common interests

▶ The Maya have lived in Guatemala for thousands of years.

2 CHECK. Choose the correct answer for each question.

1. Why is community radio important in Guatemala?
   a. It provides jobs for people.
   b. It helps the Maya culture survive.
   c. It plays a lot of music.

2. What was Angelica doing when she got her job on the radio?
   a. studying her local language
   b. traveling around Guatemala
   c. playing traditional music

3. Who was the radio station looking for?
   a. a presenter
   b. a musician
   c. a teacher

4. What was happening to some Maya languages before community radio?
   a. They were growing.
   b. They were changing.
   c. They were dying.

3 DISCOVER. Complete the exercises to learn about the grammar in this lesson.

A Read the pairs of sentences about the interview from exercise **1** and notice the verbs in **bold**. Choose the sentence in each pair that describes an action that was in progress at a certain time in the past.

1. a. The radio station **chose** Angelica.
   b. Angelica **was teaching** Tzuthil in the evenings.
2. a. The radio station **was looking** for a new presenter.
   b. They **decided** to speak to Angelica.
3. a. Several Maya languages **were dying**.
   b. Community radio stations **started** to present shows in Maya languages.

B Work with a partner. Compare your answers from exercise **A**. Which verb form is used to describe actions that were in progress at a certain time in the past?

◄ Two Guatemalan musicians sit with their instruments.

LEARN

2.3 Past Progressive: Affirmative and Negative Statements

Affirmative		
Subject	*Was/ Were*	Verb + *-ing*
I/He/She/It	was	working.
You/We/They	were	

Negative		
Subject	*Was Not/ Were Not*	Verb + *-ing*
I/He/She/It	was not wasn't	sleeping.
You/We/They	were not weren't	

1. Use the past progressive to talk about an action that was in progress at a certain time in the past.	were studying — 9:00 — now They **were studying** at 9:00 last night.
2. **Remember:** Use the simple past for completed or repeated past actions, events, states, and feelings.	Yesterday I **rode** my bike to work. She **swam** every day last week. He **didn't like** the movie.
3. **Remember:** *Non-action* verbs are not usually used with the progressive.	✓ I **saw** an accident last night. ✗ I was seeing an accident last night.

See page **A1** for spelling rules for the *-ing* form of verbs.

4 Complete each sentence with the past progressive form of the verb(s) in parentheses.

1. Angelica ___was teaching___ (teach) her local language in the evenings.
2. At 6:00 p.m. many people in town ___Were listening___ (listen) to Angelica's show.
3. The radio ___was playing___ (play) loud dance music last night.
4. We ___were talking___ (talk) to Carlos, but he ___wasn't listening___ (not listen) to us.
5. Pedro ___was looking___ (look) for a job at a radio station, but he didn't find one.
6. Tom and Karen ___were living___ (live) in Guatemala last year.
7. The people next to us ___Were speaking___ (speak) Spanish. I think they were Mexican.
8. Steve ___was sitting___ (sit) in the library, but he ___wasn't studying___ (not study). He ___was reading___ (read) a magazine.

REAL ENGLISH

The past progressive is often used to describe a scene in the past.

The café was full. A band ***was playing****, and people* ***were talking*** *loudly. Everyone* ***was enjoying*** *the evening.*

It doesn't bother me!

5 WRITE & SPEAK. Complete the sentences. Use the past progressive. Make two of your sentences negative. Then share your sentences with a partner.

1. Last night at 9:00, I was having dinner with my friends.
2. At 5:00 this morning I was studying for Our. writing class.
3. Last August, She was reading.
4. On Sunday morning he was drivg to Detroit.
5. Two years ago I was sitting in my country.

2.4 Past Progressive: Questions and Answers

Yes/No Questions			
Was/ Were	Subject	Verb + *-ing*	
Was	I/he/she	**listening**	to music?
Were	you/we/they	**eating**	dinner?

Short Answers
Yes, she **was**. / **No**, she **wasn't**.
Yes, they **were**. / **No**, they **weren't**.

Wh- Questions				
Wh- Word	*Was/ Were*	Subject	Verb + *-ing*	
What	**was**	he	**doing**	at 3:00?
Where	**were**	you	**studying**	last night?

Short Answers
He was working.
At the library.

Who or *What* as Subject			
Wh- Word	*Was*	Verb + *-ing*	
Who	**was**	**singing**	last night?
What	**was**	**making**	that noise?

Short Answers
Rita.
My car.

Remember: *Who* or *What* can take the place of the subject in a *Wh-* question.

A: **Who** was playing that loud music last night?
B: Alex and Rui.

6 Use the words in parentheses to complete the questions and answers. Use the past progressive.

1. A: What was Berta doing (Berta / do) in the evenings?
   B: She was teaching (she / teach).
2. A: Were they speaking (they / speak) Spanish?
   B: No, they weren't.
3. A: Were you waiting (you / wait) for me?
   B: Yes, I was.
4. A: Where you going (you / go) after class yesterday?
   B: I was going (I / go) home.

5. A: Who ______________ (Jane / talk) to?
   B: ______________ (she / talk) to her math teacher.
6. A: Why ______________ (those people / cheer)?
   B: Because ______________ (their team / play) really well.
7. A: What ______________ (you / do) at 8:00 last night?
   B: ______________ (I / cook) dinner.
8. A: ______________ (it / snow) last night?
   B: No, ______________.

7 **SPEAK.** Work with a partner. Take turns asking and answering questions 4, 7, and 8 from exercise **6**. Use your own answers, not the answers from the book.

A: *Where were you going after class yesterday?* B: *I was going to the gym.*

PRACTICE

8 Circle the correct verb forms to complete each situation.

1. We (1) **were listening** / **listened** to a great band last night. They (2) **were playing** / **played** three songs, and then they (3) **were stopping** / **stopped**. We (4) **were wanting** / **wanted** them to play more songs, but they didn't. We (5) **were leaving** / **left** and (6) **were asking** / **asked** for our money back.
2. Lily's watch (7) **was breaking** / **broke** yesterday morning. It (8) **was falling** / **fell** off her wrist on her way to work. She (9) **was walking** / **walked** out of the subway station at the time, and someone (10) **was stepping** / **stepped** on it. Last night after work, she (11) **was buying** / **bought** a new one.
3. I (12) **was sitting** / **sat** at the student center yesterday afternoon. Several students (13) **were studying** / **studied**. Others (14) **were using** / **used** their phones. Then I (15) **was seeing** / **saw** my friend, Phil. He (16) **was eating** / **ate** lunch alone, so (17) I **was going** / **went** over and (18) **was sitting** / **sat** with him.

9 Complete each sentence with the past progressive or the simple past form of a verb from the box.

arrive	die	open	own	see	sleep	think	walk

1. The language ______________. Only a few people spoke it.
2. I saw street musicians when I ______________ home last night.
3. Debbie ______________ a nice car, but she didn't drive it much.

4. I'm surprised Kumiko is here today. I ____________ she was on vacation.

5. Marcia ____________ to the meeting 15 minutes late. Her boss was very angry.

6. I ____________ Andy yesterday. He was talking to some friends.

7. My sister called me at midnight last night. I ____________, and she woke me up.

8. The professor ____________ the door and left the room.

10 EDIT. Read the information about Dr. Gregory Anderson's work in Siberia. Find and correct five more errors with the simple past and the past progressive.

▲ Dr. Anderson in Siberia

Dr. Anderson and his team made some interesting discoveries during a trip to Siberia in Russia. They were studying Xyzyl (*hizzle*), a local language there. They ~~were visiting~~ visited five villages during their trip, and they found that 50 to 60 people in those communities spoke Xyzyl in their daily lives. In one village, they were talking to an eleven-year-old girl called Kristina. She was knowing how to speak Xyzyl. Her grandmother was teaching her. Kristina was the youngest Xyzyl speaker in the village. Most of the other Xyzyl speakers got old. Many of them were 60 years old or older. It was clear that the Xyzyl language died. Dr. Anderson and his team studied the language, and they were making recordings to help it survive.

11 APPLY.

A Work with a partner. Write interview questions for Dr. Anderson. Use the information from exercise **10** and the words below to help you. Use the simple past or the past progressive.

1. where / your team go Where did your team go?
2. how many villages / you / visit ____________
3. who / you / talk to in the village ____________
4. what / you / do in the village ____________
5. your idea: ____________

B Role-play a radio interview with Dr. Anderson. Partner A is the interviewer. Partner B is Dr. Anderson. Use your questions from exercise **A**, the information from exercise **10**, and your imagination.

A: *So, tell us about your trip, Dr. Anderson. Where did your team go?*

B: *We went to Siberia.*

EXPLORE

CD1-11

1 READ the article about Jimmy Chin, a mountain climber and photographer. Notice the words in **bold**.

Surviving an Avalanche

▲ Jimmy Chin has climbed up and skied down Mount Everest, the world's highest mountain.

Jimmy Chin is one of the few people to survive a Class 4 avalanche—an avalanche big enough to destroy buildings. In 2011, **while he was skiing in the Teton Mountains**, an avalanche started behind him. Chin was going down the mountain **when, in his own words, "the whole mountainside came down."**

The avalanche buried Chin under tons of snow and carried him downhill. Halfway down, the rolling snow threw him to the surface. However, Chin was not safe. **When he looked up**, trees were snapping all around him. The snow was still moving fast. Soon the avalanche buried him again.

"I knew I was going to the bottom of the valley," he remembers. Amazingly,[1] **when the avalanche reached the bottom of the mountain,** Chin was pushed to the surface! He was alive and on top of the snow **when his very surprised friends reached the bottom of the valley**.

After this experience, Chin took a month off from work. "It's important to do what's meaningful to you," he says. "You don't want to take your time for granted."[2]

[1] **amazingly:** (very) surprisingly
[2] **take something for granted:** not be grateful enough for something

▼ An avalanche carries hundreds of tons of snow down a mountain.

2 CHECK. Read the statements. Circle **T** for *true* or **F** for *false*. Then correct the false statements to make them true.

1. A Class 1 avalanche can destroy buildings. **T** **F**
2. Jimmy Chin was skiing alone in the Tetons. **T** **F**
3. The avalanche buried Chin at first. **T** **F**
4. Chin's friends had to dig him out of the snow. **T** **F**
5. Chin decided to take a break after this experience. **T** **F**

3 DISCOVER. Complete the exercises to learn about the grammar in this lesson.

A Look at the two underlined events in each sentence from the article in exercise **1**. Write ***1*** above the event that started first.

1. In 2011, while he was skiing in the Teton Mountains, an avalanche started behind him.
2. When he looked up, trees were snapping all around him.

B Circle the correct answer to complete each statement.

1. The **simple past** / **past progressive** form is used for the event that starts first.
2. The **simple past** / **past progressive** form is used for the event that interrupted another event.

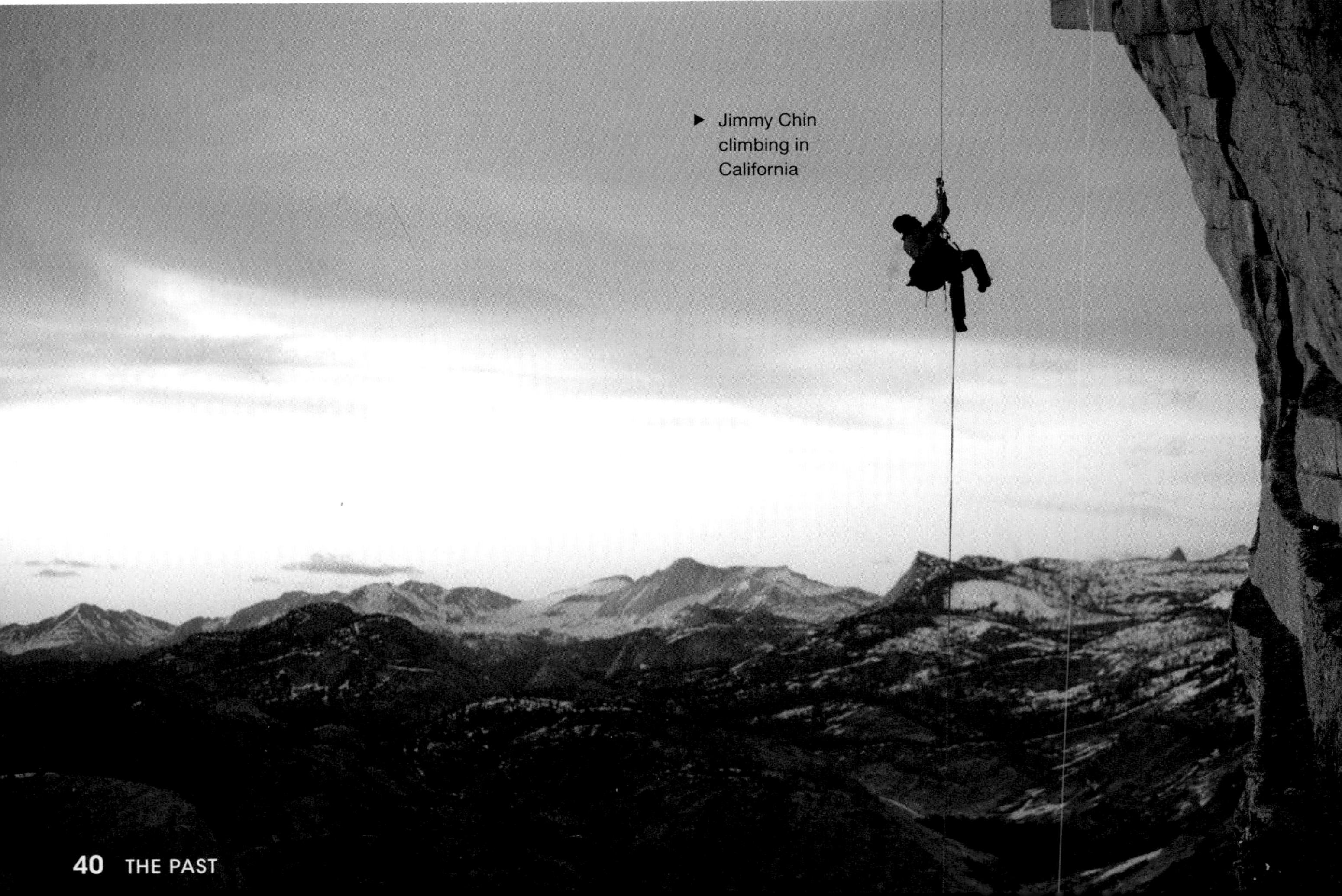

▶ Jimmy Chin climbing in California

LEARN

2.5 Past Time Clauses with *When* and *While*

When	*While*
The storm began **when I was driving home**. (Main Clause / Past Time Clause)	The storm began **while we were walking home**. (Main Clause / Past Time Clause)
When I was driving home, the storm began. (Past Time Clause / Main Clause)	**While we were walking home**, the storm began. (Past Time Clause / Main Clause)
I was sleeping **when you texted me**. (Main Clause / Past Time Clause)	You texted me **while I was sleeping**. (Main Clause / Past Time Clause)

1. A clause is a group of words with a subject and a verb. A main clause can stand alone as a complete sentence.	Elena called last night **while I was cooking dinner**. (Main Clause / Past Time Clause)
2. A past time clause tells when an action or event happened. A past time clause can come before or after the main clause.	**When it started to snow,** I was walking home. It started to snow **while I was walking home.**
3. Use *while* or *when* + the past progressive to show that one action was in progress when another action happened.	I broke my leg **when I was skiing.** (Second Action / Action in Progress) Iris called **while I was cooking dinner**. (Second Action / First Action)
4. Use *when* + the simple past for an action or event that happened at a specific point in the past.	I was painting the living room **when I fell off the ladder**. (Action in Progress / Action at a Point in the Past)
5. Use a comma when the time clause comes at the beginning of a sentence.	**When we were taking the exam,** the lights went out. The lights went out **when we were taking the exam.**

4 Circle the correct form of the verb(s) to complete each sentence.

1. Jimmy Chin **skied** / **was skiing** when the avalanche **began** / **was beginning**.
2. When Chin's friends **reached** / **were reaching** him, he **lay** / **was lying** on top of the snow.
3. Terry **lost** / **was losing** his watch when he **swam** / **was swimming** in the ocean.
4. Mark and Dan's boat **sank** / **was sinking** while they **fished** / **were fishing**.
5. I **cut** / **was cutting** my finger when I **cooked** / **was cooking** dinner.
6. While Jean **shopped** / **was shopping**, the fire alarm **went off** / **was going off** in the store.
7. Carla **found** / **was finding** fifty dollars when she **walked** / **was walking** home yesterday.
8. Andre **prepared** / **was preparing** for the party when he suddenly **felt** / **was feeling** sick.
9. My pencil **broke** / **was breaking** while I **took** / **was taking** the exam.
10. Padma **heard** / **was hearing** a strange noise when she **hiked** / **was hiking** in the woods yesterday afternoon.

2.6 Past Time Clauses with *When*: Events in Sequence

1. When two actions happened one after the other, use the simple past in the past time clause and the main clause. Use *when* to introduce the past time clause.	When her phone **rang**, she **answered** it. (Past Time Clause: When her phone rang) (Main Clause: she answered it)
2. The past time clause can come first or second in the sentence. The action or event in the past time clause happened first.	**When I got home,** I took a shower. (First Event: I got home) (Second Event: I took a shower) I took a shower **when I got home.** (Second Event: I took a shower) (First Event: I got home)
3. **Remember:** Use a comma when the past time clause comes first in the sentence.	**When Joe saw the accident,** he called the police.

5 Read each sentence. Which action or event happened first? Which action or event happened second? Write ***1*** for *first* and ***2*** for *second* below each action. Add a comma if necessary.

1. When the storm ended, the workers began to clean up.
   (1) (2)
2. When Tuan got out of the hospital he made plans for a vacation.
   (1) (2)
3. We looked out the window when we heard the noise.
   (2) (1)
4. When she saw the fire in her kitchen Michelle screamed for help.
   (1) (2)
5. My son called me when his plane landed.
   (2) (1)
6. The music started when the bride and groom walked into the room.
   (2) (1)
7. When the phone rang Isabelle turned the TV off.
   (1) (2)
8. I called my parents when I received my exam results.
   (2) (1)

6 Complete each sentence with the correct form of the verb in parentheses.

1. Eric finished his assignment when he ___got___ (get) home.
2. When Vicky ___put___ (put) her bag on the floor, a thief stole it.
3. When Max's car broke down, he ___was walking___ (walk) to the nearest gas station.
4. My sister laughed when I ___was telling___ (tell) her the joke.
5. Juanita smiled when she ___was hearing___ (hear) the good news.

6. We bought ________ (buy) our tickets when we got to the station.

7. Sylvie closed the window when it was starting (start) to rain.

8. I lit some candles when the electricity ________ (go) out.

7 SPEAK. Work with a partner. Complete the sentences.

When I woke up this morning . . . *When I woke up this morning, I called my parents.*

When I got to class . . .

When I finished my homework . . .

PRACTICE

8 Look at the time line about a mine accident in Chile. Then complete each sentence with the simple past or past progressive form of a verb from the box.

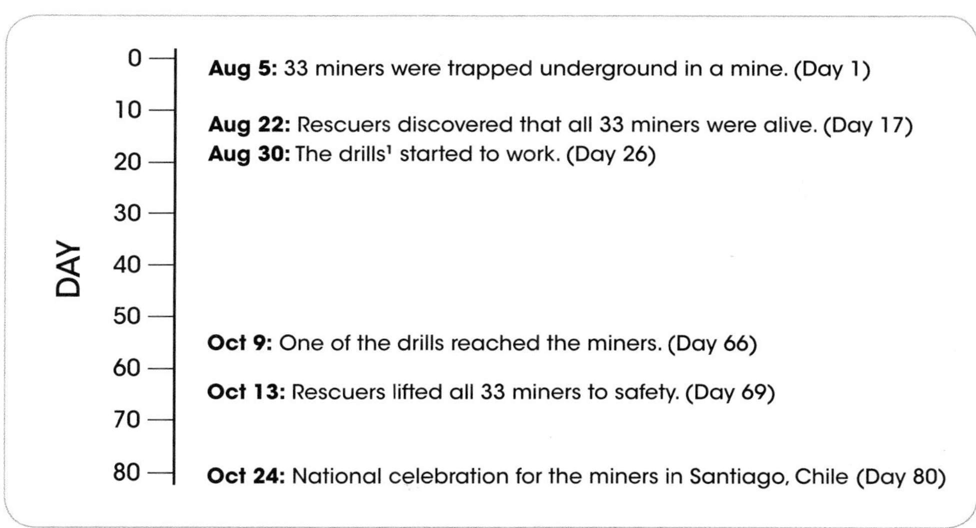

DAY
0
10
20
30
40
50
60
70
80
Aug 5: 33 miners were trapped underground in a mine. (Day 1)
Aug 22: Rescuers discovered that all 33 miners were alive. (Day 17)
Aug 30: The drills[1] started to work. (Day 26)
Oct 9: One of the drills reached the miners. (Day 66)
Oct 13: Rescuers lifted all 33 miners to safety. (Day 69)
Oct 24: National celebration for the miners in Santiago, Chile (Day 80)

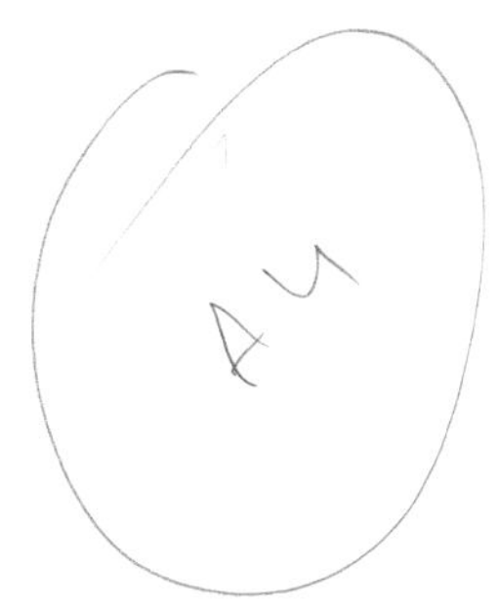

[1]**drill:** a machine that makes a round hole

arrive	attach	begin	complete	~~fall~~	read	wait	watch

1. On August 5, 2010, when 33 miners were working in a mine in Chile, the roof fell and trapped them.

2. While the miners' families were waiting anxiously for news, the mining company began its rescue attempts.

3. When those attempts failed, the government ________ a huge rescue operation.

4. When the necessary equipment ________ at the scene, the rescue team started to search for the miners.

5. When one of the drills reached the miners, the miners ________ a note to it.

6. When the rescue team ______________ the note, they discovered that all 33 of the miners were alive.

7. When the rescue team ______________ the escape route, they began to lift the miners out of the mine.

8. Millions of people all over the world ______________ on TV when the rescue workers lifted the last man out of the mine.

9 LISTEN & SPEAK.

CD1-12

A Listen to the conversation about Ernest Shackleton. Then answer the questions.

1. How many men were with Shackleton on the ship? ______________
2. In what year did Shackleton's ship become trapped in the ice? ______________
3. Did the men all survive? ______________

CD1-12

B Complete each sentence with the simple past or the past progressive form of the verb(s) in parentheses. Then listen again and check your answers.

1. The *Endurance* was approaching (approach) Antarctica in January 1915 when it ______________ (become) locked in the ice.
2. When the ocean water ______________ (freeze), ice ______________ (surround) the ship.
3. Shackleton and his men ______________ (stay) on the *Endurance* at first, and then they ______________ (make) a camp on the ice.
4. They ______________ (wait) for nine months, but the ice ______________ (not release) the ship.

▼ The crew of the *Endurance* plays soccer to pass the time. Their ship is in the background.

5. Then one day, while some of the men ______________________ (arrange) supplies on the ice, the ship ______________________ (begin) to break up.

6. When the *Endurance* ______________________ (start) to sink, Shackleton ______________________ (decide) to take his men across the ice on foot.

7. While Shackleton and five of his men ______________________ (try) to reach the island of South Georgia to find help, the others ______________________ (spend) several more months at the camp on the ice.

8. When Shackleton and his men ______________________ (arrive) in Chile, they ______________________ (receive) a hero's welcome.

10 APPLY.

A Read Marta's blog entry. Underline the past time clauses.

You won't believe what happened to me tonight! While I was crossing Newton Street, a truck went through a red light. The driver was texting when the light changed. He wasn't looking at the road. When I jumped out of the way, I fell onto the sidewalk and cut my knee. I was wearing my new jeans, too! When I got home, I took care of my knee and then called the police. Fortunately, I got the truck's license number while I was lying in the street.

B Work with a partner. Close your books and take turns retelling the story about Marta's accident. Use past time clauses.

C Think of an accident that you or someone you know had. Take notes in the chart. Use the questions to help you.

When did the accident happen?	
Where were you?	
What were you doing?	
What happened?	
What happened next?	

D In your notebook, write a paragraph about your accident. Use your notes from exercise **C** and Marta's blog entry as a model. Use at least five past time clauses. When you are finished, read your story to a partner or small group.

LESSON 4 Repeated Past Actions: *Used To* and *Would*

EXPLORE

CD1-13

1 READ the conversation between two visitors to the British Museum in London, England. Notice the words in **bold**.

Who Owns the Past?

Cho: These statues are beautiful. Where are they from?

Noriko: They're from Athens, Greece. I think they **used to be** a part of the Parthenon.

Cho: Well, it's wonderful to see them, but why are they here in London? They should be back in Greece with the rest of the Parthenon.

Noriko: A lot of people agree with you. Lord Elgin, a British diplomat,[1] brought these statues to London in the early nineteenth century.

Cho: You mean he just took them?

Noriko: Well, I don't know. I'm not sure what really happened. Back then archaeologists[2] **used to do** things like that. They **would explore** a historic site and bring objects from the site back to their home countries. Then, they **would study** them and put them on display in museums. Sometimes, that's the only reason treasures like these survived.

Cho: But didn't the Greek people try to stop Lord Elgin?

Noriko: Sure, there were a lot of complaints. Was it right or wrong to take these statues? It's a difficult question. I love to visit museums and see things from around the world and learn about them.

Cho: Hmm . . . I understand what you're saying, but it still seems wrong to me, somehow.

[1] **diplomat:** a person who acts as the official representative of his or her country in a foreign country

[2] **archaeologist:** a person who studies the past by looking at items such as buried houses, tools, pots, etc.

▶ A statue of a horse's head from the Parthenon, Acropolis, Athens, Greece 447-432 B.C.

▲ A carving from the Parthenon, Acropolis, Athens, Greece

2 CHECK. Read the statements. Circle **T** for *true* or **F** for *false*.

1. The statues are from Italy.	**T**	**F**
2. The statues came to England in the 20th century.	**T**	**F**
3. Cho thinks the statues should go back to Greece.	**T**	**F**
4. In the past, it was not unusual for archaeologists to bring discoveries home.	**T**	**F**
5. Cho and Noriko agree about the future of the statues.	**T**	**F**

3 DISCOVER. Complete the exercises to learn about the grammar in this lesson.

A Look at these sentences from the conversation in exercise **1**. Decide whether the **bold** verb in each sentence refers to a single action **(S)** or a repeated action **(R)**. Write *S* or *R*.

1. __S__ Lord Elgin . . . **brought** these statues to London in the early nineteenth century.
2. ____ You mean he just **took** them?
3. ____ Back then archaeologists **used to do** things like that.
4. ____ They **would explore** a historic site and bring objects from the site back to their home countries.
5. ____ Then, they **would study** them and put them on display in museums.

B Look at the sentences from exercise **A**. Which verb forms are used for repeated actions? Discuss your answer with your classmates and teacher.

LEARN

2.7 *Used To:* Affirmative and Negative Statements

Affirmative			
Subject	*Used To*	Base Form	
I/She/They	**used to**	study	history.

Negative			
Subject	*Didn't Use To*	Base Form	
I/She/They	**didn't use to**	study	math.

1. *Used to* expresses a habit or state in the past that no longer exists.	I **used to run** several times a week. (Now, I don't.) I **used to live** in a small town. (I live in a city now.) I **didn't use to eat** meat. (I do now.)
2. In negative statements use *use to,* not *used to.*	I didn't **use to** love math.

REAL ENGLISH

Use *used to* instead of the simple past to emphasize that the habit or state is not true now.

*When I was young, I **used to go** to the beach every day.*

4 Rewrite each sentence with *used to* or *didn't use to* and the verb in **bold**.

1. Archaeologists **removed** objects from historic sites.

   Archaeologists used to remove objects from historic sites.

2. I **went** to museums every weekend when I lived in Berlin.

   ____

3. My cousin **lived** across the street, but I didn't see him much.

   ____

4. Jim **didn't like** math when he was in school.

   ____

5. There **was** a supermarket near my home until last year.

   ____

6. Carole **played** in a band in college.

   ____

7. I **didn't drive** much when I lived downtown.

   ____

8. Mike **worked** in a bank before he got his new job.

   ____

2.8 *Used To:* Questions and Answers

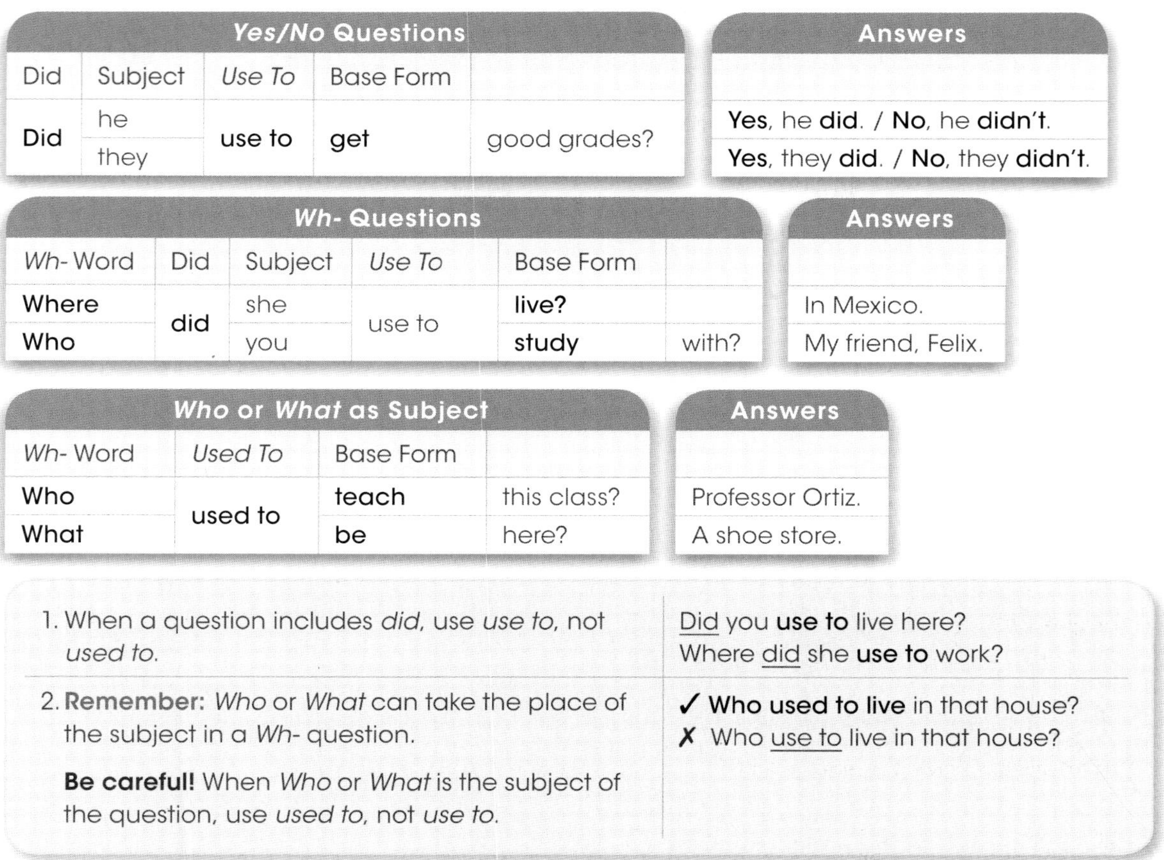

Yes/No Questions					Answers
Did	Subject	*Use To*	Base Form		
Did	he	use to	get	good grades?	**Yes**, he **did**. / **No**, he **didn't**.
	they				**Yes**, they **did**. / **No**, they **didn't**.

Wh- Questions						Answers
Wh- Word	Did	Subject	*Use To*	Base Form		
Where	did	she	use to	live?		In Mexico.
Who		you		study	with?	My friend, Felix.

Who or *What* as Subject				Answers
Wh- Word	*Used To*	Base Form		
Who	used to	teach	this class?	Professor Ortiz.
What		be	here?	A shoe store.

1. When a question includes *did*, use *use to*, not *used to*.	Did you **use to** live here? Where did she **use to** work?
2. **Remember:** *Who* or *What* can take the place of the subject in a *Wh-* question. **Be careful!** When *Who* or *What* is the subject of the question, use *used to*, not *use to*.	✓ **Who used to live** in that house? ✗ Who use to live in that house?

5 Complete each question with the words in parentheses. Use the correct form of *used to.*

1. ___Did you use to ride___ (you / ride) a bike when you were a child?
2. What ______________ (you / do) after school when you were a child?
3. ______________ (your family / live) in a different place?
4. Where ______________ (your mother / work)?
5. What ______________ (your family / do) on the weekends when you were a child?
6. Who ______________ (be) your English teacher?
7. ______________ (you / visit) your friends often?
8. Where ______________ (you / go) on vacation?

6 **SPEAK.** Work with a partner. Ask and answer the questions from exercise **5**.

A: *Did you use to ride a bike when you were a child?*

B: *Yes, I did.*

REAL ENGLISH

When the phrases *used to* or *use to* are used to talk about the past, they are often pronounced /*yustə*/.

2.9 *Would*: Repeated Past Actions

Affirmative and Negative Statements				
	Subject	*Would/ Would Not*	Base Form	
When I was in high school,	I	would 'd	ride	my bike to school.
When Scott was a child,	he	would not wouldn't	eat	any vegetables.

1. *Would* expresses a repeated past action or habit that no longer exists.	In high school, we **would play** soccer every afternoon. As a child, I **wouldn't study**, but I **would get** good grades.
2. **Be careful!** Do not use *would* for past situations or states that no longer exist. Use *used to* or *use to*.	✓There **used to be** a library on this street. ✗ There would be a library on this street. ✓He **didn't use to live** on Palm Street. ✗ He wouldn't live on Palm Street.

7 Complete each sentence. Use *would* and the verb in parentheses.

1. When I was a child, my father ________________ (take) me to the zoo about once a month.
2. In high school, my brother ________________ (not start) his homework until around midnight.
3. When Alicia was a child, she ________________ (play) with her friends after school.
4. When my parents were in school, they ________________ (eat) lunch at home every day.
5. In college, I often ________________ (not go) to bed until 3:00 a.m.
6. My grandfather used to work very hard during the week, but on the weekends he ________________ (relax).
7. In college, Sandra ________________ (study) for about six hours every day.
8. When I was in high school, I ________________ (sit) in the back of the classroom and draw in my notebook.
9. When Kyle was on the soccer team, he ________________ (run) five miles every morning before school.
10. We ________________ (go) to the market every day when we lived in France.

PRACTICE

CD1-14

8 Complete the article about the Iceman with the words and phrases from the chart. Use each word or phrase only once. Then listen and check your answers.

Used To	Would	Simple Past		
used to hunt	wouldn't come	didn't grow	didn't spend	killed
used to think	would go	~~discovered~~	found	used

The Iceman

Back in 1991, hikers in the mountains near the border of Austria and Italy (1) discovered the body of a man in the ice. Scientists soon learned that the body was over 5000 years old. They called the man the "Iceman."

Scientists (2) ______________ that the Iceman died from the cold. Five thousand years ago, people of central Europe (3) ______________ wild animals for food. They (4) ______________ up into the mountains in all kinds of weather, and sometimes they (5) ______________ back. Then, in 2001, scientists found part of an arrow in the Iceman's body. Somebody (6) ______________ the Iceman, and we will probably never know why.

After more recent tests, scientists now think the Iceman was not just a hunter. They think he probably had a higher position in society, and (7) ______________ a lot of time in the mountains. Before the most recent tests, scientists believed that people in the Iceman's community (8) ______________ crops.[1] However, they (9) ______________ small pieces of stone in the Iceman's stomach. This suggests that the Iceman's people (10) ______________ stones to grind[2] flour for some kind of bread.

Even though the Iceman died over 5000 years ago, we know a lot about his life thanks to scientific research.

[1] **crops:** plants that people grow for food

[2] **grind:** to rub something until it becomes a powder

◄ How the Iceman died used to be a mystery. Now scientists think they have the answer.

9 WRITE. Look at the information in the chart about people 5000 years ago and people today. Then write six sentences using *used to, didn't use to,* or *would.*

People 5000 Years Ago	People Today
hunt animals, gather fruit and nuts cook over fire live in caves or simple shelters use animal skins for clothing	buy food in grocery stores cook with stoves live in houses or apartments buy clothing in stores or make clothing from cloth

People didn't use to buy food in a grocery store.

1. ______________________________
2. ______________________________
3. ______________________________
4. ______________________________
5. ______________________________
6. ______________________________

10 APPLY.

A A few years ago Brian was not happy, so he made some changes. Look at the chart. What changes did he make? Discuss them with a partner.

Brian used to be unhappy, and he didn't have many friends. He joined a band last year. Now . . .

Brian		
In the Past	Change	Now
lonely, didn't have many friends	joined a band last year	happy, has new friends
unhealthy	bought a bike a few months ago	healthy
always arrived late for class and work	learned to drive last month	always arrives on time

B Think about some changes you have made in your life. In your notebook, make a chart like the one in exercise **A** and write notes about three of these changes.

C Work with a partner. Take turns talking about the changes in your life. Use *used to, didn't use to,* and *would.*

D In your notebook, write a short paragraph of four or five sentences about one of the changes you made.

A couple of years ago, I used to feel lonely all the time. I would stay home at night and watch TV . . .

UNIT 2 Review the Grammar

Charts 2.1–2.9

1 Circle the correct word(s) or phrase(s) to complete each sentence.

1. Hundreds of years ago, people **used to believe** / **would believe** that the Earth was flat.
2. My brother **put** / **was putting** the phone down while I **talked** / **was talking** to him.
3. When the plane **landed** / **was landing** safely, everyone **started** / **was starting** to clap.
4. When my grandfather was young, he **was walking** / **would walk** five miles to school every day.
5. How many reports **did Malik write** / **did Malik use to write** last week?
6. Lisa **used to live** / **would live** in Miami, but then she **moved** / **was moving** to Paris.
7. **Were you going** / **Did you use to go** to Central Park a lot when you **were living** / **would live** in New York?
8. Yuri **drove** / **was driving** home when his car **broke down** / **was breaking down**.
9. I **wanted** / **used to want** to see the show, but I couldn't get a ticket.
10. **Did you use to play** / **Were you playing** tennis when you **hurt** / **were hurting** your arm?

Charts 2.1–2.7

2 Complete each sentence or question with the word(s) in parentheses. Use the simple past, the past progressive, or *used to*. There is more than one correct answer for some items.

1. While I ___was sitting___ (sit) in the airport lounge, I ___saw___ (see) a famous actor.
2. Irina ______________ (write) poems, but now she writes short stories instead.
3. Martin ______________ (try) to turn on his computer, but nothing ______________ (happen).
4. When my brother and I ______________ (be) young, we ______________ (play) games with my parents in the evenings.
5. ______________ (you / have) trouble with the alphabet when you ______________ (learn) Arabic?
6. We ______________ (go) to the movies three times last week.
7. I ______________ (work) when you ______________ (call), so I ______________ (not answer) the phone.
8. When Stephanie was a child, she ______________ (visit) her grandparents twice a month.

Charts 2.1, 2.3, 2.5, 2.9

3 EDIT. Read the paragraph about stepped wells in India. Find and correct six more errors with the simple past, the past progressive, and *would*.

Stepped Wells in India

Northern India is very hot. The area gets a lot of rain, but the water disappears very quickly because of the heat. Around 1500 years ago, the people of northern India ~~used to begin~~ began to build stepped wells to provide water for the population. They dug deep holes to reach water underground, and they were making rock walls for the wells. In each well, they builded stone steps and passages to help people reach the water easily. They often were decorating the walls of the passages with beautiful designs.

The stepped wells were long and narrow. They were cool, dark places, and they were often having special rooms away from the heat. While people were collecting water, they would took some time out of their busy days and talk with their neighbors. The wells becomed important social centers.

▶ A visitor walks into a stepped well in northern India.

Charts 2.1, 2.3, 2.5

CD1-15

4 LISTEN & WRITE.

A Look at the photos on page 55. Then listen to the stories of four people who survived attacks by wild animals. Complete the chart with information about each person's story.

	Eric Nerhus	Ben Nyaumbe	Kootoo Shaw	James Morrow
Activity	diving			
Animal			polar bear	
Place		Kenya		
Reason for Survival				his face mask protected him

CD1-15

B Write sentences about each story from exercise **A**. Use the information in the chart, the simple past, the past progressive, and past time clauses. Then listen again and check your sentences.

While Eric Nerhus was diving in Australia, a shark attacked him. He survived because the shark bit his belt.

____

____

____

____

____

____

____

Charts 2.1–2.6

5 SPEAK.

A Think of a dangerous situation that you or someone you know was in. What happened? What did you or this person do? How did you or this person survive? Write notes in your notebook.

B Work with a partner. Take turns telling your stories from exercise **A**. Use the simple past, the past progressive, and past time clauses. Ask your partner questions for more information about his or her story.

Connect the Grammar to Writing

1 READ & NOTICE THE GRAMMAR.

A Read the story. What difficult experience did the writer have? How did she survive? Discuss the writer's experience with a partner.

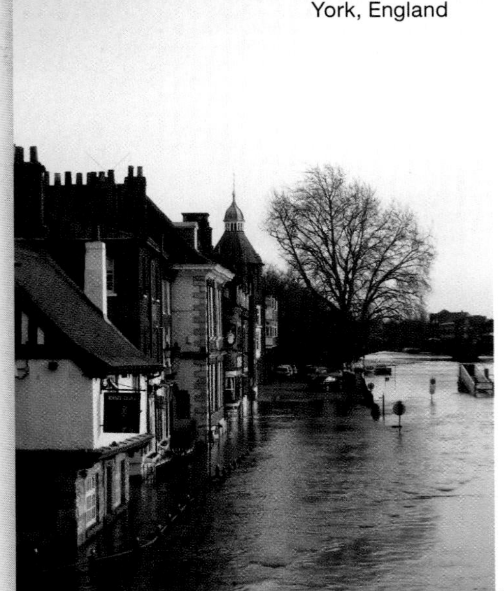

▼ A flooded river in York, England

Remembering a Spring Flood

When I was a young girl, we lived near a river. Every spring when the snow melted, it caused the river to rise a few feet. Then the level of the river would fall again. One spring, however, the river kept rising.

One day that spring, I looked out my window. The river was rising very quickly. My parents came and got me. While the water was rising higher, we climbed onto the roof of our house. From the roof, I looked down at the river. It was covering everything in its path. My family and I waited on our roof for help. I was losing hope when we were finally rescued.

GRAMMAR FOCUS

In the story, the writer uses the simple past to talk about completed actions and events.

*I **looked** out my window.*
*My parents **came** and **got** me.*

The writer uses the past progressive to describe a scene in the past.

*The river **was rising** very quickly.*

The writer uses past time clauses to describe when actions or events happened.

***When I was a young girl,** we lived near a river.*

B Read the story from exercise **A** again. Circle the simple past, underline the past progressive, and double underline the past time clauses. Then work with a partner and compare your answers.

C Complete the chart with information from the story in exercise **A**. Add more boxes to the chart if necessary.

Event 1	Event 2	Event 3	Event 4
One spring, the river near my house kept rising.	My parents came and got me.		

Write about a Difficult Experience

2 BEFORE YOU WRITE.

A Brainstorm a list of difficult experiences you have had.

B Choose one experience to write about. Use the chart below to describe your experience. Add more boxes to your chart if necessary.

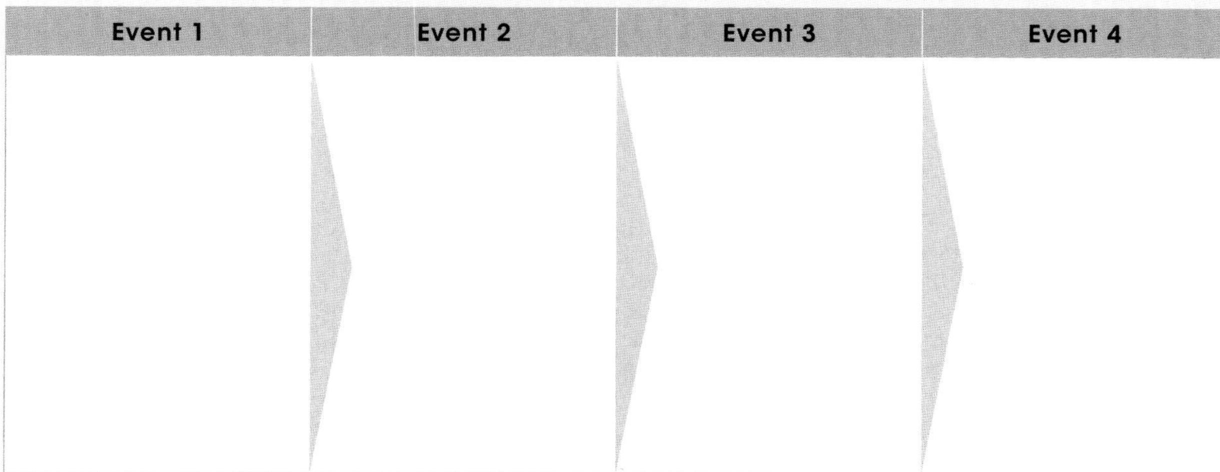

3 WRITE about your difficult experience. Use the information from your chart from exercise **2B** and the story from exercise **1A** to help you.

WRITING FOCUS Identifying and Correcting Sentence Fragments

A sentence fragment is missing an important part of a sentence, such as a subject or verb.

✓ My family and I waited on our roof for help.
✗ Waited on our roof for help. (no subject)

✓ It was covering everything in its path.
✗ Everything in its path. (no subject and no verb)

Make sure each of your sentences has a subject and a verb.

4 SELF ASSESS. Read your story and underline the simple past, the past progressive, and past time clauses. Then use the checklist to assess your work.

☐ I used the simple past to talk about completed actions and events. [2.1]

☐ I used the past progressive to describe a scene in the past. [2.3]

☐ I used past time clauses to tell when an action or event happened. [2.5, 2.6]

☐ I checked for and corrected sentence fragments. [WRITING FOCUS]

UNIT 3 Health and Fitness

Nouns

▶ Residents of Shanghai, China, exercise with fans.

EXPLORE

CD1-16

1 **READ** the article about *sangomas,* traditional African healers. Notice the words in **bold**.

Sangomas of Southern Africa

Sangomas are traditional **healers** of southern Africa. They use **plants, songs,** and **dances** to help **people** who are sick. Many people in southern Africa prefer traditional **healers** to modern medicine. **Women**, for example, may see a sangoma instead of a doctor when their **babies** are born. Often, however, modern medicine and traditional medicine work together. Using one kind of medicine doesn't mean ignoring **the other kind**.

A **sangoma's** goal is to make his or her patient[1] feel better. To help their **patients, sangomas** perform different **ceremonies**. In one ceremony, the sangoma throws **shells** and animal **bones** on the ground. The **shells** and **bones** form a pattern. The pattern helps the sangoma understand the patient. **Other methods** of helping **patients** include special **drinks**, drumming, and singing.

Scientists are studying the **methods** used by **sangomas**. They hope to learn new **ways** to keep **people** healthy.

[1] **patient:** a person who is cared for by a doctor

2 CHECK. Read the statements. Circle **T** for *true* or **F** for *false*.

1. Modern medicine has replaced traditional healers in Africa. **T** **F**
2. Sangomas perform different kinds of ceremonies. **T** **F**
3. The pattern formed by shells and bones helps patients understand the sangoma. **T** **F**
4. Sangomas sometimes sing to help their patients. **T** **F**
5. Modern scientists don't think traditional medicine is useful. **T** **F**

3 DISCOVER. Complete the exercises to learn about the grammar in this lesson.

A In the article, each of these nouns is used in the plural. Find the correct plural form of each noun in the article and write it on the line next to its singular form.

Singular	Plural
1. healer	healers
2. dance	______
3. person	______
4. woman	______
5. baby	______
6. patient	______
7. ceremony	______
8. drink	______
9. bone	______
10. scientist	______

B Notice the different ways the plural nouns in exercise **A** are formed. Discuss them with a partner.

◄ A traditional African healer

LEARN

3.1 Spelling Rules for Regular and Irregular Plural Nouns

	Singular	Plural
1. Add *-s* to most singular nouns to form the plural.	apple scientist boy	apple**s** scientist**s** boy**s**
2. Add *-es* to nouns that end in *-s, -sh, -ch,* or *-x.*	class, dish, inch, tax	class**es**, dish**es**, inch**es**, tax**es**
3. For nouns that end in a consonant + *-y,* change the *-y* to *-i* and add *-es.*	party, city	part**ies**, cit**ies**
4. For some nouns that end in *-o,* add *-s.* For other nouns that end in *-o,* add *-es.* Learn the spelling of each noun separately.	photo potato	photo**s** potato**es**
5. For most nouns that end in *-f* or *-fe,* change the ending to *-ves.* For other nouns that end in *-f,* add *-s.*	leaf, wife belief, roof	lea**ves**, wi**ves** belief**s**, roof**s**
6. Some nouns have irregular plural forms.* Irregular plural nouns include nouns with a. a vowel change b. an irregular ending c. no change (often animals)	a. man, foot, tooth b. child c. fish, deer	a. m**e**n, f**ee**t, t**ee**th b. child**ren** c. **fish, deer**

*See page **A2** for a list of common irregular plural nouns.

4 Complete each sentence with the plural form of the noun in parentheses.

1. ___Scientists___ (Scientist) are interested in traditional medicine.
2. The healer told ______________ (story) about the life of her patient.
3. In some countries, most ______________ (baby) are born at home.
4. The mother took her three ______________ (child) to the doctor.
5. Healers work to improve the ______________ (life) of their patients.
6. The dentist says my ______________ (tooth) are in very good condition.
7. The doctor told me to eat more ______________ (banana).
8. I think I eat too many ______________ (potato).
9. Our school offers healthy ______________ (lunch) every day.
10. Different cultures have different ______________ (belief) about health.

REAL ENGLISH

A few nouns have no singular form. They are used only in the plural. Some examples are: *clothes, glasses, jeans.*

*I'm wearing my new **jeans** today.*

5 Work with a partner. Partner B closes his or her book. Partner A reads a singular noun from chart 3.1. Partner B says the plural form of the word and spells it. Switch roles after five or six words.

A: *apple* B: *apples: a, p, p, l, e, s*

3.2 Possessive Nouns

Singular Noun	Possessive Form
girl	The **girl's** bicycle is blue.
child	The **child's** room is messy.

Plural Noun	Possessive Form
girls	The **girls'** bicycles are blue.
children	The **children's** rooms are messy.

1. Use possessive nouns to show ownership or a relationship.	The **writer's** house is in New York. **Mark's** father is very strong.
2. To make singular nouns possessive, add an apostrophe (') + *-s* (*'s*).	The **child's** mother is over there.
3. To make plural nouns possessive a. add an apostrophe to regular plural nouns b. add an apostrophe + *-s* to most irregular plural nouns	 a. The **boys'** parents are here. b. The **children's** teacher is kind.
4. To make a noun phrase with two nouns possessive, add an apostrophe + *-s* to the second noun only.	**John and Tina's** father is sick.

6 Circle the correct word to complete each sentence.

1. **Maria's** / **Marias'** daughter is in hospital.
2. The **nurses's** / **nurse's** name is Meg.
3. The **students'** / **students's** goal is to become doctors.
4. The **childrens'** / **children's** section of the hospital is bright and cheerful.
5. You can find many **doctor's** / **doctors'** phone numbers online.
6. My **baby's** / **babies'** cold is getting worse.
7. **Peoples'** / **People's** health is getting better.
8. The Internet has increased **parent's** / **parents'** concerns about their children.

7 Write the correct possessive form of the word in parentheses.

1. Is your ___dentist's___ (dentist) office in this building?
2. The ________________ (building) elevator is broken.
3. ________________ (Mrs. Achebe) house is across the street from the hospital.
4. The ________________ (doctors) white coats are in the closet.
5. Julian and ________________ (Amy) baby is six weeks old.
6. This ________________ (city) hospitals are excellent.
7. Marta is a coach for the ________________ (women) swim team.
8. ________________ (Mark and Sam) apartment is on the second floor.

8 Work in a small group. Take turns talking about things that belong to members of your group.

Paul's backpack is black. *Ava's hair is long.*

3.3 *Another* and *Other*

1. *Another* + a singular noun means one more person or thing of the same group.	I've already had two pieces of pizza, but I'm going to have **another** piece.
Another can also refer to a different person or thing.	This pen doesn't work. I need **another** pen.
Use *another* to refer to a person or thing that is not specific.	My car is very old. I need to buy **another** car soon.
2. *The other* + a singular noun means the second of two people or things of a specific group. *The other* + a plural noun means the rest of the people or things of a specific group.	There are two hotels in this area. One hotel is on Main Street. **The other** hotel is on Oak Street. We had three assignments. I did one last night and did **the other** assignments this morning.
3. *Other* + a plural noun means some, but not all, of the remaining people or things in a group.	Some people like to talk. **Other** people prefer to listen.
4. The pronoun *one* or *ones* can replace the noun after *another* or *(the) other.*	Lydia's watch broke, so she bought **another** one. (*one* = watch) These earrings are pretty, but I prefer **the other** ones. (*ones* = earrings)

REAL ENGLISH

Another and *the other* are also used alone as pronouns.

These pears are delicious. I'm going to have ***another****.* (*another* = pear)

Ken owns two apartments. One apartment is in Chicago. ***The other*** *is in Miami.* (*the other* = apartment)

9 Complete the sentences with *another, other,* or *the other.*

1. I took one pill early this morning. I need to take ___another___ pill after lunch.
2. Some people exercise every day. ________ people never exercise.
3. Eight nurses work here. Six of them are very experienced. ________ two are new.
4. Many doctors work in hospitals, but ________ doctors have their own offices.
5. My brother had a soccer game on Saturday, and on Sunday he had ________ one.
6. I have two exams tomorrow. One exam is the morning. ________ one is in the afternoon.
7. I saw two movies on Saturday. The first one was great, but ________ movie was terrible.
8. This glass is dirty. Could I have ________ one, please?

One month to learn Pronunciation, Vocabulary & Grammar.

English Vocabulary In Use Grammar

IELTS Speaking – Mark Clark & Mark Allen

Englishpage. com (grammar) –

- feeling : dislike, hate, love, like, miss
- senses : hear, see, sounds, feel, smell, taste
- possessions : belong, have, own
- appearance : look, seem, appear
- mental states : believe, think, undertand
- desires : hope, see, want, prefer.

10 Complete the sentences with *one* or *ones*.

1. Leyla takes one vitamin every morning and another ___one___ at night.
2. There are three hospitals in my city. One is near my apartment. The other ______ are downtown.
3. Brett doesn't like his doctor. He wants to find another ______.
4. I missed my doctor's appointment this morning, so I made another ______ for next week.
5. A few of the articles in that health magazine are about nutrition. The other ______ are about exercise.
6. Dan has two appointments next week. One is on Monday. The other ______ is on Thursday.
7. I prefer these eyeglasses. The other ______ aren't very attractive.
8. Use this elevator. The other ______ are broken.

PRACTICE

11 Circle the correct word to complete each sentence.

1. The **doctor's** / **doctors** schedule is very full this week.
2. My **babies** / **baby's** health is very important to me.
3. Doctor Chen has a lot of **patients** / **patient's**.
4. The hospital lost the **men** / **man's** x-rays.
5. The **teacher's** / **teachers** are having a meeting today.
6. Some **person** / **people** watch a lot of TV.
7. The **child's** / **children's** father took them to the park.
8. That building is over 1000 **foot** / **feet** high.

12 **PRONUNCIATION.** Read the chart and listen to the examples. Then complete the exercises.

CD1-17

PRONUNCIATION **Nouns: *-s* and *-es* Endings**

Many plural nouns and possessives end in *-s* or *-es*. The endings have one of three sounds: /s/, /z/, or /əz/.

1. Pronounce *-s* as /s/ after the consonant sounds /f/, /k/, /p/, /t/, and /θ/.	shop's, tests, beliefs, bike's, months
2. Pronounce *-s* as /z/ after the consonant sounds /b/, /d/, /g/, /l/, /m/, /n/, /ŋ/, /r/, /v/, or any vowel sound.	logs, jobs, head's, songs, wives, day's
3. Pronounce *-es* as /əz/ after /s/, /z/, /ʃ/, /ʤ/, /tʃ/, or /ks/ sounds.	kisses, diseases, wishes, judge's, watches, taxes

CD1-18

A Listen and circle the final sound you hear for each word.

1.	nurses	/s/	/z/	(/əz/)	7.	boy's	/s/	/z/	/əz/
2.	patient's	/s/	/z/	/əz/	8.	beds	/s/	/z/	/əz/
3.	doctor's	/s/	/z/	/əz/	9.	jobs	/s/	/z/	/əz/
4.	cups	/s/	/z/	/əz/	10.	bridges	/s/	/z/	/əz/
5.	book's	/s/	/z/	/əz/	11.	boxes	/s/	/z/	/əz/
6.	hospitals	/s/	/z/	/əz/	12.	dishes	/s/	/z/	/əz/

CD1-18

B Listen again and repeat each word. Pay attention to the endings.

13 Read each situation and complete the sentences about it. Use *another, the other,* or *other* and the noun in parentheses.

1. Situation: *Your father saw one of his two doctors last week.*

   He saw ___the other doctor___ (doctor) this morning.

2. Situation: *My bottle of vitamins is almost empty.*

   I need to buy ________________ (bottle of vitamins) soon.

3. Situation: *You bought six oranges. Four of them were sweet and delicious.*

   ________________ (oranges) were sour.

4. Situation: *Emma found three errors on her homework assignment. Then, she found one more.*

   Emma just found ________________ (error) on her homework assignment.

5. Situation: *I invited ten people to my party. Seven people came.*

   ________________ (people) did not come.

6. Situation: *Carol is a nurse. She doesn't have the same schedule every week. Some weeks she works during the day.*

   ________________ (weeks) she works at night or on the weekends.

7. Situation: *My coat is old, and it's not very warm.*

   I need ________________ (coat).

8. Situation: *The students at my school study different things. Some students are studying science.*

   ________________ (students) are studying history, math, or languages.

14 EDIT. Read the information about the human body in extreme situations. Find and correct eight more errors with plural nouns and possessive nouns.

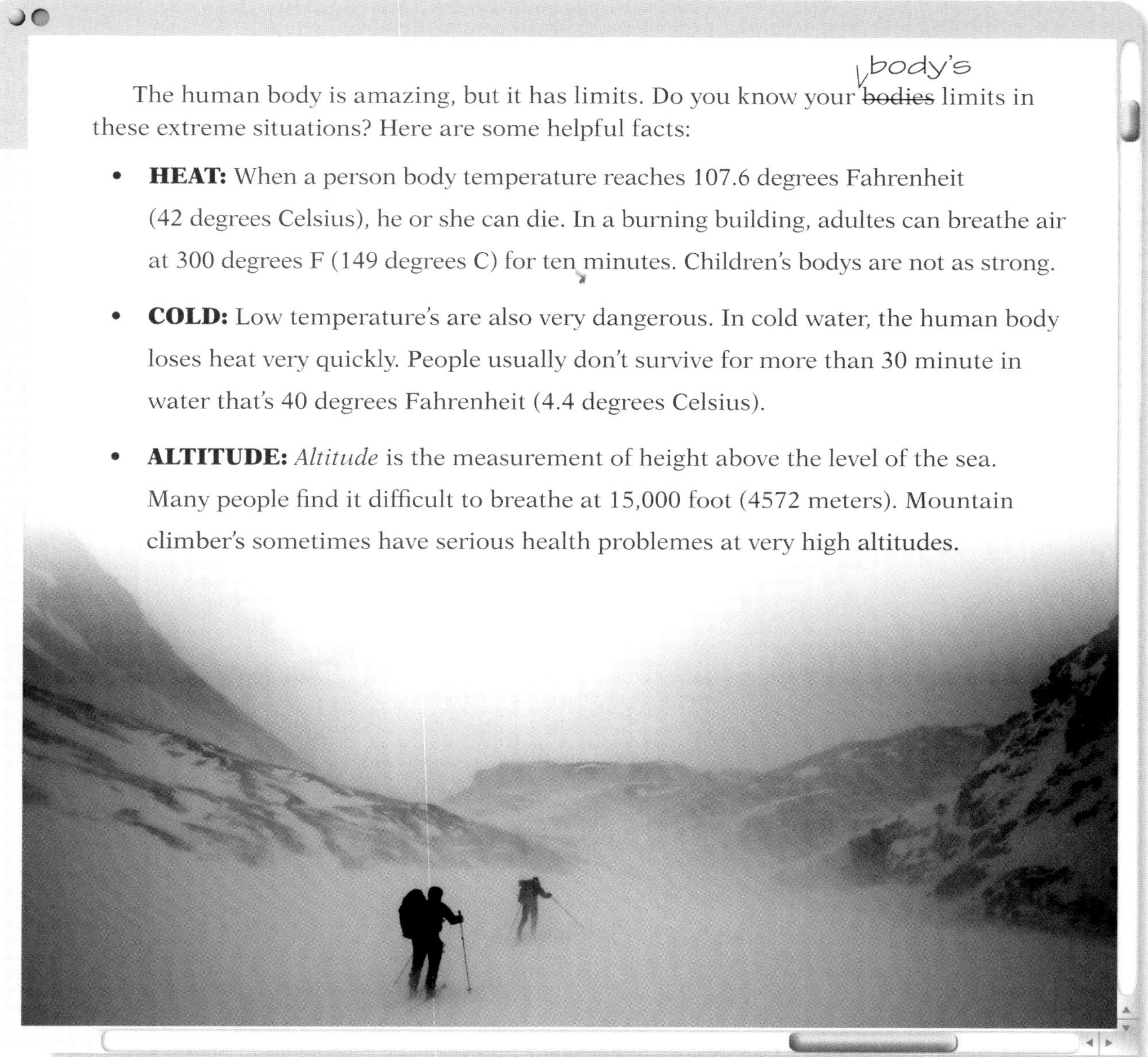

The human body is amazing, but it has limits. Do you know your ~~bodies~~ body's limits in these extreme situations? Here are some helpful facts:

- **HEAT:** When a person body temperature reaches 107.6 degrees Fahrenheit (42 degrees Celsius), he or she can die. In a burning building, adultes can breathe air at 300 degrees F (149 degrees C) for ten minutes. Children's bodys are not as strong.
- **COLD:** Low temperature's are also very dangerous. In cold water, the human body loses heat very quickly. People usually don't survive for more than 30 minute in water that's 40 degrees Fahrenheit (4.4 degrees Celsius).
- **ALTITUDE:** *Altitude* is the measurement of height above the level of the sea. Many people find it difficult to breathe at 15,000 foot (4572 meters). Mountain climber's sometimes have serious health problemes at very high altitudes.

15 APPLY.

A In your notebook, write six sentences using singular and plural nouns, and possessive nouns. Use the words from the box or your own ideas.

camera	car	children	clothes	diet	dog	health	job	sister	TV

My sister's children are in high school.

B Work with a partner. Share your sentences from exercise **A**. Ask questions to keep the conversation going. Pay attention to possessive nouns and plural nouns.

A: *My sister's children are in high school.*

B: *Where do they go to school?*

EXPLORE

CD1-19

1 READ the article about three different superfoods. Notice the words in **bold**.

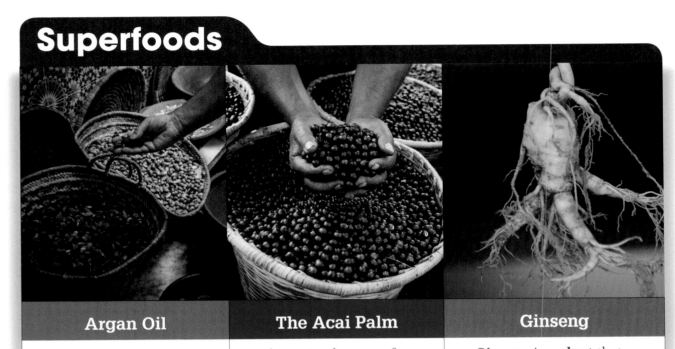

Superfoods

Argan Oil

The **oil** from argan **nuts** is very important to the **people** of southwestern Morocco. It has many different **uses**. It adds **flavor**[1] to **food**, it prevents dry **skin**, and it keeps **hair** soft. Now it is popular in other **countries**, too, and it is becoming more expensive. The **production** of argan **oil** cannot increase very quickly, because argan **trees** don't produce **nuts** until they are about 20 **years** old.

[1] **flavor:** a specific taste

The Acai Palm

The acai palm **tree** of Central and South America has round purple **fruit**. **Acai** is very important to some of the **tribes** in the Amazon **Rainforest**. In fact, it is a very large **part** of their **diet**.[2] **People** make both sweet and salty **dishes** with **acai**. Now some **companies** say that **acai** helps **people** lose **weight**.

[2] **diet:** a person's regular food and drink

Ginseng

Ginseng is a **plant** that grows in Asia and North America. There are many different **types** of ginseng **plants**. Chinese **medicine** started using **ginseng** **thousands** of **years** ago to treat all **kinds** of **diseases**. According to some scientific **studies**, **ginseng** may help manage **stress**.[3] Be careful, though! Too much **ginseng** can keep you awake at **night**.

[3] **stress:** mental or physical difficulty caused by work, worries, and so on

2 CHECK. Match each statement with the correct tree or plant. Write the letter on the line.

1. You can use it in sweet and salty meals. __b__
2. It keeps hair soft. ____
3. Tests suggest it can help you relax. ____
4. It is becoming more expensive. ____
5. According to some companies, it helps you lose weight. ____
6. Some people don't sleep well because of it. ____

a. argan oil
b. acai palm
c. ginseng

3 DISCOVER. Complete the exercises to learn about the grammar in this lesson.

A Look at these sentences from the article in exercise **1**. Notice the nouns in **bold**. Circle the nouns that name things you can count. Underline the nouns that name things you cannot count.

1. The **oil** from argan **nuts** is very important to the **people** of southwestern Morocco.
2. It adds **flavor** to **food,** prevents dry **skin,** and keeps **hair** soft.
3. Now some **companies** say that **acai** helps people lose **weight**.

B Work with a partner. Compare your answers from exercise **A**.

▶ Goats in Morocco like argan nuts so much that they climb trees to find them.

LEARN

3.4 Count Nouns and Non-Count Nouns

Count Nouns		
	Noun	Verb
A	**doctor**	is coming.
Many	**doctors**	are coming.

Non-Count Nouns		
Noun	Verb	
Health	is	important.
The coffee	tastes	good.

1. Count nouns name things that can be counted. They have a singular and plural form. Use *a* or *an* before a singular count noun or an adjective + a singular count noun.	I ate an **orange** for breakfast. I bought four **oranges** yesterday. **a** building **an** apartment **a** small apartment
2. Non-count nouns name things that cannot be counted. They do not have a plural form. Do not use *a* or *an* before a non-count noun.	happiness, beauty, information, science, snow, water ✓ Alaska gets a lot of **snow**. ✗ Alaska gets a lot of snows. ✓ I need **information**. ✗ I need an information.
3. Use singular pronouns and verb forms with non-count nouns.	✓ **Rice** is cheap, but I don't like it. ✗ Rice are cheap, but I don't like them.

REAL ENGLISH

Some nouns can be count with one meaning and non-count with a different meaning.

*She goes to the gym three **times** a week.* (count)

*I don't have **time** to go to the gym today.* (non-count)

*We had three **exercises** for homework last night.* (count)

***Exercise** is important for good health.* (non-count)

4 Circle the correct word(s) to complete each sentence.

1. Some people use argan oil to keep their **hair** / **hairs** soft.
2. Some companies **says** / **say** that acai helps people lose weight.
3. Chinese medicine **is** / **are** over 2000 years old.
4. Science **is** / **are** a difficult subject, but I enjoy **it** / **them**.
5. The **store** / **stores** on that street are sometimes expensive.
6. **Apartment** / **An apartment** is a convenient place to live.
7. Do you have any **time** / **times** to help me with my assignment?
8. Hans goes to Germany three or four **time** / **times** a year.

9. This **information is** / **informations are** incorrect.

10. Last night's homework **was** / **were** very difficult.

11. That furniture **is** / **are** ugly. I don't know why I bought **it** / **them!**

12. Did you have any interesting **experience** / **experiences** on your vacation?

3.5 More Non-Count Nouns

Categories of Non-Count Nouns	
1. Some non-count nouns name a category of related items. The related items are often count nouns.	**clothing** (pants, sweaters, shoes) **fruit** (apples, oranges, bananas) **furniture** (tables, chairs, desks) **homework** (essays, exercises, assignments) **jewelry** (necklaces, rings, bracelets) **money** (nickels, dimes, quarters) **mail** (letters, packages, postcards) **weather** (hurricanes, storms, tornadoes)
2. Some non-count nouns name things that do not have separate parts or pieces that can be counted.	air, cheese, coffee, fish, flour, hair, ice, juice, meat, milk, oil, rice, skin, soup, sugar, tea, water, wind
3. Some non-count nouns are abstract nouns. An abstract noun names an idea, a feeling, or a quality.	advice, beauty, energy, experience, fun, happiness, health, help, honesty, intelligence, knowledge, love, nature, work
4. The names of subjects of study are usually non-count nouns.	biology, chemistry, geometry, history, math, science

5 Read the sentences. Circle the non-count nouns. Then write the number of the correct category above each non-count noun. (**1** = a category of related items, **2** = something that does not have separate parts, **3** = an abstract noun, **4** = a subject of study).

1. I'm taking six classes this semester, but I'm not taking biology. (4)
2. I have a lot of homework this weekend. I have an essay due on Monday and two exams on Tuesday.
3. Please do not bring food or drinks into the museum, and please turn off your cell phones.
4. My uncle often has cheese and crackers before dinner.
5. I eat a lot of fruit. I usually have a banana, an orange, and two apples every day.
6. The café across the street has great coffee and delicious pastries.
7. For some jobs, experience isn't very important.
8. I usually call my sister when I have a problem. She always gives me good advice.
9. We need to put money in the parking machine. It takes coins and dollar bills.
10. Sarah has a lot of energy. She works six days a week and takes classes at night.
11. Your mail is on the table. You got two letters and a package today.

PRACTICE

6 Circle the correct word(s) to complete the conversations.

Conversation 1

Lori: Did you go to the supermarket?

Stan: Yes I did, but look! (1) The **fruit is** / **fruit are** rotten.

Lori: Let's see . . . Oh, yes, (2) **it smells** / **they smell** bad.

Stan: The food in that store just (3) **isn't** / **aren't** good anymore. I've been there four or five (4) **time** / **times** recently and there is always a problem.

Lori: Wait a minute, though. The bananas (5) **look** / **looks** all right.

Stan: You're right. (6) **It does** / **They do.** But I'm going to take the rest back.

Conversation 2

Tina: Are you doing your physics (7) **homework** / **homeworks,** Brendan?

Brendan: Yes, but I need some (8) **help** / **helps.** I like physics, but (9) **it's** / **they're** difficult.

Tina: Well, I have some (10) **time** / **times** now. I can help you.

Brendan: Thanks, Tina. I don't understand this (11) **exercise** / **exercises.** These instructions (12) **isn't** / **aren't** very clear.

7 Complete the conversations with the nouns from the boxes. Make the nouns plural if necessary. You will need to use one noun twice.

advice	assignment	class	fun	homework	~~time~~

Alex: Hey, Bruce. Do you want to go to the basketball game tonight?

Bruce: No, sorry. I don't have (1) ___time___. I have a lot of (2) ________ tonight.

Alex: That's too bad. How many (3) ________ are you taking this semester?

Bruce: Five. And I have an (4) ________ for each of them.

Alex: Ugh! That is a lot. You need to study less and have more (5) ________.

Bruce: That seems like good (6) ________. Enjoy the game tonight!

energy	exercise	health	time

Ellen: Hi, Junko. Where are you going?

Junko: To the gym. I was sitting in a meeting all day today. I need to get some (7) ________!

Ellen: Good for you! I'm so busy these days. I don't have (8) ________ to exercise. How often do you go to the gym?

Junko: Oh, about three (9) ________ a week. I often go early in the morning before work.

Ellen: Really? Do you feel tired afterwards?

Junko: No, I actually have more (10) ________ after I work out.

Ellen: That's great. And it's good for your (11) ________, too.

8 LISTEN, WRITE & SPEAK.

CD1-20

A Listen to an interview with a doctor about the health benefits of certain kinds of food. Check the kinds of food you hear.

☐	green vegetables	☐	beans
☐	apples	☐	lettuce
☐	oranges	☐	squash
☐	cabbage	☐	fish
☐	nuts	☐	meat

▲ Vegetables provide almost everything the human body needs.

CD1-20

B What are the health benefits of the kinds of food you heard in exercise **A**? Listen again. Then write the name of each kind of food next to the correct health benefit(s).

1. important for our eyes ______
2. good for your skin ______
3. a great source of energy ______
4. strong muscles ______
5. Vitamin K ______
6. strong bones ______

C In your notebook, write five sentences about the different kinds of food in exercise **A**.

Squash is good for your eyes.

D Work with a partner. Compare your sentences from exercise **C**. Do you know of any other kinds of food that have special health benefits? Tell your partner.

A: *Carrots are good for your eyes.* B: *Milk makes bones strong.*

9 APPLY.

A Think about the kinds of food and drink you buy. Write five items of food or drink in each column of the chart. Next to each item, write ***C*** if it is a count noun or ***NC*** if it is a non-count noun.

What items of food and drink do you buy?		
Often	Sometimes	Rarely
coffee (NC)	carrots (C)	soda (NC)

B Work with a partner. Talk about the items in your chart from exercise **A**. Pay attention to the verb forms and pronouns you use with count and non-count nouns.

A: *I sometimes buy carrots. I put them in salads.* B: *Oh, I never buy them. They taste terrible!*

C In your notebook, write five or six sentences about the items in your chart from exercise **A**. Pay attention to verb forms and pronouns you use with count and non-count nouns.

EXPLORE

CD1-21

1 READ the article about sports science. Notice the words in **bold**.

The Science of Sports

Manchester, United Kingdom

When Manchester City soccer team won the English Premier League in 2012, there were **many** reasons for its success. The owners spent **a lot of** money on star players. The team also had a very good head coach. However, one reason for the team's success was less obvious. **A lot of** teams lose their star players for weeks or months because of injuries.[1] Thanks to sports science, Manchester City players did not get hurt frequently, and did not lose **much** playing time.

During practice each Manchester City player wears a GPS monitor.[2] Sports scientists then use the information provided by the monitor. They analyze each player's movements, effort, and recovery.[3] When practice is over, each player gets **some** vitamins. They also get a large **bottle** of a special drink. Each player's drink is created especially for him. The drinks help keep the players healthy.

Some teams still do not take sports science seriously. However, spending **a little** money on sports science can greatly improve a team's performance. Manchester City's story is proof[4] of this.

[1] **injury:** damage to a person's body
[2] **GPS monitor:** a small computer that records a person's movements
[3] **recovery:** return to usual condition
[4] **proof:** something that shows that something is true

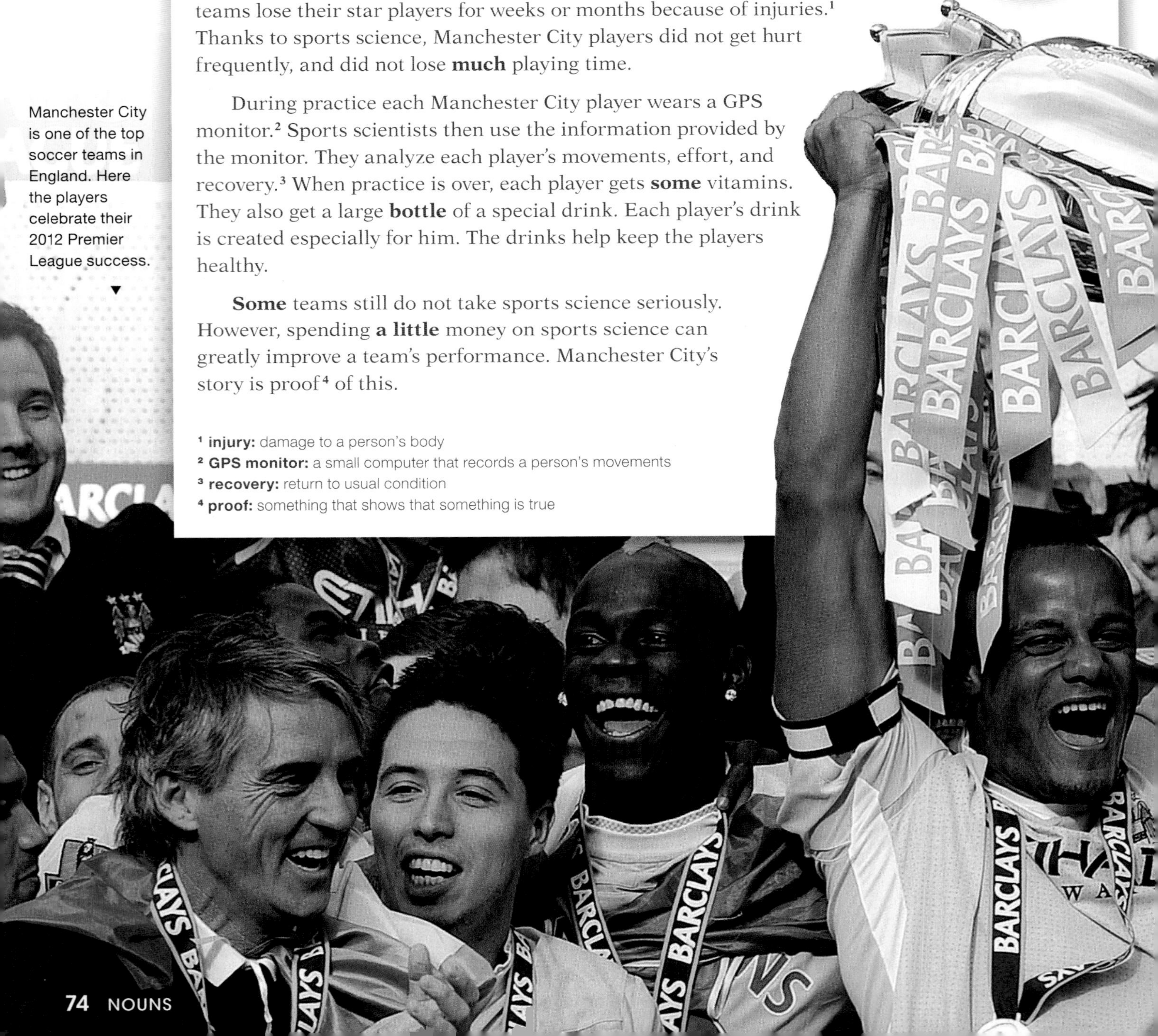

Manchester City is one of the top soccer teams in England. Here the players celebrate their 2012 Premier League success. ▼

2 CHECK. Choose the correct answer to complete each statement.

1. One reason for Manchester City's success in 2012 was ________________.

   a. having good luck b. buying star players c. playing against weak teams

2. Compared to other teams, Manchester City players ________________.

   a. were younger b. did not play as much c. had fewer injuries

3. Players wear GPS monitors to ________________.

   a. record their performance b. stop them from getting lost c. make them work hard

4. After practice, each player gets ________________.

   a. his favorite cold drink b. a bottle of a special drink c. a large bottle of water

3 DISCOVER. Complete the exercises to learn about the grammar in this lesson.

A Find these sentences in the article from exercise **1**. Write the missing words.

1. . . . there were **many** ________________ for its success.
2. The owners spent **a lot of** ________________ on star players.
3. **A lot of** ________________ lose their star players for weeks or months because of injuries.
4. . . . Manchester City players did not get hurt frequently, and did not lose **much** ________________.
5. However, spending **a little** ________________ on sports science can greatly improve a team's performance.

B Look at each sentence in exercise **A**. Is the noun after the **bold** word(s) a count noun or a non-count noun? Write **C** for *count noun* or **NC** for *non-count noun* after each sentence.

C Work with a partner. Compare your answers in exercise **B**. Then choose the correct phrase to complete each statement.

1. We use *much* with _____. a. count nouns b. non-count nouns
2. We use *many* with _____. a. count nouns b. non-count nouns
3. We use *a little* with _____. a. count nouns b. non-count nouns
4. We use *a lot of* with _____. a. count nouns b. count nouns and non-count nouns

LEARN

3.6 Quantity Words with Count and Non-Count Nouns

Count Nouns		
	Quantity Words	
We have	some a few a lot of many	dishes. flowers. glasses.
We don't have	any a lot of many	

Non-Count Nouns		
	Quantity Words	
We have	some a little a lot of	money. time. work.
We don't have	any a lot of much	

1. Use *some* with count and non-count nouns in affirmative statements.	We need **some bananas**. I left **some fruit** on the table.
2. Use *any* with count and non-count nouns in negative statements.	Maria doesn't want **any oranges**. I don't have **any homework**.
3. Use *a few* and *many* with count nouns.	I have **a few questions**. Did you buy **many apples**?
4. Use *a little* and *much* with non-count nouns.	Give the plants **a little water**. We don't have **much homework** tonight.
5. Use *a lot of* with both count and non-count nouns.	We bought **a lot of vegetables**. She eats **a lot of sugar**.

4 Circle the correct word(s) to complete each statement or question.

1. Manchester City has **some** / **any** star players.
2. **Much** / **Many** soccer teams lose players because of injury.
3. I usually go to **a few** / **a little** soccer games every year.
4. Michel didn't score **any** / **some** goals in the last game.
5. We didn't get **much** / **many** exercise last week.
6. **A lot of** / **Much** people left the game early.
7. Sally bought **any** / **some** new running shoes yesterday.
8. Marie wants to go ride her bike when she has **a few** / **some** time.
9. Were there **much** / **many** people in your yoga class this morning?
10. I didn't find **many** / **much** mistakes in your assignment.
11. There is **a little** / **a few** ice cream left in the freezer.
12. Do you have **much** / **many** homework this weekend?

3.7 Measurement Words with Non-Count Nouns

Container	Measurement	Portion	Shape	Other
a **bag** of rice	a **gallon** of milk	a **piece** of cake	a **bar** of chocolate	a **piece** of jewelry
a **bottle** of juice	a **pint** of ice cream	a **piece** of pie	a **bar** of soap	a **piece** of mail
a **bowl** of cereal	a **pound** of meat	a **slice** of bread	a **loaf** of bread	
a **box** of cereal	a **quart** of oil	a **slice** of pizza	a **sheet** of paper	
a **can** of soda	a **tablespoon** of sugar		a **stick** of butter	
a **carton** of milk	a **teaspoon** of salt		a **tube** of toothpaste	
a **cup** of coffee				
a **glass** of water				
a **jar** of jam				

1. Use a measurement word + *of* to talk about a specific quantity of a non-count noun.	He drank a **bottle of juice**. I bought three **loaves of bread**.
2. Do not use a number before a non-count noun. Use a measurement word.	✓ Put two **bars of soap** in the bathroom. ✗ Put two soap in the bathroom.

5 Circle the correct measurement word to complete each sentence.

1. Clive cut three **slices** / **bars** of pizza and put them on his plate.
2. I need to buy a new **bar** / **tube** of toothpaste.
3. Do you have a **sheet** / **slice** of paper? I need to write a shopping list.
4. Would you like a **piece** / **loaf** of pie for dessert?
5. This cake uses six **bars** / **sticks** of butter.
6. We will need three **cartons** / **loaves** of bread for the party.
7. I put a new **bar** / **stick** of soap in the bathroom.
8. Helena had a **glass** / **bowl** of cereal for breakfast.
9. Yoko is wearing five different **slices** / **pieces** of jewelry today.
10. Add two **pounds** / **gallons** of milk to the shopping list, please.
11. I didn't get a single **piece** / **sheet** of mail today.
12. The mechanic put a **quart** / **carton** of oil in my car.

6 **SPEAK.** Work with a partner. Student B closes his or her book. Student A reads measurement words from chart 3.7. Student B says any correct noun for each measurement word. Switch roles after five or six measurement words.

A: *a can of . . .*

B: *a can of beans*

PRACTICE

7 Circle the correct word or phrase to complete the blog post.

Help! What Can I Eat?

[posted by runnergirl at 8:22pm, Jan. 2]

I am a runner, so I take (1) **many** / **much** / **a lot of** interest in my diet, but sometimes it can be so confusing! For years, doctors said, "You need to drink eight 8-ounce (2) **cans** / **glasses** / **tubes** of water every day," but now (3) **some** / **a little** / **any** researchers don't agree. Also, I hear about a new diet almost every day. "To lose weight and stay healthy, don't eat (4) **much** / **a few** / **any** grains." Or, "You can eat (5) **a little** / **any** / **some** grains, but (6) **not much** / **not many** / **any**. For example, if you eat a sandwich, use only one (7) **sheet** / **loaf** / **slice** of bread." How do I do that? I already know I shouldn't eat (8) **a little** / **many** / **much** sugar. I won't drink even one (9) **bowl** / **can** / **carton** of soda because there are around nine (10) **teaspoons** / **bars** / **pieces** of sugar in each can. But what about juice? I bought a (11) **jar** / **glass** / **bottle** of juice last week, and it had more sugar than the soda. Is that OK? Please help me.

8 **SPEAK.** Work with a partner. Discuss the advice you might give to the writer. Use quantity and measurement words with the kinds of food and drink she writes about in exercise **7**.

A: *I think it's a good idea to drink a lot of water.*

B: *I agree. The writer shouldn't drink much juice. It's better to eat a piece of fruit.*

9 Complete the sentences with the words or phrases from the box.

a little	any	bowl	much	pound
~~a lot of~~	bar	jar	piece	some

1. A calorie is a measure of energy in food. High-sugar foods have ___a lot of___ calories.
2. We need to buy food with protein. How about a small __________ of peanut butter and a __________ of sliced turkey from the deli?
3. If you don't want to eat __________ grains, then you can't eat that __________ of cereal or that __________ of cake!
4. There isn't __________ milk left. I'll get __________ later.
5. I used to eat a big __________ of milk chocolate every day. Now I only eat __________ dark chocolate occasionally.

10 LISTEN, WRITE & SPEAK.

A Work with a partner. Look at the different kinds of diets and food listed in the chart. What do you know about them? Tell your partner.

CD1-22

B Listen to three friends talk about their diets. Which kinds of food are OK to eat on each diet? Put ✓ in the chart if it is OK, put ***X*** if it is not OK, and put ***?*** if you are not sure.

Do You Want to Eat Like a Caveman?				
Diet Comparisons	Low-Fat Diet	Vegetarian Diet	Vegan Diet	Paleo Diet
vegetables	✓	✓		✓
fruit		✓		
grain	✓		✓	
meat/protein			✗	
dairy				?
sugar				

C Compare your chart from exercise **B** with a partner. Then write six sentences about the diets in your notebook. Use *much, many, a few, a little, some*, and *a lot of.*

On the Paleo diet, people don't eat any grains. They eat some fruit, but they don't eat candy or other sweets.

D Share your sentences from exercise **C** with a partner. Then discuss any other information you remember from the conversation.

E Work in a small group. Discuss your thoughts and opinions about the different diets.

A: *I don't think low-fat diets are a good idea. I think eating a lot of sugar is a bigger problem.*

B: *I agree. Even organic sweets can have too much sugar. They seem healthy, but they aren't.*

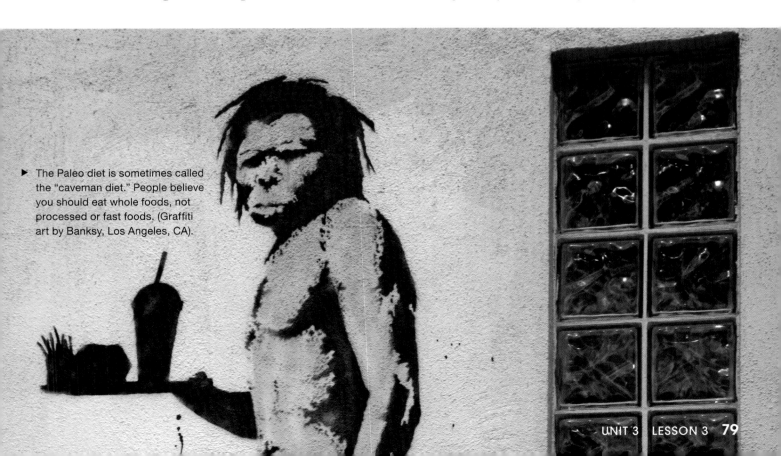

▶ The Paleo diet is sometimes called the "caveman diet." People believe you should eat whole foods, not processed or fast foods. (Graffiti art by Banksy, Los Angeles, CA).

11 EDIT & SPEAK.

A Read the paragraph about a fitness program. Find and correct seven more errors with quantity words and measurement words.

My New Fitness Program

I wasn't always fit. I used to eat ~~many~~ a lot of fast food, such as hamburgers and pizza, and I didn't get many exercise. I wasn't very happy. I wanted to lose any weight and feel fit and healthy. I didn't want to go on a special diet. Much diets have a lot of rules, and I want to enjoy a sheet of pizza or a jar of ice cream sometimes. Then, a little months ago, I found a great new fitness plan online. The plan lets me eat different kinds of food. I even have dessert a little times a week. I take a walk or ride my bike every morning. Now I'm fit and healthy, and I feel great!

B Work in a small group. Discuss the following questions.

1. Do you think the writer's fitness plan from exercise **A** sounds like a good one? Why, or why not?
2. Do you know about any special diets or fitness plans? Do you think they work? Why or why not?

12 APPLY.

A How fit and healthy are you? Complete the chart with sentences about some of your healthy and unhealthy habits. Use quantity words and measurement words.

Healthy Habits	Unhealthy Habits
I eat a lot of vegetables.	I have a bowl of ice cream for dessert every night.

B Work with a partner. Share the information from your chart in exercise **A**. Ask your partner questions for more information about his or her healthy or unhealthy habits.

A: *I eat a lot of vegetables.*

B: *What do you usually have for lunch?*

A: *A salad or a bowl of soup.*

C Form a group with another pair of students. Take turns talking about some of your partner's healthy and unhealthy habits. Use quantity words and measurement words.

Antonio gets a lot of exercise. He goes to the gym about five times a week. He also eats a lot of vegetables, but he usually drinks one or two cans of soda every day . . .

Charts 3.4, 3.6 **1** Complete the conversations with *a, an,* or *some.*

Conversation 1

Piet: I just bought (1) ___a___ new bike.

Mauro: Oh, that's (2) ________ good idea.

Piet: Yes, I really need to get (3) ________ exercise.

Mauro: Hmm, well, I have (4) ________ time off tomorrow. Do you want to go for (5) ________ ride together?

Conversation 2

June: Would you like (6) ________ cup of coffee?

Belinda: No, thanks. I just had (7) ________ coffee about fifteen minutes ago.

June: Would you like (8) ________ glass of lemonade instead?

Belinda: Yes, that would be great.

June: I also have (9) ________ fruit. I have apples, oranges, and pears.

Belinda: I'd love (10) ________ orange. Thanks, June.

Charts 3.1, 3.4–3.6 **2** Complete the sentences with one of the nouns in parentheses. Make the noun plural if necessary.

1. This gym has many new ___machines___ (machine / equipment).
2. My old gym didn't have much ________________ (machine / equipment).
3. Taylor's children don't eat much ________________ (fruit / apple).
4. How many ________________ (fruit / apple) did you use in the pie?
5. I learned an interesting ________________ (fact / information) about nutrition yesterday.
6. There was a lot of interesting ________________ (fact / information) on the website.
7. My doctor gave me a few good ________________ (advice / suggestion) about my diet.
8. Doctor Carson didn't give me much ________________ (advice / suggestion) about exercise.

Charts 3.4, 3.6 **3** Circle the correct word(s) to complete each statement or question.

1. Do you play **much** / **many** different sports?
2. My father rides his bike **a few** / **a little** times a week.
3. **Much** / **Many** people like to exercise in the morning.
4. I don't take **any** / **some** vitamins, but I have a healthy diet.
5. Elsie spends **a lot of** / **many** time at the gym. She's very fit.

6. Only **a few** / **a little** people were at the gym last night. It was almost empty.
7. She gave us **any** / **some** advice about yoga classes.
8. I found **a few** / **a little** information about that diet online, but not much.
9. I asked Paula about fitness classes. She gave me **any** / **some** good suggestions.
10. How **much** / **many** pieces of fruit do you usually eat a day?

Charts 3.4–3.6 **4** **EDIT.** Read the information about the health of Siamese crocodiles. Find and correct eight more errors with count and non-count nouns and quantity words.

Cardamom Mountains, Cambodia

Why the Health of Siamese Crocodiles Matters

~~Much~~ Many species of wild animals are dying out.[1] This is huge problem. The healths of one group of living things often depends on another group of living things. This is true for humans, too.

An good example of this is in Cambodia. In 2000, scientist Jenny Daltry took a team of scientist into Cambodia's Cardamom Mountains. She wanted to make a list of the different kinds of animals there. Daltry's team discovered much Siamese crocodiles there. There were 150!

The crocodiles live in marshes. Marshes are soft wet areas of land with much plants. The crocodiles help keep the marsh areas wet and alive. They dig mud[2] out of the marshes and help keep a water there, even during the dry season. As a result, other animals have a good source of waters. This is also helpful to humans.

[1] **die out:** disappear forever

[2] **mud:** a mixture of earth and water

▼ Siamese crocodiles are in danger of dying out.

Charts 3.1–3.6

CD1-23-27

5 LISTEN & SPEAK.

A Listen to five people talk about their fitness activities. Match the information in Column B with the correct speaker in Column A. Write the letters on the lines.

Column A		Column B
Speaker 1	c ____	a. plays many different sports
Speaker 2	____ ____	b. enjoys a dangerous sport
Speaker 3	____	c. friends do other sports
Speaker 4	____	d. roommate's father is a coach
Speaker 5	____ ____	e. is using someone else's bike
		f. gets a lot of injuries
		g. doesn't do much running
		h. isn't interested in team sports

B Work with a partner. Compare your answers from exercise **A**. Then talk about each of the speakers. Use the information from exercise **A** and any other information you remember.

Speaker 1 is starting a new sport. She rode her friend's bike three times last week.

C Look at the list of sports and other fitness activities from exercise **A** in the box below. Which of these activities do you enjoy? Do you like to watch any of these sports or activities? What do you know about them? Discuss your answers with your partner. Use quantity words, *another, other,* and *the other* when appropriate.

basketball	football	skiing	volleyball
cycling	running	swimming	yoga

I swim a few times a week. It's really good exercise. I also like to watch football. It's interesting, but there are a lot of rules. I don't understand many of them! I like a lot of other sports, too...

▶ A group of athletes competing in a triathlon

Connect the Grammar to Writing

1 READ & NOTICE THE GRAMMAR.

A Work with a partner. What do you think is the best way to stay fit? Discuss your ideas with your partner. Then read the text.

Staying Fit

Exercise is important if you want to stay fit. You don't need any fancy machines or a lot of expensive clothing. The best exercise, in my opinion, is to take a long walk every day. Walking is inexpensive, easy, and safe.

All you need for a walk are comfortable shoes, appropriate clothing, and 30 minutes to an hour of your time. If it's warm and you live near a beach, you don't even need any shoes! Walking takes very little time and money.

A walk is also a safe way to stay fit. Often people get hurt when they exercise. Some people run several miles a week and then complain of knee or back pain. Other people do a lot of drills[1] and then ache for a week. Walking is relaxing and does not put a lot of stress on your body. It provides exercise without additional pain. Walking keeps your body—*and* your mind—healthy. Go take a walk!

[1] **drill:** a practice exercise that you repeat again and again

GRAMMAR FOCUS

In the text, the writer uses singular and plural count nouns and non-count nouns both with and without adjectives and quantity words. Notice the articles and quantity words.

Count Nouns	Singular with *a/an*:	*The best exercise, . . . is to take* ***a*** *long* ***walk*** *. . .*
	Plural:	*All you need . . . are comfortable* ***shoes*** *. . .*
	Quantity word:	*You don't need* ***any*** *fancy* ***machines*** *. . .*
Non-Count Nouns	(No *a/an*):	***Exercise*** *is important if you want to stay fit.*
	Quantity word:	*You don't need . . .* ***a lot of*** *expensive* ***clothing****.*

B Read the text in exercise **A** again. Complete the chart with count and non-count nouns. Include possessive adjectives or quantity words. Find at least one more for each category.

Nouns	(Adjective) + Noun (with or without *a/an*)	Quantity Word + (Adjective) + Noun
Count	your body	any shoes
Non-Count	The best exercise	little time

C In exercise **A**, the writer states an opinion and the reasons for it. Then she uses facts to support her reasons. Complete the chart with her reasons and supporting facts.

Opinion: ***The best way to stay fit is to take a long walk.***
Reason 1: It's easy and inexpensive.
Supporting Facts: 1. You only need a comfortable pair of shoes and some appropriate clothing. 2.
Reason 2:
Supporting Facts:

2 **BEFORE YOU WRITE.**

A Work with a partner. What type of exercise or diet do you feel is best? Discuss your ideas with a partner.

B Make a chart in your notebook like the one in exercise **1C**. Complete the chart with your opinion about a good way to stay fit and your supporting facts. Use the ideas you and your partner discussed.

a an

3 **WRITE** your opinion about a good way to stay fit. Write three paragraphs and give at least two reasons for your opinion. Be sure to give support. Use the information in your chart from exercise **2B** and the text in exercise **1A** to help you.

WRITING FOCUS Subject-Verb Agreement with Count and Non-Count Nouns

When using nouns in the subject position, be sure to use the correct singular or plural form of the verb. With non-count nouns as subjects, use a singular verb.

Singular Count:	***A walk is*** *also a safe way to stay fit.*
Plural Count:	*Often,* ***people get*** *hurt when they exercise.*
Non-Count:	***Exercise is*** *important if you want to stay fit.*

4 **SELF ASSESS.** Read your paragraphs and underline the count nouns, non-count nouns, and quantity words. Then use the checklist to assess your work.

- ☐ I used *a* or *an* before singular count nouns. [3.4]
- ☐ I did not use *a* or *an* before plural count nouns and non-count nouns. [3.4]
- ☐ I used *some* in affirmative statements and *any* in negative statements. [3.6]
- ☐ I used the correct singular or plural form of verbs. [WRITING FOCUS]

UNIT 4 Going Places

Pronouns, Prepositions, and Articles

▶ Cars speed past a cowboy in North Dakota, USA.

LESSON 1 Personal Pronouns and Possessive Adjectives

EXPLORE

CD1-28

1 READ the conversation between Javier and his friends. Notice the words in **bold**.

Getting Around Mexico City

Peter: Thanks for meeting **us** at the airport, Javier. **It**'s very kind **of you**.

Javier: No problem, Peter. **I**'m just happy that **you** and Kate are back in Mexico City. How was **your** flight?

Kate: **It** was great, thanks, Javier. The only problem was that **we** wanted to sit together, but at first the airline put the children by **themselves**. **It** took a long time to find a solution, but in the end, **we** sat next to each other. Anyway, **it**'s so good to be here with **you** again.

Peter: The city looks just like **it** did when **we** visited **you** and Alicia a few years ago, but **I** don't remember all these bikes. Where did **they** come from?

Javier: Well, bikes are quite popular here now. People use **them** to commute to work.

Peter: Hmm, I used to ride **my** bike to work, but then **I** had an accident and hurt **myself** quite badly.

Javier: **I** remember . . . These bikes are mostly pretty basic. **I**'m sure **yours** went a lot faster.

Kate: Yes, **it** did. **I** was glad when **he** stopped riding.

Javier: Well, people here won't leave **their** bikes at home any time soon. Bikes make driving more difficult, but **they** are good for the environment.

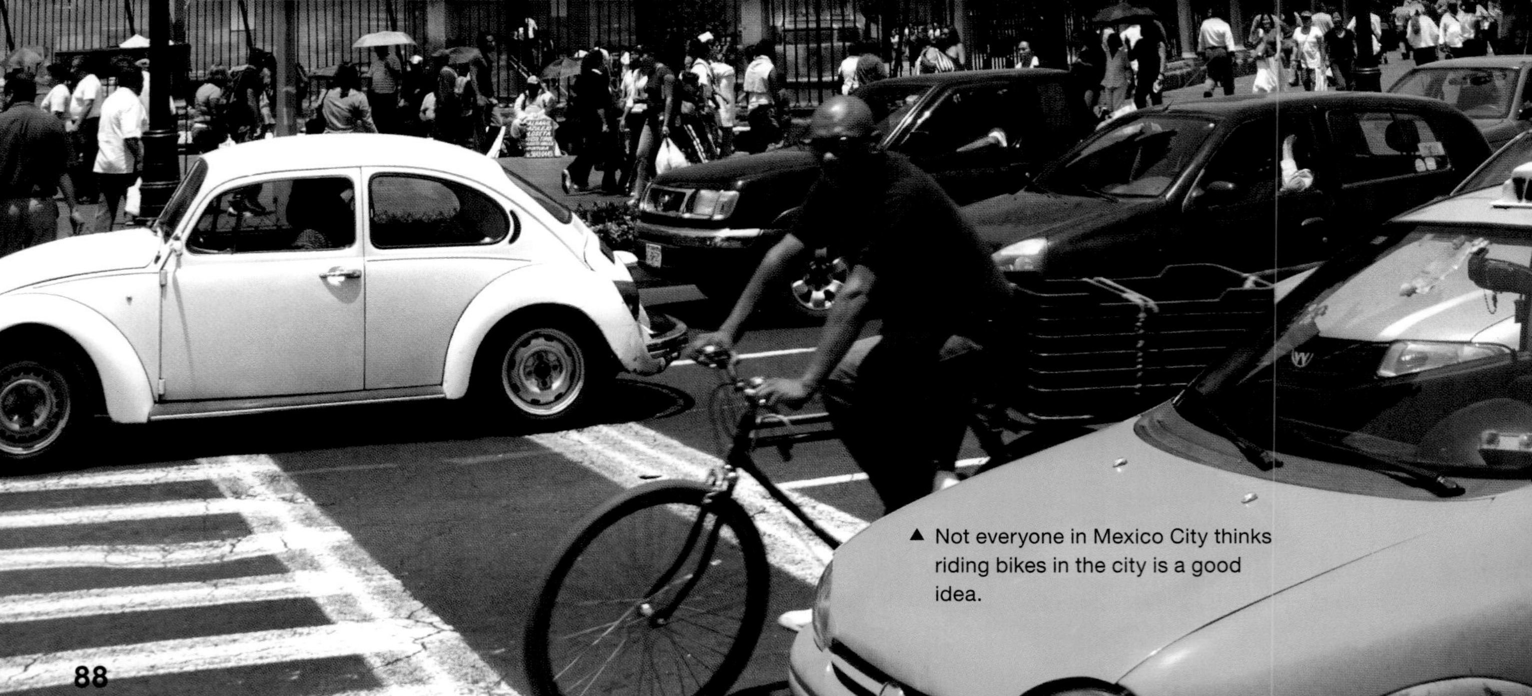

▲ Not everyone in Mexico City thinks riding bikes in the city is a good idea.

▲ Traffic on Paseo de la Reforma, Mexico City, Mexico

2 CHECK. Match each person with the correct information from the conversation. Some statements may be true for more than one person.

1. Javier ____
2. Kate ____
3. Peter ____ ____
4. Alicia ____

a. was hurt in a bike accident
b. was happy when Peter stopped riding bikes
c. lives in Mexico City
d. asks about the bikes in Mexico City

3 DISCOVER. Complete the exercises to learn about the grammar in this lesson.

A Look at the sentences from the conversation in exercise **1**. Who or what does each underlined word refer to? Write your answer on the line.

1. How was <u>your</u> flight? Peter and Kate
2. <u>It</u> was great, thanks. . . . ____________
3. . . . <u>I</u> don't remember all these bikes. ____________
4. People use <u>them</u> to commute to work. ____________
5. Well, people here won't leave <u>their</u> bikes at home. . . . ____________

B Write each underlined word from exercise **A** in the correct column in the chart.

Position in Sentence		
Subject Pronoun	Object Pronoun	Possessive Adjective
		your

LEARN

4.1 Subject and Object Pronouns

Subject Pronoun	Verb	
I You He She It We You They	arrived	late.

Subject	Verb	Object Pronoun
John	visited	me. you. him. her. it. us. you. them.

1. A pronoun takes the place of a noun or noun phrase. Subject pronouns are used as subjects.	**Elena** enjoys driving. **She** uses her car a lot. **Tom and I** went on vacation together. **We** went to Portugal. **Your suitcase** arrived. **It**'s in your room.
2. Object pronouns are used as objects of verbs or objects of prepositions.	Object of Verb: I bought **a new bike**. Do you like **it?** Object of Preposition: This ticket is for **José**. I bought it for **him**.

4 Circle the correct pronoun to complete each sentence.

1. Javier had a busy day. **He** / **Him** went to the airport to meet his friends.
2. Javier went to school with **they** / **them** years ago.
3. Did you bring your passport? You can't travel without **it** / **them**.
4. Kate couldn't find her suitcase. **Her** / **She** left **it** / **them** at home.
5. Peter and Kate have two children. **They** / **Them** are both girls.
6. Peter visits Mexico City every year. **He** / **Him** likes **it** / **them** a lot.
7. My husband and I ride bikes to work. It saves **us** / **we** a lot of money.

5 Complete the sentences. Use the correct subject or object pronoun.

1. The traffic in Mexico City is heavy. ___It___ is very slow during rush hour.
2. Some people think cyclists are a problem because there are too many of ________.
3. I drove to work with Kate. Later I met ________ at the gym.
4. These are Mario's car keys. Can you give them to ________, please?
5. I'm going for a bike ride. Do you want to come with ________?
6. This is our new car. ________ was expensive, but we love ________.

7. You look tired, Rosa. Do ________ want to go home now?

8. We were driving to work when the police stopped ________.

4.2 Possessive Adjectives and Pronouns

Possessive Adjective	Noun	
My Your His Her Its Our Your Their	coat	is black.

	Possessive Pronoun
This coat is	mine. yours. his. hers. its. ours. yours. theirs.

1. Use a possessive adjective before a noun to show that the noun belongs to someone or something.	Joe bought **his** plane ticket yesterday. The dog pushed **its** bowl across the floor.
2. Use a possessive pronoun in place of a possessive adjective + a noun.	You can use **my bike. Mine** is the blue one. That's not **your coat. Yours** is in the closet.
3. Possessive pronouns can be used as a. the subject of a verb b. the object of a verb c. the object of a preposition	a. A: Where are the bikes? B: **His** is outside. **Hers** is downstairs. b. I found their keys, but I can't find **ours**. c. Our car is nice, but look at **theirs**.
4. **Be careful!** *Its* and *it's* sound the same. *Its* is a possessive adjective, and *it's* is the contraction of *it is* or *it has*.	The team won **its** first game. A: Where is your umbrella? B: **It's** on the table.
5. **Be careful!** *Their, there,* and *they're* sound the same. *Their* is a possessive adjective. *There* refers to a place. *They're* is the contraction of *they are*.	They found **their** coats. **There** are two coats here. A: Where are the coats? B: **They're** on the chair.

6 Circle the correct word(s) to complete each sentence.

1. A: Is this **you** / **your** skateboard?
   B: No, it's not **me** / **mine**. I think it belongs to Gary.
2. **His** / **Him** car wouldn't start yesterday, so Carol let **him** / **he** use **her** / **hers**.
3. We moved here from Ohio last month. **Our** / **Ours** new apartment is beautiful!
4. My friends are unhappy because the neighbors' car is newer than **them** / **theirs**.
5. A: Is this bike **yours** / **you**?
   B: No, **my** / **mine** is green. It's over there.
6. We are going to buy a smaller house. **Ours** / **Our** is too big for us now.
7. Frank arrived here first. I parked my car behind **theirs** / **his**.

7 Complete the conversations. Use *its, it's, their, there,* or *they're.*

Conversation 1

Joan: (1) ____There____'s a postcard here from Hawaii.

Steve: Hawaii? I wonder who (2) ________________ from.

Joan: Don't you remember? Mick and Tina are (3) ________________ now. This year her company is having (4) ________________ yearly meeting in Honolulu.

Steve: Oh that's right! Well, I'm sure (5) ________________ having a great time. It was always (6) ________________ dream to visit Hawaii.

Conversation 2

Phil: I want to e-mail my friends, but I can't remember (7) ________________ e-mail addresses. I wrote them in my notebook. Have you seen it?

Mandy: I don't know. What does it look like?

Phil: (8) ________________ a small book. (9) ________________ cover is light blue.

Mandy: Oh, I think (10) ________________ over there, on the shelf by the window.

4.3 Reflexive Pronouns

Subject	Verb	Reflexive Pronoun
I	hurt	myself.
You		yourself.
He		himself.
She		herself.
It		itself.
We		ourselves.
You		yourselves.
They		themselves.

1. Use a reflexive pronoun when the subject and the object of the verb are the same.	✓ I introduced **myself** to the group. ✗ I introduced me to the group.
2. Verbs that are often followed by a reflexive pronoun include *cut, enjoy, feel sorry for, hurt, take care of,* and *tell.*	Did you **cut yourself** on the broken glass? We **enjoyed ourselves** at the party.
3. *By* + reflexive pronoun means "alone" or "without any help."	I live **by myself**. The TV turns off **by itself**.

8 Complete each sentence with the correct reflexive pronoun.

1. Hi, Stella! Did you enjoy ____yourself____ on your vacation?
2. My brother cut ________________ when he was working on his car.
3. Bye, Mike and Linda! It was nice to see you both. Take care of ________________!
4. When you are on vacation, set the timer so the lights turn on and off by ________________.
5. I felt sorry for ________________ when I fell and lost the race.
6. When we got home from the trip, we made ________________ comfortable in front of the TV.

7. There was an amazing car at the auto show. It actually drives ________________!

8. Her friends were busy, so she went to Mexico by ________________.

PRACTICE

9 Circle the correct words to complete the conversations.

Conversation 1

Bonnie: Are these keys (1) **your** / **yours**?

Hal: Yes. What's the problem?

Bonnie: (2) **Your** / **Yours** car is blocking the driveway, and I can't get (3) **my** / **mine** out. I need to move (4) **itself** / **it**.

Hal: Wait a minute, then.

Bonnie: I can't wait. If I'm late for work again, (5) **mine** / **my** boss will fire (6) **me** / **myself**.

Conversation 2

Wendy: Thanks for coming to the airport with me. I don't like to wait by (7) **mine** / **myself**.

Nick: That's OK. When are (8) **you** / **your** parents arriving?

Wendy: (9) **Their** / **There** flight is late, I'm afraid. (10) **Its** / **It's** delayed for another hour.

Nick: No problem. Where do you want to wait for (11) **they** / **them**?

Wendy: Let's get something to eat and enjoy (12) **ourselves** / **yourselves**.

10 Complete the sentences with the correct pronoun(s) or possessive adjective(s).

1. Dale broke ___his___ foot last week. Now ________'s sitting at home and feeling sorry for ________.
2. ________ need a photo of ________ for my passport. Can you take one for ________?
3. My car uses much less gas than ________. Why don't you get one like ________?
4. Margaret visits Mr. and Mrs. Cho every Sunday. This Sunday, she knocked on ________ door three times, but ________ didn't hear ________.
5. My neighbor's cat isn't feeling well. Yesterday it fell out of a tree and hurt ________. Today it didn't eat ________ food.
6. We were on a business trip, so the company paid for ________ hotel. We stay in cheaper places when we pay for ________.
7. ________'m sorry. I can't lend you ________ camera. I need ________ tonight. Ask Jim if he will lend you ________.
8. A: Do you drive to work by ________?
   B: No, I go with Susan. ________ is a coworker. We drive in my car for a week, and then the next week we drive in ________.

11 Complete Eva's story about a cruise she took with her husband and friends. Use a correct pronoun (subject, object, or reflexive) or a possessive adjective.

EUROPE
Med. Sea
AFRICA

A Cruise to Remember

A couple of years ago, (1) ____my____ husband Ricardo and (2) ________________ went on a cruise in southern Europe, on the Mediterranean Sea. (3) ________________ went with (4) ________________ friends Aaron and Lara. They love cruises, so we agreed to try one with (5) ________________. The trip was fantastic! The weather was perfect almost every day. (6) ________________ rained only once. Also, the tour company arranged special activities for (7) ________________ at each stop. From what I remember, (8) ________________ enjoyed ourselves very much!

12 LISTEN.

CD1-29

A Look at the map on page 95 and listen to Ricardo tell his story about the cruise. Notice the numbers on the map. After you listen, write the name of the person next to the number where he or she had a problem.

1. ________________ 3. ________________

2. ________________ 4. ________________

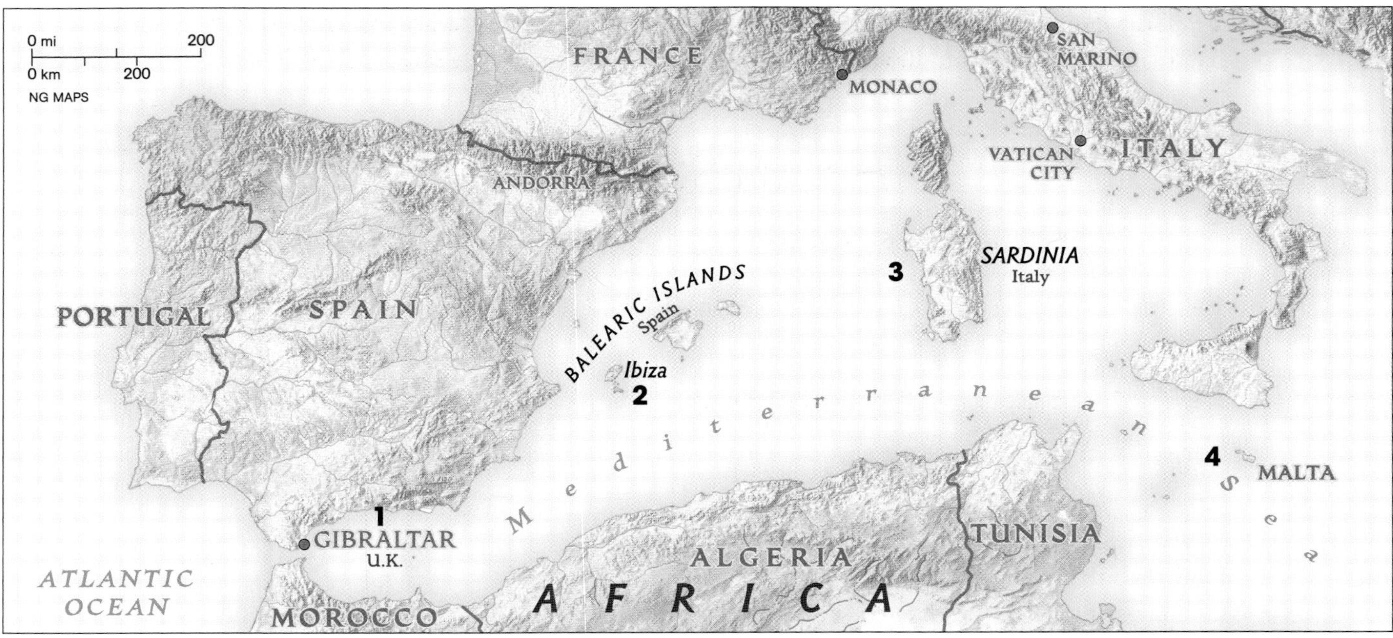

CD1-30-33

B Complete the chart with information from Ricardo's story. Listen again. Then share your sentences with a partner.

Name	What happened? Why?
1. Ricardo	He was seasick. He forgot ____________________.
2.	
3.	
4.	

13 APPLY.

A Work in a small group. Take turns telling one good or bad thing that happened on a trip you have taken. Complete the chart with information about what happened to each classmate.

Name	What happened?
1.	
2.	
3.	
4.	

B Write two or more sentences about each person in your group. Use the correct pronouns and possessive adjectives.

Dory went to the beach one day with some friends. While they were in the water, they saw a shark. It was swimming near them, but it swam away.

EXPLORE

CD1-34

1 **READ** this page from a travel website. Notice the words in **bold**.

Diving in the Bahamas

For many years, the Bahamas, a group of islands **in the Atlantic**, has been a popular vacation spot. The islands attract a lot of divers. Divers **from many countries** come to see the wide variety of fish **in the islands' clear waters**. The fish differ **from season to season**. Spring is the best time to see mahi-mahi. **In October**, manta rays are more common. **In the winter**, divers may even see hammerhead sharks.

For experienced divers, the blue holes of the Bahamas are especially interesting. **From above**. these blue holes look like deep blue ponds.[1] In fact, they are entrances **to underwater caves**.

There are over 1000 of these blue holes **in the Bahamas**. They are one of the most unusual environments **on Earth**. **At the surface**, there is a thin layer[2] of fresh rainwater. **Below that**, there is salt water because the caves open **to the sea**.

[1] **pond:** a body of water smaller than a lake

[2] **layer:** a thickness or covering

▼ A great hammerhead shark, Bahamas Islands

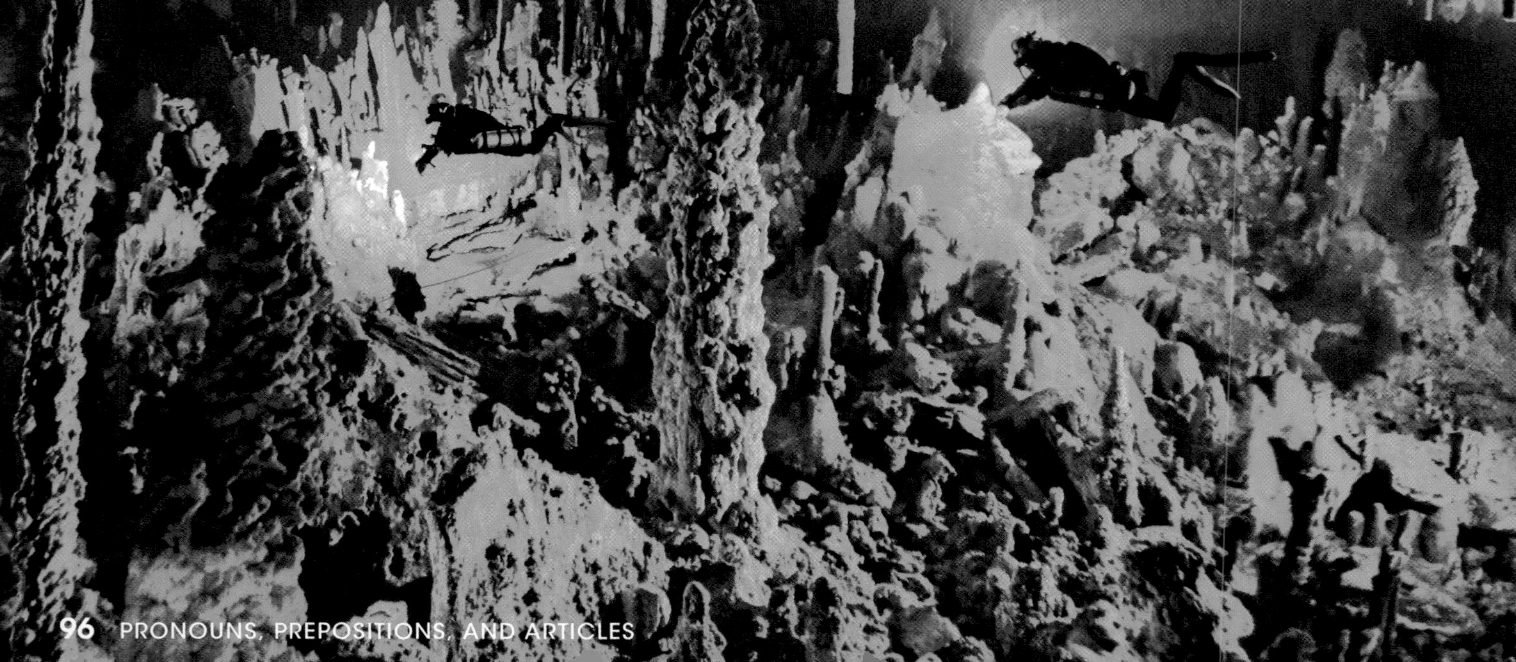

2 CHECK. Choose the correct answer for each question.

1. Where are the Bahamas?

   a. in South America b. in the Pacific Ocean c. in the Atlantic Ocean

2. In the Bahamas, divers can see ________________.

   a. the same fish all year round b. mahi-mahi in the spring c. manta rays in the spring

3. The blue holes of the Bahamas are entrances to ________________.

   a. caves on the beach b. caves in the mountains c. caves under the water

3 DISCOVER. Complete the exercises to learn about the grammar in this lesson.

A Look at the phrases in bold from the website in exercise **1**. Write each phrase in the correct column of the chart.

Phrases about Time	Phrases about Place
for many years	in the Atlantic

B Circle the word at the beginning of each phrase you wrote in the chart. Which words appear in both columns? Which words appear in only one column?

▼ Divers explore an underwater cave in the Bahamas.

LEARN

4.4 Prepositions of Time

1. Prepositions are usually part of a prepositional phrase. A prepositional phrase consists of a preposition and an object of a preposition. The object of a preposition is a noun or noun phrase.	Our train leaves **in the morning**.
2. Prepositions of time tell when something happens.	She took her vacation **in the summer.** **On Sunday** he slept late.
3. Use *at* with clock times and with *noon*, *night*, and *midnight*.	In some countries, dinner begins **at nine o'clock.** He goes out **at night.** noon, midnight
4. Use *in* with periods of time, including: a. parts of a day (except *night*) b. seasons c. months d. years	a. Sam leaves for work **in the morning.** / in the evening b. We usually take a vacation **in the summer.** c. School starts **in September.** d. I was born **in 1999.**
5. Use *on* with dates and days of the week.	My sister was born **on July 15.** I'll see you **on Sunday.**
6. Other common prepositions of time are *for, from . . . to/until,* and *during.*	We took lessons **for** three years. Stefan studies **from** six o'clock **until** ten o'clock. She likes to talk **during** class.

4 Circle the correct preposition to complete each sentence.

1. Jenny goes on vacation **for** / **in** two weeks every summer.
2. This year she decided to go **on** / **in** August.
3. She started looking at destinations online **at** / **in** the spring.
4. She took diving lessons **on** / **in** Saturdays from 9:00 **until** / **for** noon.
5. She printed her plane ticket **on** / **in** August 11 **on** / **at** midnight.
6. Her flight left **in** / **at** five **in** / **at** the evening.
7. She was on the plane **for** / **on** almost eight hours.
8. She arrived at her hotel late **in** / **at** night.

5 **SPEAK.** Work with a partner. Complete the statements so they are true about you. Then read your sentences to your partner. Ask your partner questions.

1. Last year, I went to ____________________. I was there for ____________________ days.
2. My birthday is on ____________________. I was born in ____________________.
3. In my country, students start school in ____________________. The school day starts at ____________________ and ends at ____________________.

4.5 Prepositions of Place and Direction

1. Prepositions of place tell where someone or something is.	The teacher is standing **near the window**. The parking lot is **behind the restaurant**. Let's meet **outside the cafeteria**. My car broke down **under the bridge**. I saw my friend **across the room**.
2. a. Use *in* to talk about a place inside any kind of container. b. Use *in* with names of countries, states, and cities.	a. Put the book **in a box**. I left the keys **in the car**. b. He lives **in China**. They have an apartment **in Shanghai**.
3. a. Use *on* to talk about a position on the surface of something. b. Use *on* with names of streets.	a. Put the book **on the shelf**. I left the keys **on the table**. b. The store is **on Fifth Avenue**. I got lost **on Brookline Street**.
4. a. Use *at* to talk about a specific point. b. Use *at* with addresses.	a. Go left **at the stop sign**. b. My brother lives **at 29 School Street**.
5. Prepositions of direction tell us which way someone or something is going.	We walked **toward the post office**. I drove **from Portland to Seattle**. I saw Mario on his bike **between the art and biology buildings**.

6 Complete the sentences. Use *in, on,* or *at.*

1. Michaela is on vacation ______ Ireland.
2. The travel guide is ______ the table.
3. I live ______ 21 Millbrook Road.
4. There is a restaurant ______ Walker Street.
5. Your coat is ______ the closet.
6. Barbara was very busy ______ work yesterday.
7. Were you ______ class this morning?
8. Turn right ______ the next traffic light.

REAL ENGLISH

A few common phrases with prepositions do not have *a/an/the* before the noun: *in class, in bed, at home, at school,* and *at work.*

*I stayed **in bed** until 11:00 a.m.*
*I'll call him later. He's **at work** now.*

7 Complete the sentences. Use the correct preposition from the box.

across	behind	between	from	near	outside	toward	under

1. I want to take your photo with the lake ____________ you.
2. The sun was too hot for Fiona, so she sat ____________ a beach umbrella.
3. My last apartment was ____________ the street from a restaurant. It was noisy.

4. Nilesh's hometown is ______________ two rivers.

5. We couldn't find a taxi, so we started walking ______________ the station.

6. This road goes ______________ the coast to the top of the mountain.

7. Jill was surprised when someone left flowers ______________ her front door.

8. The police station is on Lewis Street ______________ the library.

PRACTICE

8 SPEAK.

A Circle the correct preposition to complete the conversation about Ria's trip.

> **REAL ENGLISH**
>
> In most sentences, 'place' comes before 'time.'
>
> *Jemila went to Brazil* ***in January****.*
>
> But time expressions can also come at the beginning of a sentence.
>
> ***In January****, Jemila went to Brazil.*

Kim: Hi, Ria! How was your trip (1) **to** / **at** / **on** Indonesia?

Ria: It was great. Thanks!

Kim: Were you there (2) **during** / **for** / **until** a long time?

Ria: Yes, I was there (3) **from** / **at** / **on** February 28th (4) **for** / **during** / **until** March 15th.

Kim: Wow! What cities did you visit?

Ria: Well, I started (5) **on** / **at** / **in** Jakarta. I stayed (6) **on** / **at** / **in** my friend's place (7) **from** / **until** / **for** a few days. Then I traveled by bus (8) **from** / **toward** / **through** Jakarta (9) **on** / **to** / **until** Bandung. It was beautiful in Bandung, but the traffic was terrible.

Kim: I heard they drive (10) **on** / **at** / **near** the left side of the street. Is that true?

Ria: Yes, and walking (11) **under** / **across** / **between** the street can be dangerous! Cars in the U.S. stop (12) **behind** / **at** / **on** stop lights, but in Bandung I often had to walk (13) **over** / **between** / **under** cars. I was scared until I learned the secret.

Kim: Really? What's the secret?

Ria: Well, first, you put one foot (14) **at** / **on** / **over** the street and wave your hand. Then you walk quickly. People are coming (15) **on** / **toward** / **to** you in their cars, but they slow down when they see you. Easy!

B Work with a partner. Ask and answer the questions about your country. Use prepositions of time and place.

1. Is crossing the street easy? Describe the process.

   Crossing the street is very easy in my country. First, you stop at the corner. Then you wait for a few minutes, until the light is green. When it turns green, you walk to the other side.

2. How do you usually travel to your friends' houses?

3. How do you usually get to another city or town?

9 Complete the phone conversation. Use the words and phrases from the box. Add a correct preposition before each word or phrase.

a new house	three o'clock	the morning	Monday
24 Oak Road	~~May 3rd~~	the airport	night

Alex: Hi Basma! I'm looking at a flight that arrives (1) on May 3rd.
Can you pick me up (2) ________?

Basma: Sure. What time?

Alex: Well, my plane arrives (3) ________ (4) ________

Basma: What? I'll be asleep. Why are you flying so late (5) ________?

Alex: Because the ticket is half price.

Basma: Sorry, but I have to work (6) ________ morning. That might be hard.

Alex: That's OK. I can get a taxi. What is your new address? Didn't you just move (7) ________?

Basma: I live (8) ________.

Alex: Great! See you soon. Bye!

10 **EDIT.** Read the article about an unusual type of vacation. Find and correct seven more errors with prepositions of time, place, and direction.

On the Honey Road

Balyolu (pronounced bal-yoll-oo) is Turkish for "honey road." It is also the name of an unusual tour ~~on~~ in northeast Turkey.

Catherine Jaffee is a woman from Colorado in the United States. At 2008, she went to Turkey and traveled for two years. When she reached Kars, a historic region on Turkey, she thought of an idea for a tour. About 900 years ago, Kars was in the Silk Road, an important trading route from Europe and China. Kars was an important trading center in that time. Jaffee became fascinated by the way people in Kars earn their living: beekeeping and making honey.

Jaffee created a travel experience for visitors that also helped local people. On a Balyolu tour, travelers walked several miles a day at seven days. They passed under many areas with beautiful scenery. Along the way, the walkers met beekeepers and their families and tasted different kinds of honey. It was the perfect trip for anyone with a sweet tooth!

▶ A beekeeper in Turkey

CD1-35

11 **LISTEN** to a student's presentation about a creative- writing vacation in France. Answer each question with a prepositional phrase of time or place.

1. Where did the course take place? in Paris
2. When did the course begin? ________________
3. How long did the course last? ________________
4. Where did Melanie stay? ________________
5. When did the students get together? ________________
6. Where did they sit to discuss the day's work? ________________ or ________________
7. Where did the students spend time observing life? ________________
8. When did Melanie feel like a student? ________________

12 **APPLY.**

A Work in a group of three. Complete the chart. Ask and answer the questions about a place you have visited. Then ask and answer the questions about your classmates. Use prepositions of time and place.

	You	________	________
1. Where did you go?			
2. When did you go?			
3. How long were you there?			
4. Where did you stay?			
5. What was special about your trip?			

B Write about your classmates' trips. Use the chart in exercise **A** as a guide. Be sure to use prepositions correctly.

Martina went to some beautiful mountains in Slovakia a few years ago. She went in the summer. She was there for two weeks. While she was there, she stayed in a cabin on a lake and spent her days looking at the beautiful scenery. She also swam, hiked, and had a great time.

EXPLORE

CD1-36

1 READ the article about an adventure in Alaska and the Yukon. Notice the words in **bold**.

Andrew Skurka's Alaska-Yukon Expedition

On March 14, 2010, Andrew Skurka walked out of the town of Kotzebue in northwest Alaska to begin an amazing expedition.[1] He was starting **a** journey of 4678 miles (7528.5 km). He took skis and **an** inflatable raft[2] with him. His plan was to complete **the** journey mostly by hiking and skiing. He used **the** raft to cross rivers. He did not take any trains or ride in any cars or buses on his route. **The** route took him through several national parks, and he saw **some** spectacular[3] sights along **the** way.

▲ Extreme trekker Andrew Skurka in Wrangell-Saint Elias National Park, Alaska

Skurka did not carry all of his supplies with him. Instead, he got supplies at villages along **the** way.

The loneliest part of **the** trip was in **the** north. There, Skurka traveled 657 miles and didn't see **a** single village or road. During his journey, he faced **some** serious challenges. For example, in some places **the** snow was very deep and too soft for skiing. However, he managed to complete **the** journey. On September 5, 2010, he arrived back in Kotzebue. His trip took 176 days.

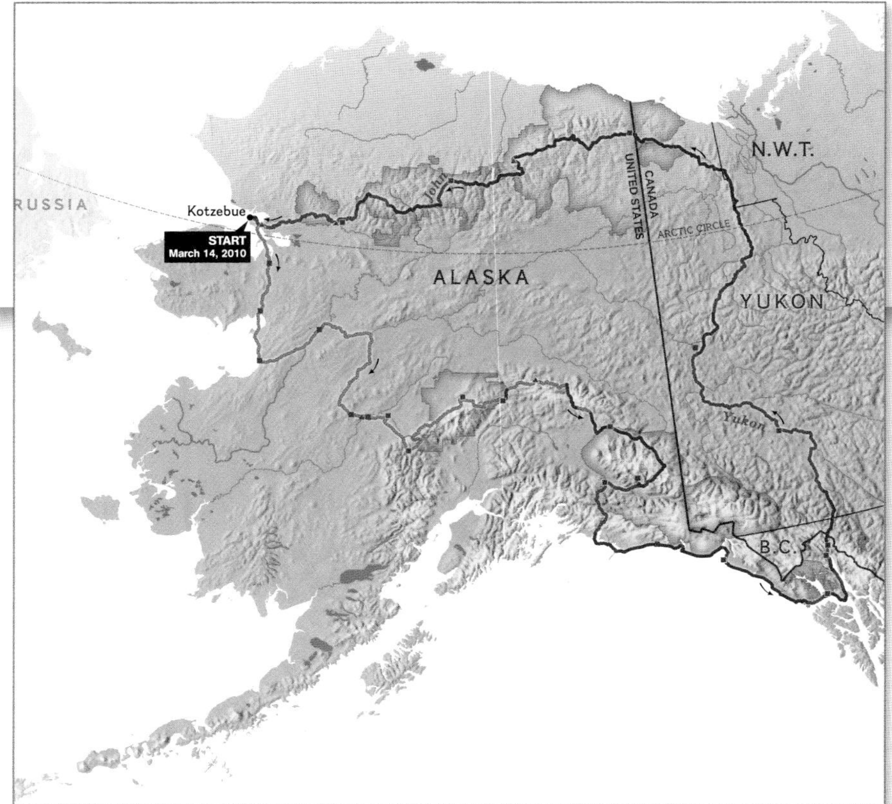

[1] **expedition:** a well-organized trip taken for a special purpose

[2] **inflatable raft:** a small, flat boat that you fill with air

[3] **spectacular:** wonderful, exciting

2 CHECK. Read the statements about Andrew Skurka. Circle **T** for *true* or **F** for *false*.

1. He used a large boat. **T** **F**
2. His journey was 2500 miles. **T** **F**
3. He stopped at villages along the way. **T** **F**
4. He didn't travel through any national parks. **T** **F**
5. There was a lot of snow in some places. **T** **F**
6. His journey took a year. **T** **F**

3 DISCOVER. Work with a partner. Look at the pairs of sentences from the reading on page 103. Notice the words in bold. Why does the second sentence in each pair use *the* instead of *a* or *an*? Discuss your answer with your classmates and teacher.

a. He was starting **a** journey of 4678 miles. His plan was to complete **the** journey mostly by hiking and skiing.

b. He took skis and **an** inflatable raft with him. He used **the** raft to cross rivers.

▲ Andrew Skurka slides across the ice in his inflatable raft.

LEARN

4.6 Indefinite and Definite Articles

Indefinite Articles: *A, An, Some,* (Ø)			
Singular Count Nouns	She needs He has	**a** **an**	coat. idea.
Plural Count Nouns	We bought I like	**some** Ø	peaches. apples.
Non-Count Nouns	She doesn't drink	Ø	tea.

Definite Article: *The*			
Singular Count Nouns	We looked at	**the**	map.
Plural Count Nouns	She opened	**the**	packages.
Non-Count Nouns	I washed	**the**	fruit.

1. Use the indefinite article *a* or *an* to talk about a person, place, or thing that is not specific. **Remember:** Use *a* before nouns or adjectives that begin with a consonant sound. Use *an* before nouns or adjectives that begin with a vowel sound.	She is at **a party**. (We don't know which party.) Where can I buy **an umbrella**? (I want to buy any umbrella, not a specific one.) **a** *college* **an** *adventure* **a** *university* **an** *important point*
2. Use *some* or no article before plural count nouns or non-count nouns to talk about something that is not specific.	There are **some motorcycles** in the parking lot. I need to buy **some gas**. He likes motorcycles. We need gas.
3. Use the definite article *the* to talk about a specific person, place, or thing.	My English course ends next week. I'm studying for **the test**. (We know which test.)
4. Use *the* before a noun when a. there is only one person, place, or thing b. the speaker and listener are thinking about the same thing c. the speaker or listener has mentioned the person, place, or thing before	a. Why are you looking at **the sun**? (There is only one sun.) b. Did you feed **the baby**? (The speaker and listener know which baby.) c. There's a woman with a child outside. **The child** is laughing. (The speaker has mentioned the child before.)

4 Circle the correct article or Ø for *no article* to complete each sentence.

1. Andrew Skurka had problems with **the** / **a** snow during his trip.
2. Skurka took **a** / **some** raft with him.
3. **A** / **The** route of Skurka's expedition went through eight national parks.
4. He bought **some** / **a** supplies for his journey.
5. **Some** / **The** trip took 176 days.

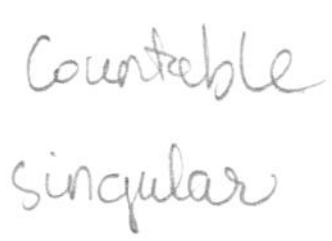

6. A: I'm flying to Alaska tonight. uncountable
   B: Really? When do you have to be at Ø / **the** airport?

7. **A** / **The** plane tickets to Alaska were very expensive.

8. We need to buy **a** / **some** map of the area.

4.7 Generalizations vs. Specific References

	Generalization	Specific Reference
Singular Nouns	**A bike** is a cheap form of transportation.	**The orange bike** is my sister's.
Plural Nouns	**Bikes** don't use any gas.	**The bikes** are in the garage.

1. A generalization is a statement about all members of a group. To make a generalization, use a singular count noun with *a* or *an* or a plural noun.	**A city** is a great place to live. **Cities** are great places to live.
2. Use *a* or *an* to make a generalization with a singular count noun.	**A car** is the best way to get around. **An icy street** is dangerous.
3. Use no article to make a generalization with a non-count noun or a plural noun.	**Chocolate** is delicious. **Vacations** are relaxing.
4. **Remember:** Use *the* to refer to a specific person, place, or thing.	**The restaurant** on Bay Street is very popular. **The people** at my office are very friendly.

5 Change each generalization from singular to plural.

1. A national park is an interesting place to visit. National parks are interesting places to visit.
2. A bike is fast and cheap. ______
3. A boat is a slow way to travel. ______
4. A cruise is expensive. ______
5. A taxi is hard to find at night. ______
6. A car is convenient, but it costs a lot. ______
7. A backpack is a useful item. ______
8. An explorer has an interesting job. ______

6 Look at the bold words or phrases. Write **S** for *specific noun* or **G** for *generalization*.

G 1. **Journeys** are often difficult and dangerous.
___ 2. **Train journeys** are often very slow.
___ 3. **The journey** took about six months.
___ 4. **The photos** in this magazine are amazing!

______ 5. **Photos** are a great way to remember a trip.

______ 6. **The national parks** in Alaska are beautiful.

______ 7. **A hike** is a great way to explore, and it's good exercise.

______ 8. **The hike** up the mountain is very difficult.

PRACTICE

7 Circle the correct article or Ø for *no article* to complete each sentence.

1. **The** / **A** / **Ø** hiking trip is a good way to relax and enjoy nature.
2. I need **a** / **the** / **some** new bike. The one I have now used to be my grandmother's.
3. When I got on the bus, I looked in my purse for **a** / **the** / **some** change.
4. Please drive carefully. **Ø** / **A** / **The** roads are very icy tonight.
5. **Ø** / **The** / **Some** people do not enjoy traveling by train.
6. **A** / **Some** / **Ø** bus tour is a great way to see the city.
7. Our tour guide showed us **a** / **some** / **an** inexpensive places to eat.
8. The hotel has **a** / **an** / **the** entrance on Water Street.
9. When I'm on vacation, **some** / **a** / **Ø** time seems to pass very quickly.
10. **A** / **The** / **Ø** weather was perfect when we were on vacation.

8 Complete the conversations with *a, an, some, the,* or Ø for *no article.*

Conversation 1

Sheila: Are you going out?

Derek: Yes, I'm going to (1) ______ train station. I need to buy (2) ______ ticket for my trip to St. Louis next week.

Sheila: Oh. Why don't you buy it online?

Derek: I tried to, but there was (3) ______ problem with (4) ______ website.

Sheila: Well, good luck. (5) ______ lines are always very long at the station.

Conversation 2

Derek: Hi there! I'd like (6) ______ information about (7) ______ trains to St. Louis, please.

Clerk: Yes, sir. What's (8) ______ date of your trip?

Derek: March 12th. I want to leave early in (9) ______ morning.

Clerk: Well, there's (10) ______ train at 6:10. Is that too early?

Derek: No, that's perfect. How much is (11) ______ round-trip ticket?

Clerk: Seventy-five dollars. We take (12) ______ credit cards or cash.

9 READ, LISTEN & SPEAK.

A Look at the photo and read the caption and the information in the chart. Then circle the correct article or Ø for *no article* to complete each sentence.

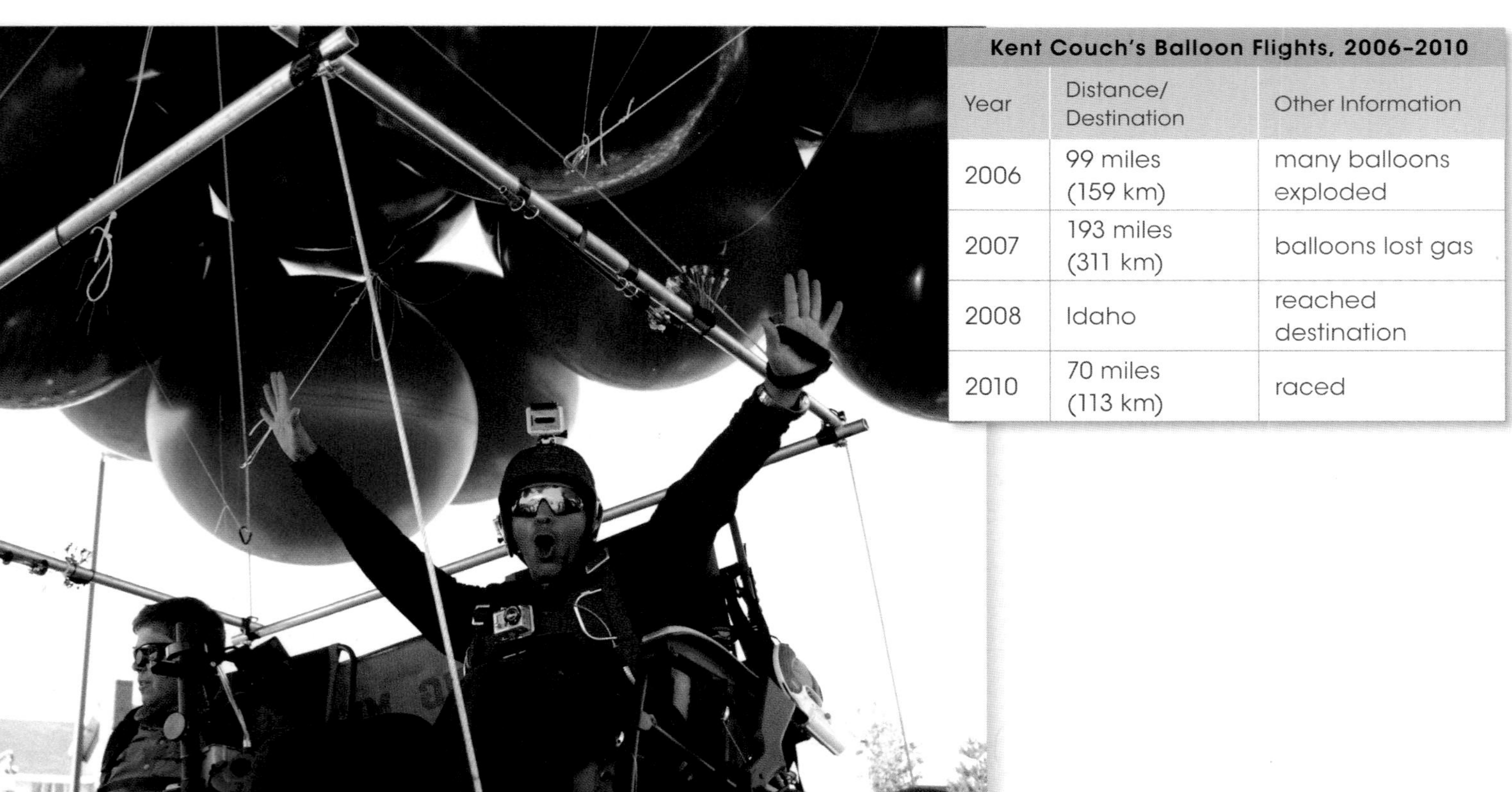

Kent Couch's Balloon Flights, 2006–2010		
Year	Distance/ Destination	Other Information
2006	99 miles (159 km)	many balloons exploded
2007	193 miles (311 km)	balloons lost gas
2008	Idaho	reached destination
2010	70 miles (113 km)	raced

▲ Kent Couch and Fareed Lafta prepare for take-off in July 2012. Their form of transportation? Over 350 balloons and a lawn chair.

1. Kent Couch made **the** / **some** / **a** balloon flight every year between 2006 and 2008.
2. Not all of **a** / **some** / **the** flights were successful.
3. In 2006, **some** / **Ø** / **the** balloons exploded, so Couch ended **Ø** / **the** / **an** flight.
4. In 2007, he had **Ø** / **a** / **an** problems with **some** / **a** / **the** gas in the balloons.
5. **The** / **Ø** / **A** 2008 flight was **a** / **some** / **the** success. Couch reached his destination.
6. In 2010, Kent Couch entered **the** / **a** / **Ø** race with another lawn-chair balloon.
7. **A** / **Ø** / **The** race was 70 miles (113 km).
8. **The** / **Ø** / **Some** flights in 2006 and 2007 were not **the** / **Ø** / **some** successes.

B Complete each statement with *a, an, the,* or Ø for *no article.*

1. Kent Couch owns _____ Italian restaurant.	**T**	**F**
2. Couch and Fareed used _____ lawn chair for their journey.	**T**	**F**
3. The balloons had _____ gas in them.	**T**	**F**
4. They expected to fly at _____ height of 5000–10,000 feet.	**T**	**F**

5. Each man had ______ small phone. **T** **F**

6. ______ weather in the north was perfect. **T** **F**

7. ______ weather report that day was not good. **T** **F**

8. Their journey was ______ success. **T** **F**

CD1-37-39

C Read the statements from exercise **B**. Then listen to the news reports. Circle **T** for *true* or **F** for *false*. Then correct the false statements to make them true.

D Work with a partner. Compare your answers from exercise **C**. What is your opinion of this form of transportation? Discuss your ideas.

10 APPLY.

A Work with a partner. Decide who will read Activity 1 and who will read Activity 2 and read about the vacation activity. Then close your book and tell your partner about the vacation activity that you read about. Pay attention to articles.

For an amazing undersea adventure, fly to the Maldives in the Indian Ocean and swim with a whale shark. Whale sharks are enormous, so don't swim in front of one!

◄ Swimming with a whale shark in the Maldives

The Nürburgring is a very dangerous racetrack to drive. It costs 35 dollars to drive around the track once. No, there isn't a speed limit!

◄ Racing at the Nürburgring in Nürburg, Germany

B Choose another vacation activity or kind of adventure. In your notebook, write a short paragraph of four or five sentences about the activity.

When I was on my last vacation, I tried scuba diving. For scuba diving, you need to use special equipment . . .

EXPLORE

CD1-40

1 READ the posts from two travel blogs. Notice the words in **bold**.

Greg's Blog

Posted: June 19

I love photography and I drive all over **the United States** and **Canada** with my camera. I live in **Portsmouth**, **New Hampshire**, so every fall I get some great photos of the leaves changing color in **New England**. I just went on a long road trip and took photos of **the Rocky Mountains**, **Mount Rushmore**, **the Mojave Desert**, **the Mississippi River**, and **San Diego**. . . . I'm posting some of my favorite photos for you to see.

Maya's Blog

Posted: July 1

I'm staying with my sister Sylvie this month. Last weekend she took me to **New York City**. We took an early train to **Grand Central Station**. Then we walked up **Fifth Avenue** to **Central Park**. Next, we went to **the Museum of Modern Art**. It was wonderful! After a delicious lunch at **the Plaza Hotel**, I wanted to see more sights. I got everything on video: **the Empire State Building**, **the Brooklyn Bridge**, and a lot of other places, too. . . . I'm having a great time!

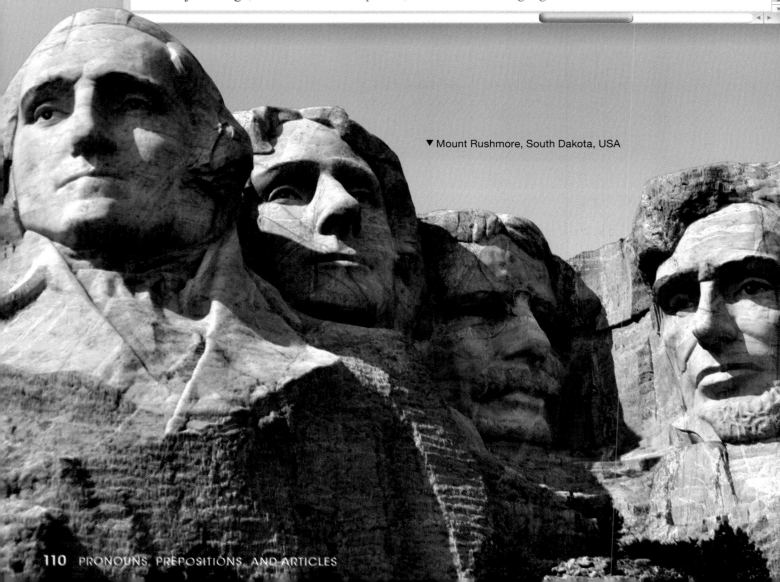

▼ Mount Rushmore, South Dakota, USA

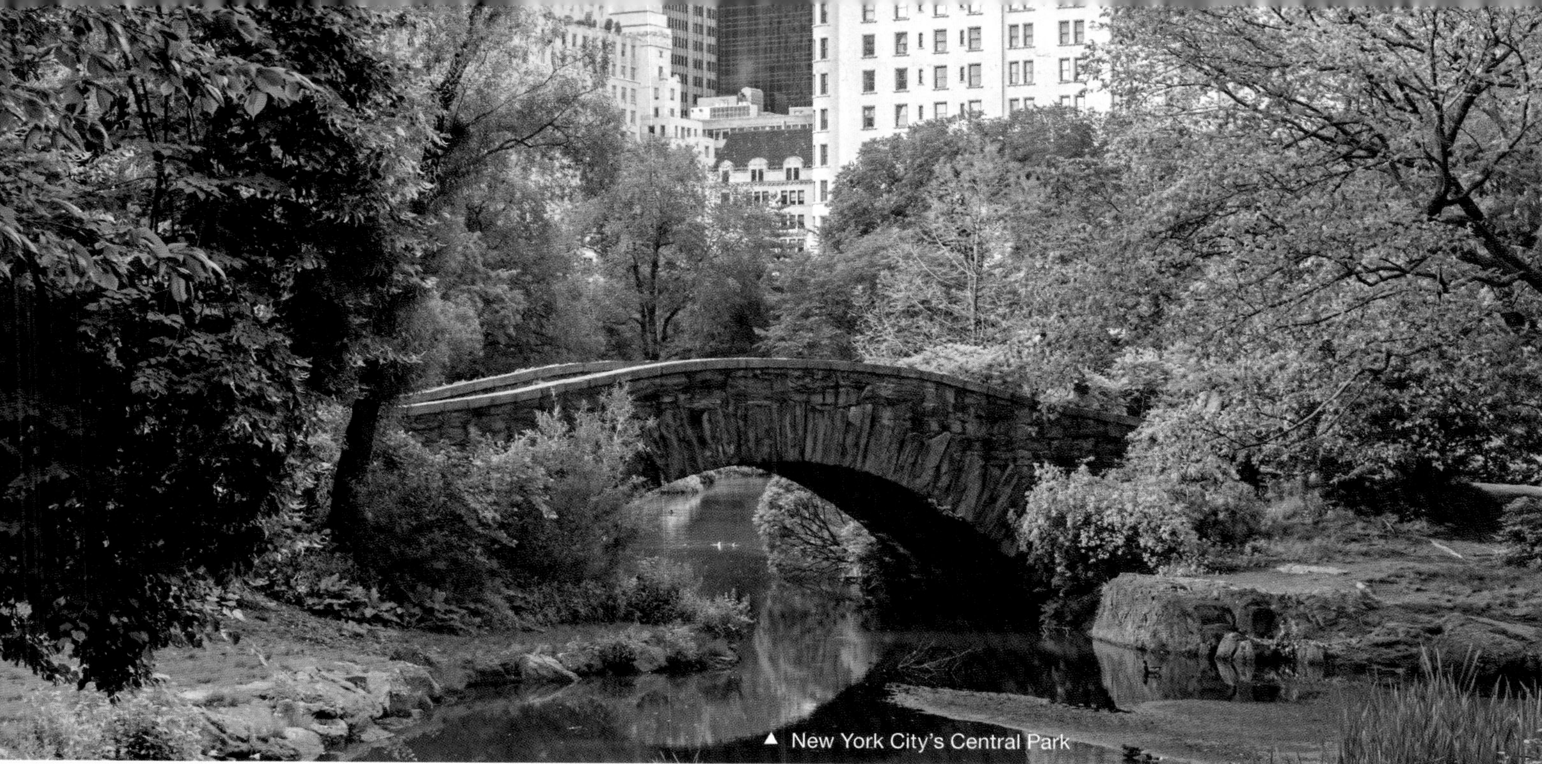
▲ New York City's Central Park

2 CHECK. Answer the questions about the blog posts from exercise **1**.

1. Where is Greg's home? ______________________________
2. Where does he drive with his camera? ______________________________
3. Which desert did Greg just visit? ______________________________
4. Which museum did Maya visit with her sister? ______________________________
5. Where did Maya and Sylvie have lunch? ______________________________

3 DISCOVER. Complete the exercises to learn about the grammar in this lesson.

A Find place names with *the* and without *the* in the blog posts from exercise **1**. Write the place names in the correct column of the chart.

Place Names with *The*	Place Names without *The*
the United States	Canada

B Work with a partner. Compare your charts from exercise **A**. When do we use *the* with place names? Discuss your answer with your classmates and teacher.

LEARN

4.8 *The* and No Article: Geographic Names

The	No Article
Baghdad is on **the** Tigris River. They live in **the** United States.	She is from Brazil. Africa is a huge continent.

1. Use no article before the names of most cities, states, countries, and continents.	Barcelona is a beautiful city. Josh lives in Texas. Morocco is in Africa.
2. Use *the* before the names of places that contain an *of-* phrase or the word *kingdom* or *republic*.	**the** District of Columbia **the** United Kingdom **the** Dominican Republic
3. Use *the* before most plural geographic names.	**the** United States **the** Philippines **the** Alps, **the** Andes **the** Hawaiian Islands
4. Do not use *the* before the names of single mountains or single islands.	Mount Everest, Mount McKinley Long Island, Maui
5. Use *the* before the names of oceans, seas, and rivers. The words *ocean, sea,* and *river* are often omitted.	They live near **the** Caspian Sea. The explorers traveled up **the** Amazon.
6. Use *the* before the names of deserts. The word *desert* is often omitted.	**The** Mojave Desert is in California. **The** Sahara is the world's largest desert.

4 Complete each sentence with *the* or Ø for *no article.*

1. My brother visited ______ Rocky Mountains last summer.
2. ______ Luzon is the largest island in ______ Philippines.
3. ______ Andorra is a small country in ______ Europe.
4. Flights from ______ Boston take about six hours to cross ______ Atlantic Ocean.
5. ______ Mount Everest is 29,035 feet (8850 meters) high.
6. ______ Atacama Desert is in ______ Chile between ______ Pacific Ocean and ______ Andes Mountains.
7. ______ Galápagos Islands are the home of many interesting kinds of animals.
8. Millions of tourists visit ______ United Arab Emirates every year.
9. ______ Sardinia and ______ Sicily are islands. They are part of Italy.
10. The city of Riyadh in ______ Saudi Arabia is located in ______ Arabian Desert.

5 **SPEAK.** Work with a partner. Take turns describing the places in chart **4.8** and other places you know. Pay attention to articles.

Mount McKinley is in Alaska. Alaska is in the United States.

4.9 Other Uses of *The* and No Article with Place Names

The	No Article
It's next to **the** Seaside Hotel. **The** Eiffel Tower is in Paris.	It's near Heathrow Airport. We live on Elm Street.

1. Use *the* before the names of most hotels, theaters, museums, and names that end in *tower, bridge,* or *building.*	**the** Savoy Hotel **the** Majestic Theater **the** Natural History Museum **the** Golden Gate Bridge **the** Empire State Building
2. Do not use an article before the names of most streets, parks, squares, airports, or bus and train stations.	Third Avenue, North Street, Steamboat Road, Friendship Park, Union Square, Logan Airport, Grand Central Station
3. Use *the* before names of most places that include *of* or *for.*	**the** Statue of Liberty **the** Center for Performing Arts

6 Complete each sentence with *the* or Ø for *no article.*

1. I am staying at _____ All Seasons Hotel, on the southwest coast of Bali.
2. When we left Florida, we flew out of _____ Miami International Airport.
3. _____ Eiffel Tower received over seven million visitors in 2011.
4. _____ Museum of Modern Art in Rio de Janeiro has an unusual design.
5. The post office is on _____ Anderson Street.
6. Terry is studying English Literature at _____ University of Mumbai.
7. My brother attends _____ Center for Performing Arts.
8. Traffic was very heavy on _____ Brooklyn Bridge this morning.
9. Do you live on _____ River Road?
10. Heidi took a great photo of _____ Bridge of Sighs in Venice.
11. I'll meet you by the statue in _____ Westridge Park at 2:00 p.m.
12. What's playing at _____ Sherman Theater this week?

PRACTICE

7 SPEAK & WRITE.

A Complete the names of the famous places and locations in the chart with *the* or Ø for *no article*. Then match each famous place with its location. Write the letter of the location on the second line in the first column.

◀ The Burj Al Arab Hotel, Dubai City, Dubai, the United Arab Emirates

Famous Place	Location
1. the Burj Al Arab Hotel d	a. Ø Japan
2. the Great Pyramid of Giza ____	b. the Himalayas
3. the Sydney Opera House ____	c. Ø Rio de Janeiro
4. Ø Mount Everest ____	d. Ø Dubai
5. ____ Copacabana Beach ____	e. Ø Egypt
6. the Louvre Museum ____	f. Ø Australia
7. Ø Haneda Airport ____	g. Ø Paris

B Work with a partner. Compare your answers from exercise **A**. Then take turns asking and answering questions about the places. Use the information in the chart and *the* or no article.

A: *Where is the Burj Al Arab Hotel?*

B: *It's in Dubai.*

C Write five sentences about other famous places and their locations. Use *the* or no article.

The Prado Museum is in Madrid.

____

____

____

____

____

8 EDIT. Read the post from a travel blog. Find and correct six more errors with articles.

I just got back from a great business trip to ~~the~~ South America. The trip started in Peru with two sales meetings in the Lima. Then, I flew to Venezuela for a meeting with clients in the Valencia. They also have an office in Philippines. I want to go there someday! The second week I was in Chile. I had some free time, so I went skiing in Andes. The scenery was amazing!

I arrived at the Logan Airport in Boston last night. I like to travel, but it's nice to be home—the New England is really beautiful this time of year. ☺

9 APPLY.

A Complete the e-mail to a friend. Write about a town or city you have visited. Use at least one place name in each numbered line. Use *the* when necessary.

Hi ____________________ (*name of your friend*),

A big hello from (1) ____________________ (*town or city*). I'm here for a few days. I decided to stay here because it's near a lot of other places in (2) ____________________ (*state, region, or country*). Yesterday, I went to see (3) ____________________ (*interesting building*) in the morning and took some photos of (4) ____________________ (*an interesting area*).

Today, I went to (5) ____________________ (*your choice of place*). Tomorrow, I am going to visit (6) ____________________ (*your choice of place*). Some other places I would like to see while I am here are (7) ____________________ and (8) ____________________ (*your own ideas*).

Well, that's all for now!

(9) ____________________ (*your name*)

B Tell a partner about the places in your email from exercise **A**. Ask and answer questions about each other's city or town. Do you know anything about the places in your partner's email? What do you know about them?

A: *Is Central Park really big?*

B: *Yes, it's the biggest park in New York City.*

Review the Grammar UNIT 4

Charts 4.1–4.6, 4.8

1 Circle the correct words to complete the conversation. Circle Ø for *no article*.

Gary: Hi, Andrea. It's Gary. Is (1) **your** / **her** / **yours** sister there?

Andrea: Sorry, (2) **they're** / **he's** / **she's** away on vacation (3) **at** / **on** / **for** a month.

Gary: A month? Really? Is she in (4) **the** / **a** / **Ø** Europe?

Andrea: No, South America. She's (5) **in** / **at** / **on** Buenos Aires right now. She's traveling around (6) **from** / **out of** / **over** country to country.

Gary: Is she traveling with (7) **the** / **Ø** / **a** friends?

Andrea: No, (8) **Ø** / **the** / **some** friends wanted to go with (9) **she** / **her** / **herself**, but they decided not to go, so she went (10) **with** / **by** / **for** herself.

Gary: Wow! That sounds exciting. I hope she's having (11) **the** / **some** / **a** great time.

Andrea: She is. I got (12) **a** / **an** / **some** e-mail from her this morning. She's having a lot of fun.

Charts 4.5–4.6

2 **EDIT.** Read the description of a vacation. Find and correct seven more errors with prepositions and articles.

My Favorite Vacation: Singapore

Last year, I took a vacation to ~~the~~ Singapore with my sister Ana. We went at September and had a great time. We stayed at nice hotel, and the food there was delicious. We visited all of a popular tourist places. We also went shopping in Orchard Road, one of the main shopping areas. At the evenings, we would sit at a outdoor café and talk until late in night. It was a wonderful vacation. I want to go back there someday!

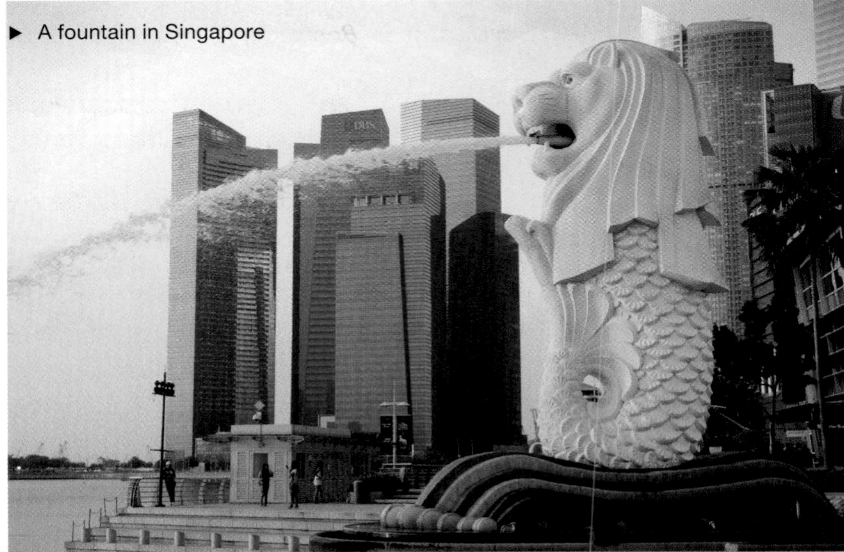

► A fountain in Singapore

Charts 4.1, 4.2, 4.4–4.9

3 LISTEN & SPEAK.

A Listen to a woman describe places in Boston. Choose the correct answer for each question.

CD1-41

1. Where does she live?
   a. on Newbury Street
   b. near the Public Garden

2. What is her favorite place in Boston?
   a. The Museum of Fine Arts
   b. Faneuil Hall Marketplace

CD1-41

B Listen again and take notes about each of the places in the chart.

The Public Garden	Newbury Street	Faneuil Hall Marketplace
beautiful in the spring and summer		

C Work with a partner. Talk about the places from exercise **B**. Use your notes and any other information you remember. Do you know anything else about Boston? Tell your partner.

The Public Garden is beautiful in the spring.

The public transportation in Boston is good.

Harvard University is near Boston. It's in Cambridge.

Charts 4.1, 4.2, 4.4–4.6

4 Work in a small group. Take turns talking about your city or hometown. Ask your classmates follow-up questions. Pay attention to articles, pronouns, and prepositions.

A: *My hometown is Tangier in Morocco. I love the Medina, the old part of the city.*

B: *What do you like about it?*

▶ The skyline of downtown Boston, Massachusetts

Connect the Grammar to Writing

1 READ & NOTICE THE GRAMMAR.

A Read the following description of a writer's favorite place.

My Favorite Place

Last summer I went to Italy with my friends Maria and Beth. One day we woke up early in the morning and drove to a town on the coast. From there, we took a boat to a small island. This island is now my favorite place in the world!

I loved the colorful fishing boats on the beach and the pretty pink houses. The weather was perfect, and the people were friendly. In fact, while we were looking at the boats, a fisherman waved to us. He and his wife invited us to have lunch with them. We had a picnic lunch by the sea. In the afternoon, we walked along the beach and had coffee at an outdoor café. When it was time to leave, I didn't want to go!

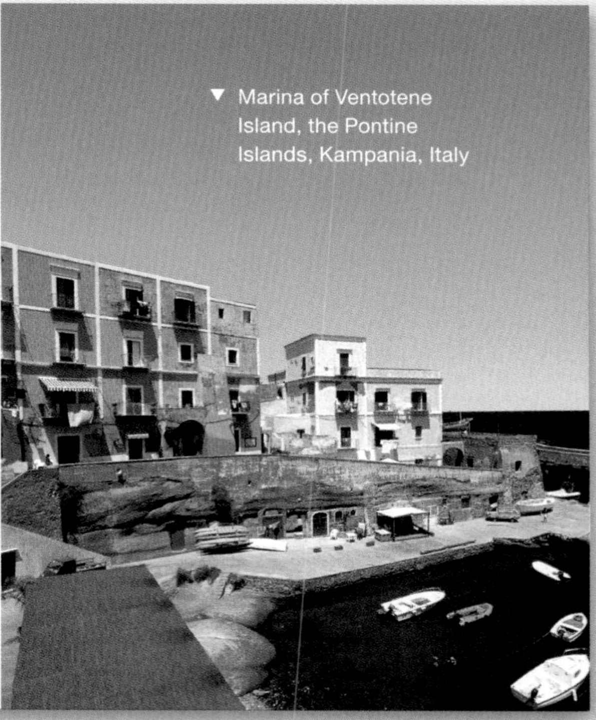

▼ Marina of Ventotene Island, the Pontine Islands, Kampania, Italy

GRAMMAR FOCUS

In the description, the writer uses prepositions of time, place, and direction to describe her favorite place.

One day we woke up early **in** *the morning and drove* **to** *a town* **on** *the coast.*
From *there, we took a boat* **to** *a small island.*

B Read the description in exercise **A** again. Underline the prepositions of time, place, and direction. Then work with a partner and compare your answers.

C Complete the chart with information from the description in exercise **A**.

Where did she go?	to an island; to Italy
When did she visit this place?	
Who was there?	the writer, her friends, a fisherman and his wife
What did she do there?	
What did she see?	

2 BEFORE YOU WRITE. Complete the chart with information about your favorite place. Use the chart from exercise **1C** as a model.

Where did you go?	
When did you visit this place?	
Who was there?	
What did you do there?	
What did you see?	

3 WRITE two paragraphs about your favorite place. Use the information from your chart in exercise **2** and the description in exercise **1A** to help you.

WRITING FOCUS Avoiding Misplaced Prepositional Phrases

When a prepositional phrase is misplaced, the meaning of a sentence is often unclear. Make sure prepositional phrases are correctly placed in your sentences.

✗ *We waited for the boat inside the café.* (Meaning: The boat is inside the café.)
✓ *We waited inside the café for the boat.*

4 SELF ASSESS. Read your description. Underline the prepositions of time, place, and direction. Then use the checklist to assess your work.

- ☐ I used subject and object pronouns correctly. [4.1]
- ☐ I used prepositions of time, place, and direction correctly. [4.4, 4.5]
- ☐ I used articles correctly. [4.6–4.9]
- ☐ I checked for and corrected misplaced prepositional phrases. [WRITING FOCUS]

UNIT 5 A Changing World

The Present Perfect

▲ Penguins on an iceberg near Antarctica

EXPLORE

CD2-02

1 READ the excerpt from a lecture about the Aral Sea. Notice the words in **bold**.

Asia's Aral Sea

Professor: . . . Now, as we'**ve just seen** in the first slide, the Aral Sea is in central Asia on the border between Kazakhstan and Uzbekistan. It used to be one of the biggest inland seas[1] in the world, but most of its water **has disappeared**. The sea **has shrunk**[2] to 10 percent of its original size.

Some people say that the water level **has gone** down because of climate change. However, we know that in the second half of the twentieth century, agricultural projects used up the water in the Aral Sea. The Aral Sea used to be home to 24 species of fish. Now, people keep cows and camels on the land next to old fishing ships.

Student 1: Have the governments of Kazakhstan and Uzbekistan **ever tried** to save the sea?

Professor: Yes, **they have**. In Kazakhstan, they built a dam[3] to help save the northern part of the Aral Sea, and the water level **has risen** again. A lot of fish are living there again, and birds **have returned**, too.

Student 2: What about the southern part in Uzbekistan? **Has** the situation there **improved**?

Professor: No, I'm afraid it **hasn't**. Unfortunately, most of the southern Aral Sea **has** probably **disappeared** forever.

[1] **inland sea:** a sea that is completely surrounded by land
[2] **shrunk:** gotten smaller
[3] **dam:** a wall that is built to keep water in a certain area

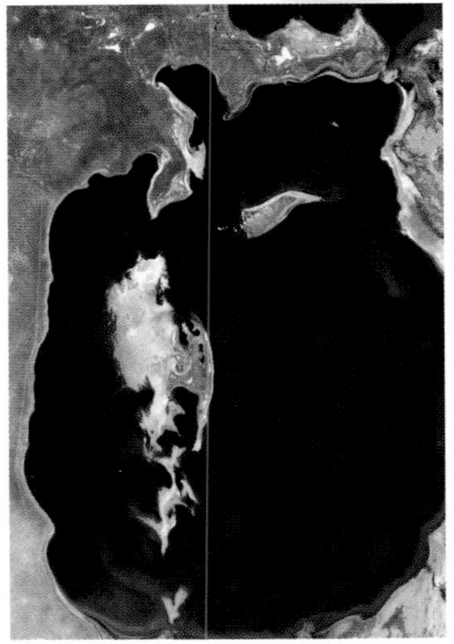

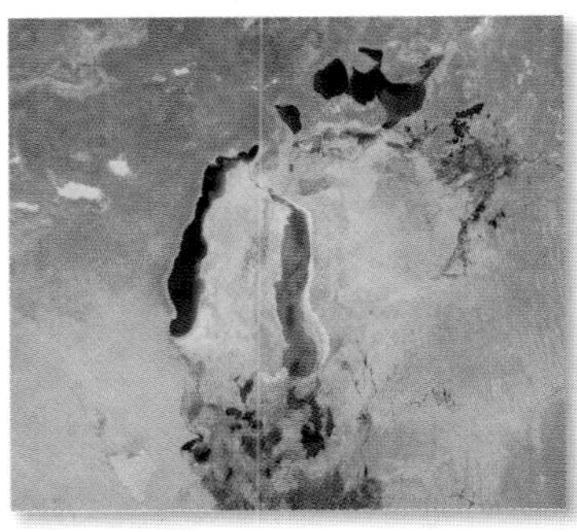

▲ The Aral Sea photographed in 1989 (top) and 2008 (bottom)

2 CHECK. Choose the correct answer for each question.

1. Which of these statements about the Aral Sea is true?
   a. It is the biggest inland sea in the world. √
   (b.) It is in two different countries.
   c. It is in eastern Asia.

2. The Aral Sea is smaller now because of ______________.

a. high temperatures   b. agricultural projects   c. building projects

3. The dam in Kazakhstan helped the ______________.

a. northern Aral Sea   b. southern Aral Sea   c. entire Aral Sea

3 DISCOVER. Complete the exercises to learn about the grammar in this lesson.

A Look at these sentences from the lecture in exercise **1**. Notice the words in **bold**. Then choose the correct answers for the questions that follow.

Most of the water **has disappeared**.
The water level **has risen**.
Birds **have returned**.

1. Which statement is true for all three sentences?
   a. The actions happened at some time in the past.
   b. The actions are happening now.
   c. The actions will happen at some time in the future.
2. Do we know the exact time of the actions or events in these sentences?   a. Yes   b. No

B Discuss your answers from exercise **A** with your classmates and teacher.

◂ The Aral Sea has dried up and left behind ships like this one.

LEARN

5.1 Present Perfect: Statements

Statements			
Subject	*Have* or *Has* (*Not*)	Past Participle	
I/We/You/They	have have not/haven't	planned	my trip.
He/She/It	has has not/hasn't	eaten	dinner.

Contractions
I have → **I've**
You have → **You've**
He has → **He's**
She has → **She's**
It has → **It's**
We have → **We've**
You have → **You've**
They have → **They've**

1. Use the present perfect: a. for a recently completed action	a. the plane arrived ——×——│ now The plane **has arrived**.
b. when a time period is not complete, such as *this morning, this afternoon, today, this week*	b. John **hasn't called** today. (It's only 4:00 p.m.)
c. for an action or event that happened one or more times at an indefinite time in the past	c. read that book ——×——×——×——│ now I **have read** that book three times.
d. Use the present perfect when the time of the past action or event is not known or important, but the result of or the experience from the action or event is.	d. I **have washed** the dishes. (They are clean now.) Nancy **has lived** in Mexico City. (She knows a lot about it.)
2. The present perfect is formed with *have* or *has* + the past participle of the verb. The past participle of regular verbs is the same form as the simple past (the base form of the verb + *-ed*).	My brother **worked** late yesterday. (simple past) He **has worked** late a lot recently. (present perfect)
3. Many verbs have irregular past participles.*	**Base** / **Simple Past** / **Past Participle** do / did / done get / got / got/gotten go / went / gone have / had / had make / made / made

*See page **A4** for a list of irregular verbs.

4 Complete each sentence with the present perfect form of the verb in parentheses.

1. The Aral Sea has become (become) ten times smaller in the last 50 years.
2. The dam has not helped (not help) the southern Aral Sea.
3. The Aral Sea has been (be) the topic of many discussions.
4. We have not heared (not hear) the latest news about the Aral Sea.

5. Our professor has gone (go) to Asia many times.

6. Maria has not read (not read) a newspaper for many years. She reads the news online.

7. The students have not spoken (not speak) to their teacher today.

8. They have done (do) all of the exercises. Now, they're taking a break.

9. David has called (call) three times this morning.

10. Joe has seen (see) every James Bond movie twice. He loves them!

11. Ellen has returned (return) from India. I want to hear all about her trip.

12. I have not eaten (not eat) lunch. Do you want to go to the cafeteria with me?

5 Complete the exercises.

A Write the missing forms of the irregular verbs from exercise **4**.

Base Form	Simple Past	Past Participle
be	was/were	been
become	became	become
hear	hear/heared	heard
go	went	gone
do	did	done
speak	spoke	spoken
see	saw	seen
read	read	read

B Work with a partner. Compare your charts from exercise **A**. Then check your answers using the irregular verb list on page **A4**.

6 **WRITE & SPEAK.** Complete the sentences. Use the present perfect. Then share your sentences with a partner.

1. I've attended classes 4 times this week.
2. I've written english many times.
3. I've not graduated, but I want to do it someday to someday.

A: *I've had pizza three times this week.*

B: *Really? That's a lot!*

REAL ENGLISH

When writing a sentence with two present perfect verbs joined by *and*, do not repeat *has* or *have* before the second verb.

*Aasim **has** recently **graduated** from college and **started** a new job.*

5.2 Present Perfect: Questions and Answers

Yes/No Questions				Short Answers
Have/Has	Subject	Past Participle		
Have	you	**driven**	before?	Yes, I **have**./No, I **haven't**.
Has	he	**worked**	in the past?	Yes, he **has**./No, he **hasn't**.

Wh- Questions				Short Answers
Wh- Word	*Have/ Has*	Subject	Past Participle	
What	**have**	they	**found?**	A map of the city.
Where	**has**	she	**gone?**	To the library.

Who or *What* as Subject				Short Answers
Wh- Word	*Has*	Past Participle		
Who	**has**	**been**	to Italy?	I **have**./Maria **has**.
What	**has**	**happened**	this week?	A lot of things.

7 Put the words in the correct order to make questions.

1. you / visited / South America / have Have you visited South America?
2. this week / what / you / have / learned What have you learned this week?
3. Bill / started / new job / his / has Has Bill started his job?
4. the news / you / read / today / have Have you read the news today?
5. have / in Europe / you / where / been Where have you been in Europe?
6. eaten / today / have / you / what What have you eaten today?
7. this week / absent / has / who / been Who has been absent this week?
8. today / she / called / has / who Who has she called today?

8 Use the words in parentheses to complete each question. Use the present perfect.

1. Have you and Scott visited (you and Scott / visit) Asia?
2. Has he read (he / read) today's newspaper?
3. What have you done (you / do) with the mail?
4. Where has she gone (she / go)?
5. Has it stopped (it / stop) raining?
6. What have they decided (they / decide) to do tonight?
7. Has she finished (she / finish) her homework?
8. Who has had (have) lunch?

5.3 Using Adverbs with the Present Perfect

1. *Already* means "sometime before now." Put *already* before the past participle or at the end of the sentence.	We've **already** seen that movie. We've seen that movie **already**.
2. *Ever* means "at any time before now." It is usually used in questions. *Never* means "at no time before now." *Ever* and *never* usually go before the past participle.	Have you **ever** read that book? I've **never** been to London.
3. *Recently* and *lately* mean "not very long ago" or "in the recent past." Put *recently* after the past participle or at the end of a sentence. *Lately* usually comes at the end of a sentence or a question.	I've read a lot of good books **recently**. Have they **recently** been to China? Have you seen any good movies **lately**? We haven't seen Sonja and Ben **lately**.
4. *Just* means "right before now." Use *just* for recently completed actions. Put *just* before the past participle.	The plane has **just** landed. We've **just** finished dinner.
5. *Still* in negative statements means "up to now." Put *still* before *haven't* or *hasn't*.	She **still** hasn't called me. We **still** haven't found the answer.
6. *Yet* means "until now." *Yet* is often used in negative statements and questions. Put *yet* at the end of the sentence.	He hasn't finished his report **yet**. Have you cleaned the kitchen **yet**?

9 Circle the correct adverb to complete each sentence.

1. Have you sent Mandy's birthday card **just** / **still** / **yet**?
2. I've **already** / **never** / **ever** heard of that restaurant. Where is it?
3. Maria has **already** / **ever** / **yet** finished her math assignment.
4. Have you seen any good movies **still** / **already** / **lately**?
5. Hal has **ever** / **just** / **still** passed his driving test.
6. I've sent Monica three e-mails but she **yet** / **never** / **still** hasn't replied.
7. We took the exam last week but we haven't received our results **never** / **already** / **yet**.
8. I haven't been to the gym **still** / **already** / **lately**.

10 **SPEAK.** Find a classmate who has done each of the activities below. Use questions with *Have you ever . . . ?* and the present perfect. Write his or her name on the line.

A: *Have you ever cooked a turkey?* B: *Yes, I have./No, I haven't.*

1. cook a turkey ______________
2. drive a truck ______________
3. paint a picture ______________
4. run in a race ______________
5. study French ______________
6. visit Mexico ______________

PRACTICE

11 WRITE & SPEAK.

A Complete each sentence with the words in parentheses. Use the present perfect.

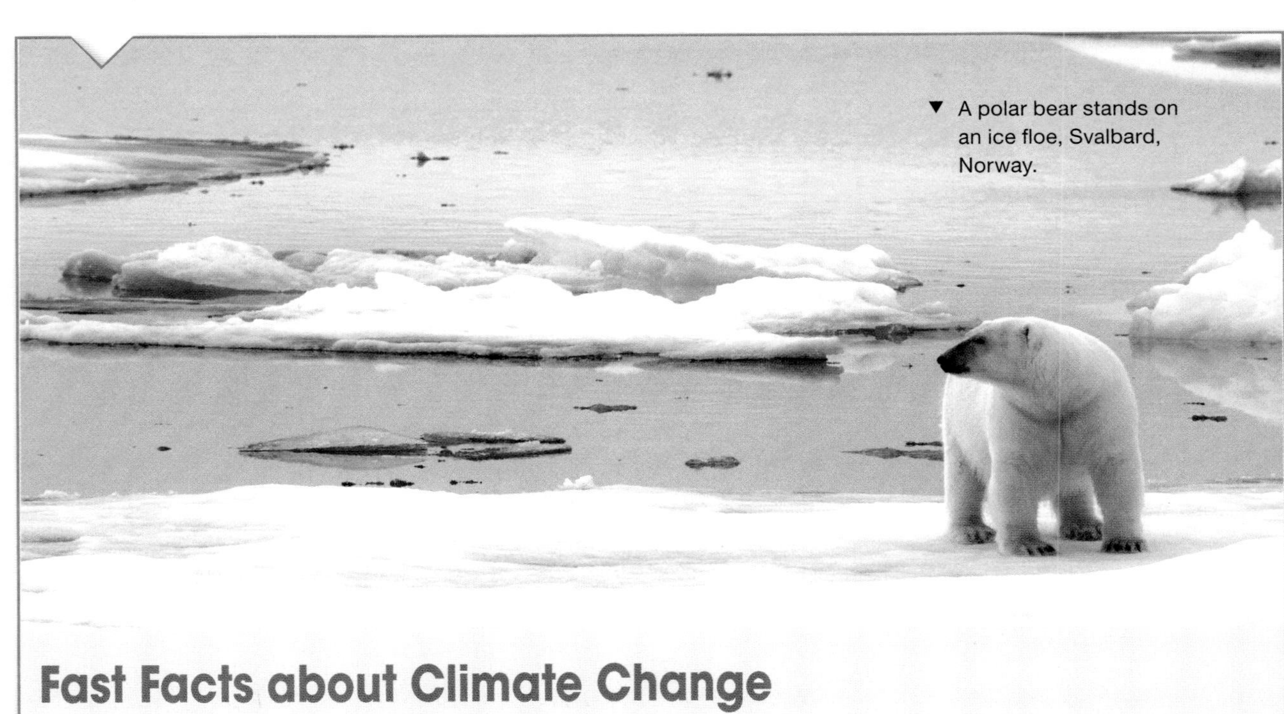

▼ A polar bear stands on an ice floe, Svalbard, Norway.

Fast Facts about Climate Change

1. In recent years the population of the Earth has grown to over seven billion.
(the population of the Earth / grow / to over seven billion)

2. In the last 200 years, human activity has caused changes in the climate. (human activity / cause / changes in the climate)

3. 0.8 degrees celsius / temperatures have rised by 1.4 degrees Fahrenheit (0.8 degrees Celsius) since 1880. (average temperatures / rise)

4. Most of this increase has happened recently., according to NASA.[1] (most of this increase / happen / recently)

5. Temperatures in the Arctic increased faster than the global average. (temperatures in the Arctic / increase)

6. The ice has began to melt at the Poles.
(the ice / begin to melt)

7. Sea levels have rised around the world.
(sea levels / rise)

8. Climate has already affected many groups of people and many types of animals. (climate change / already / affect / many groups of people)

[1] **NASA:** National Aeronautics and Space Administration

B Work with a partner. Compare your answers from exercise **A**. Then discuss the questions.

1. Do any of the facts from exercise **A** surprise you? Why or why not?
2. Have you heard or read any other facts about climate change? Tell your partner.

CD2-03

12 LISTEN and write the words you hear.

1. ________________ a new apartment.
2. ________________ jobs.
3. ________________ at that restaurant a few times.
4. ________________ all week?
5. ________________ the assignment?
6. ________________ to Alaska?
7. ________________ in a helicopter.
8. ________________ their house ________?

13 APPLY.

A Write five questions to ask a partner about activities he or she has done. Use the present perfect. Then ask and answer the questions with a partner. Write your partner's answers.

1. Q: ________________

   A: ________________
2. Q: ________________

   A: ________________
3. Q: ________________

   A: ________________
4. Q: ________________

   A: ________________

B Form a group with another pair of students. Tell your group about some of your partner's activities. Use the present perfect.

Claudia has learned about climate change this week.

C In your notebook, write eight sentences about your and your group mates' activities.

I've learned about the Aral Sea this week.

EXPLORE

CD2-04

1 READ the article about an unusual robot. Notice the words in **bold**.

Paro, the Robot Seal

▲ Dr. Takanori Shibata with Paro, the robot seal

Factories **have used** robots to build cars and other machines **for many years**. Now, the science of robotics **has reached** a new level. Robots **have now moved** from factories into people's homes.

Paro, for example, is a robot that looks like a baby seal. Paro behaves like a real pet in many ways. It responds to touch and the human voice. It also makes sounds similar to an actual baby seal. **Since Paro first appeared in 2005**, the robot **has found** a place in nursing homes[1] around the world. Nursing homes **have used** dogs and cats in pet therapy[2] **for a long time**. However, it is not always possible to have a live animal in a nursing home. Japanese scientist Dr. Takanori Shibata designed Paro to replace real pets.

Paro **has become** very popular in some countries. For example, nursing homes in Denmark **have bought** over a hundred Paro robots **since 2008**. A study found that the robot helped elderly[3] people. They felt calmer and talked more when they spent time with Paro.

Not everyone thinks that the use of robots such as Paro in nursing homes is a good idea. Some psychologists **have pointed out**[4] that relationships with robots are not *real* relationships. They believe that robots such as Paro cannot replace human connections.

[1] **nursing home:** a place where people who are sick or old can live and get care
[2] **pet therapy:** the use of trained animals to help people feel better
[3] **elderly:** old
[4] **point out:** tell someone something

2 CHECK. Read the statements. Circle **T** for *true* or **F** for *false*.

1. Paro first appeared in 2008. **T** **F**
2. Sometimes it is not possible to have pets in nursing homes. **T** **F**
3. Dr. Shibata designed Paro to help in therapy. **T** **F**
4. Paro helps elderly people to move better. **T** **F**
5. Some people think it is a bad idea to use robots in nursing homes. **T** **F**

3 DISCOVER. Complete the exercises to learn about the grammar in this lesson.

A Find these sentences in the article from exercise **1**. Write the missing words.

1. Factories **have used** robots to build cars and other machines ______________________________.
2. Nursing homes **have used** dogs and cats in pet therapy ______________________________.
3. ______________________________, the robot **has found** a place in nursing homes around the world.
4. For example, nursing homes in Denmark **have bought** over a hundred Paro robots ____________________.

B Look at the sentences in exercise **A**. Then choose the correct answer for each question. Discuss your answers with your classmates and teacher.

1. Which word is used with a length of time? a. for b. since
2. Which word is used with a point in time? a. for b. since

▼ Nursing homes in the Netherlands have used robot pets since 2008.

LEARN

5.4 Present Perfect with *For* and *Since*

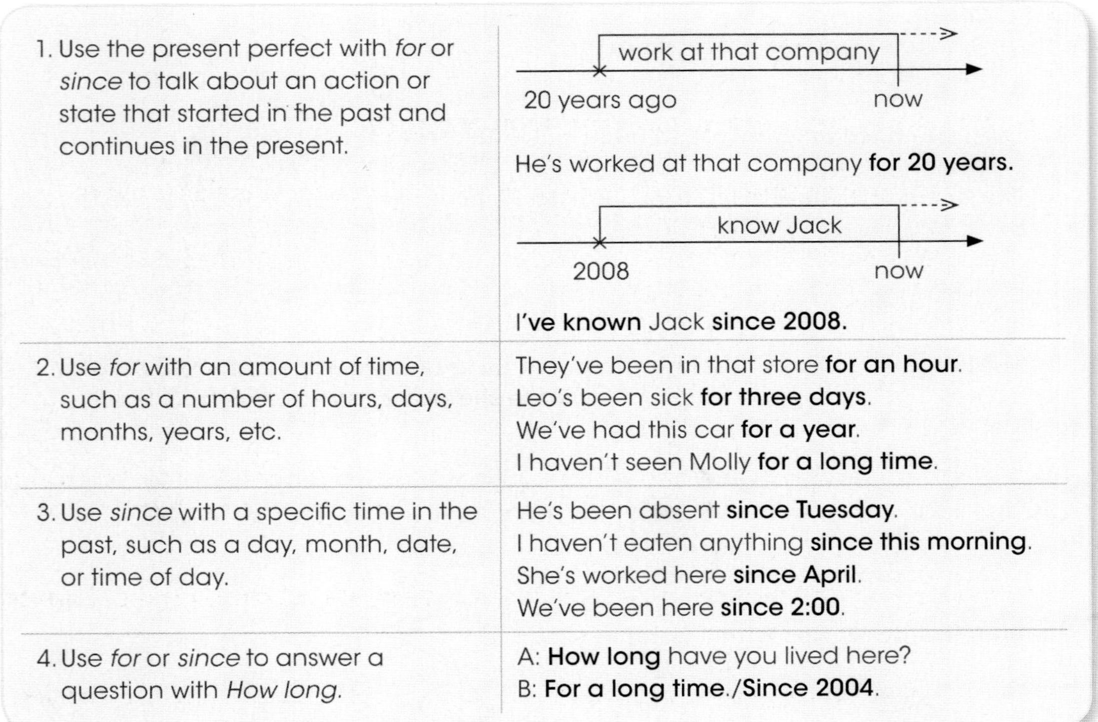

1. Use the present perfect with *for* or *since* to talk about an action or state that started in the past and continues in the present.	work at that company 20 years ago — now He's worked at that company **for 20 years.** know Jack 2008 — now **I've known** Jack **since 2008.**
2. Use *for* with an amount of time, such as a number of hours, days, months, years, etc.	They've been in that store **for an hour**. Leo's been sick **for three days**. We've had this car **for a year**. I haven't seen Molly **for a long time**.
3. Use *since* with a specific time in the past, such as a day, month, date, or time of day.	He's been absent **since Tuesday**. I haven't eaten anything **since this morning**. She's worked here **since April**. We've been here **since 2:00**.
4. Use *for* or *since* to answer a question with *How long*.	A: **How long** have you lived here? B: **For a long time**./**Since 2004**.

4 Complete each sentence with *for* or *since* and the information in parentheses.

1. Paro has been on sale in the United States since 2009. (2009)
2. Car manufacturers have used robots in their factories for a long time (a long time)
3. The university has had a robotics department Since the 1990. (the 1990s)
4. Nurses in Japan have supported the use of Paro for several yeals (several years)
5. Robots have performed dangerous jobs in factories for many years. (many years)
6. A: How long has Rita owned her car?
   B: Rita has owned her car since April. (April)
7. Matt has studied robotics for two years. (two years)
8. A: How long have you known Siri?
   B: I've known Siri for five years. (five years)

5.5 Present Perfect: Past Time Clauses with *Since*

He has been in Japan **since he graduated from college**.
Main Clause — Past Time Clause

We have lived here **since we got married**.
Main Clause — Past Time Clause

1. *Since* can introduce a past time clause. The time clause refers to a specific time in the past. Use the present perfect in the main clause and the simple past in the time clause.	I've known Rita **since I was in high school**. Main Clause — Past Time Clause
2. **Remember:** A time clause can come first or second in a sentence. Use a comma when the time clause comes at the beginning of a sentence.	She has lived in Mexico **since she was 21**. **Since she was 21,** she has lived in Mexico.

5 Use the words in parentheses to complete each sentence. Use the correct form of the verb. Add a comma when necessary.

1. (life / change / since / a lot) Life has changed a lot since the first personal computers went on sale.
2. (since / his cell phone / break) His cell phone broke since Martin has been without one.
3. Since Yvonne moved into her new apartment, we've not spoken to her (we / not / speak / to her).
4. (I / not see / Alicia) I have not seen Alicia since she got back from Spain.
5. (since / I get / a smartphone) I've got a smartphone since I haven't bought any CDs.
6. (Jack / be / to Australia / twice) Jack has been to Australia twice since his parents moved to Sydney.
7. Since the new professor arrived, the students have enjoyed all of my classes (the students / enjoy / all of the classes).
8. Since I bought my new car, I have not had any problems with it (I / not have / any / problems / with it).

PRACTICE

6 WRITE & SPEAK.

A Complete each sentence with the present perfect form of the verb in parentheses and *for* or *since*.

1. Personal computers ___have been___ (be) available ___since___ 1980.
2. People ____________ (enjoy) television ________ almost 100 years.
3. We ____________ (use) social networking sites ________ a long time.
4. Lily ____________ (have) a smartphone ________ she was in high school.
5. I ____________ (not buy) a CD ________ many years.
6. Fabian ____________ (take) three online courses each semester ________ he started college.
7. I ____________ (not receive) any emails ________ Friday.
8. Dan ____________ (send) ten text messages ________ 9:00 a.m.

B Work with a partner. Compare your answers from exercise **A**. Then talk about your own experience with technology. Use the topics below and the present perfect with *for* or *since*.

laptop	phone	social networking site	TV	DVD

A: *I've had this phone for six months.*

B: *Really? Do you like it?*

7 LISTEN.

CD2-05

A Listen to three phone conversations with an agent at an electronics company. Write the number of each conversation next to the topics below.

____ phone	____ Internet connection	____ MP3 player

CD2-06-08

B Work with a partner. Complete the excerpts from the conversations. Then listen again and check your answers.

Conversation 1

Agent: I'm sorry to hear that. How long (1) ____________ it?

Caller: I bought it in January, so I've only (2) ________ it (3) ________ about two months.

Agent: And what's the problem?

Caller: Well, (4) ________ the last week or two, the sound (5) ____________ terrible!

Conversation 2

Caller: . . . (6) ________________ some problems with my phone (7) ________________.

Agent: What's the problem, sir?

Caller: . . . Ever (8) ____________ I dropped it, the screen (9) ____________ really unclear.

Conversation 3

Caller: Finally! (10) ________________ on hold (11) ____________ twenty minutes.

Agent: Thank you for your patience. (12) ________________ a lot of calls today.

Caller: My Internet connection (13) ____________________ since (14) ________________ power yesterday.

8 EDIT. Read the conversations. Find and correct six more errors with the present perfect and past time clauses.

1. A: That's a nice watch, Paulo. I don't think I've ~~saw~~ *seen* it before.

   B: I've only had it since two weeks. It was a birthday present from my parents.

2. A: I've been on a diet for two months ago.

   B: Oh, how much weight have you lost?

   A: Not much, but I felt so much better since I started my diet.

3. A: How long are you interested in music, Anna?

   B: Oh, I've loved music since I am a child. My mother used to sing to me all the time.

4. A: Kazu, you speak French! I didn't know that.

   B: Yeah, I took it in high school. But I don't speak French for several years. I've forgotten a lot.

9 APPLY.

A In your notebook, write five facts about yourself that are true at the present time. Do not write permanent facts such as *I am Japanese*. Use the verbs in the box and the simple present.

be	have	live	own	study	want

I own a motorcycle.

B Work with a partner. Share your facts from exercise **A**. Ask questions about your partner's facts with *How long* and the present perfect. Use *for* or *since* in your answers.

A: *How long have you lived on Taylor Street?*

B: *I've lived on Taylor Street since 2010. / I've lived on Taylor Street for several years.*

C Form a group with another pair of students. Share some facts about your partner with the group.

Dalia has been married for nine years.

EXPLORE

CD2-09

1 READ the conversation about a website that creates pictures of characters from literature. Notice the words in **bold**.

The Composites

Katya: Hey, Helen, you**'ve been** on the computer for two hours! What are you looking at?

Helen: This website called *The Composites*. **Have** you **seen** it? Brian Davis, the website designer, **had** an interesting idea. He **decided** to use a computer program to create pictures of fictional[1] characters. Last year, he **put** the pictures on the website. Now you can see what the characters from books really look like.

Katya: What kind of computer program does that?

Helen: It's the same program the police use to create pictures of criminals.[2] It's used to help people when they**'ve witnessed**[3] a crime. The program lets them create a composite[4] picture of the criminal for the police. It lets them choose the right eyes, nose, hair, and so on.

Katya: OK, but why is the website using it for characters from books?

Helen: Well, in movies based on books, the characters often look very different from their description in the book, right? I'm often disappointed by that.

Katya: Yes, that's true. I **read** the novel *Dracula* last month. The main character in the book looks completely different in the movie.

Helen: OK, let's see . . . Look, here's a picture of Dracula on the website. Does he look more like the description in the book?

[1] **fictional:** not real
[2] **criminal:** a person who commits a serious crime
[3] **witness:** see or observe an event such as a crime
[4] **composite:** made up of different pieces or elements

▶ A composite illustration of Count Dracula based on the description in *Dracula* by Bram Stoker

2 CHECK. Choose the correct answer for each question.

1. What does *The Composites* website let people do?
   a. read great literature
   b. see interesting pictures
   c. write a computer program
2. Who usually uses composite pictures to create pictures of criminals?
   a. authors
   b. readers
   c. the police
3. Where does the information for the pictures on the website come from?
   a. police witnesses
   b. visitors to the website
   c. books' descriptions
4. Why is Helen disappointed by some movies that are based on books?
   a. The characters in the movies don't look right.
   b. The movies change the names of the characters.
   c. The movies change the events of the story.

3 DISCOVER. Complete the exercises to learn about the grammar in this lesson.

A Look at each sentence or phrase from the conversation from exercise **1**. Does it refer to a definite or indefinite time in the past? Put a check (✓) in the correct column.

	Definite Time	Indefinite Time
1. **Have** you **seen** it?	☐	☑
2. Last year, he **put** the pictures on the website.	☐	☐
3. . . . when they**'ve witnessed** a crime . . .	☐	☐
4. I **read** the novel *Dracula* last month.	☐	☐

B Look at the sentences from exercise **A**. Which verb form do we use to talk about an indefinite time in the past? Discuss your answer with your classmates and teacher.

◄ Count Dracula as portrayed by Bela Lugosi in the 1931 film *Dracula*

LEARN

5.6 Present Perfect and Simple Past: Indefinite or Definite Past Time

Present Perfect	Simple Past
Luis **has left**.	Luis **left** two hours ago.
I **haven't done** my homework.	I **didn't do** my homework last night.
Have you **seen** the new movie?	**Did** you **see** the new movie last weekend?

1. Use the present perfect to talk about an indefinite past action or situation. The exact time of the action or situation is not known or important, but the result is.	They **have left.** (They are not here now. When they left is not known or important.)
2. Use the simple past for an action or event that happened at a definite time in the past. The past time is stated or understood.	They **left** last night. (The past time is stated.) A: What did you do after dinner? B: I **called** my brother. (The past time is understood.)
3. We often begin a conversation with a general statement or question in the present perfect (indefinite time). Then, we provide details of time, place, and so on in the simple past (definite time).	A: **Have** you **seen** that movie? B: Yes, I **saw** it yesterday. A: What **did** you **think** of it? B: It **was** great!

4 Circle the correct form of the verbs to complete the conversation.

Christine: (1) **Have you ever visited** / **Did you ever visit** *The Composites* website?

Rose: Yes, (2) **I've looked** / **I looked** at it this morning!

Christine: What (3) **have you thought** / **did you think** of it?

Rose: It's great! (4) **I haven't seen** / **I didn't see** anything like it before. (5) **I've found** / **I found** a lot of characters on the site from books I've read. In fact, (6) **I've started** / **I started** a new novel last week, and I want to pay more attention to the descriptions from now on.

Christine: Good idea! I love the novel *Jane Eyre*, and I (7) **have read** / **read** it many times. Last year I (8) **watched** / **have watched** a movie based on the book. The actress who played Jane (9) **surprised** / **has surprised** me. She (10) **looked** / **has looked** just like the description in the book. That doesn't happen very often.

5 Complete the conversation. Use the present perfect or the simple past form of the verbs in parentheses.

Drew: (1) Have you seen (you / see) any Sherlock Holmes movies?

Joel: Yes, I (2) watched (watch) several of the old ones when I was in college, but I (3) haven't seen (not / see) one for a long time now.

Drew: (4) Did you enjoy (you / enjoy) them?

Joel: Yes, the stories (5) were (be) interesting, and I (6) liked (like) the characters a lot.

Drew: Well, it's your lucky day! There's a new TV show with a really good actor as Sherlock Holmes. (7) have you seen (you / see) it yet?

Joel: No, I (8) haven't watched (not watch) much TV recently. When is it on?

5.7 Present Perfect and Simple Past: Incomplete or Complete Time

Present Perfect	Simple Past
Meg **has had** that job since 2012. They **have lived** in Texas for a year. He **hasn't texted** me this week.	Meg **had** a bad cold last week. They **lived** in Texas for a year. He **didn't text** me yesterday.

1. a. Use the present perfect for actions or situations that started in the past and continue to the present. Use *for* or *since* to express the time period.	a. She **has worked** at the school for 10 years. (She still works there.)
b. Use the simple past for actions or situations that started and finished in the past.	b. She **worked** at the school for 20 years, but she retired last year. (She does not work there anymore.)
2. a. Use the present perfect for a time period that is incomplete.	a. I **haven't had** breakfast this morning. (It's still morning.)
b. Use the simple past for a time period that is complete.	b. I **didn't have** breakfast this morning. (It's now afternoon.)

6 Complete each sentence with the simple past or present perfect form of the verbs in parentheses.

1. This store has been (be) open for two months. It's already very popular.
2. The store was (be) open for 12 years. It closed last August.
3. Carla used (use) my laptop yesterday, but she hasn't returned it yet.
4. I've used (use) my laptop every day since I bought it.
5. We lived (live) in Florida for ten years. Then we moved to California.
6. My brother and his wife have lived (live) in this house since 2005.
7. Linda has taught (teach) for 15 years. She loves her job. / has been teaching
8. My brother taught (teach) for six years before he became a pilot.

7 Complete each sentence with the present perfect or the simple past form of the verb in parentheses. Use the time of speaking to help you.

Time of Speaking:

1. 11:00 A.M. I haven't seen (not see) George this morning.
2. 5:00 P.M. I didn't see (not see) George this morning.
3. 3:00 P.M. Did you talk (you / talk) to Julia this morning?
4. 11:00 A.M. Have you talked (you / talk) to Julia this morning?
5. 2:00 P.M. Lin has answered (answer) the phone three times this afternoon.
6. 10:30 P.M. Lin answered (answer) the phone three times this afternoon.
7. 11:00 P.M. I ate (eat) two bowls of cereal this morning.
8. 9:30 A.M. I have eaten (eat) two bowls of cereal this morning.

PRACTICE

8 READ & WRITE. Read the information about two science fiction movies. Then complete the paragraphs with the present perfect or the simple past form of the verbs in parentheses.

Science Fiction and Real Life

Science fiction movies sometimes predict the future. We looked at some science fiction movies and asked the question: *What has happened in real life?*

Movie #1: *Blade Runner* (1982) **Place and Time:** Los Angeles, California, 2019

In the movie:

In the 1982 movie *Blade Runner*, people in Los Angeles speak a combination of European and Asian languages.

What has happened in real life?

The number of Spanish speakers in the Los Angeles area (1) ________________ (increase) rapidly since 1980. At that time, the city (2) ________________ (be) home to 1.5 million Spanish speakers. Now, that number (3) ________________ (grow) to over 3.5 million. In 2012, students in Los Angeles schools (4) ________________ (speak) over 90 different languages.

▼ Los Angeles, California, USA

▲ The Terrafugia Transition car-airplane vehicle on display at the New York Auto Show

In the movie:

In *Blade Runner,* flying cars are a common form of transportation.

What has happened in real life?

Engineers (5) ________________ (design) and (6) ________________ (build) some flying cars already. A flying car (7) ________________ (appear) at the New York International Auto Show in 2012.

Movie #2: *Minority Report* (2002) **Place and Time:** Washington, DC, 2054

In the movie: 

In the 2002 movie *Minority Report,* computers don't have keyboards or mice.[1] Instead, people wear special gloves and make movements with their fingers. They use these movements to control their computers.

What has happened in real life?

Since the movie *Minority Report* (8) ________________ (come) out in 2002, touch-screen phones and computers (9) ________________ (become) very common. Also, for several years, computer games (10) ________________ (allow) users to control the action with hand and body movements.

[1] **mice:** small decives used to control computers

9 Complete the conversation with the words in parentheses. Use the present perfect or the simple past.

Elsa: Last night (1) ___I finished___ (I / finish) a really good novel about life in the twenty-third century. Do you want to borrow it?

Michel: No, thanks. I'm not very interested in science fiction.

Elsa: (2) ______________ (you / read) much science fiction?

Michel: No, not much. (3) ______________ (I / read) a few novels by Isaac Asimov.

Elsa: Oh, when (4) ______________ (you / read) those?

Michel: Um, I think (5) ______________ (I / read) the last one about two years ago.

Elsa: What (6) ______________ (you / think) of them?

Michel: Oh, (7) ______________ (I / find) the ideas about the future really interesting.

Elsa: I don't understand. (8) ______________ (you / enjoy) them, but (9) ______________ (you / not read) any other science fiction novels since then.

Michel: That's right. (10) ______________ (I / not have) much free time lately. For the last two years, (11) ______________ (I / spend) most of my time studying. Anyway, I prefer crime novels. (12) ______________ (I / borrow) one from the library last week, but (13) ______________ (I / not start) it yet.

10 WRITE & SPEAK.

A Write true sentences about yourself. Use the words in parentheses and a verb in the present perfect or simple past.

1. ___I have lived in Wisconsin since 2012.___ (since 2012)
2. ______________ (this month)
3. ______________ (since the beginning of the year)
4. ______________ (last year)
5. ______________ (a few years ago)
6. ______________ (for the past several weeks)
7. ______________ (for a few months)
8. ______________ (when I was ten years old)

B Work with a partner. Compare your sentences from exercise **A**. Then use the present perfect or the simple past to ask your partner for more information.

A: *I have lived in Wisconsin since 2012.* B: *Where else have you lived? / Where did you live before?*

11 EDIT. Read about a young software developer in Uganda. Find and correct six more errors with the present perfect and the simple past.

Abdu Sakalala: Software Developer

▲ A man talks on a cell phone west of Kampala, Uganda.

Abdu Sakalala is a 22-year-old student in Uganda. His life has changed when a phone company has run a training course for software developers[1] in Uganda last year. Sakalala attended the course and then he has started creating his own apps (programs) for mobile phones. Since then, Sakalala wrote several successful apps for cell phones. For example, he has produced a dictionary app, a translation app, and a sports app for soccer fans. Some of these apps have received international attention, and Sakalala already made almost $400,000 from his work.

But Sakalala is most proud of *Uganda Theme*. This is an app that changes the display on cell phones with pictures and sounds from his country. When it has appeared on the Internet, it immediately has become one of the most popular downloads in the world that week.

[1] **software developers:** people who create computer programs

12 APPLY.

A Read the conversation below. Underline the verbs.

Janice: Have you ever visited Europe?

Logan: Yes, I've been there several times.

Janice: Oh really? Where have you been?

Logan: I've been to Italy, France, and Spain.

Janice: When did you go to Spain?

Logan: I went last summer with some friends.

B Work with a partner. Talk about one of the activities in the box or your own idea. Use the conversation in exercise **A** as a model. Use the present perfect and the simple past.

Visit Europe/Asia/Africa	Take a cruise
Learn to play a musical instrument	Walk more than five miles
Ride a motorcycle	Your idea: ____________
Swim in a lake	

EXPLORE

CD2-10

1 READ the article about the Inuit people of the Arctic. Notice the words in **bold**.

Good Times and Bad Times for the Inuit

The Inuit are the native people of the Arctic regions of Canada, Greenland, Russia, and the United States. In recent years, climate change **has been making** life difficult for the Inuit people of the Arctic. Their traditional culture **has been** under attack. Sea ice is very important in their lives. Recently, the sea ice **has been melting**. No sea ice means no seal hunting. No seal hunting means no meat for the dogs, and dogs are very important to the Inuit. These changes **have caused** social problems in Inuit communities everywhere.

In some countries, however, life for Inuit people **has been improving**. In Alaska, many Inuit **have been earning** money from shares[1] in local companies. In Canada, changes to the law have given the Inuit more independence from the national government. They live in regions that earn money from mining and pipelines.[2] Russia, however, has no special areas or programs for its Inuit people.

For the Inuit, Greenland is special. Around 85 percent of the island's people are Inuit. The Inuit **have been driving** dog sleds across the icy land for over 700 years. Denmark used to govern Greenland. However, since 2008, the Inuit people of Greenland **have been running** their own country.

[1] **share:** an equal part of the ownership of a company
[2] **pipeline:** a system of connected pipes used to carry gas, water, or oil over long distances

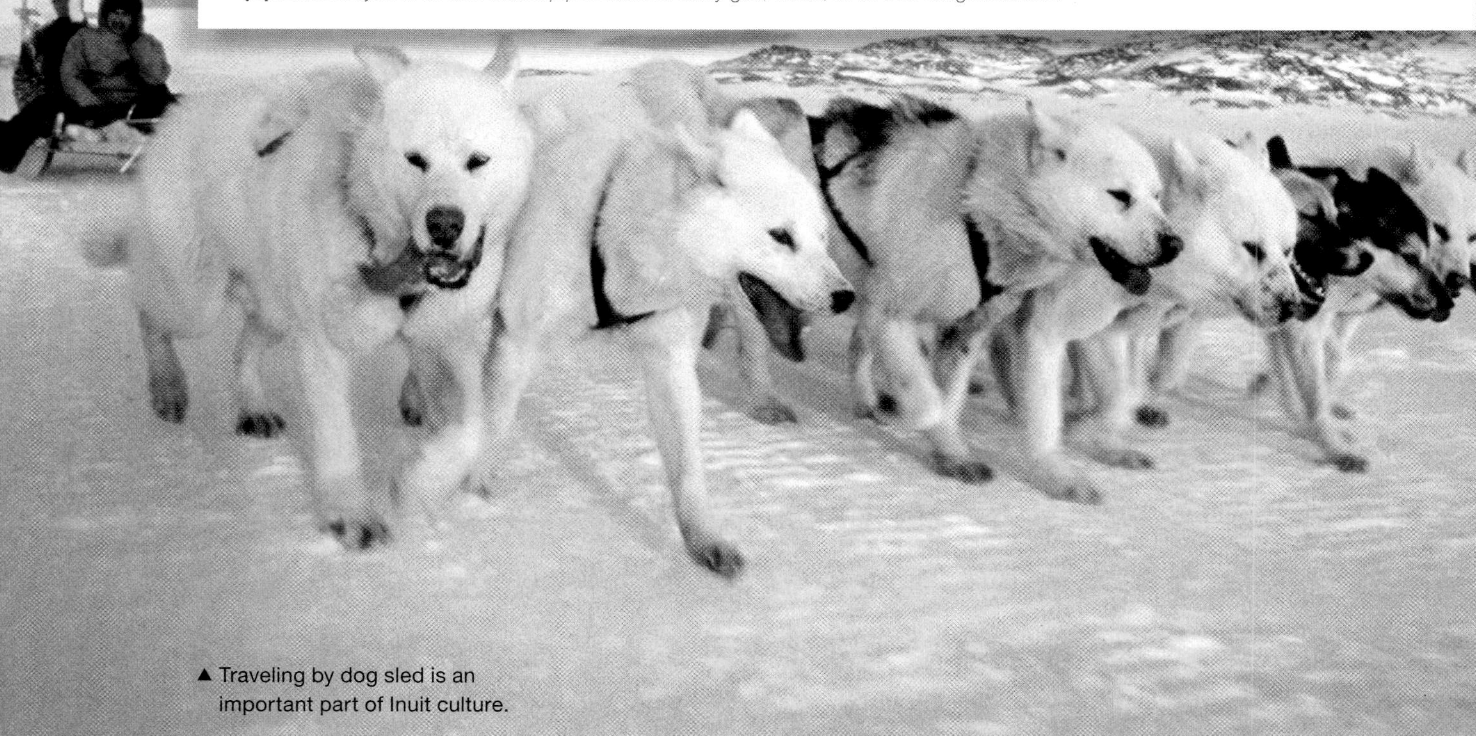

▲ Traveling by dog sled is an important part of Inuit culture.

2 CHECK. Match each Inuit group in Column A with the correct topic(s) in Column B.

Column A

1. All Inuit __b, e, g__
2. Alaskan Inuit ______
3. Canadian Inuit ______
4. Greenlandic Inuit ______
5. Russian Inuit ______

Column B

a. Increased independence
b. Climate change
c. Mining and pipelines
d. Shares in local companies
e. Social problems
f. No special areas or programs
g. Melting sea ice

3 DISCOVER. Complete the exercises to learn about the grammar in this lesson.

A Read the sentences about the article from exercise **1**. Notice the words in **bold**. Is the action finished or still happening? Put a check (✓) in the correct column.

	Finished	Still Happening
1. Climate change **has been making** life difficult for the Inuit people of the Arctic.	☐	☑
2. The sea ice **has been melting**.	☐	☑
3. Canada **has changed** some of its laws.	☑	☐
4. In other countries, life for Inuit **has been improving**.	☐	☑
5. The Inuit **have been driving** dog sleds across Greenland for over 700 years.	☐	☐

B Work with a partner. Compare your answers from exercise **A**. What do you notice about the verb form used for actions that are still happening? Discuss your answer with your classmates and teacher.

▼ Many Inuit depend on seal hunting for food and clothes. The Inuit also sell seal skins to earn money.

LEARN

5.8 Present Perfect Progressive: Statements

Affirmative and Negative Statements				
Subject	*Have* or *Has* (*Not*)	*Been*	Verb + *-ing*	
I/We/You/They	have have not/haven't	been	working	for six months. since last year. lately/recently.
He/She/It	has has not/hasn't			

1. Use the present perfect progressive: a. to talk about an action or situation that started in the past and continues in the present	a. 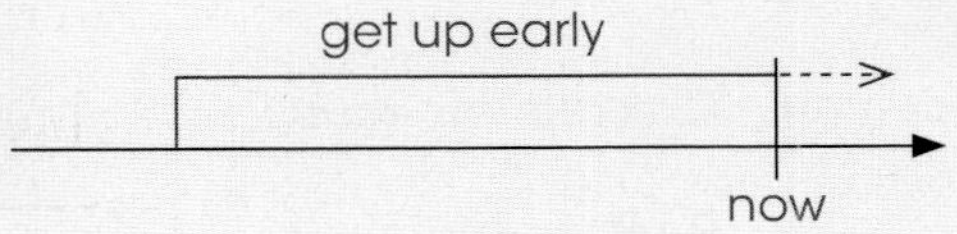 I**'ve been getting up** early lately.
b. to emphasize that a repeated action is only temporary	b. She**'s been walking** to work this week. (She usually drives, but her car is broken.)
c. to emphasize that an action or situation was completed very recently	c. A: Why is there paint on your shirt? B: I**'ve been painting** my living room. (I just finished painting it.)
2. Use *for* or *since* with the present perfect progressive to tell how long the action has been happening.	I **haven't been thinking** clearly for a few days. He **has been sleeping** since he got home.
3. **Remember:** We do not usually use non-action verbs with the progressive.	✓ They**'ve known** Ed for a long time. ✗ They've been knowing Ed for a long time.

4 Complete each sentence with the present perfect progressive form of the verb in parentheses.

1. I have been reading (read) about the Inuit for my assignment.
2. Inuit people have been living (live) in the Arctic regions for over a thousand years. have lived
3. Their way of life has been changing (change) in recent years.
4. In Canada, some Inuit have been earning (earn) money as artists.
5. Some schools haven't been teaching (not teach) children in their native languages.
6. More tourists have been visiting (visit) Greenland recently.
7. More people have been writing (write) about Inuit culture.
8. Interest in the Inuit has been growing (grow).
9. Inuit people have been useing (use) dog sleds for hundreds of years.
10. Some governments have not been helping (not help) the Inuit.

5.9 Present Perfect Progressive: Questions and Answers

Yes/No Questions					Short Answers
Have/Has	Subject	*Been*	Verb + *-ing*		
Have	you	**been**	**waiting**	for a long time?	Yes, I **have**./No, I **haven't**.
Has	he		**exercising**	lately?	Yes, he **has**./No, he **hasn't**.

Wh- Questions					Answers
Wh- Word	*Have/Has*	Subject	*Been*	Verb + *-ing*	
What	**have**	they	**been**	**doing?**	Studying.
How long	**has**	she		**sleeping?**	About an hour.

Who or *What* as Subject					Answers
Wh- Word	*Has*	*Been*	Verb + *-ing*		
Who	**has**	**been**	**helping**	you?	Maria./Maria **has**.
What	**has**		**happening**	lately?	A lot of things./Not much.

Homework #

5 Put the words in the correct order to make questions using the present perfect progressive.

1. recently / been / you / doing / what / have What have you been doing recently?
2. been / long / living / he / how / here / has How long has he been living here?
3. diet / have / healthy / eating / been / you / a Have you been eating healthy diet?
4. going / she / been / to class / has Has she been going to class?
5. shouting / he / has / been / why Why has he been shouting?
6. the piano / been / for / you / a long time / have / playing Have you been playing the piano for a long time?
7. lately / on weekends / why / Andre / been / has / working Why has Andre been working on weekends lately? dating
8. has / teaching / who / this week / been / the class Who has been teaching the class this week? lately
9. you / been / reading / lately / what / have What have you been reading?
10. been / a lot / you / have / lately / studying Have you been studying a lot lately?

6 **SPEAK.** Work with a partner. Ask and answer questions using *How long* and the present perfect progressive. Use the phrases below.

do this exercise	drive a car	go to the gym	live here
sit in this classroom	study English	take classes here	wear glasses

A: *How long have you been living here?* B: *About six months.*

5.10 Present Perfect Progressive and Present Perfect

Present Perfect Progressive	Present Perfect
I**'ve been reading** a book on Greenland. (I'm not finished.)	I**'ve read a lot of books** on Greenland. (I'm finished.)
A: How long **have** you **been driving?** B: About ten years.	A: **Have** you **ever driven** in New York City? B: No, I take the subway when I'm there.

1. Use the present perfect progressive for an action or situation that is not complete.	She **has been writing** a cookbook. (She's not finished.)
Use the present perfect for a completed action or situation.	She **has written** a cookbook. (She is finished.)
2. Use the present perfect progressive with an action verb to ask a question with *How long*.	A: **How long have** you **been studying?** B: I**'ve been studying** for two hours.
Use the present perfect with a non-action verb to ask a question with *How long*.	A: **How long have** you **known** her? B: I**'ve known** her since I was five.
3. Use the present perfect for repeated actions.	I**'ve watched** three movies this week. I**'ve watched** the news three times today.

7 Complete each sentence or question. Use the present perfect or the present perfect progressive form of the verb in parentheses.

1. Wow! You have changed (change) since I saw you last! You look great!
2. I've been working (work) on my report since this morning. I still have two sections to write.
3. How long have you owned (you / own) your car?
4. Margaret has gone (go) to Alaska twice.
5. I've been using (use) Steve's old computer this afternoon. Mine is broken.
6. How long have you been reading? (you / read) that book?
7. This assignment has been taken (take) me three hours. It's finally finished!
8. Tamara has had (have) that coat for 20 years. She needs a new one.

PRACTICE

8 Complete the conversations with the words in parentheses. Use the present perfect or the present perfect progressive.

Conversation 1

Kylie: Judy, (1) have you seen (you / see) my running shoes?

Judy: No, I haven't. I'm not surprised you can't find them. The last few weeks (2) you haven't been exerciseing (you / not exercise) like you used to.

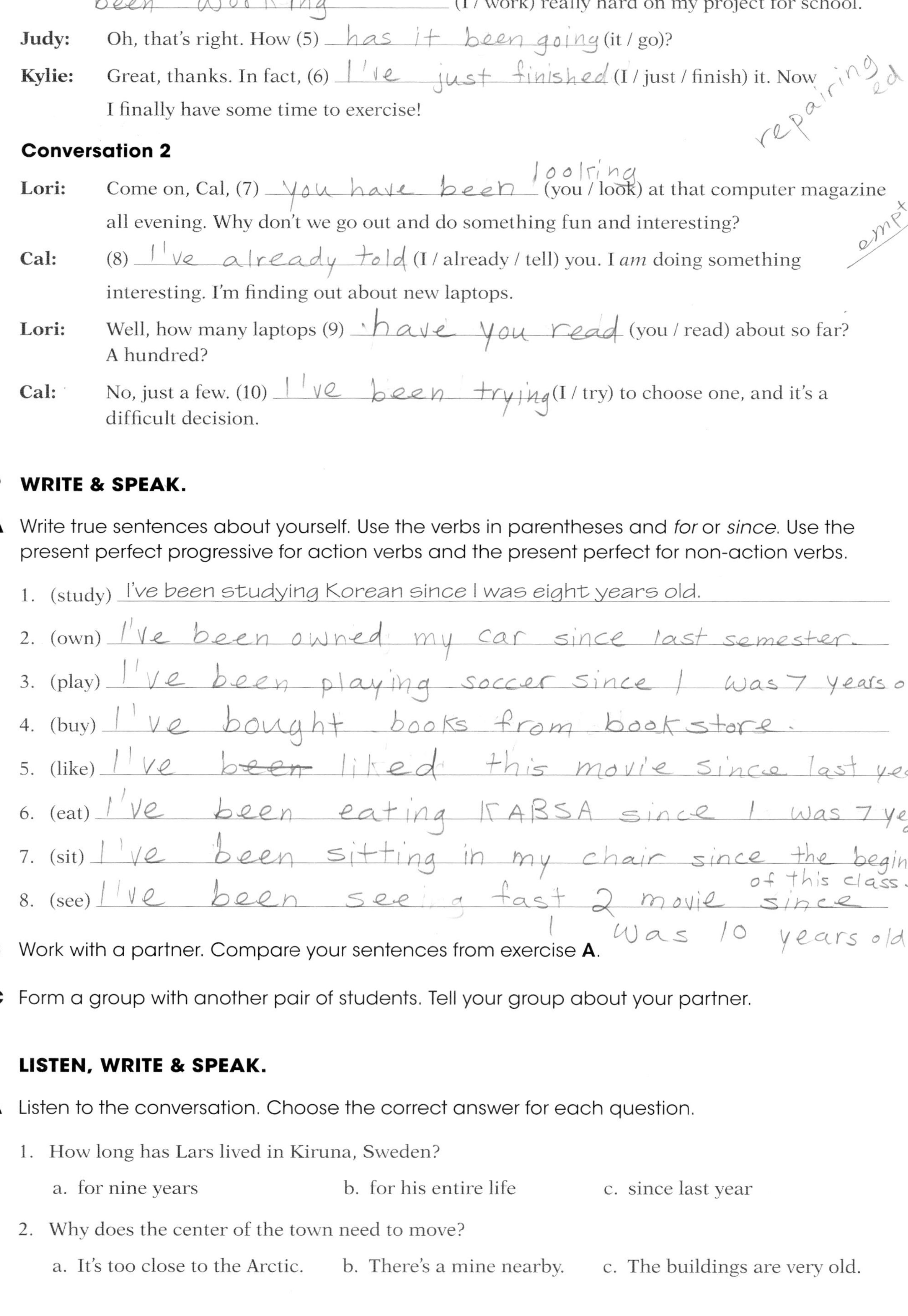

Kylie: Well, (3) I have not had (I / not have) time. (4) I have been working (I / work) really hard on my project for school.

Judy: Oh, that's right. How (5) has it been going (it / go)?

Kylie: Great, thanks. In fact, (6) I've just finished (I / just / finish) it. Now I finally have some time to exercise!

repairing ed

Conversation 2

Lori: Come on, Cal, (7) you have been looking (you / look) at that computer magazine all evening. Why don't we go out and do something fun and interesting?

Cal: (8) I've already told (I / already / tell) you. I *am* doing something interesting. I'm finding out about new laptops.

empty

Lori: Well, how many laptops (9) have you read (you / read) about so far? A hundred?

Cal: No, just a few. (10) I've been trying (I / try) to choose one, and it's a difficult decision.

9 WRITE & SPEAK.

A Write true sentences about yourself. Use the verbs in parentheses and *for* or *since*. Use the present perfect progressive for action verbs and the present perfect for non-action verbs.

1. (study) I've been studying Korean since I was eight years old.
2. (own) I've been owned my car since last semester.
3. (play) I've been playing soccer since I was 7 years old.
4. (buy) I've bought books from bookstore.
5. (like) I've ~~been~~ liked this movie since last year.
6. (eat) I've been eating KABSA since I was 7 years old
7. (sit) I've been sitting in my chair since the begining of this class.
8. (see) I've been seeing fast 2 movie since I was 10 years old.

B Work with a partner. Compare your sentences from exercise **A**.

C Form a group with another pair of students. Tell your group about your partner.

10 LISTEN, WRITE & SPEAK.

CD2-11

A Listen to the conversation. Choose the correct answer for each question.

1. How long has Lars lived in Kiruna, Sweden?

   a. for nine years b. for his entire life c. since last year

2. Why does the center of the town need to move?

   a. It's too close to the Arctic. b. There's a mine nearby. c. The buildings are very old.

◀ This Sami herder uses a snowmobile to help move his reindeer.

B Use the words to write questions about the conversation from exercise **A** on page 149. Use the present perfect or the present perfect progressive.

1. where / Lars / live / all his life ______________________
2. what / happen / to the ground under Kiruna / recently ______________________

   ____
3. what / change / in Kiruna / so far ______________________
4. what / the Sami people / do / for hundreds of years ______________________

   ____
5. how / the Sami people's lives / change ______________________

CD2-11

C Listen again. In your notebook, take notes on the answers to the questions from exercise **B**.

D Work with a partner. Ask and answer the questions from exercise **B**.

11 APPLY.

A What changes have you and the members of your family made recently? Use the chart to take notes on your ideas.

Changes that have happened	Changes that are still happening
I've made new friends. I've cooked new friends	My grandmother has been taking classes.

B Work with a partner. Talk about some of the changes you and the members of your family have made. Use the information from your chart in exercise **A**. Use the present perfect and the present perfect progressive.

I've made a lot of new friends this year. My grandmother has been taking computer classes since August.

C In your notebook, write a paragraph of four or five sentences about your family. Use your notes from exercise **B**. Use the present perfect and the present perfect progressive.

Charts 5.1–5.3, 5.4, 5.6, 5.7

1 Complete the blog post. Use the present perfect or the simple past form of the verbs in parentheses. For some items both forms are correct.

A Change in the American Dream

Sunday, January 25

For years, many Mexicans (1) ___have left___ (leave) Mexico to come to the United States. However, in recent years, more and more Mexicans in the United States (2) ____________ (return) home to Mexico. In 2011, around 400,000 Mexicans (3) ____________ (leave) the United States and (4) ____________ (return) to Mexico.

The number of people leaving Mexico for the United States (5) ____________ (fall) lately, too. According to some research, 404,000 Mexicans (6) ____________ (leave) their country for the United States in 2010. Just four years earlier, in 2006, that number (7) ____________ (be) over one million. Experts (8) ____________ (discuss) the reason for this change, but not everyone agrees on the answer.

Charts 5.1, 5.4, 5.6–5.8, 5.10

2 Circle the correct words to complete the reader's response to the blog post in exercise **1**.

Tuesday, January 27

A very interesting blog post, thank you. I actually have some personal experience with this subject. I (1) **have known** / **knew** my friend Carlos Mendoza (2) **since** / **for** 2005. He (3) **left** / **has left** his hometown in Mexico when he was 18. Like many other young Mexicans, he (4) **crossed** / **has been crossing** the Rio Grande and came to the United States because he wanted to find work. Carlos (5) **settled** / **has been settling** in Arizona in 2004, where he started his own cleaning service. His business was very successful, but Carlos (6) **didn't clean** / **hasn't been cleaning** houses for a year now. While he was in the United States, he (7) **saved** / **has saved** his money. Now, he (8) **has gone** / **has been going** back to Mexico to open his own store. Carlos (9) **sent** / **has been sending** me e-mails regularly (10) **for** / **since** several months. I wish him all the best!

Charts 5.1, 5.4–5.8, 5.10

3 EDIT. Read the article about Brendon Grimshaw. Find and correct eight more errors with the present perfect, the present perfect progressive, and the simple past.

Moyenne Island
Seychelles
Indian Ocean

Brendon Grimshaw and Moyenne Island

Moyenne Island in the Seychelles was deserted[1] and forgotten for fifty years. Then, in 1964, British newspaper editor Brendon Grimshaw ~~has~~ bought the island. He moved there nine years later, and lived there ever since.

When Grimshaw moved to Moyenne Island, it has been empty. Small trees and bushes covered the land, and there weren't any paths. Grimshaw wanted to take care of the island, so he asked a local man, Rene Lafortune, to help him. Since the two men have started work, they has planted 16,000 trees. Some of the first trees have now been growing to over 60 feet tall. The two men have also built more than three miles (5 km) of nature paths.

Grimshaw has been working hard on his project since about forty years, and today Moyenne Island is a huge success story. Since Grimshaw bought the island, it have attracted about 2000 new birds. Grimshaw has also raised over 100 giant tortoises[2] on the island.

Since 2008, Moyenne Island was a national park. It is a beautiful example of how one person's dream can change at least a small area of the world.

[1] **deserted:** empty because of no people living somewhere
[2] **tortoise:** a slowly moving land turtle with a high shell

▲ Brendon Grimshaw bought a deserted island in the Seychelles in 1964. Today, Moyenne Island is a beautiful national park.

Charts 5.1–5.9

4 LISTEN.

A Look at the words in the box. Put a check (✓) next to the words you know. Ask your teacher about any words you do not know.

☐ coworker	☐ cubicle	☐ social media	☐ software

CD2-12

B Listen to part of a radio call-in show about changes in the workplace. Which caller is more positive about technological change at work? Circle your answer.

a. Caller 1 b. Caller 2

CD2-12

C Listen again and complete the sentences from the radio show with the words you hear.

Caller 1

1. The way we work ___has changed___ a lot in recent years, but young people like me often feel that it ______________ enough.
2. Well, for example, we ______________ social media since it first ______________.
3. Some of their programs ______________ on the market before I was born!

Caller 2

4. I ______________ six e-mails in one hour from the same coworker.
5. The strange thing was that this person was sitting in the cubicle next to mine, and she ______________ one word to me the whole time!
6. For one day each week, she ______________ down the company's e-mail system.
7. Since the experiment, the change in the office ______________ amazing.

Charts 5.1–5.9

5 SPEAK.

A Think about how technology has changed your life. What are some positive and negative changes? Complete the chart with your ideas.

Positive Changes	Negative Changes
easy communication	not enough face-to-face contact

B Work in a small group. Talk about how technology has changed your lives. Use your notes from exercise **A** to help you. Ask follow-up questions for more information. Use the present perfect, the present perfect progressive, and the simple past.

Connect the Grammar to Writing

1 READ & NOTICE THE GRAMMAR.

A What kinds of changes have you read about in this unit? Discuss your ideas with a partner. Then read the text below.

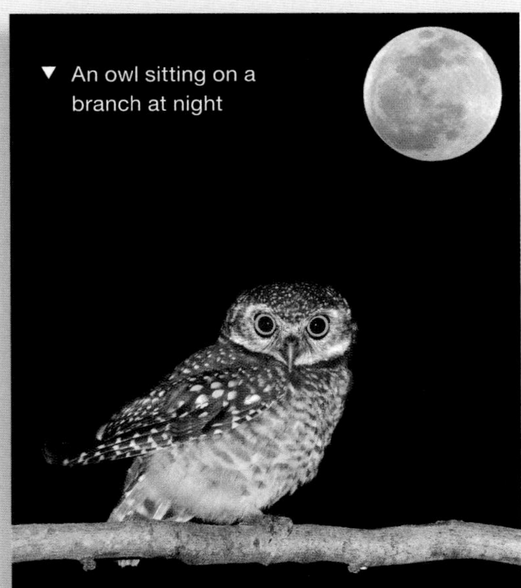

▼ An owl sitting on a branch at night

Since the Sun Went Down

The sun went down three hours ago. Since then, it's gotten very dark. The moon has risen, and the stars have been appearing in the sky.

Many birds, butterflies, and small animals have disappeared for the night. Others have become active. A raccoon is in my yard. It's been coming into my yard every night this winter. I hear an owl. I've heard it a few times before.

Since the sun went down, it's become much colder. The temperature has already dropped six degrees. I've put on a warm sweater, socks, and slippers. I like a lot of things about winter, but not the cold!

GRAMMAR FOCUS

In exercise **A**, the writer uses the present perfect to describe recently completed actions or events.

*It **has gotten** very dark.*
*The temperature **has** already **dropped** six degrees.*

The writer uses the present perfect progressive to talk about actions that started in the past and continue to the present.

*It **has been coming** into my yard every night this winter.*

B Read the text in exercise **A** again. Underline the present perfect verbs and circle the present perfect progressive verbs. Then work with a partner and compare your answers.

C In exercise **A**, the writer begins with a statement about a recent time and event. Then she describes recent changes caused by this event. Complete the chart with information about these changes.

Recent Event: The sun went down.
Changes: It's gotten very dark.

2 BEFORE YOU WRITE.

A Think of an event you have recently experienced. When did the event happen? What changes have happened because of the event? Complete the chart with information about the experience. Use the chart from exercise **1C** as a model.

Recent Event: ______________________________
Changes:

B Look at the changes in your chart from exercise **A**. Number each change in your chart *1, 2, 3,* etc., to help you plan the order of this information in your writing.

3 WRITE three paragraphs about the changes you have experienced recently. Use the information in the chart in exercise **2A** and the text in exercise **1A** to help you.

WRITING FOCUS Using Commas between Items in a Series

Use a comma between words or phrases in a series. A series is three or more related words, phrases, or clauses. Use a comma after all items in a series except the last one.

Many ***birds, butterflies, and small animals*** *have disappeared for the night.*

4 SELF ASSESS. Read your text. Underline the present perfect verbs and circle the present perfect progressive verbs. Then use the checklist to assess your work.

- ☐ I used the present perfect to talk about recently completed actions. [5.1, 5.4]
- ☐ I used *for* and *since* correctly with the present perfect. [5.4, 5.5]
- ☐ I used the present perfect progressive to talk about an action that started in the past and continues in the present. [5.8, 5.10]
- ☐ I used commas between words or phrases in a series. [WRITING FOCUS]

UNIT 6 Appearances and Behavior

Adjectives and Adverbs

▲ Madagascar's stone forest is home to several kinds of lemurs.

EXPLORE

CD2-13

1 READ the article about an attempt to steal a koala. Notice the words in **bold**.

Koalas Fight Back!

In March 2006, thieves broke into a zoo in Queensland, Australia. They planned to steal a koala. Everybody loves koalas, right? With their **big round** eyes, **flat** noses, **thick fur** coat, and **hairy** ears, these **cute** creatures have become a **popular** symbol of Australia. However, appearances can be **deceptive.**[1] The koala at the zoo was very **fierce**. Soon the thieves had **deep** scratches from the koala's **sharp** claws,[2] so they decided to steal something easier. They stole a crocodile instead!

Koalas are **interesting** animals. A **koala** mother carries her baby, called a *joey*, in a **warm** pouch, or pocket, on her stomach. Koalas eat only the **oily** leaves of eucalyptus trees. These leaves are **harmful** to many other animals, but koalas eat about two and a half pounds (just over one kilo) every night. The **water** content of these leaves is **high**, so koalas do not drink very much. In fact, in one **native Australian** language the word *koala* means "no drink."

[1] **deceptive:** causing someone to believe something that is not true

[2] **claws:** the sharp nails of an animal

▶ This baby koala is already covered in thick fur.

▲ A saltwater crocodile, Australia

2 CHECK. Read the statements. Circle **T** for *true* or **F** for *false*.

1. The thieves went to the zoo to steal a crocodile. **T** **F**
2. Koalas have small eyes. **T** **F**
3. The koala at the zoo was very calm. **T** **F**
4. Female koalas have a pouch for their babies. **T** **F**
5. Eucalyptus leaves are bad for many animals. **T** **F**
6. Eucalyptus leaves do not contain much water for koalas. **T** **F**

3 DISCOVER. Complete the exercises to learn about the grammar in this lesson.

A Complete the sentences with the words from the article in exercise **1**.

1. . . . , these ________________ creatures have become a ________________ symbol of Australia.
2. The koala at the zoo was ________________ .
3. Soon the thieves had ________________ scratches from the koala's ________________ claws.
4. These leaves are ________________ to many other animals.
5. The ________________ content of these leaves is ________________ . . . .

B Look at the adjectives you wrote in exercise **A**. Check the three answers that complete the statement *An adjective can . . .*

1. _____ come before a noun
2. _____ come after a noun
3. _____ come after a form of *be*
4. _____ look like a noun

LEARN

6.1 Adjectives

1. Adjectives describe nouns. They usually come before the noun they describe.	Did you see the **beautiful** sunset? Jack told a **funny** story.
2. Adjectives can come after *be* or another linking verb. In this case, they describe the subject. Examples: *appear, be, become, feel, get, look, seem, smell, sound,* and *taste.*	You **are amazing**! You **look tired**. The garbage **smells horrible**.
3. Adjectives do not have a plural form. Do not add *-s* to adjectives that describe plural nouns.	✓ We visited an **ancient** town in Italy. ✓ We visited some **ancient** towns in Italy. ✗ We visited some ancients towns in Italy.
4. Use *a* or *an* before an adjective + a singular count noun. Use *a* before an adjective beginning with a consonant sound. Use *an* before an adjective beginning with a vowel sound.	She goes to **a good** university. We live in **an old** apartment. Climbing Mt. Everest is **a unique** experience.

4 Underline the adjective(s) in each sentence. Then draw an arrow to the noun or pronoun that each adjective describes.

1. Koalas have thick fur.
2. Thieves didn't take the angry koala. They were afraid of its sharp claws.
3. Australia is enormous, and Australian animals are fascinating.
4. The zoo helps sick animals. The koala appeared ill, but it seems healthy now.
5. Crocodiles have sharp teeth and powerful jaws. That crocodile looks hungry.

5 Put the words in the correct order to make sentences.

1. (looks / soft / the bear's fur) The bear's fur looks soft.
2. (crocodile / is / enormous / that / an) ______
3. (have / strong / legs / kangaroos) ______
4. (pandas / shy / are / animals) ______
5. (has / exhibit / great / the zoo / a) ______
6. (an / history / interesting / Australia / has) ______

6.2 Nouns as Adjectives

1. A noun can sometimes be used as an adjective. It describes a noun that follows it.	I sat on a bench in the **park**. (Noun) I sat on a **park bench**. (Noun as Adjective)
2. When nouns are used as adjectives, they do not change form.	✓The **plane ticket** was expensive. ✓The **plane tickets** were expensive. ✗ The planes tickets were expensive.

6 Rewrite each sentence. Use the noun in **bold** as an adjective.

1. My sister works as a nurse in a **school**. My sister is a school nurse.
2. The scissors are in the drawer of my **desk**. The scissors are in my ____________.
3. I study the design of **furniture**. I study ____________.
4. Her coat is **leather**. She is wearing a ____________.
5. Have you seen the keys to my **car**? Have you seen my ____________?
6. This store sells **computers**. This is a ____________.
7. I need a bag for my **groceries**. I need a ____________.
8. This juice was made from **oranges**. It's ____________.

7 Circle the correct words to complete the sentences.

1. I need to buy a new pair of **shoe** / **shoes**. I know a very good **shoe** / **shoes** store.
2. Les enjoys watching **car** / **cars** races. He really likes fast **car** / **cars**.
3. Kate is a **movie** / **movies** star. She's been in a lot of great **movie** / **movies**.
4. Vince is a **mountain** / **mountains** climber. He's climbed seven **mountain** / **mountains** this year.
5. Erin reads a lot of **book** / **books**. Last month she started a **book** / **books** club.
6. Carl is a **restaurant** / **restaurants** manager. He manages three **restaurant** / **restaurants**.
7. My mother makes delicious **vegetable** / **vegetables** soup. She always uses fresh **vegetable** / **vegetables**.
8. We live in a huge **apartment** / **apartments** building. There are 300 **apartment** / **apartments** in our building.

6.3 Word Order of Adjectives

	Opinion	Size	Age	Shape	Color	Origin	Material	Noun as Adjective	Noun
I wore my			new		black		leather		shoes.
We made a	delicious						chocolate		cake.
We sat at a		small		round					table.
I work in an			old		red		brick		building.
We saw some	beautiful					Chinese			paintings.
He gave her a	gorgeous							wedding	ring.
That's a	great					German		soccer	team.

1. When more than one adjective is used to describe a noun, they usually follow the order in the chart.	✓We saw some **ancient Egyptian** sculptures. ✗ We saw some Egyptian ancient sculptures.
2. **Be careful!** We rarely use more than three adjectives together.	✓They live in a **big brown** house. ✗ They live in a beautiful big old brown house.
3. Use a comma or *and* between adjectives that give the same kind of information. Use *and* when the adjectives come after a linking verb.	He's a **kind, patient** person. He's a **kind and patient** person. He's **kind and patient**.
Do not use commas between adjectives that give different types of information.	I have a **big orange** cat. She has **short curly blonde** hair.

8 Put the adjectives in parentheses in the correct order to complete each sentence. Add a comma or *and* where necessary.

1. I live in a big apartment (apartment / big) building.
2. There are two ________ (Mexican / good) restaurants in my neighborhood.
3. Dani keeps her jewelry in a ________ (round / glass) box.
4. Susi bought a ________ (new / winter / nice) coat.
5. Luke knows many ________ (historical / interesting) facts about this town.
6. The restaurant was in a ________ (old / strange / stone) building.
7. Anita is wearing a ________ (silk / beautiful / green) scarf today.
8. We watched a ________ (old / great) movie last night.
9. The animals claws are ________ (long / sharp).
10. My town has many ________ (modern / impressive / beautiful) buildings.

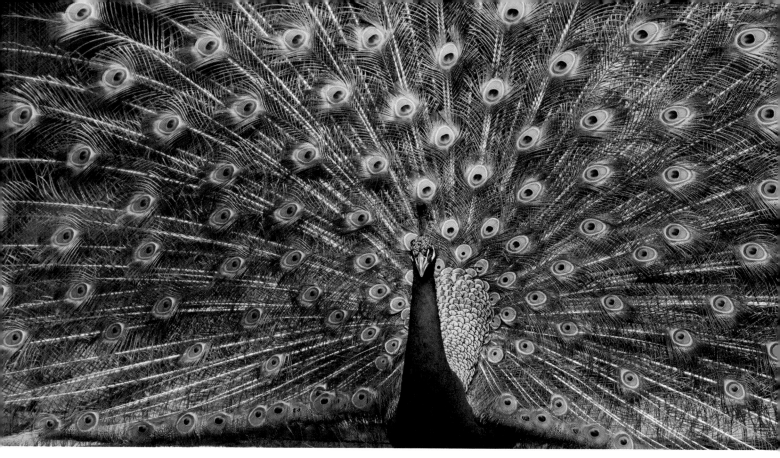

▲ A beautiful male peacock

PRACTICE

CD2-14

9 Complete the conversation with the words from the box. Then listen and check your answers.

amazing	attractive	brown	colorful	~~favorite~~	green	nice	terrible

Petra: What are you watching?

Alex: It's a documentary about birds. Look, this part is about peacocks.

Petra: Oh, good—peacocks are my (1) ___favorite___ kind of bird.

Alex: Really?

Petra: Yes. I love their feathers. The colors are (2) ____________ !

Alex: Well, yes, the males are very (3) ____________, but the females aren't. Their feather's aren't (4) ____________; they're (5) ____________.

Petra: I know, but that's the way it is with most birds: the male has beautiful feathers, so he is (6) ____________ to females.

Alex: I guess so. Well, they certainly are interesting, beautiful birds, but they make a (7) ____________ noise.

Petra: Yes, that's true. When a male calls out to the female birds, he doesn't make a very (8) ____________ sound.

10 Put the words in parentheses in the correct order to complete each sentence. Add *a, an, and,* or a comma where necessary.

1. Cows are common farm animals.
(farm / common / animals)

2. Marta has __________.
(brown / long / hair)

3. Paris is __________.
(exciting / city / interesting)

4. Georgia is __________.
(person / friendly / kind)

5. Pandas eat __________.
(leaves / green / small)

6. There was __________ in the kitchen.
(black / scary / spider)

7. We went to __________.
(shoe / new / store / wonderful)

8. That restaurant has __________.
(food / delicious / Indian)

11 **APPLY.**

A Work with a partner. Look at the nouns in the box. Each noun can be used as an adjective with all of the nouns in one of the groups below. Match each noun with the correct group.

art	computer	fire	grocery	phone	~~police~~	train	TV

1. police officer, station, car
2. __________ show, channel, star
3. __________ class, museum, student
4. __________ call, company, number
5. __________ bag, list, store
6. __________ program, game, system
7. __________ alarm, department, truck
8 __________ schedule, station, ticket

B In your notebook, write five questions. In each, use an adjective + a noun from exercise **A**.

What is your favorite TV show? What art museums have you visited?

C Take turns asking and answering your questions from exercise **B** with your partner. Explain your answers, using adjectives where appropriate.

A: *What is your favorite TV show?* B: Dr. Who. *It has interesting stories and fascinating characters.*

EXPLORE

CD2-15

1 **READ** the article about the Maori people, the first people to live in New Zealand, and their traditional tatoos. Notice the words in **bold**.

New Zealand

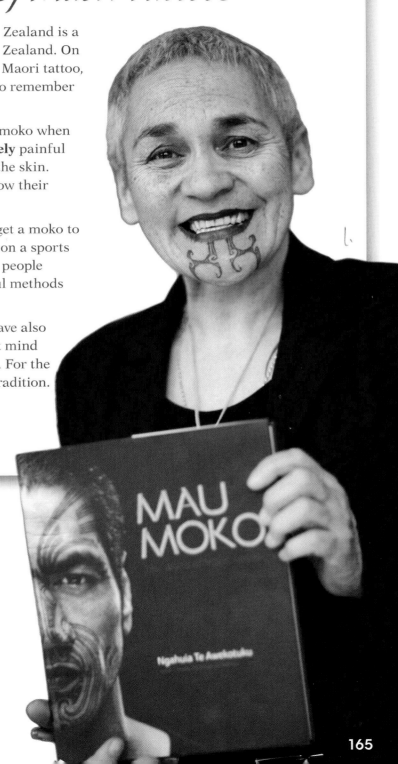

Moko—The Art of Maori Tattoos

Dr. Ngahuia Te Awekotuku of New Zealand is a leading writer on Maori issues in New Zealand. On her chin and lips she **proudly** wears a Maori tattoo, or *moko*. The purpose of her moko is to remember the Maori queen who died in 2006.

In the past, young Maori received moko when they became adults. It was an **extremely** painful process. A sharp tool was used to cut the skin. People sat **quietly** and **patiently** to show their courage.

These days, a young Maori might get a moko to mark an achievement[1] such as getting on a sports team or passing an exam. Most young people choose to get a moko using less painful methods than in earlier times.

Some people who are not Maori have also started to get moko. Some Maori don't mind this, but others are not happy about it. For the Maori, moko remains a **very** serious tradition.

[1] **achievement:** something that someone does successfully, usually as a result of much effort

MAU MOKO

▶ Dr. Ngahuia Te Awekotuku with her book *Mau Moko: The World of Maori Tattoo*.

2 CHECK. Choose the correct answer to complete each statement.

1. How does Dr. Te Awekotuku feel about her tattoo? She ______________ .

   a. doesn't like it b. is proud of it c. doesn't care about it

2. The main reason for Dr. Te Awekotuku's moko is to ______________ .

   a. decorate her face b. mark an achievement c. honor someone's memory

3. To show their courage when they received moko, young people used to ______________ .

   a. watch the sharp tool b. remain calm c. choose large designs

4. Some non-Maori people now get moko. The Maori people's feelings are ______________ about this.

   a. negative b. positive c. mixed

3 DISCOVER. Complete the exercises to learn about the grammar in this lesson.

A Find these sentences in the article from exercise **1**. Write the missing words.

1. On her lips and chin she **proudly** ______________ a Maori tattoo.
2. People ______________ **quietly** and **patiently** to show their courage.

B Work with a partner. Look at the verbs you wrote in exercise **A**. Notice the location of the bold adverbs. With a partner, discuss how to complete the statement *An adverb can come . . .*

▼ A Maori man in New Zealand

LEARN

6.4 Adverbs of Manner

Adjectives		
	Adjective	Noun
They are	**slow**	animals.
She is a	**careful**	driver.

Adverbs of Manner		
	Verb	Adverb
They	move	**slowly.**
She	drives	**carefully.**

1. Adverbs of manner describe action verbs.	He spoke **softly.** She dances **beautifully.**
2. Adverbs of manner usually come after the verb or after the verb + the object. Do not put adverbs of manner between the verb and the object.	✓ He sang **beautifully.** ✓ He sang the song **beautifully.** ✗ He sang beautifully the song.
3. Do not use an adverb after a linking verb. Use an adjective after a linking verb.	✓ She **looks happy.** ✗ She looks happily. ✓ The flowers **smell beautiful.** ✗ The flowers smell beautifully.
4. To form adverbs of manner, add *-ly* to most adjectives.* **Be careful!** Not all words that end in *-ly* are adverbs.	beautiful → beautiful**ly** cheerful → cheerful**ly** happy → happi**ly** soft → soft**ly** Adjectives: friendly, lonely, ugly, lovely Nouns and Verbs: reply, supply
5. Some adverbs of manner have the same form as the related adjective. To create an adverb, do not add *-ly* to these words: *early, fast, hard, late.*	✓ They eat fast. ✗ They eat fastly.
6. The adverb form of *good* is *well.*	✓ My new laptop works **well.** ✗ My new laptop works good.

*See page **A3** for spelling rules for adverbs ending in *-ly.*

4 Complete each sentence with the adverb form of the adjective in parentheses.

1. The professor wears her tattoo ___proudly___ (proud).
2. The young Maori sat __________ (quiet) as they got their tattoos.
3. The tattoo process was painful, but they acted __________ (brave).
4. They started the presentation __________ (early).
5. The professor explained the history of the Maori very __________ (clear).
6. He doesn't speak Maori __________ (good), but he understands it.
7. She answered all our questions __________ (honest).
8. I read her book __________ (quick).
9. She thought very __________ (hard) about her future.
10. He spoke very __________ (fast). I didn't understand everything.

5 Write the adverb form of each adjective. Then place the adverb in a correct place in the sentence. Sometimes there is more than one correct place.

1. My brother doesn't drive. (safe) *safely*
2. We worked last semester. (hard)
3. Journalists write their reports. (quick)
4. Martina walked along the beach. (slow)
5. The professor didn't answer my question. (complete)
6. The mail arrived. (early)
7. The children played in the yard. (happy)
8. I held the baby. (gentle)

6.5 Adverbs of Degree

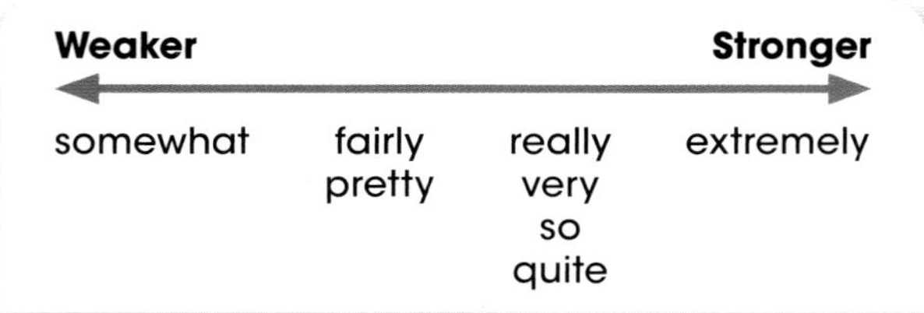

1. Use adverbs of degree to make adjectives or other adverbs stronger or weaker.	The movie was **somewhat** long. The students did **very** well on the test. Our team played **pretty** badly last night.
2. Adverbs of degree usually come before the adjective or adverb.	✓ It was **really** good. ✗ It was good really.
3. Do not use *pretty, fairly,* or *somewhat* in negative statements.	✓ She was **somewhat** tired. ✗ She wasn't somewhat tired.

REAL ENGLISH

Extremely, quite, very, and *somewhat* are more formal. *Really, pretty,* and *kind of* are less formal.

Formal: *The results of the two tests were **quite** different.*
Informal: *I'm **pretty** sad that my friend moved.*

6 Put the words in the correct order to make sentences.

1. boring / sounds / Steven's assignment / somewhat
   Steven's assignment sounds somewhat boring.
2. extremely / is / this song / popular
   ______
3. expensive / quite / looked / Elsa's shoes
   ______

4. ended / quickly / pretty / the discussion

____

5. helpful / this software / very / seem / doesn't

____

6. tired / so / last night / I / was

____

7. scary / really / was / that movie

____

8. Russian / Liza / fairly / speaks / well

____

7 Read each pair of sentences. Does the **bold** adverb of degree make the underlined adjective or adverb stronger or weaker? Put a check (✓) in the correct column.

	Stronger	Weaker
1. The article was <u>interesting</u>. The article was **pretty** interesting.	☐	☑
2. The house was in <u>poor</u> condition. The house was in **really** poor condition.	☐	☐
3. Lee studied <u>hard</u> for his exams. Lee studied **very** hard for his exams.	☐	☐
4. Andrea paints <u>well</u>. Andrea paints **fairly** well.	☐	☐
5. I'm <u>hungry</u>. I'm **so** hungry!	☐	☐
6. The professor spoke <u>slowly</u>. The professor spoke **somewhat** slowly.	☐	☐
7. Chen felt <u>tired</u>. Chen felt **extremely** tired.	☐	☐
8. The store was <u>busy</u>. The store was **quite** busy.	☐	☐

PRACTICE

8 Circle the correct word to complete each sentence.

1. Sally came into the room very **sudden** / **(suddenly.)**
2. I love your wedding photos! You both look so **happy** / **happily**.
3. The children are working very **hard** / **hardly** this semester.
4. The team played extremely **good** / **well** in the last game.
5. The new boss spoke **proud** / **proudly** about his plans for the company.
6. This pizza wasn't **cheap** / **cheaply**, but it tastes **good** / **well**.
7. I spoke to the professor **quick** / **quickly**. He explained the assignment very **clear** / **clearly**.
8. Mike had a **bad** / **badly** accident. He hurt his arm very **bad** / **badly**.

9 Complete the text with the correct form of the words in parentheses.

A Person I Admire

I just got back from a really (1) ________________ (nice) visit with my grandfather in Montana. He used to live in Florida, but he has been living (2) ________________ (happy) in Montana for almost 20 years now. He celebrated his 82nd birthday this summer, and he looks (3) ________________ (terrific). He eats a (4) ________________ (healthy) diet and exercises (5) ________________ (regular). He's extremely (6) ________________ (active) for his age. He hasn't slowed down at all since I last saw him.

My grandfather also has a lot of hobbies and interests. For example, he plays the guitar really (7) ________________ (good) and sings (8) ________________ (beautiful). When he was young, he was very (9) ________________ (curious) and loved to travel. He traveled (10) ________________ (frequent), so he has some (11) ________________ (interesting) stories. He's a (12) ________________ (great) storyteller, too! After a week with Grandpa, I didn't want to leave!

10 EDIT, LISTEN & SPEAK.

A Read the e-mail. Find and correct eight more errors with adverbs and adjectives.

Hi, Jessica and Mark,

I need some advice. I had an interview for a job as a DJ[1] at my local radio station, but I was ~~unsuccessfully~~ unsuccessful. I've had a lot of experience as a DJ, and I work very hard. I wore a new nice suit to the interview, and I felt pretty confidently when I left my house.

Before the interview, I read some interview tips and techniques online. For example, one said, "Copy the interviewer's movements close." Well, I tried that technique, but the interviewers didn't seem to like it very much. Anyway, I didn't get the job. Now I'm real confused. I know I made a few mistakes in the interview, but nothing really bad. At first, I was nervously, but that was because I arrived lately. When the interview started, I spoke loud, smiled frequently, and talked a lot—well, until they asked me to stop. Also, I didn't ask any questions, but in general, I thought it went good. Where did I go wrong?

Thanks,

Kevin in Ohio

[1]**DJ:** a person who plays recorded music on the radio or at live events

CD2-16

B Listen to the first part of the *Helping Hand* radio show and check your answers from exercise **A**.

C Look at the list of Kevin's behaviors in the chart. Then complete the second column of the chart with your opinion of his behaviors. Check (✓) *Good* or *Bad* for each behavior. Then write notes to explain your opinions.

CD2-17

D Listen to the second part of *Helping Hand*. Complete the radio expert's column in the chart.

Kevin's Behaviors	Your Opinion	Radio Expert's (Mark's) Advice
1. wore a suit	Good ☑ Bad ☐ Notes: *This shows respect.*	*Bad choice. Dress appropriately.*
2. arrived late	Good ☐ Bad ☐ Notes:	
3. copied the interviewers	Good ☐ Bad ☐ Notes:	
4. spoke loudly	Good ☐ Bad ☐ Notes:	
5. smiled frequently	Good ☐ Bad ☐ Notes:	
6. didn't ask questions	Good ☐ Bad ☐ Notes:	

E Work with a partner. Share the information in your charts from exercise **D** and discuss why you agree or disagree with the radio expert.

11 APPLY.

A Work with a partner. When is it important to make a good first impression, for example, at a job interview, your first day in a new class, your first day at a new job? Brainstorm a list of situations with your partner.

B Choose one of the situations from your list from exercise **A**. Then write a list of ways to make a good impression in that situation. Use adjectives and adverbs.

Situation: first day at a new job → dress professionally, be very polite

C Share your ideas in a small group.

D In your notebook, write five or six sentences about how to make a good first impression in the situation you chose. Use adjectives and adverbs and your ideas from exercise **B**.

On the first day of a new job, it is extremely important to dress professionally and listen carefully. You should also be very polite. . . .

Review the Grammar UNIT 6

Charts 6.1, 6.3, 6.4, 6.5

1 Circle the correct words to complete the conversation.

Neil: My sister sounded (1) **unhappy** / **unhappily** on the phone last night.

Junko: Oh, what was the matter?

Neil: Well, I think she is a little (2) **angry** / **angrily** about her grades at college.

Junko: Are they really (3) **bad** / **badly**?

Neil: I don't know. My sister works very (4) **hard** / **hardly** and does all of her assignments (5) **careful** / **carefully**. She is an extremely (6) **good** / **well** student.

Junko: So, what happened?

Neil: Well, her math exam didn't go (7) **good** / **well**. She didn't fail it (8) **complete** / **completely**, but she didn't get a (9) **pretty** / **very** good grade. When she took the exam, she didn't feel (10) **very** / **somewhat** confident.

Junko: That's too bad.

Neil: I know, but she's (11) **smart, studious** / **smart and studious**. I'm sure she will become (12) **successful** / **successfully** in the long run.

Charts 6.1, 6.3, 6.4

2 **EDIT.** Read the article about an unusual cat. Find and correct seven more errors with adverbs and adjectives.

Venus, the Two-Faced Cat

Venus is a ~~pet famous~~ famous pet cat. She even has her own social networking page. She has also appeared on national TV.

Many people are interested in Venus because she has a unusual appearance, as you can see! One half of her face is black with an green eye, and the other half has stripes orange and a blue eye. How does something like this happen?

According to Leslie Lyons, a professor at the University of California, Davis, cats like Venus are extreme rare. Cats with orange and blacks coats are not unusual. However, cats with different colored eyes are unusually. This means Professor Lyons is much more interested in the real mystery about Venus: her blue beautiful eye.

▲ Venus's face is evenly divided into two colors.

Charts 6.1–6.5

CD2-18

3 LISTEN & SPEAK.

▲ A male bowerbird stands in front of the bower he built.

A Look at the photo and read the caption. Listen to the conversation about bowerbirds. Then choose the correct answer for each question.

1. What did Ken think of the film?

   a. It was fairly interesting.

   b. It was very interesting.

2. Why did Ken watch the whole film right away?

   a. He thought the photography was good.

   b. He wanted to watch it alone.

3. Why do male bowerbirds build bowers?

   a. to prove their strength

   b. to attract females

4. The three bowerbirds' stages looked ________________ .

   a. similar   b. different

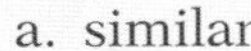

5. What does Marion say about the stage made of garbage?

   a. That sounds terrible!   b. That sounds terribly!

B Work with a partner. Compare your answers from exercise **A**. Did any of the information about bowerbirds surprise you? Discuss your answer with your partner and then the class.

Charts 6.1–6.5

4 SPEAK & WRITE.

A Think of a person you admire. The person can be someone you know or someone famous. Write notes in the chart about that person. Use adjectives and adverbs. Use the questions in the chart to help you.

	Person: ________________
What adjectives describe the person's appearance, character, and abilities?	intelligent, funny
How did/does the person behave? Speak? Move? Laugh? Work? Have fun?	works hard

B Work with a partner. Tell your partner about the person you chose. Use your notes from exercise **A**.

C In your notebook, write a short paragraph of five or six sentences about this person. Use your notes from exercise **A**.

Connect the Grammar to Writing

1 READ & NOTICE THE GRAMMAR.

A Do you know any interesting looking animals? Tell a partner about an animal you think is interesting. Then read the text.

The Yellow-Tailed Woolly Monkey

The yellow-tailed woolly monkey is a very rare animal. It has thick brown fur and white hair around its mouth. The monkey is named for the bright yellow fur underneath its long, curled tail. These monkeys live in a small area in the high mountains of Peru. With their long arms and legs and powerful tail, they move quickly through the forests.

Unfortunately, these monkeys have lost a lot of their natural habitat. Farms and cattle ranches[1] are some of the reasons for this. People are now working hard to protect these amazing animals.

[1] **ranch:** a large farm used for keeping animals

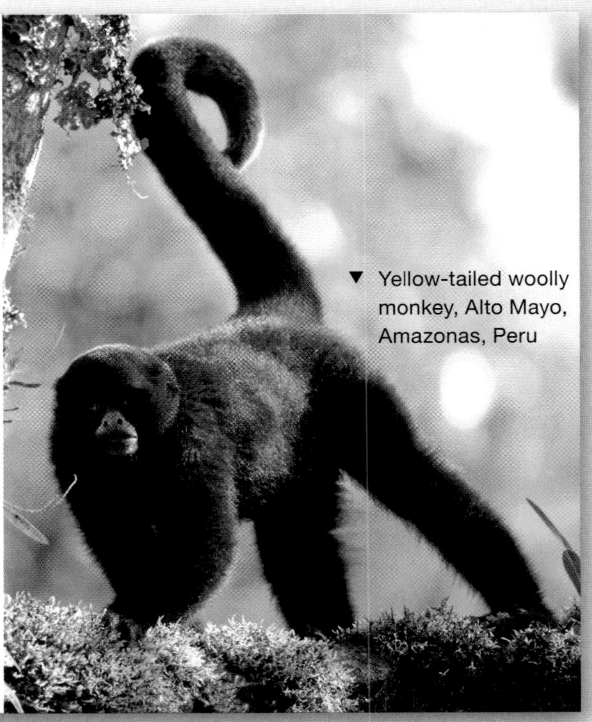

▼ Yellow-tailed woolly monkey, Alto Mayo, Amazonas, Peru

GRAMMAR FOCUS

In the text in exercise **A**, the writer uses adjectives and adverbs to describe a rare kind of monkey.

Adjectives: *It has **thick brown** fur and **white** hair around its mouth.*
Nouns as adjectives: *Farms and **cattle** ranches are some of the reasons for this.*
Adverbs of manner: *. . . they move **quickly** through the forests.*
Adverbs of degree: *The yellow-tailed woolly monkey is a **very** rare animal.*

B Read the text in exercise **A** again. Underline the adjectives and circle the adverbs of manner and degree. Then work with a partner and compare your answers.

C Complete the chart with information about the woolly monkey from exercise **A**. Write adjectives or adverbs and the words they describe.

Appearance	thick brown fur,
Habitat (where it lives)	small area,
Movements or Behavior	

2 BEFORE YOU WRITE. Choose an animal from this unit or another animal that interests you. Then complete the chart. Use the chart from exercise **1C** as a model.

Appearance	
Habitat (where it lives)	
Movements or Behavior	

3 WRITE about the animal you chose. Write two paragraphs. Use the information from your chart in exercise **2** and the text in exercise **1A** to help you.

WRITING FOCUS Using Adjectives and Adverbs

Good writers use adjectives and adverbs to make their writing more interesting.

Compare:

With their arms and legs and tail, they move through the forests.

*With their **long** arms and legs and **powerful** tail, they move quickly through the forests.*

Good writers also choose their words carefully and do not use too many adjectives or adverbs.

Compare:

*With their **long** arms and legs and **powerful** tail, they move **quickly** through the forests.*

*With their **big long** arms and **strong** legs and **powerful curled** tail, they move **quickly** and **gracefully** through the **beautiful thick Peruvian** forests.*

Make sure to choose your adjectives and adverbs carefully when you write. This is especially important in academic and business writing.

4 SELF ASSESS. Read your text. Underline the adjectives and adverbs. Then use the checklist to assess your work.

- ☐ I used adjectives correctly. [6.1–6.3]
- ☐ I used adverbs correctly. [6.4, 6.5]
- ☐ I used the correct word order with adjectives and adverbs. [6.3, 6.4]
- ☐ I used adjectives and adverbs to add interest to my writing. [WRITING FOCUS]
- ☐ I chose my adjectives and adverbs carefully. [WRITING FOCUS]

UNIT 7 Tomorrow and Beyond

The Future

A team of architects has designed a mobile hotel that lets guests sleep in pods hundreds of feet in the air. Each pod is a hotel guest room with power and water.

EXPLORE

CD2-19

1 **READ** the article about space travel for tourists. Notice the words in **bold**.

A Star-Studded Trip You'll Never Forget

Where are you planning to spend your next vacation? **Are** you **going to take** a trip to the beach? Or visit family perhaps? Do you want to travel somewhere new and different for a change? If so, try a trip to space! The following companies provide exciting trips that you **will remember** for a lifetime.

VIRGIN GALACTIC

You'**ll have** a fantastic experience, and you'**ll come back** with great stories to tell. On the VSS *Enterprise*, you and five other passengers **will fly** into space. You **won't orbit**[2] Earth, but you **will experience** zero gravity.[3] How much **will** this trip cost? About $250,000.

SPACE ADVENTURES

You'**ll fly** 250 miles above Earth, and you'**ll orbit** it every 90 minutes. It'**ll be** a spectacular experience! You **will be** the only passenger, but you **will spend** a week on the International Space Station with trained astronauts. How much money **will** you **need** for this trip? Around $50 million dollars.

No, your trip to space **is not going to be** a cheap vacation, but **it will be** a memorable one!

[1] **astronaut:** a person who travels in outer space
[2] **orbit:** to move in a path around another object in space
[3] **zero gravity:** a condition in which people and things float; happens in space

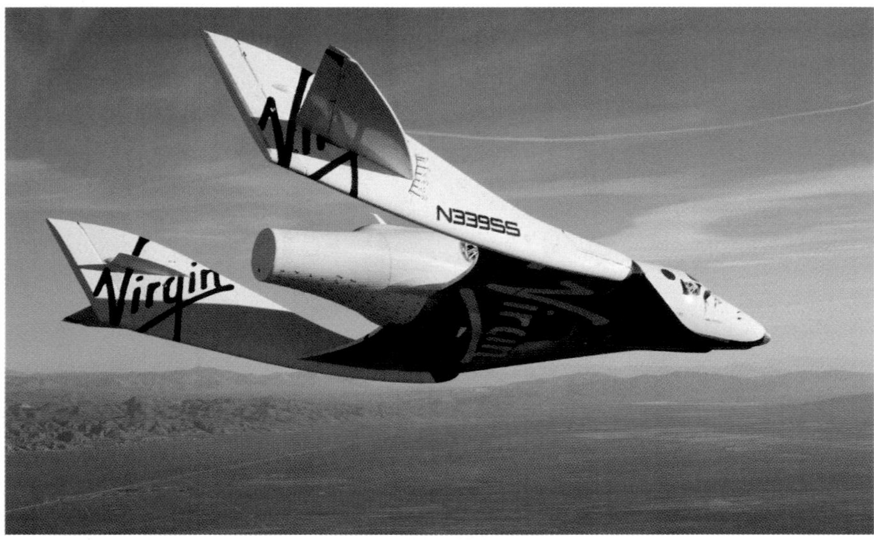

◀ **Virgin Galactic's** special WhiteKnight plane will carry the VSS *Enterprise* to 50,000 feet. Then the *Enterprise (center)* will continue into space alone.

2 **CHECK.** Read each statement. Is it true for Virgin Galactic, Space Adventures, or both? Put a check (✓) in the correct column(s).

	Virgin Galactic	Space Adventures
1. This trip is expensive.	☐	☐
2. A flight with this company costs $250,000.	☐	☐
3. This company's spaceships circle Earth.	☐	☐
4. Passengers spend a week on the International Space Station.	☐	☐

3 **DISCOVER.** Complete the exercises to learn about the grammar in this lesson.

A Find these sentences in the article from exercise **1**. Write the missing words.

1. **Are** you **going to** ________________ a trip to the beach?
2. You**'ll** ________________ a fantastic experience, . . .
3. . . . but you **will** ________________ zero gravity.
4. No, your trip to space **is not going to** ________________ a cheap vacation, . . .

B Look at the sentences in exercise **A**. Choose the correct answer to complete the statement.

The ________________ form of the verb comes after *will/won't* and *be (not) going to.*

a. base   b. simple past   c. the simple present

LEARN

7.1 Future with *Will*

Affirmative Statements		
Subject	*Will*	Base Form
I/He/We	will 'll	win.

Negative Statements		
Subject	*Will Not/ Won't*	Base Form
I/He/We	will not won't	win.

Yes/No Questions			
Will	Subject	Base Form	
Will	you/she/they	**help**	us?

Short Answers
Yes, she **will**. / No, she **won't**. Yes, they **will**. / No, they **won't**.

Wh- Questions			
Wh- Word	*Will*	Subject	Base Form
When	will	you	**arrive**?
What		she	**need**?
Who(m)		they	**see**?

Short Answers
Tomorrow night.
Her passport.
Their parents.

1. Use *will* for: a. things you are sure will happen in the future b. predictions about the future c. decisions made at the time of speaking d. offers or promises	a. The sun **will rise** at 6:00 a.m. tomorrow. b. I think **you'll do** well on the test. c. A: Someone's at the door. B: **I'll get** it. d. I'**ll call** you later.
2. The contractions *'ll* and *won't* are usually used in conversation and informal writing.	A: Do you want anything? B: Sure. **I'll** have a cup of coffee. **I won't** have time for more.
3. To express *there is (not)/there are (not)* in the future, use *there will be/there won't be.*	**There will be** a new teacher next year. A: **Will there be** time for questions? B: I'm afraid **there won't be** extra time.

4 Complete the exercises.

A Complete the information about a new space museum. Use *will* or *won't* and the verbs in parentheses.

The Space Museum
A Fantastic Journey for the Whole Family

Visitors to our grand opening in October (1) ___will get___ (get) a close look at several historic spacecrafts. Also, astronauts (2) ___will visit___ (visit) the museum a few times each year. They (3) ___will talk___ (talk) about their experiences in space, and visitors (4) ___will have___ (have) the chance to meet them personally. You (5) ___will not be___ (not be) disappointed with your visit!

The museum (6) will open (open) on October 16 with an exhibit about space tourism. This exhibit (7) will remain (remain) open until January 15. In addition, there (8) will be (be) fun activities for the whole family. Your children (9) will not want (not want) to go home!

Next year, the museum (10) will welcome (welcome) several new exhibits about the history and future of our journeys to the stars. Buy your tickets for opening day now, so you (11) won't miss (not miss) a thing!

B Read the statements. Write questions using *will*. The underlined word or phrase in each statement provides information about the answer.

1. The museum will open in October. When will the museum open?
2. Astronauts will talk about their experiences in space. What will ?
3. The new exhibits will be at the museum. Where will the new be?
4. Visitors will see historic spacecrafts. What visitors will see?
5. Yes, there will be activities for children. Will there be acivites?
6. This exhibit will close on January 15th. When will exhibit close?
7. Yes, there will be new exhibits every year. Will there ?
8. No, the museum will not be open on major holidays. ______

Astronaut John W. Young drives the Lunar Roving Vehicle (LRV) at the Decartes landing site, April 21, 1972

7.2 Future with *Be Going To*

Affirmative Statements			
Subject	*Be*	*Going To*	Base Form
I	am 'm	going to	stay.
He/She/It	is 's		
We/You/They	are 're		

Negative Statements			
Subject	*Be Not*	*Going To*	Base Form
I	am not 'm not	going to	stay.
He/She/It	is not 's not isn't		
We/You/They	are not 're not aren't		

Yes/No Questions			
Be	Subject	*Going To*	Base Form
Am	I	going to	go?
Is	he/she/it		
Are	you/we/they		

Short Answers
Yes, you **are**. / **No**, you **aren't**.
Yes, she **is**. / **No**, she **isn't**.
Yes, we **are**. / **No**, we **aren't**.

Wh- Questions				
Wh- Word	*Be*	Subject	*Going To*	Base Form
What	is	she	going to	do?
Where	are	they		go?

Short Answers
Ride her bike.
To the museum.

1. Use *be going to* for a. things you are certain will happen in the future b. things you plan to do c. predictions	a. It **is going to snow** tomorrow. b. **I'm going to watch** the news at 6:00. c. Space travel **is going to become** more popular in the future.
2. Contractions are usually used in conversation and informal writing.	A: What are you going to do this weekend? B: **I'm going to visit** my sister in Boston.

CD2-20

5 Complete the conversation with *be going to* and the subjects and verbs in parentheses. Then listen and notice the pronunciation of *be going to*.

Carl: I'm so glad it's Friday. (1) Are you going to do (you / do) anything special this weekend, Valerie?

Valerie: Yes, (2) I'm going to (I / go) to the opening of the new Space Museum. I'm sure it'll be crowded, but I really want to see it.

Carl: (3) What are going to see (you / see) there?

Valerie: Well, (4) Phil and I are going to take (Phil and I / take) the children on some of the rides. There is one called "A Trip to the Moon."

Carl: That sounds fun.

Valerie: Yeah, (5) they are going to (they / love) it.

Carl: (6) What are you and phil going to (you and Phil / do)?

Valerie: Oh, an astronaut is giving a lecture in the afternoon. (7) Are we going to attend (we / attend) that. How about you? Are you going to the game on Saturday?

Carl: No, I'm not, unfortunately. I have to study.

Valerie: That's too bad. (8) Are you going to study (you / study) all weekend?

Carl: No, on Sunday (9) I'm not going to (I / not do) any work. (10) I'm going to sleep (I / sleep) late and just relax.

Valerie: Oh, good. Well, have a great time.

6 SPEAK. Work with a partner. Ask and answer questions about your plans for the future. Use *be going to* and the time expressions in the box. Practice saying *going to* as "gonna."

this weekend	tonight
next year	after class

A: *What are you going to do this weekend?*

B: *I'm going to relax. How about you?*

REAL ENGLISH

In speaking, *going to* is often pronounced "*gonna*" when it comes before a verb. Use *going to*, not *gonna*, in writing.

Say: *We're **gonna** be late.*
Write: *We**'re going to be** late.*

PRACTICE

CD2-21

7 LISTEN and write the words and contractions you hear.

1. This book about the planets looks great. I 'm going to buy it.
2. My brother enjoyed the astronaut's lecture. He ______________ to another one next month.
3. Governments ______________ much money on space research in the near future.
4. The astronauts ______________ on the space station until the end of the month.
5. A: Don't wait for me. I ______________ here for a long time.

   B: I'm not in a hurry. I ______________ for you.
6. The museum gift shop ______________ at 10:00 a.m.
7. There ______________ any lectures next week.
8. Sarah ______________ that movie. She doesn't like science fiction.

8 WRITE & SPEAK.

A Read the statements. Write questions using *will* or *be going to*. The underlined word or phrase in each statement provides information about the answer.

1. Yes, I'm going to take classes here next semester.

   Are you going to take classes here next semester?

2. I'm going to hang out with friends this weekend.

   ____

3. No, I won't be in class on Wednesday.

   ____

4. Yes, people will visit Mars someday.

   ____

5. People will travel by flying car in the future.

   ____

6. I'm going to call my parents tonight.

   ____

B Work with a partner. Take turns asking and answering the questions from exercise **A**. Use your own ideas.

A: *Are you going to take classes here next semester?*

B: *No, I'm not. I'm going to go back to Colombia.*

9 LISTEN, WRITE & SPEAK.

CD2-22

A Listen to three people who want to become astronauts. Complete the notes in the chart.

	Glenn	Sylvia	Mark
Two Years	be ________	finish ________	join the ________
Five Years	start astronaut training	be ________	be a flight engineer
Ten Years	be ________	go on her first space mission	work for ________

B Write five questions about the information from the chart in exercise **A**. Use *When* or *What* and *will* or *be going to*.

When will Sylvia go on her first mission? What is Sylvia going to do in ten years?

1. ______________________________

2. ______________________________

3. ______________________________

4. ______________________________

5. ______________________________

C Work with a partner. Take turns asking and answering the questions from exercise **B**. Use the information from the chart in exercise **A** in your answers.

10 **EDIT.** Read about home life in the future. Find and correct seven more errors with *will* and *be going to.*

Home Life in the Future

I grew up in a house with a big yard and a lot of room to play. However, I don't think that children of the future ~~going~~ are going to be so lucky. The world's population will continues to increase, and this means all of us will live in smaller homes. I think some big cities in Asia, such as Seoul and Singapore, will be serves as models for the cities of the future. People are going live in high-rise apartment buildings. These apartment buildings going to be cheaper, safer, and more practical than separate houses.

There are going be more advances in electronics. Also, people have more entertainment choices in their homes in the future. We won't to go out very often to watch movies or concerts. Movie theaters will go out of business in the future.

11 **APPLY.**

A Write six predictions about the future with *will* or *be going to*. Use the topics from the box or your own ideas.

education	fashion	shopping
entertainment	food	work

Cars will use hydrogen for fuel.

1. ______________________________

2. ______________________________

3. ______________________________

4. ______________________________

5. ______________________________

6. ______________________________

REAL ENGLISH

The adverbs *definitely* and *probably* are common with predictions to show certainty. *Definitely* and *probably* usually come after *will* but before *won't*.

*She **will definitely** come to class.*
*She **probably won't** be late.*

B Work in a group. Share your predictions from exercise **A**. Give reasons for your ideas.

Cars will use hydrogen for fuel, because there won't be any gas in the future.

EXPLORE

CD2-23

1 READ the conversation and the excerpt from a lecture. Notice the words in **bold**.

The Future of Work

10:00 a.m.

Stuart: Hey, Bob. **Are you coming** to the lecture on the future of work?

Bob: Yes, but it **doesn't start** until twelve, so I**'m leaving** around eleven.

Stuart: No, it *was* at twelve, but Professor Miller**'s going** on vacation tonight, so she changed the schedule. The lecture **begins** at ten-thirty. Hurry up, or we'll be late!

10:50 a.m.

Professor Miller: . . . so you see, in the future, companies are not going to pay people to drive to a central building. With the money they **save**, they're going to be able to hire more qualified workers. And it probably isn't going to matter where you live. In fact, workers in different time zones[1] are going to be popular with companies.

Stuart: Why is that?

Professor Miller: Well, let's take an example, Stuart. Imagine you're a manager in the United States. It's late afternoon on Thursday. The financial[2] year **finishes** tomorrow, and you**'re giving** a presentation in the morning. You need some new information, but everyone around you is going home. You contact your researcher in Australia, and because of the time difference, you **have** the information first thing the next morning . . .

[1] **time zone:** one of 24 areas the world is divided into as measured from Greenwich, England
[2] **financial:** having to do with money

◀ Businesspeople work at futuristic control panels.

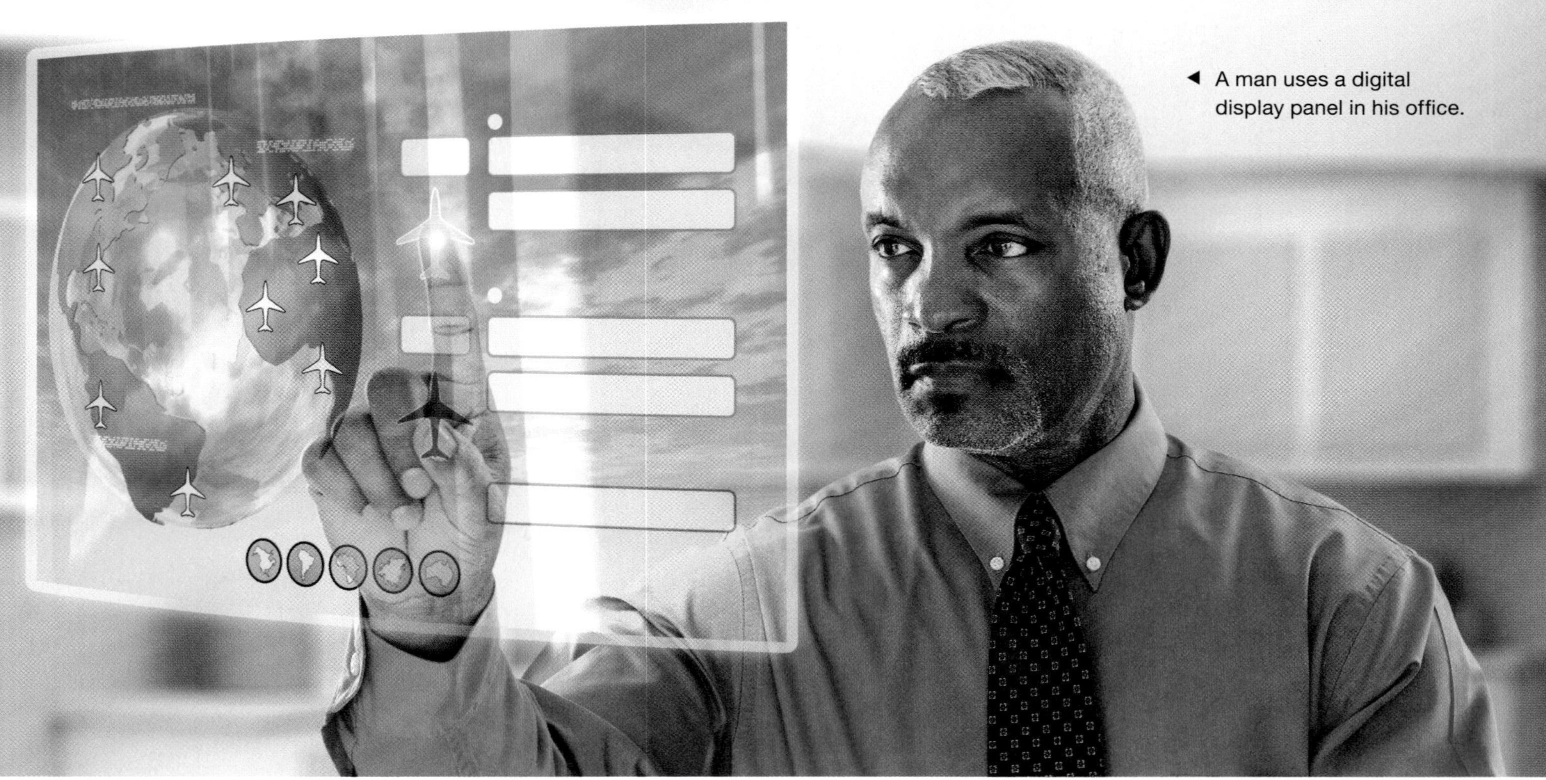

◂ A man uses a digital display panel in his office.

2 CHECK. Read the statements. Circle **T** for *true* or **F** for *false*.

1. Bob isn't going to go to the lecture.	**T**	**F**
2. The lecture is about work in the future.	**T**	**F**
3. Professor Miller changed the class schedule.	**T**	**F**
4. The class is usually at 10:30.	**T**	**F**
5. Professor Miller is going to take a vacation.	**T**	**F**

3 DISCOVER. Complete the exercises to learn about the grammar in this lesson.

A Look at the verb forms in **bold** in the conversation and excerpt in exercise **1**. Write the verbs in the correct column of the chart.

Simple Present	Present Progressive
doesn't start	

B Work with a partner. Discuss your answers to the questions.

1. Do the verb forms from exercise **A** refer to the present or future?
2. How does the meaning differ between the forms in the two columns?

LEARN

7.3 Simple Present: Future Schedules

Statements	Questions
My train **leaves** at 4:00 this afternoon. The game **doesn't start** until 3:00.	**Does** the train **leave** at 5:00? **When does** the game **start**?
The stores **close** at 6:00 this evening. They **don't close** late tonight.	**What time** do the stores **close**? **Do** the stores **close** late tonight?

1. Use the simple present to talk about future events that are scheduled or on a timetable.	Next semester **starts** on January 15. Our flight **leaves** at 10:45.
2. The simple present is often used to talk about the future with these verbs: *arrive, begin, close, end, finish, leave, open,* and *start.*	A: What time **does** the concert **end** tomorrow night? B: I think it **ends** around ten.

4 Complete the conversations with the verbs in parentheses. Use the simple present.

1. A: What time ___does___ the lecture ___begin___ (begin)?
   B: It ___begins___ (begin) at ten-thirty.
2. A: When __________ Professor Miller __________ (leave) for vacation?
   B: She __________ (leave) tonight.
3. A: Excuse me, what time __________ flight 225 from Chicago __________ (arrive)?
   B: It __________ (arrive) at 1:45.
4. A: When __________ fall classes __________ (start)?
   B: They __________ (not start) until September 20.
5. The stores __________ (not open) until noon on Sunday.
6. A: What time __________ Martha's train __________ (get) to Miami?
   B: It __________ (get) there at ten-fifteen.
7. Hurry up! The cafeteria __________ (close) in 20 minutes.
8. Our bus __________ (not leave) until one-thirty. Let's get something to eat.
9. A: When __________ Linda __________ (start) her new job?
   B: She __________ (start) next Monday.
10. A: I __________ (finish) work at six tomorrow. Do you want to have dinner?
    B: No, sorry. My son __________ (have) an important hockey game tomorrow night.

7.4 Present Progressive for Future Plans

Statements	Questions
I'm **going** to the beach tomorrow.	**Is** Olga **going** to the party tonight?
She**'s not traveling** to Norway this summer.	**What are** you **doing** this weekend?
They **are finishing** later.	**Are** they **finishing** by 5:00?
We **aren't working** tomorrow.	**What are** we **eating** for dinner?

1. Use the present progressive for definite future plans. The plan is often in the near future, or the details of the plan, such as place or time, are specific.	She**'s meeting** us at the airport. I**'m not going to** the concert tonight.
2. When the present progressive is used for the future, we often include a future time expression, such as *tonight, tomorrow, next month, this summer*, etc.	Future: I**'m working** this weekend.
When there is no future time expression or future context, the present progressive refers to the present.	Present: I'm working.

5 Complete each statement or question with the words in parentheses. Use the present progressive for future.

1. ______I'm working______ (I / work) late tonight.
2. ____________________ (when / they / leave) for Rio?
3. ____________________ (we / go) a party on Friday night.
4. ____________________ (Craig / graduate) in June?
5. ____________________ (he / not have) dinner with us tonight.
6. ____________________ (I / meet) Marla at 2:30.
7. ____________________ (where / you / go) after class?
8. ____________________ (what / you / do) tomorrow night?
9. ____________________ (you / visit) your family this weekend?
10. ____________________ (how / you / get) home today?

6 SPEAK. Work with a partner. Take turns asking and answering questions 7–10 from exercise **5**.

A: *Where are you going after class?*

B: *To the dentist.*

PRACTICE

7 Circle the correct words to complete the conversations. Then listen and check your answers.

Conversation 1

Alison: Sue, (1) **do you do / are you doing** anything tomorrow evening?

Sue: No, (2) **I just spend / I'm just spending** a quiet evening at home. Why?

Alison: Well, I bought tickets to a lecture called "Working Smart." for my sister and me, but now (3) **she doesn't come / she's not coming**. Would you like to go with me?

Sue: I'd love to! Who (4) **speaks / is speaking**?

Alison: A guy called Tim Ferriss. He (5) **talks / is talking** about ways to work less and enjoy life more. I can't wait!

Sue: I definitely need to hear that! What time (6) **does it start / is it starting**?

Alison: At eight.

Conversation 2

Terri: Hey, George, I don't really understand this week's assignment. (7) **Do you hand / Are you handing** it in tomorrow?

George: No. (8) **I don't understand / I'm not understanding** it either, and Professor Doyle's vacation (9) **starts / is starting** tomorrow. Jerry and I (10) **meet / are meeting** him tonight for coffee to discuss it. Do you want to join us?

Terri: Sure. Where (11) **do you meet / are you meeting him**?

George: At the Bridge Street Cafe at seven-thirty.

CD2-24

8 **LISTEN** to each statement or question. Is it present or future? Check (✓) present or future. Then listen again and write the words or phrases that helped you choose your answers.

1. ☐ present ☑ future Helpful words: tomorrow
2. ☐ present ☐ future Helpful words: ________________
3. ☐ present ☐ future Helpful words: ________________
4. ☐ present ☐ future Helpful words: ________________
5. ☐ present ☐ future Helpful words: ________________
6. ☐ present ☐ future Helpful words: ________________
7. ☐ present ☐ future Helpful words: ________________
8. ☐ present ☐ future Helpful words: ________________

9 APPLY.

A Look at Pedro's calendar for next week. In your notebook, write five questions about his schedule and plans. Use the present progressive and simple present for future.

When is he going to New York City?

What time does his train to New York leave?

12 Monday	Thursday 15
math exam 10:30 a.m. *meet Professor Allen—Room 204 4:00 p.m.*	*Spanish exam 3:00 p.m.* *dinner with Mom and Dad—7:00 p.m. China Garden Restaurant—28 Brown St.*
13 Tuesday	**Friday 16**
dentist appointment 8:30 a.m. *study for Spanish exam with Yuri and Keiko—library 2nd floor 5:00 p.m.*	*work at bookstore 10:00 a.m. - 4:00 p.m.* *New York City with Ted* *get tickets at train station* *train 431 6:15 p.m.*
14 Wednesday	**17 Saturday** / **18 Sunday**
tennis with Rick—sports center 4:00 p.m. *watch game—Todd's house 7:00 p.m.* *bring snacks*	Saturday: *museum* *concert—8:00 p.m.* Sunday: *1:00 p.m. baseball game* *go home—train 432 6:45 p.m.*

B Work with a partner. Ask and answer your questions from exercise **A**.

A: *When is he going to New York City?*

B: *On Friday.*

A: *What time does his train leave?*

B: *It leaves at 6:15.*

C In your notebook, create a calendar with notes about your schedule and plans for next week. Use Pedro's calendar from exercise **A** as a model.

D Work with a partner. Take turns asking and answering questions about your partner's week. Use the simple present and the present progressive for future.

A: *I'm having dinner with Alex on Wednesday night.*

B: *That's nice. Where are you going?*

EXPLORE

CD2-25

1 READ the blog post about Fatima's experience in South East Asia. Notice the words in **bold**.

Fatima's Blog: Ocean News and Views

Hi everyone! I'm on a diving tour of Southeast Asia. The diving is breathtaking! I'**ll post** some photos **when I have more time.**

In this blog I **will share** photos of my trip as well as ideas about the ocean and ways to protect it. I'm **going to write** about a new topic each week. My first post is about the future of coral reefs. *Sharks are Not Your Enemy!* **is coming** next week, so stay tuned! My goal is for everyone to enjoy the photos and learn ways to help protect our oceans and the animals in them. I hope, for example, that **after you read this first post**, you **will never use** another plastic bag and you **will avoid** all toxic sunscreens. Enjoy!

Post 1: The Future of Coral Reefs

Coral reefs are one of the most beautiful and colorful sights in nature, but according to scientists, they are in danger. We must change our behavior if we want them to survive. Some experts predict that a large percentage of the world's coral reefs **will not exist** in the year 2050. **Will** people **change** their behavior **before it's too late**? Here are some facts about coral reefs, and a few things you can do to help protect our oceans:

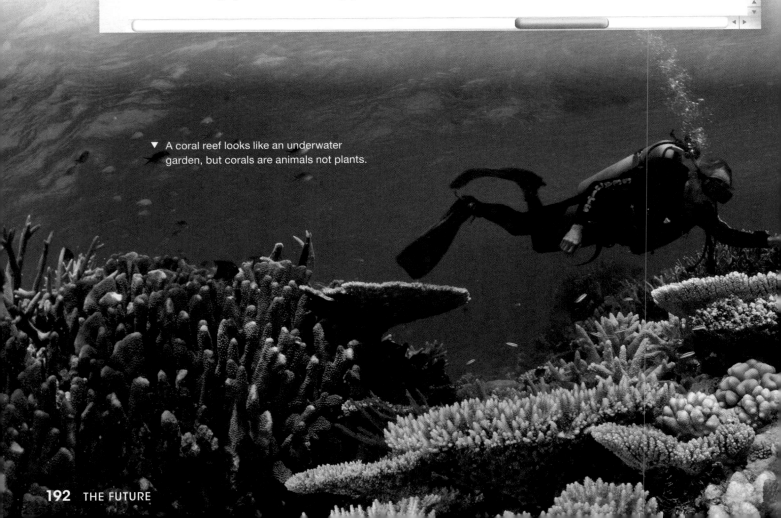

▼ A coral reef looks like an underwater garden, but corals are animals not plants.

2 CHECK. Choose the correct answer to complete each statement.

1. Fatima is in ________________.	a. Asia	b. Africa
2. Her goal is to ________________ the ocean.	a. enjoy	b. protect
3. Coral reefs are ________________.	a. in danger	b. dead
4. She thinks plastic bags are ________________.	a. good	b. bad
5. According to some experts, only ________________ of coral reefs will exist in 2050.	a. 50 percent	b. 30 percent

3 DISCOVER. Complete the exercises to learn about the grammar in this lesson.

A Look at these sentences from the blog post in exercise **A**. Circle the subject + verb that comes after each underlined time word.

1. I'll post some photos when I have more time.
2. . . . after you read this first post, you will never use another plastic bag . . .
3. Will people change their behavior before it's too late?

B Look at the verbs you circled in exercise **A**. What verb form is used in the clauses?

LEARN

7.5 Comparison of Future Forms

1. Use *will* or *be going to* for predictions and things you are certain about in the future.	Ana is smart. She'**ll get** a good job. Ana is smart. She'**s going to get** a good job.
Be careful! Use only *be going to* when you are certain about something because of evidence or information you have now.	✓ The score if 5-0. We **are going to** win! ✗ The score is 5-0. We will win!
2. Use *will* for decisions made at the time of speaking, offers, and promises.	A: You didn't mail the letter. B: I forgot! I'**ll do** it tomorrow.
3. Use *be going to* for plans or intentions.	I'**m going to play** soccer on Sunday afternoon. Lisa **isn't going to teach** next semester.
4. Use the present progressive for plans. The plans are often in the near future.	Jason **is leaving** for Hong Kong tomorrow. Rita **isn't coming** to the party tonight.
5. Use the simple present for future events that are scheduled or on a time table.	The train **leaves** at 10:35 tomorrow morning.

4 Circle the correct future form to complete each sentence.

1. Don't carry that heavy suitcase. **I'll carry** / **I'm carrying** it for you.
2. I'm going to Australia this summer. **I'm going to visit** / **I visit** the Great Barrier Reef.
3. I heard the weather report. **It's snowing** / **It's going to snow** tonight.
4. According to experts, coral reefs **are** / **will be** in serious trouble by 2050.
5. Tricia **will go** / **is going** to a concert tonight.
6. We **are going** / **go** to Alaska next month.
7. I'm tired. **I'm staying** / **I stay** home tonight.
8. Darlene **has** / **is going to have** her baby in a few months.
9. Do you need money? **I'm lending** / **I'll lend** you some.
10. **I'll take** / **I'm going to take** a photography class next semester.

5 Choose all possible correct answers to complete each sentence.

1. In the future, people ________________ to Mars.

   a. travel b. will travel c. are going to travel

2. Ten years from now, I ________________ a doctor.

   a. will be b. am c. am going to be

3. Don't forget. We ________________ dinner with my grandparents tonight.

   a. have b. are having c. will have

4. Louis ________________ to Puerto Rico to study Spanish next semester.

a. goes b. is going c. is going to go

5. My friends and I ________________ our own business after college.

a. start b. will start c. are going to start

6. Are you going to class now? ________________ you a ride.

a. I'm giving b. I'll give c. I give

7. My family ________________ a vacation in Florida next week.

a. will take b. is taking c. takes

8. ________________ early tomorrow morning. I have a meeting at 7:30 a.m.

a. I'm getting up b. I get up c. I'll get up

9. Oh, no! Look at this traffic! ________________ late.

a. We're b. We'll be c. We're going to be

10. When ________________ Friday? Let's do something afterward.

a. does your class end b. will your class end c. is your class ending

7.6 Future Time Clauses with *After, As Soon As, When, Before*

1. A future time clause tells when an action or event will happen. The time clause can come before or after the main clause.	**After I eat lunch,** I will take a nap. (Time Clause / Main Clause) I will take a nap **after I eat lunch.** (Main Clause / Time Clause)
2. Future time clauses begin with *before, after, as soon as,* or *when.*	
a. Use *after, as soon as,* or *when* to show that the action or event in the time clause will happen first.	a. **When** we **get married,** we'll buy a house. (Time Clause (First Event) / Main Clause (Second Event))
b. Use *before* to show that the action or event in the time clause will happen second.	b. **Before** we **get married,** we'll buy a house. (Time Clause (Second Event) / Main Clause (First Event))
3. Use the simple present, not *will* or *be going to,* in the time clause.	✓ After I **graduate,** I will get a job. ✗ After I will graduate, I will get a job.
4. **Remember:** Use a comma when a time clause comes at the beginning of a sentence.	**As soon as I get a job,** I'm going to move. **When I get to the office,** I'll call you.

6 Look at the underlined clauses in each sentence. Write *1* above the action that will happen first. Write *2* above the action that will happen second. Then add a comma if necessary.

1. After I finish my homework, I'm going to bed. (1 / 2)
2. When I finish this book about coral reefs I am going to write my essay.
3. Lulu is going to call the office as soon as she receives the information.
4. My sister will read all the instructions before she uses her new phone.
5. I'll start cooking dinner when you get home.
6. My brother is going to buy a new computer when he receives his next paycheck.
7. After I go to the gym I'm going to go to the supermarket.
8. I'll clean the living room before our guests arrive tonight.
9. I'll help you as soon as I send this e-mail.
10. After she graduates from college she's going to move to Toronto.

7 Circle the correct form of the verb to complete each sentence. Then add a comma if necessary.

1. After the rain (**stops**) / **will stop**, we we're going to take a walk.
2. Louise **goes** / **will go** back to work as soon as she feels better.
3. I'll let you know as soon as my plane **lands** / **will land** in Paris.
4. Andy **is** / **will be** surprised when I arrive at his birthday party.
5. Before I leave I **show** / **will show** you that website.
6. They're going to take some photos of the Alps when they **visit** / **will visit** Switzerland.
7. When my sister saves enough money she **buys** / **is going to buy** a car.
8. He'll call you as soon as he **finishes** / **is going to finish** his homework.
9. When I **see** / **will see** Sam I'll invite him to the party.
10. I'll say goodbye to you before I **leave** / **am leaving** tonight.

PRACTICE

8 Circle the correct form of the verbs to complete the conversation.

Ria: Hey Joan, what (1) **are you doing** / **do you do** this evening?

Joan: (2) **I'm going to watch** / **I'll watch** TV.

Ria: What (3) **are you going to watch / will you watch**?

Joan: There's a documentary about wildlife in Africa on tonight. It (4) **starts / will start** at nine.

Ria: Oh, that sounds interesting. What time (5) **will it end / does it end**?

Joan: Let's see . . . It (6) **ends / is ending** at ten-thirty. Why? (7) **Are you going to go / Will you go** to bed early?

Ria: Yeah, I (8) **'ll give / 'm giving** a presentation in the morning . . . but, I (9) **'ll watch / 'm watching** the first half of it with you.

Joan: Oh, good. I (10) **'m recording / 'll record** the rest of it, so you can watch it tomorrow.

9 Combine the pairs of sentences with the words in parentheses. Add a comma when necessary.

1. First: I'm going to talk to Hans. Second: I'm going to write my assignment.

   (after) After I talk to Hans, I'm going to write my assignment. OR I'm going to write my assignment after I talk to Hans.

2. First: Rui and Fatima are going to arrive. Second: We're going to have dinner.

   (when) ____________________

3. First: Barbara is going to buy a few things. Second: She's going to go home.

   (before) ____________________

4. First: Mary is going to call. Second: I'm going to ask about the test.

   (when) ____________________

5. First: She is going to finish law school. Second: She is going to move to Ohio.

   (as soon as) ____________________

6. First: I'm going to finish my homework. Second: I'm going to go for a run.

   (when) ____________________

7. First: He is going to paint it. Second: He is going to sell his house.

   (before) ____________________

8. First: I'm going to make dinner. Second: I'm going to watch the news.

   (after) ____________________

10 **SPEAK.** Work with a partner. Complete the sentences about yourself.

After I finish this English course . . .

When I retire . . .

As soon as class ends today . . .

. . . before I go home today.

After I finish this English course, I'm going to take a vacation.

11 **EDIT.** Read the article about the Great Bear Rainforest. Find and correct six more errors with future forms.

The Future of the Great Bear Rainforest

A Canadian company wants to build an oil pipeline[1] in central Canada. It ~~carries~~ will carry oil from Alberta to the coast of British Columbia, over 700 miles (1120 km) away. The pipeline will carrying oil to the coast, where big ships will to collect the oil for the next stage of its journey. The pipeline will create a new market for Canadian oil in China and other Asian countries.

Unfortunately, the plan going to take the pipeline through the Great Bear Rainforest. Many people do not want this to happen. The building of the pipeline will threatens animals such as the Kermode bear. Also, some of the local people think that the ships are going cause problems. They are afraid that one of the ships will spill[2] oil when it will travel along the coast of British Columbia.

[1] **pipeline:** a large pipe for carrying oil or gas across a country
[2] **spill:** to drop liquid by accident

◄ A Kermode bear, also known as a spirit bear, in the Great Bear Rainforest, British Columbia, Canada

12 APPLY.

A Work with a partner. Read Judy's *To Do List* for tomorrow. With a partner, take turns talking about her plans for tomorrow.

At eleven o'clock, she's going to check the monkey house.

TO DO LIST

- check monkey house 11:00
- answer e-mail 1:00
- call Frank – ask about lions and their new diet 2:00
- interview zookeeper applicant 3:00 – use new question sheet for the interview
- leave office 4:00
- buy Mom's birthday present
- get birthday cake—Sam's Bakery

B Complete each sentence with the correct form of the verbs in parentheses. Then add a comma if necessary. For some items, there is more than one correct answer.

1. Judy is going to answer (answer) her e-mail before she calls (call) Frank.
2. When she ________ (speak) with Frank she ________ (ask) him about the lions' diet.
3. She ________ (call) Frank before she ________ (interview) the zookeeper applicant.
4. Judy ________ (use) the new question sheet when she ________ (talk) to the zookeeper applicant.
5. After she ________ (finish) the interview she ________ (leave) her office.
6. As soon as she ________ (leave) her office she ________ (go) to the store.
7. When she ________ (go) to the store she ________ (buy) her mother's birthday present.
8. Judy ________ (get) a birthday cake after she ________ (do) everything else.

C In your notebook, write five or six sentences about your schedule for tomorrow. Use *before, after, as soon as,* and *when.*

After I finish class, I'm going to meet Luisa and Daniela for coffee.

D Work with a partner. Take turns talking about your schedules for tomorrow. Ask follow up questions.

A: *What are you doing after class?*

B: *I'm going to study for a grammar test.*

A: *Oh, who's your grammar teacher?*

Charts 7.1–7.6

1 Complete the conversations with the words in parentheses. Use *will, be going to,* the present progressive for future, or the simple present for future. In some cases, more than one answer is possible.

1. **Vera:** What's wrong with Erik today?

   Deng: He's upset about last month's sales report. ______________ (I / talk) to him after ______________ (I / send) this e-mail.

2. **Jamal:** What time ______________ (you / finish) work tonight?

   Larry: At six-thirty. ______________ (I / call) you when ______________ (I / leave) the office.

3. **Student:** Excuse me, ______________ (the library / close) at ten tonight?

   Librarian: No, ______________ (it / close) at eleven tonight.

4. **Scott:** Hey, Mike. ______________ (you / go) to the meeting this afternoon?

   Mike: No, ______________ (I / leave) for China today. My flight ______________ (be) at three o'clock.

Charts 7.1, 7.2, 7.6

2 **EDIT.** Read the article about a new form of identification for zebras. Find and correct five more errors with future verb forms.

Barcodes for Zebras

Counting zebras in the wild has always been difficult. However, counting zebras ~~becomes~~ will become much easier in the future thanks to a new computer program called *Stripespotter*. In the future, scientists will just take photos of zebras. After they will take photos of the zebras, *Stripespotter* is doing the rest of the work. It will to examine the stripes on each zebra. The pattern of a zebra's stripes is like the barcode on a product at the supermarket. Each one is different. After scientists are going to collect enough photos, they are having an accurate record of the zebra population.

▲ A zebra in the Okavango Delta, Botswana

Charts 7.1-3 7.5, 7.6

3 LISTEN, WRITE & SPEAK.

CD2-26-27

A Listen to two people talk about one of their future goals. Check (✓) the correct goal for each speaker.

Speaker 1: Matt

Goal: ☐ learn to cook Thai food ☐ learn to play the guitar ☐ own a music store

Plans:

________________________ at a music store

________________________ every day

________________________ music a lot

Predictions:

________________ famous ________________ very good

Speaker 2: Tammy

Goal: ☐ meet new people ☐ get in shape ☐ run a marathon

Plans:

________________________ a new pair of running shoes

________________________ a running club

________________________ some short races

Predictions:

________________ really hard ________________ in great shape

CD2-26-27

B How do the speakers plan to achieve their goals? What predictions do they have about their goals? Listen again and complete the notes for each speaker.

C Work with a partner. Compare your answers from exercises **A** and **B**. Then take turns asking and answering questions about the speakers' goals, plans, and predictions. Discuss anything else you remember about the speakers. Use future forms.

A: *Is Matt going to take a class?* B: *Yes, he is.*

Charts 7.1-7.6

4 WRITE & SPEAK.

A Think of one of your own goals for the future. Then, in your notebook, write notes to answer these questions: How do you plan to achieve your goal? What are your predictions about your goal?

B Work with a partner. Take turns talking about your goals. Use your notes from exercise **A**.

Connect the Grammar to Writing

1 READ & NOTICE THE GRAMMAR.

A What are some of your predictions about the future? Discuss your predictions with a partner. Then read the text.

Personal Transporters

In the future, more people will use personal transporters, like the one in this photo. Personal transporters will take us places quickly and safely. When they become cheaper, everyone is going to want one!

Personal transporters will also be good for the environment. They'll use less fuel than cars. They'll also take up less space, so we won't need as many large parking lots. This will mean more space for parks and trees.

We'll soon see more personal transporters at airports and in large factories. When workers at these places try them, I'm sure they will find them very helpful and convenient. Police officers, letter carriers, and security guards will also find these vehicles very useful in their work. Personal transporters are going to make the commute to work more fun. I'm going to buy one as soon as I can!

GRAMMAR FOCUS

In the text in exercise **A**, the writer uses *will* and *be going to* to make predictions.

In the future, more people ***will use*** *personal transporters like the one in this photo.*

When they become cheaper, everyone ***is going to want*** *one!*

The writer uses *future* time clauses to specify the time of future events.

When they become cheaper, *everyone is going to want one!*

B Complete the chart with four more predictions about personal transporters from the text in exercise **A**.

Topic: Personal Transporters
Predictions: 1. more people will use them

C Read the text from exercise **A** again. Underline two more future time clauses.

2 BEFORE YOU WRITE.

A Work with a partner. Brainstorm topics about the future. Write a list of your ideas in your notebook.

B Choose one of the topics from your list in exercise **A**. Then complete the chart with your predictions about this topic. How will it change life in the future?

Topic: ______________________
Predictions:

3 WRITE about your predictions for the future. Write three paragraphs. Use your topic and your notes from exercise **2B** and the text in exercise **1A** to help you. Use future time clauses.

WRITING FOCUS Using Gender-Neutral Language

Use gender-neutral language in your writing. This shows respect for both men and women. Here are some tips for using gender-neutral language in writing:

- Do not use words with *man* or *mankind* when referring to people in general or all people. For example, in the text in exercise **1A**, the writer uses *people* instead of *man* or *mankind*.
- Use job titles that refer to both men and women. For example, in exercise **1A**, the writer uses *police officers* instead of *policemen*. Here are some other examples:

Original Term:	**Gender Neutral Term:**
fireman	*fire fighter*
mankind, man	*humanity, people*
businessman	*businessperson*
policeman	*police officer*
stewardess	*flight attendant*

4 SELF ASSESS. Read your text. Underline your predictions. Then use the checklist to assess your work.

- [ ] I used *will* or *be going to* to make predictions [7.1, 7.2]
- [ ] I used future forms correctly. [7.1–7.4]
- [ ] I used the correct verb forms in main clauses and time clauses. [7.6]
- [ ] I used gender-neutral language. [WRITING FOCUS]

UNIT 8 Consumer Society

Comparatives and Superlatives

▲ Cars in a scrap yard in Canada.

TOURS

EXPLORE

CD2-28

1 READ the article about consumer societies. Notice the words in **bold**.

What is a Consumer Society?

A *consumer* is a person who buys things, and a *consumer society* is a society that encourages people to buy and use goods.[1] Some people think that a consumer society provides people with **better** lives. People in consumer societies tend to live **more comfortably**. They eat a **wider** variety of food. They go to restaurants **more often**. They also buy a lot of products, maybe more than they need.

Products such as TVs, cell phones, and computers used to be luxuries.[2] Today people can buy these things **more easily than** ever before. The market for these goods is growing **faster** all the time. Consumer societies encourage people to buy **bigger** and **better** products. For example, **"smarter"** phones come out every year. In a consumer society, people are often buying **newer** and **more advanced** products. This creates a lot of waste. Nowadays, many people are thinking **more seriously** about the effects of consumer societies on the environment, and they are trying to become **more responsible** consumers.

[1] **goods:** items that can be bought or sold
[2] **luxury:** something that is expensive but not necessary

2 CHECK. Read each statement. Circle **T** for *true* and **F** for *false.*

1. Everyone agrees that consumer products improve their lives.	**T**	**F**
2. These days, consumer goods are hard to find.	**T**	**F**
3. Many people want luxury products these days.	**T**	**F**
4. Consumer societies help the environment.	**T**	**F**

3 DISCOVER. Complete the exercises to learn about the grammar in this lesson.

A Find these sentences in the article from exercise **1**. Write the missing words.

1. They eat a ________________ variety of food.
2. . . . ., and they are trying to become ____ consumers.

B Look at the words you wrote in exercise **A**. Then circle the correct word to complete each rule.

1. For **long** / **short** adjectives, put *more* before the adjective to form the comparative.
2. For **long** / **short** adjectives, add *-er* to the end of the adjective to form the comparative.

LEARN

8.1 Comparative Adjectives

	Comparative Adjective	*Than*	
The blue car is	newer	than	the gray car.
	more expensive		

1. Use a comparative adjective + *than* to compare two people, places, or things. You can use a comparative adjective + noun when the comparison is clear from context.	Lydia is **taller than** Alex. Gorillas are **more intelligent than** cows. The **bigger house** is mine. The **more interesting shows** are on cable TV.
2. Add *-er* to the end of most one-syllable adjectives to form the comparative.* If the adjective ends in *-e*, add *-r*.	small → small**er** low → low**er** large → large**r** nice → nice**r**
3. Use *more* before most long adjectives (adjectives that have two or more syllables).	Jack is **more serious than** Nikki. Do you think math is **more important than** music?
4. Some two-syllable adjectives are used with either *-er* or *more* to form the comparative.	quiet → quiet**er** / **more** quiet simple → simple**r** / **more** simple
5. Some adjectives have an irregular comparative form.	good → **better** bad → **worse** far → **farther, further**

*See page **A3** for more information on speling rules for comparative adjectives.

REAL ENGLISH

Words such as *a little, a lot, much,* and *not much,* are often used to quantify comparative adjectives.

Tina is ***a little*** *taller than Nick.*

4 Complete each sentence with the correct comparative form of the adjective in parentheses. Add *than* when necessary.

1. New cars are much __more quiet than / quieter than__ (quiet) old cars.
2. Do you think money is __more important than__ (important) good health?
3. This coat is __nicer than__ (nice) that one.
4. My old laptop was a lot __bigger than__ (big) my new one.
5. Gas is so expensive! I want a __more efficient__ (efficient) car.
6. Many people think modern life is __better than__ (good) life in the past.
7. Communication is a lot __easier than__ (easy) it was 50 years ago.
8. The pollution in my city is much __worse than__ (bad) it used to be.
9. I prefer __hotter than__ (hot) temperatures. That's why I love summer.
10. My new school is a little __farther than__ (far) my old one.

8.2 Comparative Adverbs

	Comparative Adverb	*Than*	
Gas prices are rising	faster	than	food prices.
	more rapidly		

1. Use a comparative adverb + *than* to compare two actions.	Mark works **harder than** Jeff. Carol drives **more carefully than** Peter.
2. Add *-er* to the end of one-syllable adverbs to form the comparative.	fast ⟶ fast**er** hard ⟶ hard**er** long ⟶ long**er** high ⟶ high**er**
3. Use *more* before adverbs that end with *-ly*.	quickly ⟶ **more** quickly frequently ⟶ **more** frequently
4. Some adverbs have an irregular comparative form.	well ⟶ **better** far ⟶ **farther, further** badly ⟶ **worse**

5 Complete the sentences with the comparative form of the adverbs in parentheses + *than*.

1. My new oven works a lot better than (good) my old oven. It heats up much ___ (quick) my old oven, but it also burns food ___ (often) my old one!

2. Now that he's a manager, Gerry works a lot ___ (hard) he used to. He also travels ___ (frequent) he did before, and his trips last ___ (long) they used to.

3. People are creating garbage ___ (rapid) they used to. They are throwing away their old things because they can buy new goods ___ (easy) before. In the past, people treated their belongings ___ (careful) they do now.

6 Use the words in parentheses to complete each sentence. Use the comparative form of the adverb and the correct form of the verb.

1. This computer works more efficiently than (work / efficiently) that computer.
2. My new watch ___ (keep time / accurately) my old watch.
3. My sister ___ (call / often) my brother.
4. My phone ___ (ring / loudly) your phone.
5. Tara ___ (shop / frequently) Lori.
6. Brad ___ (type / quickly) Lynn.
7. Kate ___ (sing / badly) Deb.
8. Lila ___ (study / hard) Nora.

8.3 Completing Comparisons

1. You can use an object pronoun to complete a comparison. But in more formal speaking and writing, use a subject pronoun + an auxiliary verb.	Ed is six feet tall. Bob is taller than **him**. (Object Pronoun) Ed is six feet tall. Bob is taller than **he is**. (Subject Pronoun + Aux. Verb)
2. Use an auxiliary verb after *than*. Do not repeat the main verb.	✓ Ana runs faster **than** Pat **does.** ✗ Ana runs faster than Pat runs.
3. A possessive noun or possessive pronoun can be used after *than*.	My car was more expensive **than Ellen's**. My car was more expensive **than hers**.
4. If the comparison is clear, *than* and the second part of the comparison are not necessary.	Nowadays, smart phones are **cheaper**.
5. **Be careful!** Use *than*, not *then*, in a comparison.	✓ I work harder **than** I used to. ✗ I work harder then I used to.

7 Circle the correct word(s) to complete each sentence.

1. My computer is more efficient **than your** / **than yours**.
2. The white coat is warmer **then** / **than** the gray one.
3. Ellen buys nicer clothes **than I do** / **than I am**.
4. Cars are expensive, but houses are **more expensive** / **more expensive than**.
5. Does your new stereo play music more loudly than your old one **was** / **did?**
6. Harry's motorcycle is newer than **my** / **mine**.
7. Cho's package arrived more quickly **than Kelly's did** / **than Kelly's was**.
8. Dave is 27 years old. His sister is older **than he is** / **than he does**.

8 Complete each comparison using the information in parentheses. Do not repeat the same noun.

1. Irina's car is bigger ___than mine (is)___ (my car).
2. Tom takes better photos ___than his father___ (his father).
3. Miguel's suit is more fashionable ___than chad's suit___ (Chad's suit).
4. You finished your shopping more quickly ___than she___ (she).
5. Jeff's kitchen is larger ___than our kitchen___ (our kitchen).
6. This printer prints more quickly ___than your printer___ (your printer).
7. My apartment is more comfortable ___than their apartment___ (their apartment).
8. Alison studies harder ___than her sister___ (her sister).

PRACTICE

9 Use the words in parentheses to complete the conversation with comparative adjectives or adverbs. Add *than* where necessary. In some cases, more than one answer is possible.

Matt: My phone is working (1) worse than (badly) ever! And it's (2) ________ (old) all the other phones I see, too. I want a (3) ________ (modern) phone.

Lara: Take a look at my phone. It was (4) ________ (cheap) my last phone, and I'm much (5) ________ (happy) with it. When I'm traveling, I listen to music (6) ________ (often) I do when I'm at home, so I wanted a phone with a (7) ________ (big) memory card.

Matt: Wow, it's much (8) ________ (nice) mine! The screen is a lot (9) ________ (large), too. I want one like that!

Lara: Yeah, you need a big screen, because you watch videos on your phone (10) ________ (frequently) I do.

10 Look at the charts comparing three laptop computers. Then complete the sentences with the comparative form of the adjectives and adverbs in parentheses.

Product Details	T400	XJ7	A-50
Screen size	15 inches	17 inches	14 inches
Weight	5.5 pounds	6 pounds	6.5 pounds
Amount of time on the market	18 months	3 months	9 months
Cost	$565	$650	$499

Customer Ratings	T400	XJ7	A-50
Starts quickly	★★★	★★	★★★★
Runs reliably	★★★★★	★★★★	★★★
Operates quietly	★★★★	★★★	★★★★★
Displays pictures well	★★★	★★★★★	★★★★

1. (large / small) The screen of the T400 is larger than the A-50's, but it is smaller than the XJ7's.
2. (light / heavy) The XJ7 is ________ the A-50, but it is ________ the T400.
3. (new / old) The A-50 is ________ the T400, but it is ________ the XJ7.
4. (cheap / expensive) The T400 is ________ the XJ7, but it is ________ the A-50.
5. (quickly / slowly) The T400 starts ________ the XJ7, but ________ the A-50.

6. (reliably) The T400 runs ______________________________ the XJ7 or the A-50.

7. (quietly) The A-50 operates ______________________________ the T400 or the XJ7.

8. (well) The XJ7 displays pictures ______________________________ the T400 or the A-50.

CD2-29

11 **LISTEN** to six people deciding what to buy. Circle the choice each speaker makes. Then write the reason for each decision. Use comparative adjectives or adverbs.

	Speaker's Choice	Reason for Decision
Speaker 1	blue coat / green coat	It is more comfortable.
Speaker 2	sports car / family car	
Speaker 3	yellow roses / red roses	
Speaker 4	downtown / suburbs	
Speaker 5	brown boots / black boots	
Speaker 6	big TV / small TV	

12 **APPLY.**

A Imagine that you are going on vacation soon. Brainstorm a list of vacation ideas, for example, a camping vacation, a resort vacation, a safari, etc. Write your list of ideas in your notebook.

B Choose two of your vacation ideas from exercise **A** to compare. In your notebook, make a chart like the one below. Write notes about your vacation ideas in your chart.

A Camping Vacation	A Resort Vacation
cheap sleep on the ground fun simple food close to nature	expensive comfortable bed relaxing good food gym, pool

C In your notebook, write five sentences comparing your two vacation choices. Use the information from your chart from exercise **B** and comparative adjectives and adverbs.

A camping vacation is cheaper than a resort vacation.
Your sleep will be more comfortable at a resort.
Camping is more fun than a resort.

D Choose one of your vacation ideas from exercise **C**. In your notebook, write two or three sentences to explain why you prefer it.

I want to go on a camping vacation. It's cheaper than a resort vacation, and it's closer to nature. . . .

E Work with a partner. Share your ideas from exercise **C** and explain your decision from exercise **D**. Did your partner make a good choice? Why, or why not?

EXPLORE

CD2-30

1 **READ** the excerpt from a discussion between the professor of a business class and a guest speaker. Notice the words in **bold**.

Online Reviews: ★ or ★★★★?

Professor: So, Dennis, what changes have you seen in marketing recently?

Dennis: Well, as you know, customers love to post online reviews of products these days. These reviews are now just **as important as** traditional advertising. Maybe even more important. TV advertising is **as useful as** it was before, of course. On the other hand, newspaper ads[1] are much **less effective than** they used to be.

Professor: Hmm. That's interesting. . . . I've spoken to some marketing people who are**n't as positive as** you are about online reviews.

Dennis: Really? I'm surprised. There are certainly some concerns with online reviews. For example, satisfied customers are **less likely** to write reviews **than** people who have had a problem. This means there might be more negative reviews than positive ones. But online shoppers are wiser now. A few negative opinions are **not as harmful as** they used to be. Also, the positive reviews can be **as valuable as** ads. If a customer loves a product, he or she will endorse[2] it just **as enthusiastically**[3] **as** a TV ad does!

[1] **ad:** short for advertisement
[2] **endorse:** to say that you support or approve of someone or something
[3] **enthusiastically:** to do something in a way that shows a lot of interest and excitement

▼ A billboard, a traditional form of advertising

2 CHECK. Read each statement. Circle **T** for *true* or **F** for *false*.

1. Dennis thinks that online reviews are not very important in marketing. **T** **F**
2. Newspaper ads used to be more effective. **T** **F**
3. Some marketing people have a negative opinion of online reviews. **T** **F**
4. Customers with problems are more likely to write online reviews. **T** **F**
5. Online shoppers won't buy a product if they see a negative review. **T** **F**
6. Positive online reviews aren't very valuable. **T** **F**

3 DISCOVER. Complete the exercises to learn about the grammar in this lesson.

A Look at each phrase from the discussion in exercise **1** on page 213. Does the phrase mean *equal* or *not equal*? Circle the correct answer.

1. as useful as — **equal** / **not equal**
2. less effective than — **equal** / **not equal**
3. aren't as positive as — **equal** / **not equal**
4. not as harmful as — **equal** / **not equal**
5. as valuable as — **equal** / **not equal**
6. as enthusiastically as — **equal** / **not equal**

B Look at the phrases from exercise **A**. Then answer the questions.

1. What word follows comparisons beginning with *as* + adjective? ____________________
2. What word follows comparisons beginning with *less* + adverb? ____________________

◄ Neon signs in Nanjing Lu, Shanghai's main shopping street, China

LEARN

8.4 Comparisons with *As . . . As*

	As	Adjective	*As*	
My car is	as	big comfortable	as	your car.

	As	Adverb	*As*	
I drive	as	well carefully	as	you do.

1. Use *as* + adjective/adverb + *as* to compare two people, places, or things that are the same or equal in some way.	Adjective: Your car is **as old as** mine. Adverb: I can run a mile **as fast as** you can.
2. To complete a comparison with *as . . . as,* you can use a. a noun (+ verb) b. a subject pronoun + verb or an auxiliary verb c. a possessive noun or possessive pronoun	a. I dance as well as **my brother (dances).** b. I dance as well as **he dances.** I dance as well as **he does.** c. My computer is as old as **Rita's.** My computer is as old as **hers.**
3. In informal speaking, object pronouns are often used to complete comparisons with *as. . . . as.*	Formal: He's as tall as **I am**. Informal: He's as tall as **me**.

4 Complete each sentence with *as . . . as* and the adjective or adverb in parentheses.

1. Magazine ads are ___as effective as___ (effective) newspaper ads.
2. Mark plays the guitar ______________ (well) Nancy does.
3. Online reviews are ______________ (useful) asking friends about products.
4. I read online reviews ______________ (carefully) he does.
5. The coat was just ______________ (warm) it looked.
6. Your sofa is just ______________ (comfortable) Diane's.
7. My computer is ______________ (fast) the newer models.
8. He shops online ______________ (frequently) I do.

5 Use the words to make comparisons with *as . . . as.*

1. Desktop computers / be / popular / laptops

   ___Desktop computers are as popular as laptops (are).___

2. Microwave ovens / work / well / regular ovens

   ____

3. Motorcycles / go / fast / cars

   ____

4. This hotel room / be / big / my apartment

   ____

5. A smartphone / send messages / quickly / a laptop

____

6. My mother / speak English / well / my father

____

7. Gabi / go shopping / often / Linda

____

8. Trains / be / comfortable / airplanes

____

8.5 Comparison with *Less* and *Not As . . . As*

Less + Adjective or Adverb + *Than*				
	Less	Adjective/Adverb	*Than*	
This phone is	**less**	**expensive**	**than**	that one.
This old fan works	**less**	**efficiently**	**than**	the new fan.

Not As + Adjective or Adverb + *As*				
	Not As	Adjective/Adverb	*As*	
This phone is	**not as**	**expensive** **good**	**as**	that one.
This old fan does	**not work as**	**efficiently** **well**	**as**	the new fan.

1. The opposite of *more* is *less*. *Not as . . . as* and *less* have the same meaning.	My old car was **less efficient than** my new car. My old car was **not as efficient as** my new car.
2. Use *not as . . . as* with one-syllable adjectives or adverbs.	My apartment is **not as big as** yours. Tom does**n't** run **as fast as** Steven.
3. Use *less . . . than* or *not as . . . as* with adjectives or adverbs that have two or more syllables. The meaning is the same.	My son visits **less frequently than** my daughter. My son does**n't** visit **as frequently as** my daughter.
4. **Remember:** If the comparison is clear, the second part of the comparison is not necessary.	The food at Joe's cafe is**n't as good as** the food at Chez Claude, but it's **less expensive**. The food at Joe's cafe is **less expensive than** the food at Chez Clause, but it is**n't as good**.

See Chart 8.3 for more information completing comparisons.

6 Complete the conversations with *less* or *not as . . . as* and the words in parentheses. Do not use *not* unless it is included in the parentheses. Use *than* and the second *as* only where necessary.

1. Anita: The clothes in this store (1) ___aren't as nice as___ (not be / nice) they used to be. Look at this coat! It's much (2) ______________ (fashionable) the coat I bought here last year.

Jackie: Well, that's true. It (3) ________________ (not be / stylish), but it's also (4) ________________ (expensive).

2. Chris: Check out this new coffee machine! It looks great! Ours (5) ________________ (not be / fancy) this new one.

Mike: Well, it's definitely fancier than ours, but it (6) ________________ (not be / efficient). It (7) ________________ (not make coffee / quickly), and the coffee (8) ________________ (not taste / good).

7 Rewrite each sentence with the word(s) in parentheses.

1. My watch is less attractive than yours. (not as . . . as)

   My watch isn't as attractive as yours.

2. Sally's shoes aren't as fancy as Jill's. (less)

   Sally's shoses are't less's fancy than Jill's

3. Adam exercises less frequently than he used to. (not as . . . as)

   Adam does not exercises as frequently as he used to.

4. This supermarket isn't as expensive as the one across the street. (less)

   This supermarket is less expensive than the one accross the street

5. The actor's new movie isn't as exciting as his last one. (less)

   The actor's new movie is less exciting than his last one

6. This gym is less convenient than the one near my house. (not as . . . as)

   This gym is not as convenient as the one near my house.

7. This review is less positive than that one. (not as . . . as)

   This review is not as positive as that one

8. The new tablet doesn't start up as quickly as the old one. (less)

   The new table doesn't start up less quickly than the old car

PRACTICE

8 Complete the conversation with *less* or *(not) as . . . as* and the words in parentheses. Make the verbs negative only when *not* is given. Use *than* and the second *as* only where necessary.

Tina: Your new camera (1) isn't as big as (not be / big) your old one.

Dawn: I know. It (2) ________________ (not be / heavy) my old X-2000, and it was (3) ________________ (expensive), too.

Tina:	But you took great photos with your old one! Why did you decide to change?
Dawn:	Well, my old camera was really difficult to use, so I (4) ______________________ (not take photos / often) I wanted to. This new camera is (5) ______________________ (not be / complicated) my old one, so it's much (6) ______________________ (difficult) to use.
Tina:	And what about your photos? Are they (7) ______________________ (nice) the ones from your old camera?
Dawn:	Oh yes, they're just (8) ______________________ (good) my old ones.

9 **EDIT.** Read the online reviews of a play house for children. Find and correct seven more errors with comparisons with *less* and (*not*) *as . . . as*.

THE JOLLY ROGER PIRATE SHIP

Customer Reviews

★★★★★ **A Huge Success!**

Our family loves this! Our last playhouse was much less exciting ^than the Jolly Roger. It was also less attractive as this one. And this is really an important point: it wasn't as safe as. –**Maria**

★★★ **Hard to Build**

My kids enjoyed this, but for me, putting it together was just as hard building a real pirate ship! It's true that I probably don't build things as quickly as a lot of other people do. And maybe I'm not as good with tools as they do, but I still think this product should be less complicated than! –**Sam**

★★★★ **Fun for Younger Kids**

My four-year-old son says this play structure is fun as a real pirate ship! He plays in it as often as he can, but my six-year-old daughter isn't as enthusiastic as he is about it. I'm a little disappointed because she uses it less often then I expected. –**Lin**

10 Look at the chart comparing three Internet movie services. Then complete each sentence with the words in parentheses. Use *less* and *(not) as . . . as*. For some sentences, more than one answer is possible.

	C-Movie	MyScreen	FAB
Membership fee	$9.95	$5.00	$5.00
Monthly rate	$7.95	$8.50	$9.95
New movies	every month	every two weeks	every week
Easy to use	★★★	★★★	★★★★
Customer service	★★★	★★★★	★★★★

1. FAB's membership fee ___is as cheap as___ (be / cheap) MyScreen's.
2. Becoming a member of MyScreen ___is less expensive than___ (be / expensive) joining C-Movie. isn't as expensive as
3. C-Movie's monthly rate ___isn't as high as___ (be / high) the others'.
4. C-Movie ___adds new movies less frequently than___ (add new movies / frequently) FAB.
5. Using FAB ___is less difficult than___ (be / difficult) using the others.
6. On C-Movie, you can ___find movies as easily as___ (find movies / easily) on MyScreen. They are both pretty easy to use.
7. MyScreen's customer service ___is as good as___ (be / good) FAB's.
8. C-Movie's customer service ___is less helpful than___ (be / helpful) the other two services. isn't as helpful as

11 **APPLY.**

A Use the chart below to compare two or three similar products or services you have used. For example, transportation services, restaurants, shopping websites, etc. Choose five categories to compare. Use the chart from exercise **10** as a model.

	1: ________	2: ________	3: ________

B In your notebook, write five sentences comparing the products or services from your chart in exercise **A**. Use *less* and *(not) as . . . as*. Use the sentences in exercise **10** as models.

The TRIMET bus is less expensive than the subway or a taxi. It's not as comfortable as a taxi. . . .

C Work with a partner. Talk about how the products or services you chose compare with each other. Use *less* and *(not) as . . . as*. Does your partner agree with you?

EXPLORE

CD2-31

1 READ the article about a problem on Mount Everest. Notice the words in **bold**.

Mount Everest:
The Highest Garbage Dump in the World?

Most people know that Mount Everest is **the highest** mountain in the world. However, there is another fact that many people don't know: it has become one of **the dirtiest** mountains in the world.

Mount Everest is one of **the toughest** and **most exciting** mountains to climb on Earth. It is not **the coldest** or **the windiest** place on Earth, but it comes close! These challenges make it one of **the most attractive** mountains for serious climbers. Since 1952, over 3500 climbers have reached the top. Unfortunately, most of them have left equipment and trash on the mountain.

In fact, trash is now one of **the biggest** threats to the environment on Mount Everest. Local organizations have brought tons of trash down from the mountain. One of **the most interesting** projects handed over more than a ton of tin cans, glass bottles, and old climbing tools to artists in Nepal. The artists used the trash to create works of art. Then, they sold the art to raise money for local charities.[1] **The least expensive** work of art cost $17, and **the most expensive** one cost $2400.

[1] **charity:** an organization that raises money to help people

▶ The consumer society produces a lot of waste, even in the Himalayas. Here, a climber collects trash on Mount Everest.

2 CHECK. Circle the correct word to complete each statement.

1. According to the reading, Mount Everest is very **clean** / **dirty**.
2. Climbing Mount Everest is very **difficult** / **easy**.
3. Mount Everest is **an unusual** / **a popular** mountain for serious climbers.
4. Climbers **rarely** / **often** leave trash on Mount Everest.
5. People create **art** / **charities** from the trash on Mount Everest.

3 DISCOVER. Complete the exercises to learn about the grammar in this lesson.

A Look at the bold phrases in the reading from exercise **1**. Then write three more examples in each column of the chart.

Adjectives with *-est*	Adjectives with *most*
tall	*exciting*

B Which adjectives add *most*? Circle the correct answer. a. long ones b. short ones

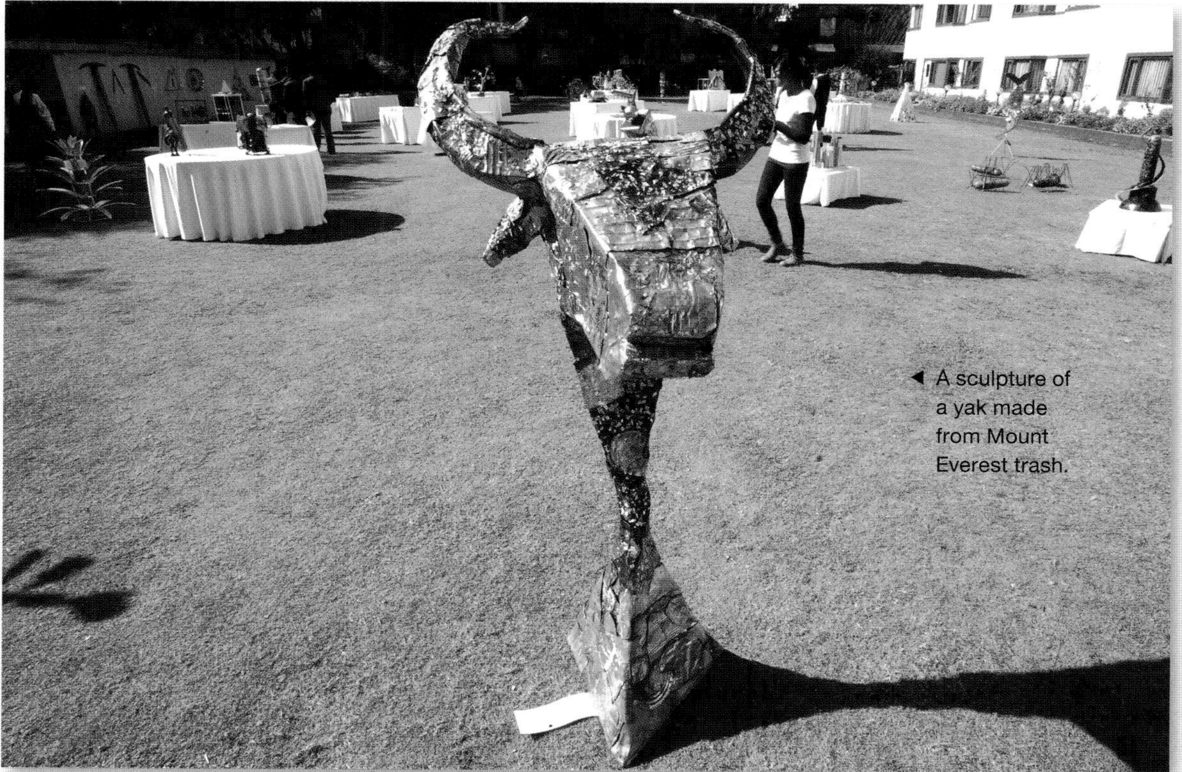

◀ A sculpture of a yak made from Mount Everest trash.

LEARN

8.6 Superlative Adjectives and Adverbs

	Superlative Adjective	
The red car is	the nicest the most expensive	car in the parking lot.

	Superlative Adverb	
She runs	the fastest the most slowly	of all the players on the team.

1. Use a superlative adjective to compare three or more people, places, or things.	Ali is **the tallest** student in our class. Prague is **the most beautiful** city I've ever seen. What's **the most interesting** book you've ever read?
2. Use a superlative adverb to compare the action of three or more people or things.	Of all my friends, Alicia calls **the most frequently**. My red shoes fit **the most comfortably** of all my shoes.
3. Add *-est* to the end of most one-syllable adjectives or adverbs to form the superlative.* Use *the* before superlative adjectives. It is not as common before adverbs.	Adjective: I bought **the longest** couch in the store. Adverb: Steve works **hardest** of all the students.
4. Use *the most* before most adjectives that have two or more syllables and adverbs ending in *-ly*.	Maria is **the most careful** climber of the group. The Grand Canyon is **the most amazing** sight I've ever seen. Of all the girls, Brenda sings **the most beautifully.**
5. For some two-syllable adjectives and adverbs, either *-est* or *the most* can be used to form the superlative.	stupid ⟶ the stupid**est**/the **most stupid** cruel ⟶ the cruel**est**/the **most cruel**
6. Some superlatives are irregular.	good/well ⟶ **the best** bad/badly ⟶ **the worst**

*See page **A3** for more information on spelling superlative adjectives and adverbs.

4 Complete the sentences with the superlative form of the adjective or adverb in parentheses.

1. The biggest (big) piles of trash on Mount Everest are on the lower areas.
2. Trash is one of ______________ (bad) problems on Mount Everest now.
3. Many climbers consider K2, a mountain between Pakistan and China, to be ______________ (difficult) mountain to climb, not Mount Everest.
4. Ted was ______________ (experienced) climber on the expedition.
5. Which climber is ______________ (far) from the top?

6. That was ______________________ (easy) mountain I've ever climbed.

7. Danny climbs __________________________ (quickly) of all of us.

8. Mount Everest is __________________________ (high) mountain on Earth.

9. That company has __________________________ (good) guides.

10. Climbing Mount Everest in a snowstorm is one of __________________________ (stupid) thing you can do. It's extremely dangerous!

5 LISTEN & SPEAK.

CD2-32

A Listen and complete each question with the superlative form of the adjective or adverb you hear.

1. At what time of day do you work ___most efficiently___?

2. Who is __________________________ person in the world?

3. What is __________________________ movie you've ever seen?

4. What kind of books do you read __________________________?

5. What is __________________________ thing to do in a storm?

6. What is __________________________ to watch?

7. What is __________________________ place to have lunch in this area?

8. Who is __________________________ person in your family?

B Work with a partner. Take turns asking and answering the questions from exercise **A**.

A: *At what time of day do you work most efficiently?*

B: *In the afternoon.*

REAL ENGLISH

A possessive adjective can replace *the* in a superlative comparison.

Zara is ***the best*** *friend I have.*
Zara is ***my best*** *friend.*

8.7 More on Superlative Adjectives and Adverbs

1. The opposite of *the most* is *the least*.	This is **the least expensive** phone in the store. All the other phones cost a lot more. She drives **the least carefully** of all my friends. All my other friends drive much more carefully.
2. A prepositional phrase with *in* or *of* is often used to complete a superlative.	The Nile is **the longest river in the world.** This hat is **the prettiest of the three.**
3. **Remember:** If the comparison is clear, it is not necessary to complete it.	This sentence is **the longest**. She won because she ran **the fastest.**
4. *One of the* often comes before a superlative adjective. The superlative adjective is followed by a plural noun.	China is **one of the biggest countries** in the world.

6 Use the words in parentheses to write superlative sentences. Use *least* when *not* is included in the parentheses. Make the nouns plural if necessary.

1. This is a state park. (not popular / in California)

   This is the least popular state park in California.

2. Canada is a country. (large / in North America)

   ____

3. Tokyo has a population. (big / in Japan)

   Tokyo has the biggest population in JAB

4. This is an apartment. (not expensive / in the building)

   This is the least. expensive in the building.

5. Alan drives. (fast / of my three brothers)

   Alan drives the fastest of my three brother.

6. Jane is a student. (one of the / intelligent / in her class)

   Jane is one of the most intelligent in her class

7. That was a class. (one of the / not interesting / I've ever taken)

   That was one of the least interesting classes I've ever taken.

8. Mel works. (not efficiently / all the people in this office)

   Mel works the least efficiently all the people in the office

9. This is a computer. (cheap / in the store)

   This is the cheapest computer in the World.

10. That's a street. (one of the / pretty / in this city)

   That's one of the most prettiest street in this city.

7 **SPEAK.** Work with a partner. Talk about people, places, and things you know about. Use the superlative form of the adjectives and adverbs from the box or your own ideas.

carefully	fast	hard	large	popular
crowded	good	interesting	old	well

My grandmother is the oldest person in my family. She's 91.

PRACTICE

8 Complete the sentences with the superlative form of the adjectives and adverbs in parentheses. Use *least* if *not* is included in the parentheses.

1. **Kelly:** I think people are too concerned about having (1) ___the most modern___ (modern) cell phones. Cell phones contain some of (2) ______ (rare) minerals on Earth, but many people just throw their old cell phones away when they buy a new one. This is (3) ______ (one of the / bad / thing) you can do! But if you recycle your old cell phones, it's (4) ______ (one of the / good / thing) you can do.

2. **Amir:** My cell phone is (5) ______ (important / thing) I own. It's (6) ______ (convenient / place) I have to keep information.

3. **Brad:** My new cell phone is a piece of junk! It was (7) ______ (not expensive) phone in the store. What a mistake! Also, the salesperson in that store was one of (8) ______ (not helpful / salesperson) I've ever spoken to.

9 **EDIT.** Read the article about trash in the desert. Find and correct eight more errors with superlatives.

Cameron's Camels

The Arabian Desert in the Middle East is one of the ~~most hot~~ hottest environments on Earth, and it has the less amount of rainfall. But to the camel, it is home. The camel is one of the most strong animals in the world. Camels can go for many days with only a little food and water. When they do find water, they probably drink the most quick of any land animal. Adult camels can drink about 25 to 30 gallons (95–114 liters) in ten minutes. Unfortunately, finding water is not the seriousest problem camels face. Most dangerous threat to camels comes from humans. Tourists in the desert leave trash behind. Camels think the trash is food and eat it. This is very dangerous for the camels, because it can kill them.

One of the most polluted part of the desert is outside the city of Abu Dhabi. Each year, many camels die there from eating trash. Cameron Oliver has been trying to change this. Since he was eight years old, Cameron has been telling people that trash is very dangerous for camels. Of all the young people in Abu Dhabi, Cameron has worked most hard to help the camels. When he was 12, Cameron became the most young person to win an Abu Dhabi award for community service.

PLEASE **STOP** KILLING ME
DON'T **LITTER**
www.cameronscamelcampaign.com

10 APPLY.

A Work with a partner. Use the words in parentheses to write superlatives. Then choose the correct answer to complete each fact on the quiz.

General Knowledge Quiz

1. ________ is *the highest mountain* ________ (high / mountain) on Earth.
   a. Mount Kilimanjaro b. Mount Everest c. K2
2. ________ is ________________ (fast / animal) in the world.
   a. the camel b. the zebra c. the cheetah
3. ________ is ________________ (long / river) in the world.
   a. The Nile River b. The Amazon River c. The Yangtze River
4. ________ is ________________ (wide / ocean) on Earth.
   a. The Pacific Ocean b. The Atlantic Ocean c. The Indian Ocean
5. ________ is ________________ (small / continent).
   a. Africa b. Antarctica c. Australia
6. ________ is ________________ (large / animal) on Earth.
   a. the elephant b. the blue whale c. the giraffe
7. ________ is ________________ (cold / place) on Earth.
   a. Antarctica b. Alaska c. Canada
8. ________ is ________________ (close / planet) to the sun.
   a. Mars b. Venus c. Mercury

B Check your answers at the bottom of this page. How many of your answers were correct?

C With your partner, write six more general knowledge facts like the ones from the quiz in exercise **A**. Use superlative adjectives and adverbs.

1. *The Nile River is the longest river in the world.*

D Use the facts from exercise **C** and quiz your classmates.

A: *This is the largest country in South America.*

B: *Is it Argentina?*

A: *No.*

C: *Is it Brazil?*

A: *Yes, it is!*

Answers: 1. b. Mount Everest, 2. c. the cheetah, 3. a. The Nile River 4. a. the Pacific Ocean, 5. c. Australia, 6. b. the blue whale, 7. a. Antarctica, 8. c. Mercury

Charts 8.1, 8.3–8.7

1 READ & WRITE.

A Read the information about the Greendex survey, and look at the chart. Then complete each sentence according to the information in the chart. Use the comparative or superlative form of the adjective or adverb in parentheses. For some sentences, more than one answer is possible.

The Greendex is a survey of 1000 consumers in several countries. It asks consumers how they spend their money. Each consumer receives a score. High scores indicate "green," or environmentally friendly, attitudes. Low scores indicate environmentally unfriendly attitudes.

Greendex: Rankings

	Overall	Housing	Transportation	Food	Goods
Americans	44.7	31.5	54.9	57.0	44.2
Brazilians	55.5	48.9	67.1	57.5	53.8
British	49.4	35.9	62.7	62.2	47.1
Canadians	47.9	35.1	57.8	60.9	45.7
Chinese	57.8	48.2	69.0	63.7	56.8
Germans	51.5	40.3	61.9	61.9	47.1
Indians	58.9	51.4	67.3	71.1	57.3
Japanese	48.5	35.3	65.9	54.7	52.7
Mexicans	53.9	48.0	62.2	53.6	54.5
Russians	53.1	44.1	66.4	60.4	47.9

Transportation

1. The Chinese make the greenest (green) choices.
2. Americans are ______ (green) consumers.
3. British consumers make ______ (green) choices than Canadian consumers.
4. Mexican consumers are ______ (green) Japanese consumers.

Food

5. The British are ______ (concerned) the Chinese.
6. Indians are ______ (concerned) consumers.
7. Russians are ______ (concerned) Brazilians.
8. Americans are ______ (concerned) Canadians.

Goods

9. Canadians don't buy goods ________________ (responsibly) Mexicans do.
10. Indians buy goods ________________ (responsibly).
11. Germans buy goods ________________ (responsibly) Brazilians.
12. Americans buy goods ________________ (responsibly).

B In your notebook, write four or five sentences based on the housing data from the Greendex chart in exercise **A** on page 227. Use comparative and superlative adjectives and adverbs. Use the sentences from exercise **A** to help you.

Mexicans make greener housing choices than Canadians.

Indian consumers are more concerned about green housing than German consumers are.

Charts 8.1–8.7

2 **EDIT.** Read the article about the results of the Greendex survey. Find and correct eight more errors with comparatives and superlatives.

The Greendex Survey: Some Overall Conclusions

- According to a recent Greendex survey, people in India were the ~~most green~~ consumers in the world. They scored lower in transportation than the Chinese were, but they scored ~~the highest~~ than the Chinese in three other categories.
- Mexicans were more concerned about green transportation as green food or goods. For them, the low score of all was in the housing category.
- Germans scored highly in the transportation category than they did in the food category. However, they were least concerned about housing than goods.
- The Japanese were one of the least concerned nationality overall. They had one of the most bad scores in the housing category.
- Americans had the lowest overall score of all the nationalities in the survey. Food was the only category in which Americans did not score lower then the other nationalities.

Charts 8.1–8.4, 8.6

3 LISTEN & SPEAK.

CD2-33

A Listen to a professor discussing the Greendex survey with her students. Then complete the students' opinions about the survey.

Martin:

1. Most people think that their country is ______________________ the results show.
2. Many people think they buy goods ______________________ they really do.
3. We like to think we're trying ______________________ we can to be green.

Karin:

4. Life in the United States is much ______________________ without a car.
5. Cars that use less gas are becoming ______________________ in the United States.
6. Attitudes about the environment aren't changing ______________________ people think.

Andrew:

7. Most people want to make life ______________________ for themselves and their families.
8. Everyone wants an ______________________ life.

CD2-33

B Look at the sentences from exercise **A**. Then listen again. Do you agree or disagree with the students' ideas and opinions? Why, or why not? Write notes on your own ideas and opinions in your notebook.

C Work with a partner. Share your ideas and opinions from exercise **B**. Use comparatives and superlatives.

I agree with Martin's opinion about goods. People don't shop as carefully as they think they do.

Charts 8.1–8.7

4 WRITE & SPEAK.

A Look at the items in the box. Then rank the items from 1 to 8, with (1 = the least important and 8 = the most important).

____ a. a big car	____ d. a smart phone	____ g. plastic bags
____ b. stylish clothing	____ e. meals in restaurants	____ h. a gold watch
____ c. a computer	____ f. a TV	

B In your notebook, write six sentences about the items from exercise **A**. Use comparatives and superlatives and your own ideas and opinions.

I think a computer is less important than a smart phone.

C Work with a partner. Share your rankings from exercise **A** and your opinions from exercise **B**.

Connect the Grammar to Writing

1 READ & NOTICE THE GRAMMAR.

A Before you buy something, do you compare it with similar products? Discuss your shopping habits with a partner. Then read the text.

The Best Sleeping Bag

I needed to buy a new sleeping bag for a winter camping trip. So, I went to a camping store and compared three different brands[1] of sleeping bags: Ultra Comfort, Snowy Down, and Northern Trek. I wanted to look at each sleeping bag very carefully. For winter camping, the Snowy Down had the highest rating. But in some ways, the other two sleeping bags were better. Of the three sleeping bags, the Snowy Down was the warmest, but it was also the most expensive. The Northern Trek cost less than the Snowy Down, but it was just as expensive as the Ultra Comfort. The Ultra Comfort was warmer than the Northern Trek. Finally, the Ultra Comfort was lighter than the other sleeping bags, so it was easier to carry.

I decided not to get the Northern Trek for camping outside. It wasn't as warm as the other sleeping bags. But we were having a mild winter, so I didn't need the warmest kind of sleeping bag. So I looked more closely at the lightest sleeping bag, the Ultra Comfort. That's the one I chose.

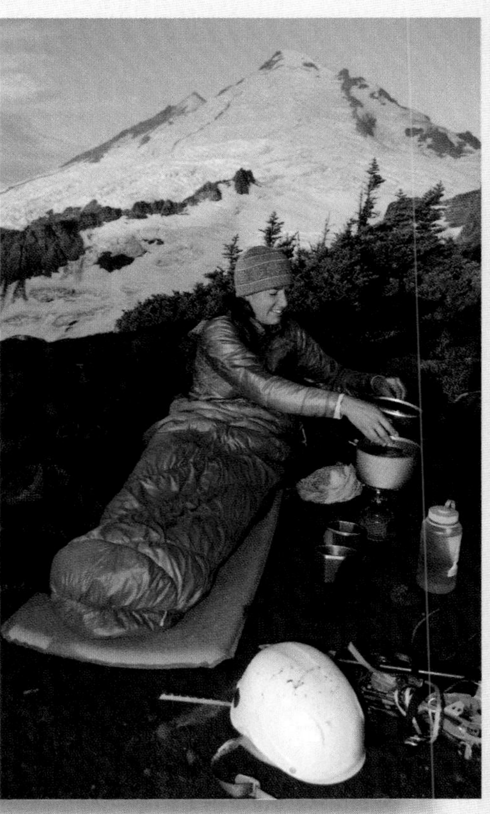

[1] **brand:** the commercial name for a product

GRAMMAR FOCUS

In exercise **A**, the writer uses comparatives and superlatives to discuss three sleeping bags.

*The Ultra Comfort was **warmer than** the Northern Trek.*

*. . . it was just **as expensive as** the Ultra Comfort.*

*Of the three sleeping bags, the Snowy Down was **the warmest** and **most expensive**.*

B Read the text in exercise **A** again. Underline the comparatives and circle the superlatives. Then work with a partner and compare your answers.

C Work with a partner. Complete the chart with information from the text in exercise **A**.

Product Details	Ultra Comfort	Snowy Down	Northern Trek
Cost	as expensive as the Northern Trek		
Warmth		the warmest	
Weight			

Write a Product Review

2 BEFORE YOU WRITE. Think of a product that you plan to buy. Compare three different brands of this product. Complete the chart with information about each brand. Use the chart from exercise **1C** as a model.

Product Details	Product #1 ______	Product #2 ______	Product #3 ______
Cost			

3 WRITE a review comparing the three different brands of the product you chose. Write two paragraphs. Use the information from your chart in exercise **2** and the article in exercise **1A** to help you.

WRITING FOCUS Correcting Run-on Sentences

A run-on sentence is an error that happens when two independent clauses are connected without a connecting word or correct punctuation.

✗ *I enjoyed my winter camping trip next year, I'll invite a few friends to join me.*

To correct a run-on sentence, you can divide the run-on sentence into separate sentences.

✓ *I enjoyed my winter camping **trip**. **Next** year, I'll invite a few friends to join me.*

You can also use a comma and a conjunction (*and, but, or*) between the two independent clauses.

✓ *I enjoyed my winter camping **trip, but** next year I'll invite a few friends to join me.*

4 SELF ASSESS. Read your review and underline the comparatives and superlatives. Then use the checklist to assess your work.

☐ I used comparative adjectives and adverbs correctly. [8.1, 8.2, 8.3]

☐ I used comparisons with *less* and (*not*) *as . . . as* correctly. [8.4, 8.5]

☐ I used superlative adjectives and adverbs correctly. [8.6, 8.7]

☐ I checked for and corrected run-on sentences. [WRITING FOCUS]

UNIT 9 The Natural World

Conjunctions and Adverb Clauses

▲ A bouvardia, Lincoln, Nebraska, USA

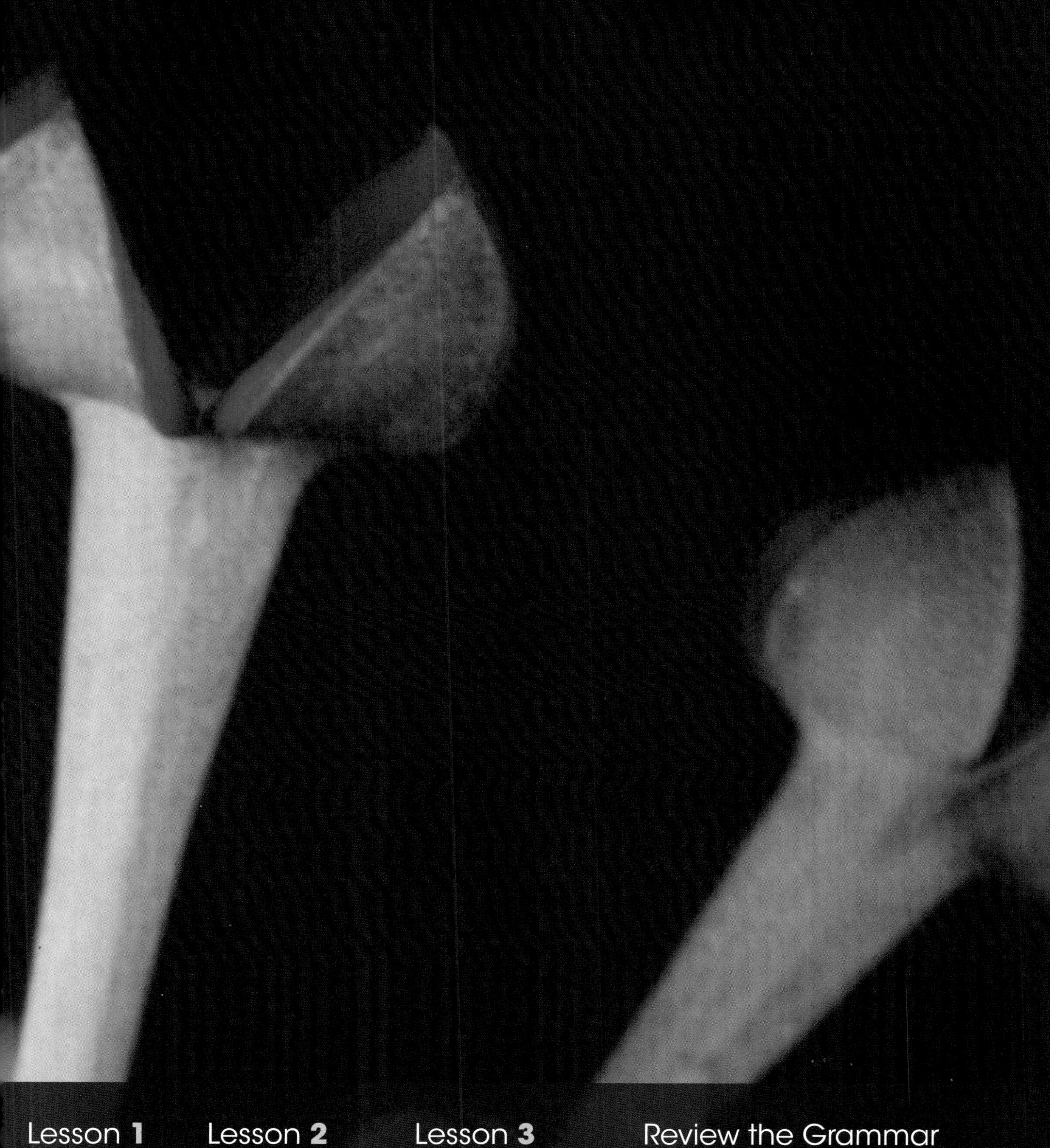

EXPLORE

CD3-02

1 READ the article about a special kind of plant. Notice the words in **bold**.

What's for Dinner?

Most plants get the nutrients[1] they need to grow from soil. Some plants, however, grow in poor soil that doesn't provide the food the plants need. These plants have to attract **and** catch insects to stay alive. Plants that trap **and** eat insects are called carnivorous, **or** meat-eating, plants.

Many plants attract insects with bright colors **and** pleasant smells, **and** carnivorous plants **do too**. Some carnivorous plants also contain tasty liquids, **so** insects will come close **and** take a drink.

However, scientists have recently discovered something else that attracts insects to some carnivorous plants. These plants shine with a blue light. The light is ultraviolet,[2] **so** people can't see it. The light can't attract humans, **but** it is bright **and** attractive to insects.

Pitcher plants are among the most interesting "ultraviolet" plants. Their leaves form tubes that hold liquids. The blue light attracts insects to the edge of the plant's leaves, **and** some of them fall in. They try to escape, **but** the leaves have special hairs that stop them from climbing out. Soon the insects become a meal for the plant.

[1] **nutrient:** something in food that is necessary for life
[2] **ultraviolet:** a blue color that the human eye cannot see

▼ Carnivorous pitcher plants in the Morne Seychellois National Park, Mahe Island, Seychelles, Africa

▼ A carnivorous plant attracts an insect.

2 CHECK. Match the beginning of each statement in Column A with the correct ending in Column B.

Column A	**Column B**
1. Ultraviolet light _____	a. does not provide enough nutrients for some plants.
2. Poor soil _____	b. keep insects inside the plant.
3. Insects _____	c. have leaves like tubes.
4. Pitcher plants _____	d. attracts insects to plants.
5. Special hairs _____	e. provide nutrients for carnivorous plants.

3 DISCOVER. Complete the exercises to learn about the grammar in this lesson.

A Read the pairs of sentences based on the article from exercise **1**. Then choose the correct answer for each question.

1. They have to attract **and** catch insects to survive.
   Many plants attract insects with bright colors **and** pleasant smells.

   How is *and* used in these sentences? a. to add ideas b. to show how ideas are different

2. The light is ultraviolet, **so** people cannot see it.
   Carnivorous plants grow in poor soil, **so** they do not get many nutrients from the ground.

   What type of idea follows *so*? a. a result b. a cause

3. The insects try to escape, **but** they are unable to get away.
   The light can't attract humans, **but** it is bright and attractive to insects.

   What type of idea follows *but*? a. a similar idea b. a different idea

B Work with a partner. Compare your answers from exercise **A**.

LEARN

9.1 Conjunctions: *And, Or, So, But*

1. Conjunctions connect words, phrases, or clauses.	Words: We're having chicken, rice, **and** broccoli for dinner tonight. Phrases: Do you want to go to Paris **or** to Rome? Clauses: I like Texas, **so** I moved to Dallas.
2. Use *and* to connect information that is similar. We also use *and* to add additional information.	You need flour, eggs, **and** sugar to make a cake. She likes to swim **and** play the drums.
3. Use *or* to talk about choices or alternatives.	Do you want pie **or** fruit for dessert? Tonight I'll watch TV **or** go to the gym.
4. Use *so* to show a result. *So* introduces a clause. Do not use *so* to connect words or phrases.	It was raining hard, **so** I took the bus. Cause / Result
5. Use *but* to show a contrast or a difference between people, places, things, or ideas.	She lived in Mexico for years, **but** she never learned Spanish.
6. Do not use a comma before a conjunction when it connects two words or phrases. Use a comma before a conjunction when it connects two independent clauses. An independent clause can stand alone as a complete sentence.	✓ Tennis is fun **but** difficult. ✗ Tennis is fun, but difficult. Mother's Day is May 11 this year**, and** it's my sister's birthday. Do you want to go out to eat**, or** do you want to stay home?

4 Circle the correct conjunction to complete each sentence.

1. Pitcher plants attract insects with bright colors, light, **and** / **so** tasty liquids.
2. Plants get nutrients from the ground **or** / **so** from insects.
3. Insects go inside plants **but** / **and** drink the liquid.
4. The Botanical Garden is closed today, **so** / **but** we can't go.
5. Jamie knows a lot about nature, **and** / **but** he hasn't heard of pitcher plants.
6. Are you going to water the plants now **but** / **or** later?
7. Tasha didn't take care of her plants, **so** / **but** they died.
8. These flowers are beautiful, **or** / **but** they do not last a long time.

5 Complete the sentences with *and, or, so,* or *but.* Add commas if necessary.

1. Are you more interested in plants ____or____ animals?
2. Bella loves flowers ____________ she doesn't have a garden.
3. These plants require a lot of sunlight ____________ water.

4. We worked hard in the garden ___________ we were very tired.

5. The fruit on that plant looks delicious ___________ it's poisonous. Don't eat it!

6. Do you want to visit the park ___________ the zoo? We don't have time for both.

7. Sam bought flowers ___________ a box of chocolates for his mother.

8. The flowers in the park were amazing ___________ I took a lot of photos.

6 SPEAK. Work with a partner. Take turns making sentences by matching the beginning of each sentence with the correct ending.

1. English is difficult, but . . .	a. tea?
2. Last week, I went shopping and ...	b. I don't play it very well.
3. Do you want coffee or . . .	c. I like it.
4. I have a headache, so . . .	d. went inside.
5. Is Rapid City in South Dakota or . . .	e. I bought some new shoes.
6. We parked the car and . . .	f. I took some aspirin.
7. I just finished a pizza, so . . .	g. Wyoming?
8. I like tennis, but . . .	h. I don't want anything to eat.

English is difficult, but I like it.

9.2 *And + Too, So, Either, Neither*

1. To show similarity in an affirmative statement and avoid repetition, use: a. *and* + subject + auxiliary verb* + *too* b. *and* + *so* + auxiliary verb + subject	 a. Linda likes to swim, **and Luc does too.** b. Linda likes to swim, **and so does Luc.**
Be careful! The word order of clauses with *too* and *so* is different.	Linda lives in Toronto, **and Luc does too.** Linda lives in Toronto, **and so does Luc.**
2. Use the same form for the auxiliary verb and the main verb.	I **went** to work, and so **did** Dante. Jackie **eats** meat, and I **do** too.
3. To show similarity in a negative statement and avoid repetition, use: a. *and* + subject + auxiliary verb + *either* b. *and* + *neither* + auxiliary verb + subject	 a. Mae doesn't eat fish, **and Kim doesn't either.** b. Mae doesn't eat fish, **and neither does Kim.**
Be careful! The word order of clauses with *either* and *neither* is different.	I don't speak Greek, **and my parents don't either.** I don't speak Greek, **and neither do my parents.**
4. Do not use a negative auxiliary verb with *neither*.	✓ I don't play golf, and **neither does my sister**. ✗ I don't play golf, and neither doesn't my sister.

* Auxiliary verbs are sometimes called *helping verbs*. *Have*, *do*, and *will* are common auxiliary verbs.

7 Complete each sentence with *so, too, either,* or *neither* and the correct form of the auxiliary verb (*do, have, be,* or *will*).

1. Ellie likes to watch nature films, and ______ her children.
2. Franco's not watching TV, and ______ Mary.
3. I don't buy flowers often, and my sister ______.
4. We grew our own vegetables, and our neighbors ______.
5. Sid has finished his assignment, and ______ Olivia.
6. Eric won't be at the meeting tomorrow, and ______ his boss.
7. Carlos is from Mexico, and Vera ______.
8. I haven't seen that TV show, and ______ Paul.

REAL ENGLISH

Use *so* + an auxiliary verb + *I* to agree with an affirmative statement.

A: *I love San Francisco.*
B: ***So do I.***

Use *neither* + an auxiliary verb + *I* to agree with a negative statement.

A: *Tina has never been to Europe.*
B: ***Neither have I.***

8 Choose the correct answer(s) to complete each sentence. For some sentences there is more than one correct answer.

1. Eddie arrived late, and ______.
   a. so did I b. I did too c. neither did I
2. I haven't lived with my parents for a long time, and ______.
   a. my sister has too b. so has my sister c. my sister hasn't either
3. Alicia was working last night, and ______.
   a. Hans was too b. neither was Hans c. so was Hans
4. The restaurant won't be open, and ______.
   a. so will the diner b. neither will the diner c. the diner will too
5. I speak French, and ______.
   a. so does my sister b. my sister does too c. neither does my sister
6. Alex wasn't enjoying the movie, and ______.
   a. so were we b. we weren't either c. neither were we
7. We like to ski, and ______.
   a. so do our children b. neither do our children c. our children don't either
8. Jack will be on vacation next week, and ______.
   a. Kate will too b. Kate does too c. so will Kate

PRACTICE

9 Complete each sentence with *and, or, so,* or *but* and a phrase or clause from the box. Add a comma if necessary.

learn to play it	go for a walk
~~the day after~~	she is free tonight
she doesn't like roses	the tickets are very expensive
I'm not hungry	a sleeping bag

1. Luisa is arriving tomorrow or the day after.
2. Usha likes most flowers, but she doesn't like roses.
3. I had lunch an hour ago, but I'm not hungry.
4. I'm going to buy a guitar and learning to play it.
5. The zoo is wonderful, but the tickets are very beautiful.
6. Before we go camping, I need to buy a tent and a sleeping bag.
7. Do you want to play tennis or go for a walk?
8. Lily has finished her project, so she is free tonight.

10 Replace the bold word in each sentence with *either, neither, so,* or *too.* Do not change the meaning of the sentence. Make any other necessary changes.

1. I've never had a garden, and **neither** has my brother.

   I've never had a garden, and my brother hasn't either.

2. Uncle Steve likes working in the garden, and **so** does Aunt Jill.

   Uncle Steve likes working in the garden, and Aunt Jill does too.

3. The yellow flowers aren't expensive, and the red ones aren't **either**.

   The yellow flowers aren't expensive, and neither ~~the~~ are the red ones

4. I've read the article about plants, and Jane has **too**.

   I've read the article about plants, and so has Jane.

5. Bill's not going to the lecture, and **neither** am I.

   Bill's not going to the lecture, and I amn't either.

6. Chan doesn't like loud music, and his brother doesn't **either**.

Chan doesn't like loud music, and ______________________________.

7. The children enjoy baseball, and **so** do their parents.

The children enjoy baseball, and ______________________________.

8. I'll have time to help you, and Sally will **too**.

I'll have time to help you, and ______________________________.

11 **EDIT.** Read the fact file about the saguaro cactus. Find and correct seven more errors with conjunctions and *too, so, either,* and *neither.*

Fact File: The Saguaro Cactus

- Saguaros can reach a height of over 40 feet (12.2 meters), so in their first ten years they only grow around one inch (2.54 cm).
- The fruit of the saguaro is red, so it contains around 2000 seeds. It is very tasty, but it is popular with local people.
- Saguaros grow arms, but they have room for a lot of flowers and fruit. This gives them a better chance to reproduce.
- The largest known saguaro is in Maricopa County, Arizona, in the United States. It is 45.3 feet (13.8 m) tall and 10 feet (3.1m) wide.
- Saguaros live in the desert. There are hardly any rivers there, and it doesn't rain much neither. When it rains, saguaros store the rainwater inside their stems.
- Old western movies show saguaros in Texas and New Mexico, but Texas does not have any saguaros, and New Mexico does either.
- The saguaro used to provide both food or shelter for Native Americans.
- Bats help spread saguaro seeds, and birds do so.

▼ The saguaro is a type of cactus plant that grows in the Sonoran Desert of California, Arizona, and Mexico.

12 LISTEN & WRITE.

CD3-03

A Listen to a podcast about giant redwood trees. As you listen, circle the correct information.

1. a. Most of the world's giant redwoods are in **California** / **Montana.**
   b. Redwood trees also grow in **Iowa** / **Oregon.**
2. a. They grow to **379 feet** / **179 feet** tall.
   b. They can have a circumference of **26 feet** / **36 feet.**
3. a. Their leaves are **long** / **short**.
   b. Their leaves are **curved** / **flat**.
4. a. Their roots are **deep** / **shallow**.
   b. Their roots are very **weak** / **strong**.
5. a. The **tallest** / **shortest** trees are in deep valleys.
   b. The **youngest** / **oldest** trees are in deep valleys.

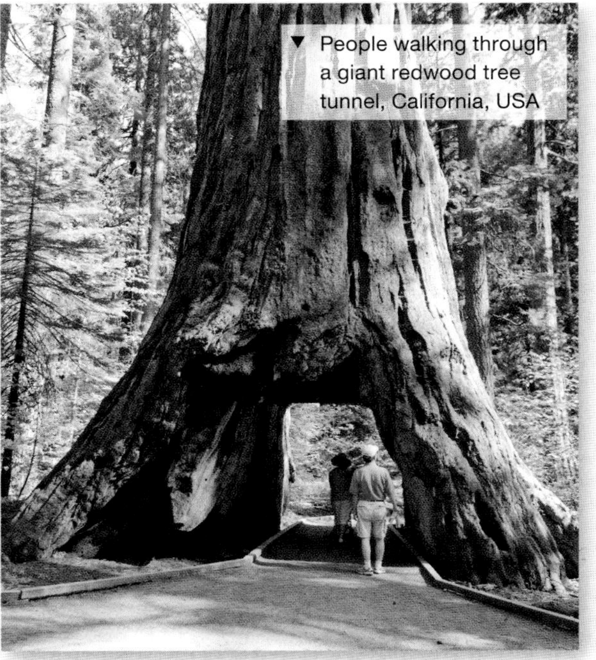
▼ People walking through a giant redwood tree tunnel, California, USA

B In your notebook, write five sentences about giant redwoods. Use the information from exercise **A** and the conjunctions from this lesson.

The giant redwood is found in California, and so are other types of redwoods.

C Work with a partner. Compare your sentences from exercise **B**.

13 APPLY.

A Complete each sentence with your own ideas.

1. I need to talk to my friend, but *I don't know where she is*.
2. Do you want to go to the movies or ______?
3. I've packed my suitcase, so ______.
4. My new neighborhood is great! There are a lot of good restaurants and ______.
5. I left work early, so ______.
6. We can go to the pool or ______.
7. My car is not very fast, but ______.
8. The children finished their homework quickly, so ______.

B Work with a partner. Share your sentences from exercise **A**.

EXPLORE

CD3-04

1 READ the article about a volcano in Africa. Notice the words in **bold**.

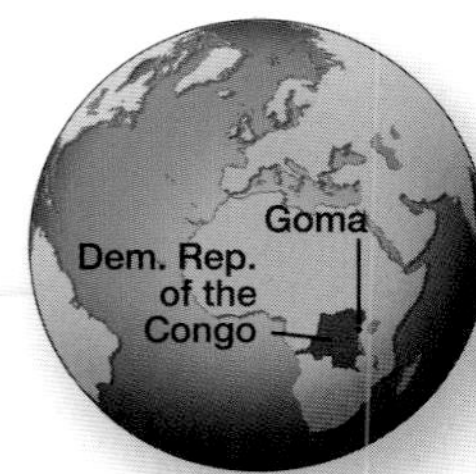

Volcano Watching

Although Mount Nyiragongo in the Democratic Republic of the Congo looks beautiful, it is very dangerous. It is dangerous **because it is an active volcano**. It erupted[1] in 1977 and again in 2002. In 2002, 147 people died because of the eruption.

Scientists are studying Mount Nyiragongo very closely. They want to know when it will erupt again. This information is very important **since nearly a million people live nearby in the city of Goma**.

Ken Sims is a scientist who studies volcanoes. **Even though it was very dangerous**, in 2010 Sims and his team climbed down into the crater[2] of Mount Nyiragongo. Sims made this journey **because he wanted to collect new lava from the volcano**. New lava tells us more about the volcano than old lava. Sims hopes that the lava he collected will help predict the next eruption.

[1] **erupt:** explode
[2] **crater:** a large hole in the ground or in the top of a volcano

▼ View of lava from Nyiragongo Volcano, Democratic Republic of the Congo, Africa.

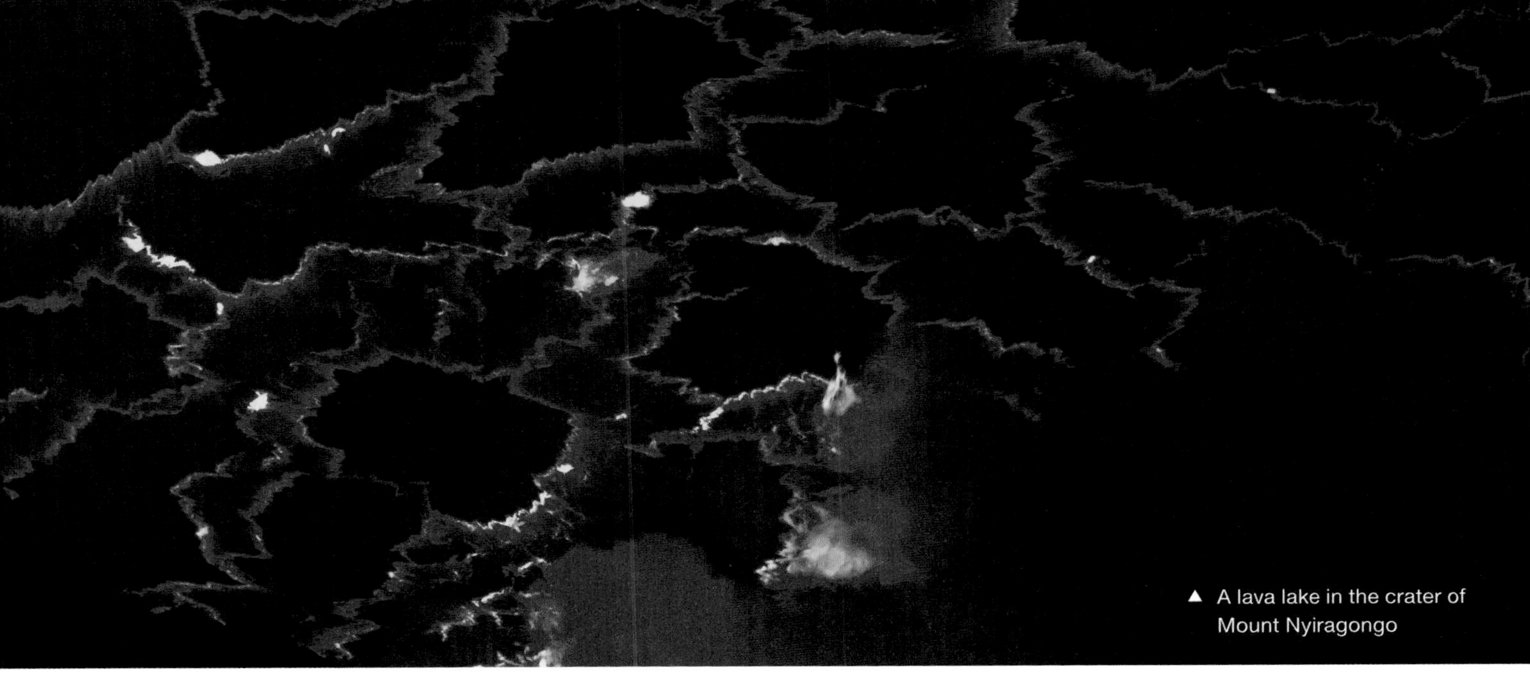

▲ A lava lake in the crater of Mount Nyiragongo

2 CHECK. Write a short answer for each question.

1. Why is Mount Nyiragongo dangerous? ______________________
2. Why are scientists studying Mount Nyiragongo very closely? ______________________
3. Who is Ken Sims? ______________________
4. What did Ken Sims do in 2010? ______________________
5. What can new lava help Ken Sims do? ______________________

3 DISCOVER. Complete the exercises to learn about the grammar in this lesson.

A Find these sentences in the article from exercise **1**. Write the missing words.

1. ______________ Mount Nyiragongo in the Democratic Republic of the Congo looks beautiful, it is very dangerous.
2. This information is very important ______________ nearly a million people live nearby in the city of Goma.
3. ______________ it was very dangerous, in 2010 Sims and his team climbed down into the crater of Mount Nyiragongo.
4. Sims made this journey ______________ he wanted to collect new lava from the volcano.

B Look at the words you wrote in exercise **A**. Then answer the questions.

1. Which words are used to introduce a contrast?

   ______________ and ______________

2. Which words are used to introduce a reason?

   ______________ and ______________

LEARN

9.3 Adverb Clauses: Cause

We got lost **because it was dark**.
Main Clause — Adverb Clause

Since it was raining hard, **we stayed home**.
Adverb Clause — Main Clause

1. An adverb clause shows a relationship, such as cause, time, or condition. It begins with a conjunction, such as *because*, *when*, or *if*.	**Since the weather was nice,** we went to the park. (Adverb Clause (Cause)) She's going to call us **when her train arrives**. (Adverb Clause (Time)) **If it's nice on Saturday**, we'll have a picnic. (Adverb Clause (Condition))
2. Adverb clauses are dependent clauses. They cannot stand alone as complete sentences. Do not use an adverb clause without a main clause.	✓ I opened the window **because it was hot**. (Main Clause / Adverb Clause) ✗ Because it was hot.
3. An adverb clause of cause begins with the conjunction *because* or *since*. It tells why an action or event happened (its cause). The main clause tells the result.	I stayed home **because it was raining**. (Result / Cause) **Since it was raining,** I stayed home. (Cause / Result)
4. **Remember:** An adverb clause can come before or after the main clause. Use a comma when the adverb clause comes at the beginning of the sentence.	**Because I didn't know the answer,** I asked Meg. **Since the train was late,** we took a taxi.

4 Look at the underlined clauses in each sentence. Label each clause **C** for *cause* or **R** for *result*.

1. Since Mount Nyiragongo is so close, the city of Goma is in danger.
2. Scientists study volcanoes because they want to predict their eruptions.
3. The people of Goma are worried since there was a lot of damage after the last eruption.
4. Because some volcanoes don't erupt often, people don't worry about them.
5. Since volcanoes are so interesting, I like to read about them.
6. The film about volcanoes was popular because it had wonderful photography.
7. Since I'm afraid of volcanoes, I don't go near them.
8. Lava is dangerous because it is extremely hot.

5 Combine the sentences with the conjunction in parentheses. Do not change the order of the information. Add a comma if necessary.

1. There are around 1900 active volcanoes on Earth. It is important to study them. (since)

   Since there are around 1900 active volcanoes on Earth, it is important to study them.

2. My friend and I were in Sicily. We saw Mount Etna. (since)

   Since my friend & I were in Sicily, we saw Mount Etna

3. Mount Etna is interesting. It erupts frequently. (because)

   Mount Etna is interesting because it erupts frequently

4. It was a hot day. We wore shorts and t-shirts. (because)

   Because it was a hot day, we wore shorts & T-shirts

5. The volcano was very high. We didn't climb to the top. (because)

   Because the volcano was very high,

6. We had a wonderful view. It was a clear day. (because)

   We had a wonderful view because

7. We climbed for several hours. We were very tired. (since)

   Since we climbed for several hours,

8. My friend was excited. He found some lava. (because)

   My friend was excited, because

9.4 Adverb Clauses: Contrast

We took a walk **even though it was raining**.
(Main Clause: We took a walk; Adverb Clause: even though it was raining)

I like that restaurant **although it is quite expensive**.
(Main Clause: I like that restaurant; Adverb Clause: although it is quite expensive)

1. An adverb clause of contrast begins with the conjunctions *although* or *even though*. It introduces a contrast that is often surprising. The surprising information is in the main clause.	**Although golf is a popular sport,** I don't like it. (Adverb Clause: Although golf is a popular sport; Main Clause: I don't like it) I went swimming **even though the water was very cold**. (Main Clause: I went swimming; Adverb Clause: even though the water was very cold)
2. **Remember:** An adverb clause can come before or after the main clause. Use a comma when the adverb clause comes at the beginning of a sentence.	**Even though I was sick,** I went to work. **Although I wanted to go out,** I stayed home last night.

6 Combine the sentences using *although* or *even though*. Put the surprising information in the main clause. Add a comma if necessary.

1. The lava was hot. The scientist picked it up.

   Even though the lava was hot, the scientist picked it up.

2. Erica looked everywhere. She couldn't find her book.

   Even though ____________________.

3. I am tired. I'm going to go to the gym.

   Although ____________________.

4. The book was useful. It was very old.

   ________________ even though ________________.

5. Marsha likes her new apartment. It's very small.

   ________________ even though ________________.

6. I went to bed early last night. I'm tired today.

   Although ____________________.

7. Mark didn't pass his math test. He studied hard.

   ________________ even though ________________.

8. The movie was exciting. A lot of people left early.

   Although ____________________.

PRACTICE

7 Match the beginning of each sentence in Column A with the correct ending in Column B.

Column A	Column B
1. I visited Australia **because** g	a. we were tired.
2. We went on a hike **even though** d	b. it's a dangerous place to swim.
3. **Although** Nanette brought her camera, h	c. it wasn't very long.
4. **Since** the river is so fast, b	d. we didn't enjoy our walk.
5. Joe returned from vacation early **because** f	e. the food isn't expensive.
6. **Although** the restaurant is famous, e	f. he was sick.
7. I didn't finish the book **even though** c	g. my favorite cousin lives there.
8. **Because** it was raining, a	h. she didn't take any photos.

8 Circle the correct conjunction to complete each sentence.

1. Keiko went to Brazil **because** / **even though** she wanted to see the Amazon rainforest.
2. **Although** / **Because** it wasn't dark in the rainforest, she couldn't see very well.
3. **Since** / **Even though** the desert is so hot and dry, not many people live there.
4. Alex went for a long walk **since** / **although** it was a beautiful day.
5. A lot of people were swimming in the lake **although** / **because** the water looked dirty.
6. **Since** / **Even though** it's warm and sunny, there are a lot of people at the beach today.
7. **Because** / **Even though** city parks are popular, they're usually crowded.
8. People like to go to city parks **although** / **since** they are easy to get to.

9 Combine each pair of sentences into one sentence with *since/because* or *although/even though*. Do not change the order of the ideas. Add a comma if necessary.

1. Marie wants to move to another city. She likes her hometown.

   Marie wants to move to another city although/even though she likes her hometown.

2. Dana likes her hometown. She wants to stay there for the rest of her life.

   ______

3. Miguel is good at basketball. He is tall and fast.

   ______

4. Alan is not very fast. He is good at basketball.

   ______

5. I studied math in college. It wasn't my best subject in high school.

   ______

6. My sister enjoyed history in high school. She decided to study it in college.

   ______

7. The children didn't eat much at the party. They didn't like the food.

____

____

8. Lin liked the food at the party. She didn't eat very much.

____

____

10 WRITE & SPEAK. Complete the sentences with your own ideas. Then share your sentences with a partner.

1. Many people like the ocean because they like blue of the water.
2. Although the mountain was high, I still climbon mountain.
3. Since volcanoes can be dangerous, I don't want to near it.
4. Computers are useful although sometimes it wastes time.
5. Even though it rained, I still went to school.
6. Because the wing blows so strongly, my family decides cancel our tour.
7. My friend likes playing guitar because it makes she feel comf
8. I don't like eat American food although I am living US.

▼ The Sahara Desert

11 LISTEN & SPEAK.

CD3-05

A Listen to part of a lecture about the Sahara Desert and its relationship to the Amazon rainforest. Choose the correct information to complete each statement.

1. People don't connect the Sahara with the Amazon since the two places ________________.

   a. have different climates b. are a long way from each other

2. Sand contains minerals because it ________________.

   a. comes from rocks b. is in the desert

3. The Amazon needs lot of minerals since ________________ there.

   a. it rains a lot b. there are many plants

4. Sand travels from Africa to the Amazon because ________________.

   a. the plants need it b. that is the usual direction of the wind

5. The Sahara is helping new life to grow even though ________________.

   a. it does not have many plants of its own. b. it is a very old desert.

B Work with a partner. Tell your partner three things about the Sahara and the Amazon. Use the information from the lecture in exercise **A** and your own knowledge. Use *since, because, even though*, and *although*.

There are very few plants in the Sahara because it is so dry.

12 APPLY.

A Look at the notes about Manuel's favorite natural place. Then think about a natural place you have visited, such as a beach, a mountain, or a lake. Write notes about it in the chart.

Manuel's Favorite Beach	My Favorite ________________
empty before 10:00 a.m.	
huge waves	
no restaurants or stores	
noisy in the afternoon	
people play games	
beautiful sunsets	

B In your notebook, write five sentences about the natural place you chose. Use your notes from exercise **A**. Use *because, since, although,* and *even though* to combine your ideas.

I usually go to the beach early because it is empty before 10:00 a.m.

Although the beach is popular, there aren't any restaurants or stores.

C Work with a partner. Share your sentences from exercise **B**. Ask follow-up questions to learn more about your partner's favorite natural place.

A: *Many people go to the beach to surf because there are huge waves.*

B: *Do you like to swim at the beach even though there are huge waves?*

EXPLORE

CD3-06

1 READ the article about the effects of noise on dolphins and whales. Notice the words in **bold**.

The Sounds of the Sea

Whales and dolphins use sound to locate food, find their way through the dark oceans, and communicate. Sometimes, however, human noise interferes with the sounds that whales and dolphins make. The result can be very harmful to these animals.

Underwater, sounds are louder and travel farther. Scientists believe that even distant noise from human activities can disturb dolphins and whales. This noise can come from ships, submarines,[1] and the equipment that is used to search for oil and gas. Underwater noise causes whales to increase how loudly they communicate. However, **if the underwater noise gets too loud, whales and dolphins will stop communicating.**

If dolphins and whales stop communicating, important information will be lost. For example, a dolphin that finds food won't be able to tell other dolphins. Mother whales will lose contact with their babies. Animals may die on the shore instead of finding their way across the sea.

What can we do to protect dolphins and whales? We can try to create less noise. Ships and submarines can avoid areas with a large number of these animals. Scientists also believe that a "curtain" of bubbles[2] around industrial sites will reduce noise underwater. **If we do nothing, dolphins and whales will suffer.**

[1] **submarine:** a kind of ship that can travel underwater
[2] **bubble:** a small ball of air found in a liquid

▲ Dolphins swimming off the coast of the Bahamas

2 CHECK. Read the statements. Circle **T** for *true* or **F** for *false*.

1. Whales and dolphins depend on sound for communication.	**T**	**F**
2. Ships cause problems for dolphins.	**T**	**F**
3. When dolphins can't hear, they can find their way correctly.	**T**	**F**
4. Mother whales don't need to be in contact with their babies.	**T**	**F**
5. Curtains of bubbles will make more underwater noise.	**T**	**F**

3 DISCOVER. Complete the exercises to learn about the grammar in this lesson.

A Find these sentences in the article from exercise **1**. Write the missing words.

1. However, if the underwater noise ________________ too loud, whales and dolphins ________________ communicating.
2. If dolphins and whales ________________ communicating, important information ________________ lost.
3. If we ________________ nothing, dolphins and whales ________________ suffer.

B Look at the words you wrote in exercise **A**. Then circle the correct answer to complete the statement. Discuss your answer with your classmates and teacher.

Will is used in ________________. a. clauses that begin with *if* b. main clauses

LEARN

9.5 Adverb Clauses: Future Conditional

If you study hard, you'll pass the test.
(If you study hard = Adverb Clause; you'll pass the test = Main Clause)

If she doesn't pass the course, she won't come back next year.
(If she doesn't pass the course = Adverb Clause; she won't come back next year = Main Clause)

1. A future conditional sentence includes an adverb clause of condition or *If-* clause and a main clause. The *If-* clause tells the possible condition. The main clause tells the result.	**If I go tomorrow,** I'll call you. (If I go tomorrow = Adverb Clause (Possible Condition); I'll call you = Main Clause (Result))
2. In a future conditional sentence, use the simple present in the *If-* clause. Use *will* or a form of *be going to* in the main clause.	If you **need** a ride, I **will drive** you. They **won't wait** if you **are** late. If you **don't leave** soon, you**'re going to miss** the train.
3. Use a comma when an *If-* clause comes at the beginning of the sentence.	**If she wants to go,** we'll wait for her.

4 Circle the correct form of the verb(s) to complete each sentence.

1. If a dolphin **will find** / **finds** food, it will call other dolphins.
2. If humans **will make** / **make** a lot of noise, whales and dolphins will lose contact with each other.
3. Dolphins and whales **continue** / **will continue** to have problems if we don't do anything to help them.
4. If scientists **don't** / **won't** find a solution to the problem, the situation will get worse.
5. If you **watch** / **will watch** that documentary, you **learn** / **will learn** a lot about dolphins.
6. We **will be** / **are** late for class if we **aren't going to leave** / **don't leave** now.
7. Carol **gets** / **will get** good grades if she **keeps** / **will keep** working hard.
8. Tony **will help** / **helps** me with my assignment this weekend if he **will have** / **has** time.

5 Complete each sentence with the simple present or a future form of the verbs in parentheses.

1. If I ___go___ (go) on the boat trip, I ___will bring___ (bring) my new camera.
2. If you ________ (have) trouble with your homework, I ________ (help) you.
3. If it ________ (snow) a lot tonight, we ________ (not have) class tomorrow.

4. If the bank ________________ (not call) me back, I ________________ (be) angry.

5. If she ________________ (go) to Singapore, she ________________ (stay) with her cousin.

6. You ________________ (miss) the bus if you ________________ (not hurry).

7. If the tickets ________________ (be) too expensive, I ________________ (not go) to the concert.

8. If you ________________ (want) to go downtown, I ________________ (drive) you.

6 SPEAK. Work with a partner. Take turns completing the sentences.

1. If we have a lot of homework, . . .
2. If I pass this class, . . .
3. If it's sunny tomorrow, . . .
4. If I go to Rome, . . .
5. If I get up early tomorrow, . . .
6. If I call my family tonight, . . .
7. If you lend me twenty dollars, . . .
8. If we study together, . . .

If we have a lot of homework, I won't go out with my friends tonight.

9.6 Adverb Clauses: *If* and *When*

If we see a bear, I'll be scared.
(Adverb Clause) (Main Clause)

When they go hiking tomorrow, they'll take a lot of pictures.
(Adverb Clause) (Main Clause)

1. Use *if* in an adverb clause to talk about situations or events you think are possible, but you are not certain about.	**If dinner costs more than $50,** I'll pay with my credit card.
2. Use *when* in an adverb clause to talk about situations or events you are certain will happen.	**When the semester ends,** I will go to Miami.
3. **Remember:** Use a comma when an *If*- or *When*- clause comes at the beginning of the sentence.	**When I go to the grocery store,** I'll get some coffee.

7 Read each sentence. Does it describe a situation or event in the future that is certain or not certain? Complete the second sentence with an *if*- or *when*- clause. Add a comma if necessary.

1. Maybe the dolphin will swim too close to the shore.

   If the dolphin swims too close to the shore, it will have problems.

2. Maybe the whale will come near the boat.

   ________________________________ we'll get some great photos.

3. I'm going to see Ray.

______________________ I'll show him the photos from our trip.

4. Maybe Noor will leave her job.

I'll be surprised ______________________.

5. My parents are going to go to Paris.

My parents are going to visit the Eiffel Tower ______________________.

6. The lecture is going to end soon.

______________________ I'll try to talk to the professor.

7. Maybe it will rain tomorrow.

______________________ we won't go hiking.

8. My brother is going to graduate.

______________________ he's going to work for my uncle.

PRACTICE

CD3-07

8 Complete the conversation using the words in parentheses. Add *if* or *when*. Then listen and check your answers.

Ivan: (1) ______________ (I / not work) late tomorrow night, my wife and I are going to go see a movie. What are you doing this weekend?

Meg: My sister Carla is coming for a visit. (2) ______________ (the weather / be) good, we're going to go hiking. (3) ______________ (it / not be) good, we'll go shopping downtown.

Ivan: The weather report said it's going to be sunny all weekend.

Meg: Great! We'll go hiking, then!

Ivan: (4) ______________ (you / get) out in the woods, you'll see a lot of wildlife, I'm sure. I always see interesting wildlife when I go hiking around here.

Meg: I know. I saw a lot of deer when I was hiking last weekend. I really hope we see some deer this weekend. Carla will be so excited (5) ______________ (we / do). She loves deer.

Ivan: Really? Does she like bears, too? I hear there are a lot of bears around this year!

Meg: Bears? That sounds dangerous.

Ivan: Don't worry. (6) ______________ (you / see) a bear, it probably won't come near you. In fact, (7) ______________ (you / make) a lot of noise, it will probably run away.

Meg: Well, (8) ______________ (we / go) hiking, we'll try to make a lot of noise, then!

9 WRITE & SPEAK.

A Read each statement. Then complete the second statement with an *If-* or *When-* clause. Add a comma if necessary.

1. Maybe there will be a storm tonight.

   If there is a storm tonight, ______ we're going to stay home.

2. It's possible that I'll miss two weeks of class.

   ______ I won't get a good grade.

3. My friend is going to arrive tonight.

   ______ I'll start cooking dinner.

4. Maybe I'll get a new job.

   I'll probably make more money ______.

5. You'll see me at the party tomorrow.

   I'll tell you all about my vacation ______.

6. I'll probably miss the train.

   I'll be late for my appointment ______.

7. My foot will probably still hurt tomorrow.

   ______ I won't play in the game.

8. The store is going to open in five minutes.

   ______ I'm going to buy a carton of milk.

9. I'm going to get home later.

   ______ I'm going to watch the news.

10. Maybe it will snow this afternoon.

    ______ our office will close early.

B Work with a partner. Compare your answers from exercise **A**. Then take turns completing the sentences with your own ideas. Use *if-* and *when-* clauses.

A: *If there's a good show on TV tonight, we're going to stay home.*

B: *If we're tired tonight, we're going to stay home.*

10 EDIT. Read the excerpt from an interview about the Sundarbans in Bangladesh and India. Find and correct five more errors with adverb clauses.

The Sundarbans

Jean: Today, I'm talking to Dr. Ruth Lowe, an expert on the Sundarbans region of Bangladesh and India. Dr. Lowe, if you ~~will be~~ are ready, we'll start the interview now. Can you explain why the Sundarbans are so important?

Dr. Lowe: Of course, Jean. First, the mangrove forests of the Sundarbans are home to wildlife such as the Bengal tiger. These forests also protect the region from serious storms that hit the coast every year. If the forests will disappear, millions of people will be in danger. Unfortunately, people are harming the Sundarbans. If they do not stop, they are in serious danger.

Jean: What exactly will happen if the mangroves will continue to disappear?

Dr. Lowe: Well, when people don't stop destroying the mangroves, the Sundarbans won't be able to protect towns and cities on the coast from storms. If the storms will hit these places, there will be a lot of damage, and people's lives will be at risk.

Jean: That sounds like a real problem.

Dr. Lowe: Well, yes, it really is . . .

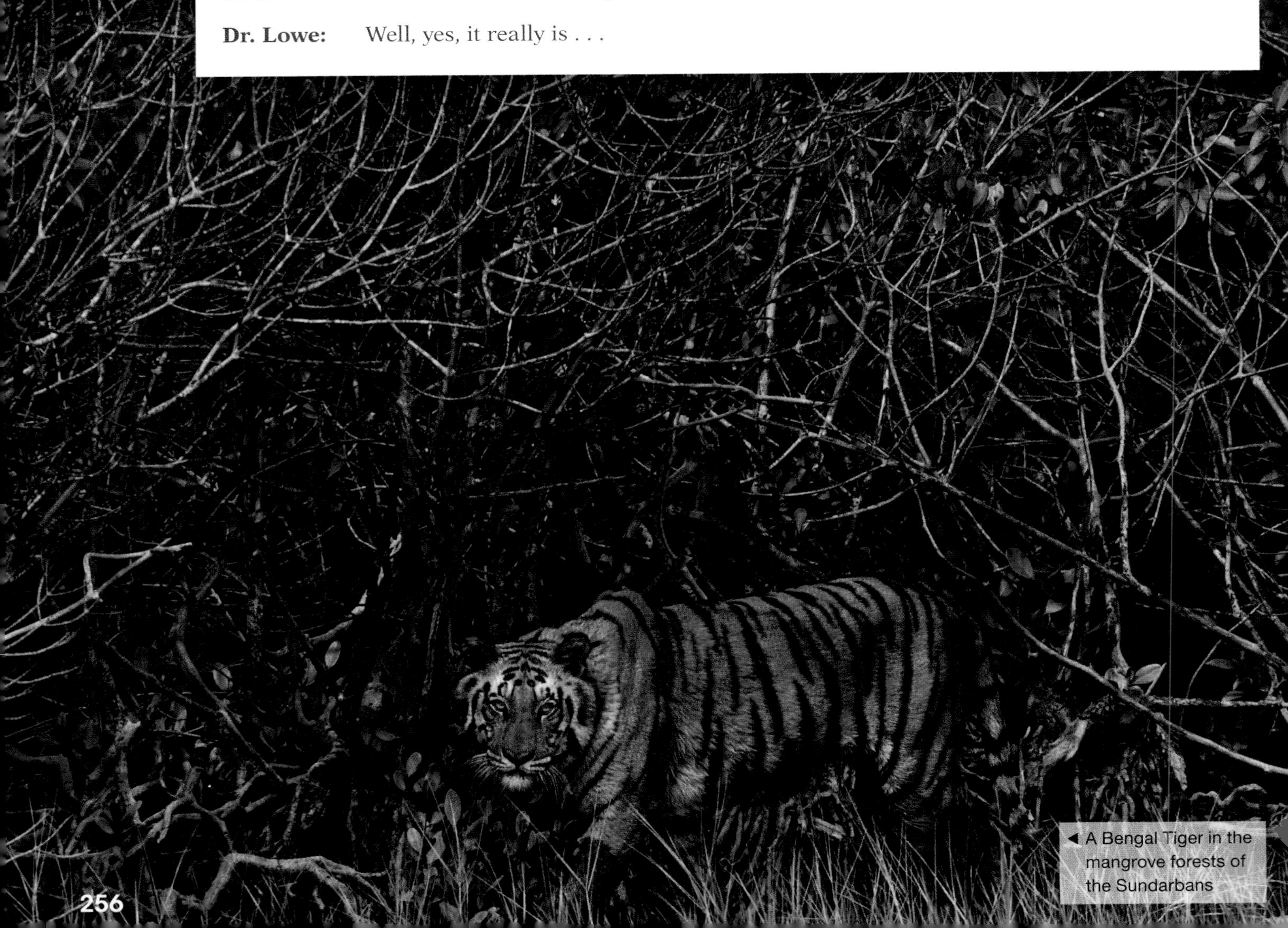

◄ A Bengal Tiger in the mangrove forests of the Sundarbans

11 APPLY.

A Think about your future. What are some things you know will happen? What are some things you think will happen but are not certain about? Complete the chart with your ideas.

Things I Know Will Happen	Things I Think Will Happen
watch the hockey game on TV	go to Japan

B Write six sentences about your future using your notes from exercise **A**. Use adverb clauses with *if* and *when*.

If I have enough money this year, I'll go to Japan.

When I get home tonight, I'm going to watch the hockey game on TV.

____

____

____

____

____

____

C Work with a partner. Share your sentences from exercise **B**. Ask your partner follow-up questions for more information.

A: *If I save enough money this year, I'll go to Japan.*

B: *Interesting. Where do you want to go in Japan?*

Review the Grammar UNIT 9

Charts 9.1, 9.5, 9.6

CD3-08

1 Complete the conversation with the conjunctions in the box. You will need to use some conjunctions more than once. Then listen and check your answers.

and	if	or	so	when

Andy: Do you want to take the afternoon off (1) ___and___ go to the beach? It's a beautiful day, (2) __________ the beach is never crowded on Tuesdays.

Kerim: I'd like to come with you, (3) __________ I don't know if I can. I need to finish my science assignment. What time are you going?

Andy: It takes an hour to get there, (4) __________ I'm going to leave here at about one o'clock.

Kerim: OK. (5) __________ I work for a few hours now, I think I'll be able to finish it by then.

Andy: OK, great! I'll make some sandwiches for us. Do you want cheese (6) __________ turkey?

Kerim: Cheese, please! I'll call you (7) __________ I'm ready.

Andy: Take your time. We'll leave (8) __________ you finish.

Charts 9.2–9.4

2 Rewrite each sentence using the word(s) in parentheses. Do not change the meaning of the sentence. Make any other necessary changes.

1. John's flight was delayed, so he was upset. (because)
   John was upset because his flight was delayed.
2. My parents are going on vacation, and I am too. (so)
   ____
3. Lin didn't pass the exam, and neither did Brian. (either)
   ____
4. It was Anne's birthday, but she didn't go out. (even though)
   ____
5. Patricia enjoyed the trip, and so did her sister. (too)
   ____
6. I have a few days off, so I'm going to visit my uncle. (since)
   ____
7. Boris was sick, but he still went to work. (although)
   ____
8. Jane didn't go to the party, and Danny didn't either. (neither)
   ____

Charts 9.1–9.4

3 EDIT. Read the facts about lightning. Find and correct five more errors with adverb clauses and conjunctions. Sometimes there is more than one way to correct an error.

1. We do not see most lightning ~~even though~~ *because/since* it happens inside clouds.
2. Lightning usually strikes near the center of a storm, because it can also strike far from the center.
3. Rubber shoes do not protect people from lightning, and so do small buildings.
4. Lightning can travel through wires, although it's dangerous to use electrical equipment during a storm.
5. Lightning doesn't just happen during thunderstorms. People have seen lightning during forest fires, snowstorms, but volcanic eruptions.

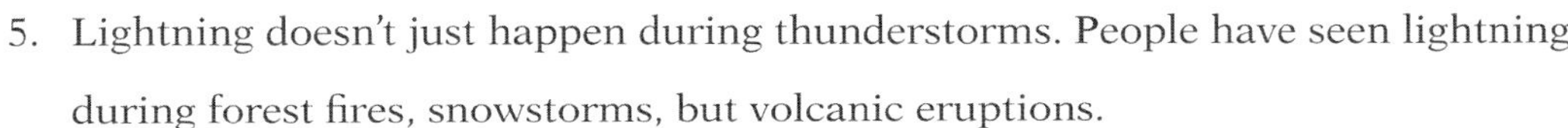

6. Many people believe that lightning never strikes in the same place twice, so that is not true. Keep away from places that attract lightning.

Charts 9.1–9.4

4 LISTEN, WRITE & SPEAK.

A Read the statements in the chart. Then listen to two students discuss the differences between gorillas and chimpanzees. Decide if each statement is true for gorillas, chimpanzees, both, or neither. Put a check (✓) in the correct column.

	Gorillas	Chimpanzees	Both	Neither
1. They live in Africa.				
2. They have tails.				
3. They are intelligent.				
4. They eat meat.				
5. They are strong.				
6. They can be aggressive.				
7. They behave in a funny way.				

B In your notebook, write five sentences about gorillas and chimpanzees. Use the information from the chart in exercise **A** and conjunctions from this unit. Then work with a partner and compare your answers.

Gorillas live in Africa, and chimpanzees do too.

Connect the Grammar to Writing

1 READ & NOTICE THE GRAMMAR.

A How does your environment affect you? Work with a partner and discuss some of the things in your environment that affect your lives, such as storms, fires, or pollution. Then read the text.

Noise Pollution

Since we can't see, smell, or touch noise pollution, many of us don't notice it. People that do notice it think it's annoying, but they don't worry too much about it. However, noise pollution is all around us, and it sometimes causes some very serious problems.

Many things that we see every day cause noise pollution. Trucks, motorcycles, airplanes, loud machines, and power tools all make a lot of noise. Even music is noise pollution when people play it very loudly.

Noise pollution can cause a number of health problems. For example, it can lead to hearing loss. It can also lead to sleep problems. Near airports, people often wake up at night because the planes are so loud. They don't sleep enough, so they get sick more easily. Noise pollution also makes people feel stressed. Stress makes it difficult for them to concentrate, so they can't do their work very well. For example, if a child goes to a noisy school, he or she will probably get lower grades than a child in a quiet school.

These are just some of the ways that noise pollution affects our daily lives.

GRAMMAR FOCUS

In the text in exercise **A**, the writer uses *and* to connect information that is similar, and *so* to show a result.

Trucks, motorcycles, airplanes, loud machines, ***and*** *power tools all make a lot of noise.*
They don't sleep enough, ***so*** *they get sick more easily.*

The writer uses adverb clauses with *because* and *since* to show cause and effect relationships.

Since *we can't see, smell, or touch noise pollution, many of us don't notice it.*
Near airports, people often wake up at night ***because*** *the planes are so loud.*

B Read the text in exercise **A** again. Circle the conjunctions *and* and *so*, and underline the adverb clauses with *because* and *since*. Then work with a partner and compare your answers.

C In exercise **A**, the writer describes a situation in his environment that affects him and other people. He describes the causes of that situation and its results, or effects. Complete the chart on page **261** with causes and effects of noise pollution that the writer describes.

Write about Causes and Effects

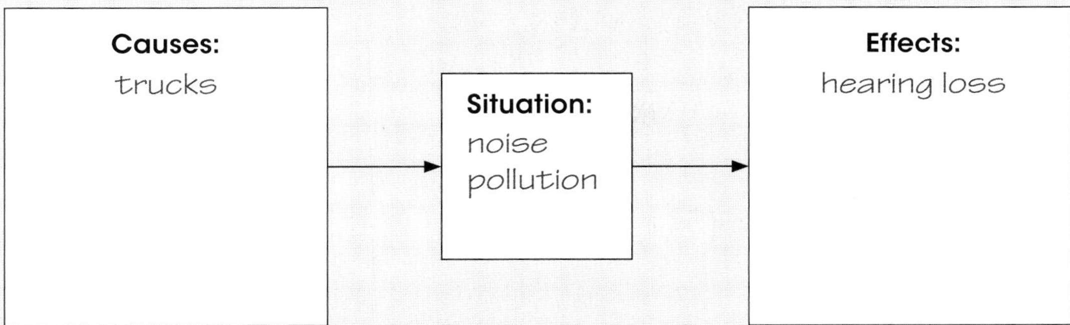

2 BEFORE YOU WRITE.

A Brainstorm a list of situations or events in your environment that affect you. Write a list of your ideas in your notebook.

B Choose one of your ideas from exercise **A** to write about. Think of the causes of this situation or event and its effects. Write notes in the chart. Use the chart from exercise **1C** as a model.

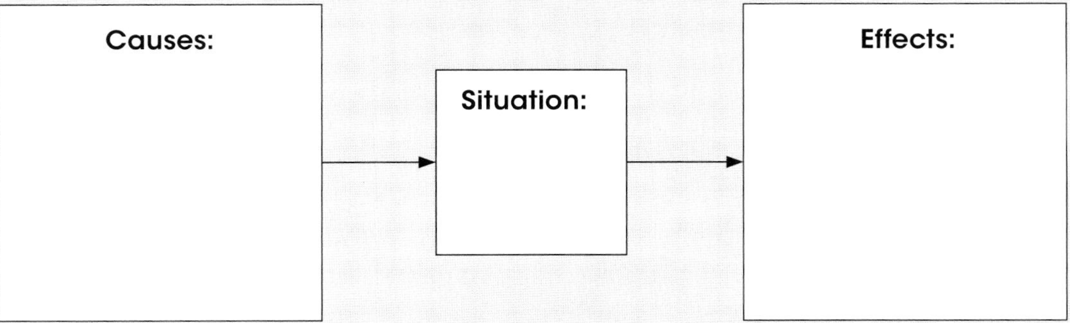

3 WRITE three paragraphs about your topic and its causes and effects. Use the notes from your chart in exercise **2B** and the article in exercise **1A** to help you.

WRITING FOCUS — Correcting Comma Splices

A comma splice is when two independent clauses are joined by a comma without a conjunction. To correct a comma splice, put a comma followed by a conjunction (such as *and, but,* or *so*) between the two independent clauses.

✗ Noise pollution is all around us, it sometimes causes some very serious problems.
(Independent Clause / Independent Clause)

✓ Noise pollution is all around us, **and** it sometimes causes some very serious problems.
(Independent Clause / Independent Clause)

4 SELF ASSESS. Read your text. Circle the conjunctions *and* and *so,* and underline the adverb clauses that show causes. Then use the checklist to assess your work.

☐ I used *and* to connect ideas and *so* to show results. [9.1]

☐ I used adverb phrases with *because* and *since* to show causes. [9.3]

☐ I used commas and conjunctions to join independent clauses to avoid comma splices. [WRITING FOCUS]

UNIT 10 Work and Play

Gerunds and Infinitives

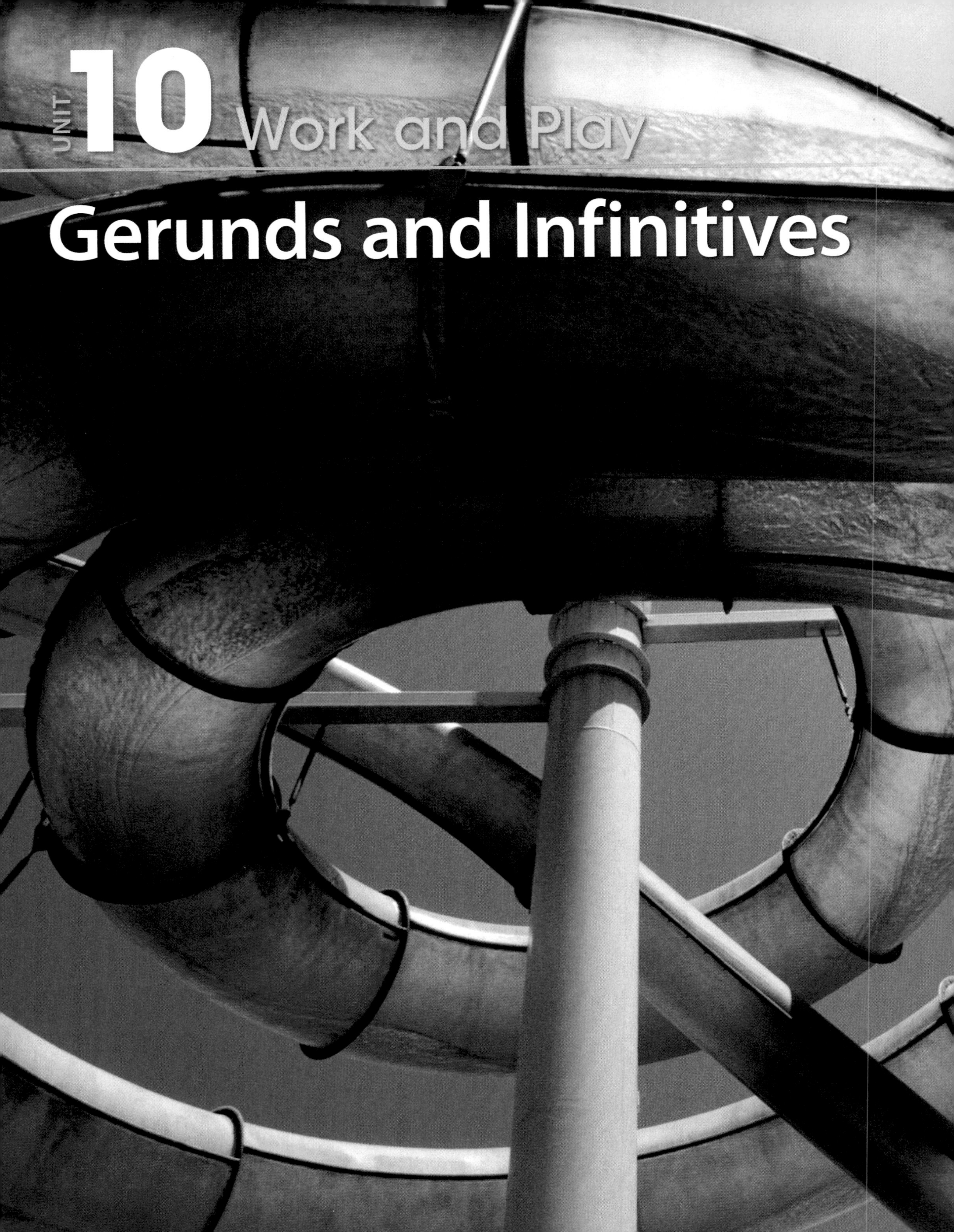

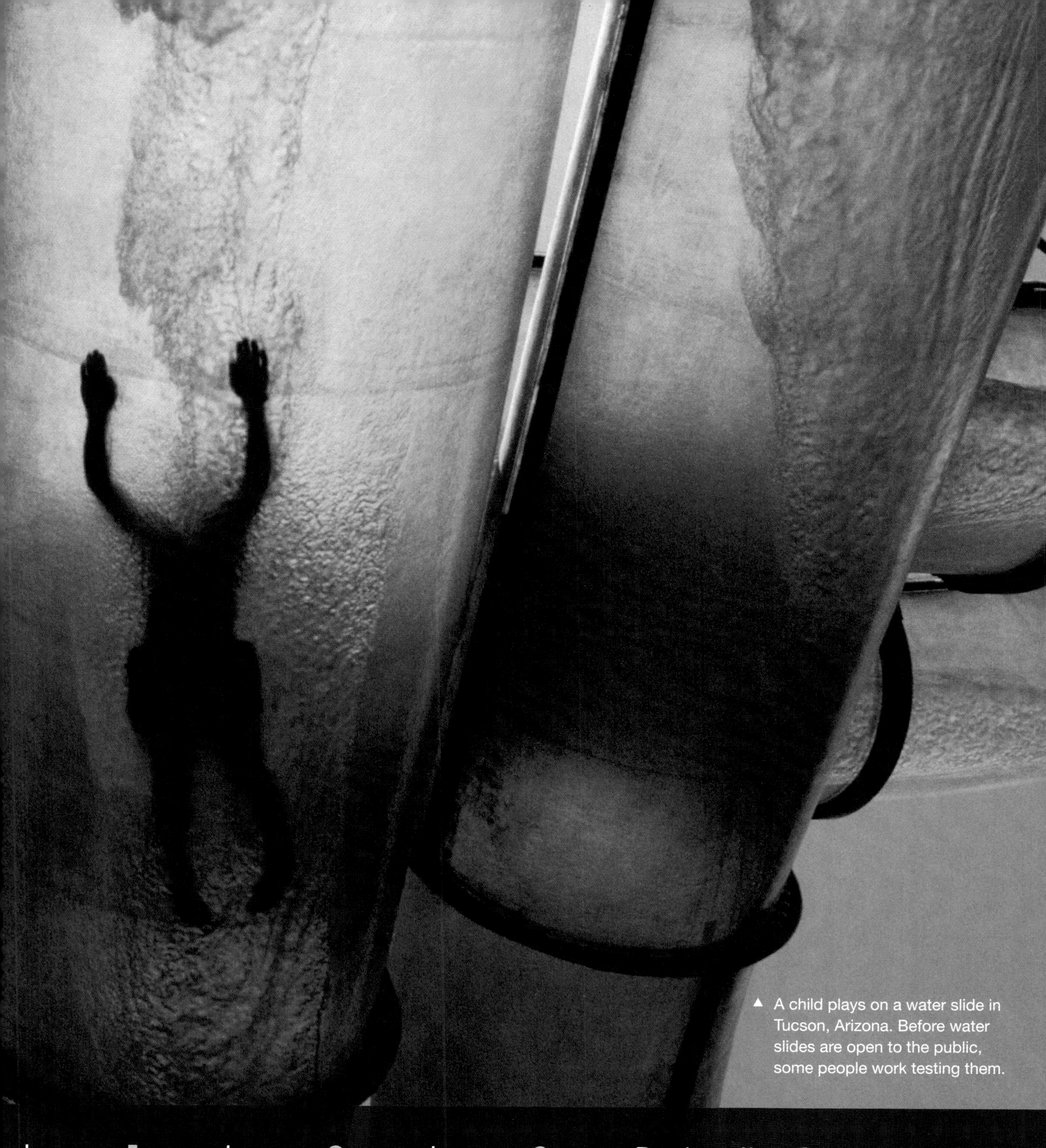

▲ A child plays on a water slide in Tucson, Arizona. Before water slides are open to the public, some people work testing them.

EXPLORE

1 READ the article about Jason deCaires Taylor. Notice the words in **bold**.

Jason deCaires Taylor

Combining work and play is not easy to do. However, British sculptor[1] Jason deCaires Taylor has succeeded **in doing** exactly that. As a child, Taylor often **went diving** for fun in Malaysia. He **enjoyed seeing** the beautiful colors of the coral reefs. He also **enjoyed swimming** with the fish that used the reefs as their home.

Over the years, more and more divers have visited coral reefs. The divers have sometimes damaged the reefs. **Saving coral reefs** became a passion of Taylor's. He has created underwater sculpture parks to draw[2] divers away from natural coral reefs. His sculptures also provided a base **for growing** new coral.

Taylor's largest work, *The Silent Evolution*, lies 30 feet (9 meters) under water near Isla Mujeres, Mexico. It consists of 400 life-size human figures. It took Taylor 18 months to create the statues. **Placing them** on the sea floor took another 120 hours. Before long, however, many different plants were growing on the figures, and Taylor's work was a success.

[1] **sculptor:** an artist who makes works of art from stone, wood, or metal
[2] **draw:** attract

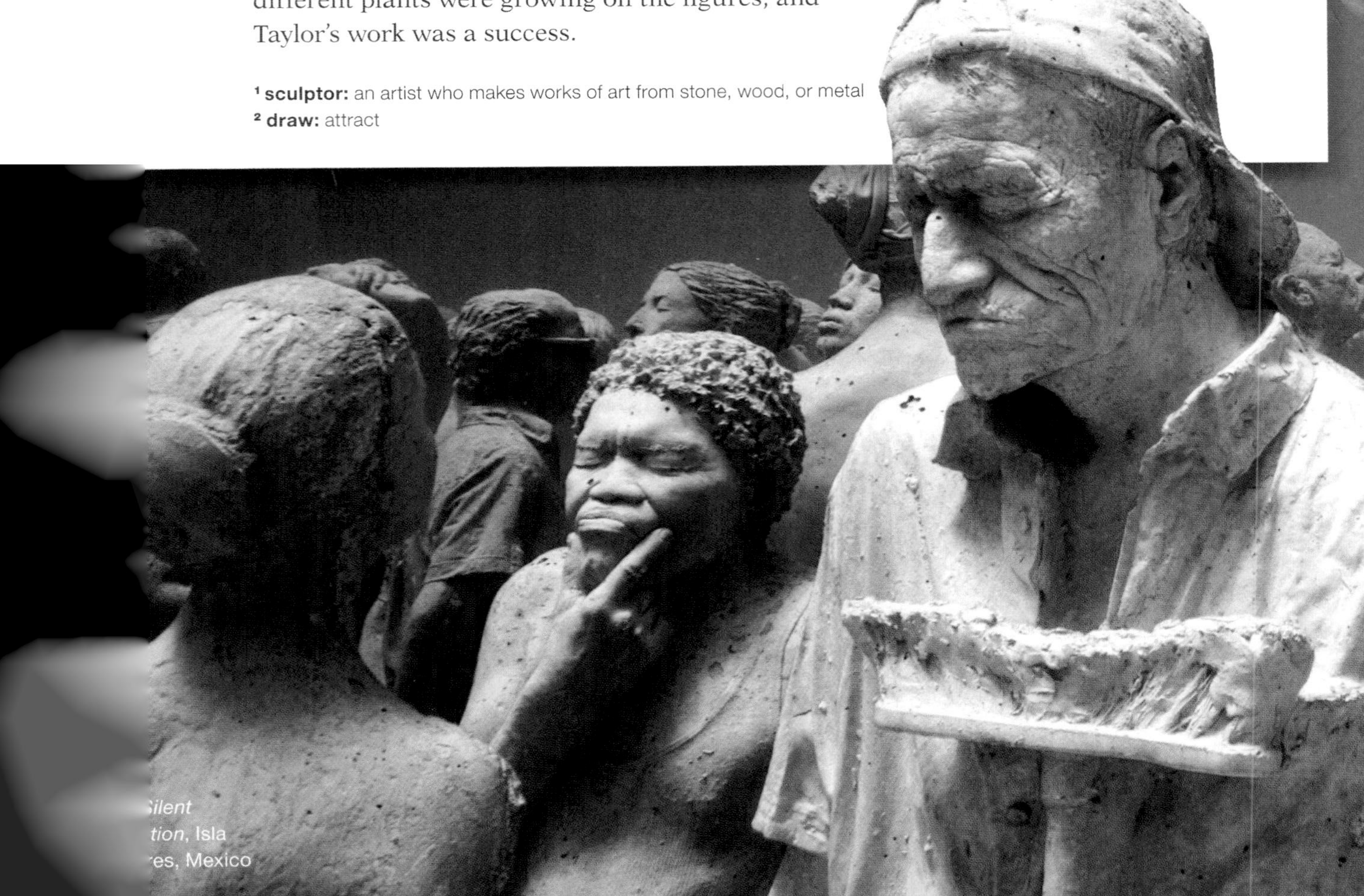

ilent tion, Isla res, Mexico

2 CHECK. Read the statements. Circle **T** for *true or* **F** for *false.*

1. Taylor combines work and play.	**T**	**F**
2. Taylor dove in Malaysia for work.	**T**	**F**
3. As a child, Taylor didn't like the ocean.	**T**	**F**
4. Taylor's sculptures helped the coral.	**T**	**F**
5. Taylor's sculpture, *The Silent Evolution,* is near Malaysia.	**T**	**F**

3 DISCOVER. Complete the exercises to learn about the grammar in this lesson.

A Find and complete these sentences in the article from exercise **1**. Write the missing words.

1. ________________ work and play is not easy to do.
2. ________________ coral reefs became a passion of Taylor's.
3. As a child, Taylor often went ________________ for fun in Malaysia.
4. He enjoyed ________________ the beautiful colors of the coral reefs.
5. His sculptures also provided a base for ________________ new coral.

B Look at the sentences in exercise **A**. Then choose all of the possible correct answers to complete the statement.

In a statement, *-ing* forms can come ________________.

a. before the main verb b. after the main verb c. after a preposition

LEARN

10.1 Gerunds as Subjects and Objects

Gerund as Subject		
Gerund	Verb	
Swimming	is	fun.
Not sleeping	was	difficult.

Gerund as Object		
Subject	Verb	Gerund
I	dislike	**camping.**
He	has stopped	**working.**

1. A gerund is the base form of a verb + *-ing*.[1] A gerund acts like a noun. It can be the subject or the object of a sentence.	Subject: **Running** is my favorite activity. Object: I enjoy **running.**
2. When a gerund or gerund phrase (gerund + object) is the subject of a sentence, the verb is always in the third-person singular.	✓ **Making new friends** takes time. ✗ Making new friends take time.
3. These are some common verbs that can be followed by gerunds: *avoid* *enjoy* *like* *consider* *finish* *mind* *dislike* *keep* *miss*	They **avoided answering** the question. I **have finished washing the dishes.** We **miss seeing** you. What do you **enjoy doing** in your free time?
4. Put *not* before a gerund to make it negative.	We considered **not going** to the party.
5. *Go* + gerund is used in many expressions about activities. *go camping* *go hiking* *go skiing* *go dancing* *go shopping* *go swimming*	Did you **go running** today? Last week, I **went swimming** in the ocean. They **are going shopping** at the mall.

[1]See page **A1** for spelling rules for verbs ending in *-ing*.
[2]See page **A5** for a longer list of verbs followed by gerunds.

4 Complete each sentence with the gerund form of the verb in parentheses.

1. Jason deCaires Taylor enjoys ____diving____ (dive).
2. ________________ (swim) around *The Silent Evolution* has become very popular.
3. We considered ________________ (visit) Isla Mujeres.
4. Jerry enjoyed ________________ (see) the underwater sculptures.
5. The divers avoided ________________ (touch) the coral reefs.
6. ________________ (take) photos underwater isn't easy.
7. We dislike ________________ (go) to the beach when it's crowded.
8. I'm not in a hurry. I don't mind ________________ (wait) for you.

5 WRITE & SPEAK. Complete the statements with a gerund. Use your own ideas. Then share your statements with a partner.

1. ____Skiing____ is my favorite sport.
2. I enjoy ________________.
3. ________________ is difficult.
4. I dislike ________________.

10.2 Gerunds as the Object of a Preposition

	Preposition + Gerund	
We believe	**in working**	hard.
He has a good reason	**for missing**	class.
They are afraid	**of making**	a big mistake.

1. A gerund or gerund phrase can be the object of a preposition.	They're **excited about going** to Hawaii. He's **good at managing** people.
2. Gerunds are used after many noun + preposition combinations. Here are some common noun + preposition combinations: *choice between* *need for* *in danger of* *reason for*	They had a good **reason for being** late. We had a **choice between taking** the test on Monday or Tuesday.
3. Gerunds are used after many verb + preposition combinations. Here are some common verb + preposition combinations: *believe in* *succeed in* *dream about* *talk about* *feel like* *think about* *plan on* *worry about*	She **worries about finding** a job after college. Do you **feel like seeing** a movie tonight? I **succeeded in not looking at** my phone for two hours.
4. Gerunds are used in many adjective + preposition combinations. The verb *be* is usually used before the combination. Here are some common adjective + preposition combinations: *afraid of* *nervous about* *excited about* *sad about* *good at* *tired of* *interested in* *upset about*	Is she **sad about leaving**? I'm **nervous about giving** the presentation. I'm **tired of not feeling** well.
5. Use *by* + a gerund to tell how something is done.	I learned how to fix my bike **by watching** a video.

*See page **A5** for different patterns with gerunds.

6 Complete each sentence with the correct preposition and the gerund form of the verb in parentheses.

1. We planned *on seeing* (see) the sights during our business trip.
2. Angela is interested ______________ (take) a photography class after school.
3. I got good grades in college ______________ (study) every night.
4. Mitchell is thinking ______________ (go) to Montreal this summer.
5. My brother had to make a choice ______________ (fix) his car or ______________ (buy) a new one.
6. Nadine is very good ______________ (solve) problems at work.

7. What was your reason ________ (leave) your job?

8. I'm tired ________ (study). Let's take a break.

9. Molly became a better tennis player ________ (practice) every day.

10. Steven likes swimming in pools, but he's afraid ________ (swim) in the ocean.

7 SPEAK. Work with a partner. Take turns completing the sentences with statements that are true about you. Use gerunds.

I feel like seeing a movie tonight.

1. I feel like . . .
2. I'm good at . . .
3. I'm not good at . . .
4. I'm afraid of . . .
5. I'm not interested in . . .
6. I'm interested in . . .
7. I worry about . . .
8. I often think about . . .

PRACTICE

CD3-11-13

8 Complete each person's story with the gerund form of the verbs in parentheses. Add a correct preposition when necessary. Then listen and check your answers.

Gail's Story

Well, I had a choice (1) between taking (take) a job at a bank in my hometown or (2) ________ (become) a ski instructor. It was a very easy decision! I love (3) ________ (ski), so (4) ________ (do) it as a job was a dream come true for me. I enjoy (5) ________ (be) outdoors and (6) ________ (help) people. I'm good (7) ________ (teach), too! I certainly don't miss (8) ________ (sit) in front of a computer all day. I feel really lucky. I've found the perfect job!

Nick's Story

(9) ________ (find) a job isn't easy these days, but I finally found one. I work for a sports website. I got the job (10) ________ (post) photos on the website. I'm really good (11) ________ (take) action photos, and they needed a photographer. When they saw my photos, they offered me the job immediately. I was very excited (12) ________ (work) as a sports photographer, so of course I said yes. It's a fun job. I really enjoy (13) ________ (get) up and (14) ________ (go) to work every day.

Miyoko's Story

I'm really interested in (15) ________ (see) the world, so (16) ________ (leave) my teaching job to become a tour guide was a good choice for me. (17) ________ (travel) is stressful sometimes, so I make sure everything goes smoothly for my clients. It's such a great job. I don't think I'll ever consider (18) ________ (go) back to teaching again!

9 READ, WRITE & SPEAK.

A Read the information and look at the chart. Then complete the statements with the correct information. Use gerunds.

> A large group of students between the ages of 11 and 16 answered the following question: *In a typical week, which of these activities are you most likely to do in your free time?* The chart below gives information about their answers.

Free-Time Activities among 11- to 16-Year-Olds

	All	Girls	Boys
Listen to music	87%	91%	83%
Watch TV/DVDs	87%	86%	87%
Go to a friend's house	84%	88%	81%
Text friends	75%	84%	66%
Talk on the phone	71%	83%	58%
Surf the Internet	68%	65%	71%
Go to the movies	66%	70%	62%
Play computer games	66%	45%	88%
Go shopping	64%	86%	41%
Read books or magazines	57%	67%	48%

Source: http://www.scotland.gov.uk/Publications/2005/09/02151404/14063 Poll figures: MORI

1. Listening to music is the most popular activity for girls.
2. ________________ is 6 percent less popular among girls than it is among boys.
3. ________________ is the least popular activity for boys.
4. ________________ is 7 percent less popular among boys than it is among girls.
5. For all 11- to 16-year-olds, ________________ (75%) is slightly more common than ________________ (71%).
6. ________________ is as popular as (87%) ________________ for all students.
7. More 11- to 16-year-olds are interested in ________________ (68%) than ________________ (57%).
8. ________________ is the most popular activity for boys and the least popular for girls.

B Work with a partner. Compare your answers from exercise **A**. Which statement in exercise **A** is the most interesting? Explain your answer to your partner.

10 LISTEN & SPEAK.

CD3-14

A Listen to eight people talk about their free-time activities. Take notes about each person's activities in your notebook.

CD3-14

B Complete each sentence with the gerund form of a verb you hear and other information about the speaker. Listen again if necessary. More than one correct answer is possible.

1. Elizabeth enjoys *going for a hike on weekends*.
2. Frank is not interested in ______.
3. Sandra doesn't mind ______ again.
4. Martin is apologizing for ______ party.
5. Roberto is afraid of ______.
6. Lucia succeeded in ______ for a couple of hours.
7. ______ on the ship is Cindy's responsibility.
8. Sam can't think of a good reason ______ any longer.

C Work with a partner. Take turns making up more sentences about the people in exercises **A** and **B**. Use gerunds.

Elizabeth loves being outside in nature.

11 APPLY.

A Complete the questions with the words in parentheses. Add prepositions when necessary.

1. What have you *missed doing* (miss / do) this year?
2. What have you stopped doing (stop / do) this year?
3. What are you interested in learning (interested / learn) to do?
4. What are you good at doing (good / do)?
5. What are you terrible at doing (terrible / do)?
6. What are you thinking about doing (think / do) tonight?
7. What do you enjoy doing (enjoy / do) on the weekends?
8. What is your main reason for taking (reason / take) English classes?

B Work with a partner. Ask and answer the questions from exercise **A**.

C In your notebook, write your own answers to the questions from exercise **B**.

I've missed seeing my friends this year.

EXPLORE

CD3-15

1 READ the article about Felix Baumgartner. Notice the words in **bold**.

The World's Highest Skydive

How **would** you **like to jump** out of a balloon way up in space? It sounds impossible, but Austrian skydiver Felix Baumgartner did exactly that! Baumgartner **wanted to become** a professional[1] skydiver from a very early age. He **learned to make** parachute[2] jumps and **started to skydive** when he was 16 years old. Baumgartner's goal was to set a record[3] for jumping from the highest altitude.[4] He also **hoped to become** the fastest skydiver of all time.

In 2012, Baumgartner got his chance. His childhood hero, the famous skydiver Joseph Kittinger, **helped** him **to prepare** for the historic jump. On October 14 of that year, Baumgartner flew a helium[5]-filled balloon to a height of 127,852 feet (about 24 miles, or 38.6 kilometers) above the surface of the Earth, and then jumped. On his trip back to Earth, Baumgartner **managed to reach** a record speed of 843.6 miles (1357.6 kilometers) per hour . . . faster than the speed of sound! After opening his parachute, the man known as "Fearless Felix" made a perfect landing on his feet, and lifted his arms in victory. His jump set new skydiving records for speed and distance.

Now Baumgartner **has decided to retire**. This will **allow** the next group of skydivers **to aim** for his records. He will soon **start using** his skills to help people in danger. He **plans to fly** rescue helicopters or **become** a firefighter.

[1] **professional:** doing something for pay rather than as a hobby
[2] **parachute:** a large, lightweight sheet attached to a falling person that unfolds in the wind and causes the person to fall slowly
[3] **record:** the best time, distance, speed, etc.
[4] **altitude:** distance above sea level
[5] **helium:** a gas that is lighter than air

▲ Felix Baumgartner jumps from a balloon 24 miles above Earth

2 CHECK. Choose the correct answer to complete each statement.

1. Felix Baumgartner became interested in skydiving ______________.
   a. when he was very young
   b. after he learned to use a parachute
   c. as an adult
2. Baumgartner became a skydiver because ______________.
   a. he wanted to learn new skills
   b. he wanted to set records
   c. he wanted to become famous
3. After Baumgartner landed, ______________.
   a. he fell over
   b. he was very happy
   c. he became a professional skydiver
4. In the future, Baumgartner ______________.
   a. won't skydive anymore
   b. doesn't know what he will do
   c. hopes to set more skydiving records

▲ Felix Baumgartner

3 DISCOVER. Complete the exercises to learn about the grammar in this lesson.

A Find these sentences in the article from exercise **1**. Write the missing words.

1. Baumgartner wanted ______________________ a professional skydiver from a very early age.
2. He learned ______________________ parachute jumps and started ______________________ when he was 16 years old.
3. He plans ______________________ rescue helicopters or become a firefighter.

B Look again at the sentences in exercise **A**. What words follow the main verbs, *want, learn,* and *plan*? ______________________

LEARN

10.3 Verb + Infinitive

Subject	Verb	Infinitive	
I	learned	to speak	German.
They	wanted	to live	in Mexico.
We	need	to buy	a new computer.

1. An infinitive is the base form of the verb + *to*. An infinitive acts like a noun. It is often the object of a verb. Sometimes it is the subject of a sentence.	They decided **to take** the bus. I want **to go** to the gym after work.
2. Certain verbs can be followed by an infinitive*: *agree* *expect* *need* *refuse* *appear* *forget* *plan* *seem* *ask* *hope* *pretend* *want* *decide* *learn* *promise* *would like*	She **hopes to visit Miami** soon. He **seems to like** his new job. I **forgot to call** Lucy.
3. Put *not* before an infinitive to make it negative.	She decided **not to go**.
4. *To* is usually not repeated when there is more than one infinitive in the sentence.	Farmers need **to wake up** early and **work** hard.

*See page **A6** for a longer list of verbs followed by an infinitive.

REAL ENGLISH

You can use *would you like* + infinitive to invite someone to do something.

***Would you like to go** to the movies?*
***Would you like to study** together?*

4 Put the words in the correct order to make sentences.

1. decided / the / jump / from / skydiver / to / space

____

2. wants / skydiving / brother / my / go / to

____

3. take / planning / is / Bruce / to / skydiving / class / a

____

4. seems / Shelly / sports / dangerous / love / to

____

5. not / pretended / be / to / Fred / about / nervous / skydiving

____

6. his / forgets / he / never / to / equipment / check

____

7. skydiving / friends / my / go / with / I / to / refused

___

8. us / Kyle / stay / and / agreed / help / to

___

10.4 Verb + Object + Infinitive

Subject	Verb	Object	Infinitive	
She	allowed	the children	to leave	early.
I	reminded	them	to arrive	on time.
They	will invite	their friends	to go	to the movies.

1. Some verbs are followed by an object + infinitive.* The object can be a noun or a pronoun. These verbs include: *advise* *invite* *teach* *allow* *order* *tell* *encourage* *remind* *warn*	They don't **allow students to use** their phones. We **invited our friends to go** to the movies. I **told you not to be** late.
2. Some verbs can be followed by an infinitive or an object + infinitive, but the meaning is different. These verbs include: *ask* *help* *pay* *want* *expect* *need* *promise* *would like*	We **expect to be** there. We **expect her to be** there. We **want to come.** We **want you to come.**

*See page **A6** for a list of verbs that can be followed by an infinitive or an object + infinitive.

5 Circle the correct words to complete each sentence. For some sentences, both choices are possible.

1. Jim and Marsha don't want **to do** / **their children to do** dangerous sports.
2. Our skiing instructor warned **not to go** / **us not to go** straight down the hill.
3. Ali's parents told **to come** / **him to come** home.
4. I would like **to stay** / **my sister to stay** a little longer.
5. The professor reminded **to finish** / **us to finish** our assignments by Thursday.
6. Irina would like **to paint** / **me to paint** the kitchen this weekend.
7. The police ordered **to leave** / **everyone to leave** the building.
8. The doctor has advised **to take** / **me to take** a few days off from work.
9. I expect **to be** / **you to be** on time for the lecture.
10. Do you allow **to borrow** / **your friends to borrow** your car?

11. This DVD teaches **to play** / **children to play** the piano.

12. They don't need **to wait** / **you to wait** any longer.

10.5 Verb + Gerund or Infinitive

Subject	Verb	Gerund	
I	started	driving	last year.
We	prefer	traveling	by train.

Subject	Verb	Infinitive	
I	started	to drive	last year.
We	prefer	to travel	by train.

1. Some verbs can be followed by a gerund or an infinitive.* Usually, there is no difference in meaning. These verbs include: *begin*, *can't stand*, *continue*, *hate*, *like*, *love*, *prefer*, *start*	I **like to swim.** = I **like swimming.** They **love to dance.** = They **love dancing.**
2. Use *and* or *or* to connect two gerunds or two infinitives. You don't need to repeat *to* when you are connecting infinitives.	I like **swimming and playing** tennis. I prefer **to swim** or **play** tennis.
3. **Be careful!** Don't connect a gerund and an infinitive with *and* or *or.*	✓ She loves **cooking** and **traveling**. ✓ She loves **to cook** and **travel**. ✗ She loves to cook and traveling.

*See page **A6** for a list of verbs that can be followed by a gerund or an infinitive.

6 Complete each sentence with the infinitive or gerund form of the verb in parentheses. Use the gerund form for sentences 1–4. Use the infinitive form for sentences 5–8.

1. I like ___playing___ (play) games.
2. I hate ________________ (wait) in line.
3. I can't stand ________________ (be) late for appointments.
4. I love ________________ (give) parties and ________________ (cook) meals for friends.
5. I've just started ________________ (exercise).
6. This is a nice pool, but I prefer ________________ (swim) in the ocean.
7. I began ________________ (play) sports when I was very young.
8. I am going to continue ________________ (live) where I am now for a long time.

7 **SPEAK.** Work with a partner. Student A reads a completed sentence from exercise **6**. Student B repeats the sentence using the alternative form, gerund or infinitive. Switch roles for each new item.

A: *I like playing games.*

B: *I like to play games.*

PRACTICE

8 Complete Lili's blog post with the gerund or infinitive form of the verbs in parentheses.

Lili's Blog | **Welcome Mountain Lovers!** Enjoy! Share your adventures. **Sunday, March 28**

I have always loved (1) ___to climb___ (climb) mountains. I'd like (2) ______________ (visit) the Alps more often, but it's expensive. I plan (3) ______________ (go) back there as soon as I can. Last year, I went to the Alps with my brothers. I always expect (4) ______________ (have) a few problems on the way up a mountain, but this time the weather was really bad. Halfway up, we met some experienced climbers. They warned us (5) ______________ (get) off the mountain as quickly as possible. My younger brother decided (6) ______________ (take) their advice. But my older brother is a very experienced climber. Together we managed (7) ______________ (reach) the top.

POSTED BY ERIK AT 10:56 PM

1 COMMENT:

Congratulations on (8) ______________ (reach) the top.
I used to love climbing, but because of an illness, my doctor has advised me (9) ______________ (not continue) climbing mountains.
I will, however, continue (10) ______________ (read) your blog!

9 PRONUNCIATION Read the box and listen to the examples. Then complete the exercises.

CD3-16

PRONUNCIATION Infinitives

In conversation, we usually pronounce the *to* of the infinitive as /tə/.

Examples:

We plan **to** visit California next year.
Have you started **to** do your homework?

CD3-17

A Listen to the sentences and repeat.

1. I hope to take drum lessons in the fall.
2. I've started to learn kung-fu.
3. I've decided to quit running.
4. My parents like to dance.
5. He encouraged us to get there early.
6. I promised to buy all my friends ice cream.
7. I asked John to show us his new boat.
8. She told us to be quiet and finish our work.

B Complete the sentences with information about yourself. Then share your sentences with a partner. Practice pronouncing the *to* in the infinitive as /tə/.

1. I hope to ______________________.
2. I've started to ______________________.
3. I've decided to ______________________.
4. My parents like to ______________________.
5. Our teacher asked us to ______________________.
6. My friend invited me to ______________________.

CD3-18

10 LISTEN to Jenna talk to a friend about her trip to Australia. Complete the sentences about her story. Use the verbs in parentheses and the infinitive or gerund form of each verb you hear.

1. Jenna's brother invited her to climb (invite) down a slot canyon with him.
2. Jenna almost ______________________ (refuse) with her brother because she didn't have the right clothes.
3. Jenna ______________________ (love) at home in Colorado.
4. Jenna ______________________ (want) with her brother. That's really why she ______________________ (agree) the trip.
5. Jenna ______________________ (need) some climbing equipment from John's wife.
6. Jenna usually ______________________ (can't stand).
7. She ______________________ (not mind) down the slot canyon.
8. Jenna enjoyed the trip, but she still ______________________ (prefer).

11 WRITE & SPEAK.

A Complete the sentences with your own ideas. Use infinitives or gerunds as appropriate.

1. I hope *to learn how to skateboard someday*.
2. When it started to rain, I decided ______.
3. My parents taught me ______.
4. On weekends, I don't mind ______.
5. I often forget ______.
6. Next year, I'm going to continue ______.
7. I enjoy ______.
8. I like ______, but I prefer ______.

B Share your sentences from exercise **A** with a partner. Ask follow-up questions where possible.

A: *I hope to learn how to skateboard someday.*

B: *Is it very difficult?*

12 APPLY.

A Choose one of your interests or hobbies and write five or six sentences about it. Use either a gerund or an infinitive in each sentence.

Baking Cakes

I love baking cakes for special occasions.

Decorating cakes teaches you to be patient.

I hope to become a professional baker.

B Work with a partner. Share your sentences from exercise **A**. Ask follow-up questions for more information.

What type of cakes do you like to make?

EXPLORE

CD3-19

1 READ the introduction and student presentation. Notice the words in **bold**.

Tiny Creatures in a Big Ocean

▲ Kakani Katija is a *National Geographic Society* Emerging Explorer.

Professor: Last week I gave you an assignment **to get** you thinking about your own future jobs. I asked you to research someone with an unusual job and gather **enough information to give** a presentation to the class. Yuri, would you like to go first?

Yuri: Sure. My hometown is **too far from the coast for me to go** there very often, but I've always loved the sea. That's why I chose a scientist who studies the oceans—Dr. Kakani Katija.

Dr. Katija researches the way warm and cold water mix and move in the oceans. She does this **to learn** more about the Earth's climate systems. The movement of water in the oceans has a big effect on our climate. So does the movement of living creatures, according to Dr. Katija.

A single whale is **too small to have** a big effect on the movement of water. However, millions of tiny creatures moving together in the same direction have **enough mass**[1] **to make** a difference. In fact, Dr. Katija believes that the movements of creatures in the ocean may influence our climate as much as the tides and wind do.

Dr. Katija's research provides important new reasons for protecting life in the oceans.

[1] **mass:** the amount of matter an object has

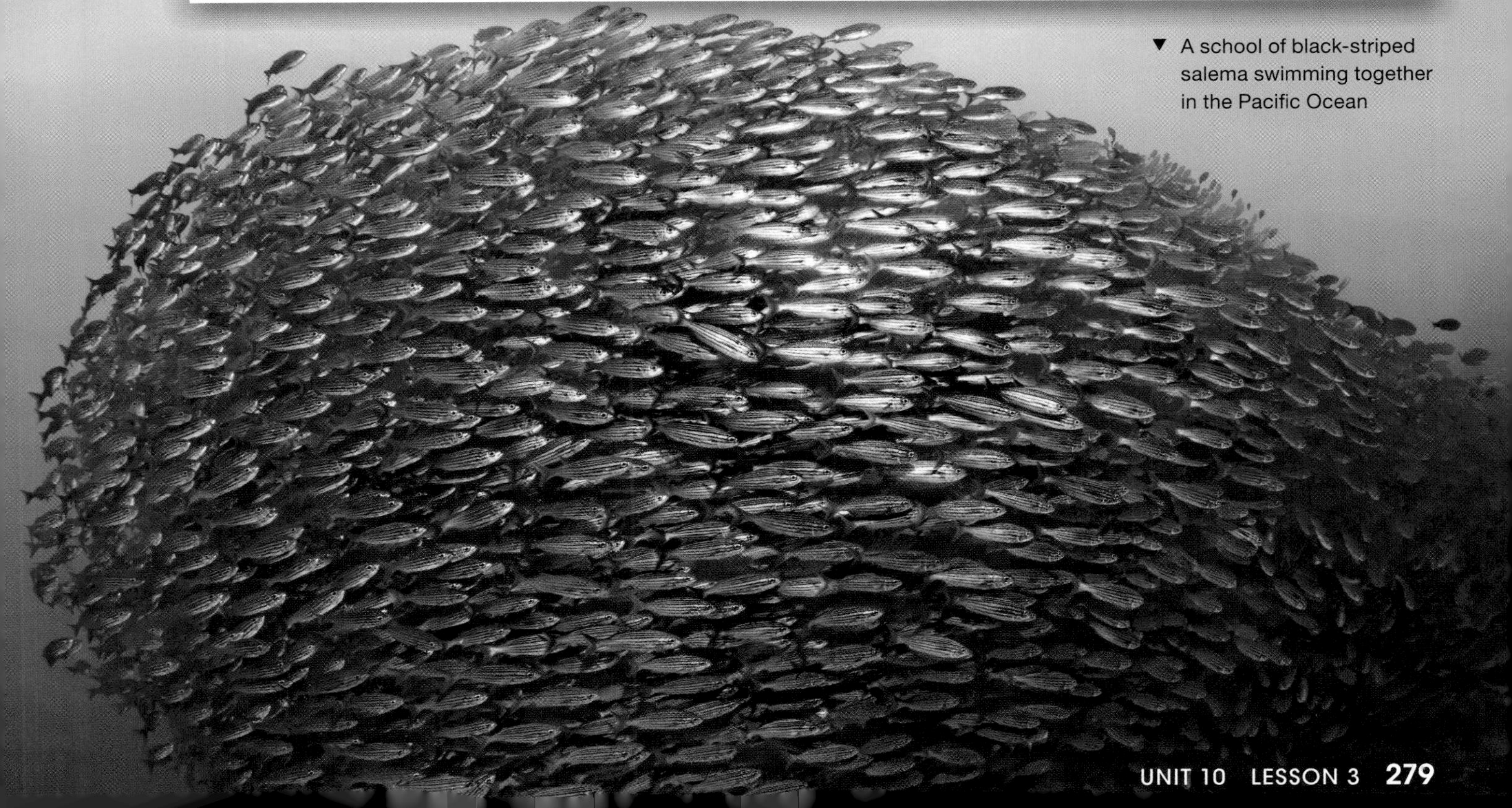

▼ A school of black-striped salema swimming together in the Pacific Ocean

2 CHECK. Choose the correct answer to complete each statement.

1. The professor gave this assignment because he wanted students ________________.

   a. to learn about the ocean b. to consider their futures

2. Yuri doesn't go to the coast often because ________________.

   a. it isn't close to his home b. he prefers to stay in town

3. Dr. Katija studies the oceans because she wants to understand ________________.

   a. how the Earth's climate works b. how sea creatures survive

4. ________________ is very important to Dr Katija's research.

   a. The movement of single large creatures b. The movement of small creatures

3 DISCOVER. Complete the exercises to learn about the grammar in this lesson.

A Look at the sentences based on the article from exercise **1**. Then answer the question that follows.

1. I gave you an assignment **to get** you thinking about your own future jobs.
2. She does this **to learn** more about the Earth's climate.

   What question does the infinitive answer in both sentences?

   a. What? b. Why? c. When?

B Look at the other bold phrases in the article. What verb form follows phrases with *too* and *enough*?

a. a gerund b. an infinitive

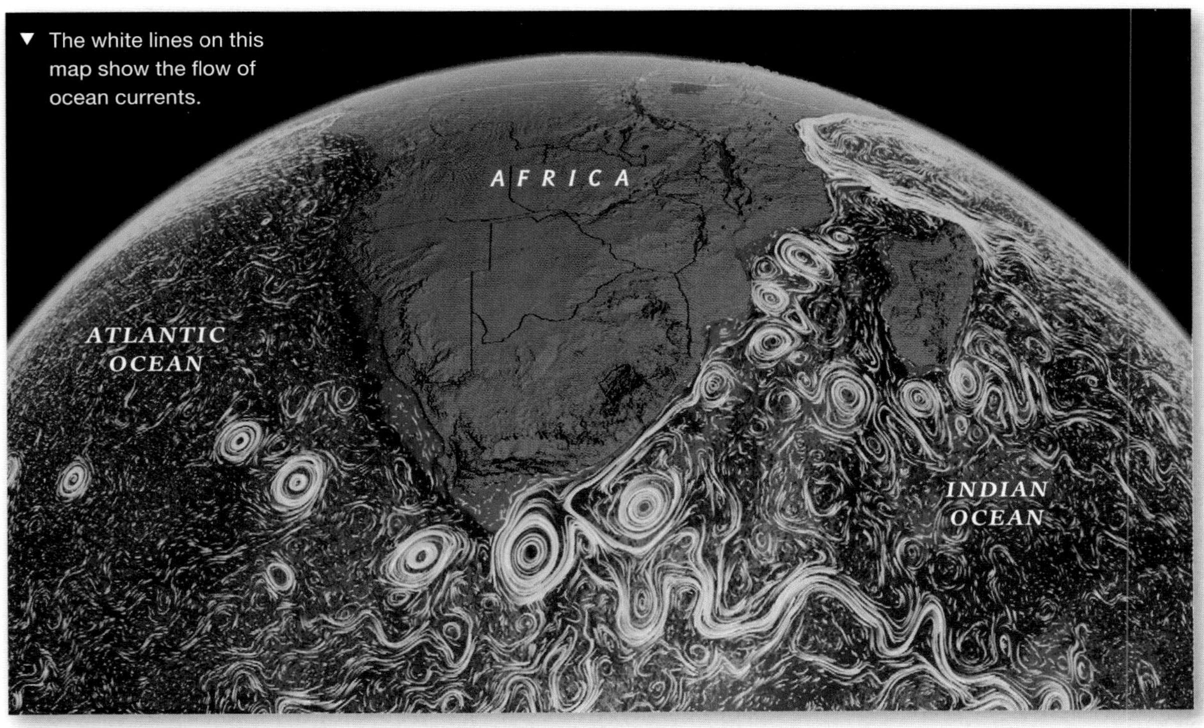

▼ The white lines on this map show the flow of ocean currents.

LEARN

10.6 Infinitives of Purpose

1. Use an infinitive to state a purpose or reason.	I went to the store **to buy** some food. (I went to the store because I wanted to buy some food.)
2. **Be Careful!** Don't use *for* + an infinitive to state a purpose.	✓ She went online to find the information. ✗ She went online for to find the information
3. We often use an infinitive in an incomplete sentence to answer questions with *Why*.	A: Why are you taking this class? B: **To learn** English.
4. **Remember:** *To* is usually not repeated when there is more than one infinitive in the sentence.	I use my phone **to talk** to people, **watch** videos, and **surf** the Internet.

4 Complete the sentences. Use infinitives of purpose.

1. The professor gave the assignment because he wanted to start a discussion about jobs.

   The professor gave the assignment *to start a discussion about jobs*.

2. Yuri chose Dr. Katija because he wanted to show his interest in the ocean.

   Yuri chose Dr. Katija __________.

3. The scientist studies the oceans because she wants to understand climate systems.

   The scientist studies the oceans __________.

4. Dani went to the library because she wanted to do some research and finish her project.

   Dani went to the library __________.

5. Because he wanted to get a good grade, Jack studied all night.

   __________ Jack studied all night.

6. Louise used the Internet because she wanted to find some answers to her questions.

   Louise used the Internet __________.

7. Everyone worked hard on their assignments because they wanted to get good grades.

   Everyone worked hard on their assignments __________.

8. Some students stayed after class because they wanted to ask the professor questions.

   Some students stayed after class __________.

5 **SPEAK.** Work with a partner. Ask and answer *why* questions about the sentences in exercise **4**.

A: *Why did the professor give the assignment?*

B: *To start a discussion about jobs.*

10.7 *Too* + Infinitive

Adjectives and Adverbs

	Too	Adjective/ Adverb	*For*	Noun or Object Pronoun	Infinitive
It's (not)	too	far	for	us	**to walk.**
It was (not)		difficult		Ken	**to understand.**
She's (not)		young			**to drive.**

Nouns

	Too Much/ Too Many	Noun	*For*	Noun or Object Pronoun	Infinitive
There was	**too much**	noise	for	me	**to study.**
There are	**too many**	books		Alex	**to carry.**
I have	**too much**	work			**to do.**

1. Use *too* + infinitive in these patterns to tell why something is not possible. a. *too* + adjective/adverb + infinitive b. *too much* + non-count noun + infinitive c. *too many* + count noun + infinitive	a. Jason is **too short to reach** the top shelf. b. I have **too much work to do** today. c. In New York, there are **too many museums to visit** in one day.
2. Use *for* + noun or object pronoun + infinitive to give information about "who."	It's too dark **for** me **to see.**

6 Complete the sentences. Use *too, too much,* or *too many* and the words in parentheses. Add any other necessary words.

1. The businessman arrived ___too late to speak___ (late / speak) at the meeting.
2. The report was ________________ (long / read) while I was on the train.
3. Many doctors have ________________ (patients / take) care of.
4. The secretary had ________________ (work / finish) before the end of the day.
5. The taxi driver drove ________________ (slowly / reach) the station in time.
6. Norman is ________________ (experienced / make) a mistake like that.
7. Francine has ________________ (e-mails / answer).
8. I have ________________ (books / carry) in my backpack.

7 Complete the sentences. Use *too, too much,* or *too many* with the words in parentheses. Use infinitives. Add any other necessary words.

1. The teacher spoke ___too quickly for me to understand___ (quickly / me / understand).
2. The students have ________________ (homework / the teacher / correct in one night).

3. My sister's job is ______________________ (work / one person / do).

4. A firefighter's job is ______________________ (dangerous / an inexperienced person / do).

5. The company received ______________________ (calls / the employees / answer).

6. A thousand dollars is ______________________ (money / John / spend) on a new camera.

7. Our teacher gave ______________________ (assignments / us / do) in one day.

8. This suitcase is ______________________ (old / me / take) on our trip.

10.8 *Enough* + Infinitive

Adjectives and Adverbs

	Adjective/ Adverb	*Enough*	*For*	Noun or Object Pronoun	Infinitive
It's (not)	easy	enough	for	students	**to understand.**
He spoke	loudly			us	**to hear.**
It's (not)	cold				**to snow.**

Nouns

	Enough	Noun	*For*	Noun or Object Pronoun	Infinitive
There was (not)	enough	time	for	me	**to finish.**
There is (not)		space			**to exercise.**

1. Use *enough* + infinitive in these patterns to tell why something is possible: a. adjective + *enough* + infinitive b. adverb + *enough* + infinitive c. *enough* + noun + infinitive	 a. I am **strong enough to lift** the heavy box. b. We will walk **quickly enough to arrive** on time. c. She has **enough talent to win** the contest.
2. **Remember!** Put *enough* after an adjective but before a noun.	✓ I'm **old enough to drive**. ✗ I'm enough old to drive. ✓ I have **enough money to buy** a car. ✗ I have money enough to buy a car.
3. Use *for* + a noun or object pronoun + infinitive to give information about "who."	The TV screen is large enough **for everyone to see** it.
4. **Be careful!** Do not use *for* + infinitive.	✓ We don't have enough time **to eat** lunch before class. ✗ We don't have enough time for to eat lunch before class.

8 Complete the sentences. Use *enough* with the words in parentheses. Use an infinitive. Add any other necessary words.

1. This store hires enough salespeople to help (salespeople / help) its customers.

2. Tim didn't do ______________________ (well / get) the job.

3. We have ______________________________ (staff / fill) the new orders.

4. The singer wasn't ______________________________ (good / win) the competition.

5. Jun earns ______________________________ (money / take) a vacation every year.

6. The children found the story ______________________________ (easy / follow).

7. Do we have ______________________________ (sugar / make) the cake?

8. The sofa was ______________________________ (comfortable / sleep) on.

9 Complete the sentences. Use *enough* with the words in parentheses. Use an infinitive. Add any other necessary words.

1. The tour guide spoke loudly enough for everyone to hear (loudly / everyone / hear).

2. There wasn't ______________________________ (time / me / finish) my report.

3. Maya's company is ______________________________ (small / everyone / know) each other.

4. The books weren't ______________________________ (light / him / carry).

5. My brother's house doesn't have ______________________________ (room / all of us / stay) overnight.

6. It was ______________________________ (warm / me / wear) shorts and a t-shirt yesterday.

7. The passengers boarded the airplane ______________________________ (quickly / the flight / leave) on time.

8. There weren't ______________________________ (books / every student / have) one.

PRACTICE

10 Complete the conversation with *enough, too, too much,* or *too many* and the words in parentheses. Use infinitives.

Anna: I applied for a job in Rome, so I need to improve my Italian. At the moment, I make (1) too many mistakes to work (mistakes / work) in Italy.

Caroline: Why don't you take an Italian class?

Anna: I am, actually, and I had my first class last night! It was tough! There was (2) ______________________________ (new vocabulary / me / remember). The teacher speaks quickly, but he is very clear.

It wasn't (3) ______________________ (fast / me / follow). He says if he speaks (4) ______________________ (slowly / us / understand) every word, it won't be realistic.

Caroline: That's true. My sister and I used to get good grades in our high school German class, but when we arrived in Berlin, everyone spoke (5) ______________________ (fast / us / understand). Luckily, we were there for a month, so we had (6) ______________________ (time / get) used to it.

Anna: There are only five students in the class, though. I'm worried there may not be (7) ______________________ (students / keep) the class going.

Caroline: That's too bad. The subject is (8) ______________________ (interesting / attract) a lot of students!

11 LISTEN & SPEAK.

A Listen to each sentence. Then choose the sentence that has a similar meaning.

1. a. The computer is too expensive for us to buy.
   b. The computer is not too expensive for us to buy.
2. a. The police arrived quickly enough to catch the criminal.
   b. The police didn't arrive quickly enough to catch the criminal.
3. a. An hour was enough time for me to read the article.
   b. An hour wasn't enough time for me to read the article.
4. a. The text on this screen isn't big enough for me to read.
   b. The text on this screen is big enough for me to read.
5. a. The TV show wasn't on early enough for the children to watch.
   b. The TV show was on early enough for the children to watch.
6. a. The patient was too sick to have visitors.
   b. The patient wasn't too sick to have visitors.
7. a. Paul is too weak to run a marathon.
   b. Paul isn't too weak to run a marathon.
8. a. The video game wasn't easy enough for my little brother to play.
   b. The video game was easy enough for my little brother to play.

B Work with a partner. Take turns making up different ways to say the sentences in exercise **A**. Try not to change the meaning. Use infinitives and different adjectives and nouns.

1. *We aren't rich enough to buy the computer.*
2. *The police arrived early enough to catch the criminals.*

12 EDIT. Read the article about langurs in India. Find and correct six more errors with infinitives.

An Unusual Job for a Monkey

In the Great Indian Desert, it's too hot and dry for langur monkeys ^to live comfortably all year round. That's why over 2000 of them come into the city of Jodhpur for to find something to eat. Local people like the langurs, so they bring food to sharing with the monkeys. It's enough easy for langurs to survive in the city, but it's not all fun and free food! Many of them have to work for a living . . . controlling other monkeys!

Langurs are welcome in Indian cities, but other kinds of monkeys aren't. There are too much of these monkeys to control, and they sometimes attack people to get food. Langurs scare other types of monkeys, so cities use them keep these monkeys away. In Delhi, for example, during a big sports event in 2010, 38 langurs patrolled[1] the streets, and the other monkeys were too much scared to stay in the area. The plan was successful enough for most people enjoying the event in peace.

▲ A langur is a type of monkey common in South Asia.

[1] **patrol:** make regular trips around an area to guard against trouble or crime

13 APPLY.

A Look at the notes in the chart about Lena's job. Then think of your job or the job of someone you know. In your notebook, make a chart like Lena's. What are the positive things about the job? What are the negative things? Write notes in your chart.

Lena's Job: Banker	
Positive Things	Negative Things
She makes enough money to take a vacation every year. *The bank is close enough for her to walk to.*	*Her schedule is very busy. She often doesn't have enough time to eat lunch.* *She is usually too tired to go out with friends after work.*

B In your notebook, write five or six sentences about the job you chose. Use your notes from exercise **A**. Use *too, enough,* and infinitives.

My job is too stressful. I often don't have enough time to finish all of my work.

C Work with a partner. Tell your partner about the job you chose.

UNIT 10 Review the Grammar

Charts 10.1–10.6, 10.8

CD3-21

1 **LISTEN** to the conversation. Write the words you hear.

Milan: Sorry I've been too busy (1) ________________ together recently.

Amy: Yeah, you need (2) ________________ more breaks!

Milan: I know. So, how is your hockey going?

Amy: Well, I'm getting better at (3) ________________ the puck,[1] but I still don't skate very fast. The coach has advised (4) ________________ more training.

Milan: So, are you going to agree (5) ________________ that?

Amy: Well, I don't mind (6) ________________ hard, but I want to avoid (7) ________________ injured. I don't want (8) ________________ my knee again. It's still not (9) ________________ for me to play at full speed.

Milan: Well, listen . . . I'm going to the park (10) ________________ some exercise tomorrow morning. Why don't you come along?

[1] **puck:** the small black disk that is used in hockey

Charts 10.1–10.3

2 Complete Nadia's blog entry about her job as a teacher. Use the gerund or the infinitive of each verb in parentheses. In some cases you can use both forms.

I had a few different jobs in mind when I was young. I thought about (1) ___studying___ (study) medicine because I love (2) ________________ (help) other people, but (3) ________________ (become) a doctor is hard work! You need (4) ________________ (study) for so many years. Also, I wasn't sure I wanted (5) ________________ (work) long hours like most doctors seem (6) ________________ (do). My final choice was between (7) ________________ (become) a nurse and (8) ________________ (work) as an elementary school teacher. Well, (9) ________________ (teach) won!

I started (10) ________________ (teach) five years ago, and I know I made the right choice. I really like (11) ________________ (work) at my school. Sometimes I don't have enough time (12) ________________ (finish) all my work, but the children are great. I love my job, and I love (13) ________________ (know) that my work makes a difference. That is very important to me.

Charts 10.1–10.5, 10.7, 10.8

3 Read each sentence. Then complete the second sentence so that it has a similar meaning to the first sentence. Use a gerund or an infinitive. If both are possible, use both.

1. I like to read magazines. I enjoy reading magazines.
2. It's fun to explore new places. ______________________ is fun.
3. The instructor told me to wait. The instructor asked ______________________.
4. Dave wants to ski this weekend. Dave is interested ______________________ this weekend.
5. I hate to be late for work. I really dislike ______________________.
6. Anna kept working. Anna continued ______________________.
7. The meeting wasn't long enough to be useful. The meeting was too ______________________.
8. I learned to swim from my father. My father taught ______________________.

Charts 10.1–10.6, 10.8

4 **EDIT.** Read the article about Barrington Irving. Find and correct seven more errors with gerunds and infinitives.

Barrington Irving

In 2007, Barrington Irving became famous ~~on~~ for being the youngest person to fly solo[1] around the world. Irving was born in Jamaica and lived there until his parents decided move to Miami. Although life was not always easy, Irving has always been good at overcome difficulties. When he was 15, Irving met a professional pilot who invited him take a look at his plane. That was when Irving became interested in learning to fly. He didn't have money enough to go to flight school, so he earned money by washing planes. He practiced to fly in video games. When he was 23, Irving built his own plane and succeeded in flying around the world in 97 days.

After this success, Irving created exciting programs for to encourage children to learn about science, math, and technology. He believes in showing children that study hard brings success. If they do their best, no goal[2] is too difficult to achieve.

[1] **solo:** alone; without help from another person
[2] **goal:** something you hope to do that requires a lot of effort and work

Charts 10.1–10.8

5 WRITE & SPEAK.

A Write eight sentences about your work and activities you do in your free time. Use the words and phrases from the box or your own ideas. Use gerunds and infinitives.

afraid of	allow(ed) me to	ask(ed) me to	can't stand	enjoy
enough time to	exercising	go/went online to	interested in	prefer
relaxing	smart enough to	start(ed)	too much money to	too old to

Exercising is one of my favorite things to do.

I started to play the piano when I was six years old.

B Work with a partner. Share your sentences from exercise **A**. Then ask and answer as many questions as you can about each of your partner's sentences. Use gerunds, infinitives, and the other grammar from this unit in your questions and answers.

A: *Exercising is one of my favorite things to do.*

B: *What kind of exercise do you like to do?*

A: *I enjoy hiking.*

B: *Why do you enjoy hiking?*

A: *I like hiking because my apartment is near a canyon, so it's not too difficult for me to hike.*

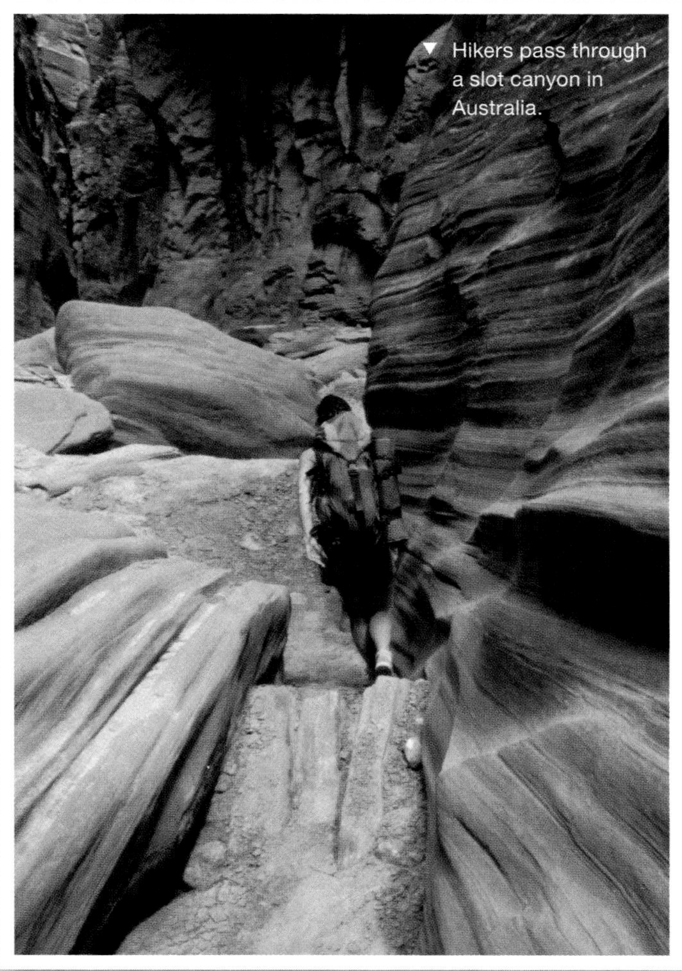

▼ Hikers pass through a slot canyon in Australia.

Connect the Grammar to Writing

1 READ & NOTICE THE GRAMMAR.

A Read the text. How did Carlos learn to do his job? Discuss your answers with a partner.

Abuela's Kitchen

When Carlos was five years old, he moved in with his *abuela*, or grandmother. She loved to cook, and Carlos spent a lot of time with her in the kitchen. Being in the warm kitchen with his grandmother was fun. She liked telling stories about her childhood, and Carlos enjoyed listening to her. He also enjoyed learning to cook by watching and helping her. In the beginning, most dishes were too difficult for him to make. First, he chopped vegetables and stirred beans. Then, he learned how to make soups and other simple dishes when he was seven. By the time he turned 13, Carlos was cooking full meals for his family and friends. He enjoyed making people happy with his food.

Eventually, Carlos realized that he had enough talent to become a chef. At the age of 18, he began working at a local restaurant. Then, 12 years later, after a lot of hard work, Carlos opened his own restaurant. He invited his family and friends to come to the grand opening. To honor his grandmother, Carlos named his restaurant Abuela's Kitchen.

GRAMMAR FOCUS

In exercise **A**, the writer uses gerunds and infinitives to explain the events of Carlos's life.

Gerunds:

__Being__ in the warm kitchen with my grandmother was fun.
He enjoyed __making__ people happy with his food.

Infinitives:

His grandmother loved __to cook__, and Carlos . . .
In the beginning, most dishes were too difficult for him __to make__.

B Read the text in exercise **A** again. Underline the gerunds and circle the infinitives. Then work with a partner and compare your answers.

C How did Carlos become a chef? Complete his timeline with the events from the text in exercise **A**.

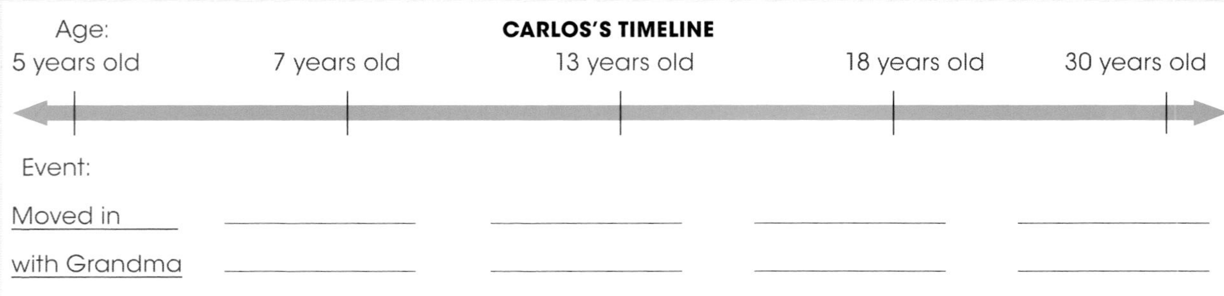

2 BEFORE YOU WRITE.

A Think of someone you know well or know a lot about. In your notebook, brainstorm a list of important events in this person's life and his or her age when the event happened.

B Choose five or more events from your list from exercise **A**. Then complete the timeline. Use the timeline from exercise **1C** as a model.

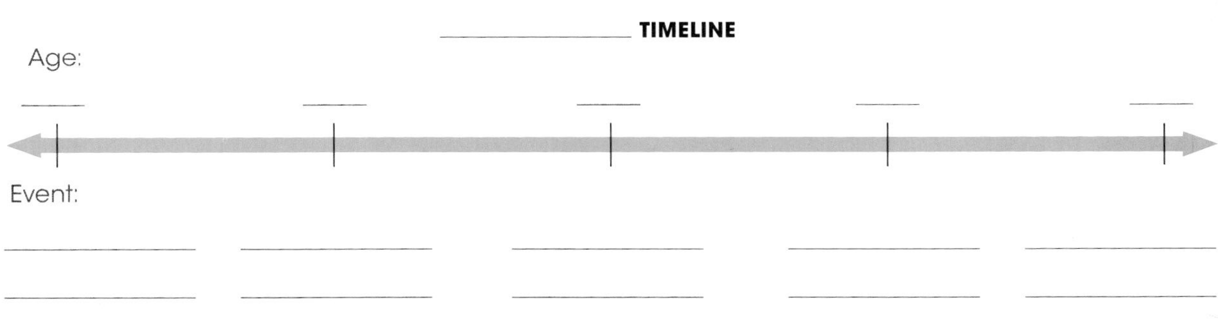

3 WRITE a short biography of the person you chose. Write two or three paragraphs. Use the information from your chart in exercise **2B** and the text in exercise **1A** to help you. Use gerunds and infinitives.

WRITING FOCUS Using *First* and *Then* to Show a Sequence

Writers often use the words *first* and *then* at the beginning of a sentence to show the sequence of events, or the order in which the events happened. Use *first* for the first event. Use *then* for a later event.

Use a comma after *first* or *then*.

> ***First,*** *he chopped vegetables and stirred beans.* ***Then****, he learned how to make soups and other simple dishes.*

4 SELF ASSESS. Read your biography. Underline the gerunds and circle the infinitives. Then use the checklist to assess your work.

- ☐ I used gerunds correctly. [10.1, 10.2, 10.5]
- ☐ I used infinitives correctly. [10.3, 10.4, 10.5]
- ☐ I used *too* and *enough* with infinitives correctly. [10.7, 10.8]
- ☐ I used *first* and *then* to show sequence in my biography. [WRITING FOCUS]

UNIT

11 People and Places

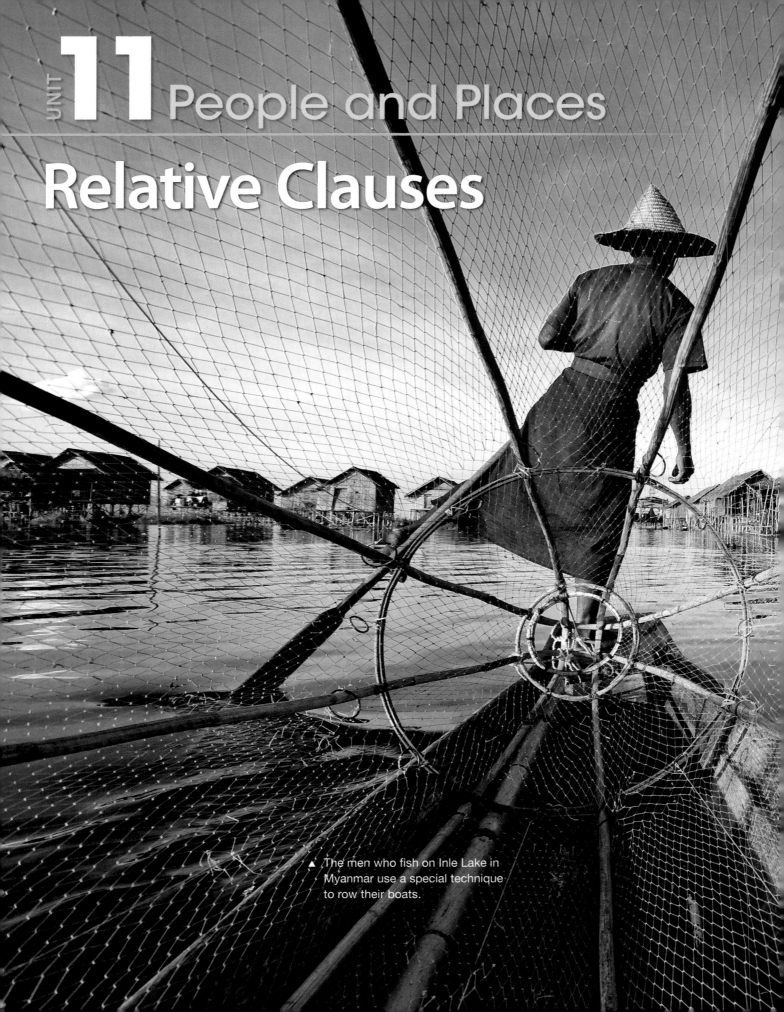

Relative Clauses

▲ The men who fish on Inle Lake in Myanmar use a special technique to row their boats.

EXPLORE

CD3-22

1 READ the conversation about the town of Petra, Jordan. Notice the words in **bold**.

Petra and the Bedul Bedouin

Petra, Jordan
AFRICA

Leo: I watched an old movie **that was on TV last night.** It was one of the Indiana Jones movies. There were wonderful old buildings in the story. They were in the Middle East somewhere, I think.

Jose: Oh, I wrote a report about those buildings for a history class. They're in Petra, Jordan. The buildings **which make up the oldest part of the city** are over 2000 years old. They are carved[1] into the hills.

Leo: Well, it certainly looks like a beautiful place. Does anyone actually live there?

Jose: Yes, I read about a Bedouin tribe **that has lived in the area for over 200 years**. They are called the Bedul. Until around 30 years ago, they had a simple life as farmers and traveled around with their animals. But Petra has become a popular tourist destination, so their lives have changed.

Leo: Oh really? How?

Jose: Well, many of the Bedul people have settled in a village. Some sell souvenirs[2] to the tourists **who visit Petra**. Others work as tour guides.

Leo: I see. Do any of them keep the old traditions alive?

Jose: Oh yes, there are still some Bedul people **who prefer to keep goats and grow crops**.

[1] **carve:** to cut from a solid material such as stone or wood
[2] **souvenir:** an object that helps people remember a place they visited

2 CHECK. Read the statements. Circle **T** for *true* or **F** for *false*.

1. Petra is a modern city. **T F**
2. The ancient buildings in Petra are on flat land. **T F**
3. The stone buildings are over 2000 years old. **T F**
4. The Bedul people have lived in the area for just a few years. **T F**
5. Many of the Bedul people have changed their jobs in the past 30 years. **T F**

3 DISCOVER. Complete the exercises to learn about the grammar in this lesson.

A Find these sentences in the conversation in exercise **A**. Write the missing words.

1. I watched an old movie that was on TV last night.
2. The buildings ________________ are over 2000 years old.
3. . . ., I read about a Bedouin tribe ________________.
4. Some sell souvenirs to the tourists ________________.
5. . . ., there are still some Bedul people ________________.

B Notice the missing words you wrote in exercise **A**. What words begin these clauses?

that, ________, ________

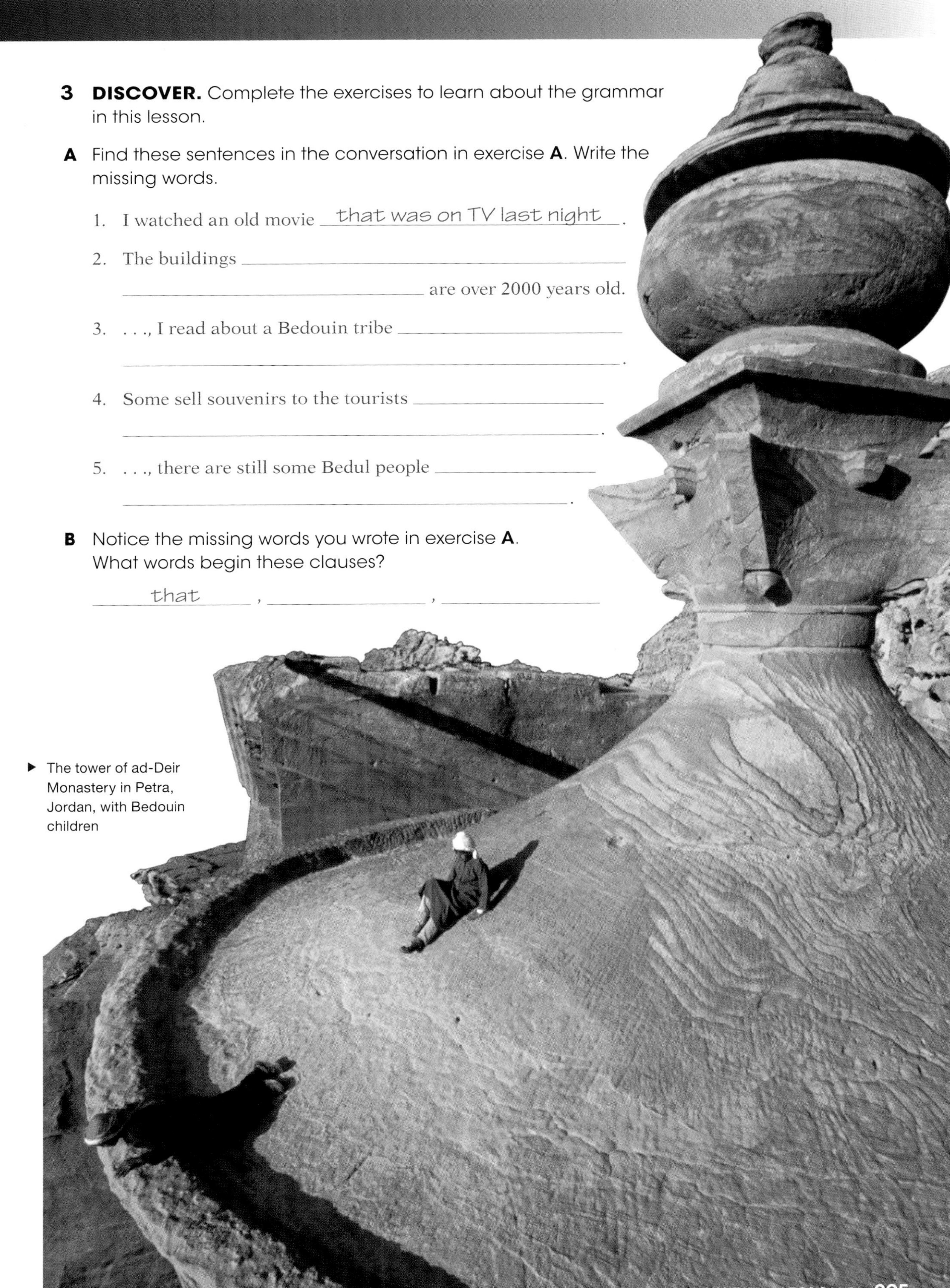

▶ The tower of ad-Deir Monastery in Petra, Jordan, with Bedouin children

LEARN

11.1 Subject Relative Clauses

After the Main Clause	Inside the Main Clause
We met the woman. She owns the shop.	The tour was great. It left at noon.
We met the woman **who owns the shop.** (Subject Relative Clause)	The tour **that left at noon** was great. (Subject Relative Clause)

1. A sentence with a relative clause* combines two sentences or ideas.	I met the man. He organized the tour. I met the man **who organized the tour.** (Relative Clause)
2. A relative clause describes a noun or a pronoun. It usually comes after the noun or pronoun it describes.	The people (Noun) **that asked me about Jordan** have left. We welcome everyone (Pronoun) **who visits our home.**
3. A subject relative clause begins with a relative pronoun (*that*, *which*, or *who*). Use *that* or *who* for people. Use *that* or *which* for places, things, and animals.	I know someone **who lives in Jordan.** Many people **that live here** speak French. The book **that's on the table** is Carla's. The photos **which show the Nile** are amazing.
4. In a subject relative clause, the relative pronoun is the subject of the clause. The relative pronoun is followed by a verb.	I like the guide **who showed** us the sites. She wants something **that will remind** her of her trip.

*Relative clauses are also called adjective clauses. Like adjectives, relative clauses describe nouns.

4 Underline the subject relative clause in each sentence. Draw an arrow from the relative clause to the noun or indefinite pronoun it describes.

1. The Bedul are people who live near Petra, Jordan.
2. Tourists that visit Petra buy souvenirs from the Bedul.
3. The Bedul used to be farmers who lived simply.
4. The building that is most popular with tourists is the Treasury.
5. The guides that show tourists around Petra are often Bedul.
6. The name *Petra* comes from the Greek word that means "stone."
7. The buildings that make up the old part of Petra are carved into the hills.
8. Anyone who wants to know more about Petra can find information on the Internet.

11.2 Subject Relative Clauses: Verb Agreement

1. The verb in a subject relative clause agrees with the noun it describes.	I have a friend **who likes traveling**. (friend = Noun; likes = Verb) I have friends **who like traveling**. (friends = Noun; like = Verb)
2. **Be careful!** The verb in the main clause always agrees with the subject of the main clause.	Main Clause: **The map** that they are looking at **looks** very old. Relative Clause: that they are looking at
3. Do not repeat the subject in a relative clause.	✓ Where's the book **that has the map of Egypt**? ✗ Where's the book that it has the map of Egypt?

5 Complete the relative clauses in each conversation. Use the simple present form of the verb in parentheses.

1. A: Have you seen the travel guide?
   B: I'm not sure. Is it the green book that ___is___ (be) on the kitchen table?
2. A: What do you want to do this afternoon?
   B: I want to find some stores that ___sell___ (sell) stone carvings.
3. A: Is there anyone who ___understands___ (understand) French?
   B: Yes. I do. How can I help you?
4. A: Oh, no. I forgot my camera.
   B: Do you have a phone that ___takes___ (take) good photos?
5. A: What kind of driver do you prefer, Ms. Jones?
   B: I prefer one who ___doesn't talk___ (not talk) too much.
6. A: What sort of clothes are you taking on your trip?
   B: I'm just taking clothes that ___are___ (be) easy to pack. I can only take one suitcase.

6 Circle the correct form of the verb to complete each sentence.

1. The guide that told funny stories **was** / **were** the tourists' favorite.
2. Restaurants that offer a fixed menu usually **has** / **have** lower prices.
3. The boat trips that include a visit to the island **costs** / **cost** a lot of money.
4. The people who are complaining about the flight **has lost** / **have lost** their baggage.
5. The train that stops at every station **doesn't arrive** / **don't arrive** until 11:00 p.m.
6. The gallery that displays the work of local artists **has been** / **have been** open for two years.

7. I have some friends who **travel** / **travels** for a month every summer.

8. The bus that stops in front of the hotel **go** / **goes** to the museum.

PRACTICE

7 Complete the sentences. Write all possible relative pronouns (*that, which,* and/or *who*). Use the simple present form of a verb from the box.

allow	attract	~~explain~~	have	live	offer	tell	visit

1. Have you found any information __that / which explains__ how Petra was built?
2. Do you know anyone ______________ in Jordan now? I need a contact there.
3. Places ______________ a lot of visitors are usually very busy on the weekends.
4. People ______________ ancient cities often learn a lot from historical tours.
5. During the holidays, it's difficult to find hotels ______________ cheap rates.
6. Sally needs a hotel ______________ guests to bring their pets.
7. Guides ______________ interesting stories are popular with tourists.
8. I want to stay in a hotel ______________ a swimming pool.

8 **PRONUNCIATION.** Read the chart and listen to the examples. Then complete the exercises.

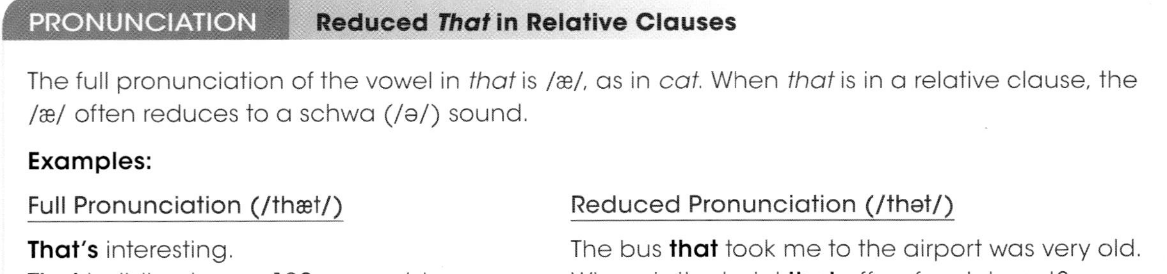
PRONUNCIATION **Reduced *That* in Relative Clauses**

The full pronunciation of the vowel in *that* is /æ/, as in *cat*. When *that* is in a relative clause, the /æ/ often reduces to a schwa (/ə/) sound.

CD3-23

Examples:

Full Pronunciation (/thæt/)	Reduced Pronunciation (/thət/)
That's interesting.	The bus **that** took me to the airport was very old.
That building is over 100 years old.	Where is the hotel **that** offers free Internet?

CD3-24

A Write the relative pronoun *that* in the correct place in each sentence. Then listen and check your answers. Notice the pronunciation of *that.*

1. I like visiting places ^that^ are warm, sunny, and relaxing.
2. I have friends don't like to fly.
3. I don't like guides talk all the time.

4. My friend likes trips allow plenty of time to shop.

5. I don't buy souvenirs break easily.

6. My classmate likes places aren't very crowded.

7. I like to stay in hotels have exercise rooms.

8. My mother likes to eat in restaurants have fixed menus.

REAL ENGLISH

That is more common than any other relative pronoun in conversation and informal situations.

B Rewrite the sentences from exercise **A** in your notebook. Change the words after *that*. Use information about yourself and people you know.

1. I like visiting places that have guided tours.

C Work with a partner. Share your sentences from exercise **B**. Pay attention to the pronunciation of *that*.

CD3-25 **9** **LISTEN** to the conversation about the World Cup in South Africa. Complete the conversation with the words you hear.

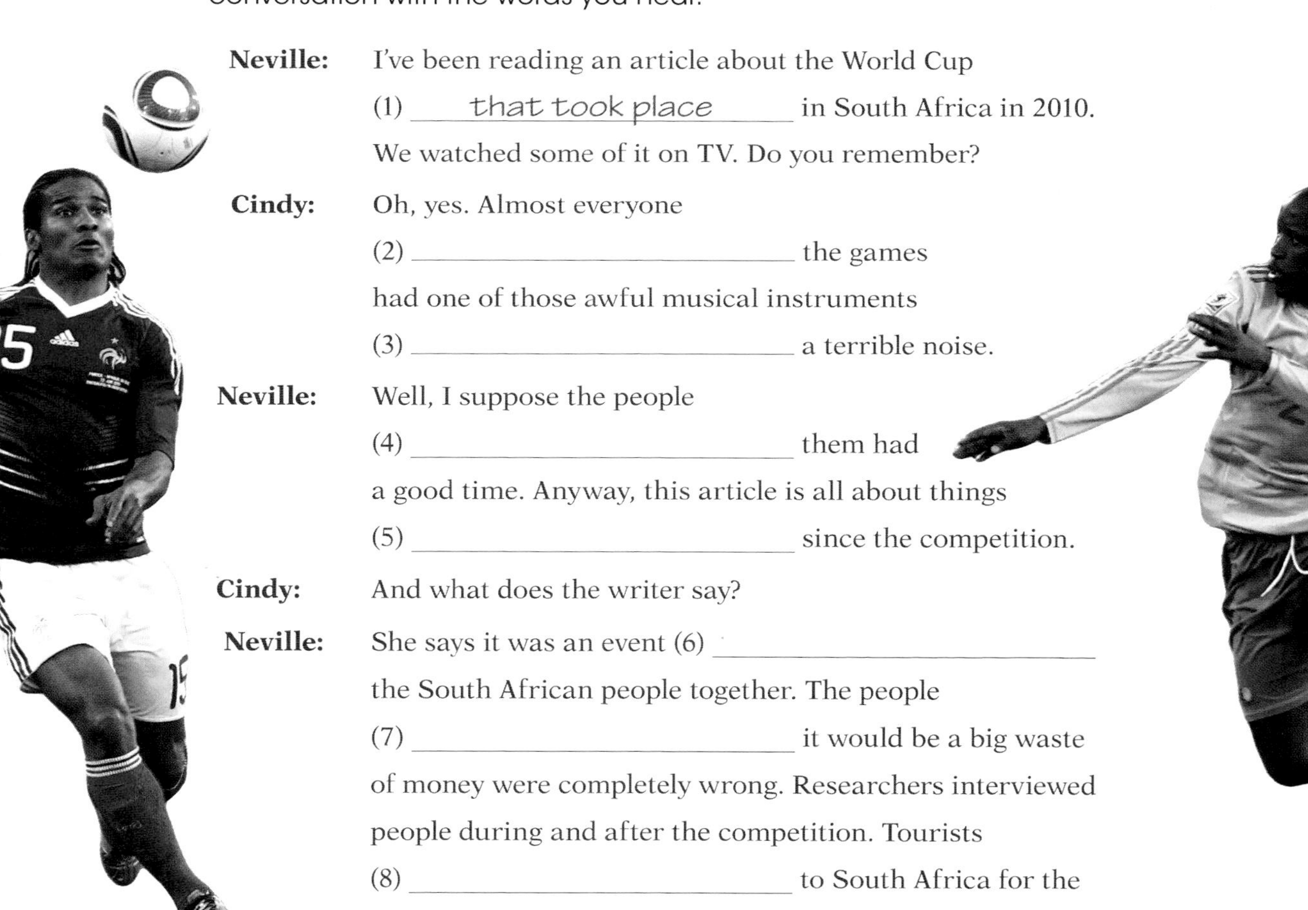

Neville: I've been reading an article about the World Cup (1) that took place in South Africa in 2010. We watched some of it on TV. Do you remember?

Cindy: Oh, yes. Almost everyone (2) __________ the games had one of those awful musical instruments (3) __________ a terrible noise.

Neville: Well, I suppose the people (4) __________ them had a good time. Anyway, this article is all about things (5) __________ since the competition.

Cindy: And what does the writer say?

Neville: She says it was an event (6) __________ the South African people together. The people (7) __________ it would be a big waste of money were completely wrong. Researchers interviewed people during and after the competition. Tourists (8) __________ to South Africa for the World Cup were very impressed, and most South Africans (9) __________ to the researchers were very proud of the way their country organized the Cup.

10 APPLY.

A Match each sentence in column **A** with the sentence from column **B** that defines the subject.

Column A	**Column B**
1. A vuvuzela is an instrument. b	a. It allows you to organize numbers or data.
2. Archaeologists are scientists. ____	~~b.~~ It is similar to a horn.
3. A magnifying glass is a tool. ____	c. It is cut from stone, wood, or another material.
4. Statisticians are scientists. ____	d. It makes small objects look bigger.
5. A carving is a piece of art. ____	e. They study historic places and objects.
6. A spreadsheet is a computer program. ____	f. They calculate and analyze numbers.

B Combine the two sentences you matched in exercise **A**. Make the second sentence a subject relative clause.

1. A vuvuzela is an instrument that is similar to a horn.
2. ______________________________
3. ______________________________
4. ______________________________
5. ______________________________
6. ______________________________

C In your notebook, write six sentences that define objects or jobs that you know about. Use subject relative clauses.

A doctor is someone who takes care of sick people.

D Work with a partner. Share your definitions from exercise **C** and let your partner guess which object or job you are defining.

A: *This is someone who takes care of sick people.*

B: *Is it a nurse? . . . A doctor?*

A: *Yes, it's a doctor. Now it's your turn.*

EXPLORE

CD3-26

1 READ the article about Lek Chailert. Notice the words in **bold**.

Lek Chailert and the Elephant Nature Park

The Elephant Nature Park is a rescue center that has taken care of sick elephants in northern Thailand since 1996. The park is in Chiang Mai Province, and the person who runs it is an extraordinary woman, Sangduen "Lek" Chailert.

Lek spent a lot of time with her grandfather as a child. He belonged to a tribe that lived in the forest. The time **that Lek spent with him** was very important to her. It helped her understand the wonders of nature. She created the Elephant Nature Park with her husband, Adam, and the organization has received international recognition.[1]

The elephants **that Lek rescues** come from all over Thailand. She often takes them from logging camps[2] when they are no longer useful. Others are sick, and some are elephants **which people have treated badly**. Lek's work also provides medical care for villagers who need it. The idea **Lek and her husband had** was to provide a safe place for elephants to live in peace. In fact, they are doing much, much more than that.

[1] **recognition:** praise and thanks for doing something good
[2] **logging camp:** a place where workers cut down trees and use elephants to move them

◀ Elephants that are born at the Elephant Nature Park will never have to work.

2 CHECK. Choose the correct answers.

1. What did Lek's grandfather help her do?

   a. create a park for elephants b. understand the natural world c. learn about his tribe

2. The Elephant Nature Park helps animals from ____________________.

   a. Chiang Mai Province only b. northern Thailand only c. all parts of Thailand

3. Some elephants at the park ____________________.

   a. are useful at logging camps b. were treated badly c. came from the Middle East

4. When does Lek take elephants from logging camps?

   a. when they can't work anymore b. when they are sick c. when they behave badly

5. What is the main purpose of the Elephant Nature Park?

   a. to teach people about elephants b. to check on logging camps c. to take care of elephants

3 DISCOVER. Complete the exercises to learn about the grammar in this lesson.

A Read the sentence. Then choose the two ideas it tells us about Lek and the elephants at the Elephant Nature Park.

The elephants that Lek rescues come from all over Thailand.

a. Lek comes from Thailand.

b. The elephants come from Thailand.

c. Lek rescues the elephants.

B Look at the sentence in exercise **A**. What is different about the word that comes after *that* in this clause and the word that comes after the relative pronoun in a subject relative clause? Discuss your answer with your classmates and teacher.

◄ Asian elephants at the Elephant Nature Park, Chiang Mai, Thailand

LEARN

11.3 Object Relative Clauses

After the Main Clause	Within the Main Clause
He is the doctor. You saw <u>him</u> last week. He is the doctor **who you saw last week**. (Object Relative Clause)	The house is blue. She bought <u>it</u>. The house **that she bought** is blue. (Object Relative Clause)

1. **Remember:** A sentence with a relative clause combines two sentences or ideas. In an object relative clause, the relative pronoun (*that, which, who,* or *whom*) is the object of the clause. The relative pronoun is followed by a subject and a verb.	The man is Vietnamese. You met him. The man **that you met** is Vietnamese. (Object Relative Clause)
2. Use *who, whom,* or *that* for people. Use *that* or *which* for places, things, and animals.	That is the woman **who / whom / that** I met last week. The book **that / which** I'm reading now is very good.
3. The subject and verb in an object relative clause agree.	I like the work **that she does**. (she = Subject, does = Verb) I like the work **that they do**. (they = Subject, do = Verb)
4. Do not repeat the object in an object relative clause.	✓ She has a job **that she loves**. ✗ She has a job that she loves <u>it</u>.

4 Complete the sentences. Write all possible relative pronouns (*that, which, who,* or *whom*) and the simple present form of the verb in parentheses.

1. The elephants ___that / which___ logging camps ___use___ (use) work very hard.
2. Many of the loggers ______________ Lek ______________ (meet) are concerned about their elephants.
3. Some of the elephants ______________ Lek ______________ (help) come from logging camps.
4. The forests of northern Thailand are not a place ______________ many tourists ______________ (visit).
5. The problems ______________ Lek and her team sometimes ______________ (find) are very serious.
6. The people ______________ the park ______________ (hire) all care about animals a lot.
7. The international recognition ______________ Lek ______________ (receive) regularly is helpful to the park.
8. Lek Chailert is a person ______________ I ______________ (admire).

11.4 Object Relative Clauses without Relative Pronouns

	Object Relative Clause			
	Object Relative Pronoun	Subject	Verb	
The people		I	**met**	were on the tour.
The film		we	**watched**	was about Indonesia.

1. The object relative pronoun (*that, which, who,* or *whom*) is often omitted from object relative clauses.	She is wearing a ring ~~**that**~~ **I like**. She is wearing a ring **I like**.
2. **Remember:** Do not omit the subject relative pronoun (*that, which,* or *who*) from subject relative clauses.	✓ I know a man **who owns ten cars**. ✗ I know a man owns ten cars.

5 Underline the object relative clause in each sentence. Then cross out the object relative pronoun.

1. Jan Peng is an elephant ~~that~~ people treated badly.
2. Jan Peng worked in a camp that loggers built.
3. The trees which Jan Peng moved were large and very heavy.
4. As Jan Peng got older, the work that she was doing became too hard for her.
5. The people whom Lek interviewed about Jan Peng promised not to make her work again.
6. Jan Peng seemed afraid when she had to go with people that she did not know.
7. The team members that Lek brought to the logging camp took good care of Jan Peng.
8. Jan Peng liked the new home that Lek and her team provided for her.

6 Complete the object relative clause in each sentence. Write all possible relative pronouns (*that, which, who, whom,* or *Ø* for no relative pronoun).

1. The book ___that / which / Ø___ I am reading now is about Laos.
2. The animals ______________ you see in zoos sometimes look sad.
3. The woman ______________ we interviewed for the job last week works at a hospital.
4. Some animals ______________ people keep as pets are dangerous.
5. The singer ______________ I saw on the street has a great voice.
6. The man ______________ we asked for directions was very helpful.
7. The doctor ______________ I saw last week was very good.
8. The article ______________ he wrote was about nature parks.

PRACTICE

7 Underline the object relative clause in the sentences. Cross out the relative pronoun when possible.

1. The notebook ~~that~~ I lost had important information in it.
2. The person that I talked to on the phone was rude to me.
3. The car that my sister bought is easy to drive.
4. Most of the people who I met on vacation speak German.
5. The doctor whom I called is not taking new patients.
6. The song which Alan was singing was beautiful.
7. The report that I'm writing is really difficult.
8. Do you have a map of the city that I can use?
9. Have you seen the books that I left on the table?
10. Meryl Streep is an actress whom I would like to meet.

8 LISTEN & SPEAK.

CD3-27-28

A Look at the photos and read the captions. Then listen to two students talk about the photos. Take notes below each photo.

Photo 1

▲ A traditional fisherman rows his boat on Inle Lake, Myanmar.

Photo 2

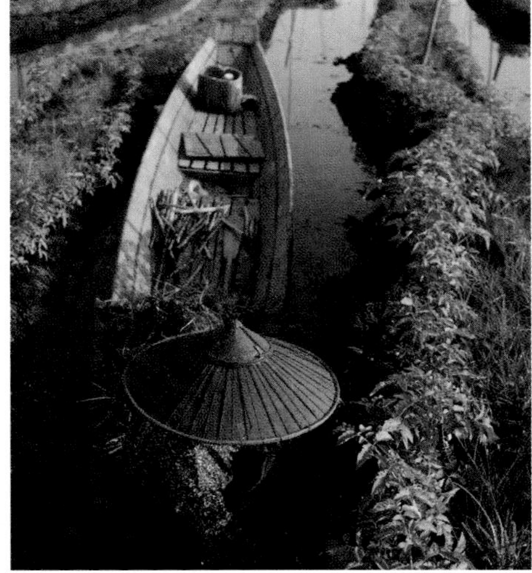

▲ A floating garden on the surface of Inle Lake, Myanmar

B Work with a partner. Compare your notes from exercise **A**.

CD3-27-28

C Read the pairs of sentences about the photos from exercise **A**. Then choose the sentence that gives the correct description of each photo. Use your notes to help you. Then listen again and check your answers.

Photo 1:

1. a. The photo the photographer bought looks like a ballet.
   (b.) The photo the photographer took looks like a ballet.
2. a. The technique the fisherman is using looks very difficult.
   b. The technique the photographer is using looks very difficult.
3. a. The boats the fisherman use are long and narrow.
   b. The boats the fishermen sell are long and narrow.
4. a. One challenge the fishermen have on Inle Lake is seeing over the tall plants.
   b. One challenge the photographers have on Inle Lake is seeing over the tall plants.

Photo 2:

5. a. The boats the local people build are made of wood and bamboo.
   b. The houses the local people build are made of wood and bamboo.
6. a. The farms the local people run produce enough food to live on.
   b. The farms the local people run produce enough food to sell in the city.
7. a. The fish they put in the lake are called Inle carp.
   b. The fish they catch from the lake are called Inle carp.
8. a. The fruits and vegetables the farmers grow come from floating gardens on the lake.
   b. The fruits and vegetables the farmers buy come from floating gardens on the lake.

D Work with a partner. Use relative clauses to tell your partner about one of the photos from exercise **A** on page 305. Use your notes from exercise **A** to help you.

The photo I'm looking at is of a fisherman on Inle Lake in Myanmar.

9 **EDIT.** Read the excerpts from a travel brochure. Find and correct five more errors with object relative clauses.

Kyoto

Kyoto was the capital of Japan for over a thousand years. It is a city which visitors find ~~it~~ fascinating.[1] In the eastern part of the city, there are many temples and gardens who you can see on a short walk. The Golden Pavilion is a beautiful building you can visit it in the northwestern hills. Another wonderful building in the center of town is Nijō-jō. This is a famous palace[2] whom every visitor wants to see.

[1] **fascinating:** very interesting
[2] **palace:** a large house that is the home of a very important person

Kuala Lumpur

The Malaysian capital, Kuala Lumpur (or "KL"), has changed a lot in the last 50 years. The historic buildings whom you can visit in Kuala Lumpur are now mixed with modern skyscrapers[1] such as the Petronas Towers. KL is a busy but friendly place, and the different cultures that you can experience them will make your visit fun.

[1] **skyscraper:** a very tall building

10 APPLY.

A Complete the sentences. Write a main clause for each object relative clause. Write true statements about yourself.

1. The last place I visited on vacation was Washington DC .
2. ______ I bought last week ______ .
3. ______ I admire most ______ .
4. ______ I met last year ______ .
5. ______ I really enjoyed ______ .
6. ______ I am looking at right now ______ .
7. ______ I owned as a child ______ .
8. ______ I called on the phone ______ .

B Work with a partner. Share your sentences from exercise **A**. Ask and answer follow-up questions.

A: *The last place I visited on vacation was Washington, DC.*

B: *How was it?*

A: *It was beautiful! Spring is the best time to visit.*

EXPLORE

CD3-29

1 READ the article about cyclists from the Isle of Man. Notice the words in **bold**.

Cycling and the Isle of Man

The Isle of Man is a small island between Great Britain and Ireland. The geography of the Isle of Man is perfect for cycling. Riding on the hills and valleys helps cyclists develop the strength **they are looking for**.

In 2011, a cyclist from the island, Mark Cavendish, became the World Road Race champion.[1] He also won several races in the famous *Tour de France*. Cavendish is an exciting cyclist **whose name is well known on the island**. He's the cyclist **everyone is talking about** now, but he's not the first to come from the island.

Rob Holden is another champion cyclist from the island. "The roads over here are difficult to ride," says Holden. "You do need to be tough."

There has been at least one successful cyclist from the island in each decade[2] since the 1950s. For an island **whose population is under 90,000**, this is an incredible[3] success story.

[1] **champion:** someone who wins an important competition
[2] **decade:** a period of ten years
[3] **incredible:** difficult or impossible to believe

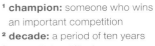

▲ Two mountain bikers descend toward Port Erin on the Isle of Man.

2 CHECK. Read the statements below. Circle **T** for *true* or **F** for *false*. Then correct the false statements to make them true.

1. The Isle of Man is between Great Britain and ~~Scotland~~ Ireland. **T** **F**
2. The Isle of Man has hills and valleys. **T** **F**
3. The roads on the Isle of Man help cyclists become strong. **T** **F**
4. Mark Cavendish became the World Road Race champion in 2012. **T** **F**
5. The population of the Isle of Man is more than 90,000. **T** **F**

3 DISCOVER. Complete the exercises to learn about the grammar in this lesson.

A Find these sentences in the article from exercise **1**. Write the missing words.

1. Riding on the hills and valleys helps cyclists develop the strength **they are looking** _____.
2. Mark Cavendish is the cyclist **everyone is talking** ____________ now.

B Look at the words you wrote in exercise **A**. Choose the correct word to complete the statement below.

These words are ____________. a. objects b. prepositions c. articles

11.5 Object Relative Clauses with Prepositions

	Object Relative Clause			
	Object Relative Pronoun	Subject	Verb + Preposition	
Did you find the book	**that / which / -**	**you**	**were looking for**?	
The man	**that / who / whom / -**	**she**	**spoke with**	is my boss.

1. A relative pronoun (*that, which, who,* or *whom*) can be the object of a preposition. The preposition usually comes after the verb in an object relative clause.	The people were customers. I met **with them.** Preposition Object The people **that I met with** were customers. Object Verb Preposition
2. **Remember:** The object relative pronoun is often omitted in conversation and informal writing.	The people ~~**who**~~ **I met with** were customers. The people **I met with** were customers. The pen ~~**that**~~ **I'm looking for** is blue. The pen **I'm looking for** is blue.
3. In formal English, the preposition can come at the beginning of the object relative clause before *whom* (for people) or *which* (for things).	The person **to whom we spoke** was helpful. The job **for which I applied** was new.
4. Do not use a preposition before *who* or *that.*	✓ The person **to whom** we spoke was helpful. ✗ The person to who you spoke is not here today. ✓ The job **for which** I applied was new. ✗ The job for that I applied was new.

4 Complete the sentences with an object relative clause. Use the words in parentheses. Only use a relative pronoun if one is given. More than one form of the verb may be correct.

1. Susanne enjoyed the race ___that she rode in___ (that / she / ride in) yesterday.
2. The sport ______________________ (that / Roberto / be / most interested in) is cycling.
3. The person ______________________ (whom / you / look for) is not in the office today.
4. Who are the students ______________________ (you / be friends with)?
5. Who was the woman ______________________ (Valerie / talk to) when we saw her this morning?
6. What's the name of the company ______________________ (your brother / work for) now?
7. The dress ______________________ (which / Sue / decide on) was very expensive.
8. He's the uncle ______________________ (I / not speak to) for many years.
9. Did you like the people ______________________ (you / work with) at your old job?
10. This is the article ______________________ (that / we / talk about) last week.

11.6 Relative Clauses with *Whose*

1. Use *whose* + noun at the beginning of a relative clause to show possession. *Whose* replaces a possessive adjective or a possessive noun (*his, her, their, its, Sam's,* etc.). *Whose* + noun can be the subject or the object of the relative clause.	The author writes beautifully. Her book won the award. The author **whose book won the award** writes beautifully. Subject Relative Clause She's the author. I just bought her book. She's the author **whose book I just bought**. Object Relative Clause
2. *Whose* can be used for people, places, animals, and things. A noun always follows *whose*.	That's the bakery. We love its cakes. That's the bakery **whose cakes we love**. Object Relative Clause
3. *Whose* often comes after *someone, anyone, no one,* and *everyone*.	She is someone **whose work interests me**. I don't know anyone **whose job involves travel**.
4. **Remember:** Do not repeat the subject or object in a relative clause.	✓ She is the artist **whose paintings are in the gallery**. ✗ She is the artist whose paintings they are in the gallery. ✓ The artist **whose painting I bought** is from Russia. ✗ The artist whose painting I bought it is from Russia.

5 Read the pairs of sentences. Circle the possessive adjective or possessive noun that the word *whose* in sentence b replaces.

1. a. Cavendish is an exciting cyclist. (His) success is not new to the island.
   b. Cavendish is an exciting cyclist **whose** success is not new to the island.
2. a. Sprinters are cyclists. Their job is to ride fast at the end of races.
   b. Sprinters are cyclists **whose** job is to ride fast at the end of races.
3. a. The cyclist lost the race. His bike wasn't working properly.
   b. The cyclist **whose** bike wasn't working properly lost the race.
4. a. The cycling team won the race. We saw the team's leader on TV.
   b. The cycling team **whose** leader we saw on TV won the race.
5. a. Is this the new bike shop? Was the bike shop's ad on the radio yesterday?
   b. Is this the new bike shop **whose** ad was on the radio yesterday?
6. a. I met a woman today. Her daughter works with my brother.
   b. I met a woman today **whose** daughter works with my brother.
7. a. We received a nice letter from the woman. We found her cat.
   b. We received a nice letter from the woman **whose** cat we found.
8. a. My sister has a dog. Its favorite food is ice cream.
   b. My sister has a dog **whose** favorite food is ice cream.

PRACTICE

6 Complete the sentences. Write a relative clause with a preposition or with *whose*.

1. The professor just walked in. You need his signature.

   The professor ___whose signature you need___ just walked in.

2. Steven Spielberg is a film producer. His movies have made millions of dollars.

   Steven Spielberg is a film producer ________________________________.

3. There's the school. My son goes to it.

   There's the school ________________________________.

4. Helen has a pet bird. Its name is Freddy.

   Helen has a pet bird ________________________________.

5. The salesperson was very helpful. Marianne spoke to her.

   The salesperson ________________________________ was very helpful.

6. The student gets sick a lot. Her mother is a doctor.

   The student ________________________________ gets sick a lot.

7. We had fun at the party. We went to it last night.

   We had fun at the party ________________________________.

8. The people are very nice. Lucy works with them.

   The people ________________________________ are very nice.

7 WRITE & SPEAK.

A Write an object relative clause with a preposition. Use the words in parentheses and an appropriate verb form. More than one verb form may be correct.

1. The sport ___Tim is interested in___ (Tim / be interested in) is hockey.
2. I haven't seen the movie ________________ (you / talk about) yesterday.
3. The job ________________ (you / apply for) last week involves a lot of travel.
4. That's the place ________________ (we / travel to) on vacation last year.
5. Everyone ________________ (we / speak to) complained about the terrible weather.

B Complete the relative clauses with your own ideas.

1. I have a good friend whose house ___is near the railroad station___.
2. I'd like to join a gym whose members ________________________.
3. The musician whose music I like the most is ________________________.
4. Anyone whose English isn't very good ________________________.
5. I know someone whose family ________________________.

8 EDIT. Read the information about the Vikings of northern Europe. Find and correct five more errors with relative clauses.

The Vikings

▲ A painting of a Viking ship from Greenland approaching Newfoundland

The people that we think of ~~them~~ as Vikings were not in fact one group of people. They were different groups of people whose native countries they were in southern Scandinavia. The areas that they lived in them are now called Norway, Sweden, and Denmark.

In addition to the violence that they are famous for it, the Vikings were explorers whose love of the sea everyone know about. The Vikings were great travelers and traders. They sailed their small wooden ships as far as Russia to the east and North Africa to the south. They were also the first Europeans to reach America. The Vikings even settled for a short time in an area who Norse name was *Vinland*. Its modern name is Newfoundland, Canada.

[1] **colony:** a country or area that is ruled by another country

9 APPLY.

A In your notebook, write five questions using the ideas in the box or your own ideas. Use relative clauses.

a musician or artist whose work you admire	something you are planning on
a restaurant whose food you enjoy	an interesting place you have been to
someone whose personality you like	a topic you know a lot about

Who's a musician or artist whose work you admire?

B Work with a partner. Take turns asking and answering your questions from exercise **A**. Use relative clauses in your conversation.

A. *Who's a musician whose work you admire?*

B. *Well, one musician whose work I have always admired is Baaba Maal.*

A. *I haven't heard of him. Where is he from?*

Review the Grammar UNIT 11

Charts 11.1–11.6

1 Combine the two sentences. Write one sentence with a relative clause.

1. These are the photos. My son took them on our vacation.
   These are the photos that my son took on our vacation.
2. That's the ancient building. I visited it yesterday.
   That's the ancient building ______.
3. The job was in Mexico City. Stefan applied for it.
   The job ______.
4. That's the man. I found his wallet.
   That's the man ______.
5. The TV show is about an archaeologist. She travels all over the world.
   The TV show is about an archaeologist ______.
6. We took a bus tour on Saturday. It was wonderful.
   The bus tour ______.
7. There's the museum. Our guide told us about it yesterday.
   There's the museum ______.
8. I bought some souvenirs for my family. They weren't very expensive.
   The souvenirs ______.

Charts 11.1–11.5

2 EDIT & SPEAK.

A Read the paragraph about Tanzania. Find and correct six more errors with relative clauses.

My country Tanzania

I come from the Tanga region of Tanzania, Africa. It is a place that is full of history and beauty. Tanga has many tourist destinations[1] such as Mount Kilimanjaro that is famous around the world. People whom go to see this mountain will never forget it. There are guides which take people up the mountain. These trips can be dangerous, so only people that they are physically fit should try to climb to the top of the mountain. Another place is Zanzibar. This is a group of islands became famous for its spices. These days, Zanzibar's economy depends more on tourism than on spices. The Serengeti National Park also attracts a lot of tourists. Here you can go on safari and see the many amazing animals live there.

[1] **destination:** a place that people go to or are going to

B Work with a partner. Use subject or object relative clauses to talk about three places in your city or country. Use the paragraph in exercise **A** as a model.

I come from Peru. It's a beautiful country that has a lot of interesting things to see. For example, . . .

Charts 11.1–11.6

CD3-30

3 LISTEN & SPEAK.

A Listen to the radio show. Complete the conversation with the relative clauses you hear.

▼ Hot-air balloon tours are the perfect way to see Cappadocia, Turkey.

Brian: Good evening, everyone. Brian Evans here with another vacation report. This week I'm in Cappadocia, Turkey, talking with some brave tourists about balloon rides. So, let's say hi to Scott from Toronto and Julie from Boston. Julie, tell us about your experience. How was the balloon ride (1) ______________________________ ?

Julie: Oh, it was incredible, Brian! The balloon was huge and so colorful. The other people (2) ______________________________ with me were really friendly and from all over the world. It was an experience (3) ______________________________ ! The views were amazing!

Brian: Well, that's one satisfied customer! Now, Scott, what did you think about the company (4) ______________________________ to go with?

Scott: Well, the pilot (5) ______________________________ our balloon was excellent, and we had a guide (6) ______________________________ from New Zealand, so his English was great.

Brian: Great! Any final words?

Julie: Yes! If you're a person (7) ______________________________ travel and photography, you'll love Cappadocia! I hope the photos (8) ______________________________ are half as beautiful as the real thing.

Brian: OK, there we have it. Thanks, and enjoy the rest of your vacation.

B Work in a small group. What kinds of activities do you like to do on vacation? Discuss your answers with your group.

Connect the Grammar to Writing

1 READ & NOTICE THE GRAMMAR.

A How do you treat a cold? Discuss your ideas with a partner. Then read the essay.

COLD TREATMENTS AROUND THE WORLD

How do you treat a cold? I asked people from all over the world this question. They had many different answers.

The first group of treatments I learned about is made up of drinks. I spoke with a neighbor who is from Italy. She makes a tea that has sage and bay leaves in it. A Native American tea that my friend Deedee drinks is made from herbs and honey. A classmate whose grandparents are from Turkey also drinks tea with herbs and honey when he has a cold.

The second group of treatments consists of different kinds of food. My neighbor Wu from China eats a hot rice cereal she calls *jook*. The chicken soup that my friend Jason's grandfather from Hungary makes works well for him. The person whose remedy was most unusual was my friend Ray from Hawaii. He chews the bark[1] of a tree that grows there.

The last group of treatments involves activities. For example, some people I know sit in a room full of steam or take a hot shower. Some people put a hot stone on the place that hurts them. And sitting or lying in the sun is a remedy that many people use, too.

[1] **bark:** the skin of a tree

GRAMMAR FOCUS

In the essay in exercise **A,** the writer uses relative clauses to describe nouns.

I spoke with a neighbor ***who is from Italy.***

He chews the bark of a tree ***that grows there.***

B Read the essay in exercise **A** again. Underline the relative clauses and draw an arrow from each clause to the noun it describes. Then work with a partner and compare your answers.

C In the text in exercise **A**, the writer first tells us the topic of the essay. Then she names three groups within this topic and gives examples for each group. Complete the chart on page 317 with information from the essay.

Topic: Cold Treatments around the World		
Group 1: drinks	Group 2:	Group 3:
Examples: tea with sage/bay leaves	Examples:	Examples:

2 BEFORE YOU WRITE.

A Work with a partner. Make a list of topics that include groups or categories.

B Choose one of the topics on your list from exercise **A** and complete the chart below with your ideas. Use the chart from exercise **1C** as a model.

Topic: ______________________		
Group 1:	Group 2:	Group 3:
Examples:	Examples:	Examples:

3 WRITE a classification essay about your topic. Write one paragraph that introduces your topic and one paragraph for each of the groups within this topic. Use the information in your chart in exercise **2B** and the essay in exercise **1A** to help you.

WRITING FOCUS Using Transition Words

Writers use transition words to lead their readers from one idea to the next. In a classification essay, the transition words *the first, the second*, and *the last* are often used.

The first *group of cures I learned about is made up of drinks.*
The second *group of treatments I learned about consists of different kinds of food.*
The last *group of treatments involves activities.*

4 SELF ASSESS. Read your classification essay. Underline the relative clauses. Then use the checklist to assess your work.

- ☐ I used subject relative clauses correctly. [11.1-11.2]
- ☐ I used object relative clauses correctly. [11.2-11.3]
- ☐ I used object relative clauses with prepositions correctly. [11.5]
- ☐ I used relative clauses with *whose* correctly. [11.6]
- ☐ I used transition words to lead my readers from one idea to the next. [WRITING FOCUS]

UNIT 12 Art and Music

Modals: Part 1

▼ Musicians in an alley covered with graffiti, São Paulo, Brazil

EXPLORE

CD3-31

1 READ the article about an artist who uses unusual material to create art. Notice the words in **bold**.

The Art of Trash

The famous French artist Edgar Degas said, "Art is not what you see, but what you make others see." In other words, art is not just something nice for you to look at. Art **is able to change** your beliefs, and maybe even your behavior.

German artist HA Schult agrees. For about four decades, Schult's art has helped to create an awareness[1] about society's wasteful consumerism.[2] One of his best-known works, *Trash People*, is an example. One thousand life-size human figures, all made of trash, make up *Trash People*. Since the 1990s, Schult has installed[3] these figures in several places around the world. Unlike many sculptors—who typically use stone, metal, or wood—his figures are made of old cans, electronics, and other kinds of everyday trash. His message is clear: people are too wasteful.

In 1999, people **were able to view** these figures in Red Square in Moscow. In 2001, visitors to the Great Wall of China **could see** them. From there, they traveled to the Pyramids of Giza in Egypt and many other places around the world. At first, some people **couldn't understand** his ideas. All they **could see** was trash. However, years later, you **can** still **find** Schult's army of trash people. If you **aren't able to see** them in person, you **can learn** a lot about them online. What do you think? Is his army winning the war?

[1] **awareness:** understanding
[2] **consumerism:** the act of spending money on goods and services
[3] **install:** to put together, put in place

▼ HA Schult's *Trash People* (2014)

2 CHECK. Circle the correct answer to complete each statement.

1. According to HA Schult, the purpose of art is to **please people** / **change people's behavior**.
2. One **hundred** / **thousand** life-size figures make up *Trash People*.
3. Schult wants people to think more about being **less wasteful** / **more creative** with trash.
4. *Trash People* is **not** / **still** traveling around the world now.

3 DISCOVER. Complete the exercises to learn about the grammar in this lesson.

A Find these sentences in the article from exercise **1**. Write the missing words.

1. Art is able to change your beliefs, and maybe even your behavior.
2. In 1999, people ______________ these figures in Red Square in Moscow.
3. In 2001, visitors to the Great Wall of China ______________ them.
4. At first, some people ______________ his ideas.
5. If you ______________ them in person, you ______________ a lot about them online.

B Write the phrases you wrote in exercise **A** in the correct place in the chart.

	Present or Future	Past
Affirmative	is able to change	
Negative		

LEARN

12.1 Ability: *Can* and *Could*

Statements			
Subject	Modal (*Not*)	Base Form	
I You She They	can can't	paint	with watercolors.
	could couldn't	speak	before the age of three.

Yes/No and *Wh-* Questions				
Wh- Word	Modal	Subject	Base Form	
	Can	Lisa	**sing**?	
	Could	you	**see**	the stage last night?
What	**can**	babies	**say**	at age one?
When	**could**	you	**speak**	English well?

Short Answers
Yes, she **can**.
No, I **couldn't**.
Not much.
A few years ago.

1. *Can* and *could* are modals. Modals add meaning to a verb. Use the base form of a verb after affirmative and negative forms of modals.	We **can watch** TV when we finish dinner. You **can't see** the board. Maybe you need glasses. They **couldn't find** the museum, so they came home.
2. Modals do not change form. Do not add *-s/-es* to the end of modals.	✓They **can see** the movie tomorrow. ✗ She cans see the sign.
3. To form questions, put the modal before the subject. Do not use *do/does*.	✓**Can** you **understand** me? ✗ Do you can understand me?
4. To form negatives, use *not* after the modal. Do not use a form of *do*.	✓He **couldn't understand** the teacher today. ✗ He didn't could understand the teacher today.
5. Use *can* to express ability or possibility in the present or future.	Larissa **can play** the violin beautifully. She **can sing** for us tomorrow night.
6. Use *could* to talk about ability in the past.	Jon **could paint** very well when he was young.

4 Complete the conversation. Use *can (not)* or *could (not)* and the words in parentheses.

1. HA Schult ___can create___ (create) beautiful art from trash.
2. ___Can we see___ (we / see) the exhibit today?
3. Beethoven ___Could not hear___ (not hear) well, but he ___could create___ (create) beautiful music.
4. Tim and Ria ___could not discuss___ (not discuss) modern art until they took an art history class. Now they ___can talk___ (talk) about different artists and movements.
5. Some people ___can not understand___ (not understand) modern art.
6. A: ___Could van Gogh write___ (van Gogh / write) beautiful music?
   B: No, but he ___could paint___ (paint) amazing pictures.

REAL ENGLISH

There are three correct ways to write *can* + *not*: *can not, cannot,* and *can't.*

7. A: What could da Vinci do (da Vinci / do) well?
   B: He could do (do) everything well!
8. Where can I buy (I / buy) guitar strings around here?

5 PRONUNCIATION. Read the chart and listen to the examples. Then complete the exercises.

PRONUNCIATION ***Can* and *Can't***

In affirmative statements and questions, the /æ/ sound in *can* is reduced to a schwa (/ə/) sound. In negative statements and short answers, the /æ/ sound is fully pronounced.

CD3-32

Examples:

I **can hear** you.	I /kən/ hear you.	**Can** you **see** me?	/kən/ you see me?
I **can't see** you.	I /kænt/ see you.	Yes, I **can**.	Yes, I /kæn/.

CD3-33

A Listen to these students. Write *can* or *can't*.

1. My teacher ________________ draw very well.
2. I ________________ understand modern art.
3. My friends and I ________________ get together often.
4. I ________________ speak more than one foreign language.
5. In my opinion, art ________________ change how people think.

B Work with a partner. Read the sentences in exercise **A** to your partner but say *can* or *can't* depending on what is true for you.

My teacher can't draw very well.

▶ HA Schult exhibition, *Under the Pyramids*, Egypt, 2002

12.2 Ability: *Be Able To*

Statements				
Subject	*Be*	*(Not) Able To*	Base Form	
I	am was	able to not able to	attend understand	the performance. the presenter very well.
You We	are were			
He She	is was			

1. You can also use *be (not) able to* + a base form of a verb to express ability.	They'**re able to read** the Chinese text. **I'm not able to hear** the speaker.
2. *Be able to* has the same general meaning as *can*, but it can be used in different past, present, and future verb forms.	We **were able to watch** the show recently. She **isn't going to be able to finish** the class. He'**ll be able to stay** until Friday.
3. Use *will be able to* for a future ability that will be new or learned; do not use *can*.	✓ We'**ll be able to speak** French after the course. ✗ We can speak French after the course.
If the ability is true or possible now, use *can* or *will be able to*.	I **can meet** you after work. I'**ll be able to meet** you after work.
4. **Remember:** To form *Yes/No* questions with *be*, put the form of *be* before the subject.	**Is** she **able to talk** now? **Were** you **able to finish** the project?
To form *Wh-* questions, put the *Wh*-word + a form of *be* before the subject.	**What are** you **able to see**? **Why wasn't** she **able to go**?

6 Complete the sentences. Use the correct present, past, or future form of *be able to* or *be not able to*.

1. Art is not what you see; it is what you __are able to__ make other people see.
2. The artist hopes his new painting __is able to__ bring attention to the problem of poverty.
3. A: What __are__ songwriters __able__ do with a three-minute song?
   B: They __are able__ make people think and feel strong emotions.
4. Beethoven __wasn't able to__ hear, but he __was able to__ create beautiful music.
5. Because of computers, artists of the future __will be able to__ work in new ways.
6. The lead actor is in the hospital, so he __isn't able to__ appear in tonight's performance.
7. The director's last movie __was able to__ influence people's opinions about the horrors of war.
8. Nowadays, people __was able to__ see operas in movie theaters for a low price. Before, many people __weren't able to__ experience them because they were so expensive.

9. After I return from my year in France, I ______________ speak French and discuss art.

10. Now he has his own piano, so he ______________ practice a lot more.

12.3 Past Ability: *Could* and *Was/Were Able To*

Could (Not)	*Was/Were (Not) Able To*
She **could walk** before she was one.	She **was able to walk** before she was one.
We **couldn't dance** before we took the class.	We **weren't able to dance** before we took the class.
A: **Could** you **draw** well as a child?	A: **Was** she **able to draw** well as a child?
B: Yes, I **could**. / No, I **couldn't**.	B: Yes, she **was**. / No, she **wasn't**.

1. Use both *was/were able to* and *could* to express general ability in the past.	Tara **could run** 10 miles when she was 20. As kids, we **were able to swim** every day.
2. Use *was/were able to* (but not *could*) to express ability related to one event in the past.	✓ She **was able to finish** the project last night. ✗ She could finish the project last night.
3. *Could* can be used to express ability related to one event in the past with: a. verbs of perception (*see, hear, understand*) b. negative forms (*couldn't*)	a. I **could understand** yesterday's lecture. b. She **couldn't finish** the project last night.

7 Circle all correct answers. Sometimes both answers are correct.

1. Nancy **was able to** / **could** sing beautifully as a child.
2. Patrice **wasn't able to** / **couldn't** go to the movies last night.
3. Bao **was able to** / **could** play the piano at the competition last year, but he **wasn't able to** / **couldn't** play in this year's competition.
4. A: **Were you able to** / **Could you** hear the speaker?

   B: No, I **wasn't** / **couldn't**.
5. George **was able to** / **could** buy a rare painting yesterday.
6. Most students **were able to** / **could** speak very well after the course.
7. When I turned ten, I **was able to** / **could** get my first laptop.
8. They **were able to** / **could** hear the doorbell even though the TV was very loud.
9. A: I need a few more tubes of this blue paint.

   B: Try the new art shop on Main Street. I **was able to** / **could** buy that color there last week.
10. I **wasn't able to** / **couldn't** finish my writing assignment during class. Luckily my teacher will let me finish it at home.

PRACTICE

8 Complete the first sentence with *can* or *could* and the verb in parentheses. Then rewrite the sentence using the correct form of *be able to*.

1. Chris ___can play___ (play) the piano fairly well.

   ___Chris is able to play the piano fairly well.___

2. My parents ________________ (not go) to the concert yesterday.

   ____

3. Tanya hasn't been practicing, so she ________________ (not dance) next week.

   ____

4. A: ________________ (you / understand) the actors last night?

   B: No, ________________

   A: ________________

   B: ________________

5. I ________________ (not find) the artist's biography on the website.

   ____

6. The children ________________ (finish) their paintings tomorrow.

   ____

7. The professor ________________ (not teach) the art class tomorrow.

   ____

8. I ________________ (not hear) the movie because people were talking.

   ____

9 **LISTEN & SPEAK.**

A Complete the conversation. Use a verb from the box with the correct form of *be able to*.

come	do	not get	relax
create	~~help~~	meet	not see

Director: Hi, Clare. I just got a call from Nomi, and she (1) ___isn't able to help___ us set up the art exhibit today. She's not feeling well. (2) ________________ you ________________ and help us?

Assistant: Sure, but I (3) ________________ there until around two o'clock this afternoon. Is that OK?

Director: Two is fine. We (4) ________________ a lot of work last night.

Assistant: Great. I'll see you then. By the way, who is the artist?

Director: His name is Yong Ho Ji.

Assistant: Oh, yes, I know his work. He (5) ______________ such amazing sculptures with those old car tires. I really look forward to seeing his work. I (6) ______________ his last exhibit because I was out of town. By the way, (7) ______________ I ______________ him? I'd love to ask him about his work.

Director: Sure. Once we set everything up, you (8) ______________ and enjoy the reception. I'll introduce you then.

CD3-34

B Listen and check your answers.

C **ANALYZE THE GRAMMAR.** Work with a partner. Change the answers in exercise **A** to *can* or *could*. Find and circle the one item that must use a form of *be able to*. Then practice the conversation twice: once more formally and once less formally. Pay attention to the pronunciation of *can/can't*.

Hi, Clare. I just got a call from Nomi, and she can't help us set up . . .

REAL ENGLISH

Be able to is often used in more formal conversations. *Can* is more common in everyday usage.

Hey Liz, I ***can't see*** *you.*
*Mr. Jones, I****'m not able to see*** *you.*

▼ Korean artist Yong Ho Ji uses recycled tires to create his sculptures. This photo is from an exhibit on endangered species.

10 EDIT. Read the passage from a podcast. Find and correct five more errors with *can (not)*, *could (not)*, and *was/were (not) able to* for ability.

ABOUT ART: Podcast 22

Host: Welcome to the Guggenheim Museum in New York. This is Ava Paterson, and I'm talking to visitors here about this week's question: Can art keeps us young? What do you think, sir? Are people able fight the effects of aging with creative activities?

Man: Yes, I think so. My grandfather was able to organize his thoughts easily, and he thought art helped him. He was a painter. A lot of older people have trouble with their memories. People with Alzheimer's disease[1] sometimes can't remember their own families, for example. My grandfather was 93 when he died, and he can remember absolutely everything! The last time I saw him, I could ask him many questions about his life.

Host: And what do you think, miss? Can art have positive effects on people as they age?

Woman: Well, research shows that people are able to live longer in the future, but is art the reason? I'm not sure. I like to believe that it can help. I love to see and create art, so I hope when I'm older, I will able to think clearly.

[1] **Alzheimer's disease:** a disease that causes a person to lose their memory

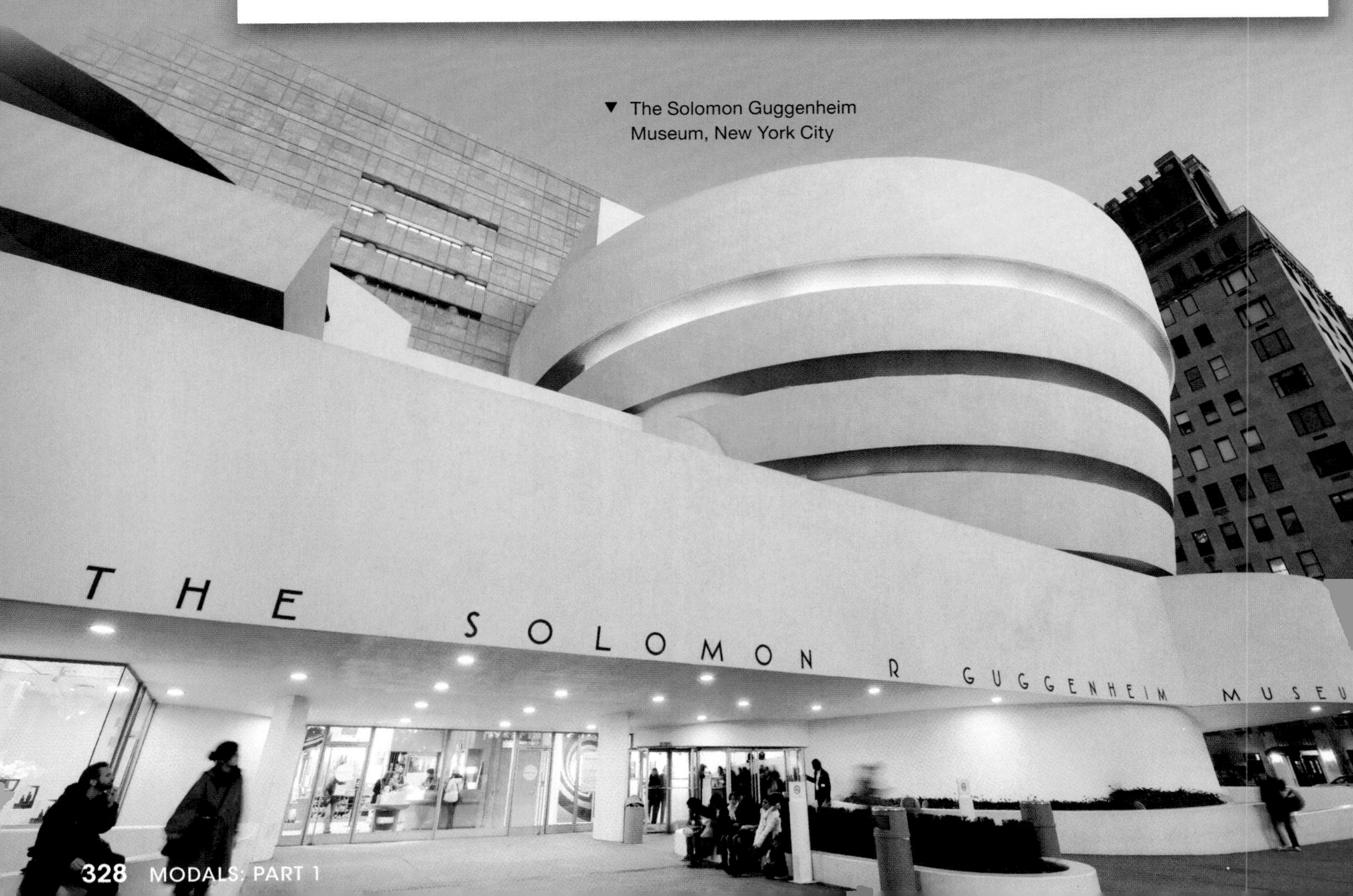

▼ The Solomon Guggenheim Museum, New York City

CD3-35

11 LISTEN.

Listen to the conversations. Circle **T** for *true* or **F** for *false*.

1. The woman was able to understand the actors. **T** **F**
2. The woman is able to go to the museum on Friday. **T** **F**
3. The man isn't able to decide. **T** **F**
4. The man thinks he could draw better as a child. **T** **F**
5. The woman was able to enjoy the ballet. **T** **F**
6. The woman was able to help the man with his photos. **T** **F**
7. The woman will be able to see the concert. **T** **F**
8. The man wasn't able to finish his art exam. **T** **F**

12 APPLY.

A Work with a partner. Discuss the situations in exercise **11** and the topics in the lesson where people talked about ability (or inability). Write as many situations or topics as you can remember in your notebook.

seeing art at a museum, famous people and their abilities

B Choose four of the situations. Write two sentences using past, present, or future forms of *can, could,* and *be able to* for ability.

1. Situation: looking at music videos online

   I could enjoy the music. I wasn't able to understand the words.

2. Situation: __________

3. Situation: __________

4. Situation: __________

C Share your sentences in a group. Be sure to ask follow-up questions.

A: *I was looking at a music video online the other day. I wanted to learn the words, but I couldn't understand the singer.*

B: *What band was it? Often you can find song lyrics online. Just do a search for "lyrics" and the name of the band.*

EXPLORE

CD3-36

1 **READ** about a popular new type of *old* music in Argentina. Notice the words in **bold**.

Old Meets New in Argentinian Music

Radio Host: Today's show is about a new form of Latin American music whose roots[1] are in traditional music. You **may be** familiar with *cumbia*, but do you know *nu-cumbia?* You **might not know** it now, but you will very soon. Before we play you some music, we'd like to take some calls from a few of our listeners. Jana in Dallas.

Jana: Thank you for taking my call. When I was younger, I lived in Colombia and studied the language and history. In a music class, I first heard about *cumbia*. *Nu-cumbia* **must be** amazing because *cumbia* itself is so good.

Radio Host: So what can you tell our guests about *cumbia*?

Jana: Well, it's a musical tradition that originated[2] in Colombia and Panama around 100 years ago. I think drums **might be** one of the main instruments. It has a great beat for dancing.

Radio Host: Thank you, Jana. That's right. *Cumbia* originated in Colombia and Panama, but its popularity has since spread all over Latin America. Recently, a new form of *cumbia*—called *nu-cumbia*—has been growing in popularity in Argentina's capital, Buenos Aires. Before we play you some of this fantastic music, we have another caller. Miro from Miami.

Miro: Hi. I'm a DJ and I just wanted to say that *nu-cumbia* is not only popular in Argentina. One woman in particular, La Yegros, has become a hit in many countries. Her music is a mix of electronic sounds and *cumbia*-style melodies. She is a great performer, too. I think with artists like her, *nu-cumbia* **may become** even bigger. Soon, it **could reach** a much larger audience.

[1] **root:** beginning, origin
[2] **originate:** to begin to happen

◀ A DJ in a popular night club in Palermo, Buenos Aires, Argentina

2 CHECK. Read the questions. Choose the correct answers.

1. Where did *cumbia* come from?
   a. Colombia and Panama
   b. Colombia and Argentina
2. When did *cumbia* start?
   a. recently
   b. 100 years ago
3. What is *nu-cumbia*?
   a. a new form of music
   b. a traditional dance
4. Who is La Yegros?
   a. a DJ from Miami
   b. a performer from Argentina

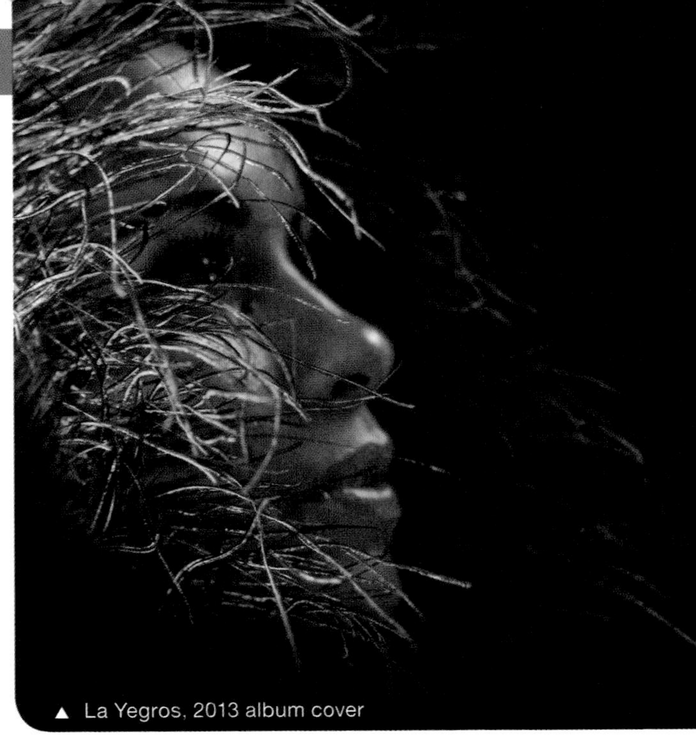

▲ La Yegros, 2013 album cover

3 DISCOVER. Complete the exercises to learn about the grammar in this lesson.

A Find these sentences in the interview from exercise **1**. Write the missing words.

1. You ________________ be familiar with *cumbia*, but do you know *nu-cumbia*?
2. You ________________ know it now, but you will very soon.
3. *Nu-cumbia* ________________ be amazing because *cumbia* itself is so good.
4. . . . *nu-cumbia* ________________ become even bigger.
5. Soon, it ________________ reach a much larger audience.

B Use the words you wrote in exercise **A** to complete the statements.

1. The speaker uses ________________, ________________, and ________________ to say something is (or isn't) possible. The speaker is not certain.
2. The speaker uses ________________ to say something is probably true.

LEARN

12.4 Possibility: *May, Might,* and *Could*

Weak Possibility or Certainty	Strong Possibility or Certainty
May (Not), Might (Not), and *Could*	*Couldn't*
The song **may become** a big hit. I don't know. We **might not go** to the show. We don't have tickets yet. He **could be** at lunch. I'm not sure. I'll check.	The song **couldn't become** a hit. It's terrible. He **couldn't be** at lunch. He's in a meeting.

1. Use *may (not), might (not),* or *could* with the base form of a verb to express weak possibility in the present or future. The speaker is not certain.	He **may like** rock music. I'm not sure. I **may not go** to the party. I **might stay** home. We **could go** to a movie instead, perhaps?
2. Do not contract *may not* or *might not.*	✓They **might not come** to the party. ✗ She mightn't call. She's been very busy.
3. **Remember:** *Could* is used for past ability as well as present and future possibility.	I **could climb** trees when I was young. We **could go** to the beach next weekend.
4. Use *could not/couldn't* when you are almost certain that an action or situation is not likely.	He **couldn't be** in Paris. He went to London. The baby **couldn't want** food. She just ate.
5. **Be careful!** Don't confuse *may be* and *maybe.* *Maybe* is an adverb and is usually at the beginning of a sentence.	✓They **may be** home. ✓**Maybe** they are home. ✗ They maybe home.

REAL ENGLISH

Use simple present or future if you are certain.

A: *Are you sure they like opera?*
B: *They **love** it. I'm sure they**'ll go** with you.*

4 Change the sentences from certain to less certain. Use *may, might,* or *could.*

1. Alisha will become a great D.J. (could)

   Alisha could become a great D.J.

2. Eric Clapton plays the guitar better than anyone else. (might)

   ____

◄ A DJ in Catalonia, Spain

3. *The Nutcracker* is the best ballet I have ever seen. (may)

____

4. That website provides free music. (might)

____

5. The art gallery will become more successful next year. (could)

____

6. His new movie will win a lot of prizes. (could)

____

7. La Yegros will soon have a lot more fans. (might)

____

8. Her latest album will surprise her followers. (may)

____

5 ANAYLYZE THE GRAMMAR. What do these sentences with *could* express? Write **PP** for *present possibility*, **FP** for *future possibility*, or **PA** for *past ability*.

1. FP Anti's new song could win the songwriting contest.
2. _____ I couldn't go to the jazz club last week.
3. _____ Could you sing well when you were a child?
4. _____ This album is awesome! It could be the best music I've ever heard.
5. _____ The movie about Mozart was confusing. I couldn't understand the story.
6. _____ This song is great. It could become a big hit.
7. _____ If you have trouble learning Romeo's lines, I could help you.
8. _____ Toni missed band practice. She could be ill.

6 SPEAK. Work with a partner. Make plans to do something after class. Use *could*, the ideas in the box, and your own ideas.

go to a movie	go to the theater
watch TV	try a new restaurant

A: *We could go to a movie.*

B: *We could do that. Or we could try that new Turkish restaurant downtown.*

REAL ENGLISH

When making suggestions about possible future activities, we often use *could*.

*We **could walk**. It's not far.*

12.5 Logical Conclusions: *Must* and *Must Not*

Facts	Logical Conclusions
Jenna's songs are beautiful.	She **must practice** a lot.
Her songs are soft and slow.	She **must not like** hard rock.

1. Use *must* to express a logical conclusion (an idea you are almost certain is true, based on facts you know).	I heard you laughing. You **must be** happy.
2. Use *must not* to express a negative conclusion.	Barbara **must not eat** meat. She never buys it.

7 Complete the logical conclusions. Use *must* or *must not.*

1. She is one of the most popular musicians around. She ___must___ perform a lot.
2. They never listen to Bob Marley. They __________ like reggae music.
3. The music teacher is shouting. He __________ be angry.
4. Brian is listening to music. He __________ have any work to do.
5. Keiko's guitar sounds great! It __________ be an expensive one.
6. That song is on the radio all the time. The singer __________ be rich.
7. Junko has seen *Cats* six times. She __________ love musicals.
8. My brother gets bad grades in his music classes. He __________ work very hard.

PRACTICE

8 Read the conversation. Circle the correct answers.

Professor: OK, class, this week we are looking at world music and how you can use it in your own music. Have you all chosen a form of world music? Todd?

Todd: I'm sorry, Professor, I thought we were doing jazz this week . . .

Leo: Todd, sometimes I think you (1) **must not** / **couldn't** listen at all!

Professor: That's OK, Leo. We all make mistakes. Chen? How about you?

Chen: Um, I'm still trying to decide between two styles. I (2) **may** / **must** choose a Russian folk song, or I (3) **maybe** / **might** use some type of Indian music.

Professor: Hmm, they're very different. That (4) **must not** / **must** be a difficult choice. Either one (5) **must** / **could** be interesting.

Chen: Indian music (6) **could be** / **maybe** difficult to work into my style of music.

Professor: (7) **Maybe** / **Might** try listening to some songs by the Beatles. You (8) **may not** / **could not** realize it, but they combined Indian music with some of their music.

9 WRITE & SPEAK.

A Read each situation and write one positive and one negative logical conclusion.

Situation	Logical Conclusion
1. Carrie loves singing and dancing.	*She must like performing for people.* *She must not be a shy person.*
2. Maryam often listens to classical music.	
3. Matsu isn't playing with the band tonight.	
4. Julie spends hours practicing the guitar.	

B Work with a partner. Share your logical conclusions from exercise **A**. Decide which sentences are the best. Then share them with the class.

10 APPLY.

CD3-37

A Listen to five clips of music from different parts of the world. Write the number (1–5) next to the country you think the music is from.

United Kingdom _____ Portugal _____ India _____ Jamaica _____ Japan _____

B Work with a partner. Compare and discuss your answers from exercise **A**. Use *may (not), might (not), could (not),* or *must (not)* to explain your thoughts.

The first clip may be a Portuguese song. I think I recognized the language. It couldn't be from the United Kingdom. It doesn't sound English.

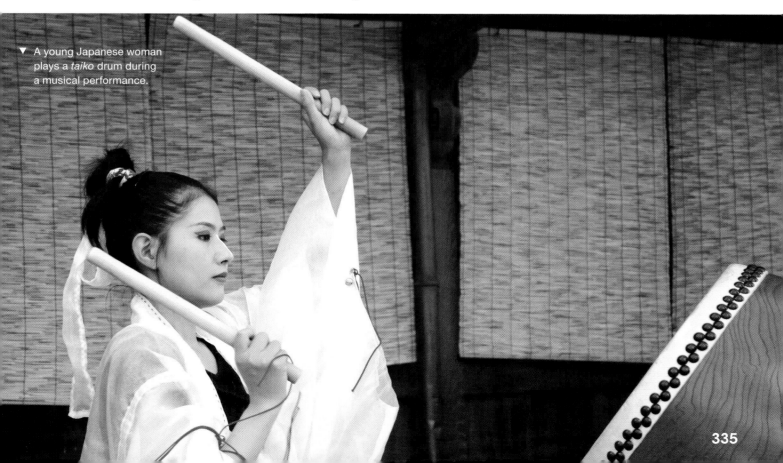

▼ A young Japanese woman plays a *taiko* drum during a musical performance.

EXPLORE

CD3-38

1 **READ** three conversations that Peter, a fan, has outside a theater after a play. Notice the words in **bold**.

After the Show

Peter: Excuse me! **May I come** through? I want to get some autographs.[1]

Security Guard: No, you **can't come** through here. This area is only for the actors.

Peter: Oh, I see. But this is the way they come out, isn't it? **Can I** wait here?

Security Guard: Yes, **you can**, but **would you stand** over there by the wall, please, so you're not in the way?

****

Peter: **May I have** your autograph, Mr. Lane?

Mr. Lane: I'm sorry. I'm afraid I don't have time tonight. **Can I get** past, please?

****

Peter: Hello, Ms. Garcia. I'm a huge fan of yours . . . I really loved the play. You were fabulous, as always! **Could I have** your autograph, please?

Ms. Garcia: Yes, of course. **Can I borrow** your pen?

Peter: Of course. Oh, and **will you sign** this program[2] for my sister?

Ms. Garcia: Sure. What's her name?

Peter: Frances. **Would you write** it on the front here?

Ms. Garcia: Of course. I'm so glad you enjoyed the show.

[1] **autograph:** a famous person's signature, given to a fan or admirer
[2] **program:** a small book with information about a play or other event

2 CHECK. Read the statements. Circle **T** for *true* or **F** for *false*.

1. Peter is standing near the actor's exit. **T** **F**
2. The security guard asks Peter to stand somewhere else. **T** **F**
3. Mr. Lane agrees to sign his autograph. **T** **F**
4. Ms. Garcia has her own pen for signing autographs. **T** **F**
5. Peter asks Ms. Garcia to sign the back of his program. **T** **F**

3 DISCOVER. Complete the exercises to learn about the grammar in this lesson.

A Find these questions in the conversations from exercise **1**. Write the missing words.

1. Excuse me! ____________ I come through?
2. Yes, you can, but ____________ you stand over there by the wall, please, so you're not in the way?
3. Yes, of course.____________ I borrow your pen?
4. Oh, and ____________ you sign this program for my sister?
5. ____________ you write it on the front here?

B Look at the questions in exercise **A**. Some questions ask for permission to do something yourself. Other questions ask someone else to do something for you. Complete the statements.

1. Questions ____ and ____ ask permission to do something yourself.
2. Questions ____, ____, and ____ ask someone else to do something for you.

LEARN

12.6 Permission: *May, Could,* and *Can*

Asking for Permission	Answers
May we **sit** in these seats?	I'm sorry. They're taken.
Could I **have** your autograph?	Sure. No problem.
Can I **borrow** your pen?	Of course.

Expressing Permission
You **may play** video games after all your homework is done.
We **can't play video games** until our homework is done.

1. Use *may, could,* or *can* + the base form of a verb to ask for permission.	**May** I sit here? **Could** he **use** this bike?
2. *Can* is less formal or polite than *may* or *could. May* is the most formal.	Hey Jim, **can** I **borrow** your bike? Doctor, **may** I **call** you at home?
3. Use *may (not)* or *can (not)* + the base form of a verb to express what is or is not permitted.	You **may watch** educational programs on TV. We **cannot watch** sitcoms or reality TV shows.
4. **Be careful!** When you use *could* to ask permission, it does not refer to the past.	**Could** I **use** your car tomorrow?
5. To answer questions using *can, could,* or *may,* use *can* or *may.* Do not use *could. Can* is more common. *May* is more formal.	A: **Could** my children **stay** at your house? B: Sure they **can**. A: **May** we **go** the library, Ms. Smith? B: Yes, you **may**. Please return by 4:00.

4 Complete the exercises.

A Circle all possible answers to complete the conversations.

1. A: Hey, Jim, **may** / **can** / **could** I ride with you to the show?
   B: Sure. I'll pick you up around six.
2. A: Excuse me, Mr. Evans, **may** / **can** / **could** I have your autograph?
   B: No, you **may not** / **can't** / **couldn't**. I'm afraid I'm in a hurry.
3. A: We **may** / **can** / **could** listen to Adele practice her new song. Her manager just said it was OK. We **may** / **can** / **could** sit to the right, over here.
   B: Great!
4. A: You **may** / **can** / **could** not go backstage tonight. The band is tired.
   B: OK.
5. A: Sam, **may** / **can** / **could** I ask your opinion about my new song?
   B: Of course, you **may** / **can** / **could**. Please play it for me.
6. A: Excuse me. You **may** / **can** / **could** not take photos here.
   B: Oh, I'm sorry. I didn't know.

B ANALYZE THE GRAMMAR. Work with a partner or your class. Discuss the possible situations in the conversations in exercise **A** and decide which modal you think is best.

In number 1, I think two friends are talking. It isn't very formal, so I would use "can" or "could."

5 SPEAK. Work with a partner. Take turns asking for and giving permission, using the words in the box. Use *May I, Can I,* and *Could I* at least once. Give affirmative and negative answers.

use your bike	sit here	change the TV channel
open a window	ask you a question	leave my car here

A: *Can I use your bike?*

B: *Sure. You can use it for an hour or so. I need it at 5:00.*

12.7 Requests: *Would, Could, Can, Will*

Questions	Answers	
Would you **call** me later?	Yes, I **will**.	Sorry, I **can't**.
Could you **move** here, please?	Of course.	I'm afraid I **can't**.
Can you **come** here, please?	Yes, I **can**.	I **can't** right now. Hold on.
Will you **tell** me the problem?	Sure, I**'ll** tell you later.	No, I'm sorry. I **can't**.

1. Use *would, could, can,* or *will* + the base form of a verb to ask someone to do something for you (i.e., to make a request).	**Would** you **help** me with this? **Could** you **wash** the dishes? **Can** you **come** to my house tomorrow? **Will** you **go** to the store for me?
2. Use *can* or *will* in short answers. Do not use *could* or *would.*	A: **Could** you **help** me with this? ✓ B: Yes, I **can**. ✗ B: Yes, I could.
3. An answer with *No* often sounds rude. Use phrases such as *I'm sorry* or *I'm afraid I . . .* to make them more polite.	A: **Can** you **help** me with this, Tim? B: **I'm sorry.** I **can't** at the moment. B: **I'm afraid** I'm busy right now.
4. *Would* and *could* are more polite than *will* and *can.*	**Could** you **tell** me my grade, Professor Ortega? **Can** you **text** me the homework, Tom?

6 Complete the exercises.

A Rewrite the informal questions with more formal modals.

1. Can you download the concert tickets?

   Could you download the concert tickets?

2. Will you help me practice my lines for the play?

   Would you help me practic...?

3. Can you listen to me play the new song I just learned?

   Could you listen to me ...?

4. Will you rent the new Wes Anderson movie?

Would you rent the new ---?

5. Can you take our picture?

could you take our picture?

B **SPEAK.** Work with a partner. Take turns asking and answering the questions in exercise **A**. Add *please* to the end of each question and use an appropriate affirmative or negative answer.

A: *Can you download the concert tickets, please?*

B: *Sure, I'll do it now.*

A: *Could you download the concert tickets, please?*

B: *Sorry, I can't. My Internet connection is down.*

REAL ENGLISH

To make any request more polite, add *please* to the end.

Can you come here, ***please****?*
Could you sign this, ***please****?*

7 **PRONUNCIATION.** Read the chart and listen to the examples. Then complete the exercises.

PRONUNCIATION ***Could You*** **and** ***Would You***

When *could* or *would* comes before *you*, the final *-d* blends with the *y-* sound in *you*, resulting in a softer /dʒ/ sound: /ˈkudʒu/ and /ˈwudʒu/.

CD3-39

Examples:

Could you tell me the time?
Could you speak a little slower, please?
Would you wait a moment?
Would you explain this word, please?

CD3-40

A Complete the polite requests with *could* or *would*. Use the ideas in the imperative sentences in parentheses. Then listen and check your answers.

1. Could you tell me your full name?
(Tell me your full name.)

2. Would __________
(Lend me five dollars.)

3. Could __________
(Repeat the last question.)

4. Would __________
(Speak more slowly.)

5. Could __________
(Tell me the time.)

6. Would __________
(Raise your hands in the air!)

B Work with a partner. Take turns asking and answering the questions from exercise **A**. Give affirmative or negative answers. Pay attention to the pronunciation.

A: *Could you tell me your full name?*

B: *Sure. It's Jennifer Ann Reynolds.*

PRACTICE

8 Complete the conversations. Use appropriate modals and responses from this lesson and the words in parentheses. More than one answer may be correct.

Conversation 1

Photographer: Excuse me, ma'am. I'm working on a story for a local magazine. (1) <u>Could I take</u> (take) your picture in front of your stand?

Farmer 1: I'm sorry, but I'm busy right now.

Photographer: Oh, OK. No (2) ________________. Have a good day.

Conversation 2

Photographer: Excuse me, sir, (3) ________________ (you / let) me take your photo?

Farmer 2: Of (4) ________________. (5) ________________ (you / try) to get my stand in the photo?

Photographer: Sure. (6) ________________ (you / stand) in front of the table? Good, uh . . . (7) ________________ (you / move) to the right a little . . . That's great! And (8) ________________ (you / smile)?

Farmer 2: Sure. So, (9) ________________ (I / see) the photo?

Photographer: Of course, you (10) ________________. Here . . .

Farmer 2: Wow, this is great! (11) ________________ (you / send) it to me, please? I know my family would love to see it.

Photographer: (12) ________________ problem. What's your e-mail address?

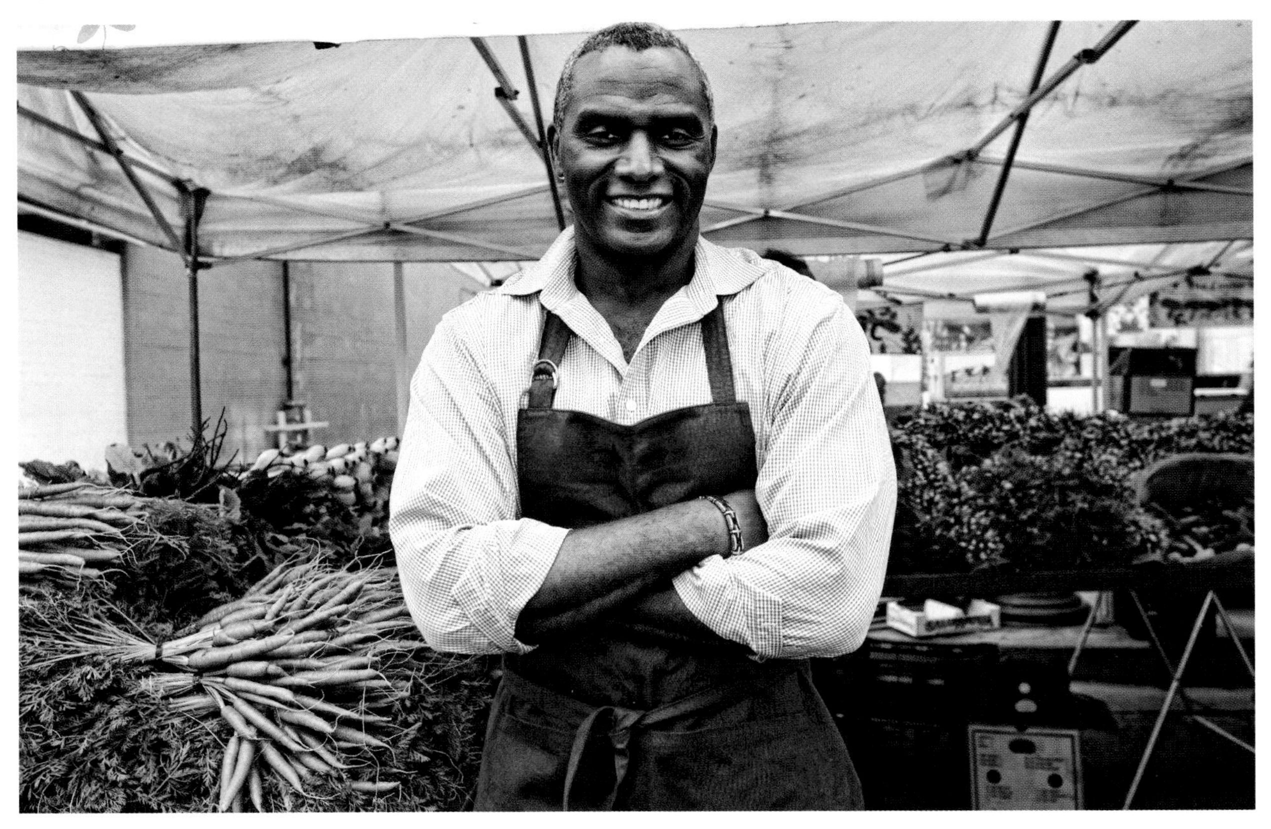

9 EDIT. Read the conversation between a student and a music professor. Find and correct five more errors with modals asking for or giving permission and making requests.

Kira:	Excuse me, Professor Howard, may I ~~to~~ speak with you?
Professor:	Yes, of course you may, Kira. What's the problem?
Kira:	Well, it's about my report on John Coltrane. I spent a lot of time researching his life. I'm surprised at the low grade I received. Would I ask you what I did wrong?
Professor:	Yes, of course. If I remember correctly, you wrote too much about his life and not enough about his music and its influence on jazz. Could you come to my office to discuss it?
Kira:	Yes, I could. May I come in tomorrow or Friday?
Professor:	Sure. May you come and see me on Friday around 1:00 p.m.?
Kira:	Um, I'm already seeing Dr. Stein then. Would we talk at 1:30?
Professor:	Yes, that's perfect, and would you please bring your report with you?
Kira:	Yes, I would. Thank you so much, Professor Howard. See you Friday.

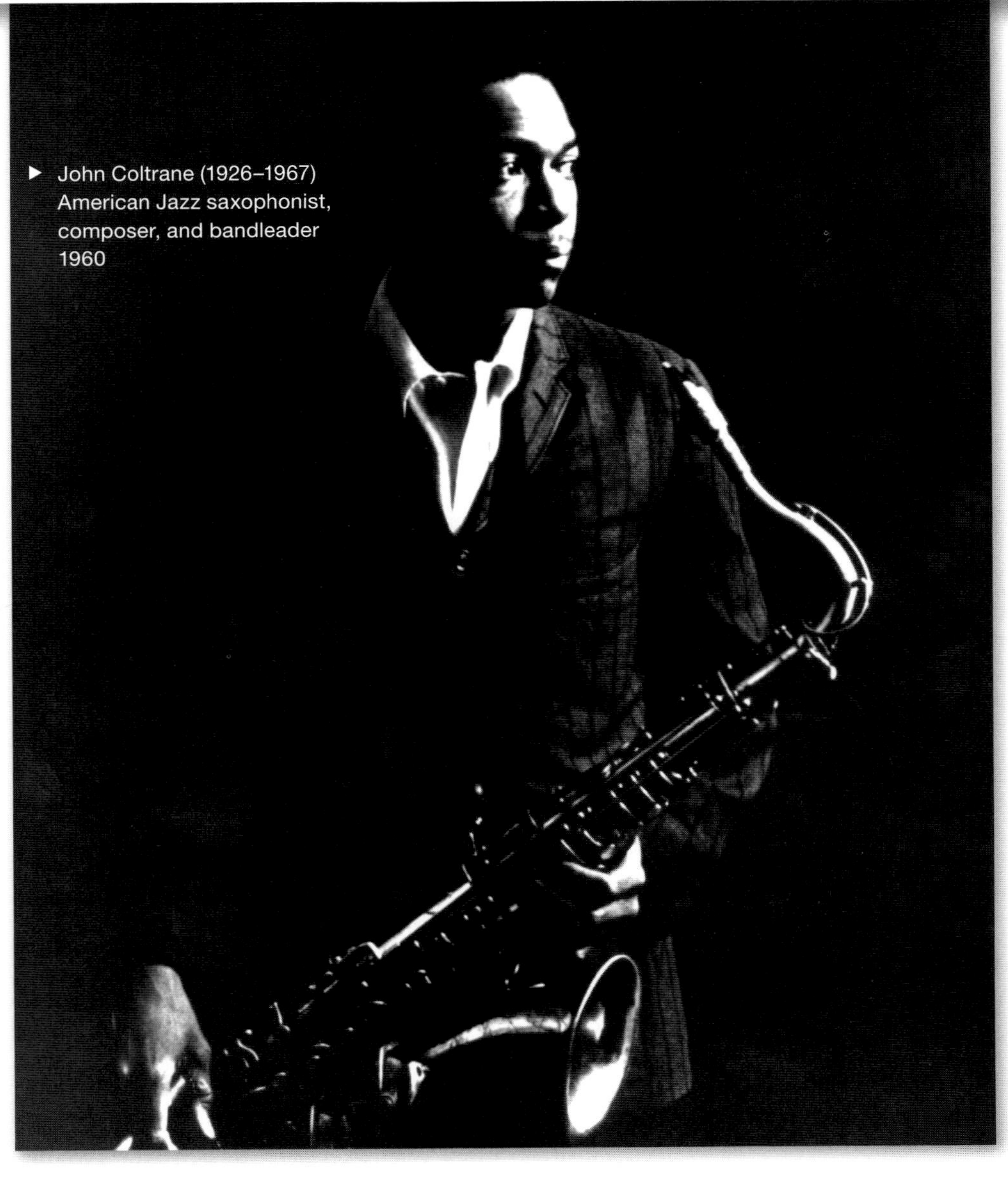

▶ John Coltrane (1926–1967) American Jazz saxophonist, composer, and bandleader 1960

10 Complete the exercises.

A Read the conversation between a musician and a fan before a concert. Underline three questions that use the grammar from this lesson.

Megan: Hey, I'm looking forward to hearing you sing. Can I help you set up your equipment?

Angel: Thanks, that'll be great. Will you put the microphone stand on the stage for me?

Megan: Sure . . . Is this all right?

Angel: Yes, uh, could you move it forward just a little? It has to be in front of the speakers.

Megan: No problem.

B **SPEAK.** Work with a partner. Look at the underlined questions in exercise **A**. Ask each question using a different modal. Discuss which modal is more polite.

A: *"May I help you set up your equipment?" is more polite, I think.*

B: *I agree. You could also say, "Could I help you set up your equipment?"*

11 **APPLY.**

A Write two questions for each situation, one asking permission and one making a request.

1. You are buying something at a concert.

____

____

2. You are with a guitar instructor learning a new song.

____

____

3. You are on a bus or train.

____

____

4. You are in a movie theater.

____

____

B Work with a partner. Role-play the situations you have chosen. Take turns asking the questions and responding. Use the conversation in exercise **10A** as a model.

A: *Can I help you?*

B: *Yes, could I have two bottles of water, please?*

A: *Sure. That'll be eight dollars.*

B: *Forget it! That's much too expensive!*

Review the Grammar UNIT 12

▲ Graffiti in Buenos Aires, Argentina

Charts 12.1–12.5, 12.7

1 Circle the correct words to complete the conversation.

Rob: I (1) **can't** / **might not** understand what's happening to this city! Everywhere you go, people are painting graffiti on the walls. It's terrible!

Devon: (2) **Will you** / **Must you** relax? Graffiti is a modern art form. When I was in Buenos Aires last year, I (3) **could** / **was able to** go on a special tour of the city's graffiti.

Rob: Really? When I look at graffiti, (4) **I may not** / **I'm not able to** see anything artistic.

Devon: Well, a lot of people (5) **can** / **must** like it, because I noticed the other day that a company here is now giving graffiti tours.

Rob: You (6) **will not** / **must not** be serious! When did *that* start?

Devon: I'm not sure exactly, but on their website, (7) **you must** / **you can** see that visitors take our city's graffiti very seriously. (8) **Will** / **May** you take the tour with me this weekend? (9) **May be** / **Maybe** after the tour (10) **you could** / **you'll be able to** appreciate graffiti a little better.

Charts 12.1–12.7

CD3-41

2 **LISTEN.** You will hear eight people. First listen and write the modal and base form you hear. Then listen again and choose the correct meaning.

1. couldn't see ______ (a.) I wasn't able to see well. b. I may not be able to see well.
2. ______ a. I don't know if he likes it. b. It's clear he doesn't like it.
3. ______ a. I'll definitely buy a novel. b. I could buy a novel.
4. ______ a. I can teach you. b. I'd like you to teach me.
5. ______ a. She might become good. b. She will become good.
6. ______ a. He will have the ability. b. He will be allowed.
7. ______ a. I might be able to hear. b. I was able to hear.
8. ______ a. Do I know how? b. Would you let me?

Charts 12.2–12.5, 12.7

3 EDIT. Read the conversation. Find and correct six more errors with modals and similar expressions expressing ability, probability, requests, permission, or logical conclusions.

Christine: What is your favorite art form, Joan?

Joan: Oh, ballet, without a doubt. I must spend ~~spending~~ half my money on ballet tickets!

Christine: Really? Could you explain why?

Joan: I appreciate the skill of the dancers. They must not work very hard to make it look so easy.

Christine: So, who is the best dancer you've seen?

Joan: Last summer, I could get tickets to see South Korean ballerina Hee Seo dance in New York. She is amazing! She is able communicate many emotions just with her movements. I think she could become one of the best ballet dancers of all time. This summer she is going to appear in *Swan Lake*, which I love. Unfortunately, I maybe out of the country then. If I'm here, I'm going to get tickets for the first night.

Christine: Would you to let me know when they go on sale? From what you say, I'm sure Hee Seo might be amazing to watch.

Charts 12.1–12.7

4 SPEAK.

A Brainstorm a list of hobbies or other activities related to art and music. Write things that you have experience with or hope to learn more about.

Visual Art	Music	Other Art Forms
painting drawing	playing guitar jazz music	ballet acting

B Work with a partner. Discuss the questions. Talk about your experience with art and/or music. Use the chart you completed in exercise **A** to help you with ideas.

1. Can you play a musical instrument? Which one? How well?
2. What could you do as a child that you can't do now? What can you do now that you couldn't do five years ago?
3. If you could make a request to a famous artist or musician, who would it be? Tell your partner your request.
4. Could you be a famous artist one day? If so, what type of artist? If not, why not?

Connect the Grammar to Writing

1 READ & NOTICE THE GRAMMAR.

A What are some different types of reviews you've read? Tell a partner. Then read a review of the movie *Gravity.*

Go See *Gravity*!

Would you like a new view of the world? Then go and see the movie *Gravity*. This powerful movie could change the way you see your world. In fact, it might turn your view of the whole universe upside down.

In *Gravity,* disaster strikes two astronauts while they are on a space walk. They aren't able to get back to their ship, and they will probably not survive. Because *Gravity* is a 3-D movie, viewers can experience floating in space along with the astronauts. You may feel off balance as you watch the screen. You will feel like you are with the astronauts and have no control.

After I saw *Gravity,* I couldn't look at the world in the same way. I was able to see my place in the world. The world is so large, and I am so small. Watch and you too might leave the movie with a new sense of your place in the universe.

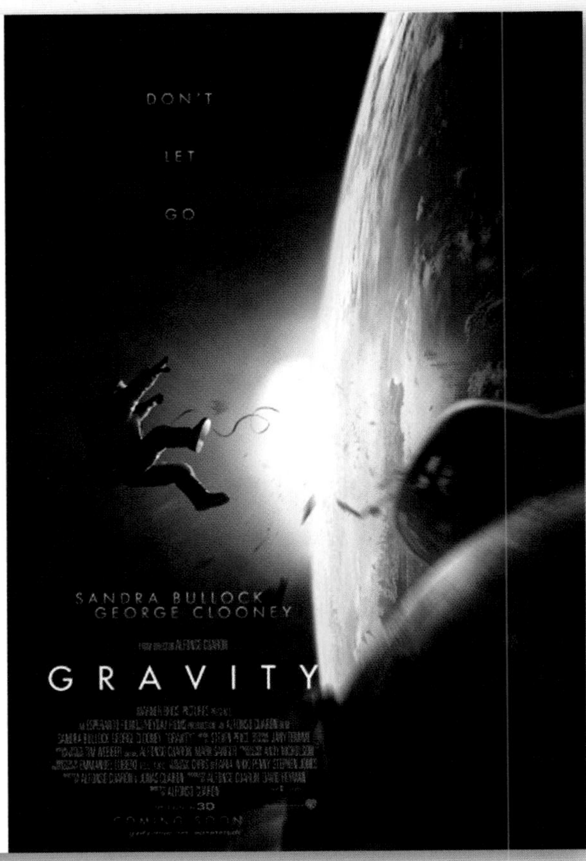

GRAMMAR FOCUS

In the review in exercise **A**, the writer uses modals to discuss ability and possibility in the past, present, and future. Be aware that each modal has different meanings and uses.

Past: *After I saw* Gravity, *I* ***couldn't look*** *at the world in the same way.*
Present: *. . . viewers* ***can experience*** *floating in space along with the astronauts.*
Future: *This powerful movie* ***could change*** *the way you see your world.*

B Read the review in exercise **A** again. Find four more modals or similar expressions used to discuss ability and possibility in the past, present, or future. Write them in the chart.

Past	Present or Future
	. . . movie could change the way you see . . .

C Complete the outline with information from the review in exercise **A**. Discuss your answers with a partner.

Title/Name: Gravity

Main characters: ______

Basic idea: Disaster strikes while they are on a mission.

Setting (place): ______

Artistic quality: 3-D movie, ______,

Possible effects on viewer: could change your view of the world,

______

______

______

______

2 BEFORE YOU WRITE.

A Think of a movie, book, or musical artist that has had an effect on your life by changing your ideas, feelings, or behavior. In your notebook, brainstorm a list of the possible effects that your chosen topic might have on other people.

B Make an outline like the one in exercise **1C**. Complete the outline with information about your movie, book, or musical artist.

3 WRITE a review. Use the information from your outline in exercise **2B** and the model in exercise **1A** to help you.

WRITING FOCUS Using Italics or Quotation Marks for Titles of Works

Use *italics* for the titles of movies, books, paintings, television series, and other longer works of art.

Then go and see the movie ***Gravity***.

Use quotation marks (" . . .") for titles of short stories, poems, songs, single television shows, and shorter works of art.

"The Journey" is a short story about space.

4 SELF ASSESS. Read your review. Underline the modals. Then use the checklist to assess your work.

- ☐ I used *can, could,* or *be able to* to discuss ability. [12.1, 12.2]
- ☐ I used *may, might,* or *could* to discuss possibility. [12.3, 12.4]
- ☐ I used *must* or *must not* to state logical conclusions. [12.5]
- ☐ I used italics and quotation marks correctly to show the titles of works. [WRITING FOCUS]

Modals: Part 2

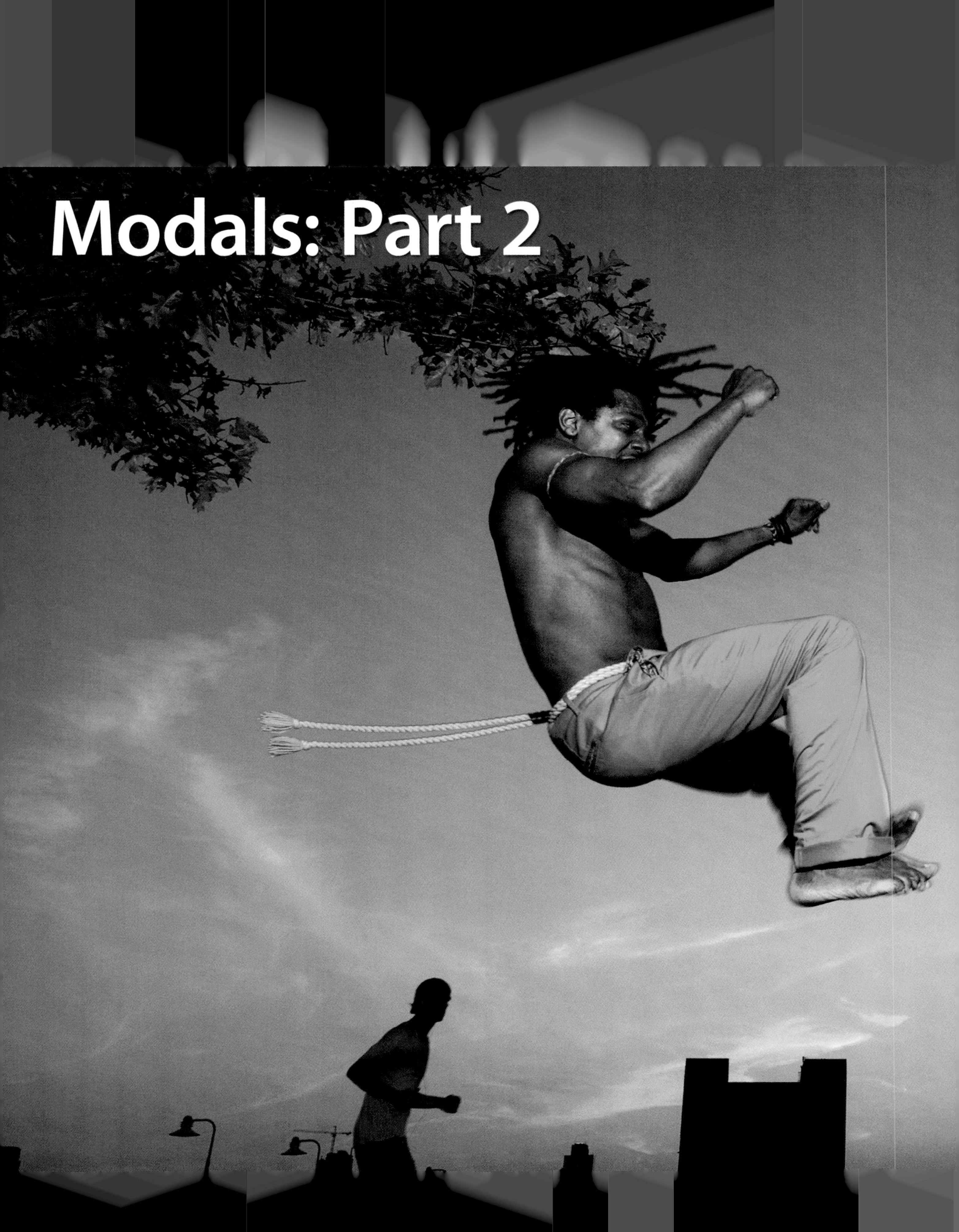

▲ Two young Brazilian men practice capoeira in a New York park at sunset.

EXPLORE

CD4-02

1 READ the conversation on an online forum about judo. Notice the words in **bold**.

I'm a FEMALE judo player. Ask me anything!

Submitted 6 months ago by Judo_Gal

Hi, forum! I am a female, and I have been practicing judo for 15 years. I'm happy to answer your questions.

Concerned Dad: Hi Judo_Gal. My daughter wants to take judo lessons, but I'm concerned about safety. Should I be?

Judo_Gal: No. You really **don't have to worry** too much. Judo means "the Gentle Way." Players do not try to hurt their opponents.[1] Of course, you **have to be** careful. Sometimes players throw each other, and accidents can happen.

Concerned Dad: Do they kick, too?

Judo_Gal: No. Judo players **cannot kick** each other. In fact, there are several moves that players **must avoid**. For example, players **may not punch**[2] each other or **touch** their opponent's face. They also **have to keep** their hands away from their opponent's legs.

Concerned Dad: Can you hold your opponent's jacket? You **can't do** this in other martial arts.

Judo_Gal: Yes, you are allowed to hold the outside of your opponent's jacket, but you **can't put** your hands inside a sleeve.

Concerned Dad: Thanks for your answers. Just one more question. Why do you think practicing judo is good for young people?

Judo_Gal: Well, it was great for me. Judo players **must be** very disciplined. I learned quickly to follow rules and manage my time. They **must not ignore** their coaches, and they **must** always **behave** respectfully. These are great lessons for people at any age!

[1] **opponent:** a person who takes the opposite side in a fight, game, or contest
[2] **punch:** to hit with a closed hand

▶ Nadia Merli (white) of Brazil and Haruka Tachimoto of Japan (blue) compete in the Judo Grand Slam on November 30, 2013, in Tokyo, Japan.

▲ Female karate players watch a karate competition during the First Women's Olympics of Afghanistan in Kabul, November 6, 2006.

2 CHECK. Read the statements. Circle **T** for *true* or **F** for *false*.

1. Judo is a sport for men only. **T** **F**
2. Judo is very dangerous. **T** **F**
3. Judo players can throw each other. **T** **F**
4. It's OK to hit each other in the face in judo. **T** **F**
5. Judo_Gal believes judo is just for fun. **T** **F**

3 DISCOVER. Complete the exercises to learn about the grammar in this lesson.

A Find these sentences in the online forum from exercise **1**. Write the missing words.

1. You really ____________________ worry too much.
2. Of course, you ____________________ be careful.
3. Judo players ____________________ kick each other.
4. For example, players ____________________ punch each other . . .
5. They ____________________ ignore their coaches, . . .
6. . . . and they ____________________ always behave respectfully.

B Look at the sentences in exercise **A**. Write the number of each sentence in the correct place according to its meaning.

1. Necessary or required action or behavior: __2__ and ____
2. Unnecessary action or behavior: ____
3. Prohibited action or behavior: ____, ____, and ____

LEARN

13.1 Necessity: *Must* and *Have To*

Must
You **must arrive** on time. They **must finish** by the end of the day.

Have To
She **has to arrive** on time. We **have to finish** by the end of the day. I **had to leave** before class ended.

Questions with *Have To*
Do you **have to leave?** **Does** she **have to go?** Why **do** we **have to** be early? What **did** he **have to do?**

Short Answers
Yes, I **do**. **No,** she **doesn't**. Because it's polite. He **had to** apologize to the coach.

1. Use the modal *must* or the similar expression *have to* + the base form of a verb to mean *need to*.	Players **must start** at the same time. A soccer team **has to score** goals to win.
2. *Must* is common in formal situations, such as when expressing rules or laws as an authority.	Drivers **must wear** seat belts. You **must be** quiet during the test.
3. *Have to* is common when talking about something you need to do yourself.	My child is sick. I **have to leave** early. We **have to be** on time. Hurry!
4. *Have got to* is an informal way to say something is necessary. It is common in conversation, and it is usually contracted.	Hurry up! We**'ve got to** go. She**'s got to leave** now or she'll be late.
5. To express that something was necessary in the past, use *had to*. *Must* and *have got to* cannot be used for the past.	✓ We **had to go** to the store earlier. ✗ We must go to the store earlier. ✗ We had got to go to the store earlier.
6. For questions, use a form of *do* + *have to*. *Must* and *have got to* are not usually used in questions.	**Do** I **have to stay** home? **Does** he **have to attend** every class?

4 Circle the correct answers to complete the conversations. In some cases, both answers are possible.

1. **Official:** Excuse me. You (1) **must** / **have to** leave cell phones in a locker.

   Player: Sorry, sir.

2. **Player:** Do we (2) **must** / **have to** join a specific group?

   Official: Yes, you (3) **must** / **have to** check this list and find your group.

3. **Player:** Excuse me, where do we (4) **must** / **have to** sign in?

   Official: You're late. You (5) **must** / **had to** sign in by 9:00 a.m. this morning.

4. **Friend 1:** Sorry, I couldn't call you. I (6) **must** / **had to** put my cell phone in a locker.

   Friend 2: Oh, yeah. Did you (7) **have to** / **had to** apologize to the coach?

   Friend 1: Yes. I (8) **have to** / **had to** do extra exercises, too. My arms hurt!

5. **Player 1:** Hey, you (9) **'ve got to** / **got to** be careful.

   Player 2: Sorry. I'm tired. I (10) **had got** / **had** to wake up early this morning.

5 Read the club rules. Then complete the five conversations. Use the words in parentheses and the correct form of *must* or *have to*.

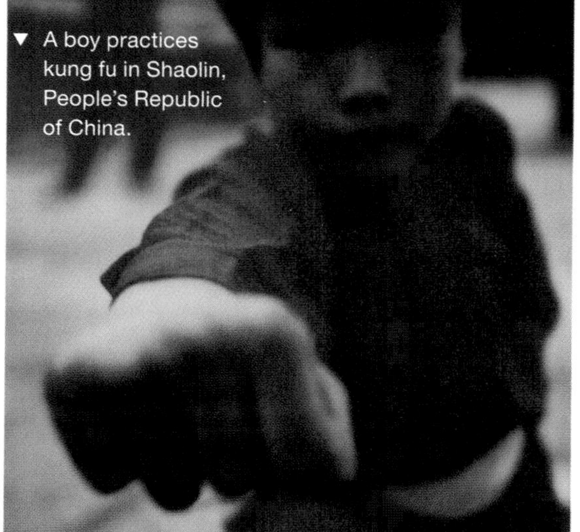
▼ A boy practices kung fu in Shaolin, People's Republic of China.

Club Rules

1. Arrive on time! Never be late for a lesson.
2. Do not wear watches or jewelry on the mat.
3. Put long hair in a braid or a ponytail.
4. Do not wear shoes on the mat.
5. Bring a clean suit to class.

1. **Instructor:** Students must arrive (students / arrive) on time.
2. **Student:** do we have to take off (we / take off) our watches?

   Instructor: Yes. you must remove have to (you / remove) jewelry, too.
3. **Lisa:** Jen, do you have a hair band? I always forget that we have to wear (we / wear) our hair up.

   Jen: I know. It has to be (it / be) in a braid or ponytail. Here's a band.
4. **John:** Tim, you must remove have to (you / remove) your shoes before practice.

   Tim: Oh yeah. Thanks. I almost forgot.
5. **Mother**: Remember, you have to bring (you / bring) a clean suit to class.

   Daughter: I forgot! Where is it? I have to hurry (I / hurry) or I'll be late.

▼ Children practice kung fu at the Ta Gou Academy, Shaolin, Henan Province, People's Republic of China.

13.2 Prohibition (*Must Not, May Not, Can't, Couldn't*) and Lack of Necessity (*Not Have To*)

Prohibition	Lack of Necessity
You **must not do** that. It's not allowed. They **must not leave** work before 5 p.m.	I **don't have to take** the test. It's not necessary. He **doesn't have to go**, but he can if he wants to.

1. To express that an action is prohibited, use *must not.*	Players **must not speak** during the match.
2. *May not* and *can't* are also used to express prohibition. *Can't* is more informal. Use *couldn't* to express past prohibition.	Players **may not start** until they hear the bell. You **can't drive** without a license. I **couldn't drive** before I was 16.
3. To express that an action is not necessary, use *don't have to.*	He **doesn't have to go** to class. It's a holiday.
4. To say that something was not necessary in the past, use *didn't have to.*	They **didn't have to** take tennis lessons because they already knew how to play.
5. **Be careful:** There is no negative or past form of *have got to,* so the expression is not used for prohibition or lack of necessity.	✗ I have not got to go. ✗ I had got to go yesterday.

6 Circle the correct answer to complete each sentence.

1. In some sports, players **must not** / **do not have to** talk during play. Silence is required.
2. Players **must not** / **don't have to** ignore the rules. It's important to play fairly.
3. Monica **must not** / **doesn't have to** go to practice this evening. It's her night off.
4. You **can't** / **don't have to** be late, or you'll be in trouble.
5. Jim **must not** / **didn't have to** play his best to beat me. I played terribly!
6. You **must not** / **don't have to** cheat! No one will want to play with you if you do.
7. In many sports, players **may not** / **don't have to** play the whole game, but often they do.
8. In the past, girls **couldn't** / **didn't have to** compete in many sports.
9. We didn't **have to** / **have got to** be at school until 8:00 yesterday morning.
10. In soccer, you **may not** / **don't have to** use your hand to score a goal. It's against the rules.

7 **WRITE & SPEAK.** Work with a partner. Write one thing that is prohibited and one thing that is not necessary in your class or school. Then share your answers with your class.

Prohibited: We must not speak while someone else is speaking.

Not Necessary: We don't have to write essays in class.

PRACTICE

8 PRONUNCIATION. Read the chart and listen to the examples. Then complete the exercises.

PRONUNCIATION **Reduced Forms of *Have To*, *Has To*, and *Have Got To***

Have to, *has to*, and *have got to* are usually reduced.

CD4-03

Pronunciation:	Examples:
have to is /ˈhæftə/	You don't **have to** go already, do you?
has to is /ˈhæstə/	She **has to** play better next week.
has got to is /sˈgatə/ or /zˈgatə/	It**'s got** to stop. He**'s got to** see that.
have got to is /vˈgatə/	We**'ve got to** leave early.

CD4-04

A Listen to the reduced pronunciation. Complete each sentence with the full form.

1. You ___have to___ practice a lot to become good at any sport.
2. My friend ______________ stop watching football! It takes up all his time.
3. I ______________ get new running shoes. Mine have a hole in them.
4. Students don't ______________ know all the answers. don't have to
5. A student ______________ be responsible.
6. Did you ______________ study a lot last weekend?

B Work with a partner. Take turns saying the sentences in exercise **A**. Then use your own ideas after *have to* and *have got to*.

You have to practice speaking a lot to become fluent.

9 Complete the exercises.

A Circle the correct answers to complete the conversation.

Sunil: Hi, Jay. It's Sunil. I can't find my schedule. When (1) **do we have to** / **have we to** be at the ice rink for tomorrow's game?

Jay: Hi, Sunil. Um, 3:15 or 3:30, I think. I'll have to check. It's right here on my phone. Hold on . . . Uh, no, I was wrong—we (2) **must not** / **don't have to** be there until 4 p.m.

Sunil: Thanks. I (3) **got** / **'ve got** to remember these things! Are you feeling confident?

Jay: To be honest, I'm nervous. We were terrible last week.

Sunil: Yeah, you're right . . . but we (4) **must** / **had to** compete without our best player.

Jay: Well, Kurt is still sick, and a sick player (5) **can't** / **hasn't got to** play. The coach says we (6) **can't** / **don't have to** stay on the team if we do badly again tomorrow.

Sunil: Why (7) **does he have** / **has he** to say things like that?

Jay: I guess it's his job! Look, I (8) **'ve got to** / **had to** go—I have a ton of homework to do.

CD4-05

B Listen to the conversation and check your answers.

10 Look at Rosa's *To Do* lists. Write six sentences. Use modals and similar expressions of necessity, lack of necessity, and prohibition.

Last Weekend

To Do List

1. ☑ New diet! No sweets all weekend!
2. ☒ Meet study group at library. CANCELLED!!
3. ☑ Work 8-noon Sat.

This Weekend

To Do List

4. ☐ No work! Day off!
5. ☐ Don't forget tennis practice!
6. ☐ Write draft of essay.

1. (eat) Rosa couldn't eat sweets all weekend.
2. (meet) ________
3. (work) ________
4. (go) ________
5. (forget) ________
6. (write) ________

11 **SPEAK.**

A Complete the chart with activities in your life. Use the *To-Do* lists in exercise **10** as a guide.

	Necessary	Not Necessary	Prohibited
Last Weekend			
This Weekend			

B Work with a partner. Share the information in your chart. Use modals and expressions of necessity, lack of necessity, and prohibition.

I have to work on Saturday this weekend.

12 LISTEN.

CD4-06

A Listen to the radio feature about Folk Racing. Choose the correct answers to complete the sentences.

Folk Racing

1. In Finland, Folk Racing drivers _____ adults.
   a. have to be
   b. don't have to be
   c. must not be

2. If your child is under five years old, she _____.
   a. can compete
   b. has to compete
   c. may not compete

3. You _____ a good driver to be in a Folk Race.
   a. must be
   b. don't have to be
   c. cannot be

4. To drive a car in a Folk Racing competition, you _____ a special license.
   a. don't have to have
   b. must have
   c. must not have

5. If you want to do Folk Racing, you _____ a car.
   a. must have
   b. don't have to have
   c. must not have

6. In 2013, the price of a car _____ more than 1400 euros.
   a. couldn't be
   b. had to be
   c. didn't have to be

B Complete the sentences about Folk Racing. Use modals and similar expressions of necessity, lack of necessity, and prohibition.

1. If you want to drive in one of these races, you ____have to____ go to Finland.
2. In Finland, a four-year-old ____________ wait very long to drive in a race.
3. Last year we forgot to get a special license, so we ____________ join the race.
4. He spent 2000 euros on his car. He ____________ compete in Folk Racing.
5. Drivers in Folk Racing ____________ spend a lot of money on their cars.
6. You ____________ forget to have fun!

13 **EDIT.** Read the article about Lynn Hill, a well-known rock climber. Find and correct five more errors with modals and similar expressions of necessity and prohibition.

You ~~may not~~ don't have to be an expert rock climber to enjoy Yosemite National Park, but it doesn't hurt. According to climbers, if you want the best views, you must to climb some of the park's famous mountains. If you are a climber, you have to visit Camp 4, the base camp where many famous climbs have started.

Lynn Hill arrived at Camp 4 for the first time as a 15-year-old in the 1970s. She was a gymnast, so she hadn't to learn to control her movements. She soon showed great ability.

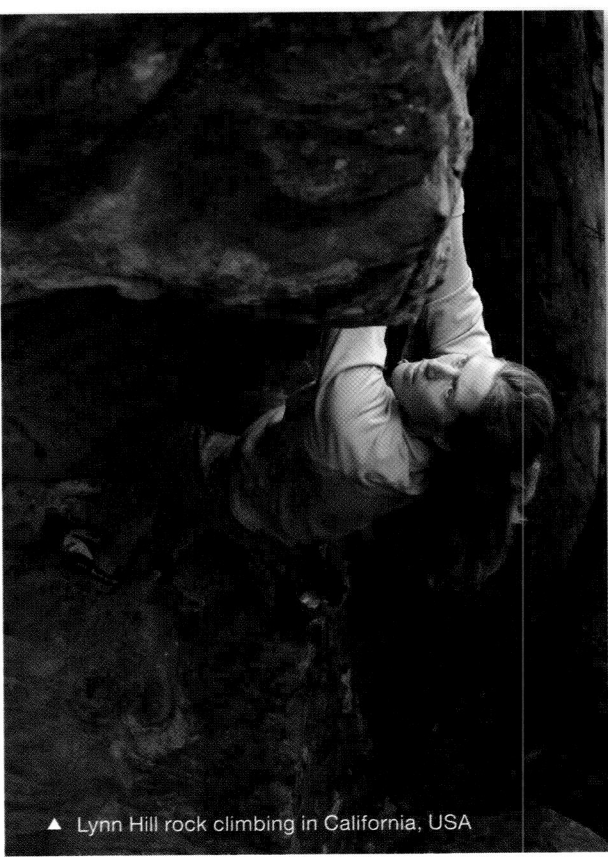

▲ Lynn Hill rock climbing in California, USA

In her thirties, she came back to Camp 4 with a goal. To reach her goal, she had got to 'free climb' the challenging route—the Nose, within 24 hours. Free climbing means it's just you and the rock. You have to put your hands and feet into cracks in the rock, and you don't have to use ropes or other equipment. At times during her climb, Hill must hang by just her fingers. She completed her famous climb in 23 hours.

14 **APPLY.**

A Work with a partner. Brainstorm other competitions you know about (e.g., marathons, car racing). Then choose one, and write 4-5 sentences about it.

You must be very healthy and strong.
You don't have to be a professional athlete.
You cannot compete if you haven't trained and qualified.
You must wear a number on your shirt.

B Read your sentences to another pair of students and let them guess what you wrote about.

A: *You must be very healthy and strong. . . .*

B: *Is it a running race, maybe a marathon?*

A: *Yes, it is!*

EXPLORE

CD4-07

1 READ the conversation. Notice the words in **bold**.

Man versus Horse

Denise: Hey, coach! I was wondering if I could ask you about my training plans. I'm **supposed to run** in the "Man versus Horse" race in Wales in a few months. I'm not sure how to prepare.

Coach: The *what*? What is the "Man versus Horse" race? That sounds crazy!

Denise: I know. It's a tough race; it's about 23 miles long. I don't think you can really beat the horses, but it**'s supposed to be** fun trying.

Coach: I've never heard of it! Sounds interesting. So what are your training plans?

Denise: The course has a lot of hills, so I'm planning to do my training on hills.

Coach: Well, you **shouldn't run** on hills all the time. Hills are important, but you **ought to run** on flat surfaces as well. And you **should take** at least one rest day a week . . . two if you include a really long run in the schedule.

Denise: OK. That's good to know. I was wondering, **should** I **run** the full race distance before the event?

Coach: Yes. In fact, you **should do** at least one run that's longer than the race. It'll be good for your confidence. So, you **are supposed to keep** away from the horses, right?

Denise: Yes, of course! They say you **shouldn't get** too close to them if you can avoid it.

▼ "The "Man versus Horse" competition takes place every year in LLanwrtyd Wells, Wales.

2 CHECK. Read the statements. Circle **T** for *true* or **F** for *false*.

1. Denise thinks the "Man versus Horse" race will be easy. **T** **F**
2. She thinks she will enjoy the race. **T** **F**
3. The race is not on flat land only. **T** **F**
4. The coach thinks training only on hills is a good idea. **T** **F**
5. The coach advises Denise to run further than 23 miles in her training. **T** **F**
6. The organizers tell runners to stay close to the horses. **T** **F**

3 DISCOVER. Complete the exercises to learn about the grammar in this lesson.

A Underline the modal or similar expression in each sentence. Then circle the main verb.

1. I'm supposed to (run) in the "Man versus Horse" race in Wales in a few months.
2. Well, you shouldn't run on hills all the time.
3. Hills are important, but you ought to run on flat surfaces as well.
4. And you should do at least one run that's longer than the race.
5. So, you are supposed to keep away from the horses, right?

B Which sentences in exercise **A** give advice? Which sentences express the speaker's belief or expectation? Write the number of each sentence according to its meaning.

1. Advice: __2__, ______, ______
2. Expectation: ______, ______

▼ Runners at the start of the "Man versus Horse" competition in Llanwrtyd Wells, Wales, UK (June 2013)

LEARN

13.3 Advisability: *Should* and *Ought To*

Should	*Ought To*
You **should exercise** regularly to stay fit. He **shouldn't play** in the game. He's sick.	You **ought to exercise** regularly to stay fit.

1. Use *should* or *ought to* + the base form of a verb to give advice or to say that something is a good idea.	People **should help** each other more. You **ought to call** your mother.
2. Use *shouldn't* to say that something isn't a good idea. It is uncommon to use *ought not to.*	You **shouldn't be** mean to your sister.
3. Use *should* in questions.* *Ought to* in questions is uncommon.	**Should** we **help** them?

*See Chart 12.1 on page **322** to review forming statements and questions with modals.

4 Read the advice sheet for runners. Then complete the sentences. Use *should, shouldn't,* or *ought to.* If there is more than one correct answer, write both.

5th Annual Hartfield 3-Mile Family Fun Run

Advice for Adult Runners

- Register online to ensure a place. Space is limited.
- Don't wait until the day of the race to register. You may be too late!
- Ask for a map if you want to check out the course.
- Wear something light; you don't need special running clothes.

Notes for Parents

- We don't advise children under five to run this distance.
- Drinking a little water before the race is a good idea.
- Walking to the finish is allowed if your child doesn't want to run all the way.
- Please don't make children train too hard for the race.

1. A: Should I sign up early to be sure to get a place in the run?

   B: Yes, you should/ought to register online.

2. You Shouldn't register on the day of the race.
3. If you want to check out the course, you ought to ask for a map.
4. This is a "fun run," so you Shouldn't buy special running clothes. You Should wear something light.
5. Children under five Shouldn't run this distance.
6. Runners should drink a little water before the race starts.
7. If your child gets tired, you Shouldn't push them. It's OK to walk.
8. Children Shouldn't train for the fun run only if they want to.

5 SPEAK.

A Match each piece of advice on the right with a situation on the left. Some advice may work for more than one situation.

Situation	Advice
1. I'm so tired! __c__	a. Join our swimming club.
2. I need information about ice hockey. ____	b. Try another sport.
3. I'm afraid of the water. ____	~~c~~. Don't train so hard!
4. I don't enjoy basketball anymore. ____	d. Look on the Internet.

B Work with a partner. Take turns reading the situations from exercise **A** and giving advice using *should* or *shouldn't*.

A: *I'm so tired!*

B: *You shouldn't train so hard.*

REAL ENGLISH

Should and *ought to* have similar meanings, but we use *should* much more frequently.

13.4 Expectations: *Be Supposed To*

Present and Future

A: You **aren't supposed to walk** on the grass.
B: Oh, I didn't realize that. I'm sorry.

She's **supposed to call** in a few minutes.
It's **supposed to rain** tonight. Bring an umbrella.

Past

A: He **wasn't supposed to arrive** until 10.
B: Well, I guess he's early. Let's say hello!

He **was supposed to call**. Maybe he forgot.
It's sunny! How nice. It **was supposed to rain**.

1. To express a future expectation, use *am/is/are* + *supposed to* + the base form of a verb.	I'**m supposed to arrive** a few minutes early. The package **is supposed to arrive** later today. You'**re supposed to use** a new ball for each game.
2. To talk about something that was expected but did not happen, use *was/were* + *supposed to* + the base form of a verb.	A: They **were supposed to be** here by noon. B: Maybe they are stuck in traffic.

6 Complete the sentences with the correct form of *be supposed to* and the verb in parentheses.

1. We __are supposed to be__ (be) at football practice early today. We should hurry.
2. You ________________ (not kick) other players in soccer.
3. A: ________ that runner ________________ (win) the race?

   B: Yes, he is. His times have been faster than everyone else's.
4. My mother ________________ (call) me tomorrow.
5. Alex ________________ (not arrive) last night, but he got on an earlier flight, and he got here at 10 p.m.

6. Peggy _______________ (go) on vacation tomorrow, but she's sick.

7. Ken is always at the gym. _______ he _______________ (train) so hard?

8. I _______________ (drive) Steve to the big game yesterday, but my car broke down.

9. We are late! We _______________ (arrive) at 7:00.

10. Players _______________ (not wear) jewelry during the game, but they sometimes do.

7 WRITE & SPEAK.

A Complete the sentences. Use your own ideas.

1. I'm supposed to _______________.
2. Students aren't supposed to _______________.
3. As a child, I was supposed to _______________, but I didn't.
4. I wasn't supposed to _______________, but I did.

B Work with a partner. Share your sentences from exercise **A**. Ask follow-up questions.

A: *I'm supposed to be on a diet this month. I'm not supposed to eat sweets or drink soda.*

B: *Why? Are you training for something?*

PRACTICE

8 Circle all correct answers. Sometimes both answers are correct.

1. A: Professional athletes **shouldn't** / **aren't supposed to** make so much money.

   B: I disagree. They **should** / **ought to** make as much as they can.
2. The game **should** / **was supposed to** start at 2 p.m., but it was delayed by half an hour.
3. If you're interested in action photography, you **ought to** / **are supposed to** borrow my camera. It's great for sports shots.
4. Dev **isn't supposed to** / **shouldn't** run on his bad ankle. He could get hurt.
5. **I'm supposed to** / **ought to** be at baseball practice in ten minutes, but I won't get there with all this traffic!
6. You **ought** / **should** not wear glasses when you play soccer.
7. I fell yesterday, and my shoulder hurts. I **ought to** / **should** see a doctor.
8. I can't believe we lost the game! That team **shouldn't** / **wasn't supposed to** be very good.

9 Look at the photo and read the caption. Complete the conversation with the phrases from the box. Use each phrase only once.

should I try	shouldn't worry	it's supposed to be
ought to learn	should I call	ought to provide
are supposed to use	should call	~~was supposed to be~~

Gina: Christine (1) was supposed to be here 15 minutes ago. Where is she? She (2) ______________ us if she is going to be late.

Myoko: We have time. You (3) ______________ so much. Our start time is an hour away.

Gina: (4) ______________ her and ask if she's changed her mind?

Myoko: Oh, Gina, you (5) ______________ to relax a bit more! She'll be here soon. So, are you looking forward to going hydrosphering for the first time?

Gina: Yes, I am. (6) ______________ really exciting when you are riding inside the ball. I'm a little bit nervous. I think they (7) ______________ more safety information.

Myoko: I agree. Don't forget that you (8) ______________ the safety straps when you are in a hydrosphere by yourself for the first ride.

Gina: I won't forget. I'm really excited about the second ride when we'll be together in the same hydrosphere. (9) ______________ to take some photos?

Myoko: Yes, of course. Oh, look. Here comes Christine now . . .

▼ Hydrosphering is a sport invented in New Zealand in the 1990s. People hydrosphere by rolling down hills inside a large, plastic ball called a hydrosphere.

10 EDIT. Read the answers to an online survey. Then find and correct six more errors with modals and other similar expressions of advisability and expectation.

Survey: Are Sports Out of Control?

This month's online survey was about the state of modern sports. Here are some of the replies we received to our questions.

1. Should top athletes ~~to~~ earn millions of dollars a year?

Tim in Texas: No, I think it's gotten crazy. There ought to be a maximum salary in every sport.

Gene in Georgia: Yes, I think so. Athletes should earn a fair amount. Sports stars are supposed provide entertainment for millions of people. That is worth a lot of money. Also, college athletes don't earn any money, but they risk a lot. They should to get paid, too.

2. Should there be so much advertising in sports?

Tim in Texas: I understand the need for advertising—sports are a very expensive business. However, there ought to be more control.

Gene in Georgia: Sports supposed to be attractive to fans, and advertising adds a lot of color to events. There shouldn't be more control.

3. Should children compete or ought they just have fun?

Tim in Texas: Small children are suppose to enjoy sports. They ought to concentrate on learning skills, not winning games.

Gene in Georgia: All sports supposed to produce stars for world championships. If we want that to happen, then competition should start as early as possible.

11 APPLY.

A Work with a partner. Discuss the questions in exercise **10**. In your notebook, take notes about your answers and your partner's answers.

Question 1

A: *All sports are different. Each sport should make its own rules about players' salaries.*

B: *I agree. Sports stars are like movie stars. They should earn as much as they can.*

B Write two sentences for each question. Write about your ideas and your partner's.

Question 1

My answer: Top athletes are supposed to be "superhuman." Their salaries should be more than the average person's, too.

My partner's answer: Top athletes . . .

Charts 13.1–13.4

1 Circle all correct answers. Sometimes more than one answer may be correct.

1. You **may not** / **can't** / **must not** bring food into the stadium.
2. Tom **can't** / **doesn't have to** / **shouldn't** join the club. He is below the minimum age.
3. We **don't have to** / **must** / **have to** return the tickets by today, or we'll lose our money.
4. Lori and her friend **didn't have to** / **shouldn't** / **weren't supposed to** play tennis yesterday. Their match was canceled.
5. I **have to** / **must** / **'m supposed to** practice tonight, but I have a headache. I might not go.
6. The team isn't very good. The coach **ought to** / **has to** / **should** find better players.
7. The referee **must** / **had to** / **has got to** act fast when a fight started during the game last night.
8. You **don't have to** / **may not** / **can't** sit there. That seat is reserved for the coach.

Charts 13.1–13.4

CD4-08

2 **LISTEN** and circle the answer that is similar in meaning to the sentence you hear.

Example: 1. You hear: *I am supposed to play softball tomorrow.*

1. **People expect me** / **I have permission** to play softball tomorrow.
2. It's **a good idea** / **necessary** for me to speak to the coach immediately.
3. We **should** / **must** buy three tickets for the game.
4. I **must** / **should** ski more often.
5. I **went** / **didn't go** swimming yesterday as planned.
6. The referee **must** / **ought to** write a report after the game.
7. The players **have got to** / **ought to** receive free tickets for their families.
8. It wasn't **necessary** / **a good idea** for us to train hard for the race.
9. Tennis players **do not have to** / **can't** touch the net.
10. Speaking while the coach is talking is **prohibited** / **not necessary**.

Charts 13.1–13.4

3 **WRITE.** Read the tennis serving tips. Then write four sentences in your notebook about the tips. Use one modal or similar expression for each of the following: necessity, prohibition, advice, and expectation.

You shouldn't practice during a game.

Tennis Serving Tips	
1. Do not practice during a game.	3. Don't throw the ball too high.
2. Don't throw the ball straight up.	4. Keep your eye on the ball.
	5. Relax and enjoy serving!

Charts 13.1–13.4

4 EDIT. Read the tips about serving. Use the information in exercise **3** to find and correct seven more errors with modals and similar expressions of necessity, prohibition, advice, and expectation.

Perhaps, like many tennis players, you love playing the game, but hate serving. Well, good news! You don't have to feel that way anymore! We asked our readers to share their advice on serving like a pro. Here are the results.

- You shouldn't practice during a competition. You ought practice your serve only when you don't have to worry about winning or losing.
- You got to relax. Serving ought to be easy, but it can be very difficult if you are nervous.
- You must take your eye off the ball! You should watch it all the way from your hand until you hit it.
- You shouldn't throw the ball too high. You're not supposed wait a long time for the ball to drop. If you do that, you are throwing it too high.
- You don't have to throw the ball straight up. Instead, you should to throw the ball slightly to your right, if you are right-handed. Left-handers should throw to the left.
- You must not be afraid of your serve. It's the only time in tennis that you have complete control of what happens. Serving supposed to be fun!

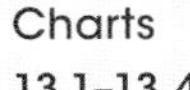
Charts 13.1–13.4

5 SPEAK.

A In your notebook, take notes about tips you would give a beginner about one of the activities in the box or your own idea. Use modals of necessity, prohibition, advice, and expectation. Use exercise **4** as a model.

Cycling: going uphill	Swimming/Running: breathing
Basketball: shooting a basket	Soccer: scoring a goal

B Work with a partner. Share your ideas from exercise **A**.

All cyclists ought to ride up hills regularly. When you approach a hill, you should increase your speed on the flat road. If the hill is steep, you must choose a low gear. On very steep hills you've got to be ready to stand on your pedals, if necessary.

Connect the Grammar to Writing

1 READ & NOTICE THE GRAMMAR.

A Think of a sport that you enjoy. Tell a partner your sport and your reasons for liking it. Then read what one student wrote about snowboarding.

Try Snowboarding!

We all know we are supposed to exercise to stay in shape, but sometimes going to the gym can become boring. That's when you have to find a new challenge. If you live in an area with mountains and snow, you definitely ought to try snowboarding.

First of all, snowboarding is great exercise. It strengthens your muscles and it's good for your heart. Of course, you must take things slowly at first; you can't expect to fly down a mountain like an Olympic snowboarder on your first day. Like any activity, you must practice to become more advanced. You shouldn't start on steep[1] hills, for example. First you have to learn to control the board on small hills.

Another great thing about snowboarding is that it is easy to get started. Instructors are easy to find, and you don't have to buy a lot of equipment. In fact, you should rent a board at first. Then, if you enjoy it, you can buy your own equipment.

With snowboarding, you don't have to worry about a lot of rules because there aren't any! Snowboarding is a fairly new sport, but it has quickly become very popular. Try snowboarding today! You won't regret it!

[1]**steep:** not flat; a steep hill will cause a skier or snowboarder to go very fast.

GRAMMAR FOCUS

In the text in exercise **A**, the writer uses modals and similar expressions to express necessity and advisability.

Necessity: *That's when you* ***have to find*** *a new challenge.*
. . .you ***must take*** *things slowly . . .*

Advisability: *. . . , you definitely* ***ought to try*** *snowboarding.*
You ***shouldn't start*** *on steep hills, for example.*

B Work with a partner. Find at least one more example for each meaning.

Necessity: ______________________________

Advisability: ______________________________

C In exercise **1A**, the writer introduces the topic and states his opinion. He gives two reasons and supports, or explains, those reasons. Complete the diagram to show his writing plan.

Topic: Snowboarding	→	Opinion:
Reason 1: great exercise	→	Support/Explanation:
Reason 2:	→	Support/Explanation: Instructors are easy to find, and you don't have to buy a lot of equipment.

2 BEFORE YOU WRITE.

A Work with a partner. Choose a sport to write about and discuss your opinion with your partner. You may decide to write about a sport you don't like.

B In your notebook, draw a diagram like the one in exercise **1C**. Complete the diagram with your topic, your opinion, and two reasons. Then support or explain your reasons.

WRITING FOCUS Writing a Clear Introduction

When writers set out to write an opinion essay, their goal is to get readers to agree with their ideas. It's a good idea to start an essay strongly by doing the following.

- **Relate to your readers**: *We all know we are supposed to exercise to stay in shape, but sometimes going to the gym or running can become boring. That's when you have to find a new challenge.*
- **State your opinion clearly:** *If you live in an area with mountains and snow, you definitely ought to try snowboarding.*

3 WRITE an opening paragraph that names your sport and states your opinion. Then write one paragraph for each reason. Use the information from your chart in exercise **2B** and the text in exercise **1A** to help you.

4 EDIT. Read your text. Underline the modals and similar expressions. Then use the checklist to assess your work.

- ☐ I used *must* or *have (got) to* for necessity and *don't* or *doesn't have to* for lack of necessity.. [13.1, 13.2]
- ☐ I used *should* or *ought to* for advisability. [13.3]
- ☐ I used *be supposed to* for expectation. [13.4]
- ☐ I wrote a clear introduction by relating to my reader and stating my opinion clearly. [WRITING FOCUS]

UNIT 14 Innovations

Verbs

▲ In 1964, people considered the AT&T picture phone to be an exciting new invention.

EXPLORE

CD4-09

1 READ the article about driverless cars. Notice the words in **bold**.

Cars without Drivers

▲ People in a driverless car

We **live** in a modern world with constant technological innovation.[1] These new ideas often **raise** difficult moral[2] questions. "Driverless" cars, which **drive** their passengers around automatically, are a good example. When the technology first **appeared**, it was just one more amazing modern invention. Now, four U.S. states **allow** driverless cars on certain roads. Nevada, Florida, California, and Michigan have all **passed** laws that **permit** them. Several cities in Belgium, France, and Italy **are** also **planning** for them.

Do you feel safe knowing that the cars around you **might** not **have** drivers? In a dangerous situation, a driver **must react**[3] instantly. A car without a driver **has** only its computer program.

So what **happens** if a child **runs** in front of a driverless car? The child's life is in danger, and the situation **requires**[4] an instant response. **Will** the driverless car **change** direction and **put** its passengers in danger? Or **will** it **continue** toward the child because that **reduces** the risk to the car's passengers? If the machine **makes** the morally wrong choice, who is to blame . . . the car company or the helpless passenger?

[1] **innovation:** the process of developing new and improved ideas, methods, and products
[2] **moral:** related to what is right or wrong
[3] **react:** speak or move when something happens
[4] **require:** need

2 CHECK. Choose the correct answer to complete each sentence.

1. In the writer's opinion, modern inventions _____.
   a. are always a good thing b. can cause new problems c. do not affect our lives
2. According to the article, driverless cars are _____.
   a. allowed everywhere b. allowed in some places c. not allowed anywhere
3. In the example of the child, the writer worries that the driverless car may not _____.
   a. realize danger b. stop c. make the right decision
4. According to the article, in an accident involving a driverless car, it is difficult to know _____.
   a. exactly what happened b. who is responsible c. if the passenger had a choice

3 DISCOVER. Complete the exercises to learn about the grammar in this lesson.

A Find the following verbs in the article in exercise **1**. Write the direct object that follows each verb. If the verb does not have a direct object, write ✗.

1. raise difficult moral questions
2. drive _____
3. appeared X
4. allow _____
5. must react _____
6. has _____
7. happens _____
8. requires _____
9. Will . . . change _____
10. makes _____

B Look at the verbs without direct objects in exercise **A**. Can you add a direct object to any of these verbs? Discuss your answer with your classmates and teacher.

LEARN

14.1 Transitive and Intransitive Verbs

Verbs				
	Subject	Verb	Direct Object	
Transitive	Jen and Joe	**rented**	**a car**	on their vacation.
Intransitive	They	**arrived**		in the evening.

1. A transitive verb is followed by a direct object (DO). The direct object is a noun or pronoun that experiences the action of the verb. It often answers questions with *who* or *what.*	Jon **lost** his car keys. (DO: his car keys) A: **What** did John lose? B: **His car keys.**
2. An intransitive verb is not followed by a direct object. It is often followed by a prepositional phrase or an adverb. Here are some common intransitive verbs: *arrive* *fall* *live* *sleep* *come* *go* *travel* *wait*	We **arrived** after dark. (Prepositional Phrase: after dark) They **waited** quietly. (Adverb: quietly)
3. Some verbs can be both transitive (T) and intransitive (I). Here are some common examples: *begin* *close* *open* *call* *continue* *start* *change* *drive* *stop*	He **is driving** his new car. She **drives** to work. He **opened** the door. The door **opened**.

4 Underline the verb in each sentence. Write ***T*** if the verb is transitive or ***I*** if the verb is intransitive. If the verb is transitive, circle the direct object.

1. __T__ Eve always tries the latest things.
2. ____ Last week, she tested a driverless car.
3. ____ She traveled to the beach in the car.
4. ____ She slept for about 30 minutes.
5. ____ Then, a dog ran in front of the car.
6. ____ Luckily, the car didn't hit the dog.
7. ____ Eve went to the store.
8. ____ She arrived safely.
9. ____ However, she didn't like the car.
10. ____ Eve won't buy a driverless car.

5 Read the pairs of sentences and notice the verbs in bold. Write ***T*** if the bold verb is used transitively or ***I*** if the verb is used intransitively. Circle the direct object of each transitive verb.

1. a. __T__ The boss **started** the meeting with an announcement about the new product.
   b. __I__ The meeting **starts** at 9:30. Don't be late.
2. a. ____ The gas station **closes** at 6 p.m.
   b. ____ **Close** the windows. It looks like it's going to rain.
3. a. ____ They **drove** the new car.
   b. ____ They **drove** carefully.

4. a. _____ My class **began** at 3:00. I'm late.
   b. _____ The teacher **began** the class a few minutes late.

5. a. _____ We **continued** the class the next day.
   b. _____ The lecture **will continue** on Wednesday.

6. a. _____ Someone **called** while you were out.
   b. _____ Someone **called** us late last night.

7. a. _____ They **opened** the car door carefully.
   b. _____ The car doors **open** automatically.

8. a. _____ **Has** the design **changed**?
   b. _____ **Have** you **changed** your tires recently?

▲ Doors open automatically in many taxis in Japan.

14.2 Direct and Indirect Objects with *To* and *For*

	Direct Object	*To/ For*	Indirect Object
He sent	an e-mail	to	his parents.
She bought	a gift	for	her brother.

1. Some transitive verbs are followed by a direct object + *to/for* + an indirect object (IO).	She showed **the article** (DO) to **her friend** (IO). I often get **the mail** (DO) for **my neighbor** (IO).
2. **Remember:** A direct object experiences the action of the verb. It often answers the question *what* or *who*.	We like **our teacher**. A: **Who** do they like? B: **Their teacher**.
3. An indirect object is usually a person who experiences the action indirectly. It answers the questions *to who(m)* or *for who(m)*.	He sent the package to **his parents**. A: **Who** did he send it to? B: **His parents**. I bought a gift for **my brother**. A: **Who** did you buy it for? B: **My brother**.
4. Here are some common transitive verbs that use *to* or *for*: a. *to: explain, give, offer, send, show, tell* b. *for: buy, fix, keep, make, get, provide* c. either *to* or *for*: *bring, take*	 a. Dr. Lin **showed** the results **to the students**. b. They **made** dinner **for their children**. c. Jim **brought** the report **to his boss**. Jim **brought** snacks **for the team**.

6 READ, WRITE & SPEAK.

A Circle the correct words to complete the article.

Nicolas Appert Changed the Way People Eat

▲ Nicolas Appert

At the end of the eighteenth century, the French general Napoleon Bonaparte needed help. He needed to provide healthy food (1) **to** / **for** his soldiers. Often food would go bad before it reached them. The French government offered a prize (2) **to** / **for** the inventor who could discover a solution, but for 15 years no one could solve the problem (3) **to** / **for** the government. Then in 1809, the French chef Nicolas Appert showed his ideas (4) **to** / **for** the government authorities. He recommended using glass bottles and high temperatures to keep food safe (5) **to** / **for** people. In 1810, after testing his idea, the government gave the prize (6) **to** / **for** Appert. Now the government could send fresh food (7) **to** / **for** the army when it was far away. Strangely, Appert didn't know why this process worked. He couldn't explain the reasons (8) **to** / **for** anyone, but his innovative ideas changed the way people eat.

▼ Modern-day canning jars

▼ An Appert canning jar

B Look at items 1–8 in exercise **A**. Write the verb and object that comes before *to* or *for*.

1. provide healthy food
2. ______
3. ______
4. ______
5. ______
6. ______
7. ______
8. ______

C In your notebook, use five of the phrases from exercise **B** and *to* or *for* to write new sentences with your own ideas. Then share your sentences with a partner.

The parents provide healthy food for their children.

14.3 Direct and Indirect Objects: Word Order with *To* and *For*

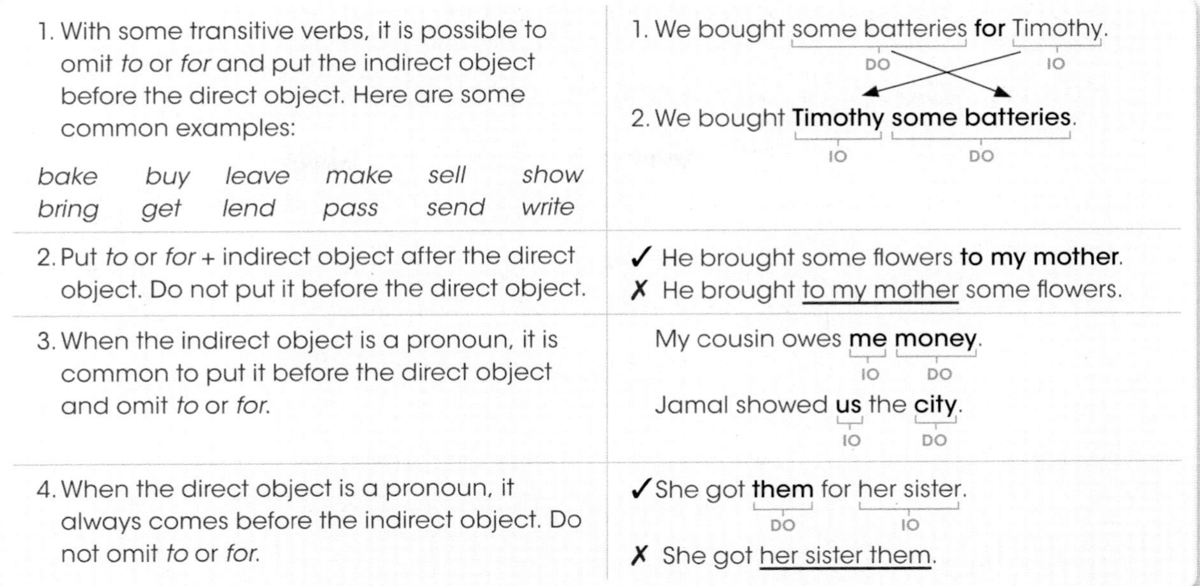

1. With some transitive verbs, it is possible to omit *to* or *for* and put the indirect object before the direct object. Here are some common examples: *bake* *buy* *leave* *make* *sell* *show* *bring* *get* *lend* *pass* *send* *write*	1. We bought some batteries (DO) **for** Timothy (IO). 2. We bought **Timothy** (IO) **some batteries** (DO).
2. Put *to* or *for* + indirect object after the direct object. Do not put it before the direct object.	✓ He brought some flowers **to my mother**. ✗ He brought to my mother some flowers.
3. When the indirect object is a pronoun, it is common to put it before the direct object and omit *to* or *for*.	My cousin owes **me** (IO) **money** (DO). Jamal showed **us** (IO) the **city** (DO).
4. When the direct object is a pronoun, it always comes before the indirect object. Do not omit *to* or *for*.	✓ She got **them** (DO) for her sister (IO). ✗ She got her sister them.

7 Rewrite the sentences without *to* or *for*. Remember to change the order of the direct and indirect objects.

1. I lent my e-book reader to my cousin.

   I lent *my cousin my e-book reader.*

2. Marie bought the latest smartphone for her husband.

   Marie bought ______________________________

3. Mike sent the new product design to his boss.

   Mike sent ______________________________

4. Did you leave the new Internet password for me?

   Did you leave ______________________________

5. Eva e-mailed her homework assignment to her professor.

   Eva e-mailed ______________________________

6. Diane showed the article about robots to her friend.

   Diane showed ______________________________

7. My parents got a new tablet for me.

   My parents got ______________________________

8. I gave the files to my coworker.

   I gave ______________________________

8 Complete the paragraphs. Put the direct object (DO) and indirect object (IO) in the correct order. Add *to* or *for* if necessary.

Paragraph 1

For graduation, my parents bought (1) ___me a car___ (DO: a car / IO: me). My brother sometimes lends (2) ______________ (DO: his car / IO: me), and he knows what I like. So my parents showed (3) ______________ (DO: it / IO: my brother) first to be sure I would like it. Of course, I loved my new car! I sent (4) ______________ (DO: a photo of it / IO: my grandfather). He wrote (5) ______________ (DO: a nice e-mail / IO: me) about his first car.

Paragraph 2

I try to make (6) ______________ (DO: a card / IO: my sister) for her birthday every year. I don't often buy (7) ______________ (DO: a card / IO: her) from a store. It takes quite a lot of thought, so I never send (8) ______________ (DO: the card / IO: her). I prefer to bring (9) ______________ (DO: it / IO: my sister) in person.

PRACTICE

9 Choose the correct ending(s) for each sentence. If no ending is necessary, choose Ø. Sometimes there is more than one correct answer.

1. Sometimes new ideas can cause _____.

   (a.) problems (b.) difficulties c. at the beginning

2. The new product appeared _____.

   a. last week b. customers c. all over the country

3. The latest computers use _____.

   a. Ø b. quietly c. less electricity

4. Alison sent _____.

   a. her friend some photos b. to her friend some photos c. some photos to her friend

5. When Hassan heard the news, he didn't react _____.

   a. immediately b. the situation c. Ø

6. The children can cook _____.

   a. their own meals b. Ø c. very well

7. The movie started _____.

   a. on time b. Ø c. an argument among my friends

8. We waited _____.

   a. Ø b. outside c. the teacher

10 READ & SPEAK.

A Circle the correct answers to complete the conversation. Circle Ø if you do not need *to* or *for*.

Drone Delivery?

Misha: What are you doing, Deena?

Deena: I'm doing some shopping online. I want to get some presents (1) **to** / **for** / **Ø** my family. There are several birthdays in my family in the next few weeks. My cousin is first. I'm going to buy (2) **to** / **for** / **Ø** her this e-reader. Oh no, wait . . . they can't deliver it (3) **to** / **for** / **Ø** her house until next week. That's too late.

Misha: Did you hear about the companies that are planning to send (4) **to** / **for** / **Ø** customers their goods by drone, sometimes even the same day?

Deena: Drones? You mean those automated flying machines? I don't believe it!

Misha: Well, it's true. Several companies are considering using drones to send orders (5) **to** / **for** / **Ø** their customers. It sounds a bit crazy, I know. Look, I'll show (6) **to** / **for** / **Ø** you the article. . . . Here's a picture of one. Amazing, huh?

Deena: Um, I'm not so sure. I'm planning to order some expensive dishes (7) **to** / **for** / **Ø** my mother. I don't think I'd ever trust one of those machines to bring it (8) **to** / **for** / **Ø** me safely!

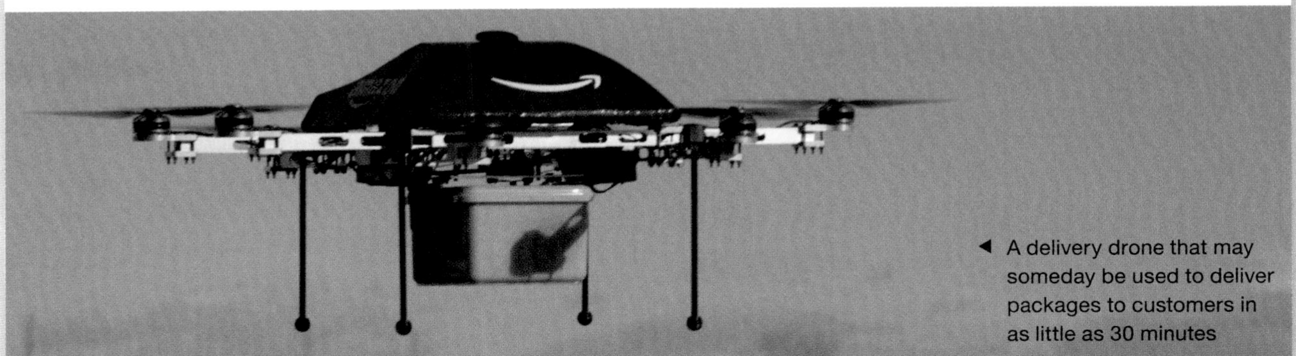

◄ A delivery drone that may someday be used to deliver packages to customers in as little as 30 minutes

B Work with a partner. Discuss the questions.

1. Do you think it's a good idea for drones to deliver things to people? Why, or why not?
2. What are possible problems with delivering things by drone?
3. Would you send people gifts by drone?

11 WRITE & SPEAK.

A Complete each sentence with a direct object and an indirect object. Use your own ideas.

1. I always go online to buy ___*food*___ for ___*my cats*___.
2. I sent ______________ a(n) ______________ recently.
3. Can you show ______________ to ______________?

4. I would like to get ______________ a(n) ______________.

5. Last week I brought ______________ to ______________.

B Work with a partner. Share your sentences from exercise **A**.

A: *I always go online to buy cat food for my cats.*

B: *Is it cheaper online?*

12 LISTEN.

CD4-10-13

A Listen to four students talk about different historical innovations. Write the correct date under each invention.

1. Rail Travel
George Stephenson

1825

2. The Dishwasher
Josephine Cochran

____

3. The Circular Saw
Tabitha Babbitt

____

4. The Printing Press
Johannes Gutenberg

____

CD4-10-13

B Listen again. Complete the chart with the verbs and objects you hear.

	Subject	Verb	Object
1. Rail Travel	Stephenson	*changed*	the way we travel
	He	operated	
2. The Dishwasher	Cochran		machines for her friends
	She	started	
3. The Circular Saw	Babbit		a large circular saw
	Men		large straight saws
4. The Printing Press	Gutenberg		books
	The printing press	changed	

C In your notebook, write sentences about each person using the verbs and objects in exercise **B**.

George Stephenson changed the way we travel.

13 EDIT. Read the conversation about a recent innovation in eyewear. Find and correct six more errors with transitive and intransitive verbs and with *to* and *for.*

Markus: Hey, Dave, I told ~~to~~ you how much I like my new phone, right? It gives me all the information I need when I'm away from my computer. Well, I just watched a video about a new pair of glasses that does the same thing. They show for you the same information as your phone, but right in front of your eyes!

Dave: Oh yeah, Mira sent me a photo of hers a couple days ago. Her parents got a pair her. I don't understand the attraction. Can you explain me it?

Markus: Well, I guess they make life easier for people.

Dave: Are you serious? . . . I'm pretty sure they'd give a headache to me, and I really don't mind checking my phone for information. Are you seriously going to get a pair? I'm sure they will cost a lot of money you.

Markus: Maybe, but I can't wait to get some.

Dave: I guess I won't need to buy a pair—you can lend to me yours!

14 APPLY.

A Read about the picture phone. Underline the verbs.

> The inventor made the picture phone for people who wanted more meaningful communication. The invention looks unusual, but nowadays people can easily talk to and see their friends and family on their phones or computers.

B Look at the photos of unusual inventions from the past and read the captions. In your notebook, write a short paragraph about each. Use the paragraph in exercise **A** as an example.

▲ Amphibious Bike, 1932

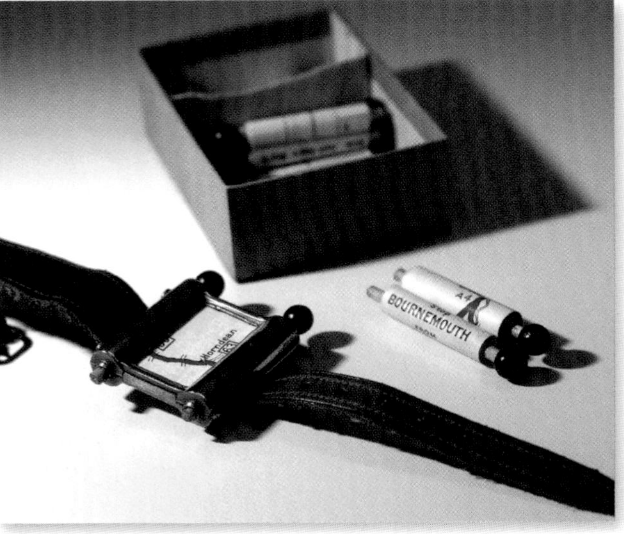

▲ Route indicator watch, 1926

EXPLORE

CD4-14 **1 READ** the transcript from a podcast about innovations in brain research. Notice the words in **bold**.

Podcast 23 Innovations: Wearable EEGs

Larissa: Hello! This is Larissa coming to you from State University with this week's *Tech Talk* podcast. On today's show, we have the president of the Tech Club here to **talk about** another exciting innovator. Welcome, Jamil!

Jamil: Thank you, Larissa. Today I'd like to tell you about a woman named Tan Le. She's a pioneer[1] and co-founder of a company that created the first ever portable[2] EEG and BCI (brain-computer interface). It's a lightweight headset that reads your brainwaves. Basically, it reads and interprets your thoughts and sends the information to a device, such as your laptop or mobile phone.

Larissa: So, anyone can **hook** their brain **up** to a device? What do we use it for?

Jamil: Well, for one thing, Tan Le hopes that it can help people who are injured or ill. For example, with this technology a person could soon be able to control an electric wheelchair[3] simply by **thinking about** turning left or right. There's a great TED talk about it online if anyone wants to **find out** more . . .

Larissa: Sounds fascinating. I'll definitely **check** that **out**. I imagine application developers[4] will **figure out** a lot of different ways to use the technology.

Jamil: Yes, definitely. That's the plan.

Larissa: So, I've heard that Tan Le's personal story is as interesting as this innovation.

Jamil: That's right. She **grew up** in Australia, but her family **comes from** Vietnam. Life was not easy when she was young, but her mother and grandmother encouraged her never to **give up**. Her experience really helped her to **get ahead**, way ahead!

[1] **pioneer:** a person who leads the way into a new area of knowledge or invention
[2] **portable:** can be carried or moved around
[3] **wheelchair:** a chair that allows people who cannot walk to move
[4] **application developer:** a computer professional who develops specialized software or applications

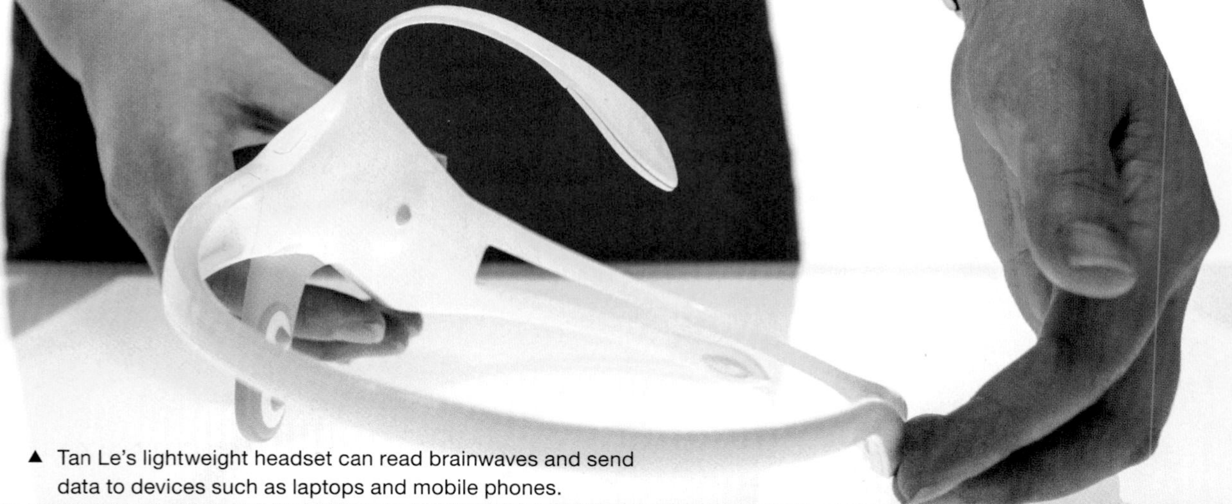

▲ Tan Le's lightweight headset can read brainwaves and send data to devices such as laptops and mobile phones.

2 CHECK. Read the statements. Circle **T** for *true* or **F** for *false*.

1. Tan Le's invention is large and heavy. **T** **F**
2. Tan Le's system can interpret people's thoughts. **T** **F**
3. Tan Le's system can only be used in hospitals. **T** **F**
4. Tan Le grew up in Vietnam. **T** **F**
5. Tan Le's family helped her succeed. **T** **F**

3 DISCOVER. Complete the exercises to learn about the grammar in this lesson.

A Look at the bold phrases in exercise **1**. Write the verb or verbs that come before each word.

about	ahead	from	out	up
talk				

B Work with a partner. Write one more words that you know in each column in exercise **A**. If you need help, see pages **A7–A9** for lists of phrasal verbs and their meanings.

A: *Another verb that goes with "out" is "watch," as in "Watch out!"*

B: *I think "look" with "out" is similar. It means "Be careful."*

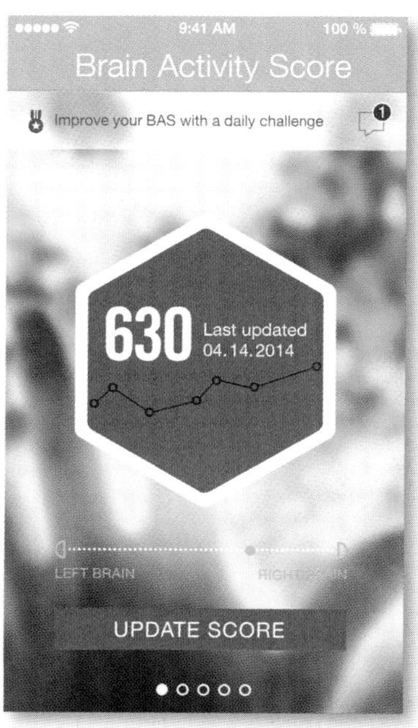

▲ Sample screen shots of brain activity and other information sent to headset users

LEARN

14.4 Phrasal Verbs

1. Phrasal verbs* usually have two words (a verb + a particle). Particles are small words (*about, over, on, in*) that look like prepositions. Unlike prepositions, however, they give a different meaning to the verb they combine with.	**Look out!** There's a dog in the road! (Phrasal Verb) I looked out the window. (Verb) (Prepositional Phrase) **look out:** be careful **out:** in a direction away from
2. Phrasal verbs are often used instead of single-word verbs that express the same meaning.	**call off** = cancel **find out** = discover, learn **get ahead** = succeed **give up** = quit, stop trying **go over** = review **hand in** = submit **run into** = meet (by accident) **talk over** = discuss

*See pages **A7–A9** for lists of phrasal verbs.

4 Underline the phrasal verb in each sentence. Then choose the correct definition. Refer to the phrasal verbs list on page **A7** for more phrasal verbs and their meanings.

1. Tan Le wants to <u>find out</u> more about how brains work.
   a. ask   b. discover
2. As a child, Tan Le learned never to give up.
   a. stop trying   b. make mistakes
3. If you want more information, you can look up Tan Le's company online.
   a. find   b. contact
4. People are thinking about the different ways to use the new technology.
   a. are considering   b. are remembering
5. Some people do not like new technology, but it isn't going to go away.
   a. continue   b. disappear
6. The world cannot go back to an age without computers.
   a. advance   b. return
7. The scientist had to call off his research because his equipment was damaged.
   a. cancel   b. repeat
8. The researcher finished the test and turned off the machine.
   a. stopped   b. started

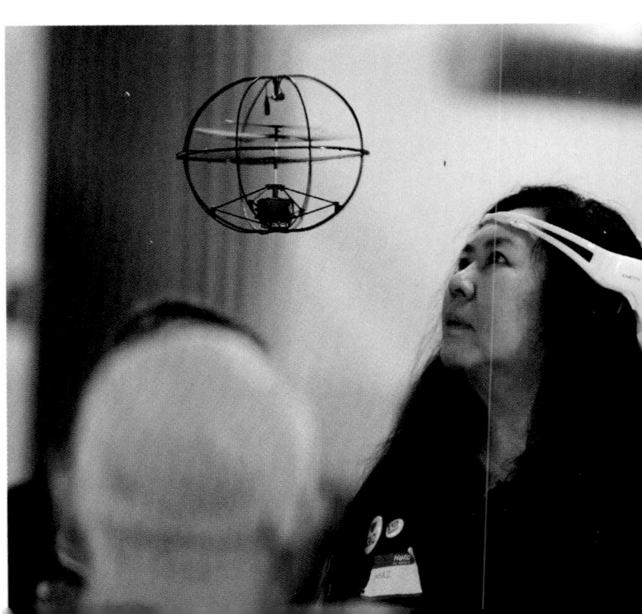

▶ A woman looks at a flying object with Emotiv Insight

14.5 Transitive and Intransitive Phrasal Verbs

Phrasal Verbs			
		Direct Object	
Transitive	Jen and Joe **got on** They **talked over**	the flight their plans	to Beijing. for the trip.
Intransitive	Nancy **showed up** Her car **broke down**	— —	ten minutes late. on the way.

1. Some phrasal verbs are transitive.* They are followed by a direct object (DO).	We **called off** the party. (DO)
2. Some phrasal verbs are intransitive.* They are not followed by a direct object.	✓ Our car **broke down**. ✗ Our car broke down it. ✗ They broke down the car.

* See pages **A7–A9** for lists of phrasal verbs.

5 READ & WRITE.

A Circle the correct particle to complete each phrasal verb.

Riverwatch

Keeping Our Rivers Clean!

Dear Neighbor,

We all live in an area that used to have beautiful rivers and ponds. Have you noticed how the standard of these areas has been going (1) **over** / **down** for the last few years? Some people throw (2) **off** / **away** their garbage carelessly, and a lot of it ends (3) **out** / **up** in the river. I went to town hall to talk (4) **out** / **over** the problem with the town officials. They clearly don't have enough staff to clean (5) **up** / **away** these areas on a regular basis.

That's when I had the idea to set (6) **in** / **up** an organization to help. This is a new idea for our community. We're called Riverwatch, and we are already making a BIG difference!

Every weekend, we send (7) **away** / **out** teams to pick (8) **up** / **on** garbage from one of the rivers. It's clear that the problem of dirty rivers and ponds will not go (9) **away** / **down** on its own. If you are concerned about the area you live in and can spend a few hours with us once a month, come (10) **over** / **by** our next meeting.

Sincerely,
Pat Siever

B Seven of the phrasal verbs in exercise **A** are transitive. In your notebook, write six more phrasal verbs from the letter and their direct objects.

throw away their garbage

14.6 Transitive Phrasal Verbs: Separable and Inseparable

Transitive Phrasal Verbs	
Separable	Jack **looked up** the word. He **looked** the word **up**. He **looked** it **up**.
Inseparable	✓ Jill **thought about** the essay. ✓ She **thought about** it. ✗ Jill thought the essay about. ✗ She thought it about.

1. Most transitive phrasal verbs are separable.* The direct object (DO) can come after the phrasal verb or between the verb and the particle. Here are some common separable phrasal verbs: *call off* *find out* *look up* *set up* *figure out* *hand in* *put on* *talk over*	I **turned off** the light (DO). → I **turned** the light (DO) **off**. I **tried on** the coat (DO). → I **tried** the coat (DO) **on**.
2. **Be careful!** When the direct object of a separable phrasal verb is a pronoun (*me, him, . . .*), it must go between the verb and the particle.	✓ She didn't **pick** it **out**. ✗ She didn't pick out it.
3. Some transitive phrasal verbs are inseparable.* The direct object must come after the particle. Here are some common inseparable phrasal verbs: *call on* *come up with* *go over* *run into* *come from* *get on* *look into* *think about*	I **ran into** an old friend (DO). I **ran into** her (DO) at the store.
4. **Be careful!** When the direct object of an inseparable phrasal verb is a pronoun, it must go after the verb and the particle.	✓ I came across **it** while doing research. ✗ I came it across yesterday.

*See pages **A7–A9** for lists of phrasal verbs.

6 Complete the phrasal verbs in the students' responses to the professor's question. Use chart 14.6 and the lists of phrasal verbs and their meanings on pages **A7–A9** to help you.

Professor: What qualities do you need to be an innovator?

1. You have to be able to ___go___ over a lot of notes and ideas.
2. You need to be good at finding ___out___ what people need.
3. It helps if you come ___from___ a family of innovators.
4. It's an advantage if you enjoy trying to ___figure___ out solutions to problems.
5. You have to be patient. Sometimes, if you go to sleep thinking ___over___ a problem, you will ___come___ (wake up) up with a solution.
6. To find the best solutions, you may need to talk ___over___ your ideas with other people.

7 Choose the option with the correct word order to replace the bold phrase in each sentence.

1. We **turned on the TV**.	(a.) turned it on	b. turned on it
2. The professor **called on Linda**.	a. called her on	b. called on her
3. We had to **call off the meeting**.	a. call it off	b. call off it
4. Don't **hand in your work** late.	a. hand it in	b. hand in it
5. **Put your shoes on**. It's time to go!	a. Put them on.	b. Put on them.
6. When did you **run into José**?	a. run him into	b. run into him
7. I can't **figure out the answer**.	a. figure it out	b. figure out it
8. I need to **look up the word *portable***.	a. look it up	b. look up it

PRACTICE

8 Circle the correct words or phrases to complete the e-mails. Sometimes both answers are correct.

Hi Frank,

My trip was terrible! I was scheduled to fly to Houston to give a speech at a conference about innovation in the workplace. When I woke (1) **up** / **out** on the day of my flight, there was a terrible storm. I had to look (2) **the flight status up** / **up the flight status** on my phone because my computer wasn't working. There was no change, so I drove to the airport. The storm got worse, and my plane took (3) **off** / **away** three hours late. Then there was a problem with the conference schedule, and they had to call (4) **off my speech** / **my speech off**. I didn't find (5) **out** / **out it** until I received a text from the conference organizers when I arrived in Houston!

Hi Silvia,

You were asking about Penny. I ran (6) **into** / **over** her last week at the train station. She invited me to come (7) **over** / **over to** her apartment for dinner. We had a great time, but she's not very happy at work. She has a new boss, and the company didn't talk (8) **it over** / **over it** with her first. Hopefully, they will get (9) **along** / **up**.

9 Complete each sentence with the phrasal verb from the box that has the most similar meaning to the bold verb. Use each phrasal verb only once.

~~hand in~~	talk about	talk over	think about	turn down

1. Anyone interested in the job may **submit** an application online.
   I need to ___hand in___ my application by tomorrow. I should get busy!
2. Please **consider** the job offer. We could use talented people like you.
   Hey, Tammy. Did you ___think about___ the job offer? What did you decide?
3. Mr. Clark, Tamara may **refuse** the offer. Other companies have offered her more money.
   What's your decision, Tammy? Are you going to ___turn down___ the job offer?
4. Mr. Clark, I'd like to **discuss** offering more money to Tamara. What do you think?
   The boss and I will ___talk about___ the possibility of offering more money to Tammy.
5. The boss will see all employees individually to **discuss** any problems.
   Ken, can we ___talk over___ the problem with this design? I'd like to find a solution.

REAL ENGLISH

Phrasal verbs are more common in informal speaking and writing. The single word verb is sometimes used in a more formal situation.

Formal: *You must **submit** your essays no later than 5 p.m. on Friday.*
Informal: *Hey Jon, when do we have to **hand in** our essays?*

10 LISTEN.

CD4-15

A Listen to the excerpt from a lecture about inventors. Complete the text with the phrasal verbs you hear.

People like to believe that inventors are brilliant people who (1) ___dream up___ new ideas on their own. In movies about innovation, an inventor often (2) ______________ with the perfect solution to a problem. At times these inventors (3) ______________ problems, but they never (4) ______________. They (5) ______________ trying to make our lives better, and eventually they succeed.

In fact, these popular ideas about inventors are far from the truth. In reality, most inventions (6) ______________ a community of people who are all trying to (7) ______________ the answer to a problem.

For example, people often (8) ______________ the name of Thomas Edison when (9) ______________ innovation. Many people believe that Edison (10) ______________ the light bulb without any help. However, Edison's light bulb was not completely new. He was just the first one to produce something that people could buy and use.

B Look at your answers from exercise **A**. Choose the best meaning for each phrasal verb. Refer to pages **A7–A9** for lists of common phrasal verbs and their meanings.

1. (a.) invent	b. want	c. own
2. a. arrives at work	b. stops sleeping	c. goes home
3. a. make	b. offer	c. meet
4. a. stop	b. change	c. wait
5. a. work	b. continue	c. win
6. a. start with	b. affect	c. belong to
7. a. describe	b. avoid	c. solve
8. a. forget	b. mention	c. criticize
9. a. discussing	b. reporting	c. finding
10. a. created	b. stole	c. changed

11 APPLY.

A Put the words in the correct order to make questions with phrasal verbs.

1. you / any problems / into / have / recently / run

   Have you run into any problems recently?

2. new ideas / think / you / do / up / how

   How do you think up new ideas?

3. you / what / about / found / have / out / inventors

   What have you found out about inventors?

4. up / what words / you / looked / have / in this lesson

   What words have you looked up in this lesson

5. count / who / do / for advice / on / you

   Who do you count on for advice?

B Work with a partner. Ask and answer the questions you wrote in exercise **A**. Then ask follow-up questions to learn more about your partner.

A: *Have you run into any problems recently?*

B: *Yes, I ran into a few problems with phrasal verbs.*

A: *Oh, which ones?*

Review the Grammar UNIT 14

Charts 14.1–14.6

1 Circle the correct words to complete the conversation. Sometimes both answers are correct. See pages **A7–A9** if necessary.

Melanie: My brother Rob (1) **sent to me** / **sent me** an interesting article last night. He's (2) **working an assignment** / **working on an assignment** about a Japanese space project called *Ikaros*.

Ross: *Ikaros?* What's that?

Melanie: It's a spacecraft that uses solar power[1] instead of rocket fuel. It has a huge sail that (3) **takes in energy** / **takes energy in** from the sun and stores it. The sail measures just over 46 square feet (14.1 square meters). Light from the sun (4) **hits to the sail** / **hits the sail** and bounces off. This allows *Ikaros* to (5) **move** / **move in** through space.

Ross: Wow! I'm sure *Ikaros* didn't get into space on its own, though . . .

Melanie: No, *Ikaros* couldn't (6) **take off** / **take away** from Earth on its own. It was launched on a rocket in 2010 and when it (7) **arrived space** / **arrived in space**, the sail (8) **carried out its task** / **carried its task out** perfectly.

Ross: And where is *Ikaros* going?

Melanie: It's already taken photos of Venus and now it's (9) **going back** / **going ahead** to the sun . . . Anyway, back to Rob — he's probably finished his assignment and he wanted me to (10) **look over it** / **look it over** for him.

[1] **solar power:** power from sun

◄ The solar yacht *Ikaros* uses a large, square sail to travel from Earth to Venus and the sun.

Charts 14.2–14.6

2 EDIT. Read the posts about 3D printers from a technology website. Find and correct seven more errors with transitive, intransitive, and phrasal verbs.

Printing in 3D

[posted @ 10:20 pm by techwizard33]

A few days ago, a friend showed ~~to~~ me his 3D printer. I wanted to see it because I might buy for my son one. The printer was smaller than I expected. It cost my friend a lot of money, too, but apparently the price is coming down. He turned on it, so I was able to see how it worked. My friend uses his computer to design items for other companies. To test his ideas, he needs to try out them. Making an item to test used to be a long process, but now my friend can make one quickly with his 3D printer. It seems incredible! I think I will buy one!

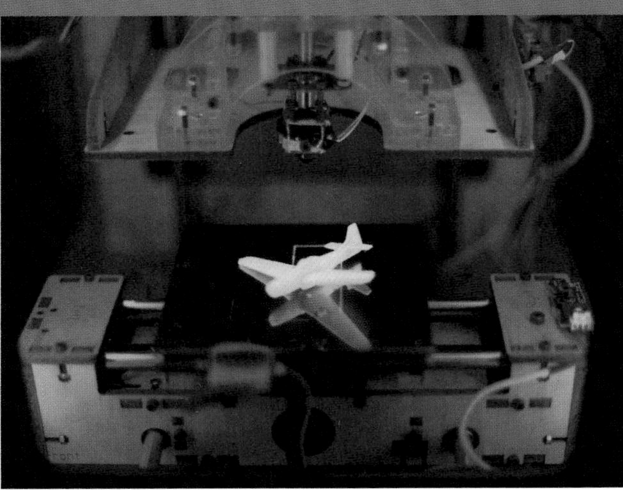

▲ A 3D printer prints a model plane.

[posted @ 10:33 pm by kbb4210]

I agree. These sound great. The other day I ran a friend into when I was downtown. She does research on historical objects. She does a lot of work to the Smithsonian Institution in Washington, DC. In the past, she had to travel twice a month to examine the real objects at the Institution, but recently she also bought a 3D printer. Now the Institution sends to her the exact measurements of an object and she prints out it at home. It's great!

Charts 14.1–14.6

CD4-16

3 LISTEN & SPEAK.

A Read the questions. Then listen to a student present her invention to her class. In your notebook, take notes about each question.

1. What did the student invent?
2. What do you use it for?
3. Who did she create the product for?
4. How did she come up with her idea?
5. Did she run into any problems?
6. Has her invention taken off?

B Work with a partner. Discuss your answers to the questions in exercise **A**.

Connect the Grammar to Writing

1 READ & NOTICE THE GRAMMAR.

A What are some innovative products you know about? Discuss your ideas with a partner. Then read the article.

Would you take a pill to remember your passwords?

Nowadays, you need a password for almost everything. Trying to remember numerous passwords is a challenge for almost everyone. Why can't it be easier?

Well, now it can. The Motorola company has come up with a pill that will remember your passwords for you. When you take the pill, it reacts with the acid in your stomach. By doing this, it is able to send an electronic signal, or "password," to your phone, laptop, or other digital device. Your device reads the signal, and automatically logs you in to your accounts. Your body *becomes* your passwords. You no longer have to write your passwords down.

This seems like the perfect product, because people hate having to remember so many passwords. But will they like the idea of a password pill? The FDA[1] has approved the pill for sale in the United States, so we may soon find out. Products come and go—will the password pill take off and be a success, or will it be just one more failed invention?

[1] **FDA:** Food and Drug Administration

GRAMMAR FOCUS

Verbs have patterns. In addition to learning the meaning, it's a good idea to record the different patterns (for example, verb + object; verb + prepositional phrase). Notice the patterns of these verbs from the article in exercise **A**.

Transitive (with object)	Verb:	*Nowadays, you **need** a password . . .*
	Phrasal Verb:	*The Motorola company has **come up with** a pill . . .*
Intransitive (no object)	Verb:	*Products **come** and **go**—*
	Phrasal Verb:	*—will the password pill **take off** and be a success . . .*

B Read the article in exercise **A** again. Underline the verbs or phrasal verbs that you want to learn more about. Write each verb and its pattern in the chart.

Verb/Phrasal Verb Pattern	Pattern
1. *react*	*verb + prepositional phrase (intransitive)*
2.	
3.	
4.	

C Complete the chart with information from the article in exercise **A**. Then work with a partner and compare your answers.

What is the problem/need?	*people have too many passwords to remember*
Who invented the product?	
How does it solve the problem?	
When is it useful?	*every day, whenever you are online, using a digital device*
Why is (or isn't) it a good idea?	

2 BEFORE YOU WRITE.

A Work with a group. Brainstorm a list of innovative products you know about or ideas you have for a new innovation. Use the innovations from the unit or your own ideas.

B Choose one of the innovative products from your list in exercise **A**. In your notebook, draw a chart like the one in exercise **1C**. Write answers about your product.

3 **WRITE** two or three paragraphs about the innovative product you chose. Write an introduction describing the problem. Then use the information from your chart in exercise **2B** and the article in exercise **1A** to help you.

WRITING FOCUS Choosing a Good Title

A title is an important part to any piece of writing. The title of the article about password pills questions a new idea. Asking a question is one way to give your writing a good title.

A good title:

- catches the readers' interest
- begins with a capital letter
- does not have a period at the end, but may have a question mark (?) or an exclamation mark (!) at the end for emphasis

4 **SELF ASSESS.** Read your text. Underline examples of transitive and intransitive verbs or phrasal verbs. Then use the checklist to assess your work.

☐ I used transitive and intransitive verbs correctly. [14.1]

☐ I used direct and indirect objects with *to* and *for* correctly. [14.2, 14.3]

☐ I used transitive and intransitive phrasal verbs correctly. [14.5]

☐ I used separable and inseparable transitive phrasal verbs correctly. [14.6]

☐ I chose a good title for my essay about an innovation. [WRITING FOCUS]

UNIT 15 Windows on the Past

Passive Voice and Participial Adjectives

▶ Rapa Nui National Park, Easter Island

LESSON 1 Passive Voice

EXPLORE

CD4-17

1 **READ** the article about a group of people who lived in South America long ago. Notice the words in **bold**.

Peru
SOUTH AMERICA

The Moche of Northern Peru

From around A.D. 100–800, mysterious people inhabited[1] northern Peru. Recently, archaeologists[2] have made some important discoveries about these people. They **are known** as the Moche. Visitors to Peru can see the remains of their pyramids, which **are called** *huacas*. For a long time, little **was understood** about Moche society or culture, but that situation has changed since some important tombs[3] **were discovered**.

One of the most interesting tombs **was found** in 2013. Archaeologists uncovered the body of a Moche woman in a large room around 20 feet (6 meters) beneath the ground. The tomb clearly belonged to an important person.

Artifacts[4] in the tomb helped to explain the woman's position in society. For example, a tall silver cup **was found** beside her body. Moche art shows that similar cups **were used** in religious ceremonies. Archaeologists believe the woman was a priestess, or an important woman who performed religious ceremonies. They think that Moche society **was ruled** by women, or at least some Moche areas were. They believe that priestesses such as this one were queens of their people. Archaeologists hope that more secrets of this fascinating culture **will be uncovered** in the future.

[1] **inhabit:** to live in an area
[2] **archaeologist:** a person who studies the past by looking at items such as buried houses, tools, pots, and so on
[3] **tomb:** a grave; a place where a dead body is buried
[4] **artifact:** an object used by humans a very long time ago

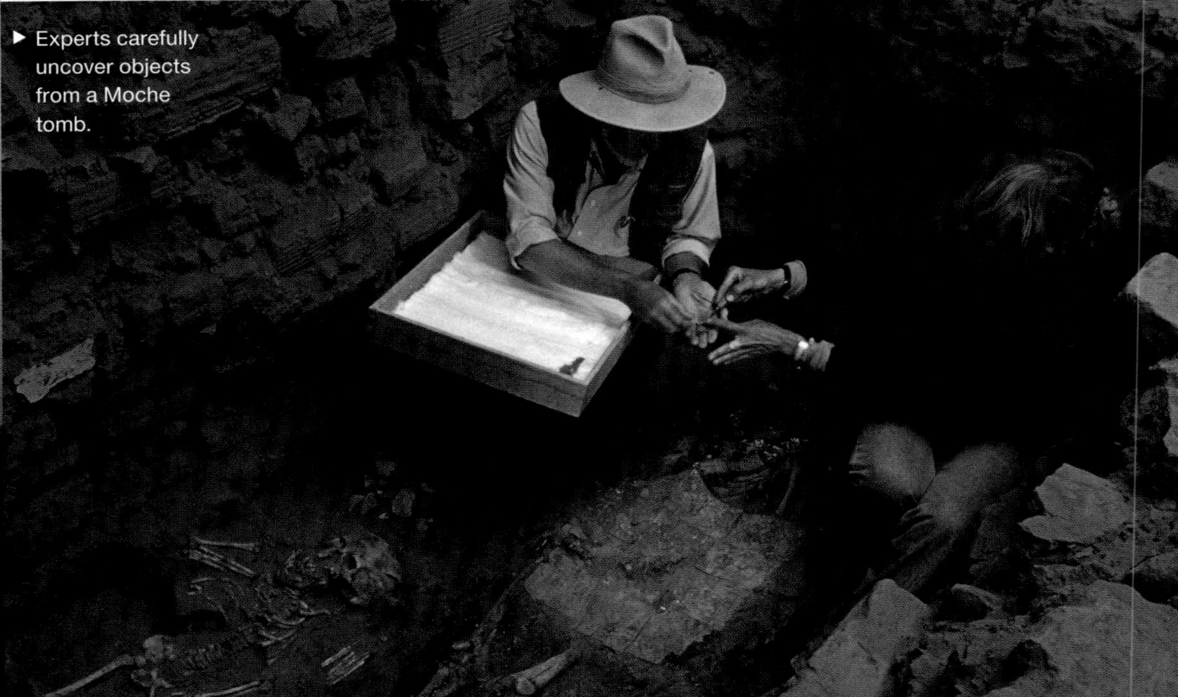

▶ Experts carefully uncover objects from a Moche tomb.

2 CHECK. Make true statements according to the article. Match the beginning of each statement with the correct ending.

1. *Huacas* are ____.
2. In 2013, researchers found ____.
3. The priestess's tomb was 20 feet ____.
4. Silver cups were important ____.
5. Women probably ruled ____.

a. in religious ceremonies
b. some Moche areas
c. an important tomb
d. beneath the ground
e. Moche pyramids

3 DISCOVER. Complete the exercises to learn about the grammar in this lesson.

A Find these sentences in the article from exercise **1**. Write the missing words.

1. They ______________________ as the Moche.
2. For example, a tall silver cup ______________________ beside her body.
3. Moche art shows that similar cups ______________________ in religious ceremonies.
4. Archaeologists hope that more secrets of this fascinating culture ______________________ in the future.

B Look at the sentences from exercise **A**. Complete the chart with the words you wrote.

Verb Form	Passive Voice: *Be* + Past Participle
Present	
Past	
Future	

◀ Dos Cabezas, the site of an important Moche *huaca* (or pyramid) in northern coastal Peru

LEARN

15.1 Active and Passive Voice

Active and Passive Voice	
Active:	A guard **locked** the doors.
Passive:	The doors **were locked** by a guard.

1. In the active voice, the subject is the *agent* or *doer*. It performs the action of the verb. The object is the receiver of the action of the verb. In the passive voice, the subject is the receiver of the action of the verb.	Active: Scientists **discovered** a lost city. (Scientists = Subject/Agent; a lost city = Object/Receiver) Passive: A lost city **was discovered** by scientists. (A lost city = Subject/Receiver)
2. A sentence in the passive voice has a form of *be (not)* + the past participle of a verb.	Oranges **are grown** in Florida. The lost objects **haven't been found**. Coal **was used** to heat buildings.
3. Only transitive verbs (verbs that can be followed by a direct object in the active voice) can occur in the passive voice.* Intransitive verbs (verbs that are not followed by a direct object in the active voice) cannot be used in the passive voice.	They **saw** bears at the camp today Bears **were seen** at the camp today. ✓ Our taxi **arrived** early. ✗ Our taxi was arrived early.
4. Sometimes *by* + the agent comes at the end of a passive sentence.	A lost city was discovered **by scientists.**

*See Chart 14.1 on page **374** for information on transitive verbs.

4 Write **A** if the underlined verb form is *active*, and **P** if it is *passive*.

P 1. Moche society around San José de Moro was ruled by women.

____ 2. Interesting objects were discovered in the tomb.

____ 3. Archaeologists found a silver cup.

____ 4. The priestess was buried in a special way.

____ 5. She wore a simple necklace of local stones.

____ 6. Several discoveries were made in Peru.

____ 7. Today's lecture on Moche society was canceled.

____ 8. The discovery of the priestess has changed the way we think about the Moche.

____ 9. Online videos about archaeology are watched by a lot of people.

____ 10. Major new discoveries will be reported in the news.

REAL ENGLISH

Use the passive voice to emphasize what happened rather than who or what performed the action.

*A cup **was found** on the ground.*
*The plans **weren't understood**.*

5 Circle the correct form of the verbs to complete the article.

▲ Burial mask of King Tut

Egypt is full of incredible ancient sites, but the most famous is the tomb of King Tutankhamun (King Tut). He (1) **ruled** / **was ruled** Egypt from around 1332 B.C.–1323 B.C. Until his tomb (2) **discovered** / **was discovered** in 1922, many details about his life (3) **didn't know** / **weren't known**. King Tut's tomb (4) **found** / **was found** in the Valley of the Kings by archaeologist Howard Carter. Carter (5) **believed** / **was believed** that Tut's tomb had to be in the area because of other nearby discoveries. When he (6) **found** / **was found** a door, he (7) **knew** / **was known** something important was behind it. Photos (8) **took** / **were taken** of the door before it (9) **removed** / **was removed**. Behind the door, Carter and his team (10) **found** / **were found** hundreds of gold objects, as well as King Tut's preserved body, or mummy.

15.2 Passive Voice: Present, Past, and Future Forms

Passive Voice				
	Subject	*Be (Not)*	Past Participle	
Present	That TV show These cars	is aren't	watched made	by millions. in Germany.
Past	The meeting The discoveries	was weren't	canceled. made	 by Dr. Jones.
Future	Our special guests The plans	will be won't be	treated changed.	well.

1. To form the passive voice, use a form of *be* with the past participle of the verb.	Gravity **was discovered** by Newton. Your bags **will be checked** by security.
2. **Remember:** The past participle of regular verbs is the same form as the simple past (verb + *-ed*). However, many verbs have irregular past participles.*	Many homes were ruin**ed**. (ruin/ruined/**ruined**) The secret was **kept**. (keep/kept/**kept**) Russian **is spoken** here. (speak/spoke/**spoken**)
3. To form questions in the simple present and past, place the appropriate form of *be* before the subject.	**Was** this car **made** in Korea? Where **were** the cars **made**?
4. To form questions with the future, put *will* before the subject.	**Will** the food **be eaten**? Where **will** the food **be kept**?

*See page **A4** for a list of irregular past participles.

6 Complete the sentences with the words in parentheses. Use the simple present, simple past, or future passive form of the verbs.

1. Before electricity was available, candles ___were used___ (use) for light.
2. The ancient site ______________ (discover) three years ago.
3. Many items ______________ (remove) for scientific study.
4. Work on the site ______________ (complete) next month.
5. The museum ______________ (not own) by the government now.
6. A: __________ Egyptian artifacts __________ (display) here?

   B: Yes, they __________. You can find them on the second floor.
7. The opening date for the Moche exhibit ______________ (not announce) until next week.
8. How __________ food ______________ (prepare) in the Middle Ages?
9. Where in the library __________ the books about ancient Greece __________ (keep)?
10. Native American history ______________ (not teach) by Professor Schulz anymore.

PRACTICE

7 Complete the exercises.

A Read the information about a common archeological procedure. Underline the verbs.

Archaeological Dig: Standard Procedure

When team members find an artifact, they follow a standard procedure.

- A student assistant places the artifact in a special container.
- The assistant writes the information about the artifact on the container label.
- The assistant records the artifact in the project's database.[1]
- Experts analyze the artifact at the laboratory.

[1]**database:** a computer program for storing information

B Complete the presentation. Use the passive voice and the verbs in exercise **A**.

Hello, my name is Liz Harrison, and I'm a team leader on the dig. I'd like to tell you a little bit about our working methods on this project. When an artifact (1) ___is found___ by team members, a standard procedure (2) ______________. First, the artifact (3) ______________ in a special container, and information about the artifact (4) ______________ on the container label. After the artifact (5) ______________ in the project's database, it (6) ______________ at the laboratory.

C Complete the conversation between two team members about something that went wrong on the project in exercise **A**. Use the simple past passive voice.

Erik: We had a problem with our new student assistants yesterday.

Kumiko: What happened?

Erik: Well, unfortunately, the standard procedure (1) ___wasn't followed___ (not follow). Some of the containers (2) ______________ (not label) properly.

Kumiko: Oh, that's not good. (3) __________ all the artifacts ______________ (place) in containers?

Erik: No, and some small pieces of pottery (4) ______________ (damage) as a result.

Kumiko: That's terrible! (5) __________ all the artifacts ______________ (record) in the database?

Erik: Yes, that (6) ______________ (do) correctly. On the bright side, the team discovered one very interesting object.

Kumiko: Oh, really? What (7) ______________ (find)?

> **REAL ENGLISH**
>
> Sometimes, the passive voice is used when the speaker does not want to blame a person or people directly.
>
> *The procedure* ***wasn't followed.***

D **WRITE & SPEAK.** Look again at the question Kumiko asks Erik at the end of exercise **C**. Write a possible reply in your notebook. Use your own ideas and three to four verbs from the box in the passive voice. Then work in a group and take turns reading your replies. Whose is the most interesting?

analyze	break	clean	find	know	make	repair	sell	steal	take	use

Erik: A long, dirty necklace was found. After it was cleaned, they saw that it was solid gold. We think it was made over 800 years ago in a small town in Italy. It might be worth over $500,000. The necklace will be analyzed early next week, so we should have more information then.

8 EDIT & SPEAK.

A Read the article about Angkor Wat, an ancient site in Cambodia. Find and correct five more errors with the passive voice.

A Restoration Success Story at Angkor Wat

The temple of Angkor Wat in Cambodia was ~~build~~ built in the 12th century by a Khmer king. It was the state temple and also the place where the king was buried. Many parts of the temple are damaged. Water and time have done much of the damage. But also, the temple constructed in a way that has not lasted. Recently, restoration work on one important part of the temple was complete by a team of specialists. Restoration is when a damaged building brought back to a good condition.

For this restoration, special techniques were required, and the Cambodian team was well trained for the job. Gradually, over a five-year period, important parts of the temple cleaned and dangerous cracks were filled. The project was a big success, and the team plans to continue its work on other buildings at the site. Hopefully, all of Angkor Wat will restore in an equally successful way.

▼ Sunrise at Angkor Wat, Cambodia

B Complete the passive questions. Use the verbs in parentheses and a correct form of the passive voice.

1. When ____was____ Angkor Wat ____built____ (build)?
2. Who ________________ (bury) there?
3. How ________________ it ________________ (damage)?
4. ____________ the rest of Angkor Wat ________________________ (restore) in the future?

C Work with a partner. Ask and answer the questions in exercise **B**. Find the answers in exercise **A**.

A: *When was Angkor Wat built?* B: *In the 12th century.*

9 APPLY.

A Read Paul's story about an item from the past. Underline the verb forms that are passive.

I have chosen a woodworking drill. It was owned by my grandfather and was used in his work as a carpenter on ships. Sadly, my grandfather was lost at sea when my father was a child, so I never knew him. His tools are kept carefully by my family. I like to do woodwork myself, so his drill is still used, and it works very well. I'm going to give the drill to my son. It's nice to think that my grandfather will be remembered through his tools.

▲ Hand drill

B Complete the chart with information from Paul's story.

	Item: Woodworking drill
Who was it owned by?	
How was it used?	
Where was it used?	
Other details	

C Choose an item from the past to write about. Complete the chart for your item.

	Item: ________________
Who was it owned by?	
How was it used?	
Where was it used?	
Other details	

D In your notebook, write a short paragraph about your item. Use the passive voice where appropriate. Then read your story to a partner.

EXPLORE

CD4-18

1 READ the article about a ship that sank in 1865. Notice the words in **bold**.

A Treasure Ship Tells Its Story: The SS *Republic*

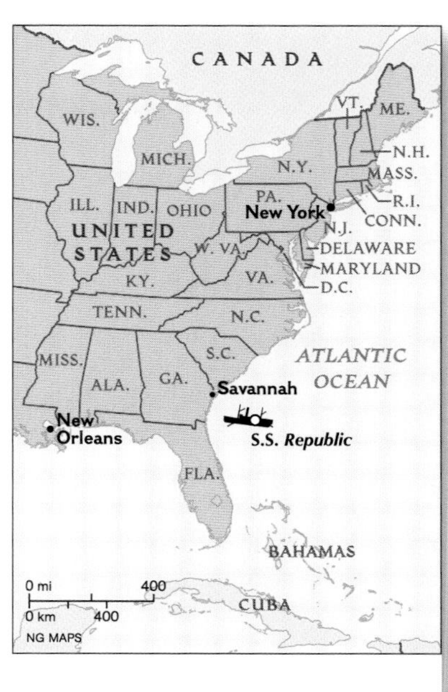

In October 1865, soon after the end of the American Civil War, the SS *Republic* left New York on a journey to New Orleans. Five hundred barrels[1] of goods and a reported $400,000 in coins were loaded onto the SS *Republic* in New York. The money was shipped **by bankers and businessmen**. Because of the situation after the war, which the southern states lost, coins from the northern states **could be used** in the South to buy almost twice as much as they could in the North.

Sadly, the SS *Republic* ran into a hurricane[2] near the Carolinas and sank about 100 miles off of the coast of Savannah, Georgia. Lifeboats and a raft were launched[3] **by the crew and passengers.** Most of the 80 people on board survived. The coins, however, sank to the bottom of the ocean along with the ship.

In 2003, the wreck of the SS *Republic* was discovered **by a company called Odyssey Marine Exploration**. Over 51,000 gold and silver coins were recovered. Thousands of everyday items were also found. Many of these items **can** now **be viewed** in public exhibitions and on Odyssey's virtual museum: www.OdysseysVirtualMuseum.com. Viewing these items is a great way to see how people lived in the 1860s.

[1] **barrel:** a large round container made of metal or wood
[2] **hurricane:** a storm with very strong winds and rain
[3] **launch:** to put a boat in the water

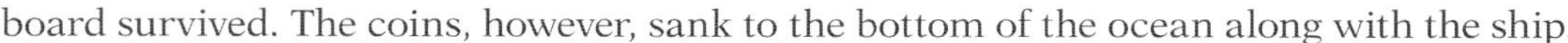

▶ Painting of the SS *Republic* by John Batchelor (courtesy of Odyssey Marine Exploration)

2 CHECK. Read the statements. Circle **T** for *true* or **F** for *false*.

1. The SS *Republic* carried only passengers and money. **T** **F**
2. The American Civil War was won by the southern states. **T** **F**
3. After the war, money could buy more in the South than in the North. **T** **F**
4. The SS *Republic* was sunk by an enemy ship. **T** **F**
5. Items from the SS *Republic* may be seen by the public. **T** **F**

3 DISCOVER. Complete the exercises to learn about the grammar in this lesson.

A Find these sentences in the article in exercise **1**. Write the missing words.

1. Five hundred barrels of goods . . . ____________ onto the SS *Republic* in New York.
2. . . . coins from the northern states ____________ in the South . . .
3. In 2003, the wreck of the SS *Republic* ____________ by a company . . .
4. Over 51,000 gold and silver coins ____________.
5. Many of these items ____________ in public exhibitions.

B Look at your answers in exercise **A**. Write them in the correct column.

Passive without Modal	Passive with Modal
were loaded	*could be used*
____________	____________
____________	

LEARN

15.3 Passive Voice with Modals

Active Voice	Passive Voice
You may return purchases with a receipt. You can't return them without a receipt.	Purchases **may be returned** with a receipt. They **can't be returned** without a receipt.

Passive Voice with Modals

	Subject	Modal (*Not*)	*Be*	Past Participle	
Past	The ship	**couldn't**		**seen**	because of the storm.
Present	The topics	**can**	**be**	**researched**	online.
Future	The report	**might not**		**finished**	on time.

1. The passive voice is often used with modals to talk about past, present, and future.	The test **can be completed** at home. Projects **must be finished** next week.
2. Use a modal + *be* + past participle to form the passive.	The building **might be closed**.
3. To form questions with modals in the passive, place the modal before the subject.	A: **Can** the test **be completed** at home? B: Yes, it can. A: **When should** the project **be finished**? B: Next week.

See Units 12 and 13 to review the meanings and uses of modals.

4 Complete the information sheet with the correct passive form of the words in parentheses.

August Archaeological Dive: Information Sheet

Welcome to this exciting dive! Over the next two weeks, many interesting items (1) ___may be found___ (may / find) at this site. Some important items (2) ______________ (might / recover) from the wreck, so care (3) ______________ (must / take) not to damage them. Please take note:

- Tools and diving equipment will be provided. Personal tools and equipment (4) ______________ (may not / use).
- New discoveries (5) ______________ (must not / move) without permission.
- New assistants (6) ______________ (could / require) to complete a training course away from the main dive site.
- Identification (7) ______________ (should / wear) at all times.
- Our dive doctor (8) ______________ (can / consult) when necessary.

Thank you all for your cooperation, and welcome to the team!

15.4 Using the *By* Phrase

Passive Voice + *By* Phrase
The sunken ship was found **by some divers.**
The passengers were rescued near the coast **by the Coast Guard.**

1. Use a *by* phrase with the passive voice to indicate who or what performed the action.	Some errors were made **by the students.** Their house was destroyed **by a tornado**.
2. Use a *by* phrase when it is important to know who or what did the action of the verb.	Our class was interrupted **by a loud noise.** The researcher is paid **by the government**.
3. Do not use a *by* phrase if the agent is a. unknown b. understood from context	a. The items **were stolen** late last night. b. The new health laws **were passed** yesterday.

5 Read the paragraph about the discovery of the SS *Republic*. Cross out four more unnecessary *by* phrases.

Treasure Found on the SS *Republic*

The wreck of the SS *Republic* was discovered in 2003 by a private company called Odyssey Marine Exploration. The ship was found ~~by the company~~ at the bottom of the ocean 100 miles southeast of Savannah, Georgia.

The remains of the SS *Republic* were around 1700 feet (518 meters) deep. New high-tech equipment was used by Odyssey to aid in the exploration and recovery effort. For example, items were removed from the wreck by a robotic craft called ZEUS.

Over 51,000 gold and silver coins were recovered by the Odyssey team from the wreck. Everyday items such as shoes, cups, and bottles were also found by the team. Photos of these artifacts are displayed on the company's website. Facts and details are also given by the company on the site for anyone who wants more information.

▶ Coins from the SS *Republic*

6 WRITE & SPEAK.

A Write passive questions about the SS *Republic* with *by* at the end.

1. (who / the SS *Republic* / discover)
   Who was the SS Republic discovered by?
2. (who / the company / start)
   ____
3. (who / the new equipment / buy)
   ____
4. (who / the ocean / search)
   ____
5. (what / the research teams / attract)
   ____

REAL ENGLISH

Passive questions with *who* and *what* ask about the agent. They often have *by* at the end.

I haven't heard of that book.
Who was it written by?

B Work with a partner. Ask and answer the questions in exercise **A**. Use the information from exercise **5** on page 407 to give answers.

A: *Who was the SS Republic discovered by?*

B: *A company called Odyssey Marine Exploration.*

PRACTICE

7 Rewrite the sentences using the bold verbs in the passive. Add a *by* phrase only when necessary.

1. People **can see** many historic items in the museum's new exhibit.
   Many historic items ___can be seen___ in the museum's new exhibit.
2. Groups **can't buy** tickets.
   Tickets ______________________.
3. Visitors to the museum **may not park** cars outside the building.
   Cars ______________________ outside the building.
4. Adults **must not use** cameras in the exhibit.
   Cameras ______________________ in the exhibit.
5. However, children on school visits **may take** photographs.
   However, photographs ______________________.
6. Visitors **should leave** their coats and bags in the coat check.
   Coats and bags ______________________ in the coat check.

7. The museum **might change** the objects on display without notice.

   The objects on display ______________________________ without notice.

8. You **can purchase** souvenirs in the gift shop.

   Souvenirs ______________________________ in the gift shop.

8 READ, WRITE & SPEAK.

A Read the information sheet about a college anthropology project. Underline the verbs.

Anthropology Project

Project Preparation and Details

Theme	What can we learn from disastrous or mysterious events?
What to do	• Choose a historical event from any period. • You can write about any country or culture. • You can do the work alone or with a partner.
What to study	• Read accounts of the event soon after it happened. • Study artifacts from the site. • Research the opinions of archaeologists and anthropologists.
Resources to use	• Visit the college library. • Use the Internet. • Interview members of the faculty (for interviews, by appointment).

Project Tasks and Due Dates

Choose a topic	January 31: Professor Lopez has to approve all topics.
Complete outline	February 7: A faculty member must sign your outline before you begin your project.
Present project	February 26: Dr. Henderson will arrange exact times.

B Complete the sentences. Use the passive voice and verbs from the information sheet in exercise **A**. Complete the *by* phrases where indicated.

1. A disaster from any period in history may ____be chosen____.
2. Any country or culture can ______________________ about.
3. The work can ______________________ alone or with a partner.
4. Accounts of events should ______________________ soon after they happen.
5. Artifacts found at the site should ______________________ and expert opinions should ______________________.
6. The Internet can ______________________ as a resource.
7. Members of the faculty may ______________________.

8. All topics must ______________________ by ______________________ on or before January 31.

9. Project outlines should ______________________ by ______________________.

10. Presentation times will ______________________ by ______________________.

C Put the words in the correct order to make passive questions. Add *by* where necessary.

1. (who / must / the outline / sign)

   Who must the outline be signed by?

2. (can / the work / do / with a partner)

   ____

3. (whose opinions / should / research)

   ____

4. (can / the Internet / use)

   ____

5. (who / must / the topic / approve)

   ____

6. (who / will / the presentations / arrange)

   ____

D Work with a partner. Ask and answer the questions in exercise **C**.

A: *Who must the outline be signed by?*

B: *A faculty member.*

9 WRITE & LISTEN.

A Complete the information about Pompeii. Write the *by* phrases from the box.

by archaeologists	~~by disaster~~	by millions of tourists	by Mount Vesuvius

In A.D. 79, the Roman city of Pompeii was struck (1) by disaster. The city was buried when tons of burning ash, stone, and deadly gases were shot into the air (2) ______________________, the nearby volcano. Sixteen thousand people were killed in one night. The disaster happened so quickly that evidence of everyday life was perfectly preserved under the ash until the city was discovered (3) ______________________ 1700 years later. Now Pompeii is visited (4) ______________________ every year.

CD4-19

B Listen to two students discuss their project on the disaster that struck the city of Pompeii. Complete the summary of what each student says with the modal verbs you hear and the passive form of the verbs in parentheses. Add *not* where necessary.

1. Juan: The research ___can be shared___ (share) if we work together.
2. Val: The stories in books and films __________ always __________ (believe).
3. Juan: Some of the photographs __________ (include) in the project.
4. Val: The people who died __________ (respect).
5. Juan: The cast of the dog __________ (show) on the official website.
6. Val: A lot of good information __________ (find) on the official website.
7. Juan: Pompeii __________ (choose) by a lot of students.
8. Val: Our project __________ (approve) if we don't hurry.

▼ A plaster cast of dog killed at Pompeii

10 EDIT. Read the extract from a student's project. Find and correct six more errors with passive modals and the use of the *by* phrase.

Mystery at Sea:
The *Mary Celeste*

I have chosen to research the mystery of the ship *Mary Celeste*. This famous story should ~~include~~ be included on any list of historical mysteries. In early November 1872, the ship left New York carrying goods to Italy. One month later, the ship was discovered in the Atlantic Ocean by another ship. There was no one on board, but the goods that the *Mary Celeste* was carrying were still on the ship.

There was no sign of trouble, but the sailors, the captain, and his family could not found. The ship's lifeboat was missing, and a long rope was attached to the back of the ship. Some versions of the story say that a fully prepared meal could see on the table, so maybe everyone left in a hurry. This, however, cannot be confirmed. Even now we don't understand exactly what happened, and the truth may never know.

In my opinion, the evidence should be examined again by people. New information might discover using modern technology. Many people don't agree with me, though. They think some things just can't be explain.

11 APPLY.

A In your notebook, brainstorm a list of rules or instructions for these places. Use passive modals.

- your school Textbooks must be purchased before classes begin.
- a library ______
- a museum ______

B Work with a partner. Share your ideas from exercise **A**. In your notebook, write more instructions for the places in exercise **A**.

EXPLORE

CD4-20

1 READ the article about an aspect of daily life in ancient Rome. Notice the words in **bold**.

What's New in Ancient Rome?

The news can be **disturbing** or even **frightening,** but throughout time people have always been **interested** in knowing what's going on around them. These days, news is reported instantly on the Internet, television, and other media. But how did people in the past find things out?

In ancient Rome, the *Acta Diurna* was a major news source. This ancient "newspaper" was first published in 59 B.C. by the Roman emperor Julius Caesar. The news was displayed on **carved**[1] sheets of metal or stone. This "newspaper" was **devoted to**[2] information from the government and was posted around the city.

One place the news was posted was in the Forum. This was Rome's business and political center. It was a favorite place for public speaking and for learning about the latest events. Here Romans could hear the serious political news of the day. They could also follow all the **amusing** stories that famous people were recently **involved** in.

People today are still **fascinated**[3] by this mix of important news and **entertaining** stories. In a modern television news program, **terrifying** events may be followed by details about the private lives of movie stars. Some things never change!

[1] **carved:** with designs or writing cut into the surface
[2] **devoted to:** used for
[3] **fascinated:** very interested

2 CHECK. Choose the correct answer to complete each sentence.

1. According to the first paragraph, some news can be ____.
   a. funny b. scary c. late
2. Compared with the news in ancient Rome, today's news ____.
   a. includes greater detail b. comes in more different ways c. talks about different topics
3. In ancient Rome, people read the *Acta Diurna* ____.
   a. in public places b. only in the Forum c. at home
4. The *Acta Diurna* reported on ____.
   a. famous people's lives b. exciting stories c. official information
5. The news in the Forum was similar to modern news; it combined serious topics with ____.
   a. amusing stories b. political statements c. government plans

3 DISCOVER. Complete the exercises to learn about the grammar in this lesson.

A Circle the correct words to complete the sentences from the article in exercise **1**.

1. The news can be **disturbed** / **disturbing** . . .
2. . . . people have always been **interested** / **interesting** in knowing what's going on around them.
3. The news was displayed on **carved** / **carving** sheets of metal or stone.
4. People today are still **fascinated** / **fascinating** by this mix of important news and **entertained** / **entertaining** stories.

B Look at your answers in exercise **A**. Check (✓) the true statements about the words you circled.

1. __✓__ They can come after *be*.
2. ____ They can come after a noun.
3. ____ They can come before a noun.
4. ____ They can be used as verbs.
5. ____ They can be used as adjectives.

▼ The Forum in ancient Rome was an important social center. Here many Romans probably received the first terrible news about the disaster at Pompeii.

LEARN

15.5 Past Participial Adjectives

1. The past participle* can be used as an adjective. The past participial adjective has a passive meaning.	The picture was painted by Da Vinci. (Past Participle (Passive)) These rooms are already **painted**. (Past Participial Adjective)
2. **Remember:** A past participle can be a. regular (the same as the simple past with *-ed*) b. irregular (different forms)	a. amaz**ed**, interest**ed** b. broke**n**, forgot**ten**
3. A past participial adjective often describes a person's feelings.	People are **fascinated** by the news. Juan was **surprised** to see the story.
4. Past participial adjectives can come before a noun or after a linking verb such as *be, look, seem,* and *sound.*	The **excited** children began to scream. The children looked **tired**.
5. Past participial adjectives often occur with certain prepositions; for example: *surprised by* and *interested in.*	Bill seemed **surprised by** his promotion. The students are **interested in** history.

***past participle:** the verb form used in the present perfect and the passive voice

4 Complete the exercises.

A Complete the e-mail with past participial adjectives. Use the verbs in parentheses. Then underline the prepositions that come after seven more of the participial adjectives.

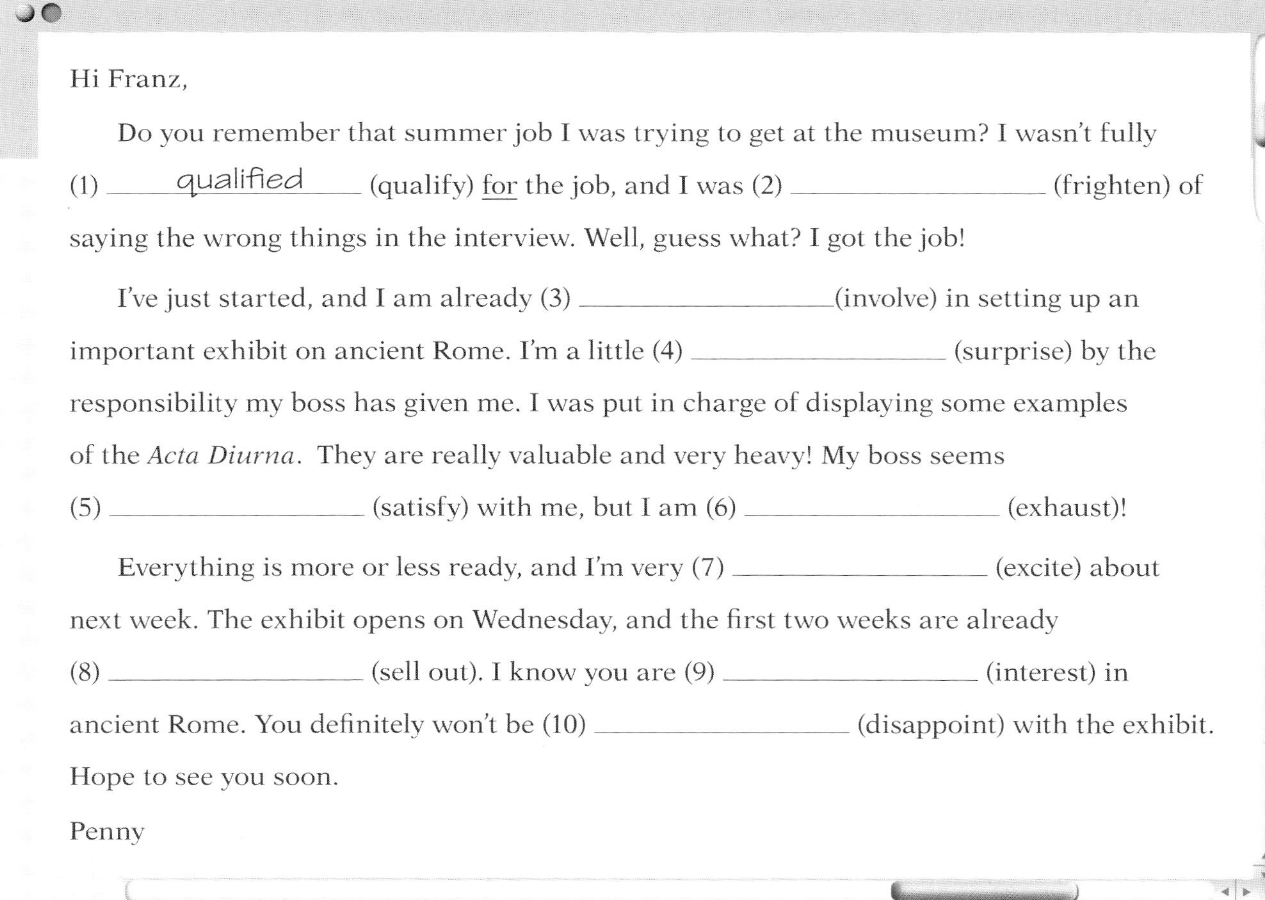

Hi Franz,

Do you remember that summer job I was trying to get at the museum? I wasn't fully (1) ___qualified___ (qualify) for the job, and I was (2) ________________ (frighten) of saying the wrong things in the interview. Well, guess what? I got the job!

I've just started, and I am already (3) ________________(involve) in setting up an important exhibit on ancient Rome. I'm a little (4) ________________ (surprise) by the responsibility my boss has given me. I was put in charge of displaying some examples of the *Acta Diurna*. They are really valuable and very heavy! My boss seems (5) ________________ (satisfy) with me, but I am (6) ________________ (exhaust)!

Everything is more or less ready, and I'm very (7) ________________ (excite) about next week. The exhibit opens on Wednesday, and the first two weeks are already (8) ________________ (sell out). I know you are (9) ________________ (interest) in ancient Rome. You definitely won't be (10) ________________ (disappoint) with the exhibit. Hope to see you soon.

Penny

B Complete the extract from Penny's interview with the correct prepositions. Look at the prepositions you underlined in exercise **A**.

Interviewer: Why do you think you are qualified (1) ___for___ this job, Ms. Browne?

Penny: I've been involved (2) ________ organizing several museum exhibits in previous jobs. My exhibits have always been popular, so the museums have been satisfied (3) ________ my work.

Interviewer: I see. And what personal qualities do you bring to your exhibits?

Penny: Well, I'm never frightened (4) ________ trying something new, so people are often surprised (5) ________ my ideas. I'm always very excited (6) ________ the exhibits myself, and I enjoy sharing that excitement with visitors. I don't want anyone to be disappointed (7) ________ their experience.

15.6 Present Participial Adjectives

1. The present participle (*-ing* form) can also be used as an adjective.	The story is **frightening.** That movie looks **terrifying.**
2. Use the present participial adjective to describe the characteristics of someone or something.	An **amusing** teacher makes a class fun. The exhibit at the museum was **interesting.**
3. Present participial adjectives can come before a noun or after a linking verb.	This is a **fascinating** movie. Her trip to China sounded **exciting.**
4. **Be careful!** When referring to people, past participial adjectives describe feelings, while present participial adjectives describe characteristics of the person.	We are **interested** in ancient history. The history teacher is **interesting.**

5 Complete Jana's blog with present participial adjectives. Use the verbs in parentheses.

My Blog about Chinese History

When I was a child, I loved to read about Chinese history, and I still do. On my blog, I talk about China's past and some of the (1) ___amazing___ (amaze) objects that have survived to the present day. Last week, for example, I wrote about a cosmetics case I saw at the museum. Everyday objects are more (2) ________ (interest) to me than famous pieces of art. They show you how average people lived in ancient times.

▲ An ancient cosmetics case that was discovered in a Han dynasty tomb

I also review historical Chinese films on my blog. For example, the movie *The Last Emperor* is about the life of Pu-Yi, the last emperor of China before the Chinese

Republic. It's a (3) ________________ (fascinate) movie. I sometimes review (4) ________________ (disappoint) movies, too. Some directors have made (5) ________________ (excite) events from Chinese history seem (6) ________________ (bore).

Every week, I post new content on my blog. It's (7) ________________ (exhaust), but I enjoy it. I let people make comments, too. Sometimes we disagree, but I enjoy hearing other people's thoughts about my blog.

COMMENTS (1)

JTC59: I enjoyed reading the Chinese folktales you talked about last week. Thanks for an (8) ________________ (entertain) blog!

PRACTICE

6 Circle the correct participial adjectives to complete the article.

Lewis Chessmen Found 600 Years Later

In 1831, Malcolm Macleod was walking along the coast on the Isle of Lewis in the north of Scotland when he found something special. Some unusual objects were (1) **burying** / **buried** in the sand. When he looked closer, he made an (2) **exciting** / **excited** discovery. Macleod found 78 (3) **carving** / **carved** figures. These figures are now (4) **knowing** / **known** as the Lewis Chessmen.

The pieces are (5) **making** / **made** of ivory and date back to the 12th century. They are (6) **interesting** / **interested** because of the expressions on their faces.

The figures have large, oval eyes and their expressions seem (7) **disappointing** / **disappointed** or (8) **worrying** / **worried**. For this reason, they are (9) **amusing** / **amused** to many people these days. Copies of these famous pieces are very popular with chess players, and are even owned by people who think the game itself is (10) **boring** / **bored**.

▼ Lewis Chessman, from a collection found on the Isle of Lewis, Scotland

7 LISTEN, WRITE & SPEAK.

CD4-21

A Listen to the three short conversations between students taking part in a special archaeology project. What type of project is it? Discuss your answer with a partner.

CD4-21

B Listen again. Circle the correct words.

Conversation 1

1. Jessie is **disgusted** / **disgusting**.
2. Tom is **annoyed** / **annoying**.

Conversation 2

3. Sue thinks the work is **interested** / **interesting**.
4. Dave thinks studying garbage is **bored** / **boring**.
5. Dave would like to do something more **excited** / **exciting**.

Conversation 3

6. Rick isn't **satisfied** / **satisfying** with the amount of work they have done.
7. Angela is **excited** / **exciting**.
8. Rick thinks their information is **surprised** / **surprising**.

C Write five questions based on the sentences in exercise **B**. Use *Why* and the correct participial adjective.

1. Why is Jessie disgusted?
2. ______
3. ______
4. ______
5. ______
6. ______
7. ______
8. ______

CD4-21

D Listen to the conversations again. In your notebook, take notes on the answers to your questions. Then work with a partner. Take turns asking and answering your questions from exercise **C**.

A: *Why was Jessie disgusted?*

B: *She didn't like the smell of the garbage.*

8 EDIT. Read the article about garbology. Find and correct five more errors with past and present participial adjectives.

Garbology: The Past through Trash

Most people think garbage is not very interesting, but archaeologists are ~~fascinating~~ fascinated by it. When archaeologists found 2000-year-old waste from Rome, they were excited about it. The waste taught them about the diet and daily life of people in ancient Rome. You can learn a lot about a culture by studying its trash.

Garbology can be described as the study of garbage to learn about a culture. Professor William Rathje and his students in Arizona invented the term when they were studying waste in modern America. Rathje and his students studied a number of landfill sites[1]. Sorting through garbage can be a tired and sometimes disgusted activity, but when the information from their research was collected, they were not disappointing with the results. The project led to some interested discoveries. It was clear that some popular ideas about modern American garbage were mistaken. For example, the team discovered that almost half of the garbage in the landfills is paper—a fact that many people found surprised.

[1] **landfill site:** a place where garbage is taken and buried

9 APPLY.

A Brainstorm all the things that you and people you know throw away. Then write short answers to the questions.

1. Are you surprised by the amount of trash you or others throw away? Why, or why not?
2. Are you worried about the amount of plastic or electronics you throw away?
3. What might people find fascinating about our trash in 100 years?
4. What topic in this lesson (or unit) did you find the most interesting?

B Work in a group. Discuss your answers to the questions from exercise **A**.

A: *I am surprised by the amount of trash my family throws away. We throw away a lot of plastic and food.*

B: *In my country, we reuse things a lot more. Everything is recycled.*

Review the Grammar UNIT 15

Charts 15.1–15.4

1 Complete the sentences with the words in parentheses. Use the active or passive form of the verbs.

1. Theories about history __should be supported__ (should / support) by evidence.
2. This TV series about the Romans ______________ (make) last year. It ______________ (film) all over Europe.
3. Last night, Dr. Canas ______________ (give) a lecture about the Middle Ages.
4. Your assignment on Gandhi ______________ (must / complete) by Friday.
5. I ______________ (might / finish) the job today.
6. ______________ (the mail / deliver) before noon? I'm expecting a package.
7. Bikes ______________ (must not / leave) outside the library.
8. Students ______________ (can / obtain) further information from the dean's office.
9. Unfortunately, my watch ______________ (can't / repair).
10. Where ______________ (you / keep) your garbage bags?

Charts 15.1–15.6

2 **EDIT.** Read the article about unusual artifacts in Costa Rica. Find and correct seven more errors with the passive voice and participial adjectives.

An Ancient Mystery from Costa Rica

The giant stone balls of Costa Rica are one of the most (1) ~~fascinated~~ fascinating human artifacts. The balls made in prehistoric times and are perfectly round. The stone comes from local mountains. It's likely that stone tools were use to make the balls. The biggest ball is eight feet across and it is weighed 16 tons.

Unfortunately, we may never be discovered the true purpose of the stones, since only a small number of stones can be studied in context. Many of the stones were removed from their original place.

Archaeologists are annoying about this situation. They say that when artifacts are found by members of the public, they must not be moved. Photos can take, but the artifacts should not be pick up.

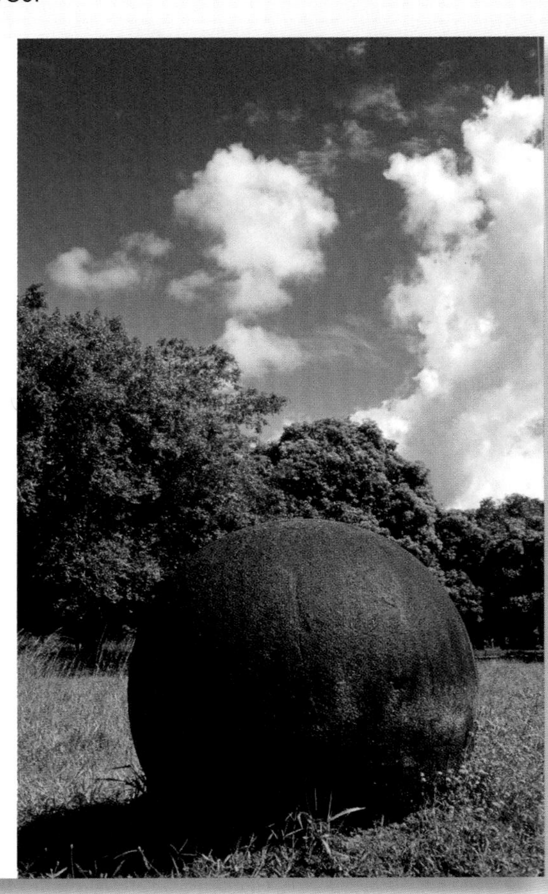

Charts 15.1–15.3

3 WRITE & LISTEN.

A Use the words to complete the questions for a history quiz show. Use the simple past passive.

1. where / the first public baths / build *Where were the first public baths built?*
2. when / the first moon landing / complete ______
3. where / scissors / invent ______
4. when / the first airplane / fly ______
5. who / popcorn / invent / by ______
6. when / the first CDs / sell ______

CD4-22

B Read the questions from exercise **A** and choose the answer you think is correct. Then listen to an extract from a quiz show and check your answers.

1.	a. India	b. Ancient Greece	(c.) Ancient Rome
2.	a. 1967	b. 1968	c. 1969
3.	a. Ancient Egypt	b. Japan	c. Germany
4.	a. 1898	b. 1903	c. 1907
5.	a. Native Americans	b. Australians	c. Europeans
6.	a. 1975	b. 1979	c. 1982

C Review the answers to the questions in exercise **A** and write a passive sentence in your notebook about each item or event.

1. The first public baths were built in ancient Rome.

Charts 15.1–15.6

4 WRITE & SPEAK.

A In your notebook, write answers to the questions. Then write three similar questions to ask your classmates. Write about the topics in this unit.

1. What was displayed in the Forum in ancient Rome?
2. Can the ruins of Pompeii be visited?
3. What are the giant balls of Costa Rica made of?
4. Which story in this unit were you most interested in?
5. Which story was the least interesting?

B Work in a group. Take turns answering the questions from exercise **A**.

Connect the Grammar to Writing

1 READ & NOTICE THE GRAMMAR.

A Can you remember a special event that happened to you when you were a child? Tell a partner about the event. Then read the text.

My Grandfather's Gift

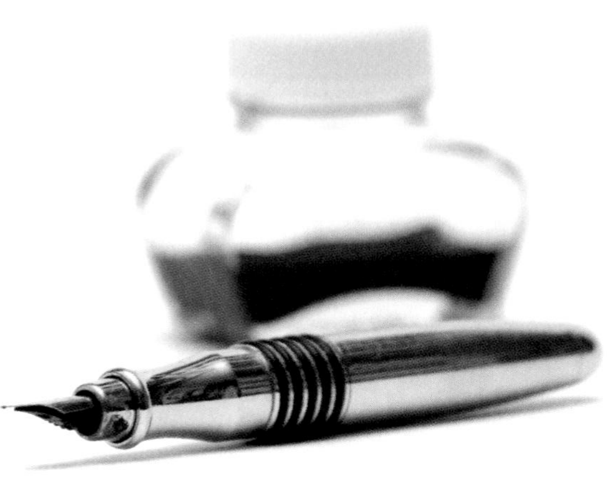

When my grandfather was a boy in Poland, fountain pens[1] were used for writing. All of his school work was done with a fountain pen. His first short story was written with a special silver fountain pen that his mother, my great grandmother, gave him for his tenth birthday. His name was engraved[2] on the pen. Sadly, his mother was killed in a car accident soon after this birthday. He was raised by his father. In an old photograph, my grandfather is dressed in a school uniform, and his fountain pen can be seen through the front pocket of his shirt. It seems he was rarely without his pen.

No one was really surprised when Grandpa became a writer. Now, most of his work has been translated from Polish to English. His stories can now be enjoyed by people all over the world, including me.

When I was ten, my mother and I went to Poland to visit him. It was an exciting time for me. He showed me his writing desk, and I remember deciding then that I wanted to be a writer, too. On the last day of our visit, my grandfather asked me to close my eyes. He gently placed his pen in my hands. I was stunned[3] and incredibly happy. I will never forget the connection I felt with my grandfather that day. It is one of the most important memories of my life.

[1] **fountain pen:** a type of pen that is filled from an ink bottle
[2] **engraved:** carved into; names or initials are often engraved in jewelry or other metallic items
[3] **stunned:** surprised or shocked

GRAMMAR FOCUS

In the text in exercise **A**, the writer uses the passive voice without the *by* phrase to focus on objects or events, not the agents.

*When my grandfather was a boy in Poland, fountain pens **were used** for writing.*
*All of his school work **was done** with a fountain pen.*

The writer uses the passive voice with the *by* phrase when the information about the agent is necessary.

*He was **raised** by his father.*

B Look at the chart. Find each example of passive voice in the text in exercise **A**. Is the agent in the text or not? Check the correct column and complete the information. Then look at paragraph 1 of the text again, and add two more examples to the chart.

Passive Voice	Agent in text (necessary information)	Agent not in text (clear from context)
1. fountain pens were used		✓ (by people)
2. his name was engraved		
3. his mother was killed		
4. he was raised		
5. his stories can . . . be enjoyed		

C Complete the chart with information from the text in exercise **A**. Discuss your answers with a partner.

	Event: Receiving gift from grandfather
What is the memory?	Receiving a special pen from my grandfather
Why is this event important?	
Details	

2 BEFORE YOU WRITE. Decide on an event from your past to write about. Make a chart like the one in exercise **1C** in your notebook. Complete the chart with your own ideas.

WRITING FOCUS **Writing Strong Concluding Sentences**

It is important to end each paragraph with a strong sentence. This lets the reader know the paragraph is ending and a new idea is coming. A good concluding sentence often states an opinion or makes a summary statement about the ideas in the paragraph. Notice the examples from the text.

It seems he was rarely without his pen.
His stories can now be enjoyed by people all over the world, including me.
It is one of the most important memories in my life.

3 WRITE two or three paragraphs about the memory you selected. Use the information from your chart in exercise **2** and the text in exercise **1A** to help you.

4 SELF ASSESS. Read your paragraphs and underline examples of the passive voice. Then use the checklist to assess your work.

- ☐ I used the passive voice correctly. [15.1, 15.2]
- ☐ I used the passive voice with the *by* phrase correctly. [15.4]
- ☐ I used the passive voice with modals correctly. [15.3]
- ☐ I used present and past participial adjectives correctly. [15.5, 15.6]
- ☐ I wrote strong concluding sentences. [WRITING FOCUS]

Noun Clauses and Reported Speech

▲ Before 1984, astronauts on spacewalks used a long, thick wire called a tether to attach themselves to their spacecraft. In February 1984, astronaut Bruce McCandless left the space shuttle *Challenger* and performed the very first untethered spacewalk.

LESSON 1 Noun Clauses with *That*

EXPLORE

CD4-23

1 READ the article about the discovery of a long lost Egyptian city. Notice the words in **bold**.

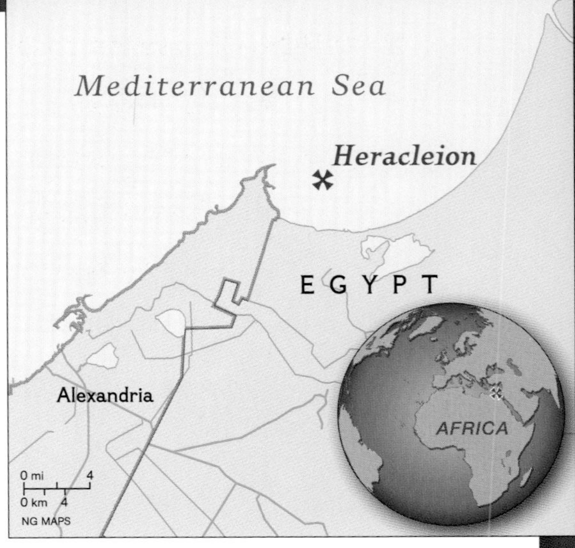

Discovering a Lost City

History books sometimes tell us about towns and cities that no longer exist. Where did they go? Stories suggest **that some of these places are lost beneath the sea**. Franck Goddio is a French underwater explorer who has discovered such places. His work has shown **that these lost places can be found**.

One of Goddio's most important discoveries is the Egyptian port of Thonis-Heracleion. At one time, historians thought **that Thonis and Heracleion were two separate cities**. However, Goddio and his team proved **that they were in fact two different names for the same city**. It is now accepted **that *Thonis* was the Egyptian name and *Heracleion* was the Greek name**.

Historians think **that the city was founded[1] in the 8th century B.C.** It was a center of trade and had religious importance because of its many temples. Experts believe **that the city was hit by several natural disasters** before it finally sank into the Mediterranean Sea in the 8th century A.D. In the ruins of the city, Goddio's team found statues, jewelry, coins, and inscriptions[2] that have added greatly to our understanding of life in ancient Egypt.

[1] **found:** to start or create a city or organization
[2] **inscription:** a piece of writing carved into an object

▲ Franck Goddio with an inscribed Heracleion stone from B.C. 378-362

2 **CHECK.** Choose the correct answer to complete each statement.

1. Franck Goddio has _____.
   a. found cities under the sea
   b. written stories about lost cities
   c. discovered a lost city on land

2. Thonis and Heracleion _____.
   a. were two separate cities
   b. were very close to each other
   c. were the same place

3. According to historians, Heracleion _____.
   a. was founded in the 8th century B.C.
   b. experienced only one disaster
   c. had no important buildings

4. The ruins of Heracleion _____.
   a. contained nothing of interest
   b. provided a lot of information
   c. were difficult to explore

3 **DISCOVER.** Complete the exercises to learn about the grammar in this lesson.

A Look at the chart. Find the sentence in the article that contains each clause with *that.* Then fill in the subject and verb.

Subject	Verb	Clause with *That*
Stories	suggest	that some of these places are lost beneath the sea.
		that these lost places can be found.
		that Thonis and Heracleion were two separate cities.
		that the city was founded in the 8th century B.C.
		that the city was hit by several natural disasters . . .

B Check the one true statement about the clauses with *that* in exercise **A**.

1. _____ They take the place of a verb.
2. _____ They take the place of a noun.
3. _____ They take the place of an adjective.
4. _____ They take the place of an adverb.

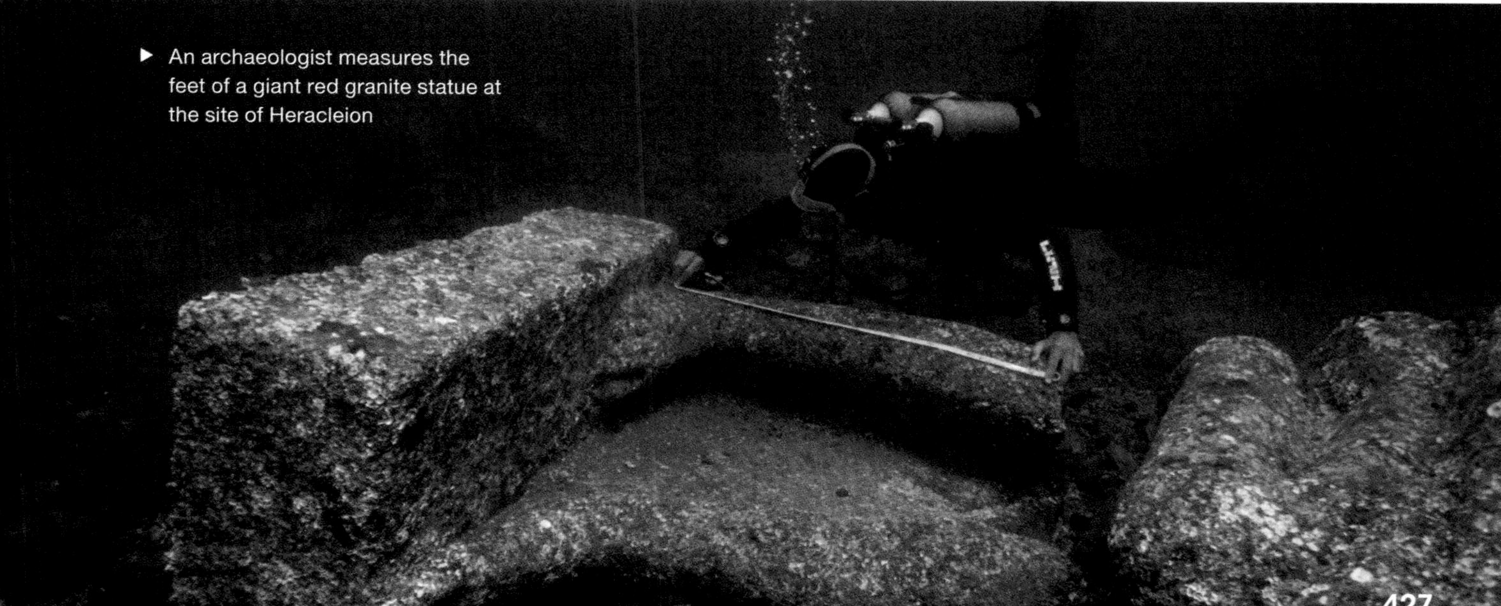

▶ An archaeologist measures the feet of a giant red granite statue at the site of Heracleion

LEARN

16.1 Noun Clauses with *That*

Noun as Object of Verb	Noun Clause as Object of Verb
Jennifer realizes the problem. (Noun: the problem)	Jennifer realizes **that her grades are falling**. (Noun Clause: that her grades are falling)

1. A noun clause takes the place of a noun in a sentence. *That* can introduce a noun clause.	Louis (S) believed (V) **the professor** (Noun/Object). Louis (S) believed (V) **that the professor was telling the truth.** (Noun Clause/Object)
2. **Remember:** A clause always has a subject and a verb.	Ann forgot **that her sister** (S) **had borrowed** (V) her keys.
3. A noun clause often follows verbs that suggest thinking or mental activity, such as *decide, think,* or *believe.*	I've **decided** that I will work harder next year. (Noun Clause: that I will work harder next year)
4. In speaking and informal writing, *that* is often omitted.	I dreamed **that I was flying**. I dreamed **I was flying**.

4 Read the sentences. Underline the noun clauses with *that.* Then circle and label the subject and verb of each noun clause.

1. Explorers always hope that they (S) will make (V) discoveries.
2. Goddio decided that he wanted to look for Heracleion.
3. He thought that he and his team could find the city.
4. They discovered that the city was near the coast.
5. The team realized that the ruins were very old.
6. The divers noticed that the ruins contained statues and jewelry.
7. Archaeologists know that the site is very important.
8. They believe that it will help our understanding of ancient Egypt.

REAL ENGLISH

Here are more verbs that suggest thinking or mental activity.

discover	*hope*	*realize*
dream	*know*	*remember*
find out	*learn*	*suggest*
forget	*notice*	*understand*

5 Complete the exercises.

A Put the phrases in order to make complete sentences. Add *that* to the beginning of the noun clauses.

1. the lecture on ancient Egypt / found out / the students / was canceled

The students found out that the lecture on ancient Egypt was canceled.

2. the city / learned / archaeologists / was important

____

3. discovered / were over 2000 years old / the statues / scientists

____

4. I / found a lost city / dreamed / I

____

5. hope / some explorers / will be famous / their discoveries

____

6. believe / I / has information on ancient Greece / her book

____

B Work with a partner. Cross out *that* in the sentences in exercise **A**. Take turns reading each sentence with and without *that*.

REAL ENGLISH

As in relative clauses, the pronunciation of *that* in noun clauses is often reduced. The /æ/ is pronounced /ə/.

6 WRITE & SPEAK.

A Complete the noun clauses with the words in the box.

~~it is under the sea~~	it has improved a lot
they are the same	it was a little boring

1. What do you remember about Heracleion?

   I remember that it is under the sea.

2. What did you learn about Thonis and Heracleion?

   I learned that ______________________________

3. What did you think about history when you were younger?

   I thought that ______________________________

4. What have you realized about your English recently?

   I've realized that ______________________________

B Use the information in the article from exercise **1** on page 426 and your own ideas to complete the noun clauses in exercise **A** in a different way. Write the sentences in your notebook, and then share them with your class mates.

1. I remember that Heracleion was hit by several natural disasters.

16.2 Noun Clauses with *That:* More Expressions

1. A noun clause with *that* can follow *be* + certain adjectives that express how someone feels, such as: *be afraid* *be happy* *be surprised* *be certain* *be glad* *be sure* *be disappointed* *be sorry* *be worried*	The students **were afraid** that the test was today. (Noun Clause: that the test was today) We **are sorry** that you didn't find your necklace. (Noun Clause: that you didn't find your necklace) **I'm sure** that my answer is correct. (Noun Clause: that my answer is correct)
2. A noun clause with *that* can follow certain common expressions, such as: a. *It is true . . .* b. *It is a fact . . .*	a. **It is true** that he worked in Egypt. b. **It is a fact** that Egypt is in Africa.
3. **Remember:** In a noun clause, *that* is often omitted.	Students were afraid **that the test was today**. Students were afraid **the test was today**.

7 Read the conversation. Underline seven more noun clauses and insert *that* in the correct place.

Ben: Is it true [that] you're leading the search tomorrow?

Lucia: Yes, it is. I'm surprised you know about it already.

Ben: News travels fast! Anyway, I'm glad you've been chosen. You'll be a great team leader. Dave doesn't have enough experience. I was afraid we were going to get lost today.

Lucia: I know. I was worried someone might get lost when he split us up into pairs. In my opinion, we should all stay together.

Ben: Yes, I agree. Professor Kim is disappointed we haven't found any sign of the city yet. He's sure we're in the right place, though.

Lucia: Well, it's true people have been looking for it for years . . .

8 **SPEAK.** Complete each sentence with a noun clause with *that*. Use your own ideas. Then share your sentences with a partner.

1. I am afraid ______________________________
2. I am glad ______________________________
3. I am sure ______________________________
4. I am disappointed ______________________________

I'm glad that tomorrow's Friday.

PRACTICE

Yonaguni
Japan
AUSTRALIA

9 READ, WRITE & SPEAK.

A Look at the photo and read the caption. Then read the conversation. Find seven more noun clauses (without *that*) and underline them.

Professor: Great dive, everyone! So what do you think after seeing the Yonaguni monument for yourselves? Do you think it's natural or man-made? Is it a pile of rocks or the remains of an ancient civilization?

Kenji: Well, I can understand all the excitement. It's true the rocks look like they have been carved. The edges are so straight . . .

Pam: I agree. And I'm sure I saw some steps. They seemed to lead to the top of the monument.

Michaela: Hmmm. I'm not sure I agree. The rocks looked natural to me.

Kenji: What about the head-shaped rock? Did you see that, Michaela?

Michaela: No, I had to go back to the surface because I had a problem with my diving equipment. I was afraid I didn't have enough air.

Pam: I'm sorry you didn't see it.

Kenji: I know there are some Japanese scientists who agree with us, Pam.

Michaela: But the Japanese government doesn't agree. Don't forget the monument is officially considered a natural site.

▼ Divers explore the Yonaguni Monument off the coast of Japan.

B Complete the sentences about the students in exercise **A**. Use the information in the conversation and your own words.

1. Kenji and Pam seem to believe that Yonaguni was man-made.
2. Michaela thinks ______.
3. Kenji suggests ______.
4. Some scientists are sure ______.
5. The students' professor hopes ______.
6. The professor is happy ______.
7. I believe ______.
8. My partner thinks ______.

C Work with a partner. Compare your answers from exercise **B**. Then share your opinions about Yonaguni with your class.

I believe that Yonaguni was once on land. My partner thinks so, too. We aren't sure whether it's natural or man-made.

10 LISTEN & WRITE.

CD4-24

A Listen to a podcast about exploring the ancient city of Machu Picchu in Peru. For each statement, circle **T** for *true* or **F** for *false*.

Machu Picchu
Peru
SOUTH AMERICA

1. Machu Picchu was built by Europeans. **T** **F**
2. Archaeologists first visited Machu Picchu over 100 years ago. **T** **F**
3. The number of visitors per day is limited. **T** **F**
4. Walking the Inca Trail to Machu Picchu takes ten days. **T** **F**
5. The only way to the city is on foot. **T** **F**

CD4-25

B Read the questions. Then listen to extracts from the podcast. How would the speaker answer the questions? Take notes on the answers in your notebook.

1. What is the best time of day to visit?
2. What is the quietest day to visit?
3. When is the best time to buy your ticket?
4. Is it difficult to get to Machu Picchu?
5. What is the best way to get to Machu Picchu?

C Write sentences in your notebook based on your notes in exercise **B**. Use noun clauses. Begin with *The speaker believes . . . , The speaker suggests . . . ,* or *It is a fact that . . .*

The speaker believes that early morning or late afternoon is the best time.

11 APPLY.

A Complete each sentence with a noun clause with *that*. Make true statements about yourself.

1. I'm sure that I will visit Machu Picchu one day.
2. I was disappointed ________________.
3. It's a fact ________________.
4. When I was young, I dreamed ________________.
5. My friends are sometimes surprised ________________.
6. In ten years' time, I hope ________________.

B Work in a group. Share your sentences from exercise **A**. Ask your classmates questions about their sentences.

A: *I'm sure that I will visit Machu Picchu one day.*

B: *Why do you want to go there?*

LESSON 2 Noun Clauses with *Wh-* Words and *If/Whether*

EXPLORE

CD4-26

1 READ part of a lecture about early exploration around the world. Notice the words in **bold**.

The Voyage of the *Kon-Tiki*

▲ Thor Heyerdahl's craft, the *Kon-Tiki*, at sea

Professor: Today we're going to discuss **where the people of the Polynesian Islands came from**.

Chen: Excuse me, Professor, I'm not sure **where the Polynesian Islands are**.

Professor: They are way out in the Pacific Ocean. Anyhow, in the mid-20th century, most scientists believed they knew **where the islanders came from**. They thought the first islanders arrived from Asia over 5000 years ago. However, one man wasn't convinced. He was an explorer named Thor Heyerdahl.

Indira: I've heard of him, Professor, but I don't remember **whether he was Norwegian or Danish** . . .

Professor: Norwegian, Indira. Heyerdahl had a theory that the Polynesian Islanders actually came from South America. He wanted to see **if his theory was possible**. So, in 1947, he sailed his balsa wood[1] boat, the *Kon-Tiki*, west from Peru to Polynesia.

Chen: Why balsa wood?

Professor: Well, it was a light-weight material that was probably used by early South American boat makers. He wanted to demonstrate **how early South Americans traveled**. After 101 days, Heyerdahl successfully reached the Tuamotu Islands in Polynesia. However, many scientists still didn't believe that his theory was correct. But now, decades later, new scientific research shows that some early Polynesians had South American DNA.[2]

Indira: So he was right?

Professor: Well, actually, we still can't be sure **whether or not early South Americans sailed west to Polynesia**. It's possible the Polynesians sailed to South America, too.

[1] **balsa wood:** a very light wood from South America that floats well
[2] **DNA:** an acid that carries genetic information in the cells of each living thing

2 CHECK. Choose the correct answer to complete each sentence.

1. The Polynesian Islands are located in the _____ Ocean.
   a. Atlantic b. Pacific c. Indian
2. Most scientists thought the first people in Polynesia came from _____.
   a. Peru b. South America c. Asia
3. Thor Heyerdahl planned his voyage because he wanted to _____.
   a. test his theory b. prove scientists were correct c. visit the Tuamoto Islands
4. Heyerdahl used a balsa wood boat because he wanted to _____.
   a. have a slow journey b. save some money c. travel like the early sailors
5. Recent scientific research has shown that Heyerdahl _____.
   a. was wrong b. was right c. might be right

3 DISCOVER. Complete the exercises to learn about the grammar in this lesson.

A Find these sentences in the lecture from exercise **1**. Write the missing words.

1. Today, we're going to discuss __where__ the people of Polynesia are from.
2. Professor, I'm not sure __________ the Polynesian Islands are.
3. He wanted to demonstrate __________ early South Americans traveled.

B Look at the sentences in exercise **A**. Circle the correct answers.

1. The words you wrote in exercise **A** are usually used in **statements** / **questions**.
2. The word order after the missing words is like a **question** / **statement**.

◀ Aerial view of Paoaoa Point and Marina Point, Bora Bora, French Polynesia

LEARN

16.3 Noun Clauses with *Wh-* Words

Wh- Questions
How did you know that?
Where is the museum?
What did the guide say?

Noun Clauses with *Wh-* Words		
I don't understand	how	you knew that.
Do you know	where	the museum is?
No one knows	what	the guide said.

1. A noun clause can begin with a *Wh-* word: *when, how, which, where, who/whom, whose, why, what.*	I don't know **when she will arrive.** Did you notice **where I put my bag?** I forget **how this machine works.**
2. **Remember:** A noun clause takes the place of a noun in a sentence.	Find out her name. (Noun) Find out **what her name is.** (Noun Clause)
3. Use statement word order in noun clauses with *Wh-* words. Do not use question word order.	What did **he** say? ✓ I understood **what he said.** ✗ I understood what did he say.
4. **Be careful!** Be sure to change the verb form in the noun clause to match *do/does/did* in the question.	When **did** he leave? I don't know when he **left.** Where **does** he **go**? I'm not sure where he **goes.**
5. A noun clause with a *Wh-* word can be used in a statement or a question. Do not use a question mark when it is in a statement.	I don't know (Statement) **when she will arrive.** Do you know (Question) **when she will arrive?**

4 Circle the correct answers.

1. I'm not sure where **is Polynesia** / **Polynesia is.**
2. Can you remind me who **was Thor Heyerdahl** / **Thor Heyerdahl was**?
3. I don't know how **the *Kon-Tiki* was built** / **was the *Kon-Tiki* built**.
4. I've forgotten when **Heyerdahl sailed** / **did Heyerdahl sail** to Polynesia.
5. Can you tell me where **was Heyerdahl** / **Heyerdahl was** from?
6. Do you remember what **he was trying** / **was he trying** to prove?
7. Do you know which islands **the *Kon-Tiki* sailed to** / **did the *Kon-Tiki* sail to**?
8. I don't understand what **does the new research show** / **the new research shows**.

5 Complete the exercises.

A Complete the noun clause in each sentence. Use the underlined part of the questions.

1. When did people start living in Polynesia?

   Do you know ___when people started___ living in Polynesia?

2. <u>Where are the islands</u>?

Can you show me ______________________________ on the map?

3. <u>How many days did the *Kon-Tiki* take</u> to get there?

Do you remember ______________________________ to get there?

4. <u>What did the DNA results show</u>?

Do you understand ______________________________?

5. <u>Who do you believe</u>?

Have you decided ______________________________?

B Work with a partner. Ask and answer the questions from exercise **A**. Use the map to help you.

A: *Do you know when people started living in Polynesia?*

B: *Over 5000 years ago. / No, I don't remember.*

REAL ENGLISH

People often use noun clauses to be less direct and more polite when asking questions.

Excuse me. Do you know ***what time it is?***

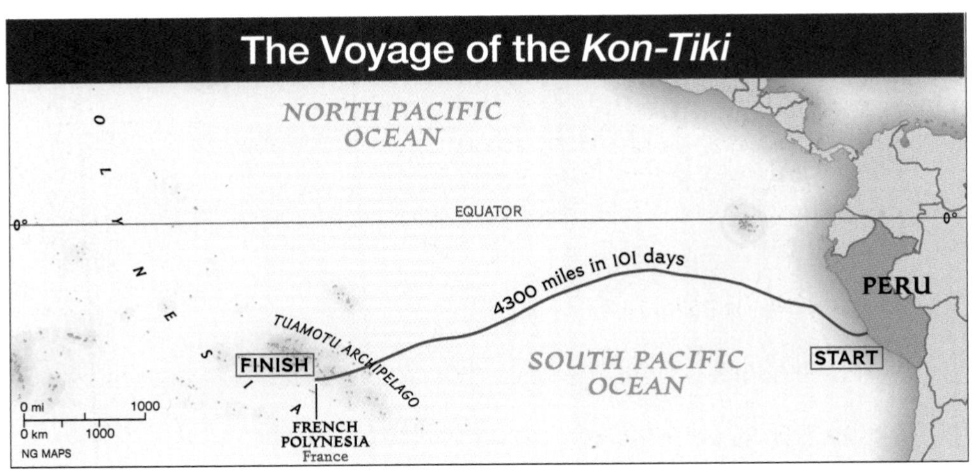

16.4 Noun Clauses with *If/Whether*

Yes/No Questions	Noun Clauses with *If/Whether*		
Are the workers busy?	I'm not sure	if whether	the workers are busy.
Did they see the e-mail?	We don't know	if whether	they saw the e-mail.

1. Use *if* or *whether* to change a *Yes/No* question to a noun clause.	Does she have class? I'm not sure **if she has class.** Do you know **whether she has class?**
2. Use statement word order with a noun clause beginning with *if* or *whether*.	✓ I don't know **if she is absent today.** ✗ I don't know if <u>is she absent today</u>.
3. When *if* or *whether* begins a noun clause, *or not* is sometimes added to the end of the clause. It is also possible to add *or not* directly after *whether*.	I don't know **if** he is right **or not.** I'm not sure **whether** she knows **or not.** I'm not sure **whether or not** she knows.

6 Finish each sentence by adding a period (.) or a question mark (?).

1. I can't remember whether Heyerdahl was Norwegian or not
2. Do you remember if the Polynesians came from South America
3. Mae wasn't certain if the lecture on Polynesia was canceled
4. I wonder whether Heyerdahl was right
5. Do you know if the professor wants us to write about Polynesia
6. Can you tell me whether the assignment is due this week

7 Complete the exercises.

A Look at the *Yes/No* questions. Then complete the noun clauses. Add a period (.) or a question mark (?) to the end of each noun clause.

1. Does Diego speak Japanese?

   Do you know whether Diego speaks Japanese?

2. Did I turn the TV off?

   I can't remember if ______________________

3. Is Alex on vacation?

   I'm not sure if ______________________

4. Was Joanne at the lecture?

   I wonder whether ______________________

5. Does the bus go to the park?

   Kai's not sure whether ______________________

6. Is the concert tonight?

   Can you tell me if ______________________

7. Did Shari leave?

   We're not certain if ______________________

8. Are they happy?

   No one knows whether ______________________

B Work with a partner. Take turns reading the completed sentences from exercise **A**. Add *or not* in an appropriate place.

Do you know whether or not Diego speaks Japanese?

PRACTICE

Mumbai (Bombay), India

8 Read the questions about exploring the city of Mumbai in India. Change the questions to noun clauses to complete the sentences.

1. Where is the Gateway to India?

   Jared wants to know ___where the Gateway of India is___.

2. Is there time to explore the old part of town today?

   Joan isn't sure ________________ to explore the old part of town today.

3. Is it a long way to the national park?

   Anna can't remember ________________ to the national park.

4. How can we get to Film City?

   I don't know ________________ to Film City.

5. Will we be able to see actors making a movie there?

   I wonder ________________ actors making a movie there.

6. Which street goes to the harbor?

   Louise isn't sure ________________ to the harbor.

7. Where is Crawford Market?

   Rick has forgotten ________________.

8. Do we need to bring the GPS?

   I want to know ________________ to bring the GPS.

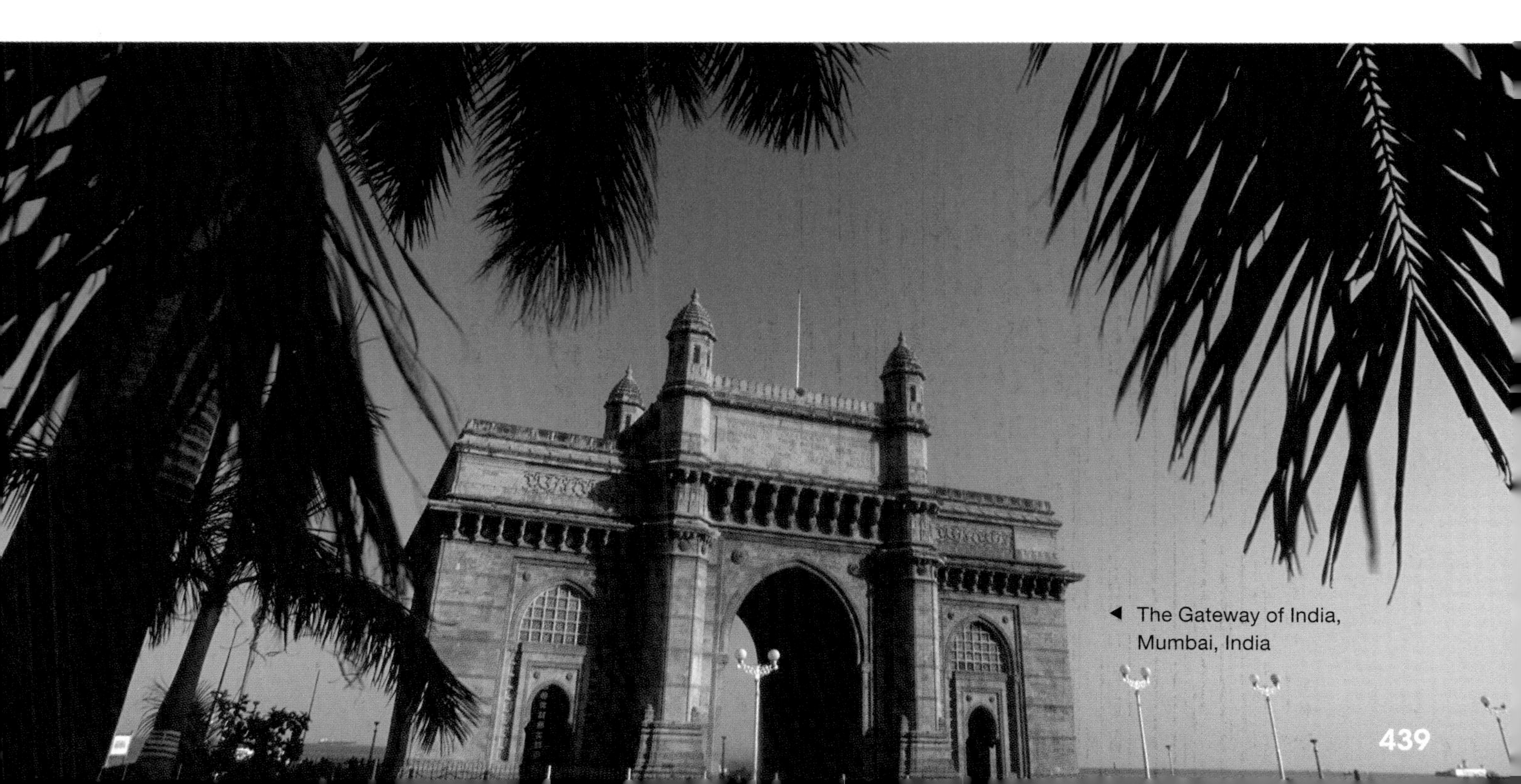

◀ The Gateway of India, Mumbai, India

9 LISTEN & WRITE.

CD4-27

A Look at the map and listen to the first part of a museum recording. Then listen again and choose the correct answers.

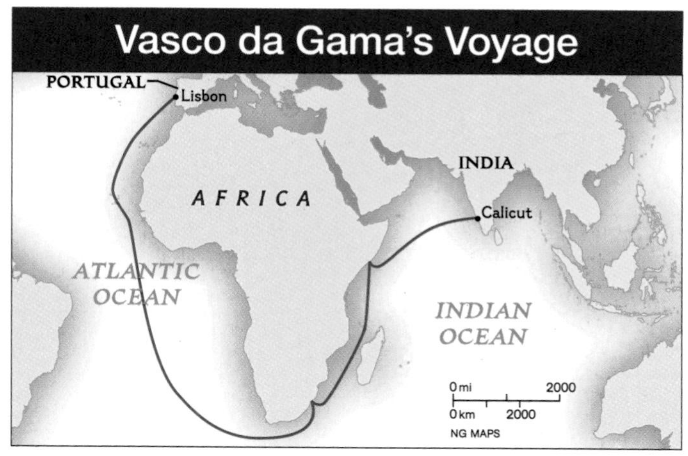

1. When did Vasco da Gama sail to India for the first time? a. 1497 b. 1597
2. What country's king sent da Gama to India? a. Spain b. Portugal

B Read more questions about da Gama and his voyage. Guess the answers by choosing *a* or *b*.

1. What was the reason for the voyage? a. trade b. exploration
2. Where did da Gama sail from? a. Portugal b. India
3. Was da Gama Italian? a. yes b. no
4. How many ships did da Gama take with him? a. two b. four
5. What did da Gama discover? a. a sea route to India b. Indian spices
6. What else is da Gama remembered for? a. his kindness b. his cruelty

C Write sentences about the questions in exercise **B**. Use noun clauses and the expressions from the box.

I'm not sure	I don't know	I don't remember	I'm not certain	I wonder

1. I'm not sure what the main reason for the voyage was.
2. ______
3. ______
4. ______
5. ______
6. ______

CD4-28

D Listen to the complete recording and check your answers to exercise **B**.

10 WRITE & SPEAK.

A Use the words in parentheses to complete the polite questions.

1. (where / the zoo / be)

   Can you tell me *where the zoo is?*

2. (how / I / can / get / to the theater)

   Could you tell me ______________________

3. (if / there / be / a good bookstore / near here)

   Do you know ______________________

4. (when / the bus to the castle / leave)

   Can you tell me ______________________

5. (what time / the stores / close)

   Do you know ______________________

6. (whether / the museum / be / open today)

   Could you tell me ______________________

B Work with a partner. Ask and answer your questions from exercise **A**. Use the information in Castletown Visitor Highlights to guide your answers.

A: *Excuse me. Can you tell me where the zoo is?*

B: *Sure. It's on Highway 15, just outside of town.*

Castletown Visitor Highlights
• Visit the castle at the north end of Castle Road. Free buses every hour, starting at 10 AM.
• See a play about a famous local explorer at Main Street Theater, Main St. & 7th Ave.
• Be sure to visit the famous Old Town Bookstore at Main Street and 4th Ave. Hours 10–8.
• Learn all about our town at Castletown Museum. Tues–Fri: 10–6; Sat–Sun: 9–5.
• For family fun, visit our local zoo! It's located just outside of Castletown, on Highway 15.

11 APPLY.

A In your notebook, draw a simple map of the place where you grew up or a place you know well. Mark an *X* on four places of interest, but do not tell your partner what they are.

B Work with a partner. Give your partner a list of the places and your map. Take turns asking and answering polite questions with noun clauses about each other's maps. Try to locate the places on the map.

A: *Can you tell me where the Museum of Modern Art is?*

B: *Sure, it's on 53rd Street, just off 5th Avenue.*

LESSON 3 Quoted and Reported Speech

EXPLORE

CD4-29

1 READ the blog about space exploration. Notice the phrases in **bold**.

Is space exploration still a good idea?

▲ Valentina Tereshkova, the first woman sent to space, June 16, 1963, Moscow

Russian cosmonaut Valentina Tereshkova made the first space flight by a woman. She **said, "Once you've been in space, you appreciate how small and fragile[1] Earth is."** Several years after Tereshkova's three-day flight, my grandparents watched the first man walk on the moon. My grandmother **told me that it was an incredible moment**. She said that she remembered when Neil Armstrong **said, "That's one small step for a man, one giant leap[2] for mankind."** In those days, everyone thought that these were amazing achievements, but is space exploration still a good idea today?

Nowadays some leading politicians **say that space exploration is too expensive**. They **argue that the money should be used to deal with problems on Earth**. On the other hand, scientists **tell us that we have learned a lot from space travel**. Some people even **say the survival of humankind may depend on space exploration**. Obviously, the question is a serious one. In my opinion, the answer is clear. As Carl Sagan **said, "We have a basic responsibility to our species[3] to venture[4] to other worlds."**

[1] **fragile:** easily broken
[2] **giant leap:** a very big step
[3] **species:** a grouping of living things, such as the human species
[4] **venture:** to act with risk or possible danger

"We have a basic responsibility to our species to venture to other worlds."
—**Carl Sagan**

◄ Astronaut Buzz Aldrich on the moon (July 1969)

◀ First-ever image of Earth from space, sent by *Voyager 1*

2 CHECK. Read the statements. Circle **T** for *true* or **F** for *false*.

1. Valentina Tereshkova was the first woman in space.	**T**	**F**
2. In the beginning, many people thought that space exploration was too expensive.	**T**	**F**
3. Some politicians think that problems on Earth are more important than exploring space.	**T**	**F**
4. Scientists believe that space travel has had practical benefits.	**T**	**F**
5. Carl Sagan thought that we should not explore space.	**T**	**F**

3 DISCOVER. Complete the exercises to learn about the grammar in this lesson.

A Circle the forms of *say* or *tell* in each of these sentences from the blog in exercise **1**. Underline the clause or sentence that follows.

1. My grandmother (told) me that it was an incredible moment.
2. . . . Neil Armstrong said, "That's one small step for a man, one giant leap for mankind."
3. . . . , scientists tell us that we have learned a lot from space travel.
4. Some people even say the survival of humankind may depend on space exploration.
5. Carl Sagan said, "We have a basic responsibility to our species to venture to other worlds."

B Look at the words you underlined in exercise **A**. Write the sentence numbers on the lines to complete the statements.

1. Sentences __2__ and ____ give the speaker's exact words.
2. Sentences ____, ____, and ____ have noun clauses.

LEARN

16.5 Quoted Speech

Exact Words	Quoted Speech
Rena: I feel sorry for you.	Rena **said, "I feel sorry for you."**
Chad: Where is Lucy going?	Chad **asked, "Where is Lucy going?"**
Tom: Is the train arriving soon?	Tom **asked, "Is the train arriving soon?"**

1. In quoted speech,* the speaker's exact words are written in quotation marks. Quotes are often introduced by the verbs *say* and *ask*.	He **said, "The buses are running late."** Lina **asked, "Where is the bus stop?"**
2. Notice the punctuation of quoted speech. a. Put a comma after the verb *say* or *ask*. b. Use quotation marks at the beginning and end of the exact words. c. Begin the quote with a capital letter. d. Put a period (.) or question mark (?) before the final quotation mark.	Quotation Marks Mr. Gomez said, **"Math is not difficult."** Comma Liam asked, **"Where are we?"** Capital *W* — Before Final Quotation Mark
3. The phrase with *said* or *asked* can come at the end of the quoted speech. When it does, put a. a comma (not a period) at the end of a statement b. a question mark if the quote is a question	a. "Your paper is late," **the Professor said.** b. "Why are we here**?" they asked.**

* *Quoted speech* is sometimes called *direct speech*.

4 Read each pair of sentences. Then choose the sentence with the correct punctuation and capitalization.

1. a. Martin asked "Did you read the blog about space exploration?"
   (b.) Martin asked, "Did you read the blog about space exploration?"
2. a. Rita said, "Yes, I read it last night."
   b. Rita said, "yes, I read it last night."
3. a. Sally asked, "Have you finished your assignment about astronauts"?
   b. Sally asked, "Have you finished your assignment about astronauts?"
4. a. "Yes. It took me a long time." said Alfredo.
   b. "Yes. It took me a long time," said Alfredo.
5. a. "New photos of Jupiter have just been published," the reporter said.
   b. New photos of Jupiter have just been published," the reporter said.
6. a. "Have you seen the new photos, Mary," Alex asked.
   b. "Have you seen the new photos, Mary?" Alex asked.

5 Complete the exercises.

A Add the necessary capitalization and punctuation to complete the quoted speech.

1. Julie said, "I'd love to be an astronaut."
2. why is that Hector asked
3. Julie said I want to see the Earth from space
4. Hector said yes, that must be an amazing sight
5. are you worried about the dangers Ratna asked
6. it's worth the risk Julie said
7. Ratna said I don't like the idea of spacewalks
8. I think they sound amazing said Hector

B Rewrite the sentences from exercise **A**. Move the information about the speaker to the other end of the sentence.

1. "I'd love to be an astronaut," Julie said.
2. ______
3. ______
4. ______
5. ______
6. ______
7. ______
8. ______

◀ Astronaut Tracy Caldwell Dyson looks through a window of the International Space Station.

16.6 Reported Speech

Quoted Speech	Reported Speech: Subject	Reporting Verb	Noun Clause
Rena said, "Ben likes traveling."	Rena	**said**	**(that) Ben liked traveling.**
Tom said, "Jill's at home."	Tom	**said**	**(that) Jill was at home.**
Chad asked, "Where is Luz going?"	Chad	**asked**	**where Luz was going.**

1. You can report what someone says indirectly (i.e., without the exact words) by using a reporting verb + a noun clause.	Harry **said that the bus was late.** Jim **asked what time it was.**
2. If the main verb in quoted speech is in the present, it usually shifts to the past in reported speech.*	Julie said, "Running **is** great exercise." Julie said that running **was** great exercise.
3. Personal pronouns and possessive adjectives** often need to change in reported speech.	Joe: "**I** don't see **your** map." Joe said **he** didn't see **my** map.
4. **Remember:** In conversation and informal writing, *that* is often omitted. In academic or formal writing, *that* is often not omitted.	He said **that** the bus is late. He said the bus is late. The leader said **that** schools were important.

**Reported speech* is sometimes called *indirect speech.*

See Unit 4, pages **90–91 to review personal pronouns and possessive adjectives.

6 Complete the conversations. Change the quoted speech in parentheses to reported speech. Remember to shift the verbs from present to past, and to change the pronouns and adjectives as necessary.

1. A: Where is Sam?

   B: I don't know. He said that ___*he was coming*___.
   ("I am coming.")

2. A: Did you see the professor?

   B. Yes. I asked her if ______________________.
   ("Is the assignment due on Friday?")

3. A: The weather doesn't look too good.

   B: No, it doesn't. Chris said that ______________________.
   ("There's going to be a storm.")

4. A: What did you say to Larry on the phone?

   B: I asked him what ______________________.
   ("What are you doing?")

5. A: Why didn't Diane help us yesterday?

   B: She couldn't. She said that ______________________.
   ("I'm too busy.")

6. A: Did you ask Scott to come to the party?

   B: Yes. He said that ______________________.
   ("I have too much work.")

7. A: Why did Irina go home?

   B: She said that ________________________________.
   ("I'm not enjoying the movie.")

8. A: Is Juan going to Australia?

   B: He said that ________________________________.
   ("I don't think so.")

7 SPEAK. Work with a partner. Imagine that you are in a noisy place. Repeat the question or statement using reported speech. Do not shift to the past tense.

A: *Do you want some coffee?*

B: *I'm sorry? What did you say?*

A: *I asked if you want some coffee.*

1. Do you want some coffee?
2. What time is it?
3. Are you enjoying the concert?
4. This restaurant is noisy.

REAL ENGLISH

When the situation is very recent or informal, speakers often do not shift the verb to the past in reported speech.

I said ***that I am hungry****.*

16.7 Reporting Verbs

Subject	Reporting Verb	Object	Noun Clause
Larry	said		(that) it's time for lunch.
	told	them	
	asked		when we were starting.
	asked	us	

1. To report a statement, use a. *said* + a noun clause b. *told* + object + a noun clause	a. Harry **said** (that) the bus was late. b. Jen **told me** (that) dinner was ready.
2. **Be careful!** You must include an object with *told*.	✓ Jen **told us** dinner was ready. ✗ Jen told dinner was ready.
3. To report questions and answers, use: a. *ask* + noun clause b. *ask* + object + noun clause c. *answer* or *reply* + noun clause	a. They **asked** if the movie was still playing. b. They **asked Joe** if it was a good movie. c. He **answered** that it was.

8 Circle all correct answers. Sometimes both answers are correct.

1. Jerry **asked** / **asked me** what my book was about.
2. I **told** / **replied** that it was about early space travel.
3. He **told me** / **asked** he knew several astronauts.
4. I **asked** / **said** I didn't believe him.

5. Jerry **told me** / **said** his uncle worked on the space program.

6. I **asked** / **said** if he ever went to watch flights take off.

7. He **answered** / **told** that he did.

8. I **asked him** / **told him** which astronauts he knew.

9 Change the speakers' exact words to reported speech. Use an appropriate reporting verb in the simple past. Add or change pronouns as necessary.

1. **Will:** What are you watching, Mei?

   Will asked Mei what she was watching.

2. **Mei:** It's a video from the space station.

   ____

3. **Will:** Who's talking?

   ____

4. **Mei:** The mission commander is giving a report.

   ____

5. **Will:** Why is the woman's hair like that?

   ____

6. **Mei:** It's because of zero gravity.

   ____

▲ Astronauts Luca Parmitano (above) and Karen Nyberg (left) on the International Space Station, August, 2013

PRACTICE

10 Complete the exercises.

A Look at the photo and read the caption. Then read the conversation about insects in space. Rewrite the conversation as quoted speech.

Spidernauts?

Hong: What are you watching?

Tina: It's a video about insects in space.

Hong: Are you serious?

Tina: Yes, astronauts sometimes take spiders and ants into space.

Hong: Oh, why do they do that?

Tina: They study their movements and feeding habits.

▲ Nefertiti, the first jumping spider in space, spent more than three months in orbit and circled the Earth over 1500 times.

1. Hong asked, "What are you watching?"
2. ______________________________ Tina replied.
3. Hong asked ______________________________
4. Tina said ______________________________
5. ______________________________ Hong asked.
6. Tina said ______________________________

REAL ENGLISH

Speakers often use "filler" language, such as *um, well,* and *hmm*. This language is not included in reported speech. *Yes* and *no* are also not reported.

Exact Words	**Reported Speech**
Um, I like traveling.	*She said she liked traveling.*
No, I don't mind.	*He said he didn't mind.*

B Review the conversation in exercise **A**. Then complete the reported speech.

1. Hong asked Tina what she was watching.
2. Tina replied that ______________________________
3. Hong asked ______________________________
4. Tina said ______________________________
5. Hong asked ______________________________
6. Tina said ______________________________

11 SPEAK.

A Work with a partner. Discuss the questions and make notes on your partner's ideas.

1. Do you know about other animals that have traveled to space?
2. Do you think that we can learn anything useful from these experiments? Explain.
3. Do you think that it's fair to send animals into space? Give your reasons.

B Report your partner's ideas to a small group or the class.

Maya told me that a cat went into space. She said that the cat was from France.

12 EDIT. Read the student's assignment. Find and correct six more errors with quoted and reported speech.

A Person I Admire

For this assignment, I watched an interview with Ellen Ochoa, who became the first Hispanic American woman in space in 1991. She went on to make several more flights and has spent over 950 hours in space.

When the interviewer asked her what ~~was~~ NASA training was like, Ochoa replied that everything was harder in training than in space. Next, the interviewer asked Ochoa how did it feel to float in zero gravity. She replied that it was fun to be weightless. She told there was really nothing to compare it to on Earth. She said the closest activity was probably swimming. Ochoa said her that astronauts had to pepare for all sorts of problems and accidents. The interviewer then asked the former asronaut did she miss her family when she was in space. Ochoa said it is difficult. She said the interviewer she used e-mail to communicate with her husband when she was in space.

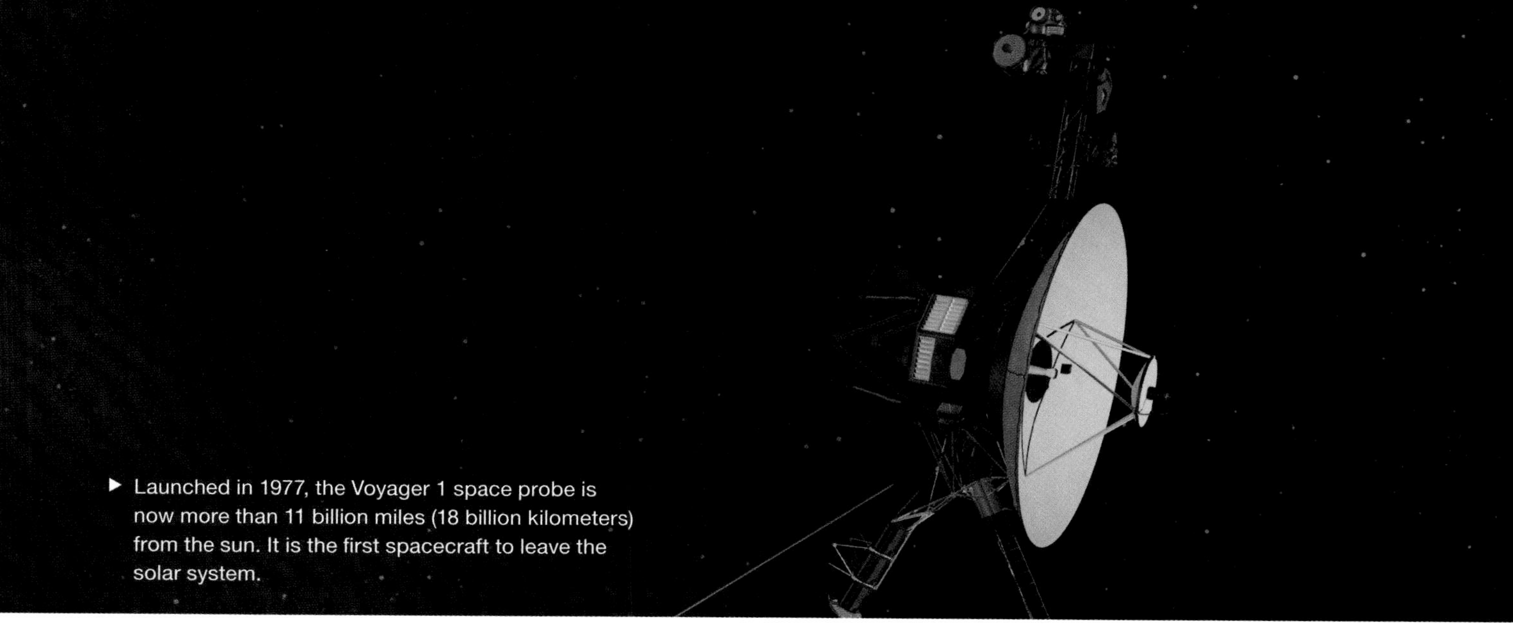

▶ Launched in 1977, the Voyager 1 space probe is now more than 11 billion miles (18 billion kilometers) from the sun. It is the first spacecraft to leave the solar system.

13 LISTEN.

CD4-30

A Listen to two students discuss a project. Circle the correct answers.

1. Maria **asked** / **told** Phil how his research was going.
2. Phil told Maria that he **was reading** / **read** about the Voyager 1 space probe.
3. Maria **asked if** / **said that** it was a useful article for the assignment.
4. Phil **asked if** / **said that** the mission was at a very exciting stage.
5. Maria asked **why it** / **what** was exciting.
6. Phil **replied** / **told** that the probe was no longer in the solar system.[1]
7. Maria wanted to know **how** / **if** a man-made object was flying around the galaxy.[2]
8. Phil **told** / **answered** that it was the first time in history.

[1]**solar system:** the sun, the moon, the eight other planets, and moons that move around the sun
[2]**galaxy:** a large system of stars; Earth's solar system is in the Milky Way galaxy

B Use the sentences from the conversation in exercise **A** to write quoted speech. Remember to use the correct tense and punctuation.

1. Maria asked , "How is your research going?"
2. Phil said ______________________________
3. ______________________________ Maria asked.
4. Phil said ______________________________
5. Maria asked ______________________________
6. ______________________________ Phil replied.

7. ______________________________ Maria asked.

8. Phil said ______________________________

CD4-30

C Listen again and check your answers from exercise **B**.

14 APPLY.

A Work with a partner. Ask and answer the questions. Take notes about your partner's answers.

1. Do you think space exploration is a good thing?

____

____

2. Do you think the money should be used for other things?

____

____

3. Do you want to go into space?

____

____

4. Do you think there is life on other planets?

____

____

B Form a group with another pair of students. Take turns reporting what your partner said on one of the topics from exercise **A**. Use reported speech.

I asked Rosa if space exploration was a good thing. She said it was worth the money and had many advantages for everyone.

UNIT 16 Review the Grammar

Charts 16.1–16.7

1 Circle all correct answers. Sometimes both answers are correct.

1. I don't know **when** / **whether** the expedition left.
2. It is a fact **that** / **why** exploration is often a dangerous activity.
3. The explorer said, "I've found **the city". / the city."**
4. **I think** / **I'm not sure** if the mission was a success.
5. **I believe** / **I believe that** the report is true.
6. The clerk **said** / **told** the tickets were sold out.
7. Do you know **if** / **how** this machine works?
8. Can you tell me **if** / **whether** or not the train is on time?
9. Are you glad **why** / **that** you came back?
10. We **asked** / **asked them** whether they had a good vacation.

Charts 16.1–2, 16.5–16.7

CD4-31

2 LISTEN & WRITE.

A Look at the photo and read the caption. Then listen to two people talk about the Hang Son Doong caves in Vietnam. Choose the correct answers.

1. (a.) Brad said the pictures were fantastic.
   b. Brad asked Sylvie what she thought of the pictures.
2. a. Sylvie asked what was so special about the caves.
   b. Sylvie asked if the caves were special.
3. a. Brad asked if the caves were the largest anywhere.
   b. Brad said the caves formed the largest cave system anywhere.

◄ A caver explores the Hang Son Doong cave system in Vietnam.

4. a. Sylvie said she didn't agree with Brad.
   b. Sylvie said he was right.
5. a. Brad said that he didn't like going in caves.
   b. Brad said that he might go into a cave.
6. a. Sylvie said she disliked caves.
   b. Sylvie asked Brad why he disliked caves.
7. a. Brad said it was easy to have an accident.
   b. Sylvie told Brad that it was easy to have an accident.
8. a. Sylvie said that the risk doesn't worry her.
   b. Sylvie told Brad the risk worried her.

B In your notebook, write a conversation using quoted speech between Brad and Sylvie. Use your answers from exercise **A** and your own ideas. Remember to use correct punctuation.

Brad said, "Hey, Sylvie, these pictures are amazing! Take a look." Then Sylvie said, . . .

C Work with a partner. Read your partner's conversation. Comment on anything that you think is incorrect.

Charts 16.1–16.4, 16.5,16.6

3 **EDIT.** Read the student's presentation. Find and correct five more errors with noun clauses, quoted speech, and reported speech.

Why Are We Here?

Often we ask ourselves why we are ~~we~~ here. This semester, I have learned a lot about this question. After learning about fossils from different parts of the world, I am convinced that humans began a great journey out of eastern Africa around 60,000 years ago. Evidence shows that early humans explored all areas of the globe. How did they survive? Scientists say us that these early humans discovered plants and animals to eat and found ways to stay warm. But, they are not certain how did they move across wide oceans and over rough terrain. I'm sure many didn't survive.

The question is why they did it? I believe the reason is that humans have an innate[2] desire to explore, learn, and take risks. The author T.S. Eliot said, "only those who will risk going too far can possibly find how far one can go." This suggests that being an explorer and taking risks helps us to survive and succeed. We should all ask ourselves, "What I am doing to improve life for the people who will live after me?"

The Human Journey

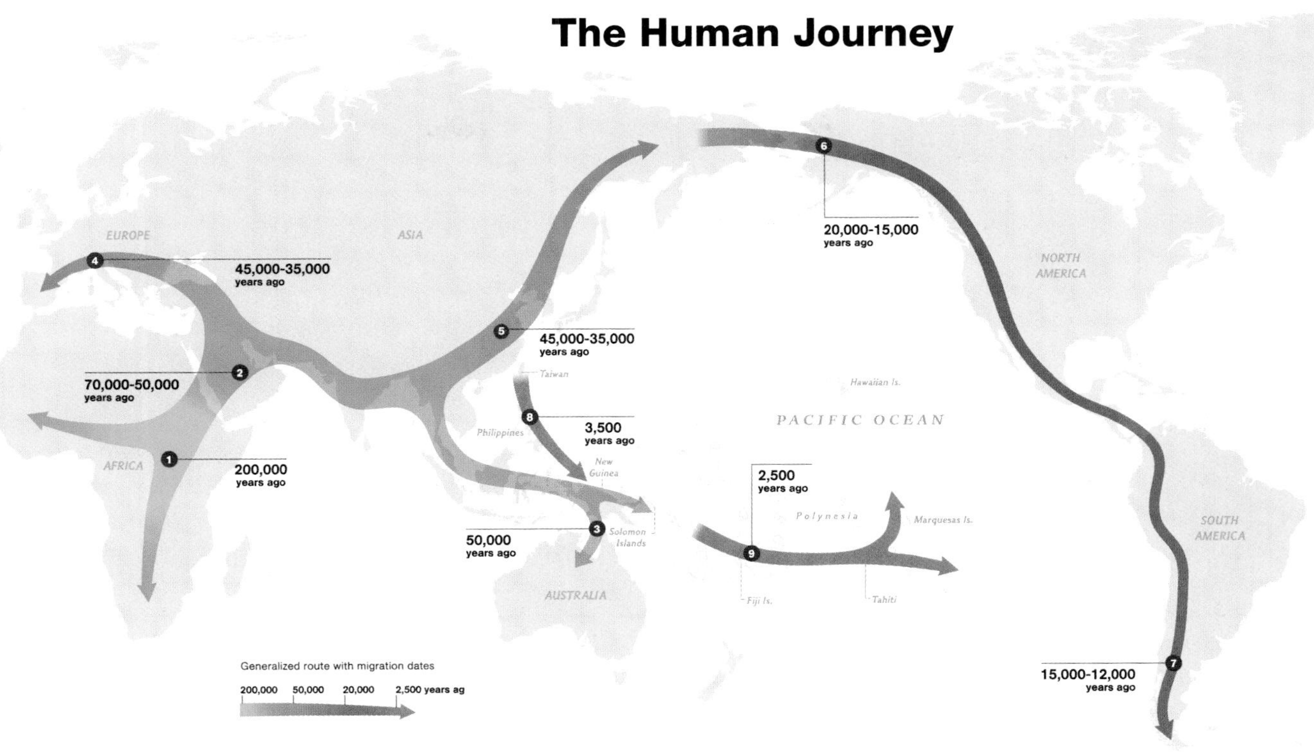

Charts 16.1–16.4, 16.6,16.7

4 WRITE & SPEAK.

A Look at the map and review the student essay in exercise **3**. Then interview a partner about exploration and risks. Ask and answer these questions. Take notes in your notebook.

1. How long ago did the first humans settle in the place where your ancestors lived?
2. Do you think that people take fewer risks today than in the past? Why, or why not?
3. Do you consider yourself an explorer? Why, or why not?
4. What risks do you take? Give examples.

B Report your partner's ideas from exercise **A** to the class.

I asked Kerim if he thought people take fewer risks today. He said he thought so. He thought people in the past were more adventurous and willing to risk a lot.

▼ A camel caravan crosses the Danakil Depression. Eritrea, Africa, where our ancestors began their journey 60,000 years ago.

Connect the Grammar to Writing

1 READ & NOTICE THE GRAMMAR.

A Think of a special trip or journey you have taken. Tell a partner the place and one thing you learned. Then read the text.

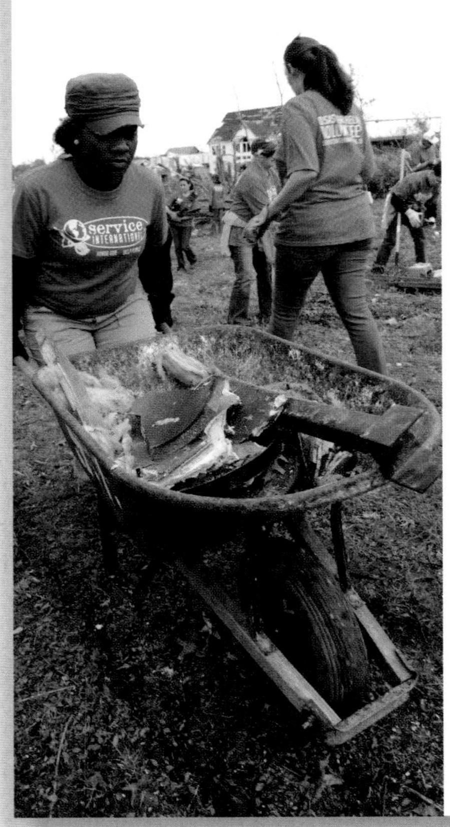

My Journey

One day my friend Bo asked me if I wanted to take a trip to Illinois. He said that some volunteers at the university were going to help people affected by a terrible tornado. Bo is a good friend and I could not say no.

My journey began on the plane. During the trip, I learned details of the storm. I also learned that we had a lot of work to do. From the plane, I saw the destruction of the storm. I was amazed that complete neighborhoods were flattened. I didn't have to ask if we were really needed. I knew we were.

We got to work right away. We cleared broken furniture, bricks, papers, and pieces of cars and household appliances. We moved branches and fallen trees. We talked with people whose homes were gone. I was surprised that many of them could still laugh. I couldn't imagine losing my home, my photos, my memories, but the people there really made me think. One man said, "My family is safe; nothing else really matters." An older woman said, "Life is too short to be sad for too long. We will rebuild and make new memories." I wanted to believe that I could be that strong. My journey was meant to help others, but I believe it helped me just as much.

GRAMMAR FOCUS

In the text, the writer uses noun clauses to describe thoughts and emotions. Noun clauses come after verbs, such as *learn, know, believe,* and after *be* + adjective.

I also learned ***that we had a lot of work to do.***
I was surprised ***that many of them could still laugh.***

The writer uses quoted and reported speech to tell the reader about conversations.

One man said, "My family is safe; nothing else really matters."
One day my friend Bo ***asked me if I wanted to take a trip to Illinois.***

B Read the text in exercise **A** again. In your notebook, write an example of a sentence with a noun clause in each category:

1. after verbs of thought
2. after *be* + adjective
3. reported speech
4. quoted speech

1. I also learned that we had a lot of work to do.

C Complete the chart with information from the text in exercise **1A**.

Where did she go?	*to Illinois, to a town hit by a horrible tornado*
What did she do?	
What did she learn?	
Quotes	*"My family is safe; nothing else really matters."*

2 BEFORE YOU WRITE.

A Work with a partner. Choose a journey that taught you something. It can be a long trip (e.g., to another country) or a short journey (e.g., to a local museum). Discuss your idea with your partner and take notes.

B In your notebook, make a chart like the one in exercise **1C**. Complete the chart with information about your journey. Use your notes from exercise **2A** and the chart from exercise **1C** as a model.

3 WRITE about your journey. Use the information from your chart in exercise **2B** and the text in exercise **1A** to help you.

WRITING FOCUS Using Quoted Speech to Add Impact

Writers use quoted speech for various reasons. One way is to make readers feel more connected or "in the moment." Notice the quotes in the text in exercise **1A**.

One man ***said, "My family is safe; nothing else really matters."***
An older woman ***said, "Life is too short to be sad for too long. We will rebuild and make new memories."***

4 SELF ASSESS. Read your text and underline the noun clauses. Then use the checklist to assess your work.

- ☐ I used noun clauses with *that* correctly. [16.1–16.2]
- ☐ I used noun clauses with *Wh-* words and *if* correctly. [16.3–16.4]
- ☐ I used quoted speech correctly. [16.5]
- ☐ I used reported speech and reporting verbs correctly. [16.6–16.7]
- ☐ I used quoted speech effectively. [WRITING FOCUS]

1 Spelling Rules for Verbs Ending in *-s* and *-es*

1. Add *-s* to most verbs.	like-like**s** sit-sit**s**
2. Add *-es* to verbs that end in *-ch, -s, -sh, -x,* or *-z.*	catch-catch**es** miss-miss**es** wash-wash**es** mix-mix**es** buzz-buzz**es**
3. Change the *-y* to *-i* and add *-es* when the base form ends in a consonant + *-y.*	cry-cr**ies** carry-carr**ies**
4. Do not change the *-y* when the base form ends in a vowel + *-y.*	pay-pay**s** stay-stay**s**
5. Some verbs are irregular in the third-person singular *-s* form of the simple present.	be-**is** go-**goes** do-**does** have-**has**

2 Spelling Rules for Verbs Ending in *-ing*

1. Add *-ing* to the base form of most verbs.	eat-eat**ing** do-do**ing** speak-speak**ing** carry-carry**ing**
2. When the verb ends in a consonant + *-e,* drop the *-e* and add *-ing.*	ride-riding write-writing
3. For one-syllable verbs that end in a consonant + a vowel + a consonant (CVC), double the final consonant and add *-ing.*	stop-stop**ping** sit-sit**ting**
Do not double the final consonant for verbs that end in CVC when the final consonant is *-w, -x,* or *-y.*	show-show**ing** fix-fix**ing** stay-stay**ing**
4. For two-syllable verbs that end in CVC and have stress on the first syllable, add *-ing.* Do not double the final consonant.	ENter-enter**ing** LISTen-listen**ing**
For two-syllable verbs that end in CVC and have stress on the last syllable, double the final consonant and add *-ing.*	beGIN-begin**ning** ocCUR-occur**ring**

3 Spelling Rules for Verbs Ending in *-ed*

1. Add *-ed* to the base form of most verbs that end in a consonant.	start-start**ed** talk-talk**ed**
2. Add *-d* if the base form of the verb ends in *-e*.	dance-danc**ed** live-liv**ed**
3. When the base form of the verb ends in a consonant + *-y*, change the *-y* to *-i* and add *-ed*. Do not change the *-y* to *-i* when the verb ends in a vowel + *-y*.	cry-cr**ied** worry-worr**ied** stay-stay**ed**
4. For one-syllable verbs that end in a consonant + a vowel + a consonant (CVC), double the final consonant and add *-ed*. Do not double the final consonant of verbs that end in *-w*, *-x*, or *-y*.	stop-stop**ped** rob-rob**bed** follow-follow**ed** fix-fix**ed** play-play**ed**
5. For two-syllable verbs that end in CVC and have stress on the first syllable, add *-ed*. Do not double the final consonant. For two-syllable verbs that end in CVC and have stress on the last syllable, double the final consonant and add *-ed*.	ORder-order**ed** HAPpen-HAPpen**ed** ocCUR-occur**red** preFER-prefer**red**

4 Common Irregular Noun Plurals

Singular	Plural	Explanation
man woman tooth foot goose	men women teeth feet geese	Vowel change
sheep fish deer	sheep fish deer	No change
child person mouse	children people mice	Different word forms
	clothes groceries glasses jeans/pants/shorts scissors	No singular form

5 Spelling Rules for Adverbs Ending in *-ly*

	Adjective	Adverb
1. Add *-ly* to the end of most adjectives.	careful quiet serious	carefu**lly** quiet**ly** serious**ly**
2. Change the *-y* to *-i* and add *-ly* to adjectives that end in a consonant + *-y*.	easy happy lucky	eas**ily** happ**ily** luck**ily**
3. Keep the *-e* and add *-ly* to some adjectives that end in *-e*.	nice free	nice**ly** free**ly**
4. Drop the final *-e* and add *-y* to adjectives that end with a consonant followed by *-le*.	simple comfortable	simp**ly** comfortab**ly**
5. Add *-ally* to most adjectives that end in *-ic*.	basic enthusiastic	basic**ally** enthusiastic**ally**

6 Spelling Rules for Comparative and Superlative Forms

	Adjective/ Adverb	Comparative	Superlative
1. Add *-er* or *-est* to one-syllable adjectives and adverbs.	tall fast	tall**er** fast**er**	tall**est** fast**est**
2. Add *-r* or *-st* to adjectives that end in *-e*.	nice	nice**r**	nice**st**
3. Change the *-y to -i* and add *-er* or *-est* to two-syllable adjectives and adverbs that end in *-y*.	easy happy	eas**ier** happ**ier**	eas**iest** the happ**iest**
4. Double the final consonant and add *-er* or *-est* to one-syllable adjectives or adverbs that end in a consonant + a vowel + a consonant (CVC).	big hot	big**ger** hot**ter**	big**gest** hot**test**

7 Common Irregular Verbs

Base Form	Simple Past	Past Participle
be	was, were	been
beat	beat	beaten
become	became	become
begin	began	begun
bend	bent	bent
bite	bit	bitten
blow	blew	blown
break	broke	broken
bring	brought	brought
build	built	built
buy	bought	bought
catch	caught	caught
choose	chose	chosen
come	came	come
cost	cost	cost
cut	cut	cut
dig	dug	dug
dive	dived/dove	dived
do	did	done
draw	drew	drawn
drink	drank	drunk
drive	drove	driven
eat	ate	eaten
fall	fell	fallen
feed	fed	fed
feel	felt	felt
fight	fought	fought
find	found	found
fit	fit	fit/fitted
fly	flew	flown
forget	forgot	forgotten
forgive	forgave	forgiven
freeze	froze	frozen
get	got	got/gotten
give	gave	given
go	went	gone
grow	grew	grown
hang	hung	hung
have	had	had
hear	heard	heard
hide	hid	hidden
hit	hit	hit
hold	held	held
hurt	hurt	hurt
keep	kept	kept
know	knew	known

Base Form	Simple Past	Past Participle
lay	laid	laid
lead	led	led
leave	left	left
lend	lent	lent
let	let	let
lie	lay	lain
light	lit/lighted	lit/lighted
lose	lost	lost
make	made	made
mean	meant	meant
meet	met	met
pay	paid	paid
prove	proved	proved/proven
put	put	put
quit	quit	quit
read	read	read
ride	rode	ridden
ring	rang	rung
rise	rose	risen
run	ran	run
say	said	said
sit	sat	sat
sleep	slept	slept
slide	slid	slid
speak	spoke	spoken
spend	spent	spent
spread	spread	spread
stand	stood	stood
steal	stole	stolen
stick	stuck	stuck
strike	struck	struck
swear	swore	sworn
sweep	swept	swept
swim	swam	swum
take	took	taken
teach	taught	taught
tear	tore	torn
tell	told	told
think	thought	thought
throw	threw	thrown
understand	understood	understood
upset	upset	upset
wake	woke	woken
wear	wore	worn
win	won	won
write	wrote	written

8 Patterns with Gerunds

Verb + Gerund

They ***enjoy dancing***.
She ***delayed going*** to the doctor.

admit	detest	mind	regret
advise	discuss	miss	remember
anticipate	dislike	permit	resent
appreciate	enjoy	postpone	resist
avoid	finish	practice	risk
can't help	forbid	put off	stop
complete	imagine	quit	suggest
consider	keep	recall	tolerate
delay	mention	recommend	understand
deny			

Verb + Preposition + Gerund

He ***succeeded in winning*** *the prize.*
Are you ***thinking about taking*** *another course?*

apologize for	concentrate on	object to	thank (someone) for
argue about	dream about/of	plan on/for	think about
believe in	insist on	succeed in	warn (someone) about
complain about	keep on	talk about	worry about

Noun + Preposition + Gerund

What's the ***purpose of doing*** *this exercise?*
I don't know his ***reason for being*** *late.*

benefit of	interest in	purpose of
cause of	problem with	reason for

Adjective + Preposition + Gerund

I'm ***excited about studying*** *abroad.*
Are you ***interested in going****?*

accustomed to	excited about	nervous about	tired of
afraid of	famous for	responsible for	upset about/with
bad/good at	(in)capable of	sick of	used to
concerned about	interested in	sorry about/for	worried about

9 Patterns with Infinitives

Verb + Infinitive			
They ***need to leave****.* *I* ***am learning to speak*** *English.*			
agree	claim	know how	seem
appear	consent	learn	swear
arrange	decide	manage	tend
ask	demand	need	threaten
attempt	deserve	offer	try
be able	expect	plan	volunteer
beg	fail	prepare	want
can afford	forget	pretend	wish
care	hope	promise	would like
choose	intend	refuse	

Verb + Object + Infinitive			
I ***want you to leave****.* *He* ***expects me to call*** *him.*			
advise	convince	hire	require
allow	dare	instruct	select
appoint	enable	invite	teach
ask*	encourage	need*	tell
beg*	expect*	order	urge
cause	forbid	pay*	want*
challenge	force	permit	warn
choose*	get	persuade	would like*
command	help**	remind	

*These verbs can be either with or without an object. (*I* ***want [you] to go.***)
After *help*, *to* is often omitted. (*He* ***helped me move.*)

Verb + Infinitive or Gerund		
I ***love to swim****.* *I* ***love swimming****.*		
begin	continue	love
(not) bother	hate	prefer
can't stand	like	start

10 Phrasal Verbs and Their Meanings

Transitive Phrasal Verbs (Separable)

*Don't forget to **turn off** the oven before you leave the house.*
*Don't forget to **turn** the oven **off** before you leave the house.*

Phrasal Verb	Meaning	Example Sentence
blow up	cause something to explode	*The workers **blew** the bridge **up**.*
bring back	return	*She **brought** the shirt **back** to the store.*
bring up	1. raise from childhood 2. introduce a topic to discuss	*1. My grandmother **brought** me **up**.* *2. Don't **bring up** that subject.*
call back	return a telephone call	*I **called** Rajil **back** but there was no answer.*
call off	cancel	*They **called** the wedding **off** after their fight.*
cheer up	make someone feel happier	*Her visit to the hospital **cheered** the patients **up**.*
clear up	clarify, explain	*She **cleared** the problem **up**.*
do over	do again	*His teacher asked him to **do** the essay **over**.*
figure out	solve, understand	*The student **figured** the problem **out**.*
fill in	complete information	***Fill in** the answers on the test.*
fill out	complete an application or form	*I had to **fill** many forms **out** at the doctor's office.*
find out	learn, uncover	*Did you **find** anything **out** about the new plans?*
give away	offer something freely	*They are **giving** prizes **away** at the store.*
give back	return	*The boy **gave** the pen **back** to the teacher.*
give up	stop doing	*I **gave up** sugar last year. Will you **give** it **up**?*
help out	aid, support someone	*I often **help** my older neighbors **out**.*
lay off	dismiss workers from their jobs	*My company **laid** 200 workers **off** last year.*
leave on	allow a machine to continue working	*I **left** the lights **on** all night.*
let in	allow someone to enter	*She opened a window to **let** some fresh air **in**.*
look over	examine	*We **looked** the contract **over** before signing it.*
make up	say something untrue or fictional (a story, a lie)	*The child **made** the story **up**. It wasn't true at all.*
pay back	return money, repay a loan	*I **paid** my friend **back**. I owed him $10.*
pick up	1. get someone or something 2. lift	*1. He **picked up** his date at her house.* *2. I **picked** the ball **up** and threw it.*
put off	delay, postpone	*Don't **put** your homework **off** until tomorrow.*
put out	1. take outside 2. extinguish	*1. He **put** the trash **out**.* *2. Firefighters **put out** the fire.*
set up	1. arrange 2. start something	*1. She **set** the tables **up** for the party.* *2. They **set up** the project.*
shut off	stop something from working	*Can you **shut** the water **off**?*
sort out	make sense of something	*We have to **sort** this problem **out**.*
straighten up	make neat and orderly	*I **straightened** the messy living room **up**.*
take back	own again	*He **took** the tools that he loaned me **back**.*
take off	remove	*She **took off** her hat and gloves.*
take out	remove	*I **take** the trash **out** on Mondays.*
talk over	discuss a topic until it is understood	*Let's **talk** this plan **over** before we do anything.*
think over	reflect, ponder	*She **thought** the job offer **over** carefully.*
throw away/ throw out	get rid of something, discard	*He **threw** the old newspapers **away**.* *I **threw out** the old milk in the fridge.*
try on	put on clothing to see if it fits	*He **tried** the shoes **on** but didn't buy them.*
turn down	refuse	*His manager **turned** his proposal **down**.*
turn off	stop something from working	*Can you **turn** the TV **off**, please?*
turn on	switch on, operate	*I **turned** the lights **on** in the dark room.*
turn up	increase the volume	***Turn** the radio **up**, so we can hear the news.*
wake up	make someone stop sleeping	*The noise **woke** the baby **up**.*
write down	write on paper	*I **wrote** the information **down**.*

Transitive Phrasal Verbs (Inseparable)		
We'll ***look into*** *the problem.*		
Phrasal Verb	**Meaning**	**Example Sentence**
come across	find something	*I* ***came across*** *this novel in the library.*
come from	be a native or resident of	*She* ***comes from*** *London.*
come up with	invent	*Let's* ***come up with*** *a new game.*
count on	depend on	*You can always* ***count on*** *good friends to help you.*
drop out of	quit	*Jin* ***dropped out*** *of the study group.*
follow through with	complete	*You must* ***follow through with*** *your promises.*
get off	leave (a bus/a train)	*I forgot to* ***get off*** *the bus at my stop.*
get on	board (a car/a train)	*I* ***got on*** *the plane last.*
get out of	1. leave (a car/a taxi) 2. avoid	1. *I* ***got out of*** *the car.* 2. *She* ***got out of*** *doing her chores.*
get together with	meet	*I* ***got together with*** *Ana on Saturday.*
get over	return to a normal state	*I just* ***got over*** *a bad cold. I feel much better now!*
go over	review	*Let's* ***go over*** *our notes before the exam.*
look after	take care of	*He has to* ***look after*** *his sister. His parents are out.*
look into	investigate	*The police* ***looked into*** *the crime and solved it.*
run into	meet accidentally	*She* ***ran into*** *Mai on campus.*

Intransitive Phrasal Verbs (Inseparable)		
My car **broke down** *again!*		
Phrasal Verb	**Meaning**	**Example Sentence**
add up	make sense	*What he says does not* **add up**.
break down	stop working	*This machine* **breaks down** *all the time.*
break up	separate	*Their marriage* **broke up** *after a year.*
dress up	put on more formal clothes	*He* **dressed up** *to attend the wedding.*
drop in	visit without an appointment	**Drop in** *when you can.*
drop out	leave or stop	*She never liked school, so she decided to* **drop out**.
eat out	eat in a restaurant	*She hates to cook, so she* **eats out** *frequently.*
fool around	play with	*He* **fools around** *with old cars for fun.*
get ahead	succeed, improve oneself	*Now that she has a new job, she is* **getting ahead**.
get along	have a friendly relationship	*My coworkers and I* **get along** *well.*
get up	awaken, arise	*I* **got up** *late this morning.*
give up	stop trying	*I played the piano for seven years but then* **gave up**.
go ahead	begin or continue to do	*You can* **go ahead**. *We'll wait for Jane.*
go away	leave, depart	*The rabbits in the garden finally* **went away.**
go down	decrease	*Prices of cars have* **gone down** *recently.*
go on	continue	*How long do you think this speech will* **go on**?
go out	leave one's home	*Jon has* **gone out**. *He should return soon.*
go up	rise, go higher	*The price of gasoline has* **gone up**.
grow up	become an adult	*Our daughter has* **grown up** *now.*
hang on	wait	**Hang on** *while I change my shoes.*
hold on	struggle against difficulty	**Hold on** *just a little longer. It's almost over.*
look out	be careful	**Look out**! *You'll fall!*
make up	agree to be friends again	*They had a fight, but soon* **made up**.
move in	go live in	*We* **moved in** *last week. We love the area!*
move out	leave a place permanently	*When is your roommate* **moving out**?
run out	use all of something	*Is there more paper for the printer? We ran out.*
sign up	join, agree to do something	*The course looked interesting so I* **signed up**.
sit down	seat oneself	*The restaurant*
speak up	talk louder	*Will you* **speak up**? *I can't hear you.*
stand up	get on one's feet	*The teacher asked the students to* **stand up**.
stay up	keep awake	*The student* **stayed up** *all night to study.*
take off	1. go up into the air 2. increase quickly	1. *After a long wait, the airplane finally* **took off**. 2. *Sales of the new product have* **taken off**.
watch out	be careful	**Watch out!** *There's a lot of ice on this road.*
work out	exercise	*The football player* **works out** *three times a week.*

11 Guide to Pronunciation Symbols

Vowels		
Symbol	**Key Word**	**Pronunciation**
/a/	hot	/hat/
	far	/far/
/æ/	cat	/kæt/
/aɪ/	fine	/faɪn/
/aʊ/	house	/haʊs/
/ɛ/	bed	/bɛd/
/eɪ/	name	/neɪm/
/i/	need	/nid/
/ɪ/	sit	/sɪt/
/oʊ/	go	/goʊ/
/ʊ/	book	/bʊk/
/u/	boot	/but/
/ɔ/	dog	/dɔg/
	four	/fɔr/
/ɔɪ/	toy	/tɔɪ/
/ʌ/	cup	/kʌp/
/ɛr/	bird	/bɛrd/
/ə/	about	/əˈbaʊt/

Consonants		
Symbol	**Key Word**	**Pronunciation**
/b/	boy	/bɔɪ/
/d/	day	/deɪ/
/ʤ/	just	/ʤʌst/
/f/	face	/feɪs/
/g/	get	/gɛt/
/h/	hat	/hæt/
/k/	car	/kar/
/l/	light	/laɪt/
/m/	my	/maɪ/
/n/	nine	/naɪn/
/ŋ/	sing	/sɪŋ/
/p/	pen	/pɛn/
/r/	right	/raɪt/
/s/	see	/si/
/t/	tea	/ti/
/tʃ/	cheap	/tʃip/
/v/	vote	/voʊt/
/w/	west	/wɛst/
/y/	yes	/yɛs/
/z/	zoo	/zu/
/ð/	they	/ðeɪ/
/θ/	think	/θɪŋk/
/ʃ/	shoe	/ʃu/
/ʒ/	vision	/ˈvɪʒən/

Source: The *Newbury House Dictionary Plus Grammar Reference, Fifth Edition*, National Geographic Learning/Cengage Learning, 2014

12 Conversion Charts

Length		
When You Know	**Multiply by**	**To Find**
inches (in)	25.44	millimeters (mm)
feet (ft)	30.5	centimeters (cm)
feet (ft)	0.3	meters (m)
yards (yd)	0.91	meters (m)
miles (mi)	1.6	kilometers (km)
Metric:		
millimeters (mm)	0.039	inches (in)
centimeters (cm)	0.03	feet (ft)
meters (m)	3.28	feet (ft)
meters (m)	1.09	yards (yd)
kilometers (km)	0.62	miles (mi)

Weight		
When You Know	**Multiply by**	**To Find**
ounces (oz) pounds (lb)	28.35 0.45	grams (g) kilograms (kg)
Metric:		
grams (g) kilograms (kg)	0.04 2.2	ounces (oz) pounds (lb)

Volume		
When You Know	**Multiply by**	**To Find**
fluid ounces (fl. oz) pints (pt) quarts (qt) gallons (gal)	30.0 0.47 0.95 3.8	milliliters (mL) liters (L) liters (L) liters (L)
Metric:		
milliliters (mL) liters (L) liters (L) liters (L)	0.03 2.11 1.05 0.26	fluid ounces (fl. oz) pints (pt) quarts (qt) gallons (gal)

Temperature		
When You Know	**Do This**	**To Find**
degrees Fahrenheit (˚F)	$(F^\circ - 32) \times \frac{5}{9}$	degrees Celsius (˚C)
degrees Celsius (˚C)	$1.8C^\circ + 32$	degrees Fahrenheit (˚F)

Sample Temperatures	
Fahrenheit	**Celsius**
0	-18
10	-12
20	-7
32	0
40	4
50	10
60	16
70	21
80	27
90	32
100	38
212	100

GLOSSARY OF GRAMMAR TERMS

action verb: a verb that shows an action.

➢ *He **drives** every day.*

➢ *They **left** yesterday morning.*

active voice: a sentence in which the subject performs the action of the verb. (See *passive voice.*)

➢ *Michael ate the hamburger.*

adjective: a word that describes or modifies a noun or pronoun.

➢ *She is **friendly**.*

➢ *Brazil is a **huge** country.*

adjective clause: see *relative clause.*

adverb: a word that describes or modifies a verb, an adjective, or another adverb.

➢ *He eats **quickly**.*

➢ *She drives **carefully**.*

adverb clause: a kind of dependent clause. Like single adverbs, they can show time, reason, purpose, and condition.

➢ ***When the party was over,** everyone left.*

adverb of frequency: (see *frequency adverb.*)

adverb of manner: an adverb that describes the action of the verb. Many adverbs of manner are formed by adding *-ly* to the adjective.

➢ *You sing **beautifully**.*

➢ *He speaks **slowly**.*

affirmative statement: a statement that does not have a verb in the negative form.

➢ *My uncle lives in Portland.*

article: a word that is used before a noun: *a, an, the.*

➢ *I looked up at **the** moon.*

➢ *Lucy had **a** sandwich and **an** apple for lunch.*

auxiliary verb: (also called *helping verb.*) a verb used with the main verb. *Be, do, have,* and *will* are common auxiliary verbs when they are followed by another verb. Modals are also auxiliary verbs.

➢ *I **am** working.*

➢ *He **won't** be in class tomorrow.*

➢ *She **can** speak Korean.*

base form: the form of the verb without *to* or any endings such as *-ing, -s,* or *-ed.*

➢ *eat, sleep, go, walk*

capital letter: an uppercase letter.

➢ *New York, Mr. Franklin, Japan*

clause: a group of words with a subject and a verb. (See *dependent clause* and *main clause.*)

➢ *We watched the game.* (one clause)

➢ *We watched the game after we ate dinner.* (two clauses)

comma: a punctuation mark that separates parts of a sentence.

➢ *After he left work, he went to the gym.*

➢ *I can't speak Russian, but my sister can.*

common noun: a noun that does not name a specific person, place, thing, or idea.

➢ *man, country, book, help*

comparative: the form of an adjective used to talk about the difference between two people, places, or things.

➢ *I'm **taller** than my mother.*

➢ *That book is **more interesting** than this one.*

conditional: a structure used to express an activity or event that depends on something else.

➢ ***If the weather is nice on Sunday,** we'll go to the beach.*

conjunction: a word used to connect information or ideas. *And, but, or,* and *because* are conjunctions.

➢ *He put cheese **and** onions on his sandwich.*

➢ *I wanted to go, **but** I had too much homework.*

➢ *We were confused **because** we didn't listen.*

consonant: a sound represented by the letters *b, c, d, f, g, h, j, k, l, m, n, p, q, r, s, t, v, w, x, y,* and *z.*

contraction: two words combined into a shorter form.

➢ *did not → **didn't***

➢ *she is → **she's***

➢ *I am → **I'm***

➢ *we will → **we'll***

count noun: a noun that names something you can count. Count nouns are singular or plural.

➢ *I ate an **egg** for breakfast.*

➢ *I have **six apples** in my bag.*

definite article: the word *the.* It is used before a specific person, place, or thing.

➢ *I found it on **the** Internet.*

➢ ***The** children are sleeping.*

demonstrative pronoun: a pronoun that identifies a person or thing.

➢ ***This** is my sister, Kate.*

➢ ***Those** are Jamal's books.*

dependent clause: a clause that cannot stand alone as a sentence. It must be used with a main clause.

➢ *I went for a walk* ***before I ate breakfast****.*

direct object: a noun or pronoun that receives the action of the verb.

➢ *Aldo asked a* ***question****.*

➢ *Karen helped* ***me****.*

direct quote: a statement of a speaker's exact words using quotation marks.

➢ *Our teacher said,* ***"Do exercises 5 and 6 for homework."***

exclamation point: a punctuation mark that shows emotion (anger, surprise, excitement, etc.) or emphasis.

➢ *We won the game!*

➢ *Look! It's snowing!*

formal: describes language used in academic writing or speaking, or in polite or official situations rather than in everyday speech or writing.

➢ *Please do not take photographs inside the museum.*

➢ *May I leave early today?*

frequency adverb: an adverb that tells how often something happens. Some common adverbs of frequency are *never, rarely, sometimes, often, usually,* and *always.*

➢ *I* ***always*** *drink coffee in the morning.*

➢ *He* ***usually*** *leaves work at six.*

frequency expression: an expression that tells how often something happens.

➢ *We go to the grocery store* ***every Saturday****.*

➢ *He plays tennis* ***twice a week****.*

future: a form of a verb that expresses an action or situation that has not happened yet. *Will, be going to,* the present progressive, and the simple present are used to express the future.

➢ *I* ***will call*** *you later.*

➢ *We****'re going*** *to the movies tomorrow.*

➢ *I****'m taking*** *French next semester.*

➢ *The show* ***starts*** *after dinner.*

future conditional: expresses something we believe will happen in the future based on certain conditions; the *if*-clause + simple present gives the condition, and *will* or *be going to* + the base form of the verb gives the result.

➢ *If you don't go to practice, the coach will not let you play in the game.*

gerund: an *-ing* verb form that is used as a noun. It can be the subject of a sentence or the object of a verb or preposition. See page **A5** for lists of common verbs followed by gerunds.

➢ ***Surfing*** *is a popular sport.*

➢ *We enjoy* ***swimming****.*

➢ *The boy is interested in* ***running****.*

gerund phrase: an *-ing* verb form + an object or a prepositional phrase. It can be the subject of a sentence, or the object of a verb or preposition.

➢ ***Swimming in the ocean*** *is fun.*

➢ *I love* ***eating chocolate.***

➢ *We are thinking about* ***watching the new TV show.***

helping verb: (see *auxiliary verb.*)

if **clause:** a clause that begins with *if* and expresses a condition.

➢ ***If you drive too fast,*** *you will get a ticket.*

imperative: a sentence that gives an instruction or command.

➢ ***Turn*** *left at the light.*

➢ ***Don't use*** *the elevator.*

indefinite article: the words *a* and *an.* They are used before singular count nouns that are not specific.

➢ *We have* ***a*** *test today.*

➢ *She's* ***an*** *engineer.*

indefinite pronoun: a pronoun that refers to people or things that are not specific or not known. *Someone, something, everyone, everything, no one, nothing,* and *nowhere* are common indefinite pronouns.

➢ ***Everyone*** *is here today.*

➢ ***No one*** *is absent.*

➢ *Would you like* ***something*** *to eat?*

independent clause: a clause that can stand alone as a complete sentence. It has a subject and a verb.

➢ ***I went for a walk*** *before breakfast.*

infinitive: *to* + the base form of a verb.

➢ *He wants* ***to see*** *the new movie.*

infinitive of purpose: *to* + the base form of the verb to express purpose or to answer the question with *why. (*also *in order to)*

➢ *Scientists studied the water* ***in order to learn*** *about the disease.*

➢ *We went to the store* ***to buy*** *milk.*

informal: language that is used in casual, everyday conversation and writing.

➢ *Who are you talking to?*

➢ *We'll be there at eight.*

information question: (see *Wh-* question.)

inseparable phrasal verb: a phrasal verb that cannot have a noun or a pronoun object between its two parts (verb + particle). The verb and the particle always stay together.

➢ *I* ***ran into*** *a friend in the library.*

➢ *Do you and your coworkers* ***get along****?*

intonation: the rise or fall of a person's voice. For example, rising intonation is often used to ask a question.

intransitive verb: a verb that cannot be followed by a direct object.

- ➢ *We didn't* ***agree****.*
- ➢ *The students* ***smiled*** *and* ***laughed****.*

irregular adjective: an adjective that does not change form in the usual way .

- ➢ *good ⟶ better*
- ➢ *bad ⟶ worse*

irregular adverb: an adverb that does not change form in the usual way.

- ➢ *well ⟶ better*
- ➢ *badly ⟶ worse*

irregular verb: a verb with forms that do not follow the rules for regular verbs.

- ➢ *swim ⟶ swam*
- ➢ *have ⟶ had*

main clause: a clause that can stand alone as a sentence. It has a subject and a verb. (See *independent clause.*)

- ➢ ***I heard the news*** *when I was driving home.*

main verb: the verb that is in the main clause.

- ➢ *We* ***drove*** *home after we had dinner.*

measurement word: a word that is used to talk about a specific amount or quantity of a non-count noun.

- ➢ *We need to buy a* ***box*** *of pasta and a* ***gallon*** *of milk.*

modal: an auxiliary verb that adds a degree of certainty, possibility, or time to a verb. *May, might, can, could, will, would,* and *should* are common modals.

- ➢ *You* ***should*** *eat more vegetables.*
- ➢ *Julie* ***can*** *speak three languages.*

negative statement: a statement that has a verb in the negative form.

- ➢ *I* ***don't have*** *any sisters.*
- ➢ *She* ***doesn't drink*** *coffee.*

non-action verb: a verb that does not describe an action. Non-action verbs indicate states, sense, feelings, or ownership. They are not common in the progressive.

- ➢ *I* ***love*** *my grandparents.*
- ➢ *I* ***see*** *Marta. She's across the street.*
- ➢ *They* ***have*** *a new car.*

non-count noun: a noun that names something that cannot be counted.

- ➢ *Carlos drinks a lot of* ***coffee****.*
- ➢ *I need some* ***salt*** *for the recipe.*

noun: a word that names a person, place, or thing.

- ➢ *They're* ***students****.*
- ➢ *He's a* ***teacher****.*

noun clause: a clause that can be used in place of a noun, a noun phrase, or a pronoun.

- ➢ *I didn't know* ***that she was here****.*
- ➢ *I'm not sure* ***if the store is open yet****.*

object: a noun or pronoun that receives the action of the verb.

- ➢ *Mechanics fix* ***cars****.*

object pronoun: a pronoun that takes the place of a noun as the object of the sentence: *me, you, him, her, it, us, them.*

- ➢ *Rita is my neighbor. I see* ***her*** *every day.*
- ➢ *Can you help* ***us****?*

participial adjective: an adjective that is formed like a present participle (*-ing*) or past participle (*-ed*) form of a verb.

- ➢ *Martin had* ***tired*** *eyes.*

particle: a short word that combines with a verb to form a phrasal verb; examples include *on, out, over, into, up, through,* and *back.*

- ➢ *I looked* ***up*** *the definition.*
- ➢ *The students ran* ***into*** *their teacher at the store.*

passive voice: when the focus of a sentence is on the object of the verb instead of the subject. The active voice focuses on the subject.

- ➢ *My wallet* ***was stolen****.*

past participle: the form of the verb used in perfect and passive. It usually ends in *-d* or *-ed.*

- ➢ *Jemila has* ***worked*** *here for a long time.*

past progressive: a verb form used to talk about an action that was in progress in the past.

- ➢ *He* ***was watching*** *TV when the phone rang.*

period: a punctuation mark used at the end of a statement.

- ➢ *She lives in Moscow****.***

phrasal verb: a verb and a particle that function as a single verb. See pages **A7–A9** for lists of common phrasal verbs.

- ➢ ***Turn off*** *the light when you leave.*
- ➢ *She's* ***figured out*** *the answer.*

phrase: a group of words that go together but are not a complete sentence (i.e., does not have both a subject and a verb).

- ➢ *He lives* ***near the train station****.*

plural noun: a noun that names more than one person, place, or thing.

- ➢ *He put three* ***boxes*** *on the table.*
- ➢ *Argentina and Mexico are* ***countries****.*

possessive adjective: an adjective that shows ownership or a relationship: *my, your, his, her, its, our, their.*

> *__My__ car is green.*
> *__Your__ keys are on the table.*

possessive noun: a noun that shows ownership or a relationship. To make most singular nouns possessive, use an apostrophe (') + *-s*. To make plural nouns possessive, add an apostrophe.

> *__Leo's__ apartment is large.*
> *The __girls'__ books are on the table.*

possessive pronoun: a pronoun that shows ownership or a relationship: *mine, yours, his, hers, ours, theirs.* Possessive pronouns are used in place of a possessive adjective + noun.

> *My sister's eyes are blue. __Mine__ are brown. What color are __yours__?*

preposition: a word that describes the relationships between nouns. Prepositions show space, time, direction, cause, and effect; often they occur together with certain verbs or adjectives.

> *I live __on__ Center Street.*
> *We left __at__ noon.*
> *I'm worried __about__ the test.*

prepositional phrase: a phrase that has a preposition + a noun or a noun phrase.

> *I live __in New York City.__*
> *We saw the movie __at the new theater.__*

present continuous: (see *present progressive.*)

present participle: the form of the verb that ends in *-ing.*

> *She is __sleeping__.*
> *They are __laughing__.*

present perfect: a verb form that connects the past to the present.

> *I __have washed__ the dishes.*
> *John __hasn't called__ today.*

present perfect progressive: a verb form used for a situation or habit that began in the past and continues up to the present or an action in progress that is not yet completed.

> *I've __been getting up__ early.*
> *__Have__ you __been waiting__ for a long time?*

present progressive: (also called *present continuous.*) a verb form used to talk about an action or event that is in progress at the moment of speaking; the form can also refer to a planned event in the future.

> *That car __is speeding__.*
> *I __am taking__ three classes this semester.*
> *We __are eating__ at that new restaurant Friday night.*

pronoun: a word that takes the place of a noun or refers to a noun.

> *The teacher is sick today. __He__ has a cold.*

proper noun: a noun that names a specific person, place, or thing

> *__Maggie__ lives in a town near __Dallas__.*

punctuation: a mark that makes ideas in writing clear. Common punctuation marks include the comma (,), period (.), exclamation point (!), and question mark (?).

> *John plays soccer**,** but I don't.*
> *She's from Japan**.***
> *That's amazing**!***
> *Where are you from**?***

quantifier: a word used to describe the amount of a noun.

> *We need __some__ potatoes for the recipe.*
> *I usually put __a little__ milk in my coffee.*

question mark: a punctuation mark used at the end of a question.

> *Are you a student__?__*

quoted speech: a statement that includes the exact words someone said. Quotation marks ("/") are used around the exact words.

> *She said, __"I'm not feeling well."__*

regular: a noun, verb, adjective, or adverb that changes form according to standard rules.

> *apple → apple__s__*
> *talk → talk__ed__/talk__ing__*
> *small → small__er__*
> *slow → slow__ly__*

relative clause: a clause that describes a noun or indefinite pronoun in a sentence. It comes after the noun or pronoun it describes. It is also called an *adjective clause.*

> *The student __that I am sitting next to__ is from Peru.*
> *I know everyone __who lives in my building__.*

relative pronoun: a pronoun that introduces a relative clause. Common relative pronouns are *who, whom, whose, that,* and *which.*

> *We met the woman __who__ owns the shop.*
> *Here's the book __that__ you were looking for.*

reported speech: a statement of what someone said that does not have quotation marks.

> *Adele said __that she was sick__.*

reporting verb: a verb used to report what people say, either in quoted or reported speech *(say, tell, asked).*

> *Tomo __said__, "Hi, how are you?"*
> *Jennifer __asked__ if we were busy.*

sentence: a thought that is expressed in words, usually with a subject and verb. A sentence begins with a capital letter and ends with a period, exclamation point, or question mark.

➢ *The bell rang loudly.*

➢ *Don't eat that!*

separable phrasal verb: a phrasal verb that can have a noun or a pronoun (object) between its two parts (verb + particle).

➢ ***Turn** the light **off**.*

➢ ***Turn off** the light.*

short answer: a common spoken answer to a question that is not always a complete sentence.

➢ A: *Where are you going?*

➢ B: ***To the store.***

simple past: a verb form used to talk about completed actions.

➢ *Last night we **ate** dinner at home.*

➢ *I **visited** my parents last weekend.*

simple present: a verb form used to talk about habits or routines, schedules, and facts.

➢ *He **likes** apples and oranges.*

➢ *Toronto **gets** a lot of snow in the winter.*

singular noun: a noun that names only one person, place, or thing.

➢ *They have **a son** and **a daughter**.*

statement: a sentence that gives information.

➢ *My house has five rooms.*

➢ *He doesn't have a car.*

stress: we use stress to say a syllable or a word with more volume or emphasis.

subject: the noun or pronoun that is the topic of the sentence.

➢ ***Patricia** is a doctor.*

➢ ***They** are from Iceland.*

subject pronoun: a pronoun that is the subject of a sentence: *I, you, he, she, it*, and *they*.

➢ *I have one brother. **He** lives in Miami.*

subordinating conjunction: a conjunction that is used to introduce an adverb clause, such as *because, since, even though*, and *although*. (See *conjunction*.)

➢ ***Even though** he ate all his dinner, he is still hungry.*

➢ *She is late **because** she got lost.*

superlative: the form of an adjective or adverb used to compare three or more people, places, or things.

➢ *Mount Everest is **the highest** mountain in the world.*

➢ *Evgeny is **the youngest** student in our class.*

syllable: a part of a word that contains a single vowel sound and is pronounced as a unit.

➢ *The word **pen** has one syllable.*

➢ *The word **pencil** has two syllables (pen-cil).*

tense: the form of the verb that shows the time of the action.

➢ *They **sell** apples.* (simple present)

➢ *They **sold** cars.* (simple past)

third-person singular: in the simple present, the third-person singular ends in *-s* or *-es*. Singular nouns and the pronouns *he, she*, and *it* take the third-person singular form.

➢ *She **plays** the piano.*

➢ *Mr. Smith **teaches** her.*

time clause: a clause that tells when an action or event happened or will happen. Time clauses are introduced by conjunctions, such as *when, after, before, while*, and *since*.

➢ *I have lived here **since I was a child**.*

➢ ***While I was walking home,** it began to rain.*

➢ *I'm going to call my parents **after I eat dinner**.*

time expression: a phrase that tells when something happened or will happen. Time expressions usually go at the end or the beginning of a sentence.

➢ ***Last week** I went hiking.*

➢ *She's moving **next month**.*

transitive verb: a verb that is followed by a direct object.

➢ *We **took** an umbrella.*

verb: a word that shows action, gives a state, or shows possession.

➢ *Tori **skated** across the ice.*

➢ *She **is** an excellent athlete.*

➢ *She **has** many medals.*

voiced: a sound that is spoken with the vibration of the vocal cords. The consonants *b, d, g, j, l, m, n, r, v, w, z*, and all vowels are typically voiced.

vowel: a sound represented in English by the letters *a, e, i, o, u*, and sometimes *y*.

***Wh-* question:** (also called *information question*.) a question that asks for specific information, not *"Yes"* or *"No."*

➢ *Where do they live?*

➢ *What do you usually do on weekends?*

***Wh-* word:** a word such as *who, what, where, when, why*, or *how* that is used to begin a *Wh-* question.

***Yes/No* question:** a question that can be answered with *"Yes"* or *"No."*

➢ *Do you live in Dublin?*

➢ *Can you ski?*

INDEX

Note: All page references in blue are in Split Edition B.

Q

R

S

13: ©uniquely india/Getty Images; **17 left:** ©Scott Heppell/AP Images, **right:** ©Robin Smith/Getty Images; **19:** ©Walter Zerla/Cultura Travel/ Getty Images; **20:** ©Fernando Vergara/AP Images; **21:** ©Fernando Bustamante/AP Images; **22:** ©AFP/Getty Images; **24–25:** ©Panoramic Images/ National Geographic Creative; **26–27:** ©Mark C. Ross/National Geographic Creative; **27:** ©Bill Hatcher/National Geographic Creative; **27 top:** ©Doug Allan/Getty Images, **bottom:** ©Biosphoto/SuperStock; **32:** ©iStockphoto/Thinkstock; **33:** ©GILLARDI Jacques/Getty Images; **34:** ©Pete McBride/National Geographic Creative; **38:** ©Dr. K. David Harrison/Living Tongues Institute for Endangered Language; **39 top:** ©Jim Webb/ National Geographic Creative, **bottom:** © StockShot/Alamy; **40:** ©Mikey Schafer/National Geographic Creative; **44:** ©Royal Geographical Society (with IBG); **45:** ©pkchai /Shutterstock; **46:** ©CM Dixon/Glow Images; **47:** ©Art Media/Glow Images; **51:** ©Kazuhiko Sano/National Geographic Creative; **54:** ©Ajit Solanki/AP Images; **55 top left:** ©TexPhoto/iStockphoto, **top right:** ©Reinhold Leitner/Shutterstock, **bottom left:** ©Pieter De Pauw/fotolia, **bottom right:** ©iStockphoto/Thinkstock; **56:** ©Charlie Edward/Shutterstock; **58–59:** ©Keren Su/Getty Images; **60–61:** © Chris Johns/National Geographic Creative; **67:** ©Michael Christopher Brown/National Geographic Creative; **68 left:** ©Nikki Bidgood/ Getty Images, **middle:** ©Rogerio Assis/SambaPhoto/Getty Images, **left:** ©picture alliance/Frank May/Newscom; **69:** ©AFP/Getty Images; **73:** ©rachel dewis/iStockphoto; **74–75:** ©Peter Powell/EPA/Newscom; **79:** ©Simon Woodcock/Alamy; **82:** ©suttisukmek/iStockphoto; **83:** ©GlobalStock/iStockphoto; **84:** ©Russell Sadur/Getty Images; **86–87:** ©Justin Guariglia/National Geographic Creative; **88:** ©David Bank/Getty Images; **89:** © Rafael Ben-Ari/Chameleons Eye/Newscom; **95:** ©Lledo/Shutterstock; **96–97:** © Wes C. Skiles/National Geographic Creative; **96 top:** ©International Mapping Inc/National Geographic Creative, **bottom:** ©Brian J. Skerry/National Geographic Creative; **101:** ©Catherine de Medici Jaffee; **103, 104:** ©Michael Christopher Brown/National Geographic Creative; **108:** ©Jeff Barnard/AP Images; **109 top:** ©Helmut Corneli/ imageBROKER/age fotostock, **bottom:** ©Robert Clarke/Alamy; **110:** ©AHPix/shutterstock; **111:** ©John A. Anderson/Shutterstock; **114:** ©Alison Wright/National Geographic Creative; **116:** ©joyt/iStockphoto; **117:** ©Philippe Michel/Thinkstock; **118:** ©Franco Banfi/Getty Images; **120–121:** ©Colin Monteath/Hedgehog House/Getty Images; **122–123:** ©imagebroker/Alamy; **122 both:** ©NASA; **128:** ©Nobert Rosing/National Geographic Creative; **130:** © AFP/Getty Images; **131:** ©Horizons WWP/Alamy; **136:** "Dracula," from the series The Composites. Courtesy of the artist; **137:** ©Moviepix/Getty Images; **140:** ©Craig Hudson/Getty Images; **141:** ©Bloomberg via Getty Images; **143:** ©Charles Sturge/Alamy; **144:** © Kristjan Fridriksson/Glow Images; **145:** ©Danita Delimont/Alamy; 150: ©Emma Wood/Alamy; **152:** ©Martin Barraud/Getty Images; **154:** ©Butterfly Hunter/Shutterstock; **156–157:** ©Stephen Alvarez/National Geographic Creative; **158:** ©Gerard Lacz/age fotostock; **159:** ©ARCO/W Layer/age fotostock; **163:** ©Praisaeng/Shutterstock; **165:** Photo: University of Waikato; 166: © Fran Lanting/National Geographic Creative; **170:** ©sergio pitamitz/Marka/ SuperStock; **172:** ©NBCU Photo Bank via Getty Images; **173:** ©FLPA/David Tipling/age fotostock; **174:** ©Mark Bowler/ Alamy; **176–177:** ©Rex Features via AP Images; **178–179:** ©Maria Starovoytova/Shutterstock; **178:** ©Mark Greenberg/AFP/Getty Images/ Newscom; **181:** ©NASA; **186:** ©Blend Images/ SuperStock; **187:** ©MixAll Studio/Getty Images; **192–193:** ©David Doubilet/National Geographic Creative; **198:** ©Sylvain Cordier/Getty Images; **200:** ©Beverly Joubert/National Geographic Creative; **202:** ©Christian Science Monitor/Getty Images; **204–205:** ©Pete Ryan/National Geographic Creative; **206:** ©ULTRA.F/Getty Images; **207:** ©PhotoStock-Israel/age fotostock; **203:** ©Robert Landau/Alamy; **214:** ©SuperStock; **218:** Photo courtesy of Pirate Play Ships, LLC; **220, 221:** ©AFP/Getty Images; **225:** Courtesy of Camerons Camel Campaign; **230:** ©Kennan Harvey/Getty Images; **232–233:** ©Joel Sartore/National Geographic Creative; **234:** ©Werner Lang/imagebroker/Newscom; **235:** ©Helmut Hess/imagebroker/age fotostock; **240:** ©Nelson Sirlin/Shutterstock; **241:** © B Christopher/Alamy; **242:** ©Martin Rietze/age fotostock; **243:** ©imagebroker/Alamy; **248:** ©Galyna Andrushko/Shutterstock; **250–251:** ©Watt Jim/Getty Images; **256:** ©Steve Winter/National Geographic Creative; **259:** ©Mike Theiss/National Geographic Creative; **260:** ©AFP/Getty Images; **262–263:** ©Peter Essick/Getty Images; **264–265:** ©Jason deCaires Taylor; **271:** ©Red Bull Stratos/ZUMA Press/Newscom; **272:** ©Marco Grob/National Geographic Creative; **276:** ©LehaKoK/Shutterestock; **278:** ©Cavan Images/Getty Images; **279 top:** ©Mark Thiessen/National Geographic Creative; **bottom:** ©Norbert Probst/imagebroker/SuperStock; **280:** ©NASA Goddard Scientific Visualization Studio/National Geographic Creative; **286:** ©Harish Tyagi/EPA/Newscom; **287:** ©David Stoecklein/age fotostock; **288:** ©Marco Grob/National Geographic Creative; **289:** ©Ace Kvale/Aurora Open/ Superstock; **290:** ©Juanmonino/Getty Images; **292–293:** ©LEMAIRE StÃ©phane/Getty Images; **295:** ©Richard Nowitz/National Geographic Creative; **299:** © Juan Soliz/PacificCoastNews.com; **301:** ©Anthony C. LoBaido; **302:** ©Karen Kasmauski/National Geographic Creative; **305 left:** ©Alan Tobey/Getty Images, **right:** ©Alex Treadway/National Geographic Creative; **306:** ©Tim Laman/National Geographic Creative; **307:** ©LaserLens/iStockphoto; **308–309:** ©Seb Rogers/Alamy; **313**: ©Hervey Garret/National Geographic Creative; **314:** ©Guido Bissattini/ Shutterstock; **315:** ©1001nights/iStockphoto; **316:** ©Fotosearch/Getty Images; **318–319:** ©John Warburton Lee/Superstock; **320–321:** ©Lior Mizrahi/Getty Images; **323:** ©Gamma-Rapho via Getty Images; **327:** Courtesy of Yong Ho Ji; **328:** ©Robert Harding Picture Library Ltd/Alamy; **330:** ©Christian Kapteyn/Alamy; **331:** ©Hamza Djenat; **332**: ©Lonely Planet Images/Getty Images; **335:** ©CulturalEyes—AusGS2/Alamy; **336–337:** ©JTB Photo/Glow Images; **341:** ©Blend Images/Getty Images; **342:** ©Granamour Weems Collection/Alamy; **344:** ©Inger Hogstrom/ Danita Delimont Photography/Newscom; **346:** ©Moviestore collection/Alamy; **348–349:** ©Pete McBride/National Geographic Creative; **350:** ©Atsushi Tomura /Getty Images; **351:** ©Xinhua/Landov; **353 both:** ©Xpacifica/National Geographic Creative; **357:** ©Ladi Kirn/Alamy; **358:** ©Bill Becher/ZUMAPRESS/Newscom; **359:** ©Rex Features via AP Images; **360:** Graham M. Lawrence/Alamy; **364:** © Frans Lemmens/ SuperStock; **367:** ©NotarYES/Shutterstock; **368:** ©Mark Thiessen/National Geographic Creative; **370–371:** © Bruce Dale/National Geographic Creative; **372–373:** ©JG Photography/Alamy; **372 top:** © AFP/Getty Images; **375:** © John W Banagan/Getty Images; **376 top:** © Hulton Archive/ Getty Images, **bottom left:** © Boyan Dimitrov/Shutterstock**, bottom right:** © Jean-Paul Barbier; **379:** ©AMAZON/UPI /Landov; **380 left to right:** © Hulton Archive/Getty Images, ©UIG via Getty Images, ©Sebastien Bergeron/Getty Images, ©North Wind Picture Archives/Alamy; **381 left:** ©North Wind Picture Archives/Alamy, **right:** ©AFP/Getty Images; **382–383 background:** ©Hyena Reality/Shutterstock; **382–383 all others:** ©Tan Le/National Geographic Creative; **384:** ©Tan Le/National Geographic Creative; **390:** ©Andrzej Mirecki; **391:** ©David Stock/Alamy; **392 left:** © Lana K/Shutterstock, **right:** ©mishooo/iStockphoto; **394–395:** © Jim Richardson/National Geographic Creative; **396 both:** © Kenneth Garrett/National Geographic Creative; **399:** ©Jacques Alexandre/age fotostock; **400:** © Michael Melford/National Geographic Creative; **402:** © Martin Gray/National Geographic Creative; **403:** ©Image Farm Inc./Alamy; 404–405: Original Artwork by John Batchelor. Courtesy of Odyssey Marine Exploration; **407:** ©St Petersburg Times/ZUMAPRESS/Newscom; **411:** ©Christian Goupi/age fotostock; **412:** ©De Agostini/Getty Images; **413:** © Oligo/Shutterstock; **414:** © Romaoslo/iStockphoto; **416:** ©pzAxe/Alamy; **417:** ©Heritage Images/Glow Images; **419:** ©Denver Post via Getty Images; **420:** ©Chris Cheadle/All Canada Photos/SuperStock; **422:** ©Gamma/Glow Images; **424–425:** ©NASA; **426, 427:** Photo: Christoph Gerigk; ©Franck Goddio/Hilti Foundation; **431:** ©JTB Photo/age fotostock; **432–433:** © Ben Robson Hull Photography/Getty Images; **434–435:** ©DeAgostini/Getty Images; **343:** ©AFP/Newscom; **439:** ©Michael Melford/National Geographic Creative; **442 top:** Photo by Universal History Archive/UIG/Getty Images, **bottom:** ©NASA/National Geographic Creative; **443:** ©NASA/National Geographic Creative; **445, 446:** ©NASA; **449:** Photo by Ricky Carioti/The Washington Post via Getty Images; **450:** ©NASA; **451:** ©JPL-Caltech/NASA; **453:** ©Rex Features via AP Images; **455 top:** ©International Mapping Inc./National Geographic Creative, **bottom:** ©Volkmar K. Wentzel/National Geographic Creative; **456:** ©R. Gino Santa Maria/Shutterstock.

MAP

4, 9, 11, 26, 33, 38, 43, 46, 74, 82, 88, 94, 95, 103, 122, 144, 152, 158, 165, 220, 242, 264, 294, 301, 308, 330, 396, 404, 413, 426, 431, 432, 437, 439,440: National Geographic Maps

ILLUSTRATION

22, 23, 199: Cenveo Publisher Services